The Blackwell Guide

─────────Blackwell Philosophy Guides─────────

Series Editor: Steven M. Cahn, City University of New York Graduate School

Written by an international assembly of distinguished philosophers, the *Blackwell Philosophy Guides* create a groundbreaking student resource – a complete critical survey of the central themes and issues of philosophy today. Focusing and advancing key arguments throughout, each essay incorporates essential background material serving to clarify the history and logic of the relevant topic. Accordingly, these volumes will be a valuable resource for a broad range of students and readers, including professional philosophers.

The Blackwell Guide to EPISTEMOLOGY *edited by John Greco and Ernest Sosa*

The Blackwell Guide to ETHICAL THEORY *edited by Hugh LaFollette*

The Blackwell Guide to the MODERN PHILOSOPHERS *edited by Steven M. Emmanuel*

The Blackwell Guide to PHILOSOPHICAL LOGIC *edited by Lou Goble*

The Blackwell Guide to SOCIAL AND POLITICAL PHILOSOPHY *edited by Robert L. Simon*

The Blackwell Guide to BUSINESS ETHICS *edited by Norman E. Bowie*

The Blackwell Guide to the PHILOSOPHY OF SCIENCE *edited by Peter Machamer and Michael Silberstein*

The Blackwell Guide to METAPHYSICS *edited by Richard M. Gale*

The Blackwell Guide to the PHILOSOPHY OF EDUCATION *edited by Nigel Blake, Paul Smeyers, Richard Smith, and Paul Standish*

The Blackwell Guide to PHILOSOPHY OF MIND *edited by Stephen P. Stich and Ted A. Warfield*

The Blackwell Guide to the PHILOSOPHY OF THE SOCIAL SCIENCES *edited by Stephen P. Turner and Paul A. Roth*

The Blackwell Guide to CONTINENTAL PHILOSOPHY *edited by Robert C. Solomon and David Sherman*

The Blackwell Guide to ANCIENT PHILOSOPHY *edited by Christopher Shields*

The Blackwell Guide to the PHILOSOPHY OF COMPUTING AND *INFORMATION edited by Luciano Floridi*

The Blackwell Guide to AESTHETICS *edited by Peter Kivy*

The Blackwell Guide to AMERICAN PHILOSOPHY *edited by Armen T. Marsoobian and John Ryder*

The Blackwell Guide to PHILOSOPHY OF RELIGION *edited by William E. Mann*

The Blackwell Guide to the PHILOSOPHY OF LAW AND LEGAL THEORY *edited by Martin Golding and William A. Edmundson*

The Blackwell Guide to
Ethical Theory

Edited by

Hugh LaFollette

Blackwell
Publishing

BLACKWELL PUBLISHING
350 Main Street, Malden, MA 02148-5020, USA
9600 Garsington Road, Oxford OX4 2DQ, UK
550 Swanston Street, Carlton, Victoria 3053, Australia

First published 2000

6   2005

Library of Congress Cataloging-in-Publication Data

The Blackwell guide to ethical theory / edited by Hugh LaFollette.
    p.   cm. — (Blackwell philosophy guides)
Includes bibliographical references and index.
ISBN 0-631-20118-1 (hb : alk. paper) — ISBN 0-631-20119-X (pbk. : alk. paper)
1. Ethics.   I. LaFollette, Hugh, 1948- . II. Series.
BJ1012.B536   2000
170—dc21   99-33934
                                                                              CIP

ISBN-13: 978-0-631-20118-2 (hb. : alk. paper) — ISBN-13: 978-0-631-20119-9 (pbk. : alk. paper)

A catalogue record for this title is available from the British Library.

Set in 10 on 13 pt Galliard
by Ace Filmsetting Ltd, Frome, Somerset
Printed and bound in the United Kingdom
by TJ International, Padstow, Cornwall

The publisher's policy is to use permanent paper from mills that operate a sustainable forestry policy, and which has been manufactured from pulp processed using acid-free and elementary chlorine-free practices. Furthermore, the publisher ensures that the text paper and cover board used have met acceptable environmental accreditation standards.

For further information on
Blackwell Publishing, visit our website:
www.blackwellpublishing.com

Contents

Contributors

Simon Blackburn is Edna J. Koury Distinguished Professor at the University of North Carolina, Chapel Hill. He is the author of *Reason and Prediction* (1973), *Spreading the Word* (1986), *Essays in Quasi-Realism* (1993), and *Ruling Passions* (1998). Blackburn has written extensively on philosophy of mind, philosophy of science, metaphysics, and metaethics, and is currently completing, with Keith Simmons, a collection on Truth for the "Oxford Readings in Philosophy" series.

John D. Caputo is David R. Cook Professor of Philosophy at Villanova University. His most recent publications are *The Prayers and Tears of Jacques Derrida: Religion without Religion* (Indiana, 1997) and *Deconstruction in a Nutshell: A Conversation with Jacques Derrida* (Fordham, 1997). Among his earlier publications are *Against Ethics* (Indiana, 1993), *Demythologizing Heidegger* (Indiana, 1993) and *Radical Hermeneutics* (Indiana, 1987). He is also editor of the Fordham University Press Series "Perspectives in Continental Philosophy" and is Executive Co-director of the Society for Phenomenology and Existential Philosophy.

R. G. Frey is Professor of Philosophy at Bowling Green State University and Senior Research Fellow in the Social Philosophy and Policy Center there. His graduate education was at the University of Virginia and Oxford University. His most recent book is *Euthanasia and Physician-Assisted Suicide* (Cambridge University Press), jointly authored with Gerald Dworkin and Sissela Bok. Forthcoming are books on utilitarianism and on the moral philosophy of Butler, Shaftesbury, and Hume.

Thomas E. Hill, Jr. is Kenan Professor, Philosophy, University of North Carolina, Chapel Hill. His books include *Autonomy and Self-Respect* (Cambridge University Press, 1991) and *Dignity and Practical Reason in Kant's Moral Theory* (Cornell University Press, 1992).

Brad Hooker is now in the Philosophy Department at the University of Reading.

He previously taught at Virginia Commonwealth University. His book-length exploration of rule-consequentialism is forthcoming under the title, *Ideal Code, Real World: A Rule-Consequentialist Theory of Morality*. He is now writing a history of twentieth-century moral philosophy for Blackwell Publishers.

Alison M. Jaggar is Professor of Philosophy and Women Studies at the University of Colorado at Boulder. She is author of *Feminist Politics and Human Nature* (1983), co-author (with James P. Sterba) of *Morality and Social Justice* (1995), and has edited five books. She is currently writing *Sex, Truth and Power: A Feminist Theory of Moral Justification*. Jaggar was a founding member of the Society for Women in Philosophy, past chair of the American Philosophical Association Committee on the Status of Women, and past co-president of the North American Society for Social Philosophy.

F. M. Kamm is Professor of Philosophy at New York University. She is author of *Morality, Mortality*, vol. 1, *Death and Whom to Save From It*, and vol. 2, *Rights, Duties and Status* (Oxford University Press, 1993–6), as well as *Creation and Abortion: A Study of Moral and Legal Philosophy* (Oxford University Press, 1992). She is also author of numerous essays in ethics and the philosophy of law.

Hugh LaFollette is Professor of Philosophy at East Tennessee State University. He is co-author, with Niall Shanks, of *Brute Science: Dilemmas of Animal Experimentation* (Routledge, 1997), author of *Personal Relationships: Love, Identity, and Morality* (Blackwell Publishers, 1996), and is currently working on a book that integrates ethical theory and practical ethics (forthcoming, Blackwell Publishers).

Jeff McMahan teaches at the University of Illinois, Urbana-Champagne. He has written *British Nuclear Weapons: For and Against*, and *Reagan and the World: Imperial Policy in the New Cold War*, and is author of numerous essays in practical ethics and ethical theory. He is currently writing two books, *Killing at the Margins of Life* and *The Ethics of War*.

David McNaughton is Professor of Philosophy and Head of Department at Keele University, and is the founding President of the British Society for Ethical Theory. He is the author of *Moral Vision* (Blackwell Publishers, 1988), and, with Piers Rawling, is currently writing a book on the distinction between agent-neutrality and agent-relativity. He is also working, with Eve Garrard, to determine if concepts like forgiveness, hypocrisy, evil, guilt, and redemption can play a moral role in a secular society.

Jan Narveson, a naturalized Canadian citizen, is Professor of Philosophy at the University of Waterloo. His books include *Morality and Utility* (Johns Hopkins Press, 1967), *The Libertarian Idea* (Temple University Press, 1989), *Moral Matters* (Broadview Press, 1993; 2nd edition, 1999), and an anthology, *Moral Issues*

(Oxford University Press, 1983). He also co-authored, with Marilyn Friedman, *Political Correctness* (1995), and co-edited, with Jack Sanders, *For and Against the State* (1996).

Phillip L. Quinn is John A. O'Brien Professor of Philosophy at the University of Notre Dame. He is the author of *Divine Commands and Moral Requirements* and of numerous papers in the philosophy of religion, philosophy of science, ethics, metaphysics, and the history of philosophy. He served as Editor of *Faith and Philosophy* from 1990 to 1995 and is co-editor of the *Blackwell Companion to the Philosophy of Religion*.

James Rachels is University Professor of Philosophy at the University of Alabama at Birmingham. His books include *Can Ethics Provide Answers?* and *Created from Animals: the Moral Implications of Darwinism*.

Geoffrey Sayre-McCord, Bowman and Gordon Gray Professor of Philosophy at the University of North Carolina, Chapel Hill, works in moral theory, metaethics, epistemology, and the history of modern philosophy. He is co-editor of *Essays on Moral Realism* (Cornell University Press). He is currently working on moral realism, on Hume's moral philosophy, and contemporary contractarianism.

William R. Schroeder teaches at the University of Illinois, Urbana-Champagne. He is author of *Sartre and His Predecessors: The Self and the Other*, and is currently completing *Continental Philosophy: The Basic Positions* for publication. He is also co- editor of the *Blackwell Companion to Continental Philosophy*.

Michael Slote is Professor of Philosophy and Chair of the Philosophy Department at the University of Maryland, College Park. The author of several books and many articles in ethics, he has recently finished a book (*Morals from Motives*) that develops and defends a sentimentalist-inspired form of virtue ethics.

Elliott Sober is Hans Reichenbach Professor of Philosophy at the University of Wisconsin-Madison. He is the author of *The Nature of Selection*, *Reconstructing the Past*, *Philosophy of Biology*, and, most recently, *Unto Others – the Evolution and Psychology of Unselfish Behavior*, co-authored with David Sloan Wilson.

Michael Smith is Professor of Philosophy at the Research School of Social Sciences, Australian National University. He is the author of *The Moral Problem* and the editor of *Meta-Ethics*.

James P. Sterba is Professor of Philosophy at the University of Notre Dame. He has written more than 150 articles and published 18 books, most recently *Justice for Here and Now* (Cambridge University Press). He has lectured widely in the United States, Europe, and the Far East.

L. W. Sumner is Professor in the Department of Philosophy and Faculty of Law, University of Toronto. He is the author of *Abortion and Moral Theory* (1981), *The Moral Foundation of Rights* (1987), and *Welfare, Happiness, and Ethics* (1996), as well as numerous articles in ethics and political philosophy. He is currently working on a book on freedom of expression.

Laurence Thomas is Professor in the Maxwell School of Citizenship and Public Affairs at Syracuse University. He is the author of *Living Morally: A Psychology of Moral Character* (Temple University Press, 1990), and *Vessels of Evil: American Slavery and the Holocaust* (Temple University Press, 1993).

Introduction

Contemporary ethicists entertain theories about human nature, explore the nature of value, discuss competing accounts of the best ways to live, ponder the connections between ethics and human psychology, and discuss practical ethical quandaries. Broadly conceived, these are the same issues ancient philosophers discussed. However, the precise questions contemporary philosophers ask, the distinctions we make, the methods we employ, and the knowledge of the world and of human psychology we use in framing and evaluating ethical theories, often only faintly resemble those of our philosophical predecessors.

Nonetheless, current ethical theories are shaped by our predecessors. We wrestle with the questions they posed. We ask the questions we ask, in the ways we ask them, because of their philosophical successes and failures. Their debates were likewise shaped by the questions posed by their predecessors. The connection between our, their, and their predecessors' questions explains why we have a history of ethics, why we all participate in the same debate. The differences between their debates and ours reflect the ways ethics has evolved. This is as it should be: the debates are similar because we are all looking for better ways to relate to and with each other; different because with time (and the benefits of hindsight), we should better understand ourselves, our place in the world, and our relationships to others.

We can divide their questions and ours into three broad categories: meta-ethics, normative ethics, and practical ethics. Here are examples of each.

Meta-ethics: What is the status of moral claims? Are claims about morality just statements of the society's standards or individual choices? Are they objective in some sense? If they are objective, what makes them so? Is ethics a viable intellectual enterprise? What is the connection, if any, between our psychological makeup and the nature of moral judgments?

Normative ethics : What is the best way, broadly understood, to live? Are there general principles, rules, guidelines that we should follow, or virtues that we should inculcate, that help us distinguish right from wrong and good from bad?

Practical ethics: How should we behave in particular situations: when should we tell the truth, under what circumstances can or should we go to war, what is the best way to organize society, how should we relate to the environment and to animals?

Part I contains essays in meta-ethics: they discuss the nature and status of ethics and the relationship between ethics and human psychology. Part II contains essays in normative ethics: they offer competing accounts of how we should live.

This idea that ethics, like Gaul, is divided into three parts, reveals the ways in which ethics as a discipline has evolved. For this is not a distinction the ancients made. Likely they would have seen it as a contrivance, carving non-existent joints in the moral universe. Still, I think we can, without undue violence to their views, classify their discussions into these three camps. Plato's theory of the forms (as traditionally understood) could be seen as the first attempt at defending moral realism and offering an objective ground for moral truths. Aristotle's account of the virtues could be seen as one of the first sustained inquiries in normative ethics. And Plato's proposed structure of the state could be envisaged as an early exercise in practical ethics. As long as we use these distinctions as simply a convenient way of distinguishing the kinds of questions they asked, then likely they would not take umbrage.

Philosophers earlier this century, however, did not see these distinctions as merely part of a useful classificatory scheme, but as separating ethics into three wholly distinct disciplines, where only the first (and perhaps the second) were "real" philosophy. In the mid-1950s, P. H. Nowell-Smith proclaimed that:

> The moral philosopher's task is now conceived, not to be one of conducting a theoretical inquiry into practical wisdom, but to be one of investigating questions, judgements, doubts, and beliefs that are themselves theoretical. The moral philosopher not only makes theoretical statements about his subject matter; his subject-matter consists of theoretical statements. (1957: 24)

Thus, most philosophers at that time thought they could fruitfully engage in meta-ethics without the slightest interest in or acquaintance with normative or practical ethics. Indeed most, like Nowell-Smith, would not even consider normative ethics as part of ethics. Not surprisingly, virtually no one then would have envisioned practical ethics as we now know it. Still less would they be tempted to think of it as philosophy.

These views of ethics were connected with the then-dominant view of philosophy, which emerged from developments in Britain and on the Continent. Ayer had boldly proclaimed in the 1940s that philosophy did not depend on *any* empirical fact; since "the propositions of philosophy are not factual, but linguistic . . . " (1952/1946: 57). That is why then, and for decades after, most philosophers thought they could do philosophy of science without the slightest acquaintance with any science, and that they could do philosophy of mind without the slightest acquaintance with psychology, cognitive science, or artificial intelligence.

Present-day philosophers, unlike the ancients, still employ these categories to roughly distinguish the types of inquiry in which they engage. But, unlike their mid-century predecessors, they reject the idea that philosophy simply concerns "theoretical statements . . . about theoretical statements." They are thus disinclined to think of these ethical categories as separate – as three wholly independently inquiries. For instance, Stephen Darwall rejects any clear separation between meta-ethics and normative ethics (1998: 12), while Shelly Kagan not only eschews the distinction between meta-ethics and normative ethics (1998: 7), he also renounces any firm distinction between normative and practical ethics (5). Furthermore, as you will notice when reading the essays, distinctions between the types of normative theory are likewise blurry and should not be taken as indicating more than a vague family resemblance.

The Essays

Meta-ethics

Part I begins with two essays discussing the status of ethics. Are moral claims objective? Do they identify "real" features of the world? How? If not, is ethics relative to individuals or cultures?

Many who claim ethics is objective have historically embraced some form of **"Moral Realism"**. *Michael Smith* describes realism as the belief that (a) moral claims are capable of being true and false, and that (b) some of those claims are, in fact, true. Realism is best understood in contrast with two alternatives: nihilism and expressivism. Both alternatives hold that moral claims cannot be true or false. They disagree, however, about the appropriate response to living in a fundamentally value-free world.

Although realists reject both nihilism and expressivism, some, *Smith* argues, dismiss them prematurely either (a) by arguing that in making moral claims we indicate our belief that such claims are capable of being true or false, or (b) by embracing a "minimalistic" conception of truth. Neither move can defeat these views. We can reject nihilism and expressivism only by embracing a robust realism. Although expressivism, like that endorsed by *Blackburn*, is unacceptable, *Smith* thinks that expressivists are right about one thing: there *is* standardly a connection between our moral claims and our proclivity to act in certain ways. This insight, however, is best captured not by expressivism, but by an internalist naturalistic moral realism.

Simon Blackburn disagrees. In **"Relativism"** he argues that one does not have to be a realist to believe that ethical judgments are objective. If we recognize that ethics is primarily a matter of practice (a point echoed by *LaFollette*) – and not a matter of abstract moral knowledge – then we do not need ethical facts embedded in the world to reject moral relativism. Such facts would serve no purpose. For although moral judgements are fallible, we can offer arguments supporting our judgements – arguments others can see, understand, and criticize. That is all the objectivity we need. Expressivism also has a decided advantage over realism: it makes better sense of the fact that we can have some moral disagreements, without assuming that one party must be mistaken.

Although these are the only essays explicitly debating whether ethics is objective, this theme is discussed, to varying degrees and in different ways, by several essays in Part II (Normative Ethics), most especially the essays on **"Contractarianism,"** **"Continental Ethics,"** and **"Pragmatic Ethics."**

The next three essayists offer different explanations of the grounds of objectivity. In **"Divine Command Theory,"** *Philip L. Quinn*, defends the claim that morality depends on God. His aim is not to convince atheists of the truth of his view – that would depend on his first convincing them of the existence and nature of god. His aim is more modest: to show that such beliefs constitute a defensible theory of ethics.

He offers and refines a version of the **"Divine Command Theory,"** and then responds to assorted criticisms which purportedly show that the very idea of a divine command ethic is indefensible. He ends by offering what he sees as a "cumulative case argument" for the suggestion that categorical moral requirements cannot exist unless there is a deity that intends them.

James Rachels explores the most prominent alternative to **"Divine Command Theory."** **"Naturalism"** is the belief that ethics is contiguous with, and understandable in light of, science, broadly understood. By the nineteenth century naturalism was the most prominent position in ethics. But earlier this century, many philosophers thought that G. E. Moore's "open-question" argument demonstrated that no form of naturalism was tenable. There were two very different reactions. Some philosophers concluded that ethical claims merely expressed our attitudes toward actions and toward others. In contrast, others, like Moore, advocated ethical non-naturalism (a position advocated here by *McNaughton*). Naturalistically inclined philosophers thus faced two tasks: (1) they had to rebut Moore's open question argument, and (2) they had to explain how they could derive ought statements from claims about what is. This derivation is difficult, in part, because "ought" statements (for example, moral claims) are thought to be motivating, while "is" statements are not.

Rachels agrees that factual statements are not, by themselves motivating. But this does not defeat naturalism. It provides a mechanism for showing how naturalism can be true. Moral statements – being ought statements – can be motivating if paired with desires or attitudes. However, the only desires and attitudes morality countenances are those evoked and sustained by deliberation. Some people might fear (or assume) that this would lead to **"Relativism"** since different people have different desires. Not so. Given of our shared biological inheritance, *Rachels* claims, most of us have the same *fundamental* interests, values, and desires. These undergird morality. In fact, evolution can easily explain how morality arose and is sustained.

Of course even if we think there are moral truths, we must still determine how to discover those truths. Many essayists offer some explanation of how we discern moral truth. Most views – even many that are not, strictly speaking, intuitionistic – give **"Moral Intuition"** a central role in moral reasoning. *Jeff McMahan* discusses that role.

Although *McMahan* thinks intuitions play a crucial role in ethical deliberations, he wishes to separate that belief from two beliefs with which intuitionism has historically been entangled: (1) the belief that we identify intuitions through some special organ of knowledge, a way of perceiving unique moral properties, and, relatedly, (2) that such intuitions, once grasped, cannot be doubted. Neither view, he argues, is credible. We can reject them both, while still maintaining the conviction (a) that intuitions provide wise guidance on how we ought to behave, and (b) that we can never be sufficiently certain about any theory for it to lead us to completely reject the intuitions with which it clashes. In fact, he argues, a theory that does not give ordinary intuitions a prominent place would not be a moral theory at all. And, since intuitions concern practical cases, then careful reflection on practical ethical issues helps drive the development of a plausible moral theory. He ends by suggesting that the most viable moral theory would be a foundationalist theory that gives prominence to moral intuitions.

In **"The End of Ethics,"** *John D. Caputo*, challenges the overarching aim of this volume. Ethical theories, he claims, strive to provide guidance in making ethical decisions. Yet that is something they cannot do. We must make ethical decisions, even if we have no theory supporting them. Moreover, most ethical decisions are particular, and for such decisions generalized theories offer no guidance. But there is no reason to despair. Recognizing that ethical theories cannot solve our day-to-day moral problems frees us from the constraints those theories place upon our thinking. It helps us see the full range of available possibilities, and offers a chance for growth, insight, progress. Finally, standard ethical theories suggest that there is only one way everyone should live. They imply that all people, in all cultures, must march to the same moral drummer. Such a view is objectionable.

Caputo's approach to ethics, like that advanced by *Schroeder* in **"Continental Ethics,"** notably differs from that taken by most essayists in this volume, essayists who represent the analytic (Anglo-American) tradition. Nonetheless, I think all the essayists are engaged in the same moral debate. For although *Caputo* and *Schroeder* are leery of standard analytic ethical theory, many of their themes are echoed by other authors, even if described in different language. For instance, *Blackburn* argues that one of the benefits of expressivism is its ability to countenance some variation in proper moral behavior, while both *McNaughton* and *LaFollette* claim the same feature is an advantage of their respective accounts. And several authors (*McNaughton* and *Slote*) reject, in their own ways, the claim that morality provides a set of rules to solve particular moral issues.

The section on Meta-ethics closes with two essays on psychology and morality. Our current understanding of both theoretical and practical ethics has been significantly shaped by our understanding of human psychology. The first essay, by *Elliott Sober*, discusses the long-standing worry about **"Psychological Egoism."** Philosophers since Socrates worried that humans might be capable of acting only to promote their own self-interest. But if that is all we can do, then it seems morality is impossible.

The character of the debate about psychological egoism has changed dramatically in the past two millennia – as we would expect. *Sober* argues that most of the standard refutations of psychological egoism fail. However, evolutionary biology can now reveal why egoism is untenable. Humans can grow, learn, and flourish only if they are given suitable parental care and guidance. A pure hedonist will be a less reliable parent than either a pure altruist or a parent acting from multiple motives (both altruism and egoism).

If egoism is implausible, what, then, is the relationship between morality and psychological health? Many people think the aim of morality is to constrain humans: to require that they act in ways that conflict with their own self-interest. Certainly that is a view endorsed by *Quinn*, and *Caputo* claims this is a presupposition of most analytic ethical theories. *Laurence Thomas* disagrees. In **"Moral Psychology,"** he argues that psychologically healthy people are usually deeply moral. Here's why. Each of us develops a proper sense of self-worth – we come to value ourselves as human beings – only to the extent that we are unconditionally loved by our parents. If parents love a child, Thomas argues, then the child learns that she is valued as a human being, by other human beings who are themselves valuable. The child thus comprehends how valuable people should be treated.

As a child who is loved matures, she comes to understand what it is to be a moral self who can be wronged by (and can wrong) others. Thus, psychologically healthy individuals will find the idea of harming others offensive. Of course psychological health is a matter of degrees, and hence, we should not expect that psychologically healthy people always act morally. That's unrealistic. Nonetheless, the connection is sufficiently strong that psychologically healthy people will be generally inclined to act morally.

Normative ethics

Large portions of the history of normative ethics have been dominated by two traditions: consequentialism and deontology. So that is where I shall begin. However, the character of these theories has evolved. The lines between them – and between them and the alternatives – have become increasingly blurry. But with that caveat in place, the first of three subsections features two essays on consequentialism; the second subsection, six essays on deontology; the third, five essays exploring alternatives to these two main traditions.

The most dominant forms of consequentialism have been utilitarian. Utilitarianism has played a pivotal role in the history of ethics. Not only has the theory enjoyed considerable support among philosophers, it has played a central role as a foil for other theories. Many deontological theories were developed and refined through their attempts to distinguish themselves from utilitarianism. Historically the most widely advocated form of utilitarianism was **"Act-Utilitarianism."** *R .G. Frey* explains that the original appeal of act-utilitarianism was the belief that the theory offers an (a) relatively simple and (b) easily applied moral theory, and hence, could be used by most people to make everyday moral decisions.

Partly because of its once dominant role, act-utilitarianism was subject to fierce criticism by its detractors, and subsequent scrutiny and revision by its defenders. It became clear to both that the theory was neither simple nor easily applied. In its aim to avoid critics and satisfy adherents, the theory has undergone substantial change. One of most interesting developments was R. M. Hare's indirect utilitarianism, which distinguishes between judgments at the critical and at the intuitive level. Utilitarianism is supposed to direct judgment at the critical level, but not at the intuitive (everyday) level. These modifications were supposed to make act-utilitarianism simpler and more usable, and therefore, more defensible. Although this move is well-motivated, in the end, *Frey* argues, it does not work. Nonetheless, it points in the right direction: utilitarians must distinguish between the theory as an account of the right and as a decision procedure. Act utilitarianism, properly understood, is simply an account of right. It is not a decision procedure. However, it does show us how we should think about morality, and thus, helps us understand the need to develop character traits that makes us most likely to promote the greatest utility.

The second prominent form of consequentialism is **"Rule-Consequentialism,"** which claims that actions are right, not because they have the best consequences, but because they spring from a set of rules that have the best consequences. Such a theory, *Brad Hooker* claims, captures the insights of utilitarianism, without its untoward consequences. The rule nature of the theory avoids many of the problems facing the use of act-utilitarianism as a decision procedure – problems which prompted the revisions *Frey* advocates. Its emphasis on consequentialism, rather than utility, allows it to admit non-utility considerations into the moral picture, especially considerations about the best distribution of utilities.

Hooker spends some time criticizing act-utilitarianism and act consequentialism for their inability to square with many of our most cherished moral intuitions and rejects some well-known arguments that any defensible rule consequentialism must ultimately collapse into act consequentialism. He then tackles one of the significant problems facing rule-consequentialism, namely, deciding how widely accepted the rules must be before they are justified. We cannot expect virtually everyone to internalize the principles; certainly we cannot demand their complete compliance. Nonetheless, the rate of internalization has to be sufficiently high to justify the rules. In the end rule consequentialism is plausible because it avoids (a) the absolutist's claim that we can never break the moral rules, not even to achieve a great good, and (b) the act utilitarian's claim that we can break the moral rules, even to achieve a mere marginal gain in utility.

The appeal of deontology is often best seen in contrast with consequentialism. So the subsection on deontology begins with *F. M. Kamm*'s **"Nonconsequentialism."** She argues that all forms of consequentialism fail since morality is concerned not just with the states of affairs produced by our actions, but by our actions' intrinsic character. Specifically, consequentialism fails because it does not treat humans as ends-in-themselves but as mere means to maximizing overall utility.

On *Kamm's* view morality is best understood as (1) setting constraints on what we can do in our quest to pursue either the impersonal or our own good, and as (2) granting prerogatives for each individual to pursue her own interests rather than to maximize the good. She then explains how those features are incorporated into the best nonconsequentialist account. She ends by explaining the unique way in which nonconsequentialists understand giving aid to others.

In the following essay, *Thomas E. Hill, Jr.* tries to disentangle the central elements of **"Kantianism"** from the more peripheral ones. Kant's moral writings are standardly studied as major works in the history of moral philosophy. Yet in the first half of this century his ideas were largely rejected and often ridiculed. During the past quarter century, however, **"Kantianism"** has reemerged as a prominent moral theory, in no small measure because of a string of commentators who have infused new life into his thought. The problem, *Hill* notes, is that Kant has often been interpreted as advocating rather radical ideas, including the ideas that (a) empirical evidence is irrelevant to moral deliberation and that (b) the only actions of moral worth are those done from duty and against the agent's inclinations. To many, such ideas seem psychologically untenable, epistemologically uninformed, and morally odious.

Perhaps Kant holds these views – although *Hill* is far from sure that he does. Nonetheless, they are not the core of Kant's thought. And that core should not be lost because of squabbles over Kant's more radical views. These core ideas survive intact. They are significant developments in moral thought: the important but limited role of the *a priori* method, the basic contours of Kant's account of duty, the nature of the categorical imperative, and the idea that morality presupposes that we are autonomous agents.

Kant is also a pivotal figure in the history of **"Contractarianism."** *Geoffrey Sayre-McCord* chronicles the development of contractarianism from its ancient beginnings to the current day. Although the theory appears in many guises, all versions share the conviction that moral norms or political institutions are legitimate only if they are accepted by those whom they govern. What differentiates the theories are disagreements about the ways that, and the conditions under which, people accept those norms or institutions. Those differences reveal that, despite contractarianism's deep Kantian roots, it has developed in ways that interest not only deontologists, but also consequentialists and "alternative" theorists.

After surveying the history of contractarianism, especially Kantian and Hobbesian versions, *Sayre-McCord* suggests that a Humean account is the most plausible. Humean versions do not seek to identify a particular set of rules emerging from the contract, but to generally explain why and how morality would have naturally emerged in human society. The point is not necessarily to show how altruism would have arisen, but to show how the sorts of creatures we are would develop the kinds of institutions, and employ the evaluative concepts, that we do.

Although intuitions in one form or another play an important role in most people's understanding of morality, **"Intuitionism,"** as a formal theory fell into disrepute mid-century. Yet, in the last dozen years it made a theoretical comeback. The theory always had one enormous asset: it appeared to accommodate ordinary moral thinking. Despite this asset, many philosophers thought (and still think) the theory is plagued with insurmountable difficulties, most especially that it is non-explanatory and wholly unsystematic. *David McNaughton* claims these criticisms are unfounded. He traces the intuitionist's beginnings from the work of W. D. Ross, and shows that Ross's work is much more systematic than most philosophers suppose.

A full-blown **"Intuitionism,"** like that defended by *McNaughton*, differs from the more limited role given intuitions by *McMahan*. For unlike *McMahan*, *McNaughton* claims that the *prima facie* moral principles *are* self-evident, known *a priori*. But to say they are self-evident does not mean they are obvious, or understandable by the most uneducated and morally unenlightened dolt. Rather, self-evident truths can be discerned only by intelligent and experienced people, who have appropriately reflected on moral matters. This partly explains why the best theory does not seek to exhaust moral truth by giving a list of general moral principles, but understands that moral judgements are inevitably particularistic.

In the next essay, *L. W. Sumner* explores the leading role that **"Rights"** play in many deontological theories. Rights set constraints on attempts to maximize the social good (*Kamm*), and they thereby safeguard individuals against the intrusive interests of society or other individuals. Rights focus on their possessors – on the agents whose interests they protect – rather than the agents who must respect those rights. This focus, *Sumner* argues, gives theories that accommodate rights a significance absent from theories without them.

Sumner provides a scheme for classifying rights, and tries to show precisely what rights require and what they protect. He condemns the popular tendency to assert rights to everything we want, a tendency that has led to a senseless proliferation of, and thereby a diminution of the significance of, rights. Rights are not moral toys we construct at will; they require a theory that explains and grounds them. The best ground for rights is provided – somewhat surprisingly – by a goal-based theory rather than a deontological one.

Jan Narveson agrees with *Sumner* that rights are an important moral currency. But, unlike Sumner, **"Libertarianism"** holds there is only one moral right – the right to liberty. And that right is (virtually) inviolable. Thus, libertarians share the basic presupposition of other nonconsequentialists, namely, that we should not override individuals' rights to maximize the good. But libertarians think that most nonconsequentialists have too broad an understanding of right and wrong, and therefore, are too willing to override constraints against violating rights.

The central notion of libertarianism is self-ownership. The proper moral order has one goal: to protect individuals' rights to themselves. Coercion is justified only to control actions aggressing against others. Nonetheless, *Narveson* claims, libertarianism need not be seen as a selfish, narrowly individualistic theory. Libertarians can establish and support communities that urge their members to help others in need. Indeed, libertarians will not be averse to saying that each of us has a duty to provide mutual aid, as long as we understand that this is not an enforceable duty.

One of the most notable theoretical developments of the past three decades has been the emergence – or re-emergence – of theoretical alternatives that challenge, or dramatically diverge from, consequentialism and deontology. The last subsection of the book includes essays exploring five of those alternatives. The first is not actually new: the roots of **"Virtue Ethics"** go back to the beginning of western philosophy. Still, it has only recently reappeared on the contemporary theoretical stage. Although some people might suspect that the gap between virtue ethics and the standard alternatives is slight, *Michael Slote* claims the theories are different to the core. Whereas both consequentialism and deontology treat deontic concepts of "ought," "right," "duty," and "obligation" as the central moral concepts, virtue theorists hold that aretaic notions like "excellence" and "admirable" are key. More specifically, virtue theorists are especially concerned about inner states of character and motivation. Although deontologists or consequentialists may also be concerned about character, their concern is derivative: character matters only because it makes people more likely to promote the good or to follow moral rules. Consider, for instance, *Frey*'s argument that character plays a central role in the proper understanding of **"Act-Utilitarianism."** In contrast, virtue theorists see virtue as primary and deontic notions as derivative.

Before developing his positive account, *Slote* identifies what he sees as the pervasive flaws of consequentialism and deontology, for these flaws help explain the appeal of virtue ethics. *Slote* argues that the most defensible virtue ethic is an ethic of caring resembling that discussed by *Jaggar*. Such a view is preferable to the idea of universal benevolence since it permits more intensive interest in and care for family and close friends. However, it is a mistake to think that a virtue ethic is confined to the personal realm; it can also offer a satisfactory account of social justice.

In the next essay – **"Feminist Ethics"** – *Alison M. Jaggar* argues that all western ethical theories have consistently devalued women. This devaluation has been captured and rationalized in these theories' central concepts and reasoning. Even after ethical theorists acknowledged the basic equality of men and women, they still refused to criticize or challenge the myriad ways in which women have been and continue to be disadvantaged, or the ways in which standard theories support that disadvantage.

How are these disparities to be remedied? Minimally, standard ethical categories must be expanded to give due attention to significant issues affecting women. Some women have also proposed that women's ethical experience should be explicitly given a central role in ethical theory. Most notably this is seen in the development of the care ethic, like that advocated by *Slote*. Although *Jaggar* thinks the care ethic has been a significant development, in part because it exposes some central flaws in modern ethical theory, the theory is inadequate. The care perspective must be supplemented by a capabilities approach that first arose in, and now informs, debates about Third World development.

In the next essay, *William R. Schroeder* explains the nature of **"Continental Eth-**

ics." He notes, as did *Caputo* earlier, that Continental thinkers are suspicious of conventional morality. Yet many current developments in analytic ethical theory – especially the search for alternatives to consequentialism and deontology and the renewed interest in moral realism – have their roots in Continental thought. Perhaps the most notable difference between continental and analytic ethics, *Schroeder* claims, is the continentalist's emphasis on personal growth, authenticity, and creativity.

He shows how these ideas were developed in the work of several pivotal continental thinkers: Hegel, Nietzsche, Scheler, Sartre, and Levinas. *Schroeder* then explores ongoing questions about whether values are found or created by humans, questions about the priority of liberty, and he challenges what he claims is a guiding assumption of most analytic ethical theories: that the main job of ethics is to suppress people's basic selfishness.

In "**Pragmatic Ethics**," *Hugh LaFollette* argues that the thought of the American pragmatists, especially John Dewey, can illuminate long-standing disagreements about the nature of ethics and the conduct of a moral life. A pragmatic ethic does not categorically reject the insights of traditional ethical theories. Insights like those discussed by other essayists can help us better understand how we ought to live. The problem is that those moral theories begin with a defective view of human inquiry, misguided accounts of human rationality and psychology, and thus, inappropriate expectations for what an ethical theory should provide.

A proper understanding of human psychology, and especially the rich notion of habit, provides a way to have a morality (a) that employs criteria without being criterial, (b) that is objective without being absolutist, (c) that understands that ethical judgements are relative without embracing relativism, and (d) that tolerates – indeed, welcomes – some moral differences without being irresolute.

The volume ends with "**Toward Reconciliation in Ethics**" by *James P. Sterba*. *Sterba* claims that despite the apparent deep differences between competing normative ethical theories, many theories significantly overlap. He identifies three commonalities. First, he argues that libertarians, with their austere moral universe, are committed to recognizing basic rights to welfare for all individuals. He then argues that consequentialists, especially given their recent penchant for employing contractarian methodology, can be shown to place constraints on attempts to maximize utility, constraints not unlike those that nonconsequentialists endorse. Finally, he discusses feminist critiques against standard western moral philosophy. He claims that an appropriately modified contractarianism can satisfy feminist criticisms, while maintaining contractarianism's inherent plausibility.

Prospects for Future Ethical Theory

Although this volume does not explicitly discuss the history of ethics, some elements of that history are evident in the discussions of individual authors. Nor does this volume pretend to discuss all the relevant issues or to provide a final solution to the questions that have plagued philosophers for thousands of years. Its aim is more modest: to provide a way-station on the long and distinguished journey of ethical theory. My hope is that it not only reliably captures the current state of debate, but will prompt further productive work in ethics.

References

Ayer, A. J.: *Language, Truth, and Logic* (2nd edn.) (New York: Dover Publications, 1952/ 1946).

Darwall, S.: *Philosophical Ethics* (Boulder, CO: Westview Press, 1998).

Kagan, S.: *Normative Ethics* (Boulder, CO: Westview Press, 1998).

Nowell-Smith, P. H.: *Ethics* (New York: Philosophical Library, 1957).

Rachels, J.: "Introduction: Moral Philosophy in the Twentieth Century." In S. Kahn and J. G. Haber (eds.), *20th Century Ethical Theory* (Saddle River, NJ: Prentice-Hall, 1997).

Part I

Meta-Ethics

Chapter 1

Moral Realism

Michael Smith

In the past twenty years or so the debate over moral realism has become a major focus of philosophical activity. Unfortunately, however, as a glance at the enormous literature the debate has generated makes clear, there is still no consensus as to what, precisely, it would take to be a moral realist (Sayre-McCord 1988a). My aims in this essay are thus twofold: first, to clarify what is at stake in the debate over realism, and, second, to explain why, as it seems to me, the realist's stance is so much more plausible than the alternatives.

Moral Realism vs. Nihilism vs. Expressivism

What do moral realists believe? The standard answer is that they believe two things. First, they believe that the sentences we use when we make moral claims – sentences like "Torturing babies is wrong" and "Keeping promises is right" – are capable of being either true or false, and, second, they believe that some such sentences really are true. Moral realism thus contrasts with two quite distinct kinds of view.

The first view shares realism's first commitment, but rejects the second. According to this first alternative, when we make claims about acts being right and wrong we intend thereby to make claims about the way the world is – we intend to say something capable of being either true or false – but none of these sentences really are true. When we engage in moral talk we presuppose that rightness and wrongness are features that acts could possess, but we are in error. There are no such features for acts to possess. This view generally goes under the name of Nihilism or the Error Theory (Nietzsche 1887; Mackie 1977).

The second more radical view shares neither commitment. According to this view, the sentences we use when we make moral claims are not used with the intention of saying something that is capable of being either true or false. We do not use them in an attempt to make claims about the way the world is. By contrast with

Nihilism, we therefore do not presuppose that rightness and wrongness are features that acts could possess. Rather we use moral sentences to express our feelings about acts, people, states of the world, and the like. When we say "Torturing babies is wrong" it is as if we were saying "Boo for torturing babies!" This view generally goes under the name of Expressivism or Non-Cognitivism (Hare 1952; Gibbard 1990; Blackburn 1994).

Expressivism and Nihilism share a conception of the world as value-free and so devoid of any moral nature. However they differ in a crucial respect as well. Because Nihilism insists that moral thought and talk presupposes that rightness and wrongness are features of acts, it sees the value-free nature of the world as something that demands a reform of moral practice: we can hardly sincerely continue to assert falsehoods once we know them to be falsehoods. Moral thought and talk thus has the same status as religious thought and talk once we become convinced atheists. By contrast expressivism holds that the value-free nature of the world has no such consequence. It holds that moral thought and talk can proceed perfectly happily in the knowledge that the world is value-free because, in making moral claims, we never presupposed otherwise.

The upshot is that there are therefore two fundamental – if rather abstract and general – questions that need to be answered to resolve the moral realism debate. The first is whether sentences that ascribe rightness and wrongness to actions are capable of being true or false: if we answer "yes" to this question then we thereby refute Expressivism. And the second question, which presupposes an affirmative answer to the first, is whether any sentences ascribing rightness and wrongness to actions really are true: if we answer "yes" to this second question then we thereby eliminate the Nihilist option as well. We thereby commit ourselves to the truth of moral realism.

An Initial Difficulty

So described, moral realism looks to be a very demanding doctrine. It can go wrong in two distinct ways: perhaps it wrongly supposes that sentences ascribing rightness and wrongness to actions are capable of truth and falsehood; or, granting that it is right about that, perhaps it wrongly supposes that some of these sentences really are true. However, as we will see, the real danger is that moral realism, so understood, is insufficiently demanding.

The distinctive feature of the two abstract and general questions just asked is that they each involve semantic ascent: that is, they each speak of a feature that must be possessed by the sentences we use when we make moral claims, or a relation that must obtain between these sentences and the world. But the fact that they each involve semantic ascent poses an initial difficulty. If a commitment to the truth of moral realism comes by answering "yes" to these two abstract and general questions, then it looks like such commitment might come cheaply, at least to competent speakers of English who have any moral commitments at all. Let me illustrate the difficulty.

Like most people reading this essay, I have various moral commitments. For example, I am quite confident that torturing babies is wrong. As a competent speaker of English, I am therefore willing to say so by using the English sentence "Torturing babies is wrong". Imagine me saying this out loud:

Torturing babies is wrong.

Moreover, as a competent speaker of English, I am also willing to say so by not just *using* this sentence of English, but also by *mentioning* it. Imagine me saying this out loud:

"Torturing babies is wrong" is true.

or even

"Torturing babies is wrong" is really true.

This is because, in common parlance, mentioning this sentence, and saying of it that it is true, is simply an alternative way of saying what I could have said by using the sentence.

" 'Torturing babies is wrong' is true" and " 'Torturing babies is wrong' is really true" are simply long-winded ways of saying that torturing babies is wrong, ways that involve semantic ascent.

Given the initial characterization of what it takes to be a moral realist, it therefore seems to follow that I am a moral realist. After all, since I willingly assert the truth of "Torturing babies is wrong" it follows that I think that the sentences I use when I make moral claims – sentences like "Torturing babies is wrong" – are both capable of being true or false and that some of these sentences really are true . . . Something has clearly gone wrong. Perhaps a commitment to moral realism follows from the mere fact that I have moral commitments, together with the fact that I am a competent speaker of English, but it seems very unlikely. But what exactly has gone wrong?

An obvious suggestion is that the surface grammar of moral sentences is potentially misleading, masking some deeper metaphysical fact. Though we *say* that these sentences are true and false, this is loose talk. What moral realists really believe, the suggestion might be, is that the sentences we use when we make moral claims are capable of being true or false *strictly speaking*, rather than merely *loosely speaking*. Everything thus turns on what it is to speak strictly, as opposed to loosely, when we say of sentences that they are true or false.

Minimalism

What do the words "true" and "false" mean, strictly speaking? One very popular view nowadays is *minimalism about truth* (Horwich 1990; Wright 1992). According to this view, the role of the words "true" and "false" in our language is simply to enable us to register our agreement and disagreement with what people say without going to the trouble of using all the words that they used to say it.

For example, suppose A says "Snow is white, and grass is green, and roses are red, and violets are blue", and that B wants to register his agreement. If the word "true" wasn't a part of our language then, in order to do so, B would have to quote what A said and then disquote. He would have to say "A said 'Snow is white' and snow is white, and A said 'Grass is green' and grass is green, and A said 'Roses are red' and roses are red, and A said 'Violets are blue' and violets are blue." But that requires B to use more than twice the number of words that A used. The role of the word "true", according to minimalism, is simply to allow B to register his agreement more efficiently. Because we have the word "true" in our language, B can quantify over all of the things that A said and then say, all at once, "Everything B said is true."

The upshot, according to minimalism, is that all there is to say about the meaning of the words "true" and "false" strictly speaking is precisely what we said when we noted the initial difficulty. All there is to know about the meaning of the word "true" is that, when "s" is a meaningful sentence of English, and when "s" is true" is also a meaningful sentence of English, someone who says " 's' is true" could just as well have disquoted and said instead "s". When you mention or quote an English sentence, and meaningfully append "is true" to it, that is just another way of saying what could have been said by using or disquoting that English sentence. Minimalism about truth thus suggests that when I say " 'Torturing babies is wrong' is true", rather than "Torturing babies is wrong", I *am* speaking strictly, for I thereby register the appropriateness of disquotation.

Accordingly, it seems to me that we should therefore put a very first realist option on the table. *Minimal Moral Realists* believe three things. First, they believe that the sentences we use when we say that actions are right and wrong are true or false strictly speaking, rather than merely loosely speaking; second, they believe that some of these sentences really are true; and third, they believe that, strictly speaking, the meanings of the words "true" and "false" are fully explained by the minimalist's story.

Minimal Moral Realism is a very cheap doctrine indeed: if you accept the minimalist's story about truth then, if you have any moral commitments at all, you are a moral realist – or, at any rate, you are a Minimal Moral Realist. Nihilism and Expressivism are eliminated in one fell swoop. The obvious question to ask is thus whether we should all be Minimal Moral Realists. The answer depends on something orthogonal to the moral realism debate itself: the plausibility of the minimalist's story about truth. As I will now argue, however, the minimalist's story is seriously inadequate.

The Main Problem with Minimalism

Minimalists about truth tell us that all there is to know about the meaning of the word "true" is that, when "s" is a meaningful sentence of English, and when "s" is true" is also a meaningful sentence of English, someone who says " 's' is true" could just as well have disquoted and said instead "s". But this story – at least in the form in which it has just been told – buries an extra, crucially important, piece of information about truth, for it fails to tell us the conditions that need to be satisfied by "s" in order for " 's' is true" to be a meaningful sentence of English. In other words, it fails to tell us what it is about a sentence that is capable of truth and falsehood that *makes* it capable of truth and falsehood. Let me spell out this problem in greater detail (Jackson, Oppy, and Smith 1994).

Everyone agrees that "Snow is white" and " 'Snow is white' is true" are both meaningful sentences of English. Moreover, everyone also agrees that though "Hooray for the Chicago Bulls!" is a meaningful sentence of English, " 'Hooray for the Chicago Bulls!' is true" is not. But why is there this difference between the two sentences? What do the meaningful strings of English words that are truth-apt have in common, that they don't have in common with those strings of English words that are non-truth-apt? What feature of the truth-apt sentences of English makes them truth-apt? Minimalism about truth, as so far characterized, does not provide us with an answer. Yet surely an answer to this question is part of what we need to know, when we know all there is to know about the meaning of the word "true".

Minimalists about truth typically insist that they can provide a suitably minimal answer to this question (Wright 1992; Horwich 1992). Consider three strings of English words: "Snow is white", "Torturing babies is wrong" and "Hooray for the Chicago Bulls!" The standard minimalist suggestion is that the first two strings of English words are truth-apt, and the third isn't, because of a purely *syntactic* feature that they possess and the third lacks. The first two strings of English words, they suggest, are of an appropriate grammatical type to figure in a whole array of contexts: the antecedents of conditionals (for example, "If snow is white, then it is the same color as writing paper" and "If torturing babies is wrong then I will support the existence of a law against it" are both well-formed sentences), propositional attitude contexts ("John believes that snow is white" and "John believes that torturing babies is wrong" are both well-formed sentences), and so on and so forth. But the third, by contrast, is not of the appropriate grammatical type to figure in these contexts (neither "If hooray for the Chicago Bulls then I will get tickets to see them play next season" nor "John believes that hooray for the Chicago Bulls" are well-formed sentences). It is this syntactic feature of the first two sentences that, according to the minimalists, makes it appropriate for them to figure in " '_____' is true" contexts, and it is the fact that the third lacks this feature that makes it incapable of figuring in such contexts. So, at any rate, minimalists typically argue.

However, for reasons Lewis Carroll made plain in his wonderful poem *Jabberwocky*, this minimalist account of truth-aptitude is unsatisfactory (1872). "'Twas brillig, and the slithy toves did gyre and gimble in the wabe" looks like a conjunction of sentences which, syntactically, are of the appropriate grammatical type to figure in the antecedents of conditionals (thus, for example, "If the toves are gyring and gimbling in the wabe then I will watch them" looks for all the world to be a well-formed sentence), to be embedded in propositional attitude contexts ("I believe that the toves are gyring and gimbling" looks to be a well-formed sentence), and so on. Indeed, it looks like these sentences can have "true" predicated of them ("'The toves are gyring and gimbling in the wabe' is true" looks to be a well-formed sentence). But it doesn't follow that these sentences are truth-apt. Indeed, we know that they aren't truth-apt because, notwithstanding their syntax, they are nonsense sentences, sentences without any meaning whatsoever. They are therefore incapable of being either true or false. The idea that mere syntax is sufficient to establish truth-aptitude is thus absurd.

We must therefore ask what a sentence with the right syntax must have added to it in order to make it truth-apt. For example, what feature would Carroll's sentence "The slithy toves did gyre and gimble in the wabe" have to have added to it, in order to make it truth-apt? The answer is both straightforward and commonsensical: the sentence would have to be meaningful, rather than nonsense, and for this to be the case the constituent words in the sentence – words like "tove", "gyre", "gimble" and "wabe" – would have to be associated with patterns of usage which make it plain what information about the world people who use the words in those ways intend to convey when they use them.

But if this is right then it seems to follow immediately that truth-aptitude cannot be a minimal matter. If sentences which are truth-apt have to be sentences that could, in principle at least, be used to convey information, then they must be sentences that could, in principle, be used to give the content of people's beliefs (or, in order to avoid Moorean problems with meaningful sentences like "I have no beliefs", they must be sentences that are suitably related by some grammatical transformation to sentences that could, in principle, be used to give the contents of people's beliefs (I will ignore this complication in what follows)). But no minimalist story could be told about the sentences that are suited to play this role. It is a substantive fact about a sentence that its constituent words are associated with patterns of usage that allow them to convey information about particular aspects of the world. It is this substantive fact about a sentence that we discover when we discover which belief it can be used to express. And it is therefore this substantive fact about a sentence that we need to discover in order to establish that it is truth-apt.

We are now in a position to identify the main problem with Minimal Moral Realism. Minimal Moral Realism assumes the truth of minimalism about truth, and so buys into the minimalist's assumption that truth-aptitude is itself a minimal matter. But this assumption is mistaken. "Keeping promises is right" may indeed be a meaningful sentence of English of the appropriate grammatical type to figure in the antecedents of conditionals, propositional attitude contexts, and the like, but it does not follow from this alone that it can be used to give the content of people's beliefs. Indeed, as we will see, many argue that there is a principled reason for supposing that such a sentence could not give the content of anyone's belief.

Expressivism and Internalism

We now know what would have to be the case for sentences like "Torturing babies is wrong" and "Keeping promises is right" to be capable of being true or false, strictly speaking. The words contained in these sentences – words like "right" and "wrong" – would have to be associated with patterns of usage that make it plain what information about the world people's use of them is intended to convey. The question to ask is therefore whether the patterns of usage associated with the words "right" and "wrong" have this striking feature. Can we give an account of the information about the world that the use of such words is intended to convey? Many people argue that we cannot.

They begin by noting the very striking fact that people's moral views tell us something about their dispositions to action. For example, it would be extremely puzzling if, having announced your firm conviction that the right thing to do is to give money to Oxfam, you then claimed utter indifference to actually giving money to Oxfam when the opportunity arose. Perhaps your indifference could be explained away. Depression and weakness of will can, after all, sap our desire to do what we think is right. But, absent some such explanation, it seems that your indifference would give the lie to your announced conviction. It would reveal you to be a hypocrite. This is why, when it comes to expressing moral views, actions speak louder than words.

This striking fact is called the *internalism constraint* (Hare 1952, ch.1; Blackburn 1984, pp. 187–9). According to internalists, there is an internal or necessary connection between the moral judgements we make and our motivations. If true, internalism places a constraint on the proper use of moral sentences. It tells us that it is a constraint on the proper use of "Torturing babies is wrong" that someone who sincerely utters it is averse to torturing babies, at least other things being equal (in other words, absent depression, weakness of will, and the like). Likewise, it tells us that it is a constraint on the proper use of "Keeping promises is right" that someone who sincerely utters it desires to keep promises, at least other things being equal.

Expressivists seize on the truth of internalism and ask the obvious question. How could the proper use of moral sentences be constrained by the truth of internalism if they could be used to give the contents of people's beliefs? After all, when we consider sentences that can uncontroversially be used to give the contents of people's beliefs – sentences like "Snow is white", "London is north of Paris", "If you waste your time in school then you will diminish your life prospects in the future", and the like – we note that they can all be used by people perfectly sincerely *no matter what* pattern of desire and aversion these people have. Why should there be any difference with moral sentences?

For example, it is not a constraint on the proper use of the sentence "If you waste your time in school then you will diminish your life prospects in the future" that someone who sincerely utters this sentence desires people to waste their time in school, or is averse to people wasting their time in school, or is indifferent to people wasting their time in school. The belief that wasting your time in school will diminish your life prospects in the future can quite happily coexist with any of these attitudes. Moreover, we find this same pattern of possibilities when we consider any other sentence that can uncontroversially be used to express the content of people's beliefs. So, Expressivists ask, why don't we find that same pattern of possibilities in the case of the sentences "Torturing babies is wrong" and "Keeping promises is right", if they too express beliefs? Why can't the belief that keeping promises is right co-exist perfectly happily with the desire to keep promises, aversion to keeping promises, and indifference to keeping promises? What is it about this belief, if there is any such belief, that makes it require the presence of a desire to keep promises? Isn't that an astonishingly peculiar feature for this particular belief to have?

The answer, according to Expressivists, is that we don't find that same pattern of possibilities because the sentences "Torturing babies is wrong" and "Keeping promises is right" *cannot* be used to give the contents of anyone's beliefs (Jackson, Oppy, and Smith 1994). They cannot be used to give the contents of anyone's beliefs because there are no such beliefs for anyone to express. Beliefs are states that give information about the world. As such, they can coexist with any pattern of desire, indifference and aversion. So since people's moral views cannot coexist with any pattern of desire, indifference and aversion, it follows that the proper role of the sentences people use when they tell us about their moral views cannot be to express such states. The proper role of "Torturing babies is wrong" is rather to express aversion to torturing babies, and the proper use of "Keeping promises is right" is to express the desire to keep promises, not to express any belief.

Accordingly, Expressivists hold that moral sentences, when properly understood, are really on a par with other uncontroversially non-truth-apt sentences, sentences like "Hooray for the Chicago Bulls!" The latter sentence is non-truth-apt not because of its surface syntax, according to Expressivism, but rather because it is properly used to express a pro-attitude towards the Chicago Bulls, rather than any belief about the Chicago Bulls. Likewise, sentences about actions being right and wrong are non-truth-apt because they are properly used to express desires and aversions with regard to those actions, not beliefs about them. When we say of moral sentences that they are true or false, and when we talk of moral beliefs, we are therefore at best speaking loosely, not strictly. Strictly speaking, moral sentences cannot be true or false. They cannot be true or false; they cannot be used to convey information about the way anything is. Strictly speaking, there are no moral beliefs for anyone to express.

Expressivists are thus best seen as offering a challenge to both moral realists and Nihilists. They challenge both these theorists to explain how the use of moral sentences could be constrained by the truth of internalism if their proper use was to convey information. What information is it such that, in order to possess that information, you have to have certain desires or aversions? Expressivists intend this question to be rhetorical. Even so, many opponents of Expressivism – both moral realists and Nihilists – have tried to answer the challenge. But in order properly to answer the challenge we can now see that they must do more than simply stamp their feet and insist that moral sentences *can* be used to give the contents of beliefs. They must specify, in precise terms, what the content of these beliefs is. Let's focus in on a particular example of an attempt to do just that.

Naturalistic Moral Realism

As I said at the outset, I am quite confident that torturing babies is wrong, and I am quite willing to say so by using the English sentence "Torturing babies is wrong". But if my use of this sentence expresses some belief I have about torturing babies, then it is fair and reasonable to ask what the content of that belief is. What feature of the world would make it true that torturing babies is wrong? It might be thought that we could just give the glib answer: torturing babies would have to have the feature of being wrong. But it turns out that I have to be able to say much more than this.

If there is some feature of torturing babies that makes it true that torturing babies is wrong, then, in giving an account of that feature, we are constrained by our conception of the world in which we live. This means, in turn, that we are constrained by the truth of *naturalism*, the view that the world is amenable to study through empirical science. This is because, given the success of the empirical sciences in providing explanations of various aspects of the world, it is extremely plausible to hold that the world is *entirely* amenable to study through the empirical sciences. Naturalism accordingly entails that the only features we have any reason to believe objects have are one and all naturalistic features, features which are themselves posits, or composites of posits, of empirical science. The upshot is therefore that, if any form of moral realism is true at all, then it must be a form of Naturalistic Moral Realism (Railton 1993a, 1993b).

Naturalistic Moral Realism holds not only that some of the sentences that we use to make moral claims are capable of being true and false, and that some really are true, but also that what makes the true ones true are naturalistic features of the world, features amenable to understanding in scientific terms. If moral features exist at all then, given the truth of naturalism, it follows that they too must be features that can be discovered either directly by observation, or by inference from observational information. Moral beliefs must therefore have naturalistic contents, for only so could they be made true by naturalistic features of the world.

We can now ask a more specific version of the question we asked earlier. If, as Naturalistic Moral Realists suppose, the sentence "Torturing babies is wrong" can be used to give the content of a belief, then what *naturalistic feature* does someone with this belief thereby believe torturing babies to have? This is the question Naturalistic Moral Realists must answer. Moreover, they must answer this question by appealing to some constraint on the way in which we use moral words. There must be some constraint on our use of moral words that makes these words apt to pick out a natural feature of acts. It is not difficult to see what that constraint might be.

By all accounts it is a conceptual truth that the moral features of acts *supervene* on their naturalistic features: two acts which are identical in all of their natural features must be alike in their moral features as well. It thus follows that if we acknowledge that a particular act is right, but insist that another act, exactly the same in every naturalistic respect, isn't right, then we thereby mis-use the word "right". Likewise for "wrong". When we apply "right" and "wrong" to acts, we are thus constrained to do so in the belief that the acts in question have some naturalistic feature that *warrants* the ascription of "right" or "wrong". This is the *supervenience constraint* (Jackson 1997).

The fact that we are constrained to use moral words in the way just described – the fact that we are constrained to ascribe moral features in virtue of naturalistic features – requires an explanation, however. Why can't we say that acts are alike in all naturalistic respects, and yet differ morally? Why can't moral features float free of naturalistic features altogether? The obvious answer, the answer favored by Naturalistic Moral Realists, is that this is because moral features *are* natural features.

If this is agreed, then the only question left to answer is *which* natural features warrant the ascription of various moral features to acts. Once we know the answer to this question then, according to Naturalistic Moral Realists, we should simply conclude that moral features are those natural features. For example, if the naturalistic feature of acts that warrants the ascription of rightness turns out to be utility maximization, then, according to Naturalistic Moral Realists, rightness *is* utility maximization. The answer to the question 'Which naturalistic feature does someone with the belief that torturing babies is wrong thereby believe torturing babies to have?' will then turn out to be the feature of failing to maximize utility.

The Open Question Argument

Elegant though this suggestion might be, it faces a serious objection. The objection was first put forward by G. E. Moore (1903). To stick with our example, Moore agreed that acts of utility maximization might always have the feature of being right, but he insisted that we resist concluding that the properties of maximizing utility and being right are the same property. They are, he insisted, quite distinct properties. The argument he gave for this conclusion is his famous Open Question Argument.

Suppose, for reductio, that rightness and utility maximization were indeed one and the same feature of acts. Then, according to Moore, it would follow that "rightness" and "utility maximization" are analytically or a priori equivalent. But it is quite clear that "rightness" and "utility maximization" are not analytically equivalent. After all, if they were analytically equivalent then the question "This act maximizes utility, but is it right?" would have to be one whose answer is immediately obvious to anyone who understands the meanings of the words used, being equivalent to the question "This act maximizes utility, but does it maximize utility?" However, as a moment's reflection reveals, the questions clearly are not equivalent. We can, without self-contradiction, agree that an act maximizes utility but deny that it is right. It therefore follows that the question "This act maximizes utility, but is it right?" is not a *closed question* – one whose answer is immediately obvious to anyone who understands the meanings of the words – but is rather an *open question* – one whose answer is open to reasoned argument. "Rightness" and "utility maximization" are thus not analytic equivalents. They do not pick out the same feature.

If the Open Question Argument is sound then it delivers a very strong conclusion indeed. For, as Moore pointed out, it doesn't seem to matter which of the various natural features of acts we consider. It would always be open to reasoned argument whether an act with any of the various natural features we might care to consider is right. It is, for example, an open question whether an act of keeping a promise is right, an open question whether an act which advances my own well-being is right, an open question whether acts that I desire to perform are right, and so we could go on and on. No matter which natural features we choose, it seems that it is never obvious whether an act with such features is right. It is always open to reasoned argument. So, if sound, the Open Question Argument seems to show that rightness is not identical with any natural feature of acts at all. It thus constitutes a decisive refutation of Naturalistic Moral Realism. But if we shouldn't accept Naturalistic Moral Realism, then which theory should we accept instead?

Non-Naturalistic Moral Realism

Moore himself thought, on the basis of the Open Question Argument, that we should reject naturalism altogether and admit a realm of extra, *sui generis*, non-natural properties into our ontology. Moore thus embraced *Non-Naturalistic Moral Realism*. He believed not only that some of the sentences we use to make moral claims are capable of being true and false, and that some really are true, but also that what makes the true ones true are non-naturalistic states of the world, states that elude understanding in scientific terms. Beliefs about which acts are right and wrong are thus beliefs about the non-natural features possessed by acts. Moreover, according to Moore, some such beliefs represent the world to be the way it really is. Moore was no naturalist.

However the problems with Non-Naturalistic Moral Realism are evident and overwhelming (Blackburn 1984, ch. 6). The first problem is that it must explain how we come by knowledge of these extra, spooky, non-natural properties. Unsurprisingly, however, Moore had no explanation. He could hardly claim that we come by knowledge of them via observation, for any property knowable in that way is, by definition, naturalistic. But neither could he claim that we come by knowledge of them via inference from any of the naturalistic features of acts, for that is precisely what the Open Question Argument (allegedly) shows to be impossible. The only options left seem to multiply the mysteries. For example, we might suppose that there is some non-empirical sort of observation, a sort of spooky sixth sense which allows us to detect the presence of spooky non-natural properties. But as soon as the idea is stated it is plain that it is, in reality, too absurd even to contemplate.

The second problem for Non-Naturalistic Moral Realism is that it must explain why there aren't possible worlds in which the non-natural properties that Moore supposes to be identical with moral properties float free of the natural properties with which they are coinstantiated in actuality. And again, unsurprisingly, Moore had no explanation of why this possibility is ruled out. If non-natural properties are distinct from natural properties then, it seems, we should be able to pull them apart modally. But, given that moral properties supervene on natural properties, it follows that we cannot pull them apart modally. He was thus forced to view the supervenience of the non-natural on the natural as a brute mystery.

The Open Question Argument, Nihilism and Expressivism

By and large, philosophers have therefore tended to think that even if it is sound, the Open Question Argument, properly understood, gives no support whatsoever to Non-Naturalistic Moral Realism. However there has been no great consensus as to what, precisely, it shows instead.

One possibility is that though the argument succeeds in establishing the conceptual truth that we *conceive* of moral features as non-naturalistic, and hence succeeds in showing that our beliefs about which acts are right and wrong are one and all beliefs about the non-natural features possessed by acts, Moore went wrong in supposing that any such features are instantiated. Viewed in this light, what the three problems just described show is that such non-natural features are nowhere instantiated in actuality. No acts have such non-natural features, and hence all our moral beliefs are false. Accordingly, on this way of thinking about it, the proper conclusion of the Open Question Argument is not a form of moral realism, but rather Nihilism. The problem with this way of thinking about Moore's argument, however, is that it concedes the intelligibility of Moorean non-natural properties, whereas the three problems just described make it look like non-natural properties aren't really intelligible at all.

Another, and more popular, suggestion has therefore been to suppose that the Open Question Argument constitutes a reductio of the very idea that there are moral features (Hare 1952; Blackburn 1994). According to this suggestion, the reason we can't come by knowledge of the moral features of acts via an inference from knowledge of their naturalistic features is because that would require that there are two distinct ways the world could be – a naturalistic way and a moral way – which stand in a certain logical relation to each other. But aren't two ways the world could be, there is only one way, a naturalistic way. The upshot, according to this suggestion, is that the claim that the world is a certain way morally isn't true, strictly speaking. The role of a moral claim isn't to represent the world as being a certain way, and hence isn't to give the content of any belief, but is rather to express desires or aversions. Thus, according to this way of thinking, the Open Question Argument constitutes a second, and many think decisive, line of argument for Expressivism.

The problem with this alternative way of thinking about Moore's Open Question Argument, however, is that it assumes that Expressivism itself somehow manages to escape the clutches of the Open Question Argument (Smith 1998). In fact, however, Expressivism itself is extremely vulnerable to a version of the argument. This is because, though Expressivism sets itself against the view that (say) "Torturing babies is wrong" is analytically equivalent to some naturalistic claim about the way the world is – for that would assume something Expressivism takes to be false, namely that wrongness is a feature of acts – it does so by insisting that sentences like "Michael judges that torturing babies is wrong" *is* analytically equivalent to some naturalistic claim: specifically, it is analytically equivalent to "Michael expresses his aversion to torturing babies". But now it seems that we can run a version of the Open Question Argument. Here is how it goes.

If "Michael judges that torturing babies is wrong" and "Michael expresses his aversion to torturing babies" were analytically equivalent then the question "Michael expresses his aversion to torturing babies, but does he judge that torturing babies is wrong?" would have to be one whose answer is immediately obvious to anyone who understands the meanings of the words used. However, as a moment's reflection reveals, the questions clearly are not equivalent. We can, without self-contradiction, agree that Michael expresses his aversion to torturing babies, but deny that he thereby judges it to be wrong. But, if this is right, then it follows that the question "Michael expresses his aversion to torturing babies, but does he judge it to be wrong?" is not a closed question – one whose answer is immediately obvious to anyone who understands the meanings of the words – but is rather an open question – one whose answer is open to reasoned argument. "Michael expresses his aversion to torturing babies" and "Michael judges that torturing babies is wrong" are thus not analytically equivalent. They do not pick out the same feature of the world.

Moreover, as with the earlier application of the Open Question Argument, it doesn't seem to matter which of the various natural features of Michael we consider. It would always be open to reasoned argument whether, when Michael expresses any of the various natural features we might care to consider – various complexes of desire, second-order desires, or whatever – he is thereby judging that torturing babies is wrong. If sound, the Open Question Argument therefore seems to show that Michael's judging it wrong to torture babies isn't analytically equivalent to any natural feature of Michael either. It thus constitutes a decisive refutation of Expressivism.

But now we have surely proved too much. After all, we said at the outset that the only options available are Nihilism, Expressivism, or some form of moral realism: that is, either Naturalistic or Non-Naturalistic Moral Realism. Yet what we have just seen is that, if sound, the Open Question Argument, together with ancillary premises, rules out *all* these options. That surely cannot be. The only conclusion to draw is therefore that, properly understood, the Open Question Argument is *unsound*. But where-in lies the mistake in the argument?

The Naturalistic Moral Realist's First Response to the Open Question Argument

Many contemporary Naturalistic Moral Realists argue that the flaw lies in the assumption that it somehow follows from the fact, conceding it to be a fact, that "rightness" and "the property of maximizing utility" are not analytically or a priori equivalent, that these terms pick out different features. That this is a flaw is, they insist, evident from examples with which we are familiar in empirical science (Brink 1989; Darwall, Gibbard, and Railton 1992).

For example, "Water" is not analytically or a priori equivalent to "H2O", but empirical science teaches us that water is just H_2O. "Redness" is not analytically or a priori equivalent to "surface reflectance property α, but empirical science teaches us that redness is just a certain surface reflectance property that we will, for convenience, call "a". So, in this particular case, they argue that the Open Question Argument assumes, wrongly, that if rightness and the property of maximizing utility were one and the same property, then it would have to be an a priori truth, one discovered by reflection on the meanings of the words "rightness" and "the property of maximizing utility", but it thereby overlooks the possibility that it may be an a posteriori truth, one discovered through observation and inference. Naturalistic Moral Realists who offer this reply to the Open Question Argument therefore face a challenge. They must show how it could be an a posteriori truth that these terms pick out the same feature. Unfortunately, however, those who face up to this challenge find that they simply run into the Open Question Argument all over again.

According to many Naturalistic Moral Realists, for example, the reason it is an a posteriori truth that rightness is the property of maximizing utility is that we invoke rightness and wrongness in order to explain various empirical phenomena, and then we discover, a posteriori, that the maximization of utility occupies the relevant explanatory role. For example, they argue that since, contingently, right actions have certain effects – they are causally responsible for a tendency towards social stability, for example – so it follows that we can fix the reference of the term "right" via the description "the property of acts, whatever it is, that is causally responsible for their tendency towards social stability."

Equipped with this reference fixing description, we can then investigate acts with this effect in order to find out which feature explains this tendency. If, say, we discover that the feature that is causally responsible is the maximization of utility, then we can conclude that rightness is the property of maximizing utility. Our conclusion will then be a posteriori, not a priori.

The answer is supposed to be straightforward because the explanation involved has the same structure as those we give in other less controversial cases. Since, contingently, red objects have certain effects – they cause those objects to look red to normal perceivers under standard conditions – so it follows that we can fix the reference of "redness" via the description "the property of objects, whatever it is, that causes them to look red to normal perceivers under standard conditions". Equipped with this reference fixing description we can then investigate the acts which have this effect in order to find out which feature explains this tendency. If, say, we discover that the feature that is causally responsible is surface reflectance property α, then we can conclude that redness is surface reflectance property α.

Unfortunately, however, this reply to the Open Question Argument is inadequate, and the reason why is perhaps already evident (Jackson 1997). Consider again the case of colors. True enough, we will not find a justification for thinking that redness is surface reflectance property α merely by reflecting on the meanings of the words "surface reflectance property α" and "redness". The fact that redness is surface reflectance property α is clearly something we discover a posteriori through empirical investigation. But in explaining how we come to make this discovery a posteriori, it is clear that we do in fact appeal to an a priori truth about redness. For we simply assumed that we can fix the reference of "redness" via the description "the property of objects, whatever it is, that causes them to look red to normal perceivers under standard conditions". But what sort of justification can we give for this claim? It clearly isn't supposed to be yet another a posteriori truth. Rather it is supposed to be an a priori truth, one which is either stipulated in the act of reference fixing itself or else discovered by reflection on the everyday meaning of the word "red". Either way, it is because we accept this claim a priori that we can move straight from the discovery that surface reflectance property α is the property that causes objects to look red to normal perceivers under standard conditions to the conclusion that surface reflectance property α is redness.

By analogy, then, even though it may well be an a posteriori truth that rightness is the property of maximizing utility, in the very argument we gave in support of this claim it is clear that we in fact appealed to another truth, but this time one which is supposed to be known a priori, about the relation between rightness and certain natural properties. For we simply assumed that we could fix the reference of "rightness" via the description, "the property of acts, whatever it is, that is causally responsible for their tendency towards social stability". But what sort of justification can be given for this claim? It clearly isn't supposed to be another a posteriori truth. Rather, it is supposed to be an a priori truth, one which is either stipulated in the act of reference fixing or else discovered by reflection on the everyday meaning of the word "right". Either way, it is precisely because we accept this claim a priori that we can move straight from the discovery that the property of maximizing utility is the property acts possess when they tend towards social stability to the conclusion that the property of maximizing utility is rightness.

This is an extremely important point, one which is quite devastating to those Naturalistic Moral Realists who think they can reply to Moore's Open Question Argument by insisting that, even though the terms "rightness" and "the property of maximizing utility" are not analytically or a priori equivalent, these terms none the less pick out the same feature of acts. For what they fail to remember is that Moore's Open Question Argument is supposed to refute *all* claims to the effect that "rightness" is analytically or a priori equivalent to a term ascribing natural features to acts, no matter which natural features are in question. If sound, it thus even refutes the claim that it is a priori that rightness is the property acts possess when they tend towards social stability. The alleged refutation goes like this: we can agree that an act has the property which is causally responsible for the tendency of acts towards social stability and yet, apparently without self-contradiction, deny that it is right, for it is an open question whether such acts are right, a matter for reasoned argument. "Rightness", we should thus conclude, cannot be a priori equivalent to "the property acts possess when they tend towards social stability".

This teaches us a valuable lesson. Naturalistic Moral Realists have no alternative but to face head-on the claim that we can, via the Open Question Argument, refute the claim that there is some naturalistic analytic or a priori equivalent for "rightness".

The Naturalistic Moral Realist's Second Response to the Open Question Argument

Moore claims to show that there is no naturalistic claim that is analytically or a priori equivalent to any moral claim by pointing out that it is always an open question whether an act with whichever naturalistic features we care to choose has some moral feature. It is always open to reasoned argument. In order to see where this argument goes wrong, we need to think more generally about the project of conceptual analysis (Smith 1994, ch. 2; Jackson 1997).

When we try to analyze a concept, what are we trying to do? The answer is roughly this. There are all sorts of constraints on the way we use various words. Consider color words as an example. It is a constraint on the proper use of color words that we use them to pick out properties that cause us to have certain visual experiences; a constraint that we use them to pick out features that are more reliably detected in daylight than in the dark; a constraint that people's use of them is especially likely to be defective if there is something wrong with their eyes; and so on and so forth. When we try to come up with an analytic equivalent of "x is red", our task is to come up with something that captures this complex set of constraints: that is, to come up with an account of what "redness" means that entails them. When we say that "redness" and "the property of objects that causes them to look red to normal perceivers under standard conditions" are analytically or a priori equivalent this is what we have in mind.

If this is right, however, then the success or failure of an analysis is to be judged accordingly. It is not to be judged by the obviousness of the analysis, and nor is it to be judged by whether the analysis is open to reasoned argument. Indeed, if what we have just said is right then it will of course be open to reasoned argument whether or not an analysis is successful because it will be open to reasoned argument what the complex set of constraints on the use of the word being analyzed is and whether or not this complex set is entailed by the proposed analysis.

If an account of the project of conceptual analysis along these lines is right, however, then Moore's argument evidently fails altogether to refute the claim that "rightness" has a naturalistic analytic or a priori equivalent. Consider, for example, the claim that "rightness" is analytically equivalent to "the property of acts that is causally responsible for their tendency towards social stability". It is irrelevant whether or not it is obvious that this is so; irrelevant whether it is open to reasoned argument. The only relevant question is whether, on reflection, we think that this analysis entails the complex set of constraints on the way in which we use the word "right". If it does, then it is analytically equivalent, notwithstanding the fact that it isn't obvious.

In many ways this brings us to where we are today in the moral realism debate. The Open Question Argument isn't sound, but it does make clear the enormous task that lies before Naturalistic Moral Realists. To repeat, Naturalistic Moral Realists must give a naturalistic account of the contents of moral beliefs; an account of the naturalistic feature that they take to be identical with various moral features. But what the Open Question Argument brings out is that, in doing so, they must find naturalistic features that are analytically – or, anyway, a priori – equivalent to those moral features. It need not be obvious that the naturalistic features and moral features are analytically equivalent, of course. It may be open to reasoned argument. But, at the end of the day, it must be demonstrable, on the basis of reflection on the ways in which we use moral words, that the naturalistic features they identify are one and the same as moral features.

Externalist Naturalistic Moral Realism

The naturalistic theories that have been claimed to fit this bill fall into two quite distinct categories. The first are versions of Externalist Naturalistic Moral Realism (hereafter "Externalist Realism" for short) (Sturgeon 1985; Railton 1986; Brink 1989). This is the view that though we can, by reflecting on the ways in which we use moral words, find a naturalistic equivalent for the term "rightness", the naturalistic equivalent we come up with will leave it completely open whether someone who believes an act to be right will desire to perform that act, or be indifferent to performing it, or be averse to performing it. The sort of theory described earlier which claims that rightness fills a distinctive explanatory role, the role of underwriting a tendency towards social stability, is an example of such a theory. Externalist Realists thus face a dual task.

On the one hand, they must come up with an explanation of why, when we reflect on the way in which we use moral words, we should conclude that rightness has the naturalistic equivalent they posit. For example, if we consider again the theory which holds that rightness is the property of acts, whatever it is, that is causally responsible for their tendency towards social stability, Externalist Realists must tell us what is it about the way in which we use moral words that is supposed to make this particular claim seem credible. The vast literature on moral explanations is perhaps best seen as addressing this issue (Harman 1977; Sturgeon 1985; Railton 1986; Boyd 1988). As I understand it, the claim Externalist Realists make in that literature is that "rightness" is a term whose meaning is fixed by a causal explanatory theory which assigns rightness a certain characteristic explanatory role. "Rightness" is thus, in a sense, much like the term "electron". Both terms serve to pick out a feature in virtue of the characteristic causal role that that feature occupies.

On the other hand, however, Externalist Realists must also try to explain away the fact that so many people have been inclined to think that our use of moral words is subject to the internalist constraint. If what we believe, in believing an act to be right, is (say) that the act has the feature that is causally responsible for a tendency towards social stability, then why have so many people been inclined to think that possession of this belief requires a desire to perform such an act, at least other things being equal: that is absent depression, weakness of will, and the like? It is surely an entirely contingent matter whether someone with such a belief will desire to perform such an act, whether they are depressed and weak of will or not. So how did so many philosophers get it wrong for so long? For many, the very fact that Externalist Realism is incapable of capturing the internalist constraint is a decisive reason to reject the theory. But though I am inclined to agree with this objection, I do not want to rest the case against Externalist Realism wholly on it.

Suppose we grant the idea that "rightness" picks out a property in virtue of its explanatory role. Still, mustn't the explanatory role in question be one that somehow guarantees the possibility of giving a justification for acting in the way that is deemed to be right (Sayre-McCord 1988b)? After all, by all accounts, the fact that an act is right implies that there is at least some justification for performing it. Someone who says "Though it would be right to act in that way, there is no justification at all for doing it" mis-uses the word "right". Yet the most remarkable feature of Externalist Realism is that it makes this connection altogether mysterious. Focus again on the version of Externalist Realism developed above. The most remarkable feature of the suggestion that rightness is that property, whatever it is, possessed by acts that tend towards social stability must surely be that an act may conduce towards to social stability but be one that there is no justification *at all* for anyone's performing. Explanatory role and justificatory potential just seem to be quite different things.

At the end of the day the really difficult task facing Externalist Realism is thus to come up with an account of the explanatory role of rightness which makes that role connect in some constitutive way with the possibility of giving a justification. Until Externalist Realists come up with such an account, their theory will look like it fails to capture one of the most important constraints on the way in which we use moral words.

Internalist Naturalistic Moral Realism

This brings us to what seems to me to be the most plausible version of moral realism. Internalist Naturalistic Moral Realists (hereafter "Internalist Realists" for short) agree with Externalist Realists that we can characterize rightness in terms of its distinctive explanatory role, but they hold that the explanatory role characteristic of rightness is, broadly speaking, that of eliciting desire under certain idealized conditions of reflection. Consider a specific version of the theory, by way of illustration (Smith 1994).

According to this version of the theory, rightness is that feature, whatever it is, that we would desire our acts to possess if our desires formed a set that is maximally informed, coherent and unified. The Internalist Realist's claim is that this analysis of rightness finds support in the way in which we use moral words. Nor is it difficult to see what reasons they might give. After all, as we have just seen, when we say that acting in a certain way in certain circumstances is right we thereby imply that there is some justification for our acting in that way in those circumstances. But facts about what there is a justification for doing, in various circumstances, are in turn plausibly thought to be facts about what we would advise ourselves to do if we were better placed to give ourselves advice: that is, more precisely, they are plausibly thought to be facts about what we would desire ourselves to do in those circumstances if our desires were immune to rational criticism. That is just what the theory says.

Of course, it might be thought that there are other ways of thinking about justification. But Internalist Realists argue that this particular analysis of the notion is amply supported by various other ways in which we use moral words. For example, it is agreed on nearly all sides that moral knowledge is a relatively a priori matter, at least in the following sense: if you equip people with a full description of the circumstances in which someone acts, then they can figure out whether the person acted rightly or wrongly by just thinking about the case hand. Someone who claimed that it would be impossible to figure out what is right by just thinking about the circumstances of action would be mis-using the word "right". Internalist Realists argue that this is well explained by the analysis just offered. It is because we can subject our desires about what is to be done in various circumstances to critical evaluation by just reflecting on our desires that moral knowledge seems to be such a relatively a priori matter.

Internalist Realists also claim that the fact that there is a connection between what it is right to do and what there is a justification for doing in turn explains the internalist constraint on the use of moral words. Suppose you believe that a certain act available to you is one which you would desire yourself to perform if you had a set of desires that was maximally informed and coherent and unified. You are then arguably under some rational pressure to have a corresponding desire. After all, desiring to act in the way you believe you would want yourself to act if you had a maximally informed and coherent and unified desire set coheres better with, or fits better with, or makes more sense in the context of, that belief, than would either being averse or indifferent to acting in that way. The coherence of your psychology thus seems to demand the desire of you.

Internalist Realists insist that it should therefore come as no surprise at all that those who believe that acting in a certain way would be right will desire to act in that way, at least absent the effects of depression, weakness of will and the like. Indeed, they argue that their analysis serves to reveal the essential nature of depression, weakness of will and the like. As psychological conditions that can undermine the connection between moral belief and desire, depression, weakness of will and the like share a common feature: they are all conditions with the inbuilt potential to create psychological incoherence. No surprise that, absent the conditions that make for that sort of incoherence, people will desire to act in the ways that they believe they would want themselves to act if they had a maximally informed and coherent and unified desire set.

Should an Internalist Naturalistic Moral Realist be a Relativist?

For these and other reasons, Internalist Realists think that their own theory is therefore a vast improvement on Externalist Realism. There is, however, an important ambiguity in the Internalist Realist's theory that still needs to be addressed. This touches on the issue of relativism.

Rightness is supposed to be that feature, whatever it is, that we would desire our acts to possess if our desires formed a set that is maximally informed, coherent and unified. But is the idea supposed to be that the "we" referred to in the analysis includes all rational creatures? In other words, is the idea that we would all converge in the desires we would have under idealized conditions of reflection? Or does the "we" include only some subset of the rational creatures? Does it include, say, me and those who desire things similar to the things that I actually desire? In other words, are contingent and rationally optional culturally induced differences in our actual desires supposed to make convergence in the desires we would have under conditions of idealized reflection impossible?

If the latter, then the theory is relativistic (Harman 1975, 1985). According to Relativistic Internalist Naturalistic Moral Realism, when we say that actions of a certain sort are right what we are really saying is a subset of rational creatures – those who have desires like our own – are such that they would desire that we act in that way if they had desires that formed a maximally informed, coherent, and unified set. However we thereby allow that other perfectly rational creatures may differ from us. This needn't force us to think that their acting in that way wouldn't be right as well. If we believe that we would desire them too to act in that way under idealized conditions of reflection then of course we will believe that acting in that way would be right for them too. The crucial point is simply that their having corresponding desires as part of their idealized desire set is no part of what makes our claim that it is right for them so to act true. On the alternative analysis, by contrast – that is, according to Non-Relativistic Internalist Naturalistic Moral Realism – their possession of such desires too is required for the truth of our claim (Smith 1994).

But of these two versions of the Internalist's theory it seems to me that the relativistic version is manifestly implausible as conceptual analysis. How could whether or not an act is right or wrong, and hence is justified or unjustified, the paradigm of a non-arbitrary fact about an act, be grounded in something so arbitrary as whether or not someone happens to have certain contingent and rationally optional culturally induced desires? The very idea seems to involve a contradiction. Yet this is the conclusion to which the Internalist who buys into relativism is committed.

The non-relativistic version of the theory, by contrast, holds that such facts are grounded in something that is itself appropriately non-arbitrary. Acts are right or wrong depending on whether, notwithstanding any contingent and rationally optional culturally induced differences in our actual desires, we would all desire or be averse to the performance of such acts if we had a set of desires that was maximally informed, coherent and unified. Underlying this form of Internalism is thus a wonderful picture of ourselves and our relations to other people. At the very deepest level – that is, in that idealized possible world in which we all have a set of desires that is maximally informed, coherent and unified – we share common aims simply in virtue of our nature as rational beings. No one is beyond the pale, not, at any rate, if they remain susceptible to rational argument. Even the most wretched may be reachable.

Notwithstanding how wonderful this picture is, however, it may be mere illusion. The truth of the non-relativistic version of Internalism depends on more than mere conceptual analysis, it depends, as well, on the substantive fact that *there is* a set of desires that we would all converge upon if we had a set of desires that was maximally, informed, coherent and unified. Even if the conceptual analysis is impeccable, absent the power of rational argument – that is, absent the power of information, together with considerations of coherence and unity – to elicit common desires in us, the non-relativistic version of Internalism entails that there are no moral facts at all.

The proper conclusion to draw is thus that even the very best version of moral realism is sub judice, something about which we will be convinced only to the extent that we are confident that the arguments we give ourselves for desiring as we do are arguments that should convince the arbitrary rational person to desire likewise. And, of course, experience teaches that that kind of confidence is difficult to maintain. The unfortunate tendency of the media to portray people from other cultures as radically different from each other, as though they don't even share a common tendency to believe and desire on the basis of reflection as opposed to superstition, let alone a common tendency to desire alike after reflecting, doubtless plays a significant role. Even convinced Non-Relativistic Internalist Naturalistic Moral Realists will therefore continue to feel the pull of Nihilism in their more pessimistic moments.

References

Blackburn, S.: *Spreading the Word* (Oxford: Oxford University Press, 1984).

——: "Circles, finks, smells and biconditionals", *Midwest Studies in Philosophy Volume XII: Realism and Anti-Realism*, ed. P. A. French, T. E. Uehling Jr. and H. Wettstein (Atoscadero: Ridgeview Press, 1994), pp. 259–81.

——: *Essays in Quasi-Realism* (New York: Oxford University Press, 1994).

Boyd, R.: "How to be a moral realist", *Essays on Moral Realism*, ed. G. Sayre-McCord (Ithaca: Cornell University Press 1988), pp. 181–228.

Brink, D.: *Moral Realism and the Foundations of Ethics* (Cambridge: Cambridge University Press, 1989).

Carroll, L. (1872): *Alice's Adventures in Wonderland and Through the Looking Glass*, ed. R. L. Green (Oxford: Oxford Paperbacks, 1998).

Darwall, S., Gibbard, A., and Railton, P.: "Toward *fin de siècle's* ethics: some trends," *Philosophical Review (1992): 115–89.*

Gibbard, A: *Wise Choices, Apt Feelings* (Oxford: Clarendon Press, 1990).

Hare, R. M: *The Language of Morals* (Oxford: Oxford University Press, 1952).

Harman, G.: "Moral relativism defended," *Philosophical Review* (1975): 3–22.

——: *The Nature of Morality* (Oxford: Oxford University Press, 1977).

——: "Is there a single true morality?" *Morality, Reason and Truth*, ed. D. Copp and D. Zimmerman (Rowman and Allanheld, 1985).

Horwich, P.: *Truth*, (Oxford: Blackwell, 1990).

——: "Gibbard's theory of norms," *Philosophy and Public Affairs* (1992): 67–78.

Jackson, F.: *From Metaphysics to Ethics* (Oxford: Oxford University Press, 1997).

Jackson, F., Oppy, G., and Smith, M: "Minimalism and truth-aptness," *Mind* (1994): 287–302.

Mackie, J. L.: *Ethics: Inventing Right and Wrong* (Harmondsworth: Penguin, 1977).

Moore, G. E.: *Principia Ethica* (Cambridge: Cambridge University Press, 1903).

Nietzsche, F: *The Genealogy of Morals* (1887); trans. W. Kaufman and R. J. Hollingdale, *On the Geneology of Morals and Ecce Homo*, ed. W. Kaufman (New York: Random House Vintage Books, 1967).

Railton, P.: "Moral realism," *Philosophical Review* (1986): 163–207.

——: "What the noncognitivist helps us to see the naturalist must help us to explain," *Reality, Representation and Projection*, ed. J. Haldane and C. Wright (Oxford: Oxford University Press 1993a), pp. 279–300.

——: "Reply to David Wiggins," *Reality, Representation and Projection*, ed. J. Haldane and C. Wright (Oxford: Oxford University Press, 1993b) pp. 315–28.

Sayre-McCord, G.: "The many moral realisms," *Essays on Moral Realism*, ed. G. Sayre-McCord (Ithaca: Cornell University Press, 1988a).

——: "Moral theory and explanatory impotence," *Essays on Moral Realism*, ed. G. Sayre-McCord (Ithaca: Cornell University Press, 1988b), pp. 256–81.

Smith, M.: *The Moral Problem* (Oxford: Blackwell, 1994).

——: "Ethics and the a priori: a modern parable," *Philosophical Studies* (1998): 149–74.

Sturgeon, N.: "Moral explanations," *Morality, Reason and Truth*, ed. D. Copp and D. Zimmerman (Rowman and Allanheld, 1985), pp. 49–78.

Wright, C.: *Truth and Objectivity* (Cambridge, MA: Harvard University Press, 1992).

Chapter 2

Relativism

Simon Blackburn

Relativism in ethical theory is the doctrine that ethical truth is somehow relative to a background body of doctrine, or theory, or form of life or "whirl of organism". It is an expression of the idea that there is no one true body of doctrine in ethics. There are different views, and some are "true for" some people, while others are true for others.

This should be distinguished from what it is sometimes thought of in ethics itself, a practical stance that encourages toleration of different societies or different approaches to practical living. This toleration could in principle coincide with an absolutist theory of ethics, according to which there is just one correct body of ethical doctrine. For that one correct body of doctrine could, in principle, include the view that it is permissible or even obligatory to tolerate people who do things differently. Nevertheless the practical attitude of fairly universal toleration is often felt to be a *consequence* of the theoretical stance that there is no one truth. That is, once the theorist takes the view that there are pluralities of ethical truths, each relative to the different positions of people, it becomes quite natural to draw the conclusion that toleration is the only warranted stance. For if "they have their truth" and we have ours, it would seem at best a brute exercise of power to coerce them into our ways, or ostracize them or go to war with them for doing it differently. Thus the postmodernist Richard Rorty takes himself to have dismantled any conception of absolute ethical truth, and indeed draws the conclusion that only a light, ironic, aesthetic stance to practical problems is justified.[1] Rorty is not unique in this. Many people, and many ethical theorists, believe that without some "robust" or "objective" conception of moral truth, our *right* to hold judgments with a sufficient degree of conviction evaporates. If we want to oppose cruelty, or defend free speech, or outlaw child sex, we need the conviction that it is not "just us", voicing a contingent or accidental aspect of how we feel. We want to hold that truth is on our side: absolute truth, even God's truth. This is why relativism is usually seen as a disturbing challenge to moral authority: a challenge that it is the business of a proper moral theory to answer.

In this essay I shall compare a number of approaches to ethical theory, in terms of how they react to relativism. I shall start with the theory I myself defend, which is a kind of "projectivism" or "expressivism". I shall argue in the next section that, perhaps surprisingly, this metaphysically undemanding view of ethics in fact puts us in a very strong position to make the right reaction to relativism. I then say how certain other approaches, while superficially better able to defend themselves against relativism, in fact open up disturbing relativistic options. While ostensibly protecting our authority, they in fact undermine it.

Expressivism holds that the key to ethics lies in the practical stances that we need to take up, to express to each other, and to discuss and negotiate. As the expressivist tradition has always emphasized, ethics is at bottom about practice. It is about choices and actions. Ethics concerns what to do, and what not to do; who to admire and who to avoid; where to draw lines, and where not to; what feelings to cultivate, and which ones to repress. Our ethic is shown in our cluster of dispositions to encourage and to discourage various choices, characters, and feelings. A sincere moral opinion is the expression of one of these dispositions. For this reason ethics can, fundamentally, be expressed in terms of prescriptions, and in some systems, like that of the Old Testament, this is indeed how it is given: thou shalt do this, and not do that. But prescriptions only get us part of the way. Attitudes need comparison and ranking as well as simple expression. "This is better than that" can get expression as "admire this more than that", but the replacement would be strained. And we have an ethical language that goes beyond simple imperatival forms for good and sufficient reason, namely to bring to the business of systematizing and reasoning about attitude the elegant framework of propositional logic.

Because practice is so important, these dispositions need discussion. They need to be queried, and sometimes qualified and rejected and replaced. These queries can take the form of asking whether a particular opinion is *true* or *right*. But the appearance should not mislead us. As Wittgenstein often reminds us, p is true means that p.[2] Asking whether a moral judgment is true or right is no more than asking whether to accept it. And asking that is asking which attitude or policy or stance to endorse.

All this should be platitudinous. But in fact in many peoples' minds it rings all kinds of alarm bells. It sounds to them to be an invitation to some alarming downgrading of ethics. It seems to undermine the "absolute" or binding or authoritative character that we associate with moral and ethical imperatives.[3] Some people who share the basic orientation have encouraged these anxieties. Bernard Williams believes that ethics cannot be what it seems.[4] And famously, John Mackie, in his "error theory" supposes that there are elements in our ethical practice that could only be justified if something more were true: some kind of "objectivity" or "authority" or "to-be-doneness" built into the frame of the world. But this something more is not true, so first-order ethical practice is founded on a mistake.[5]

I take these views to be natural, but also to be rejected. I don't think first-order ethical practice embodies any mistake at all. Particular ethical views, of course, may be mistaken. But the categories of ethics and the states of mind of those who find they need them and express themselves in terms of them are quite in order. Or rather, if they are not (as some people think that the concept of a "right", for example, is of doubtful use) then it is an ethical problem, not one of logic or metaphysics or the theory of what ethics is. One sign of this is that Mackie himself never showed what a practice of expressing and comparing and encouraging and discouraging practical stances would look like if it were *free* of the mistake. I would suppose that it would come to look exactly like ours (even if started somewhat differently, in some impoverished form). And this shows that there is no mistake embedded in the very structure of our reasonings.

Expressivism and Relativism

There is no problem of relativism for the expressivist, because there is no problem of moral truth. Since moral opinion is not in the business of *representing* the world, but of assessing choices and actions and attitudes in the world, to wonder which attitude is right is to wonder which attitude to adopt or endorse. Suppose, then, to take a real-life example, that I adopt and express an attitude: say, that women should be educated. Suppose I meet a member of the Afghan Taliban, who holds the reverse. This may certainly pose me a practical problem: in fact at least two practical problems. First, I would like to be able to change his attitude. And second, even if I can't do that, I would like to be able to stop him from implementing it. But I may not know how to go about either of these things, and there lie my practical difficulties.

The relativist will get up at this point and say, "well, it is true for the Taliban that women should not be educated". But what can that mean? Surely it is just a bad way of saying that the Taliban *hold* that women should not be educated, which we already knew. It is not a way of putting that opinion in a favorable light. "True for them" sounds a qualified kind of truth, like "it is true in Greenland that it freezes all winter", as opposed to "it is not true in Carolina that it freezes all winter". But seeing the Taliban's view as true in *any* kind of way must involve putting it into a *favorable* light. And if anyone *wants* to put that opinion in a favorable light, he has some very hard work to do, and we can promise in advance that he will fail. Why? Because nothing worth respecting speaks in favor of the view. There is no favorable light in which it can be put; it is a view that can only appear attractive when the light is very dim. If you think otherwise, I am against you and I will express this by saying that you are wrong. I reject your opinions, and this I voice by word and deed.

The relativist will try again. He will say: "well, it is *merely* your attitude against his". Part of this is right: it is indeed my attitude against his. That is what ethical conflict is. The part that is wrong is the "merely". What is "mere" about a conflict of attitude? The world's worst conflicts are those of policy, choice, and practice. They are the most important conflicts there are. By comparison, mere conflicts of opinion can fade into insignificance. It need not matter at all to me that you hold that the distance to the moon is half a million miles, although I hold that it is nearer a quarter of a million. The difference need not translate into actions that bother me. But if your attitude to me is contempt or disgust, that matters a great deal.

No doubt this mistakes the intended import of the word "mere". It is not that conflict of attitude is unimportant. The relativist will say "it is your attitude against his and *neither of you can show that the other is wrong*". The conflict is "merely" a conflict of attitude in the sense that there is no proof procedure. This, I should say, contains a grain of truth, although only a very small grain. For, after all, it is strictly false. I can show that the Taliban is wrong by the simplest means: any educated female is a perfectly good illustration of his error. My wife shows how wrong he is, and so do millions of other women. Probably the complaint is that I cannot *show the Taliban himself* that he is wrong for, after all, he is blind to the illustration or takes it the wrong way. But even this is not axiomatic. It may be possible to show the Taliban himself that he is wrong. We may be able to increase his experience of women, to undermine the delusive authorities on which he relies, to enlarge his sympathies and so on. It is unlikely to be a *quick* process, but whoever thought that it should be? It is also probably a process that is more likely to be successful if attempted by someone nearer to the Taliban's frame of mind: a more liberal Muslim, for example.

The only grain of truth in the remark is that there is no algorithm for success. There is no proof procedure nor any empirical process of working on the Taliban that is *guaranteed* in advance to bring him to my opinion. But that's just how it is. It is always contingent, and sometimes chancy, whether we can move a dissident towards concurrence with our own sympathies and attitudes. If that worries anyone, they would do well to reflect that the same is true in empirical and even mathematical or logical cases. The problem with the Taliban is that he is blind to what illustrates his error, and that may be true of people in these other cases. I can show that daffodils are yellow, but I cannot necessarily show to some particular dissident that they are yellow, if he refuses to look, or looks but is blind to colors. I can show that contradictions are false, but I cannot necessarily show it to some enthusiast who holds in advance that all logic is a patriarchal plot of which I am a part.

One formula that has attracted some admiration in recent discussions of relativism, is that on such an issue we can simply say "there is nothing else to think".[6] This may just be a flowery way of nailing our colors to the mast, but otherwise it strikes me as overdoing it. I think it is unfair to the Taliban to deny that he indeed thinks something else. It dehumanizes him, making him into some kind of mad dog, unable to think about choice, action, and ways of life at all. Whereas in fact he voices a genuine attitude, and a practical policy, for which he has his delusive reasons. That is why we are in conflict. Otherwise he would represent nothing but a kind of obstacle to our own policies, something, in Strawson's words, to be "managed or handled or cured or trained".[7] I have no sympathy with the Taliban, but I would not myself wish to put him outside the pale of human thought. We cannot conjure away attitudes of separatism and divisiveness, either of class or race or gender, by a kind of legislation that the people who hold them are beyond interpretation.

Well now, says the relativist as a last resort, but isn't expressivism usually classed as an anti-realist view of ethics (denying that ethical facts or properties have the same kind of status as real facts or real properties)? And doesn't this mean that *there are no facts* of an ethical or normative kind? And then aren't all attitudes fundamentally on an equal footing? The answers are: yes, expressivism is usually characterized as anti-realist; but no, this does not mean that there are no facts of an ethical or normative kind, and finally, even if it did, this would not mean that all attitudes are on all fours.

Anti-realism, or as I prefer to call it quasi-realism, refuses to give ethical facts a typical explanatory role. This is already heralded when we turn our backs on ethical representation. A representation of something as F is typically explained by the fact that it is F. A representation *answers to* what is represented. Expressivism holds that ethical facts do not play this explanatory role. We cannot, except by analogy, talk of ethical perception. If we want a slogan we can say that the way of the world, and that includes the mental world, is independent of the normative. Oughts do not explain is's. Our moral understandings are not explained by independent moral structures, to which we are lucky enough to be sensitive.

Why does this not imply that there are no moral facts? Minimalism shows us why not. I have already given you a moral opinion of mine: women should be educated. Here is another way of putting it: it is true that women should be educated. Here is another: it is a fact that women should be educated. If we like we can go further up this progression, which I call Ramsey's ladder: it is true that it is a fact . . . ; it is really true that it is a fact . . . ; and, soon, but not quite yet, I shall suggest that we can add objectivity to the list.[8]

And why does that not imply that divergent moral opinions are on an equal footing? Well, all the expressivist can hear that as meaning is that they are all *equally good*. And that is just not true. The Taliban's opinion on the education of women is not as good as mine. In fact, it is diametrically wrong, wrong root and branch. But notice that this would be so even if we were less minimalist than I have been about facts. Suppose a substantive or robust theory of truth were developed, giving us some notion of correspondence. Suppose it proceeds by isolating some metaphysical category of Facts (note the upper-case). And suppose finally that for the kinds of reason I have outlined, there are no normative or ethical Facts (all these doctrines belong to the *Tractatus Logico-Philosophicus*). This would be a metaphysical result. So it clearly could not imply that all moral opinions are on an equal footing. It could not imply, for instance, that it is permissible to hold that women should not be educated. It could at best imply that in holding this you do not trespass against the upper-case Facts. But that is all right. It was not *that* (or, not simply that) that is wrong with the Taliban view. The main thing that is wrong with the view is that it is inhumane, cruel, arbitrary, and so on. The metaphysics cannot imply that it is all right to be like that!

I have said that there is no problem of relativism, and tried a little to explain why this is so. I shall finish this part of the discussion by entering a very small concessive remark, something that can perhaps serve to salvage a little pride for the relativist.

There are cases like that of the Taliban, but there are also cases where travel broadens the mind. We might start off by thinking that our attitude is the only permissible attitude, or our ways are the only permissible ways, and that all others are wrong. But exposure to other people, or other cultures or times can make us change our minds. They do it differently – yet we cannot condemn them, or find it in our hearts to maintain the superiority of our ways. So we become a degree more tolerant. And this is often exactly as it should be.

I suspect that the relativist generalizes too rapidly from this kind of progression, assuming that because it is as it should be in some cases, it must be so in all cases. So that simple exposure to alternative opinion should be enough to dissolve any allegiance we hold to our own attitudes or principles. The error comes in forgetting the qualification that we "cannot condemn them, or find it in our hearts to maintain the superiority of our ways". When this is true, toleration is indeed the right upshot. But it is not always true.

If I go to other countries, I find other funerary practices. This might shock me, initially. But I learn that the essential human practices of dealing with death and grief and survival share their core function beneath their surface diversities. After this I cannot find it in my heart to maintain the superiority of our ways: it becomes a matter of choice whether we cremate, or bury, or leave for the vultures, and a good thing too. But if I go to Afghanistan, the situation is different. I can, and should, maintain exactly what I started with. If I become infected by the Taliban attitude to women, that is unfortunate and represents a deterioration in my own moral fibre. If the Taliban are seductive enough in other ways, I may have to be on my guard against this.

Clearly, then, there remain moral problems connected with multiculturalism. There is no moral problem of relativism. But there are particular problems of when to tolerate and when to oppose, and the answers to these may not all be easy, or all given in advance. We have to ask whether we are faced just with an alternative, equally good, solution to some problem of living, that can cheerfully be acknowledged in the spirit of an alternative convention, or whether, on the other hand, we are faced with something that must be opposed. Slavery, the oppressions of caste systems, the systematic degradation of women, child labor and many other facets of societies are not alternative equally good solutions to problems of living. They are things that must be opposed.

So the expressivist or quasi-realist approach gives a complete defense against relativism, acknowledging only particular problems that have to be solved, when they come up, like all moral problems. We have to approach them deploying the beliefs and attitudes that we hold, and bringing them to bear as best we can. If I am worried about whether, say, to tolerate lesbian parenthood or the use of cannabis as alternative lifestyles of whether to oppose them as impermissible aberrations, this is what I have to do. They may get put in the same category as the divergent funerary rites, or they may go with the Taliban. But each issue has to be fought on its merits. There is no problem of relativism, but only individual problems of living.

Approaches that have Problems with Relativism

Why do I think it an advantage of quasi-realism that it solves this issue so easily? Cannot other approaches say the same things? The difficulty is this. Many philosophical attempts to understand the nature of ethics look for more "robust" or "substantive" conceptions of ethical truth. Frequently they try to model ethical truth on other areas: science and a teleology for human beings in the case of some kinds of naturalism; mathematics, in the case of *a priori* and constructivist approaches; secondary qualities in the case of some contemporary "moral sense" theories. Such theories typically arise in response to a felt need for some substantive conception of moral truth. Now where there is a need, there is also a danger. The danger is that what you get actually fails to fill the need in the right way. It is here that relativism becomes a problem. I shall illustrate the threat with three examples.

The first example is the kind of theory associated with John McDowell, that uses the rule-following considerations to defend a close analogy between ethics and secondary-quality perception. This gets into difficulties over relativism, because both the rule-following considerations *and* the analogy with secondary quality perception encourage relativism. Roughly, in each case we can envisage a situation in which there are different "whirls of organism". There are organisms that whirl the Taliban way, and see women as inferior beings whose highest purpose is passively to serve the pleasures of men, and organisms that whirl the Western or enlightenment way. There are organisms that whirl the way dogs do when it comes to smells, and organisms that whirl our way. If truth was found in the "responses" or the "practice" or the "shared consensus" of organisms, then it is very hard to see why these individual communities of shared response are not generating their own truths. This is how we do think of it in the case of secondary qualities. The dog inhabits, literally, a different world of smells from the human being. And there is no saying that just one of us is "right". So relativism becomes a real threat, because the theory looks as if it has to allow for a plurality of truths. There are defensive moves possible (one can always remark that one element of our whirl of organism is to set ourselves against those who whirl another way) but the danger is very real.

For a second theory that courts danger, consider the very different view of Christine Korsgaard – a kind of constructivism.[9] Korsgaard fears the contingent, changeable world of desire and attitude enough to want an entirely different source of normativity, which she finds in such notions as self-legislation, and the nature of practical identity. Now although Korsgaard herself believes that there is a kind of Kantian straightjacket on the shape our self-legislations must take, the problem of relativism is more impressive than this solution to it. For on the face of it, you can have pluralities of self-legislating persons whose identities are happily bound up in various constraints they set themselves under, but who unfortunately find these constraints in entirely different places. Some conceive it their duty to privilege men over women, others do not. Some would find their identities threatened if they broke certain dietary prohibitions, while others do not care at all. If the "construction" or self-legislation generated moral truth, once more we seem to have a plurality of truths, and relativism strikes. And I should say that the same result awaits the less rationalistic, more political, version of constructivism that seems visible in some of Rawls's more recent work. That is, whereas in Rawls's original work we might have thought that the framework of a decent society emerged as the necessary consequence of rational choice, in the later work we have a more relativized conception of the kinds of structure that we can justify to each other, given conditions of political dialogue that are themselves contingent and local. The shift in emphasis seems to me wholly admirable, but it leaves the door open to relativistic fears that the more ambitious Kantian coloring once closed.[10]

Finally, the same kind of result looks to threaten any neo-Aristotelian theory that seeks to tie moral choice to some conception of "flourishing". The problem is again that there is a plurality of ways in which flourishing can be had. Some flourish one way, some another. It is not just that there is, as Bernard Williams memorably put it, no particular tie between behaving admirably and flourishing "by the ecological standard of the bright eye and the glossy coat". It also remains disappointingly true that in such a flexible animal as the human being, entirely different conceptions of flourishing will support entirely different conceptions of what to do and what to admire. We have only to think of the Taliban conception of what it is in a woman to flourish (a conception, incidentally, that we can easily envisage being shared by their women, at least after a generation or two). Once more if moral truth is found "in" such ideas, then given the plurality of ideas, we have the relativistic plurality of truths.

It is, then, a distinct advantage of quasi-realism that it keeps free of all that. Of course, this is not to deny that conceptions of what counts as flourishing should *inform* our attitudes. But when the conceptions are contestable, we are under no pressure at all to think that they generate different and contesting systems of ethical truth. They only generate the need to choose, and to defend our choice with the best story we can find.

Objectivity and Relativism

Objectivity is very important to many philosophers of ethics. Can the view I have sketched defend a sufficiently robust concept of objectivity to satisfy us? Here too I shall urge that there is no problem.

Objectivity, I say, is desirable. It is a virtue. But what does it mean? We can think of this by considering the flaws and failures that denote its absence. First, there are flaws of *bias*. Two considerations are equal, but the biased judge weighs one more heavily than the other. Two people have equal claims, but one is preferred to the other. The most obvious cases are ones in which only a certain range of considerations *ought* to affect an issue, but others are surreptitiously introduced. Thus, I hold that some restricted range of considerations ought to influence a hiring decision. If my college introduces another – say, trying to reject a candidate because of age or gender or haircut – then he is not being objective. He is indulging his bias. Famously, we are not good at knowing when this is true of ourselves, and the mechanisms of self-deception are familiar enough. The colleague may not actually advance age or gender or haircut as a reason. But if, sufficiently often or sufficiently predictably, the reasons he does advance all turn out to discriminate against those of the wrong age or gender, or unusual haircuts, we know what is going on. And we may know it before he does.

Worse, epistemologically at any rate, than bias is blindness. For as well as objective decisions, we talk of objective views of things. A person may fail to give an objective appreciation of the situation because he fails to see the situation at all. A person who does not appreciate what is going on cannot give an objective view of a situation. To be objective, our view has to have taken enough into consideration. It has to be sensitive to what matters.

In the case of both decisions and views this formula seems to work. To be objective is to be sensitive to the right aspects of the situation, and in the right way. This means that normativity is built into the concept at the center, and of course we can expect disagreements. My colleague may believe that he is *right* to discriminate as he does. That is, he has some story defending his discriminations, and he may try to get us to listen to it. Then once more we have a practical problem. We may find ourselves listening to him, or we may know in advance that it is no use doing so. It is not given that we never budge from our antecedent opinions, but it is not given that we simply roll over and agree with his either.

Can the expressivist or quasi-realist select an appropriate range of considerations as the *right* range? Can he privilege the decision-making of the unbiased judge, or the point of view of the informed, large-minded spectator who sees the situation in its entirety? Of course. I am against my colleague who lets his hiring decision be influenced by the age, gender or haircut of the applicant, and I express this by saying that he is sensitive to the wrong considerations. He is biased, not objective. I am impatient with people who get their opinions from the gutter press, because that press does not give a full enough selection of facts to justify their attitudes. I privilege the better-informed.

Let us return to the Taliban. You have already heard me saying that the Taliban are wrong. But can the expressivist or quasi-realist say that there is anything *objectively* wrong about their views? They are certainly sensitive to the wrong considerations – that is given by the fact that they let educational policies get decided by gender. I should also say that they are blind to the nature of women and the possibilities open to them. They are insensitive to most of the important aspects of women's lives. So certainly, it is a plain fact they show deficiencies of objectivity. They are objectively wrong.

What else might the worry about objectivity be? It might be a way of reintroducing the demand for proof, that we met in the last section. Someone might, I suppose, seek to use the notion so that someone is objectively wrong if and only if there is a guarantee in advance that there is a cognitive procedure for changing his opinion to coincide with ours. But this would be an unfortunate usage: witness my illustration that there is no such procedure even in the straightforward empirical cases where people are happiest talking of objective error.

One thought people may have in mind, when they hanker after objectivity, is this. If we are wrong about literal objects, such as what lies in our path, we expect to be tripped up. Objects make themselves felt. The Captain of the Titanic was wrong about an object, and as a result lost his ship. We might hope to show that if the Taliban are "objectively" wrong, then there is disaster lying in wait for them: an equivalent to being tripped up. This is one side of the thought that we have already met, that associates ethical truth with flourishing, and issues in Aristotelianism. The idea will be that the objectivity of the Taliban mistake will be manifested in the relative impoverishment or loss of flourishing lives. Just as people think that the economic errors of communism were finally exhibited in the collapse of eastern European communism, so they might hold that errors of morality will be illustrated in the collapse of lives built on those errors.

If that is the idea, the expressivist tradition certainly does not have to oppose it, although I myself would not believe it for a moment. It *may* be true that there are such tight constraints on flourishing that any deviation from a good ethic destroys it. Or rather, we should say, it *could* have been true. For it is not really a sensible thought to keep open, after all we know about human beings. It is much better to think of the alignment between flourishing and behaving well as highly contingent, and not only contingent, but *politically* contingent. That is, it is up to a society to create an alignment between behaving well and flourishing. As Hume argues in the third book of the *Treatise*, commercial societies implement attitudes and procedures so that people who renege on their word get tripped up.[11] If they do not get tripped up, because, for instance, transactions are not repeated, then the alignment breaks down, and we get individual cases in which the cheat flourishes.

It would be up to the world community to ensure that a society that refuses to educate its women is tripped up – that is, somehow penalized in ways that eventually result in reform. When it comes to things like caste systems or oppression of minorities, I see no reason at all for thinking that *nature* puts into place mechanisms for tripping up those who hold the wrong attitudes. It is "set us as a task", in Kantian terms, to put into place the sticks and carrots that will hopefully introduce improvement.

Here, many modern options in moral philosophy are hopelessly impoverished by their Aristotelian and Kantian trappings. Those trappings enable one group to believe piously that the Taliban will not flourish, and that this is the bottom line: this is what is wrong with them. They enable the other group to think that they have transgressed against some rational constraint on practical reasoning, and that this is the bottom line: this is what is wrong with them. Whereas the real truth is that what is wrong with them is neither of these things. So far as I can predict the Taliban might well flourish, again by the ecological standard of the bright eye and the bushy coat, if the rest of the world does nothing about it. They may flourish by any stand-ards they themselves would recognize (and as already mentioned, that could include female members of the society). And it is pie-in-the-sky to believe that there is some theorem of practical reasoning against which they trespass, or that this is what is wrong with them. (In fact, in current Kantian versions, it is pie-beyond-the-sky, since subjection to the categorical imperative arises from a transcendental autonomy: something like an act of self-legislation that happens at no time and no place). What is truly wrong with the Taliban is more straightforward than either of these things. What is wrong with them is that they oppress their women, impoverish their lives, and keep them in a state of ignorant superstition. Why should we feel any urge to say *more* than that? Isn't it bad enough?

The idea behind saying "they are objectively wrong" on this suggestion was that they are wrong in the kind of way that those who are wrong about objects are: they get tripped up. The world itself contains the mechanisms for correcting their ways, and preferably in ways that they cannot ignore. I have suggested that this is too optimistic. And again, we might reflect that it is pretty optimistic even in many empirical cases. Certainly if I am wrong about whether there is a cliff or iceberg in front of me, the world will trip me up. But it I am wrong about less immediate matters, I can go happily with my errors to the grave. If you disagree with me about the O. J. Simpson verdict, one of us is objectively wrong, but neither of us is particularly likely to suffer because of it. The connection between objectivity and flourishing is not so very close in everyday empirical cases, so it is unwise to ask for it to be closer in the delicate cases of ethics.

So we should not hear the word "objectivity" as any kind of stick with which to beat the expressivist. Looking at it the other way, if someone calls our opinion about an ethical issue "subjective" we can hear the charge in a number of ways that matter. He may be imputing hidden bias. He may be imputing lack of knowledge, or lack of ability to deploy the right knowledge. He may think that the issue is genuinely one on which it is possible to be in two minds, and that any more definite attitude is only one option, or one unattractive option. All these are charges we may have to listen to, and on occasion they may be justified. But there is no single general charge, always waiting to be made. My judgment, like that of others, will doubtless show particular flaws of this kind in particular situations, and it is then up to the critic to press the particular charge he has in mind. And that too is just part of the human situation.

Authority: The Last Word

In his recent book of that title, Thomas Nagel sets up and considers a "relativist" challenge to the authority of norms, not only in ethics but potentially in other areas too, such as logic, mathematics, or science. His hate-figure is the postmodernist or relativist who hears the right opinion, and even echoes it, but adds always the qualification or rider: that is just us. Nagel opposes to the bitter end this last word. He even invokes a kind of Platonic image of harmony between our ways and the normative orders that govern the universe. If that is to be the alternative, it is preferable to the relativism, whatever metaphysical anxieties it provokes. Nagel's anxiety, and the cost he is prepared to pay for a remedy for it, and undoubtedly widely-shared. Yet the angst is unfounded, and the cost does not have to be paid. This is fortunate, for I believe it cannot be paid: there is no proof awaiting us that our normative attitudes harmonize with the normative order governing the universe, whatever that might be.

I agree with Nagel that there is something flattening or dispiriting about the relativistic last word. And it is surely intended by many postmodernists as a debunking signal: a flag showing that they have *seen through* the authority of whatever norms are in question. They may go on to *voice* acceptance of the norms, but, to Nagel's ear, the protestation will sound hollow. They can't give the norms the *authority* they really deserve. And in Nagel's view, only the Platonist can do that.

This dialogue mistakenly assumes there to be One Big Question, when in fact there are only a lot of little questions. Nagel thinks the relativist challenge points us towards a large metaphysical hole: a gap in our ontology or view of the world that we must desperately try to overcome. I believe, instead, that it amounts at best to an attempt to undermine our *first order* confidences, and that such attempts are to be met piecemeal, depending upon the case in hand.

Here is an illustration from recent work by the late Jean Hampton. Consider the scientific norm of insisting upon double blind tests for the efficacy of new drugs (so that nobody involved knows which is a real drug and which is a placebo). Suppose some half-hearted experimentalist, who says "we like to do double blind tests", and then adds "but that is just us". Surely the right response is to ask what the little word "just" is doing. It insinuates the double blind methodology is *optional*, so that there would be nothing wrong about doing the tests without it. But that, we suppose, is a shocking mistake. Tests conducted without it have a high probability of saying that a drug is efficacious when it is not, or vice versa, and this is what we wanted to avoid. If our experimentalist denies this, he had better have a story, and most scientists would bet in advance that he will not have one.

Another good way of putting it is this. Let us give the dissident that it is just us. But let us add some words of self-awareness. It is just us, able as we are to conduct reliable tests. Or, it is just us, forearming ourselves against misleading results. There is nothing to be *ashamed* of in these words of self-description. On the contrary, there is something to be *proud* of, because learning to avoid the experimental pitfalls presumably took some doing. So we can agree with Nagel that better last words than "that is just us" should be found. But we stay within our first-order normative space as we find them. This makes it plain that the issue with the relativist is fundamentally one of confidence. But if our last words are happy enough, our confidence is well-founded, and no challenge to it exists.

My response is the same if an ethical attitude is challenged. I am in favor of education for women. Suppose now not a Taliban, but some weary postmodernist, saying "I am in favor of it too. But that is just us". Again the "just" insinuates that this is somehow an optional attitude, that there is *nothing wrong* with people such as the Taliban who happen to whirl the other way. But I am unsympathetic to this degree of toleration – the kind of open mindedness that comes when all one's brains have fallen out, as it is sometimes put. Putting it positively I can add words of self-description: it is just us, free from the politics of arbitrary discrimination, free from culturally embedded misogyny, maintaining ideals of equality and freedoms of self-development for all. These words ring well in my ear: it is just us, and we are doing well. Putting it negatively, I can expound as I have done on the way the Taliban attitude is not optional. There is indeed something wrong with it and them, and I can go on to detail some of what it is.

Of course in all this I am speaking in my own voice. That is inevitable. But so long as my own voice is not one to be embarrassed by, it is also of no interest.

Notice that this is not an open invitation to be smug. Suppose I announce my hostility to legalized cannabis. Someone comes along and, perhaps pointing to countries where cannabis is legal and things seem to go on fine, says "we may hold it right to criminalize cannabis, but that is just us". I try for words of self-description: just us, aware of the dangers; just us, able to discriminate harmless drugs from harmful ones. And here, suddenly, the words may not ring all that happily. Either the descriptions are unjustified or false, or they are not things to be proud of. They may even be things about which to be embarrassed "just us, ignorant of the real consequences, or just us, believing what we are told in the gutter press". When this happens something has to give. We either have to find better words, or change our habit of being embarrassed by ignorance or gullibility, or come to soften our opposition to cannabis. Or, perhaps, "carelessness and inattention" can provide a remedy, for one human response to finding that the last words of self-description are embarrassing is, unfortunately, just to kick over the table, refusing to listen. But that too is an embarrassing last description of our state.

We can conclude by noticing one final issue that perhaps troubles people who think about these things. I suspect it lies behind the kind of moral imperative people feel to transcend quasi-realism. It may partly explain why, as I put it in my book *Ruling Passions* they think quasi-realism smells of sulphur.

As we have seen, people hanker after algorithms, or procedures guaranteed in advance to prove that their opponents are wrong, or preferably to prove to them that they are wrong. They want this security. But suppose, as I am afraid is true, they cannot always find such procedures. Well, in fact attitudes and politics are going to continue. In practice, however much a Professor beats his breast about the need for an algorithm in the class room, out of the study he will discipline his children, sit as a magistrate, campaign for one party or another, lament the Taliban, just as if he had one. But one strand from Kant will lead the Professor to be embarrassed about some of this. For the attitudes and the politics will eventually have a coercive edge. There will come a case in which he is wrong to do it. And people think that this trespasses against the *respect* due to persons, or against the *dignity* of persons – and this worries them. People thinking like this fear that they can only be justified in coercive measures if, at least in principle, the object of those measures ought to be assenting to them, and this in turn would only be so if somewhere there is the missing algorithm. It is as if, when I lock you up, if what I do is just, then you must be tacitly in possession of thoughts that would lead to you assenting to your fate. You could reason to my conclusion, even if in fact you choose not to. Otherwise, so the line goes, I fail to respect you as a person, or infringe your dignity and even your rights.

I do not have too much sympathy with this line of thought. It seems to me only in fairy-land that everyone has at some deep level an appreciation of the right and the good. It is wishful thinking to suppose that at the end of every just piece of sentencing there is a prisoner who tacitly accepts the justice of the sentence.

Human beings do dirty things, and their cultures let them get away with them. If a Taliban living in a western jurisdiction is indicted for the not-uncommon crime of burning his wife to death for some petty shortcoming or misdemeanor, he may feel unjustly treated. His whole culture may back him in this resentment. He may feel it atrocious that his crime attracts the same penalty as if he had killed a male relative. And he may have no principles within him that could even ideally be deployed to change his feelings. But that does not give me, the westerner, the least reason either for changing the judgment, or for feeling guilty about enforcing the penalty. Nor do I trespass against dignity and due respect. The Taliban deserves no respect for his attitude to women or for his action. Nor does his self-justification express any kind of dignity. He brought it all upon himself, by himself refusing to treat half of humankind with due dignity and respect.

A weaker and more plausible requirement is that coercion should only be exercised against someone if it would be *reasonable* to expect people to agree that this is a case where coercion is necessary. The agreement sought after would not necessarily be that of the criminal, for as we have already described, the criminal may be blind to what shows the error of his ways. But so long as reasonable people see the error of his ways, coercion may be justified. This seems to be right, but it really amounts to little more than an equation between behavior being justified, and it being seen by reasonable people that it is justified. "Reasonable" is here functioning in what we might call a Hume-friendly sense. It does not mark the delivery of pure practical reason, uncontaminated by our contingent concerns, and sympathies and attitudes. It means an appeal to people who are objective, in the sense described above, and who having thought the matter through, sifted and refined their attitudes, decide that the criminal should indeed be subject to coercion. Perhaps it does trespass against the dignity or respect due to a person if we coerce him or her although our policy does not meet this condition. But that means only that we trespass against these things when our policy is unjustified. I am quite prepared to believe that this is true, but it is not as substantive a truth as we might have hoped to find.

It would, of course, be nice if all criminals were penitents, and if the dignity of people and the respect due to them were always so great that there was no need for coercive measures in the first place. And no doubt these things are true in fairyland. In the real world, we have to do the best we can, and here, as elsewhere, the task of the philosopher is partly to enable us to do this without the confusions and guilt that so often bedevil practical reasonings.

Notes

1 Richard Rorty, *Contingency, Irony and Solidarity* (Cambridge: Cambridge University Press, 1989), pp. xv, 173.
2 Most famously, at *Philosophical Investigations* (Oxford: Blackwell, 1953), §136.
3 Some writers make a distinction, whereby the moral is a subset of the ethical. Ethics is concerned with the whole field of evaluation, choice, and action, whereas morality is concerned more with obligations and duties. In this essay the distinction is not important, and I shall talk indifferently of the moral and the ethical.
4 Bernard Williams, *Ethics and the Limits of Philosophy* (London: Fontana, 1985).
5 John Mackie, *Ethics: Inventing Right and Wrong* (Harmondsworth.: Penguin Books, 1977).
6 David Wiggins, "Moral Cognitivism, Moral Relativism, and Motivating Beliefs," *Proceedings of the Aristotelian Society*, 91 (1990–91): 61–86.
7 Peter Strawson, "Freedom and Resentment" in *Studies in the Philosophy of Thought and Action* (Oxford: Oxford University Press, 1968), p. 79.
8 For more on Ramsey's ladder, see my *Ruling Passions* (Oxford: Oxford University Press, 1998), 78, 294–7.
9 Christine Korsgaard, *The Sources of Normativity* (Cambridge: Cambridge University Press, 1996).
10 The major works contrasted here are of course *A Theory of Justice* (Cambridge, MA.: Harvard University Press, 1972), and *Political Liberalism* (New York: Columbia University Press, 1993).
11 David Hume. *Treatise of Human Nature,* ed. L. A. Selby Bigge (Oxford: Oxford University Press 1888), III, ii, 5, p. 516ff.

Chapter 3

Divine Command Theory

Philip L. Quinn

Judaism, Christianity, and Islam share the view that the Hebrew Bible has authority in matters of religion. They therefore have reasons for sympathy with a divine command conception of morality. Both Exodus 20:1–17 and Deuteronomy 5:6–21, which recount the revelation of the Decalogue, portray God as instructing the Chosen People about what they are to do and not to do by commanding them. One might, of course, understand these divine commands as merely God's endorsement of a moral code whose authority is independent of them. But it seems natural enough to suppose that the authority of the Decalogue depends in some manner on the fact it is divinely commanded or the fact that the commands express God's will. So the major monotheisms have reasons to develop accounts of morality according to which it depends upon God. A long tradition of theological voluntarism in moral theory has evolved from this natural starting point.

During roughly the last quarter of the twentieth century, there has been a revival of interest in divine command morality within the community of analytic philosophers of religion. Attention has been paid to three important questions. How can the idea that morality depends upon God best be spelled out and given a precise theoretical formulation? How can the theory thus formulated be supported by argument? And how can that theory be defended against objections? In the three sections of this essay, I propose answers to these questions.

Formulating the Theory

Settling on a precise theoretical formulation of the idea that morality depends upon God involves addressing three issues. The following schema can be used to indicate what they are:

(S) Moral status M stands in dependency relation D to divine act A.

The first issue is the specification of the moral statuses that the theory will claim are dependent on God. The second is specifying the nature of the dependency relation the theory will assert holds between God and those moral statuses. And the third is specifying the divine acts on which the moral statuses will be said by the theory to depend. Each of the three specifications involves a choice among options.

There is general agreement that the theory should claim that some or all of the deontological moral statuses depend upon God. Those statuses are moral requirement (obligation), moral permission (rightness), and moral prohibition (wrongness). This agreement is understandable if one thinks of God's will or commands as creating moral law, for then the deontological moral statuses are analogous to the ordinary categories of legal requirement, permission, and prohibition. I once proposed a theory according to which the axiological statuses of moral goodness, moral badness, and moral indifference also depend upon God (Quinn 1978: 67–73). Other theorists, however, have restricted their attention to the deontological moral statuses. In the present discussion, I will follow their lead and formulate a theory in which only deontological moral statuses depend upon God.

Several accounts of the dependency relation have been proposed in recent years. In the seminal paper that started the revival of interest in divine command morality, Robert M. Adams (1973) proposed a theory in which being contrary to the commands of a loving God is part of the meaning of being morally wrong in the discourse of some Jewish and Christian believers. My initial proposal in Quinn (1978) was that divine commands and moral requirements are necessarily coextensive. Adams (1979) records a switch to the view that the property of moral wrongness is identical to the property of being contrary to the commands of a loving God.

I think all these proposals are flawed in one way or another. There may be Jews and Christians in whose discourse being morally wrong means, in part, being contrary to the commands of a loving God. But this is not the case in my discourse, and so the initial proposal made by Adams does not present a divine command theory I could accept. The flaw in my initial proposal is that it fails to capture the asymmetry of the dependence of moral requirements on divine commands because necessary coextensiveness is a symmetrical relation. And it seems clear to me that being morally wrong and being contrary to the commands of a loving God are distinct properties. Perhaps being morally wrong supervenes on being contrary to the commands of a loving God. Since supervenience relations are supposed to be asymmetrical, this possibility is worth exploring, though, as far as I know, no one has formulated a divine command theory in supervenience terms.

My second proposal in Quinn (1979) was a theory in which divine commands are necessary and sufficient causal conditions for moral requirements. Edward R. Wierenga (1989) has formulated a theory in which, by commanding a person to bring about a state of affairs at a time, God brings it about that it is obligatory that the person bring about the state of affairs at the time. My current view is that dependence of morality on God is best formulated in terms of a relation of bringing about, though care must be taken to distinguish this relation from various causal relations familiar from science and ordinary life. In particular, the divine bringing about in question will have the following marks: totality, exclusivity, activity, immediacy, and necessity. By totality, I mean that what does the bringing about is the total cause of what is brought about. By exclusivity, I mean that what does the bringing about is the sole cause of what is brought about. By activity, I mean that what does the bringing about does so in virtue of the exercise of some active power. By immediacy, I mean that what does the bringing about causes what is brought about immediately rather than by means of secondary causes or instruments. And by necessity, I mean that what does the bringing about necessitates what is brought about.

There is controversy about which divine acts bring about moral requirements, permissions, and prohibitions. As I see it, it is at the deepest level God's will, and not divine commands, which merely express or reveal God's will, that determines the deontological status of human actions. But Adams (1996) has recently objected to replacing divine commands with God's will in formulating the theory. It is therefore incumbent on me to respond to his objections. There are two of them.

The first derives from a problem about how to think about God's will. Theologians often distinguish between God's antecedent will and God's consequent will. As Adams understands the distinction, "God's antecedent will is God's preference regarding a particular issue considered rather narrowly in itself, other things being equal. God's consequent will is God's preference regarding the matter, all things considered" (Adams 1996: 60–1). It is commonly held that nothing happens contrary to God's consequent will, which is partly permissive. But since wrong actions do occur, wrongness cannot be specified in terms of contrariety to God's consequent will. Nor, according to Adams, can the ground of obligation be identified with God's antecedent will because we are sometimes morally obliged to make the best of a bad situation by doing something that a good God would not antecedently have preferred, other things being equal. And if we identify the ground of obligation with God's revealed will, we are in effect identifying it with divine commands.

My response to this objection is to deny that divine antecedent preferences, other things being equal, exhaust God's antecedent will. Following a suggestion by Mark Murphy (1998), I also attribute to God's antecedent will intentions, and I think divine antecedent intentions can be used to account for obligations to make the best of bad situations. Suppose I make a promise. God surely prefers that I keep it, other things being equal. Assume God also antecedently intends that I keep my promise, which makes it obligatory for me to keep it. If I break my promise, I create a bad situation by violating an obligation. But assume that God, in addition, antecedently intends that I apologize if I break my promise, which makes it obligatory for me to apologize if I break it. If I am in the bad situation of having broken my promise, then my obligation is to apologize. If I fail to apologize, I violate a second obligation. Of course, if I both break my promise and fail to apologize, then God neither consequently intends that I keep my promise nor consequently intends that I apologize, for nothing happens contrary to God's consequent intentions. My conclusion is that a sufficiently rich account of God's antecedent will allows us to identify the ground of obligation with some of its activities.

But Adams has a second objection. Replacing divine commands with the divine will as the ground of obligation makes sense only on the assumption that God's will can be what it is without being revealed. According to Adams, this has three undesirable consequences. First, it yields an unattractive picture of divine-human relations "in which the wish of God's heart imposes binding obligations without even being communicated, much less issuing in a command" (Adams 1996: 61). Second, "basing obligation on unrevealed as distinct from revealed divine will deprives God of the freedom to choose whether or not to impose an obligation" (Adams 1996: 61). And third, "it closes off the possibility of supererogation, important in some theistic ethical theories, the possibility of an action that is preferable from God's point of view but not ethically required" (Adams 1996: 61–2).

However, even if divine antecedent intentions impose binding obligations without being communicated, we can be confident that a good God will communicate many of these divine antecedent intentions by means of commands. As Murphy points out, God need not communicate all of them because we can infer some of them from the express divine commands, using principles of rational intending. Moreover, even if God's preferences, other things being equal, or the wishes of God's heart are not freely chosen, there is no reason to believe that God lacks freedom of choice with respect to the formation of the antecedent intentions that impose obligations. And it seems possible for there to be an action that is preferable from God's point of view whose performance is not antecedently intended by God. Hence I do not think placing the ground of obligation in the divine antecedent will has undesirable consequences if we operate with a sufficiently nuanced conception of God's antecedent will.

Thinking both of the objections set forth by Adams can be answered, I stick with my intuition that God's will determines the deontological status of actions. Revising some principles found in Wierenga (1989: 216–17) to reflect this option, I propose that the best theoretical formulations of the idea that the deontological part of morality depends upon God consists of the following three principles:

(P1)　For every human agent x, state of affairs S, and time t, (i) it is morally obligatory that x bring about S at t if and only if God antecedently intends that x bring about S at t, and (ii) if it is morally obligatory that x bring about S at t, then by antecedently intending that x bring about S at t God brings it about that it is morally obligatory that x bring about S at t;

(P2)　For every human agent x, state of affairs S, and time t, (i) it is morally permissible that x bring about S at t if and only if God refrains from antecedently intending that x not bring about S at t, and (ii) if it is morally permissible that x bring about S at t, then by refraining from antecedently intending that x not bring about S at t God brings it about that it is morally permissible that x bring about S at t;

(P3)　For every human agent x, state of affairs S, and time t, (i) it is morally wrong that x bring about S at t if and only if God antecedently intends that x not bring about S at t, and (ii) if it is morally wrong that x bring about S at t, then by antecedently intending that x not bring about S at t God brings it about that it is morally wrong that x bring about S at t.

Of course, this theory is not, strictly speaking, a divine command theory; it is instead a divine intention theory. It is, however, a version of theological voluntarism, and it pictures divine commands as expressing or revealing God's antecedent intentions. So when we speak loosely, I suppose no harm is done if we conduct the discussion in terms of divine commands. In what follows, I will do this, occasionally reminding the reader that it is the divine intentions lying behind the divine commands that really make a moral difference.

Supporting the Theory

I know of no deductive argument that is a proof of the theory I have formulated or of any of its near neighbors. In Quinn (1990a), I constructed a valid deductive argument, from premises widely acceptable among theists, for the conclusion that many obtaining deontological states of affairs are metaphysically dependent on the will of God; but I noted that this argument could not provide good reasons for holding that all such states of affairs are so dependent. I am now inclined to doubt that constructing deductive arguments is the most promising way of supporting theological voluntarism. I think a more fruitful approach is to support it by a cumulative case argument. In Quinn (1990b) and Quinn (1992), I began to construct a cumulative case for theological voluntarism. In the present discussion, I will summarize and extend my previous arguments. My cumulative case now has four parts. They support theological voluntarism in way analogous to that in which the legs of a chair support the weight of a seated person. No one leg supports all the weight, but each leg contributes to supporting the weight. I do not claim that my cumulative case for theological voluntarism is a complete case or the strongest case that could be made. I think all parts of my cumulative case should have some attractiveness for Christians. One of its parts will appeal only to Christians; two others may appeal to both Christians and some other theists; and the final part should appeal to all monotheists. I do not expect my cumulative case to persuade any non-theists to become theological voluntarists; however, I hope it will convince some non-theists that theological voluntarism is an attractive option for theists. I begin with the part with narrowest appeal and end with the part with broadest appeal.

2.1 *Commanded Christian love.* It is a striking feature of the ethics of love set forth in the New Testament that love is commanded. In Matthew's Gospel, Jesus states the command in response to a question from a lawyer about which commandment of the law is the greatest. He says: "You shall love the Lord your God with your whole heart, with your whole soul, and with all your mind. This is the greatest and first commandment. The second is like it: You shall love your neighbor as yourself" (Matthew 22:37–39). Mark 12:29–31 tells of Jesus giving essentially the same answer to a scribe, and Luke 10:27–28 speaks of a lawyer giving this answer to a question from Jesus and being told by Jesus that it is correct. In his last discourse, recorded in John's Gospel, Jesus tells his followers that "the command I give you is this, that you love one another" (John 15:17). So the authors of these books concur that the Christian ethics of love for one another is expressed in the form of a command. If Jesus is God the Son, this command and the intention behind it are divine.

Is there a reason for love of neighbor being made a matter of obligation or duty? I think there is. It is that the love of neighbor of which Jesus speaks is extremely difficult for humans in their present condition. It does not spontaneously engage their affections, and so, if it were merely permissible, they would not love their neighbors. It is therefore no accident that the love of neighbor Jesus endorses is a commanded love.

In my view, no one has seen with greater clarity than Kierkegaard just how radical the demands of love of neighbor are. In *Works of Love*, his discourse on Matthew 22:39 draws a sharp distinction between erotic love and friendship, on the one hand, and Christian love of neighbor, on the other. Both erotic love and friendship play favorites; the love of neighbor Christians are commanded to display is completely impartial. Kierkegaard says: "The object of both erotic love and friendship has therefore also the favorite's name, *the beloved*, *the friend*, who is loved in distinction from the rest of the world. On the other hand, the Christian teaching is to love one's neighbor, to love all mankind, all men, even enemies, and not to make exceptions, neither in favoritism nor in aversion" (Kierkegaard 1847: 36). His shocking idea is that the obligation to love imposed by the command places absolutely every human, including one's beloved, one's friend, and one's very self, on the same footing as one's worst enemy or millions of people with whom one has had no contact. Perhaps it is easy to imagine God loving all humans in this undiscriminating way. It is hard to see how it could be either desirable or feasible for humans to respond to one another in this fashion. But if Kierkegaard is right, this is exactly what the command to love the neighbor obliges us to do.

According to Kierkegaard, there is another way in which love of the neighbor differs from erotic love and friendship. Erotic love and friendship depend on characteristics of the beloved and the friend that are mutable. If the beloved loses the traits that made him or her erotically attractive, then erotic love dies. If the friend who was prized for having a virtuous character turns vicious, then the friendship is not likely to survive if one remains virtuous. Love of neighbor, however, is supposed to be invulnerable to changes in its object. Kierkegaard puts the point this way: "No change, however, can take your neighbor from you, for it is not your neighbor who holds you fast – it is your love which holds your neighbor fast. If your love for your neighbor remains unchanged, then your neighbor also remains unchanged just by being" (Kierkegaard 1847: 76). If there is to be such a love that alters not where it alteration finds, it cannot depend on mutable features of the neighbor and ways in which they engage our spontaneous affections and natural preferences. For Kierkegaard, it can have the independence it needs only if it is obligatory, for only then can it be motivated by a stable sense of duty rather than by changeable affections or preferences. In this way, he says, "the 'You shall' makes love free in blessed independence; such a love stands and does not fall with variations in the object of love; it stands and falls with eternity's law, but therefore it never falls" (Kierkegaard 1847: 53). We are obliged to obey eternity's law.

Kierkegaard thus has two reasons for thinking that Christian love of neighbor has to be a matter of obligation. The first is that only a love which is obligatory can be sufficiently extensive in scope to embrace everyone without distinction. Erotic love and friendship are always discriminating, partial, and exclusive. The second reason is that only a love which is obligatory can be invulnerable to alterations in its objects. Erotic love and friendship change in response to changes in the valued features of their objects. As I have argued in more detail in Quinn (1996), they are powerful reasons.

My view is that this commanded love is foundational for Christian ethics; it is also what sets Christian ethics apart from rival secular moralities. The stringency of the obligation to love is likely to give offense. In that respect, it resembles the requirements of impartial benevolence or utility maximization in secular moral theories, which are criticized for setting standards impossibly high or not leaving room for personal projects. Kierkegaard wants his readers to see just how demanding the obligation is and to accept it as binding them. "Only acknowledge it," he exhorts them, "or if it is disturbing to you to have it put in this way, I will admit that many times it has thrust me back and that I am yet very far from the illusion that I fulfill this command, which to flesh and blood is offense, and to wisdom foolishness" (Kierkegaard 1847: 71). I concur with Kierkegaard about the importance of highlighting rather than downplaying the stringency of the obligation to love the neighbor even if, as a result, many people are thrust back or offended. Christians who believe that humans in their present condition are fallen should not find this response surprising. It is only to be expected that people in such a condition will feel comfortable with moral laxity and be offended by moral stringency. There is, however, no reason for Christians to believe that fallen humans have no obligations whose stringency makes them uncomfortable. Loving everyone as we love ourselves is, I think, obligatory in Christian ethics, and it has that status, as the Gospels show us, because of God. It seems to me that Christians who take the Gospels seriously are not in a position to deny that they teach us that God intends us to love the neighbor and has commanded us to do so or that these facts place us under an obligation to love the neighbor. So I find in what is most distinctive about the Christian ethics of love in the Gospels a reason for Christians to favor a divine command conception of moral obligation.

2.2 *Lex orandi, lex credendi*. According to an old saying, the law of prayer is the law of belief. The old saying probably should not be regarded as an exceptionless generalization, for popular devotion sometimes contains superstitious elements. But often enough in Christianity what is professed in religious practice is a good guide to what ought to be contained in sound religious theory. Janine M. Idziak (1997) has shown that Christian practice emphasizes the theme of conformity to the divine will.

This theme occurs in classics of Christian spirituality and in the thought of Christian saints. In the late medieval treatise *The Imitation of Christ*, Thomas à Kempis portrays Christ as counseling a disciple "to learn perfect self-surrender, and to accept My will without argument or complaint" (quoted in Idziak 1997: 457). The colonial American saint Elizabeth Seton says that "the first purpose of our daily work is to do the will of God; secondly, to do it in the manner he wills; and thirdly, to do it because it is his will" (quoted in Idziak 1997: 457).

Nor is the theme of conformity to God's will characteristic of only the thought of extraordinary Christians. It is also found in traditional hymns: "Father, who didst fashion man/ Godlike in thy loving plan/ Fill us with that love divine/ And conform our wills to thine" (quoted in Idziak 1997: 457). And it is found in books of worship such as the Presbyterian *Daily Prayer*: "Eternal God, send your Holy Spirit into our hearts, to direct and rule us according to your will . . ."; "God of love, as you have given your life to us, so may we live according to your holy will revealed in Jesus Christ . . ." (quoted in Idziak 1997: 457). These examples, and others like them, make it clear that conformity with the divine will is an important theme in Christian spirituality. Theological voluntarism in ethics expresses this theme at the level of moral theory. There seems to me to be nothing superstitious in this aspect of Christian practice. So I regard it as providing some support for theological voluntarism in moral theory in accord with the principle of *lex orandi, lex credendi*. In other words, the fact that conformity to the will of God is an important theme in Christian devotional and liturgical practices is a good reason for Christians to adopt a moral theory in which the will of God is a source of obligations.

I am no expert on the religious practices of Judaism and Islam. What I know about Jewish and Islamic religious thought suggests that Jews and Muslims regard conformity to the will of Yahweh and the will of Allah, respectively, as very important. So I tend to think Jews and Muslims have available to them arguments similar to my argument in the case of Christianity. If so, arguments of this kind will have some appeal not just for Christians but also for some adherents of the other two major monotheisms.

2.3 *The immoralities of the patriarchs.* A Christian tradition of interpreting some stories in the Hebrew Bible serves as the basis for an argument to the conclusion that the deontological status of at least some actions depends upon God. These stories recount the incidents sometimes described as the immoralities of the patriarchs. They are cases in which God commands something that appears to be immoral and, indeed, to violate a prohibition God lays down in the Decalogue. Three such cases come up over and over again in medieval discussions. The first is the divine command to Abraham, recorded in Genesis 22:1–2, to sacrifice his son Isaac. The second is the divine command reported in Exodus 11:2, which was taken to be a command that the Israelites plunder the Egyptians. And the third is the divine command to the prophet Hosea, stated first in Hosea 1:2 and then repeated in Hosea 3:1, to have sexual relations with an adulteress. According to these stories, God has apparently commanded homicide, theft and adultery (or at least fornication) in particular cases, and such actions are apparently contrary to the prohibitions of the Decalogue. What should the patriarchs do? How are we to interpret these stories?

The tradition of biblical exegesis I am going to discuss takes the stories to be literally true; it presupposes that God actually did command as the stories say God did. It also assumes that these commands were binding on those to whom they were addressed. In *The City of God*, Augustine uses the case of Abraham to make the point that the divine law prohibiting killing allows exceptions, "when God authorizes killing by a general law or when He gives an explicit commission to an individual for a limited time." Abraham, he says, "was not only free from the guilt of criminal cruelty, but even commended for his piety, when he consented to sacrifice his son, not, indeed, with criminal intent but in obedience to God" (*The City of God* 1, 21). Augustine thinks God explicitly commissioned Abraham to kill Isaac and then revoked the commission just before the killing was to have taken place. It is clear that Augustine believes Abraham did what he should do in consenting to kill Isaac because the killing had been commanded by God. He also believes that Abraham's consent, which would have been wrong in the absence of the command, was not wrong given its presence. So Augustine holds that divine commands addressed to particular individuals (or the divine intentions they express) determine the deontological status of actions those individuals perform in obedience to them.

The connection of these cases to divine command ethics is made explicit in the work of Andrew of Neufchateau, a fourteenth-century Franciscan who is judged by Idziak to have conducted "the lengthiest and most sophisticated defense of the position" (Idziak 1989: 63). Andrew claims that there are actions which, "known per se by the law of nature and by the dictate of natural reason, appear to be prohibited, actions such as homicides, thefts, adulteries, etc. But it is possible that such actions not be sins with respect to the absolute power of God" (Andrew 1997: 91). Abraham, he goes on to say, "wished to kill his son so that he would be obedient to God commanding this, and he would not have sinned in doing this if God should not have withdrawn his command" (Andrew 1997: 91). For Andrew, not only did Abraham do no wrong in consenting to kill Isaac, he would have done no wrong if the command had not been withdrawn and he had killed Isaac. On his view, God's absolute power is such that acts such as homicides, thefts, and adulteries, which are seen to be prohibited and so sins when known by means of natural law and natural reason, would not be sins and so would not be wrong if they were commanded by God, as some in fact have been. He shares with Augustine the view that divine commands (or the divine intentions they express) can and do determine the deontological status of actions.

Thomas Aquinas too shares this view. He treats the three cases in the following passage, which deserves to be quoted in full:

> Consequently when the children of Israel, by God's command, took away the spoils of the Egyptians, this was not theft; since it was due to them by the sentence of God. – Likewise when Abraham consented to slay his son, he did not consent to murder, because his son was due to be slain by the command of God, Who is Lord of life and

death: for He it is Who inflicts the punishment of death on all men, both godly and ungodly, on account of the sin of our first parent, and if a man be the executor of that sentence by Divine authority, he will be no murderer any more than God would be. – Again Osee, by taking unto himself a wife of fornications, or an adulterous woman, was not guilty either of adultery or of fornication: because he took unto himself one who was his by command of God, Who is the author of the institution of marriage. (*Summa Theologica* I–II, q.100, a.8, ad 3)

Aquinas reasons in the following manner. Because God commanded the Israelites to plunder the Egyptians, what the Israelites took was due to them and not to the Egyptians. Since theft involves taking what is not one's due, the plunder of the Egyptians was not theft. Similarly, because God, who is lord of life and death, commanded Abraham to slay Isaac, Isaac was due to receive the punishment of death all humans deserve in consequence of original sin. Since murder involves slaying someone who is not due to be slain, the slaying of Isaac would not have been murder. And because God, who is the author of marriage, commanded Hosea to take the adulteress as his wife, she was his wife, and so he was guilty of neither adultery nor fornication in having intercourse with her.

Andrew and Aquinas differ in some respects about what the divine commands do. Andrew seems to think that God's command to Abraham brings it about that the slaying of Isaac would not be wrong while remaining a murder. Aquinas clearly supposes that God's command to Abraham brings it about that the slaying of Isaac would be neither wrong nor a murder. But such disagreement should not blind one to the ways in which they agree. Both hold that the slaying of Isaac by Abraham, which would be wrong in the absence of the divine command, will not be wrong in its presence if Abraham obeys it. We might sum up the agreement by saying that what divine commands do is to make obligatory patriarchal actions that would have been wrong in their absence. And because divine commands do this in virtue of something necessarily restricted to God alone, such as absolute power or lordship over life and death, human commands could not make a moral difference of this sort.

It is worth noting that agreement with Augustine, Andrew, and Aquinas about such cases need not be restricted to Christians who share their belief that there actually were the divine commands reported in the scriptural stories. Some may choose to think of such cases as merely possible but concur with the tradition of exegesis I have been describing in believing that divine commands would make a moral difference of the sort our medieval interpreters thought they in fact did make. I think there would be enough agreement about such cases among reflective Christians to make it fair to claim that Christian moral intuitions about scriptural cases support the conclusion that God is a source of moral obligation. What is more, it appears to be only a contingent fact that there are at most a few such cases. The properties, such as absolute power or lordship over life and death, in virtue of which divine commands have their moral effects, would still be possessed by God even if such commands were more numerous. So it is hard to resist the conclusion that any act of homicide, plunder, or intercourse with a person other than one's spouse would be obligatory if it were divinely commanded. Thus the intuitions underlying this tradition of exegesis also support the conclusion that whether any action is morally obligatory or not depends on whether it is divinely commanded (or divinely intended) or not.

I cannot speak with authority about how the exegetical traditions of Judaism and Islam treat the incidents known as the immoralities of the patriarchs. It does seem to me, however, that Jews and Muslims have available to them the strategy of interpretation made use of by Augustine, Andrew, and Aquinas. Those among them who adopt this strategy will be able to use scriptural cases to support the view that Yahweh or Allah is a source of moral obligation.

2.4 *Absolute divine sovereignty.* There are several reasons why theists of all stripes – Jews, Christians, and Muslims alike – would favor including a strong doctrine of divine sovereignty in their philosophical theology. Two of the most important pertain to creation and providence. Theists customarily wish to insist on a sharp distinction between God and creation. According to traditional accounts of creation and conservation, each contingent thing depends on God's power for its existence whenever it exists. God, by contrast, depends on nothing external for existence. So God has complete sovereignty over the realm of contingent existence. Theists also usually wish to maintain that we can trust God's eschatological promises without any reservation. Even if God does not control the finest details of history because God has chosen to create a world in which there is microphysical chance or libertarian freedom, God has the power to insure that the created cosmos will serve God's purposes for it and all its inhabitants in the long run. So God also has extensive sovereignty over the realm of contingent events. Considerations of theoretical unity then make it attractive to extend the scope of divine sovereignty from the realm of fact into the realm of value. It is an extension of this sort that we find in the remark by Andrew of Neufchateau that, with respect to God's absolute power, it is possible for homicides, thefts, and adulteries not to be sins. More controversially, the same considerations make it tempting to extend the scope of divine sovereignty from the realm of the contingent into the realm of the necessary.

How far can such extensions be pushed? In recent work in philosophical theology, Thomas V. Morris (1986) has argued for a view of absolute creation according to which God is the creator of necessary as well as contingent reality. As he sees it, in order to be absolute creator, God must be responsible somehow for the necessary truth of all propositions that are necessarily true. If this view is tenable, he notes, "moral truths can be objective, unalterable, and necessary, and yet still dependent on God" (Morris 1987: 171). Thus, for example, even if it is necessarily true that murder, theft, and adultery are morally wrong, God is responsible, according to the absolute creationist, for the necessary truth of the proposition that murder, theft, and adultery are morally wrong. But how could God be responsible for the necessary truth of a proposition?

Michael J. Loux (1986) has made an interesting suggestion about how necessary truths might depend upon God. It involves the idea that there is an asymmetrical relation of metaphysical dependence between certain divine beliefs and facts being necessarily as they are. Taking notions of believing and entertaining as primitives, Loux defines a concept of strong belief as follows: a person x strongly believes that p if and only if x believes that p and does not entertain that not-p. Since God is omniscient, divine beliefs correlate perfectly with truth and divine strong beliefs correlate perfectly with necessary truth. But there is more than mere correlation between divine strong beliefs and necessary truth. According to Loux, "God is not in the relevant strong belief states because the facts are necessarily as they are. On the contrary, the facts are necessarily as they are because God has the relevant strong beliefs. So it is the case that $2 + 2 = 4$ because God believes that $2 + 2 = 4$; and it is necessarily the case that $2 + 2 = 4$ because God strongly believes that $2 + 2 = 4$" (Loux 1986: 510). And, of course, this idea can be extended to the moral realm. It is the case that murder, theft, and adultery are wrong, on this view, because God believes that murder, theft, and adultery are wrong; and if it is necessarily the case that murder, theft, and adultery are wrong, this is so because God strongly believes that murder, theft, and adultery are wrong.

Loux's idea can also be modified to fit the sort of theological voluntarism previously discussed. Suppose that divine strong antecedent intentions are antecedent intentions that God, being essentially perfectly good, could not have failed to form. According to our theory, it is the case that murder, theft, and adultery are morally wrong because God antecedently intends that no one ever bring about the state of affairs of an act of murder, theft, or adultery being performed. It is by antecedently intending that no one ever bring about the state of affairs of an act of murder, theft, or adultery being performed, according to (P3), that God brings it about that it is the case that murder, theft, and adultery are morally wrong. The extension into the realm of the necessary is straightforward. If it is necessarily the case that murder, theft, and adultery are morally wrong, this is so because God strongly antecedently intends that no one ever bring about the state of affairs of an act of murder, theft, or adultery being performed. It is by strongly antecedently intending that no one ever bring about the state of affairs of an act of murder, theft, or adultery being performed, according to the natural extension of (P3), that God brings it about that it is necessarily the case that murder, theft, and adultery are morally wrong. And (P1) and (P2) can be extended in similar ways.

Less formally but more generally, the idea is that moral facts about deontological status are as they are because God has certain antecedent intentions concerning the actions of creaturely moral agents, and necessary moral facts about deontological status, if there are any, are as they are because God has certain strong antecedent intentions concerning the actions of creaturely moral agents. This idea gets support from the doctrine of divine sovereignty because it extends God's sovereignty to cover both the contingent part and, if there is one, the necessary part of the deontological realm.

I think the strength of my cumulative case for theological voluntarism derives in part from the diversity of sources to which it appeals. The ethical demands set forth by Jesus in the Gospels, considerations drawn from religious practice, commentary on incidents portrayed in the Hebrew Bible, and considerations from philosophical theology converge in supporting the position. Further support may be available from arguments to be found in medieval and early modern discussions of divine command ethics. Idziak (1989) contains a catalogue of such arguments. Perhaps some of these arguments can be updated and made parts of a contemporary cumulative case for theological voluntarism.

Defending the Theory

Before the recent revival of interest in divine command theory began, many philosophers were convinced that objections sufficient to refute theological voluntarism were known. So particularly during the earlier phases of the revival a lot of energy went into defending the theory against objections. A successful defense shows that the objection fails to establish the falsity of the theory. Each objection must be considered on its own merits, and objections must be replied to one by one. I have replied to a total of fourteen such objections in Quinn (1978) and Quinn (1979). Adams (1973) and Wierenga (1989) have replied to others. Richard J. Mouw (1990) has replied to yet others. I do not have space in this article even to summarize all these objections and replies. I will, however, present and reply to five objections. They are the ones that, in my experience, many people find most troubling.

3.1 *The trivial natural theology objection.* According to this objection, if we accept theological voluntarism, the task of proving the existence God is trivialized. Consider the following argument:

(1)   It is morally wrong for some human agents to bring about some states of affairs at some times.
(2)   For all human agents, states of affairs, and times, if it is morally wrong for an agent to bring about a state of affairs at a time, then God antecedently intends that the agent not bring about the state of affairs at the time.
(3)   Hence, God antecedently intends that some human agents not bring about some states of affairs at some times.
(4)   Therefore, God exists

This argument is deductively valid. Almost everyone will admit the truth of its first premise. It would be hard to defend the claim that there are no wrong actions. The second premise is a consequence of (P3), our theory's principle of wrongness. So if there are wrong actions and our theory is true, the argument is sound. It thus looks as if the theological voluntarist has a simple way to prove the existence of God. However, it does not seem reasonable to believe that this argument proves the existence of God. Nor does it seem reasonable to deny that there are morally wrong actions. So it must be unreasonable to believe that the argument's second premise is true. And therefore it must be unreasonable to believe that our theory, from which that premise follows, is true.

In response to the objection, a theological voluntarist can point out that not every sound argument is a successful proof of its conclusion. Consider, for example, this argument:

(5) There are humans.
(6) Either there are no humans or God exists.
(7) Hence, God exists.

As in the previous case, the argument is deductively valid, and almost every one will admit the truth of its first premise. If one then acknowledges the truth of its second premise, one is committed to admitting its soundness and the truth of its conclusion. But even a theist, who will, of course, believe that this argument is sound, need not concede that it is a successful proof of the existence of God. It is not easy to say precisely why the argument is not a successful proof. Perhaps the reason is that, even for a theist, the second premise cannot have, apart from the argument, more epistemic justification than the conclusion, in which case the argument cannot, as a successful proof must, transmit epistemic justification from its premises to its conclusion.

It is open to the theological voluntarist to say similar things about the previous argument. The theological voluntarist will believe that it is sound but need not consider it a successful proof of the existence of God. The reason the argument is not a successful proof, it can be claimed, is that its second premise is not, apart from the argument, better justified epistemically, even for the theological voluntarist, than its conclusion. We would not expect anyone who believes that there are wrong actions to think that theological voluntarism has more epistemic justification than theism itself. It does not follow, as the objection has it, that it is unreasonable to believe that the argument's second premise is true. The lesson to be learned is that the argument's second premise cannot antecedently be more reasonable than its conclusion for anyone who holds that there are wrong actions. Hence the argument cannot, as a proof must, make it more reasonable to believe its conclusion than it otherwise would be. More generally, theological voluntarism does not contribute to the epistemic justification of theism; the order of epistemic justification goes in the other direction.

It is worth noting that sound arguments which do not prove their conclusions are ubiquitous. Here is one: (a) Horses exist; (b) Either there are no horses or oysters exist; hence, (c) Oysters exist. This argument is obviously sound, but it is no proof of the existence of oysters. Presumably the reason it is not a proof is that, given that we know (a), our justification for believing (b) is our independent knowledge of (c). Such examples show that the theological voluntarist's response to the objection does not rely on an esoteric feature of argument in natural theology.

3.2 *The moral skepticism objection.* It is sometimes thought that theological voluntarism inevitably leads to moral skepticism. An argument in support of this view might go along the following lines. According to theological voluntarism, we can come to know what is morally obligatory, permissible, and wrong only by first coming to know certain facts about the divine will. But we cannot, at least in this life, come to know such facts, for God's will is inscrutable. Hence, we cannot in this life come to know what is morally obligatory, permissible, and wrong. A more modest version of this objection is the complaint that, according to theological voluntarism, only people who have religious knowledge can have moral knowledge. As Eric D'Arcy puts it, "if immoral actions are immoral merely because God so wills it, merely because God legislates against them, it would be sheer coincidence if someone who knew nothing of God or his law happened to adopt the same views about particular actions as God did" (D'Arcy 1973: 194). And, of course, mere coincidence of our views with God's views, though it would give us true beliefs, would not suffice for moral knowledge.

One reply to the objection is to deny that the divine will is inscrutable. The theological voluntarist can appeal to scripture, religious tradition, personal revelation, and even natural law as sources of knowledge concerning what God has willed. But then the skeptical worry will shift to the disagreements among religious people about what the deliverances of those sources are. Another reply gets closer to the heart of the matter. Our theory asserts that divine antecedent intentions bring it about that certain things are morally obligatory, others are permissible, and others are wrong. It makes no claims in moral epistemology, and so it makes no claims about how we might come to know what God's antecedent intentions are. It does not entail that we can come to know what is morally obligatory, permissible, and wrong only by first coming to know what God's antecedent intentions are. It is consistent with the view that we can only come to know what God's antecedent intentions are by first coming to know what is morally obligatory, permissible, and wrong. This is as it should be. The subject matter of our theory is a certain kind of metaphysical dependency of deontological status on divine intentions. The order of epistemic access may run in the opposite direction from the order of metaphysical dependency. After all, though effects are metaphysically dependent on their causes, in ordinary life we often come to know causes by first coming to know their effects. It is not a consequence of our theory that only people who have religious knowledge can have moral knowledge. Hence, the objection fails.

Whether or not agreement of the views of those who know nothing of God with God's views about the morality of actions is mere coincidence depends on the explanation of the agreement. An explanation available to theological voluntarists is that God has benevolently endowed normal human creatures with a moral faculty such as conscience that, when functioning properly in appropriate circumstances, reliably tracks, unbeknownst to those who know nothing of God, divine antecedent intentions. If that explanation is correct, the agreement is not mere coincidence; and, on reliabilist accounts of knowledge, those who know nothing of God are not precluded from having moral knowledge.

3.3 *The uselessness objection*. It is sometimes argued that theological voluntarism is useless as an ethical standard. Jeremy Bentham says: "We may be perfectly sure, indeed, that whatever is right is conformable to the will of God: but so far is that from answering the purpose of showing us what is right, that it is necessary to know first whether a thing is right, in order to know from thence whether it be conformable to the will of God" (Bentham 1948: 22). So his view is that we can come to know what is conformable to the divine will only by first coming to know what is right. Many theological voluntarists would disagree with this view and argue that sometimes we can come to know what is conformable to the will of God from such sources as revelation. But Bentham's view is consistent with our theory. If it is correct, our theory does not provide a decision procedure for the deontological part of ethics, a way of deciding or determining what is right. However, our theory makes no claim to provide a decision procedure. Ethical theories can perform functions other than teaching us how to decide what is right. It would be of theoretical interest to find out that what is morally obligatory, permissible, and wrong depends on divine antecedent intentions, even if this knowledge were not of any practical use. So even if Bentham's view were correct, it would not constitute a successful objection to our theory. Moreover, it is worth noting, by way of an ad hominem against Bentham, that his brand of utilitarianism would be in trouble if this objection were cogent. No one is in a position to calculate the exact hedonic values of all the consequences of all the alternative actions open to an agent in many circumstances in which moral decisions must be made. Nonetheless, a utilitarian may reply, it would be of theoretical interest to find out that hedonistic act-utilitarianism is true, even if applying it to generate solutions to moral problems is often not a practical possibility.

3.4 *The divisiveness objection*. Another objection is that theological voluntarism is bound to be a divisive point of view. William K. Frankena puts the point this way:

> However deep and sincere one's own religious beliefs may be, if one reviews the religious scene, contemporary and historical, one cannot help but wonder if there is any rational and objective method of establishing any religious belief against the proponents of other religions or of irreligion. But then one is impelled to wonder also if there is anything to be gained by insisting that all ethical principles are or must be logically grounded on religious beliefs. For to insist on this is to introduce into the foundation of any morality whatsoever all of the difficulties involved in the adjudication of religious controversies, and to do so is hardly to encourage hope that mankind can reach, by peaceful and rational means, some desirable kind of agreement on moral and political principles. (Frankena 1973: 313)

Though Frankena is in this passage discussing views in which the relation between religion and morality is logical, presumably he would have a similar worry about our theory in which the relation is metaphysical. And, of course, Frankena is correct in pointing out that religious disagreement has in the past given rise to moral disagreement and continues to do so.

But religious disagreement does not inevitably give rise to disagreement about moral principles. A theological voluntarist can agree with a secular Kantian deontologist on the principle that torture of the innocent is always morally wrong. They will, to be sure, disagree about why torture of the innocent is always wrong. A theological voluntarist who adopts our theory will say that it is wrong because God antecedently intends that no one ever bring about the torture of an innocent person. A secular Kantian deontologist may say that it is wrong because it involves failing to treat the humanity in another as an end in itself. Disagreement at the level of the metaphysics of morals is consistent with overlapping consensus at the level of moral principles. So despite religious disagreement, there are grounds for hope that we can reach, by peaceful and rational means, agreement on at least some moral and political principles.

It would, I think, be unrealistic to expect overlapping consensus on all matters of moral and political principle as long as disagreement in moral theory persists. But as Adams (1993) points out, nothing in the history of modern secular moral theory gives us reason to expect that general agreement on a single comprehensive moral theory will ever be achieved or that, if achieved, it would long endure in a climate of free inquiry. His conclusion, with which I agree, is that "the development and advocacy of a religious ethical theory, therefore, does not destroy a realistic possibility of agreement that would otherwise exist" (Adams 1993: 91). Philosophers should respond to disagreement in the area of moral theory in the same way they respond to theoretical disagreement in other areas, namely, as an opportunity to search for reasons that will reduce it. Their goal at every stage of the search should be agreement only to the extent that it is supported by the best available reasons. The mere fact that a moral theory provokes disagreement gives us no reason not to accept or advocate it. Nor does the fact that such theoretical disagreement may be an obstacle to reaching agreement on how to solve practical problems give us such a reason. So even if theological voluntarism is, to some extent, a divisive point of view, this does not show that it is false or unworthy of serious consideration by moral theorists. And, to be fair, I should note that Frankena would probably agree with this conclusion; he acknowledges that if the view that morality is dependent on religion rests on good grounds, we must accept it (Frankena 1973: 314).

It is also worth noting that not all moral disagreement is divisive. A Kierkegaardian Christian may think that Mother Teresa is only doing her duty toward her neighbor as specified by the Love Commandment and regret that he fails to live up to the standards she sets. One of her secular admirers may believe that much of the good she does is supererogatory. But if they agree that she does a great deal of good and that the world would be a better place if it contained more people like her, their disagreement about whether some good things she does are obligatory or supereorgatory is not apt to be especially divisive.

3.5 *The anything goes objection.* Perhaps the most troublesome objection to theological voluntarism was clearly stated by Ralph Cudworth. He said:

> divers Modern Theologers do not only seriously, but zealously contend . . ., *That there is nothing Absolutely, Intrinsically, and Naturally Good and Evil, Just and Unjust, antecedently to any positive Command of God; but that the Arbitrary Will and Pleasure of God*, (that is, an Omnipotent Being devoid of all Essential and Natural Justice) *by its Commands and Prohibitions, is the first and only Rule and Measure thereof.* Whence it follows unavoidably that nothing can be imagined so grossly wicked, or so foully

unjust or dishonest, but if it were supposed to be commanded by this Omnipotent Deity, must needs upon that Hypothesis forthwith become Holy, Just and Righteous. (Cudworth 1976: 9–10)

Consider some foully unjust state of affairs, say, an innocent child's being tortured to death. Translated into the idiom of our theory, Cudworth's complaint would be that theological voluntarism has as a consequence the following conditional:

(8) If God were antecedently to intend that someone at some time bring about the torture to death of an innocent child, then it would be morally obligatory for that person at that time to bring about the torture to death of an innocent child.

Cudworth is right about this point. Our theory's principle of obligation, (P1), has (8) among its consequences. But this will yield a successful refutation of our theory only if it can be shown that (8) is false. In order to show that (8) is false, one must show that its antecedent is true and its consequent is false. Can this be done?
    There is a very plausible claim that entails the falsity of the consequent of (8). It is this:

(9) There is no possible world in which it is morally obligatory for anyone at any time to bring about the torture to death of an innocent child.

And the following claim entails the truth of the antecedent of (8):

(10) There is a possible world in which God antecedently intends that someone at some time bring about the torture to death of an innocent child.

But a theological voluntarist who accepts (9) can reject (10). A theological voluntarist can consistently reject the claim Cudworth makes parenthetically that God is an omnipotent being devoid of all essential and natural justice. If God is essentially just, there will be constraints on the antecedent intentions God can form. If it is unjust to bring about a certain state of affairs, it is also unjust to intend that anyone else bring it about. Hence, a theological voluntarist can maintain that there is no possible world in which God antecedently intends that someone at some time bring about the torture to death of an innocent child.
    Theological voluntarists who are convinced that God is essentially just thus have a straightforward response to the objection. It is to admit that (8) is a consequence of their view but to insist that its antecedent is impossible. According to most theories of counterfactual conditionals, counterfactuals with impossible antecedents are trivially true. Thus theological voluntarists can accept (8) and hold that it is true. So the objection fails to refute theological voluntarism. In morality, it is not the case that anything goes if morality depends on the will of an essentially just God.
    It might seem that it is not legitimate for theological voluntarists to appeal to

divine justice. This would be the case if the only way to understand divine justice were in terms of obedience to certain self-addressed divine commands or fulfillment of certain intentions for divine action, for such things provide no constraints on the antecedent intentions God can form. But an alternative view is open to the theological voluntarist. It is that, while in the human case justice is both good and made obligatory by God, in the divine case justice is good but not obligatory. God's essential perfect goodness entails God's essential justice. So though God is not under an obligation to be just, God is just by a necessity of the divine nature. It is the divine nature itself, and not divine commands or intentions, that constrains the antecedent intentions God can form.

Of course a theological voluntarist can also consistently accept (10) and reject (9). The discussions of the immoralities of the patriarchs by Augustine, Andrew, and Aquinas provide a precedent for this move. A theological voluntarist who takes this tack can accept (8) and hold that it is true because both its antecedent and its consequent are true at the appropriate possible world or worlds. In my opinion, this response to the present objection is less plausible than the response previously considered. However, I think it would be a mistake to generalize to the conclusion that it is an implausible kind of response in every possible case, including all the cases of the immoralities of the patriarchs. Hence I do not think the contribution those examples make to my cumulative case for theological voluntarism is undercut by my preference for the first response to Cudworth's objection.

My strategy in responding to objections has been to rebut them one at a time. This seems to me fair because they are presented in this fashion by authors who criticize theological voluntarism. But, of course, someone might try to build a cumulative case against theological voluntarism by combining several objections. For example, I think Cudworth's objection would show promise of contributing to such a cumulative case if the second response to it I have discussed were the only response available to the theological voluntarist. However, I do not think the other objections I have considered show similar promise. So while I acknowledge that it is incumbent on defenders of theological voluntarism to give a hearing to and to try to rebut a cumulative case argument against their position if one is presented, I do not think that there is at present such a case to answer.

In sum, theological voluntarism is a view of the deontological part of morality that can be formulated with precision, supported from within a monotheistic worldview by a strong cumulative case argument, and defended against numerous objections. Thus our theory should be very attractive to ethical theorists who are monotheists. It should also command respect from ethical theorists who, while not themselves monotheists, are not hostile to monotheism.

Acknowledgment

I am grateful to Hugh LaFollette for helpful comments.

References

Adams, R. M.: "A modified divine command theory of ethical wrongness," *Religion and Morality*, ed. G. Outka and J. P. Reeder, Jr. (Garden City, NY: Anchor, 1973), pp. 318–47.

——: "Divine command metaethics modified again," *Journal of Religious Ethics*, 7 (1979): 66–79.

——: "Religious ethics in a pluralistic society," *Prospects for a Common Morality*, ed. G. Outka and J. P. Reeder, Jr. (Princeton, NJ: Princeton University Press, 1993), pp. 93–113.

——: "The concept of a divine command," *Religion and Morality*, ed. D. Z. Phillips (London: Macmillan, 1996), pp. 59–80.

Andrew of Neufchateau (1514); trans. J. M. Idziak, *Questions on an Ethics of Divine Commands* (Notre Dame, IN: University of Notre Dame Press, 1997).

Aquinas, T. (1273); trans. Fathers of the English Dominican Province, *Summa Theologica* (New York: Benziger, 1948).

Augustine of Hippo (426); trans. G. G. Walsh, D. B. Zema, G. Monahan, and D. J. Honan, *The City of God* (Garden City, NY: Image, 1958).

Bentham, J.: *An Introduction to the Principles of Morals and Legislation* (1789); (New York: Hafner, 1948).

Cudworth, R.: *A Treatise Concerning Eternal and Immutable Morality* (1731); (New York: Garland, 1976).

D'Arcy, E.: "'Worthy of worship': a Catholic contribution," *Religion and Morality*, ed. G. Outka and J. P. Reeder, Jr. (Garden City, NY: Anchor, 1973), pp. 173–203.

Frankena, W. K.: "Is morality logically dependent on religion?," *Religion and Morality*, ed. G. Outka and J. P. Reeder, Jr. (Garden City, NY: Anchor, 1973), pp. 295–317.

Idziak, J. M.: "In search of 'good positive reasons' for an ethics of divine commands: a catalogue of arguments," *Faith and Philosophy*, 6 (1989): 47–64.

——: "Divine command ethics," *A Companion to Philosophy of Religion*, ed. P. L. Quinn and C. Taliaferro (Oxford: Blackwell, 1997), pp. 453–9.

Kierkegaard, S. (1847); trans. H. V. Hong and E. H. Hong, *Works of Love* (New York: Harper, 1964).

Loux, M. J.: "Toward an Aristotelian theory of abstract objects," *Midwest Studies in Philosophy 11*, ed. P. A. French, T. E. Uehling, and H. K. Wettstein (Minneapolis, MN: University of Minnesota Press, 1986), pp. 495–512.

Morris, T. V.: *Anselmian Explorations* (Notre Dame, IN: University of Notre Dame Press, 1987).

Mouw, R. J.: *The God Who Commands* (Notre Dame, IN: University of Notre Dame Press, 1990).

Murphy, M.: "Divine command, divine will, and moral obligation," *Faith and Philosophy*, 15 (1998): 3–27.

Quinn, P. L.: *Divine Commands and Moral Requirements* (Oxford: Clarendon Press, 1978).

——: "Divine command ethics: a causal theory," *Divine Command Morality: Historical and Contemporary Readings*, ed. J. M. Idziak (New York and Toronto: Edwin Mellen Press, 1979), pp. 305–25.

——: "An argument for divine command ethics," *Christian Theism and the Problems of Philosophy*, ed. M. D. Beaty (Notre Dame, IN: University of Notre Dame Press, 1990a), pp.

289–302.

——: "The recent revival of divine command ethics," *Philosophy and Phenomenological Research*, 50 (1990b): 345–65.

——: "The primacy of God's will in Christian ethics," *Philosophical Perspectives* 6, ed. J. E. Tomberlin (Atascadero, CA: Ridgeview, 1992), pp. 493–513.

——: "The divine command ethics in Kierkegaard's *Works of Love*," *Faith, Freedom, and Rationality*, ed. J. Jordan and D. Howard-Snyder (Lanham, MD: Rowman & Littlefield, 1996), pp. 29–44.

Wierenga, E. R.: *The Nature of God: An Inquiry into Divine Attributes* (Ithaca, NY: Cornell University Press, 1989).

Chapter 4

Naturalism

James Rachels

Twentieth-century philosophy began with the rejection of naturalism. Many modern philosophers had assumed that their subject was continuous with the sciences, and that facts about human nature and other such information were relevant to the great questions of ethics, logic, and knowledge. Against this, Frege argued that "psychologism" in logic was a mistake. Logic, he said, is an autonomous subject with its own standards of truth and falsity, and those standards have nothing to do with how the mind works or with any other natural facts. Then, in the first important book of twentieth-century ethics, *Principia Ethica* (1903), G. E. Moore also identified naturalism as the fundamental philosophical mistake. Moore argued that equating goodness with any of the natural properties of things is "inconsistent with the possibility of any Ethics whatsoever" (Moore 1903: 92).

Frege, Moore, and other like-minded thinkers inaugurated a period in which logic and language were the dominant philosophical subjects and confusing conceptual with factual issues was the greatest philosophical sin. During this period, philosophy was thought to be independent of the sciences. This may seem a strange notion, especially where ethics is concerned. One might expect moral philosophers to work in the context of information provided by psychology, which describes the nature of human thinking and motivation; sociology and anthropology, which describe the forms of human social life; history, which traces the development of moral beliefs and practices; and evolutionary biology, which tells us something about the nature and origins of human beings. But all these subjects were counted as irrelevant to the philosophical understanding of morality.

Of course, naturalism never disappeared completely – John Dewey was the century's most influential naturalist – and in the latter part of the century it has made a comeback even among analytical philosophers. Naturalistic theories of mind, knowledge, and even logic are once again being defended. In ethics, naturalism remains under suspicion. Almost a hundred years after Moore, books of moral philosophy still routinely explain why it cannot be true.

I

Ethical naturalism is the idea that ethics can be understood in the terms of natural science. One way of making this more specific is to say that moral properties (such as goodness and rightness) are identical with "natural" properties, that is, properties that figure into scientific descriptions or explanations of things. Ethical naturalists also hold that justified moral beliefs are beliefs produced by a particular kind of causal process. Thus C. D. Broad observed that "If naturalism be true, ethics is not an autonomous science; it is a department or an application of one or more of the natural or historical sciences" (Broad 1946: 103).

The most plausible form of ethical naturalism begins by identifying goodness with satisfying our interests, while "interests" are explained in turn as the objects of preferences. Protecting our eyesight, for example, is in our interests because we have desires that would be frustrated if we could not see; and that is why unimpaired eyesight is a good thing. Again, protecting children is a good thing because we care about children and we do not want to see them hurt. As Hobbes put it, "Whatever is the object of any man's appetite or desire, that is it which he for his part calleth good" (Hobbes 1651: 28). Reasoning about what to do, therefore, is at bottom reasoning about how to satisfy our interests. In what follows, I will elaborate this view and consider its merits.

Moore believed that no such view can be correct, for two reasons. First, he said, if we focus our attention on what we mean by "good" and what we mean by "satisfies our interests" we will see that they are not the same. We need only to think clearly about the two notions to realize they are different. Second, Moore devised an argument against naturalism that came to be known as the "open question" argument. The question "Are the things that satisfy our interests good?" is an open question, and to say that those things are good is a significant affirmation. But, the argument goes, if goodness and interest-satisfaction were the same thing, this would be like asking "Do the things that satisfy our interests satisfy our interests?" An analogous argument can be given with respect to any other natural property with which goodness is identified. This seems to show that goodness cannot be identical with anything other than itself, and so, Moore concluded, ethical naturalism cannot be right.

Are these arguments effective? It depends on what, exactly, we take naturalism to be. Naturalism can be construed as a thesis about the meaning of words – that, for example, the word "good" means "satisfies our interests." If this is how we understand the theory, Moore's arguments are plausible. (I will not discuss whether in fact they are sound.) But ethical naturalism can also be understood, more interestingly, as an idea about what goodness *is* – that it is, for example, the same thing as the property of satisfying our interests. Moore's arguments do not touch this idea at all. Consider that, if his arguments were sound, they would also show that the Morning Star cannot be identical with the Evening Star. If we focus our attention on what we mean by those terms, we will see that they are not the same – the first is a star seen in the morning, while the second is a star seen in the evening. And the question "Is the Morning Star the Evening Star?" was an open question the answer to which was unknown for many centuries. But in fact the two are identical. (The same could be said about water and H_2O and about Lee Harvey Oswald and the man who shot John Kennedy.) So Moore's arguments cast no doubt on ethical naturalism, understood as a thesis about the nature of things.

There is, however, another argument that many philosophers believe is devastating to ethical naturalism. David Hume is credited with first observing that we cannot derive "ought" from "is." In perhaps the most famous passage in modern moral philosophy, Hume wrote:

> In every system of morality, which I have hitherto met with, I have always remark'd, that the author proceeds for some time in the ordinary way of reasoning, and establishes the being of a God, or makes observations concerning human affairs; when of a sudden I am surpriz'd to find, that instead of the usual copulations, *is*, and *is not*, I meet with no proposition that is not connected with an *ought*, or an *ought not*. This change is imperceptible; but is, however, of the last consequence. For as this *ought*, or *ought not*, expresses some new relation or affirmation, 'tis necessary that it shou'd be observ'd and explain'd; and at the same time that a reason should be given, for what seems altogether inconceivable, how this new relation can be a deduction from others, which are entirely different from it. (Hume 1739: 468)

Max Black dubbed this idea "Hume's Guillotine": factual judgments and evaluative judgments are fundamentally different, and no amount of purely factual information can logically entail any evaluation. It is commonly assumed that, if this is true, the naturalistic project is doomed.

But is it true? On the face of it, it appears that sometimes evaluative conclusions can be drawn from factual premises. P entails Q if and only if there is no possible world in which P is true and Q is false. But consider:

P: The only difference between doing A and not doing A is that, if we do A, a child will suffer intense prolonged pain. Otherwise, everything will be the same.

Q: Therefore, it is better not to do A.

It certainly seems that, in any world in which P is true, Q will also be true. Therefore, P entails Q. Why, then, do philosophers think there is an "unbridgeable chasm" between facts and values?

Hume himself believed that the gap between is and ought is a consequence of the fact that ought-judgments have a connection with conduct that factual judgments (and other deliverances of reason) do not have:

> Since morals, therefore, have an influence on the actions and affections, it follows, that they cannot be deriv'd from reason; and that because reason alone, as we have already prov'd, can never have any such influence. Morals excite passions, and produce or

prevent actions. Reason of itself is utterly impotent in this particular. The rules of morality, therefore, are not conclusions of our reason. (Hume 1739: 457)

When a person has a moral belief – a belief that a certain way of acting is right or wrong, or that an action should or should not be done – this necessarily involves the person's being motivated to act accordingly. Suppose, for example, I say that gambling is wrong. But then you discover that I play in a high-stakes poker game every Friday night. You might find this puzzling. What is to be made of it?

There are several possibilities. (1) Maybe I lied; I do not really believe that gambling is wrong. Perhaps I was teasing you or speaking sarcastically. (2) Another possibility is that I was only reporting what other people believe – in saying "Gambling is wrong" I only meant something like "Most people think it is wrong." I did not mean to be expressing my own view of the matter. (3) Or it may be that I am morally weak. Although I think it is wrong, and I resolve not to gamble, when Friday comes around I am overcome by temptation. Afterwards I kick myself for having succumbed. (The kicking can be avoided, however – it may be that I escape self-reproach by refusing to think very carefully about what I am doing. I want to gamble, so I do it but without giving it any thought. This is a common pattern: people often believe, for example, that they should give money to feed the starving rather than spending it on luxuries for themselves. So it is convenient for them to put the starving out of mind; then they can have their luxuries without self-reproach. Later we will see that this sort of cognitive disengagement makes moral perception impossible.)

Other explanations might be tried. But the point is that my conduct requires *some* such explanation; otherwise it is unintelligible. I cannot gamble happily, without hesitation, and reflect on my conduct with no sense of self-recrimination, if it is true that I believe gambling is wrong. It is not necessary, of course, that I always do what I think is right, but it is necessary that I have at least some motivation to do it. This motivation need not be so powerful that it cannot be overcome by other desires. But it must supply some inclination, however slight, so that there is something there for the other desires to overcome.

Beliefs about what should be done, then, are necessarily motivating, to at least some extent. But aren't purely factual beliefs also motivating in the same way? Suppose I believe the room is on fire and I rush out. We might say that I left because of that belief. This explanation, however, is incomplete. It must be added that *I didn't want to be burned*. If I did not have that desire, the fire would have been a matter of indifference to me. Of course we may think it is too obvious for words that I don't want to be burned. But its obviousness should not cause us to overlook its importance in the explanatory scheme. Knowledge of facts together with appropriate attitudes prompts action; knowledge of facts alone does not.

This is why Hume thought that ought-judgments are "entirely different" from judgments of fact. Ought-judgments are motivating; factual judgments by themselves are not. But this is itself a puzzling feature of ought-judgments that requires explanation. What is it about ought-judgments that gives them this peculiar power "to produce or prevent actions?" How is their motivational content to be explained? Hume believed, sensibly enough, that we can account for this only by understanding moral beliefs to be associated with "sentiments," or feelings. Sentiments alone have the right kind of connection with conduct. If they are not expressions of sentiment, the motivational force of moral beliefs is inexplicable.

This, however, has a surprising implication for the idea that we cannot derive "ought" from "is." Rather than explaining why such derivations are impossible, it helps to explain how they are possible. In 1964 Max Black offered this example:

> Fischer wants to mate Botwinnik.
> The one and only way to mate Botwinnik is for Fischer to move the Queen.
> Therefore, Fischer ought move the Queen.

Black argued that this is in fact a valid chain of reasoning: if the premises are true, the conclusion must be true also. But the premises concern only matters of fact. They include no "ought" judgments. The conclusion, however, is about what ought to be done. Thus it seems that we can derive "ought" from "is."

One might wonder whether the example commits some sort of subtle logical error. Perhaps the conclusion should be rewritten to say only "Therefore, Fischer *wants* to move the Queen," since the major premise concerns only what Fischer wants and not what he ought to do. But this would render the argument obviously invalid. (Fischer may not want to move the Queen because he may not realize that this move would lead to mate.) Or one might wonder whether a premise about what ought to be done needs to be added. To satisfy the maxim "No ought in the conclusion without an ought in the premises," the argument might be rewritten:

> Fischer ought to mate Botwinnik.
> The one and only way to mate Botwinnik is for Fischer to move the Queen.
> Therefore, Fischer ought to move the Queen.

But the notion that Fischer *ought* to mate Botwinnick is decidedly peculiar. And even if this different argument is valid, how does that show that the original example was invalid? Why couldn't the original one be valid as well?

We can, in fact, explain why Black's example works, by attending to the relationship between ought-judgments, reasons, and preferences. Any judgment about what should be done requires reasons in its support. If I say you should get out of the room, you may ask why. If there is no reason, then it isn't true that you should leave – my suggestion is merely strange. Suppose, however, I tell you the room is on fire. That provides a reason; and if you believe me, you will no doubt leave at once. But whether this *is* a reason for you will depend on your attitudes. If you want to avoid being burned, then the fact that the room is on fire is a reason for you to leave. In the unlikely event that you don't care whether you are burned, this fact may have no importance for you. It will not provide a reason for you to leave.

Other examples come easily to mind. Suppose you and I are sitting in a movie theater; we have come to see *The General*. I realize, however, that we are in the wrong theater. So I say we should move next door. Why? Because *The General* is being shown there, not here. Again, this is a reason for you to move only if you want to see that movie. If you don't care which movie you see, it is not a reason for you to move.

These examples illustrate one common type of practical reasoning. In each case, there is a judgment about what should be done (You should leave the room, We should change theaters) and a reason is supplied why this should be done (The room is on fire, *The General* is being shown next door). The fact that you have a certain desire (to be safe, to see *The General*) explains why the reason cited *is a reason* for you to do the indicated action. There is no mystery, then, why this pattern of reasoning is valid:

> You do not want to be burned.
> The room is on fire, and the only way you can avoid being burned is to leave.
> Therefore, you should leave.
>
> We want to see *The General*.
> The only way we can see *The General* is to go next door.
> Therefore, we should go next door.

One qualification needs to be added. It may be objected that these conclusions do not follow because there may be reasons not yet noticed why you should not leave the room, or why we should not go next door. Perhaps, for example, we should not go next door because a maniac is there shooting people. So it would not follow that we should go next door simply because we want to see *The General*. But this observation, while it is true enough, requires no fundamental change in our analysis. The new information will only form part of another argument of the same form: We don't want to be shot; there is a maniac next door shooting people; therefore we should not go next door. Whether we should go next door "all things considered" will just depend on whether we prefer missing the movie to being shot.

Black's example trades on the same features of practical reasoning. It says that Fischer should move the Queen, a judgment that is true only if there are good reasons in its support. Then just such a reason is provided (because moving the Queen is the only way to mate Botwinnik). And finally, the relevance of this reason is secured by asserting that Fischer has the required attitude (he wants to mate Botwinnik). If Fischer wants to mate Botwinnik, there is a good reason for him to move the Queen. So it follows that he should move the Queen.

Hume was wrong, then, to say that we can never derive "ought" from "is." But he was wrong for a reason that his own analysis exposes. If our premises include information about a person's relevant desires, we may validly draw conclusions about what he or she should do. This result is not out of keeping with the spirit of Hume's view. Indeed, it is probably better to express Hume's view as the idea that we cannot derive ought-judgments from facts about how the world is *independently of our desires and other attitudes regarding it*. That is the point of Hume's Guillotine.

II

We now have the rudiments of a naturalistic theory of reasons. According to this theory, attitudes are not themselves reasons, but they explain why facts are reasons. The reason you should leave the room is simply that it is on fire; but your desire to avoid being burned explains why this *is a reason* for you to act rather than its being a matter of indifference.

Sometimes "following reason" is just a matter of adopting the appropriate means to achieve what one already wants to achieve. The examples about the fire and *The General* are like this. Reflecting on such examples, we might be tempted to conclude that reason only directs action toward goals that are already fixed by pre-existing attitudes. We may call this *The Simple Picture*. According to the Simple Picture, each of us begins with a set of attitudes that are simply "given," independently of thought and reflection. We want (or approve, or care about) some things and we don't want (or approve, or care about) others. Then, reason comes in to tell us what we must do in order for those attitudes to be satisfied. Hume seemed to accept The Simple Picture when he wrote that "Reason is, and ought only to be the slave of the passions, and can never pretend to any other office than to serve and obey them" (Hume 1739: 415).

But The Simple Picture is mistaken, because what people care about is itself sensitive to pressure from the deliberative process. The process of "thinking through" the facts surrounding an issue can affect one's attitudes regarding it. Thinking things through can have the effect of strengthening the feelings one already has, but it can also cause feelings to weaken, to be modified, or to disappear; and it can cause new feelings to form. Thus our cognitive capacities can play a significant part in forming, shaping, and sustaining our attitudes. They need not merely "serve and obey" whatever attitudes we already happen to have.

This is a common phenomenon. Prior to deliberation, a person might have all sorts of attitudes, including, say, a love of smoking cigarettes, a hatred of Jews, and a resentment of demands that he contribute to charities. But then – if he is the sort of person who is willing to think seriously about such matters – he might consider that cigarette smoking can shorten his life; that contrary to the anti-Semitic stereotypes, Jews are people much like everyone else; and that there are, after all, children starving. As a result, his feelings about such things might change.

Thinking through the facts is not a simple matter. Philosophers from Aristotle to David Falk have emphasized that after "the facts" are established, a separate cognitive process is required for one to understand fully the import of what one knows. It is necessary not merely to know the facts, but to rehearse them carefully in one's mind in an impartial, nonevasive way. Aristotle even suggested that there are two distinct kinds of knowledge here: first, the sort of knowledge had by one who is able to recite facts "as a drunken man may mutter the verses of Empedocles," but without understanding their meaning; and second, the sort of knowledge that one has when one has carefully thought about what one knows (Aristotle [1147b] 1931).

We all know, for example, in an abstract sort of way, that many children in the world are dying from starvation and easily preventable diseases; yet for most of us this makes no difference to our conduct. We will spend money on trivial things for ourselves, rather than using it to help them. How are we to explain this? The Aristotelian explanation is that we "know" the children are dying only in the sense in which the drunkard knows Empedocles's verses – we simply recite the fact. Suppose, though, that we thought carefully about what life is like for those children. Our attitudes, our conduct, and the moral conclusions we reach might be substantially altered.

Thus moral judgments express attitudes, but not just any attitudes: they express attitudes that are evoked and sustained by the deliberative process. Thus, to say that an action is morally required is to say that one cannot help but feel a "sentiment of approbation" (to use Hume's term) toward it when the full range of our cognitive capacities are functioning as well as they can.

III

This apparently leads to relativism. Because people's preferences could differ, even when they are being attentive and thoughtful, what counts as a reason for one person need not be a reason for another. However, naturalists emphasize that people do share many of the same values, because people are basically alike in their interests, needs, and psychological makeup. (This is an empirical matter; it could have been otherwise.) To complete this thought, naturalists have appealed to the idea of a common human nature, shared by all people – or at least, the vast majority of people – that gives rise to our basic values. Thus Hume wrote that "When you pronounce any action or character to be vicious, you mean nothing, but that *from the constitution of your nature* you have a feeling or sentiment of blame from the contemplation of it" (Hume 1739: 469; italics added).

What is "the constitution of our nature" like, and what motivational structure does it sustain? Since Darwin, one of the most fruitful sources of information about human nature has been evolutionary theory. The most pervasive and general features of human psychology – our attitudes, dispositions, and cognitive capacities – can be viewed as the products of natural selection. This helps us to understand how those psychological features work and why we have them. Simply put, we have the psychological characteristics that enabled our ancestors to win the competition to survive and reproduce.

What is moral behavior like, viewed from this perspective? Moral behavior is, at the most general level, altruistic behavior, motivated by the desire to promote not only our own welfare but the welfare of others. Can we understand this as the product of natural selection? Darwin realized early on that this is not easy.

The problem is that altruism involves acting for the good of others even at some cost to oneself. Therefore the tendency to behave altruistically seems to work *against* reproductive success. The altruist increases the chances of others' surviving, by helping them, while at the same time decreasing the chances of his own survival, by giving something up. Therefore we would expect natural selection to eliminate any tendency toward altruism. Darwin saw this and wrote:

> It is extremely doubtful whether the offspring of the more sympathetic and benevolent parents, or of those which were the most faithful to their comrades, would be reared in greater number than the children of selfish and treacherous parents of the same tribe. He who was ready to sacrifice his life, as many a savage has been, rather than betray his comrades, would often leave no offspring to inherit his noble nature. The bravest men, who were always willing to come to the front in war, and who freely risked their lives for others, would on an average perish in larger numbers than other men. Therefore it seems scarcely possible (bearing in mind that we are not here speaking of one tribe being victorious over another) that the number of men gifted with such virtues, or that the standard of their excellence, could be increased through natural selection, that is, by the survival of the fittest. (Darwin 1871: 163)

Nevertheless, the "social instincts," as Darwin called them – the impulse to help others, even at some cost to oneself – obviously do exist, not only in humans but in other animals as well. It is most conspicuously manifested in the behavior of family members toward one another. What accounts for the selfless devotion of parents, when their sacrifices decrease their own chances of survival? Darwin was mystified. "With respect to the origin of the parental and filial affections," he wrote, "which apparently lie at the basis of the social affections, it is hopeless to speculate" (Darwin 1871: 80–1).

The mystery remained unsolved until 1964 when W. D. Hamilton announced the theory of kin selection. Hamilton's idea was based on the observation that many individuals are genetically similar to one another – typically, one shares half the genes of one's siblings, one-eighth the genes of one's cousins, and so on. Therefore, acting in such a way as to increase the chances of a genetically similar individual's surviving is a way of increasing the chances of one's own genes being passed on to later generations. This being so, we would expect natural selection to favor a tendency to altruism toward one's near kin. This fits well with the phenomenon of altruism as we commonly observe it: individuals do behave far more solicitously toward their relatives than toward strangers.

Viewed in this light, there is nothing mysterious about the self-sacrificial altruism shown by parents and siblings. It is no more than we should expect, given how natural selection operates. Of course, the point is not that individuals calculate how to ensure the propagation of their genes – no one does that. The point is that these are types of genetically-influenced behavior that will be preserved by the same mechanism that preserves any other beneficial characteristic.

But not all altruism is kin altruism. Animals may be observed to sacrifice their own interests to help others who are not closely related to them, and this is more difficult to explain. To deal with this problem, evolutionary psychologists have turned to the idea of "reciprocal altruism." The idea is that an individual performs a service for another because doing so increases the likelihood that a similar service will be performed for him – a monkey picks the external parasites off the back of another monkey, and then the favor is returned. It is easy enough to see that such reciprocal aid, when practiced by all (or even most) members of a group, will work to the advantage of all; but it is not so easy to see how, on the principles of natural selection, this sort of cooperative behavior could become established in the first place.

Perhaps the problem could be solved if we could regard the Darwinian "struggle for survival" as a competition between groups. Then we could argue that social cooperation gives the members of a group a competitive advantage – we could say that the members of groups that cooperate are more likely to survive and reproduce than members of groups that do not cooperate. But ever since Darwin, the standard way of understanding the struggle for survival has been as a competition between individuals, not groups. (This is reflected in the quotation from Darwin above, in which he says we must bear in mind that "we are not here speaking of one tribe being victorious over another.") Some observers see no justification for such an exclusive emphasis on the individual as the unit of selection. R. C. Lewontin views it as merely an "article of ideological orthodoxy, virtually unchallenged at present by any student of evolution, . . . that the individual organism is the object seen directly by natural selection":

> What is being explicitly denied is that characteristics favorable to the population as a whole will evolve by natural selection, except as a secondary consequence of the greater fitness of individuals over others within the population. So, for example, we are not allowed to claim that linguistic communication between humans was favored by natural selection by arguing that a group of protohumans who could talk to each other would be at an advantage in warfare or hunting over other groups who were without language. (Lewontin 1998: 60)

Why not? Sober and Wilson (1998) have argued that group selection has an important place in the explanation of cooperative behavior. Meanwhile, other investigators have gone in a different direction, arguing that to explain cooperation we must consider "units of selection" *smaller* than the traditional individual organisms – genes, for example, or maybe even cells (see Dawkins 1976 and 1982; and Ridley 1996). The field is crowded with competing proposals.

Many of these proposals, however, draw inspiration from a single, surprising source. The Prisoner's Dilemma, a problem studied by game theorists, has implications for a variety of issues in ethical theory, and it figures into various attempts to explain the origins of social cooperation.

In the Prisoner's Dilemma, two players must choose whether to cooperate or defect, with neither knowing what the other will do. For each player the payoff for defecting is higher than for cooperating, no matter what the other does. Therefore, it seems that the winning move must be to defect. But if both defect, the payoff is less than if both cooperate. The payoffs are stipulated as:

> *Both cooperate*: both get 3
> *Both defect*: both get 1
> *One cooperates and one defects*: the defector gets 5, the cooperator gets 0

So each player is tempted to defect because he gets the highest payoff if he defects while her "opponent" cooperates; while at the same time, both fear cooperating because if the opponent defects they end up with zero. Nonetheless, both will be better off cooperating than defecting.

The Prisoner's Dilemma models a deep problem about social cooperation. Like the monkeys who need to have their backs groomed, we will all be better off cooperating than if each of us goes it alone. Yet, if any one of us could become a "free rider," gaining the benefits of other people's cooperation without cooperating ourselves, we would be even better off (while those provide us the benefits would be worse off).

In such circumstances, what is the best strategy? The social theorist Robert Axelrod investigated this question by setting up an Iterated Prisoner's Dilemma tournament in which players had to decide repeatedly whether to cooperate. In each round, a player and his opponent would play the game 200 times. Each would decide, privately, whether to cooperate; and then the choices would be revealed and the payoffs noted. Then the process would be repeated.

Obviously, many strategies are possible. You could always cooperate or always defect; you could alternate cooperating and defecting; you could always do the opposite of what your opponent did on the previous move; and on and on. The possibilities are infinite. Axelrod arranged for his tournament to be played on computers and invited professional game theorists to submit programs that would play against one another. The winning program, called Tit-for-Tat, was submitted by Anatol Rapoport of the University of Toronto. After it was known that Tit-for-Tat had won the first tournament, a second was held and 62 programs were submitted in the attempt to find a better strategy; but again Tit-for-Tat was victorious.

Tit-for-Tat was surprisingly simple. It contained only two instructions: On the first move, cooperate. On each subsequent move, do whatever the other player did on the previous move. It is remarkable how these instructions correspond to common moral feelings. It is a "nice" strategy, in that it begins by cooperating, and it will continue to cooperate as long as the opponent is cooperating. It will never try to "take advantage" by being the first to defect. But it will not allow itself to be exploited more than once: when the opponent stops cooperating, Tit-for-Tat stops immediately. On the other hand, Tit-for-Tat is also a "forgiving" strategy. When the other player resumes cooperating, Tit-for-Tat resumes cooperating immediately.

Ethical theorists have found this result to be important for various reasons. Contract theorists, who see moral requirements as arising from agreements of mutual self-interest, have cited the Prisoner's Dilemma as exemplifying the kind of social situation which requires us to "bargain our way into morality" – we agree to cooperate by telling the truth, not harming others, and so on, so long as others obey those rules as well (Gauthier 1986). Utilitarians, meanwhile, have taken the victory of Tit-for-Tat as indicating the kind of approach we should adopt in our dealings with other people if we want everyone to be as well-off as possible. (Singer 1995: 142–52, draws a number of conclusions of this kind.) For naturalists, however, it has a different significance.

Axelrod's work might help us to understand how reciprocal altruism could have evolved. Suppose, as Axelrod's research indicates, that in a wide range of social settings Tit-for-Tat players end up better off than individuals who adopt other strategies. Then, in Darwinian terms, Tit-for-Tat players are more likely than others to survive and reproduce; and this means that any genes that dispose one to play Tit-for-Tat will be more likely to be represented in future generations. Thus we would have evolved as Tit-for-Tat players.

It would be a mistake, however, to think that because Tit-for-Tat won Axelrod's tournaments, it has been shown to be the best strategy in any environment. Axelrod's tournaments featured programs following a large number of strategies. But suppose there were only two strategies, Tit-for-Tat and a player (or players) who invariably defected. Then, Tit-for-Tat would lose every time. This poses a problem for the idea that social cooperation evolved because the tendency to play Tit-for-Tat was individually advantageous. It would be advantageous only if the environment already included other individuals disposed to cooperate. (And the problem is even more serious: we cannot sensibly speak of Tit-for-Tat, or any other strategy, as being best in all environments. Which strategy will win always depends on what the other competitors are like.) At this point some supplementary idea seems required – perhaps that individuals with different behavioral dispositions have appeared as Darwinian "variations," with Tit-for-Tat, or something similar to Tit-for-Tat, prevailing in the familiar way that advantageous variations prevail.

At any rate, none of this means that we consciously play the game. Rather, it would mean that we come equipped with a set of emotions that dispose us to deal with others as though we were playing the game. At least three kinds of emotions are involved. Friendliness and a general beneficence dispose us to be helpful to others so long as they return our good will. But we take offense when others are hostile; we resent bad treatment from them and we stop treating them well. And finally, we are disposed to forgive people their past misdeeds, so long as they express remorse and take the first step toward reform. Together, these emotions cause us to make the major moves in Tit-for-Tat. It is this combination of emotional dispositions that natural selection preserves, in the same way that it preserves any characteristics that contribute to reproductive fitness.

Evolutionary naturalism has been an important option in recent philosophy, not only in ethics but in epistemology and philosophy of mind. Naturalists have sometimes made exaggerated claims about the importance of evolution for ethics. E. O. Wilson, for example, has argued that moral philosophy in the traditional sense is no longer needed, because biology explains ethics "at all depths" (Wilson 1975: 3). The naturalistic theory we are considering here, however, is content with a more modest claim. An evolutionary understanding of the origins of altruism – whatever the details of that account might turn out to be – fills in some of the details of our conception of human nature. It helps us to understand what human beings are like, and why; and that in turn enables us to discern the values that human beings will normally have in common.

IV

Ethical naturalism says that goodness, rightness, and other such properties are "natural" properties. According to the version of ethical naturalism we are considering, which natural properties are they?

Moral properties turn out to be similar to what John Locke called "secondary qualities." The distinction between primary and secondary qualities is tricky , but for our purposes it may suffice to say, paraphrasing Locke, that secondary qualities are powers that objects have to produce effects in the consciousness of observers. Color is the classic (if disputed) example of a secondary quality. Primary qualities, such as a box's shape and mass, are what they are independently of observers. The box's shape and mass would be the same even if there were no conscious beings in the universe. But what of its color? Color is not a thing spread upon the box like a coat of paint. Rather, the box's surface reflects light-waves in a certain way. Then, this light strikes the eyes of observers, and as a result the observers have visual experiences of a certain character. If the light-waves falling on the box were different, or if the visual apparatus of the observer were different, then the box would have a different color, and this would no more be the box's "real" color than any other. The box's color, then, just consists in its power, under certain conditions, to cause a certain kind of observer to have a certain kind of visual experience.

Much the same may be said about other powers of things to induce other sorts of experiences in us. What does it mean for something to be sour? A lemon is sour because, when we put it to our tongues, we experience a certain kind of taste. What is sour for humans might not be sour for animals with different kinds of sense-organs; and if we were made differently, lemons might not be sour for us. Moreover, what is sour for one human being may not be sour for another – although we do have a notion of what is normal for our species in this regard. But despite all this, to say that lemons are sour is not a "subjective" remark. It is a perfectly objective fact that lemons have the power to produce the sensation in us. Whether they are sour is not merely a matter of opinion.

On the version of ethical naturalism we are considering, moral properties are properties of this kind – they are powers to cause us to have certain sorts of attitudes or emotions (see McDowell 1985). Being evil consists in having what it takes to provoke a thoughtful person to such responses as hatred, opposition, and contempt. When we think of a murderer and his victim, the (ordinary) facts of the matter are such that they evoke feelings of horror in us; the evil is simply the power to call forth this reaction. Similarly, being good would consist in being so constituted as to evoke our support and approval.

Dewey compares "desirable" with "edible," and the analogy is illuminating (Dewey 1929: 166). Whether something is edible is a matter of fact; if something is not edible, we cannot simply decide to make it so by adopting a positive attitude toward it. Yet whether something is edible for us depends as much on the kind of creature we are as on the kind of thing it is. If we were different, what is edible for us might be different too. However, we would not say that a certain food was inedible simply because, for special reasons, it could not be eaten by a few people. We have a conception of what is normal for humans, given the kind of creature a human being is, and what is edible for humans is what may be eaten by the representative human being, whether or not it can be eaten by everyone.

It may be thought that the analogy with "edible" breaks down at a crucial point. "Edible" means, roughly, "capable of being eaten," whereas "desirable" (in the sense relevant to ethics) means, again roughly, "worthy of being desired." So it may be thought that Dewey's theory trades on a confusion between two senses of "desirable" – "capable of being desired" and "worthy of being desired." The charge is that he thinks he has defined the latter, ethically relevant, sense of "desirable," but really he has only given a definition of the former sense of the term, which is not relevant to ethics. But this charge is not well-founded. The essence of this sort of view is that to be worthy of being desired is to be capable of being desired, under the circumstances of thought and reflection. Perhaps this is not correct, but it is not a confusion of the theory: it is the theory itself.

This sort of view is, in an obvious way, a compromise between objective and subjective views of ethics. It is objective in that identifies good and evil with something that is really "there" in the world outside us, but at the same time, what is there is the power to produce feelings inside us.

V

Arguments against philosophical theories often turn out to be nothing more than thinly disguised descriptions of the theory, together with the insistence that it cannot be true. Naturalists have suffered from this treatment more than most. Despite his eminence as a logician, when John Stuart Mill said that "The sole evidence it is possible to produce that anything is desirable is that people do actually desire it" (Mill 1861: 34), he was accused of committing a simple fallacy: it does not follow from the fact that something is desired that it is desirable. But Mill was only expressing the basic naturalistic idea that desirability is an empirical matter. We learn that a lemon is sour by tasting it; the proof of the sourness is the taste in our mouths. Similarly, we learn that something is desirable by contemplating it and as a result experiencing desire.

Complications arise, however, because such feelings can have other sources – a feeling might be the product of prejudice or cultural conditioning rather than pro-ceeding from what Hume called "a proper discernment of its object." The problem is how to distinguish between sentiments that indicate the presence of moral prop-erties and those that do not. Moral properties are powers to provoke sentiments in us. But might we not have the sentiment in the absence of such properties?

The problem will be solved if there is a way to conduct the process of deliberation that eliminates those other sources – if we can set aside prejudice and other influ-ences and take an objective look at the matter under consideration, in such a way that we will be justified in concluding that it is the thing itself that evokes our response. As Hume knew, doing this might require a considerable expenditure of cognitive energy:

> But in order to pave the way for such a sentiment and give a proper discernment of its object, it is often necessary, we find, that much reasoning should precede, that nice distinctions be made, just conclusions drawn, distant comparisons formed, compli-cated relations examined, and general facts fixed and ascertained. (Hume 1752: 73; also see Dewey 1939: 31–2; and Falk, 1986)

A sentiment indicates the presence of moral qualities only to the extent that it results from this kind of thinking. Otherwise, we cannot infer that the object itself has what it takes to cause the feeling.

The secondary quality view also fits well with the facts of ethical agreement and disagreement. There is, of course, a vast amount of agreement in ethics. We agree about good and evil for the same reason we agree about what is sour. Lemons affect most of us in the same way because we have similar sense organs; and murder affects us in the same way because we are similar in what Hume called "the constitution of our natures." The similarity is not hard to understand: we have evolved, by natural selection, not only as moderately altruistic beings, but as creatures with common desires and needs. We all want and enjoy friends. We take pleasure in our children. We respond to music. We are curious. We all have reason to want a peaceful, secure society, because only in the context of such a society can our desires be satisfied. Such facts support large-scale agreements about respect for life and property, truth-fulness, promise-keeping, friendship, and much more.

All this is compatible, however, with a degree of disagreement. As we have al-ready observed, what is sour for one human being may not be sour for another – although we do have a notion of what is normal for our species. As a practical matter, however, we need never assume that moral disagreements are expressions of intractable differences between people. More mundanely, and more frequently, disa-greement will be the result of ignorance, prejudice, self-deceit, and the like. Our working hypothesis may be that we are enough alike that we could be brought to agree about most things, if only the sources of error could be eliminated.

VI

The most important objection to ethical naturalism is that it leaves out the normative aspect of ethics. Since the whole point of ethics is to guide action, there could hardly be a more serious complaint. The objection can be expressed in various ways. One way, which we have already considered, is to say that we cannot derive "ought" from "is." Another is to say that ethical assertions are prescriptive, whereas their naturalistic translations are merely descriptive. Or it may just be said: look at the whole naturalistic account and you will find nothing that tells you what to do.

Is this objection sound? On the one hand, the version of ethical naturalism that we have considered does incorporate normative elements. On this view, ethics is action-guiding because of its connection with our desires and interests. Ethical reasoning engages our preferences, and the ethical "properties" of things are powers they have to influence our preferences. So we have some explanation of the normative aspect of ethics. Somehow, though, this does not seem to dispel the worry.

There is another way to put the complaint, due to Thomas Nagel (1997), that explains why the worry persists. We may compare our naturalistic account of ethics with naturalistic accounts of other subjects, such as mathematics. Why did Frege object to psychologistic theories of mathematics? Mathematics, he insisted, is an autonomous subject with its own internal standards of truth. Consider Euclid's famous demonstration that there are an infinite number of primes:

> Take any list of prime numbers you like, and multiply them together. Then add one. Call the resulting number n. n is not evenly divisible by any of the numbers on your list, because there will always be a remainder of one. Therefore, either n is itself a prime number, or it is divisible by some prime not on your list. Either way, there is at least one prime not on your list. Since this will be true no matter what list you begin with, it follows that there are an infinite number of primes.

If you think through this reasoning, and understand it, then you know that there are an infinite number of primes. But notice that the reasoning makes no reference to you, your cognitive capacities, your brain, your education, the social setting that produces and sustains mathematicians, the mathematical beliefs of people in your culture, the English language, or your understanding of the English language. And no information about any of those things needs to be added to the proof: it is sufficient as it is. Moreover, no information about those other matters can cast doubt on the conclusion that the primes are infinite. That could be accomplished only be showing that there is something wrong with the proof itself. As Nagel puts it, in so far as the primes are concerned, the proof is "the last word."

Now consider this example of ethical reasoning:

> If we perform the operation on the child without first administering the anesthetic, she will be in agony. The anesthetic will have no ill effects on her; it will simply render

her temporarily unconscious and insensitive to pain. Therefore, the anesthetic should
be administered.

If you think through this reasoning, and understand it, then you know that the anesthetic should be administered. But like Euclid's proof, this reasoning makes no reference to your cognitive capacities, your emotions, the beliefs of people in your society, and so on. And no information about these other matters can cast doubt on the conclusion that the anesthetic should be used. That could be accomplished only be showing that there is something wrong with the reasoning itself. This is the sense in which ethics is autonomous: the other matters do not figure into the reasoning about what should be done. In so far as the anesthetic is concerned, the reasoning is the last word.

If the reasoning is sufficient unto itself, what does our naturalistic account add? The naturalistic account explains what is happening as you think through the reasoning: you are considering facts that have the power to influence your attitudes, considering, in Hume's words, "the constitution of your nature." Your nature, formed by natural selection, includes feelings of protectiveness toward children and a disposition to care about other people, at least until they give you reason to resent them. Therefore, the result of thinking through the facts is a "sentiment of approbation" toward administering the anesthetic, which is expressed by the conclusion that it should be done. But this is what the process looks like when viewed from the outside. From the outside, we see your human nature, your feelings, the operation of your cognitive capacities, and the interaction of all these with the facts about children and anesthetics. From the inside, however, you do not consider such things: you simply think through the argument.

This is the sense in which naturalism leaves out the normative. Naturalism provides a view from the outside, and from that perspective, it provides all sorts of interesting information. But it misses something that can be experienced only from the inside, namely the normative force of the reasoning. Examined from the outside, the normative aspect disappears, because when we begin to talk *about* the reasoning – quoting it, commenting on it – we cease to say anything that compels action.

So a naturalistic account of ethics seems deficient. But should we say it is wrongheaded and reject it altogether, or should we say only that it is incomplete? If we reject it altogether, we forego a great deal of understanding and insight into the nature of ethics. So long as we confine ourselves to thinking through ethical arguments "from the inside," we can say nothing about the relation between moral thinking and the emotions, the nature of the properties to which moral terms apparently refer, or any of the other matters that have traditionally engaged moral philosophers. Indeed, we can say nothing *about* ethics at all – we cannot even say, along with the critics of naturalism, that it is autonomous. Perhaps our conclusion should be that, while moral thinking itself is done from the inside, moral philosophy is done from the outside.

References

Adams, E. M.: *Ethical Naturalism and the Modern World-View* (Chapel Hill: University of North Carolina Press, 1960).

Aristotle: *Nicomachean Ethics*, trans. W. D. Ross, in *The Basic Works of Aristotle* (New York: Random House, 1931).

Axelrod, Robert: *The Evolution of Cooperation* (New York: Basic Books, 1984).

Black, Max: "The Gap Between 'Is' and 'Should'," *The Philosophical Review*, 73 (1964): 165–81.

Broad, C. D.: "Some of the Main Problems of Ethics," *Philosophy*, 31 (1946): 99–117.

Darwin, Charles: *The Descent of Man, and Selection in Relation to Sex* (London: John Murray, 1871).

Dawkins, Richard: *The Selfish Gene* (Oxford: Oxford University Press, 1976).

——: *The Extended Phenotype* (Oxford: Freeman, 1982).

Dewey, John: *The Quest for Certainty* (New York: Capricorn Books, 1960; originally published in 1929).

——: *Theory of Valuation* (Chicago: University of Chicago Press, 1939).

Falk, W. D.: *Ought, Reasons, and Morality* (Ithaca: Cornell University Press, 1986).

Gauthier, David: *Morals By Agreement* (Oxford: Oxford University Press, 1986).

Hamilton, W. D.: "The Genetical Evolution of Social Behavior," *Journal of Theoretical Biology*, 12 (1964): 1–16, 17–32.

Hobbes, Thomas: *Leviathan*, ed. Edwin Curley (Indianapolis: Hackett, 1994; originally published in 1651).

Hume, David: *An Enquiry Concerning the Principles of Morals*. Reprint ed. L. A. Selby-Bigge (Oxford: Oxford University Press, 1902; originally published in 1752).

——: *A Treatise of Human Nature*, ed. L. A. Selby-Bigge (Oxford: Clarendon Press, 1888; originally published in 1739–40).

Lewontin, R. C.: "Survival of the Nicest?" *New York Review of Books* (October 22, 1998): 59–63.

McDowell, John: "Values and Secondary Qualities," *Morality and Objectivity*, ed. Ted Honderich (London: Routledge and Kegan Paul, 1985), pp. 110–29.

Mill, John Stuart: *Utilitarianism*, ed. George Sher (Indianapolis: Hackett, 1979; originally published in 1861).

Moore, G. E.: *Principia Ethica* (Cambridge: Cambridge University Press, 1903).

Nagel, Thomas: *The Last Word* (New York: Oxford University Press, 1997).

Ridley, Matt: *The Origins of Virtue* (Harmondsworth: Penguin Books, 1996).

Singer, Peter: *How Are We To Live?* (Amherst, NY: Prometheus Books, 1995).

Sober, Elliott, and David Sloan Wilson: *Unto Others: The Evolution and Psychology of Unselfish Behavior* (Cambridge, MA: Harvard University Press, 1998).

Wilson, E. O.: *Sociobiology: The New Synthesis* (Cambridge, MA: Harvard University Press, 1975).

Chapter 5

Moral Intuition

Jeff McMahan

Moral Inquiry

Suppose we wish to understand a particular moral problem – for example, abortion. How should we proceed? One approach, which I favor, is to reason on the basis of our existing substantive moral beliefs. We may, however, suspect that our moral beliefs about abortion, insofar as we have any prior to serious reflection, are unreliable. It might be, for example, that our beliefs about abortion reflect the lingering influence of a religious education that we now repudiate, or that our sensitivity to the status of the fetus is somewhat numbed by our feminist sympathies. Thus we may take as our starting point certain related moral beliefs about which we are more confident: for example, that killing an innocent person (where "person" is not synonymous with "human being" but instead refers to any individual with a mental life beyond a certain threshold of complexity and sophistication) is seriously morally objectionable, whereas painlessly killing a lower nonhuman animal (for example, a frog) is only mildly morally objectionable. There is, of course, divergence of opinion even about these cases. Some people believe that killing an innocent person can never be justified, while others believe that it can be justified whenever it is necessary to save the lives of a greater number of innocent persons. And, while some believe that there is no objection whatever to killing a frog independently of the effects this might have on human interests, others believe that killing a frog is seriously objectionable just because of the effect on the frog and requires a substantial justification in order to be permissible. Nevertheless, everyone agrees that killing an innocent person is significantly more objectionable morally than killing a frog, other things being equal.

We could therefore initiate our inquiry into abortion by exploring our confident sense that there is an enormous moral difference between killing persons and killing lower animals – so that, for example, the killing of a lower animal might be justified by appeal to considerations that would not constitute even the beginning of a justification for killing a person. With these beliefs as our starting point, we could work our way toward a better understanding of abortion. We could proceed by trying to understand why killing people is generally wrong and why it is generally so much more seriously wrong than killing lower animals. What are the relevant differences between persons and lower animals? Are the properties of persons that make killing them generally worse all intrinsic properties? Or is part of the explanation of the greater wrongness of killing persons that we bear certain relations to other people that do not exist between ourselves and animals? In addressing these questions, we may consult our intuitions about a range of particular cases and this may yield provocative results. We may notice, for example, that the extent to which an act of killing an animal seems wrong varies with the degree of harm the animal suffers in dying. Thus it seems more objectionable to kill a dog than to kill a frog; and the explanation seems connected with the fact that the future life that the dog loses would have been a better or more valuable life. But we may also notice that the extent to which it is wrong to kill a person does *not* seem to vary with the extent to which death is bad for the victim. Thus it seems no less wrong, other things being equal, to kill a dullard than to kill a genius, or to kill an elderly person with a reduced life expectancy than to kill a person in the prime of life, even though in each case the latter victim would seem to lose a better future life than the former. Further inquiry is necessary to understand the significance of these findings.

As our understanding of the morality of killing in general increases, we can begin to extract from our findings various implications for the morality of abortion. Suppose, for example, that we discover that there are certain properties that persons generally possess that lower animals do not that seem to help explain the difference between killing people and killing animals. We can then consider whether these properties are possessed by human fetuses (which are human beings but not persons, according to the way this term is used here). If they are, then in that respect abortion is relevantly like killing an adult human being; if not, there is reason to suppose that abortion should instead be assimilated to the paradigm of killing animals.

These remarks about abortion are intended only to provide a sketchy illustration of a certain approach to practical ethics, a certain general pattern of reasoning about moral problems. Its most conspicuous feature is that it treats certain substantive moral beliefs that we already have as reliable starting points for moral inquiry. It presupposes that at least some of our moral intuitions have a certain prima facie normative authority.

Intuitions

What are moral intuitions? As I will understand the term, a moral intuition is a spontaneous moral judgment, often concerning a particular act or agent, though an intuition may also have as its object a *type* of act or, less frequently, a more general moral rule or principle. In saying that a moral intuition is a spontaneous judgment, I mean that it is not the result of conscious inferential reasoning. In the first instance at least, the allegiance the intuition commands is not based on an awareness of its relations to one's other beliefs. If one considers the act of torturing the cat, one judges immediately that, in the circumstances, this would be wrong. One does not need to consult one's other beliefs in order to arrive at this judgment. This kind of spontaneity, I should stress, is entirely compatible with the possibility that a fair amount of cognitive processing may be occurring beneath the surface of consciousness.

Also, to say that intuitions arise spontaneously is not to imply that they must arise instantaneously, in the manner of a sense perception, when one is presented with a certain act or a description of a certain type of act. If, for example, a case is described in which there is considerable complexity of detail, one may have to explore it at length in order to distinguish and assimilate its various relevant features – in much the same way that one might have to examine the many details of a highly complex work of art in order to have any aesthetic response at all. Just as it may take time to summon an aesthetic response even when the process of contemplation involves only the assimilation and appreciation of all the elements of the piece, so moral reflection may take time even when it does not involve conscious inferential reasoning.

The belief I cited as one of the possible starting points for an inquiry about abortion – namely, that killing an innocent person is in general seriously wrong – may not or may not count as an intuition according to this understanding, though for most of us it has an intuitive basis. It counts as an intuition if one finds it immediately compelling that this particular type of act is wrong, but not if one accepts the generalization as an inductive inference from one's intuitively finding the killing of a person wrong in a succession of particular instances. Notice, too, that this case illustrates the difficulty that sometimes arises in distinguishing an intuition about a type of act from an intuition about a moral principle. The killing of an innocent person is a type of act but the claim that killing an innocent person is wrong is also a reasonably general moral principle. So an intuitive apprehension that killing an innocent person is wrong may be interpreted as having either an act-type or a moral principle as its object.

In the history of moral philosophy, the idea that moral intuitions have normative authority has been associated, unsurprisingly, with a cluster of theories that have traveled under the label "Intuitionism." Those doctrines are many and various and I do not propose to disentangle them. But two claims associated with certain historically prominent variants of Intuitionism have done much to discredit the appeal to intuitions. One of these is that intuitions are the deliverances of a special organ or faculty of moral perception, typically understood as something like an inner eye that provides occult access to a noumenal realm of objective values. The other is often regarded as a corollary of the first – namely, that intuitions are indubitable (that is, that their veridicality cannot be doubted) as well as infallible (that is, that they cannot in fact be mistaken). But numerous considerations – such as the diversity of moral intuitions, the fact that people do often doubt and even repudiate certain of their intuitions, and the evident origin of some intuitions in social prejudice or self-interest – make it untenable to suppose that intuitions are direct and infallible perceptions of moral reality.

There are other features that are occasionally attributed to intuitions that are in fact inessential. It is sometimes said, for example, that intuitions are "pretheoretical." If all this means is that they are not derived inferentially from a moral theory, then it of course follows from the stipulation that they are not the products of any sort of inferential reasoning. If, however, it means that intuitions must be untutored or entirely unaffected by a person's exposure to moral theory, then the requirement is evidently too strong. Just as many people's moral intuitions have been shaped by their early exposure to religious indoctrination, so some people's intuitions are gradually molded by their commitment to a particular moral theory. The stipulation that intuitions are not the products of conscious inference does not entail that they cannot be affected by learning. That they arise spontaneously is compatible with their having sources in one's nature that are malleable.

Theory

Many philosophers reject the idea that moral intuitions have normative authority. Peter Singer, for example, suggests that we should assume "that all the particular moral judgments we intuitively make are likely to derive from discarded religious systems, from warped views of sex and bodily functions, or from customs necessary for the survival of the group in social and economic circumstances that now lie in the distant past." On this assumption, he notes, "it would be best to forget all about our particular moral judgments" (Singer 1974: 516). It is, of course, possible to be rather less dismissive of intuitions and yet still regard them as lacking in normative authority. Some philosophers, for example, concede that intuitions may be tolerably reliable guides to action in most circumstances (since morality must ensure that people are equipped with dispositions to believe and act in certain ways in situations in which deliberation and reflection are not possible) but deny that they are a source of moral knowledge or have any proper role in reasoning about moral problems. They believe that practical reasoning about a moral problem must consist in determining what some favored moral theory implies about the problem. It is the theory that is the source of our moral knowledge concerning particular problems and cases. And the theory is itself validated by means other than the conformity of its implications with our intuitions.

According to this approach, if our concern is to understand the morality of abortion, our first task must be to discover the correct moral theory. Moral inquiry is initially and primarily theoretical; only at the end of the day is it possible to consider moral problems such as abortion, bringing the theory to bear and extracting from it the knowledge that we initially sought. This general approach therefore contrasts markedly with the first approach I sketched, according to which moral inquiry initially focuses on intuitions about problems and cases rather than on matters of abstract moral theory. According to the first approach, a moral theory about which we are entitled to be confident is something that we can hope to have only near the end of the process of inquiry into problems of substantive morality.

Let us refer to the two broadly defined patterns of moral inquiry that I have sketched as the *Intuitive Approach* and the *Theoretical Approach*. Both are richly represented in the history of moral philosophy. The Socrates of Plato's dialogues is an admirable exemplar of the Intuitive Approach, while Hobbes and Kant exemplify the Theoretical Approach. Each of the latter begins with a conception of the nature of morality that he believes dictates a certain method for arriving at moral judgments about particular problems and cases (although Hobbes also seems to treat certain substantive judgments – e.g., that promise-keeping is obligatory – as fixed points in the process of developing his theory). In recent years, most philosophers working on problems of practical ethics have largely followed the Intuitive Approach – though most (like Hobbes in the other camp) are not purists: they typically find occasion to consult the available theories for guidance or illumination. The Theoretical Approach also has many distinguished contemporary exponents, among them Richard Hare, Richard Brandt, and an assortment of theorists in one or another of the various traditions of contractarianism – though in general they tend to be more preoccupied with defending and elucidating the pet theory than with applying it to the problems of practical ethics.

The Theoretical Approach is usually reformist in a rather radical way. People have always reasoned and argued about substantive issues in morality. According to adherents of the Theoretical Approach, however, people have been misguided insofar as their reasoning has diverged from the forms and patterns of moral reasoning prescribed by the correct moral theory. Brandt, for example, suggests that "is morally wrong" means "would be prohibited by any moral code which all fully rational persons would tend to support, in preference to all others or none at all, for the society of the agent, if they expected to spend a lifetime in that society" (Brandt 1979: 194). Assuming that this definition also states a test for determining whether an act is wrong, it seems clear that any convergence of the conclusions of most people's actual moral reasoning and the conclusions that might result from Brandt's proposed mode of reasoning would be fortuitous or coincidental. According to the Theoretical Approach, therefore, philosophical ethics is utterly different from, say, the philosophy of science. While the philosopher of science may criticize certain aspects of the practice of science, and may urge scientists to revise their understanding of the nature of their practices or the status of their conclusions, the philosopher does not presume to tell scientists that they have all along been utilizing the wrong methods and would do better to adopt a wholly different approach. The Intuitive Approach is in general more respectful of the modes of moral reasoning that people actually employ – though only because people in fact tend to reason about moral problems in the way it recommends. It too can be revisionist – for example, in its condemnation of one very common mode of reasoning: namely, the deduction of moral conclusions from the supposedly infallible dicta found in one or another sacred text.

Theory Unchecked by Intuition

Could we really conduct our thinking about morality and moral problems in the way suggested by the Theoretical Approach, without building up from our moral intuitions or consulting those intuitions to test the plausibility of the implications of proposed moral theories? Even those who most vehemently deny that intuitions have any independent credibility nevertheless often build their arguments on the basis of appeals to common intuitions (for example, Rachels 1986: 112–13 and 134–5, and Singer 1993: 229). But, although this is suggestive of the difficulty of getting persuasive arguments off the ground without propelling them with our preexisting moral beliefs, it is merely an *ad hominem* point and as such does little to support the appeal to intuition. An alternative point that may be urged against the Theoretical Approach is that our intuitions often *compel* belief in a way that, for most of us, no moral theory does. If an intuition that is highly compelling cannot be reconciled with what seems to be the best supported moral theory, can it be rational to abandon the belief in which we have greater confidence at the behest of the less compelling one?

It is important to be clear about the nature of this challenge. The claim is not simply that moral intuitions often strike us as more obvious or less open to doubt than it seems that any moral theory is. By itself, this would not be a strong consideration in favor of the intuition. The theories of modern physics tell us that many of our common sense beliefs about the nature of the physical world are mistaken. Many of these beliefs seem overwhelmingly obvious while the theory that disputes them may be so recondite and arcane as to be unintelligible to all but a few. Yet most of us recognize that at least certain scientific theories that overturn aspects of our common sense conception of the physical world are so well established by their powers of explanation and prediction and by the control they give us over the forces of nature that we readily acquiesce in their claims and concede that our common sense views must be illusory. If a moral theory could command our allegiance by comparable means of persuasion, we might yield our intuitions to it without demur, even if it had none of the immediate obviousness in which our intuitions tend to come clothed. But the challenge to the Theoretical Approach is that no moral theory, at least at the present stage of the history of philosophical ethics, can have anything like the authority or degree of validation that the best supported scientific theories have. The lamentable truth is that we are at present deeply uncertain even about what types of consideration support or justify a moral theory. There are no agreed criteria for determining whether or to what extent a moral theory is justified. So when an intuition, which may be immediately compelling, comes into conflict with a moral theory, which can have nothing approaching the authority of a well grounded scientific theory, it is not surprising that we should often be profoundly reluctant to abandon the intuition at the bidding of the theory. We can, indeed, be reasonably confident *in advance* that none of the moral theories presently on offer is sufficiently credentialed to make it rationally required that we surrender our intuition.

It is instructive to consider how most of us respond when, on inquiring into a particular moral problem, we find that a moral theory has implications for the problem that clash with our intuitions. Our response is not to question how well grounded the theory is, on the assumption that we should be prepared to acquiesce if we find that the theory is well supported. If the theory generates its conclusion via a distinct argument, our tendency is to detach the argument from the parent theory and consider it on its own merits. According to R. M. Hare, for example, his universal prescriptivist theory of morality implies that we should reason about the morality of abortion by applying a variant of the Golden Rule: "we should do to others as we are glad that they did do to us" (Hare, 1975: 208). When we discover that this principle implies (according to Hare) not only that abortion is wrong (if other things are equal) but also that remaining childless is wrong (again if other things are equal), we do not go back to Hare's earlier books to check the arguments for universal prescriptivism. Instead we undertake an independent inquiry to try to determine whether and, if so, to what extent it matters to the morality of abortion that, when an abortion is not performed, there will typically later be a person who is glad to exist who would not have existed if the abortion had been performed. That is, if we are serious about understanding the morality of abortion, we will take seriously the considerations identified as relevant by the theory; and we may be grateful to the theory for helping us to see whatever relevance these considerations may in fact have; but we are generally not overawed by the fact that these considerations have been identified as relevant *by the theory*. Their provenance in the theory fails to impress.

One may even entertain a certain skepticism about whether the norms and principles extracted from a moral theory with foundations wholly independent of our intuitions can claim to be constitutive of morality at all. Recall, for example, Brandt's claim that an act is morally wrong if it "would be prohibited by any moral code which all fully rational persons would tend to support, in preference to all others or none at all, for the society of the agent, if they expected to spend a lifetime in that society." (Note that Brandt cannot make antecedent knowledge of right and wrong a component of rationality, for that would make the account circular.) The sort of code that might be chosen by rational persons to govern their association (assuming that rational people could agree to accept the same code) might be very pleasant to live under, but is there any guarantee that it would coincide with what we would recognize as *morality*? Although I cannot demonstrate this, I suspect that any such code would omit a very great deal of what seems to be universal, or nearly so, in human morality.

For example, every society of which I am aware, past and present, has generally discriminated morally, across a range of particular cases, between acts of killing and acts that involve allowing people to die. In other words, people everywhere tend to believe, intuitively, that killing a person is normally worse than an otherwise comparable act that involves letting a person die. But fully rational people, unencumbered by any prior moral ideas, who set out to devise a code to regulate their relations with one another might be unlikely to settle upon one that distinguished between killing and letting die, at least in anything like the way that people's actual moral beliefs have done. For they would presumably find it more to their advantage to adopt a code that would generally permit the killing of innocent people when this would be necessary to save the lives of a greater number of others. There is, of course, scope for debate about this. Perhaps rational people would prefer a code that would give protection of their autonomy priority over protection of their lives. But even if that were so, there are numerous other elements common to most moral actual moral codes that would be unlikely to occur to Brandt's rational moral architects: the notion of honor, various of the virtues, the idea that it is worse if a harm is an intended effect of one's action than if the same harm is a foreseen but unintended effect, the idea that one has duties of respect and beneficence to persons who are not members of the society governed by the code, and so on.

It is possible, of course, that some of these common elements of actual moral codes are in fact irrational – for example, a concern with honor or intention. Or, if they are not irrational, perhaps there is some reason that may be obscure to us but would be evident to rational moral architects, why it would be to their advantage to include these elements in their code. It seems to me, however, that these features of the codes that people actually live by are not obviously irrational and that there is reason to expect that they would have no appeal to rational choosers drained of all prior moral conviction. And if in fact these or other common features of our actual moral codes would *not* be included in the code that would be chosen, what reason would we have to recognize the chosen code as *morality* rather than as just the collection of rules that would make us all most comfortable? Is there really nothing more to morality than a set of rules the function of which is to facilitate smooth interaction and cooperation to mutual advantage among the members of a particular society? The phenomenology of moral experience certainly suggests that this is an altogether shallow and reductive understanding of the nature of morality.

I have focused on Brandt's theory for the purpose of illustration; but similar points could be urged against all moral theories with foundations independent of our moral intuitions. To the extent that a theory leaves out major features of what most of us would recognize as morality, there is reason to wonder whether the theory is really a theory about morality at all.

Moral Epistemology

The remarks in the previous section are meant only to suggest certain reservations we might have about the Theoretical Approach; they are far from providing decisive reasons for rejecting that approach. Moreover, even if we had stronger grounds for skepticism about the Theoretical Approach than those I have offered, this would still be insufficient to throw us into the arms of the Intuitive Approach. For it is hardly a ground for confidence in our intuitions that there are reasons for doubting the approach to moral inquiry that denies them a role. Something more positive has to be said on behalf of our intuitions themselves. At a minimum, more needs to be said about the role they are supposed to have in the structure of justification in ethics. In what follows I will first offer a few general remarks about moral episte-mology, after which I will briefly sketch an account of moral inquiry that offers an explanation of the role that intuitions should have in our moral thought. I will then conclude by noting that there is a conception of the nature of moral knowledge that has independent plausibility and, if correct, offers a deeper understanding of the epistemological status of moral intuitions. I should stress that the issues I will be addressing are deep and difficult, so that I can do little more here than skim the surface.

Theories in epistemology may be theories either of truth or of justification. I will focus on the issue of justification and simply assume that there is a tight connection between justification and truth. Accounts of justification tend to be divided into two major approaches: coherentism and foundationalism. This is the case in the narrower area of *moral* epistemology as well: accounts of moral justification tend to be either coherentist or foundationalist.

Coherentist accounts of moral justification hold that a moral belief is justified solely in terms of its relations, particularly its inferential relations, with other beliefs. It is justified to the extent that it coheres well with a set of beliefs that together form a coherent whole. By contrast, foundationalist accounts hold that some beliefs are self-justifying – at least in the sense that they are justified independently of their relations to other beliefs. According to foundationalist accounts, a moral belief is justified if and only if it is either self-justifying or bears an appropriate inferential relation to a belief that is self-justifying.

Of the two types of account, coherentism is generally thought to be more hospi-table to the Intuitive Approach. The most commonly endorsed method of moral inquiry among contemporary moral philosophers is the method described by John Rawls under the label "reflective equilibrium" (Rawls 1972: 19–21 and 46–51). According to the method of reflective equilibrium, we begin with a set of moral intuitions about particular acts or types of act, filter out those that are the obvious products of distorting influences, and then seek to unify the remaining intuitions under a set of more general principles. We seek principles that imply our particular judgments and also explain them, in the sense of showing how apparently disparate judgments may have common sources in more general values. (Actually, we could equally well start with candidate principles and then test them for compatibility with a range of intuitions. Nothing hinges on whether we collect intuitions to-gether first or start off instead by gathering principles.) But the match between principles and intuitions will inevitably be very imperfect in the first instance. A candidate principle may imply a great many of our intuitions and yet have some implications that conflict with other intuitions. In that case we may modify or even abandon the principle; but, if the principle has considerable explanatory power with respect to a wide range of intuitions and cannot be modified to accommodate deviant ones without significant sacrifice of this power, we may instead decide to reject the recalcitrant intuitions. In this way we move back and forth between intuitions and principles, making reciprocal adjustments until our beliefs at the various levels of generality are all brought into a state of harmony or reflective equilibrium. This method is generally interpreted in coherentist terms, in that it is understood to make coherence with other beliefs the sole criterion of a belief's credibility. Yet it obviously treats intuitions as potential sources of moral knowledge. Although intuitions arise noninferentially and thus, in coherentist terms, have no prima facie credibility on their own, those that survive the initial filtration and are compatible with the principles that emerge in the process of seeking reflective equilibrium turn out to be justified moral beliefs.

Foundationalist theories of moral justification tend to be favored by proponents of the Theoretical Approach. Typically, the foundational beliefs (that is, those that are not justified in terms of their relations to other beliefs) are held to be nonmoral; justified moral beliefs are all ultimately derivable via some process of reasoning that is based on the foundational nonmoral beliefs (for examples, see Timmons 1987). Those who attribute authority to our moral intuitions tend, understandably, to be more reluctant to embrace foundationalism. This is mainly because it seems implausible to regard our intuitions themselves as foundational. This seems to attribute to them too exalted a status. While our intuitions do seem to have a certain initial credibility, it seems exorbitant to suppose that they are self-evident or self-justifying. We recoil from the suggestion (advanced, as I noted earlier, by various traditional Intuitionists) that intuitions are the unshakable basis on which all moral knowledge rests.

There are, however, at least two ways of overcoming this ground of reluctance to combine foundationalism with the Intuitive Approach. The first is to recognize that a belief may be of the foundational *sort* and yet be defeasible. Suppose, for example, that sense perceptions are the foundations of empirical knowledge. Even if all empirical knowledge is derived immediately from sense perceptions or is ultimately traceable by chains of inference to sense perceptions, it does not follow that *all* sense perceptions are sources of empirical knowledge. Some may be distorted, illusory, or otherwise erroneous. And there is no reason why the same may not be true, *mutatis mutandis*, in the case of moral intuitions. It is, of course, paradoxical to claim that a belief that is self-justifying may actually be unjustified or mistaken. But the idea that a belief is self-justifying is not meant to entail that the belief is necessarily justified. To say that a belief is self-justifying is to say only that, insofar as the belief is in fact justified, it is not justified by virtue of its inferential relations with other beliefs (for a more detailed account, see Gaus 1996, ch. 7).

Second, a foundationalist account of moral knowledge may treat intuitions as reliable sources of moral knowledge without treating them as foundational or self-justifying. It is this possibility that I wish to explore in more detail.

Sketch of a Foundationalist Conception of Moral Justification

It seems to me that the method of reflective equilibrium, or a process very much like it, is the best or most fruitful method of moral inquiry. Of the known methods of inquiry, it is the one most likely to lead to justified moral beliefs. It does not, however, have to be interpreted within the coherentist framework. It is compatible with a foundationalist conception of moral justification.

Let me outline in more detail how the method works. Again, we may begin with intuitions about particular problems, acts, types of act, and so on. If our initial interest is in a problem about which we have no intuitions, or about which our intuitions are weak or conflicting, we should, as I have suggested with reference to the problem of abortion, find closely related cases about which we have confident intuitions and work from these. The question immediately arises, however, why we should carry the inquiry any further. Why cannot we rest content with our intuitions, allowing ourselves to be guided by them on a case-by-case basis? Part of the answer, of course, is that there are many moral problems about which we have no intuitions, or about which the intuitions we have are weak, conflicting, or obviously suspect or dubious. We need a method for determining what we should believe and what we should do in cases such as these.

There are many reasons why an intuition may appear tainted or suspect, even to the person who has it. It may, for example, seem to be a remnant of a religious or metaphysical system accepted during childhood but now rejected; it may be an obvious product of social prejudice or self-interest (e.g., the belief among slave owners in the acceptability of slavery); it may reflect the operations of an aberrant state of mind; and so on. If one's intuition about a particular moral problem is doubtful for any such reason, one will need a method of addressing the problem other than merely consulting one's intuition.

Even if one's intuition presents itself compellingly, one knows (from observing the phenomenon in others, of course) that even overmasteringly cogent moral intuitions may be mistaken and that it is thus imperative to subject them to scrutiny. One should seek to determine whether the intuition can be justified or defended. How should one proceed? When one's moral intuition is challenged by another person, it is natural to respond by appealing to claims of a higher level of generality that imply or explain the intuition. The assumption here is that the credibility of the intuition is enhanced if the intuition can be subsumed under a plausible moral principle. So, for example, the intuitive judgment that it would be wrong to torture the cat for fun might be defended by appealing to the principle that it is wrong to cause suffering without good reason. Private moral reflection may follow the same dialectical pattern as moral disagreement between persons. We should challenge our own intuitions in much the way that an opponent might challenge them; but we may also respond in much the same way, by trying to bring them within the scope of a plausible principle.

But why suppose that the credibility of one's intuition is enhanced when it is shown that the intuition follows from a moral principle (together with the facts of the case)? One suggestion is that the principle may elucidate the intuition by identifying the features of the case that are morally salient. If, for example, one feels intuitively that it is wrong to kill animals for sport, one's objection is sharpened or focused if it is seen to follow from the more general view that it is wrong, other things being equal, to deprive any individual of a good that that individual would otherwise have. The principle brings out more clearly exactly what one finds intuitively objectionable.

It is also important to note that no one supposes that just any principle will do. For the principle to support the intuition, it must have independent credibility. (The principle itself may have intuitive appeal. Presumably it does if one is inclined to accord it some initial credence – that is, if it counts as a *belief.*) According to coherentism, of course, the *mere* fact that the principle implies the intuition provides some minimal epistemic support for each; for mutual coherence among beliefs is the criterion of justifiability. But, even according to coherentism, the principle will provide no more than token support for the intuition unless it is itself well integrated within a larger network of mutually coherent beliefs. Hence the method of reflective equilibrium demands that the principle itself be tested for consistency and coherence with other moral beliefs. Its implications about particular cases should not conflict with one's intuitive judgments about those cases and, to the greatest extent possible, its implications should not contradict the implications of other principles one accepts. It is, of course, too much to require that moral principles not have conflicting implications: conflict is the price of pluralism. But conflicts should, in principle, be resolvable, in that one recognizes the necessity of one value's yielding to another, though not without some irreducible loss.

So the defense of one's initial intuition by subsuming it under a more general principle is only the beginning of moral inquiry. The principle must itself be assessed by testing its implications for consistency with one's other beliefs. One need not accept coherentism in order to appreciate the importance of this test. There are practical reasons why inconsistent moral beliefs are problematic: they may, for example, provoke indecision and, ultimately, paralysis of the will. More importantly, the achievement of greater coherence among one's beliefs diminishes the likelihood of error by helping one to identify and weed out moral beliefs spawned by self-interest, faulty reasoning, failure of imagination, illusory metaphysical beliefs, impaired faculties, and other sources of distorted or mistaken belief.

But there is a deeper basis for trying to subsume an intuition under a principle that is itself supported by its power to unify and explain a range of other intuitions. This is that the process of achieving increasing coherence among principles and intuitions facilitates the discovery of one's deeper values and also brings one's surface beliefs about particular cases into alignment with those deeper values in a way that reveals and illuminates the connections between them. When one seeks to formulate a moral principle that implies and illuminates one's intuition about a particular problem or case, one is in fact groping or probing for one's own deeper values. The expectation that the principle will illuminate and explain the force of the intuition assumes that the intuition is in fact an expression or manifestation, in a particular context, of a moral belief that is deeper, more basic, and more general than the intuition itself. One's efforts to formulate the principle and to revise and refine it in a way that brings more and more of one's intuitions within its scope are attempts to capture or articulate some core moral belief in its full generality, to get its form exactly right, omitting nothing, however subtle.

This process, as I have described it, is indistinguishable from that endorsed by the coherentist practitioners of reflective equilibrium. One seeks support for an intuition by appealing to a principle, then seeks to support the principle by demonstrating its compatibility with other intuitions, and so on. Why not understand the method as most people do, in coherentist terms?

There are various general objections to coherentist accounts of justification in ethics (e.g., Gaus 1996, ch. 6). There are also, of course, general objections to foundationalism. I cannot rehearse those debates here. I will simply note two problems with coherentism that I find particularly disturbing. One is that, according to coherentism, no belief is immune to rejection, no matter how compelling it may be. If its elimination from the network of beliefs would enhance overall coherence within the network, the belief must go. Indeed, it seems possible, though not likely, that a coherentist approach to the pursuit of reflective equilibrium could lead ultimately to the rejection of every belief with which one started. Both these suppositions, however, are utterly alien to moral life and moral reflection. There are some moral beliefs that we simply cannot give up just for the sake of greater coherence. Sometimes we must hold tenaciously to certain convictions even at the cost of diminished coherence or systematicity.

It may seem that coherentism could require the rejection of a compelling belief only if it were in conflict with an even more compelling belief, in which case it would not seem unreasonable to abandon it. But this assumes that coherentism gives some weight to what might be called the inherent cogency of a belief; but this, it seems, is a misapprehension. According to coherentism, the credibility of a belief is a function only of its relations to other beliefs. If a single powerfully compelling belief clashes with a larger number of individually weaker but tightly interlocking beliefs, coherentism seems committed to rejecting the stronger belief.

According to coherentism, one's moral beliefs are like pieces in a game: one shuffles them around, sacrifices some, and acquires others, all for the sake of achieving certain relations among them. No piece has any significance in itself; it has significance only in relation to the other pieces and in particular in the contribution that it makes to the patterned whole of which it is a part. If moral reflection were really a game like this, in which our moral beliefs had no claim to our loyalty and thus were readily expendable in the service of coherence, coherence would be fairly easily and painlessly achievable. It is because some of our moral beliefs compel our allegiance independently of their inferential relations to other beliefs that coherence always seems a distant, perhaps impossible goal.

A closely related worry about coherentism is that it assigns the same epistemic status to our intuitions about particular cases as it does to the deeper principles of which the intuitions are expressions. They stand in relations of reciprocal support: the principles imply the intuitions and we can therefore infer our way to the principles on the basis of the intuitions. But in fact the relations of reciprocal support seem asymmetrical: the principles seem to be epistemically more basic, more secure. They articulate our core values which unify, explain, and justify our intuitive judgments. Our intuitions do not so much justify the principles as provide evidence of their existence and guidance as to their nature. In short, the principles are foundational with respect to the intuitions. Insofar as our intuitions are reliable sources of moral knowledge, they are so because they are expressions of, and point back to, a range of deeper, more general values that lie at the core of our nature as moral beings.

As I noted earlier, foundationalism is distinguished by the view that some beliefs – the "foundational" ones – are justified independently of their relations to other beliefs. Among those who accept a foundationalist moral epistemology, there is a rough division between those who take certain nonmoral beliefs to be foundational and those who identify certain moral beliefs as foundational. Among the latter, there is a further division between those who take intuitions to be foundational (e.g., Ross 1930; Gaus 1996) and those who take some general principle or principles to be foundational (e.g., Sidgwick 1907). Thus, according to Geoffrey Sayre-McCord, "many have treated the privileged [i.e., foundational] moral beliefs as roughly on a par with perceptual judgments and suggested that the justification of our various moral principles parallels the kind of justification our scientific principles receive from perception. Others have thought that our privileged moral beliefs concern, instead, the most general and abstract principles of morality, and that these in turn serve to justify (or not) our other beliefs deductively" (Sayre-McCord 1996: 150).

The view that I have suggested is of this second sort. But it is distinguished from many views of this sort in that it does not regard the foundational principles as self-evident or accessible through the exercise of intuition. Many philosophers (e.g., Sidgwick 1907; Unger 1996) have regarded our intuitive apprehensions of principles of a fairly high order of generality as more reliable than our intuitions about particular cases. But, insofar as a moral principle is substantive in character rather than merely formal (for example, "treat like cases alike"), I believe that it is unwise to have high degree of confidence in our intuitive apprehension of the principle. To be justified in accepting a moral principle, we must first understand what it commits us to in particular cases. As William James noted in a letter written long before he became a practicing philosopher, "no one sees farther into a generalization than his own knowledge of the details extends" (Barzun 1983: 14). So, while I regard the principles rather than our intuitions as foundational, I deny that moral inquiry proceeds by deducing conclusions about particular cases from self-evident moral principles. Rather, it seems to me that *the order of discovery is the reverse of the order of justification.* Although the deeper principles are explanatorily prior, we have to work our way to them via our intuitions in much the way that scientists work towards general principles via our perceptual data. The process of discovering and formulating the more general principles is evidently difficult and intellectually demanding, rather in the way that discovering the syntactic structures that govern our use of language is. As this familiar analogy suggests, as we grope our way towards the principles, we are discovering what we antecedently believe, albeit below the level of conscious awareness. The principles that we hope to uncover express deep dispositions of thought and feeling that operate below the level of consciousness to regulate our intuitive responses to particular cases.

If this is right, it explains why we experience the process of moral inquiry as a process of discovery rather than an exercise of choice or will. It also explains why the foundationalist approach I am describing should coincide with coherentism in holding that we may expect to arrive at a moral theory, if at all, only near the end of reflection about particular problems and cases rather than coming to the problems with a theory ready to be "applied". It explains why it is more than a little suspicious when philosophers emerge from graduate school already believing themselves to be in possession of the correct moral theory.

Challenges

This brief sketch of an account of moral justification raises far more questions than can be answered, or even addressed, in the remainder of this short essay. The central question is, of course, what reason there is to suppose that the principles that might emerge through the pursuit of reflective equilibrium are credible. One response, which is hardly satisfying but may nevertheless be true, is that they are simply ultimate: there is nothing more basic, nothing by reference to which they can be justified. When we have worked our way back to the principles or values that underlie and best explain the countless judgments we make about particular problems and cases, there is simply nowhere deeper to go.

This would perhaps be easier to accept if the principles at which we might arrive would be luminously self-evident; but there is no guarantee that they would be. Indeed, if experience is any guide, there is even reason to suspect that they may often not be. Consider, for example, our intuitions about the moral differences between doing harm and allowing harm to occur, or, more specifically, between killing and letting die. Various philosophers have sought to trace these intuitions, which emerge very strongly in particular cases, to their source in certain deeper principles. In no instance of which I am aware do the principles cited have anything approaching the immediate plausibility of the intuitive judgments that they were supposed to explain. The principles are too abstract, too schematic, to carry immediate conviction. But perhaps the problem is that the principles that have been identified are not really ultimate; perhaps there is a deeper layer of explanation that has yet to be uncovered.

There is reason to conjecture that at least some of our foundational or core values are biologically based. One piece of evidence for this is the surprising uniformity of our intuitions about particular cases. We have been impressed for so long by the claims of anthropologists, English professors, undergraduates, and others about the diversity of moral opinion that we are inclined to overlook how much agreement there actually is. Interestingly, what one finds is that moral disagreements tend to widen and intensify the more we abstract from particular cases and focus instead on matters of principle or theory. (They also widen, of course, when religious considerations become engaged.) When the partisans of different schools of moral thought turn their attention to particular cases, there is far more intuitive agreement than their higher-level disputes would lead one to suspect. Although this is merely anecdotal, those who teach courses in moral philosophy will, I think, recognize in the following observation a familiar phenomenon. When I teach a course on normative ethics, my students tend to be ethnically quite heterogeneous. Many were raised in remote parts of the world and speak with a discernible accent from their native language. Yet, in spite of having been raised in diverse cultures, they tend to have the same intuitive responses to the cases we discuss (which is, of course, the expectation of those writers in ethics who appeal to intuitions about cases; otherwise, if a case fails to elicit the same intuitive response from most readers, it provides no basis for moral argument).

Here is a pair of examples that teachers often employ:

(1) *Trolley*: A runaway trolley is careering down the mainline track where it will soon hit and kill five people trapped on the track. A bystander can flip a switch that would divert the trolley onto a branchline track before it reaches the five; but it would then hit and kill a single person who is trapped on the branchline track.

(2) *Transplant*: Five people in the hospital need organ transplants to survive. It would be possible to save them by killing a healthy patient and dividing his organs among them.

In both of these cases there is a choice between letting five innocent people die and killing one innocent person. Virtually all of my students agree that it would be permissible to kill the one to save the five in the Trolley case; but virtually all also agree that it would be impermissible to do this in the Transplant case. There are two considerations that make this consensus rather remarkable. First, while the students discriminate intuitively between the two cases, the basis of their own discrimination typically eludes them; they are unable to identify the factors that distinguish the two cases morally. (As those familiar with the relevant literature are aware, it is possible to introduce variations into these cases that challenge the ability of even the most subtle philosophers to identify the bases of their own intuitive discriminations. This is not just a game one plays with undergraduates.) Second, the cases are beyond the range of the students' experience. Choices of these sorts are, indeed, very rare and it is unlikely that the students have ever previously thought about them at all. Yet their intuitive responses tend to be both immediate and strong. This, together with the fact that the students tend to come from widely divergent cultural backgrounds, suggests that the intuitions are not learned responses.

An alternative explanation appeals to the analogy, noted earlier, between the deep values that we unconsciously consult in making intuitive moral judgments and the deep syntactical structures that govern our use of language. Colin McGinn attributes this conception of moral knowledge to Noam Chomsky, who originally formulated the parallel account of our knowledge of language. "According to Chomsky," McGinn writes, "it is plausible to see our ethical faculty as analogous to our language faculty: we acquire ethical knowledge with very little explicit instruction, without great intellectual labor, and the end-result is remarkably uniform given the variety of ethical input we receive. The environment serves merely to trigger and specialize an innate schematism. Thus the ethical systems of different cultures or epochs are plausibly seen as analogous to the different languages people speak – an underlying universal structure gets differentiated into specific cultural products" (McGinn 1993: 30).

McGinn goes on to speculate that "perhaps the innate system of commonsense psychology, installed to negotiate our social relations, contains the resources for generating the basic principles of ethics" (McGinn 1993: 30). Certainly the sociobiological literature has familiarized us with accounts drawn from evolutionary biology that purport to explain the presence of those deep values that give rise to our intuitions about such matters as parental responsibilities, marital fidelity, and so on.

But this kind of account leaves ample room for skepticism. Even if we are biologically programmed to think and feel in a certain ways, we can still ask whether it is morally right or even defensible to think and feel in those ways. There is, for example, no obvious reason why natural selection would have left us with much concern for the lives and well-being of nonhuman animals: evolutionary biology would thus predict that our attitudes towards animals and our practices that involve them would be "speciesist" – that is, would give little or no weight to the interests of animals simply because animals are unrelated to us in certain ways. And indeed our beliefs and practices are speciesist, for the most part. But only for the most part. Many reflective people who have tried to work through their moral beliefs about animals in the way recommended by the method of reflective equilibrium have concluded that our traditional beliefs and practices are unconscionable. A plausible account of moral epistemology must be able to accommodate and make sense of our ability to make radical revisions of moral beliefs that are apparently quite deeply situated in our biological nature.

Another worry about the innatist conception of our core values is that it may suggest a disturbingly subjectivist conception of value. If our moral judgments are merely the products of biologically programmed dispositions of thought and feeling, then it may seem that values are entirely within us rather than in the world – that, as various subjectivists have put it, values are projections of our minds onto a world in which value is otherwise entirely absent. On this view, values, like tastes, are essentially arbitrary and ultimately uncriticizable. This is, of course, a common enough position, but many of us are strongly inclined to resist it.

The innatist conception does not, however, lead inevitably to a subjectivist account of value (Brody 1979). It is not out of the question that our minds have evolved in such a way that our moral sensibilities are capable of apprehending what is actually there. It is true that our sensibilities contribute something to our apprehension of value (positive or negative). Some philosophers have suggested that our apprehension of value is analogous to our perception of secondary qualities (colors, tastes, etc.). They have argued that, just as color is a real property of surfaces that is nevertheless analyzable in part in terms of its disposition to produce certain sensations in individuals with appropriate perceptual faculties in certain conditions, so too value may be a genuine feature of acts, events, and so on that is nevertheless analyzable in part in terms of its tendency to evoke certain characteristic responses in those endowed with an appropriately sensitive and discriminating moral sensibility. According to this view, we do not create value any more than we create color. Although we may be innately disposed to respond with approval or disapproval to acts and events of various kinds, it does not follow that value is created only by the act of valuing. (The analogy between values and secondary qualities is of course highly controversial and the relevant literature is extensive. See, for example, McDowell 1985 and 1997; Wiggins 1991; Wright 1988; Goldman 1988; and Johnston 1989.)

A further concern about the foundationalist account I have sketched is that, if our intuitive judgments are traceable to deeper principles that are themselves articulations of dispositions of thought and feeling that are at least in part innate, one would expect there to be greater harmony and consistency among the intuitions of each individual than one in fact finds. One's intuitions, indeed, seem bewilderingly chaotic and one finds, as soon as one begins to try to unify them under principles of greater generality, that conflicts and inconsistencies abound.

There are several explanations for this. One is that our moral intuitions undoubtedly stem from numerous diverse sources: while some derive from biologically programmed dispositions that are largely uniform across the species, others are the products of cultural determinants, economic or social conditions, vagaries of individual character and circumstance, and so on. Given the heterogeneity of these sources, it is hardly surprising that there are conflicts. The process of achieving greater consistency and coherence is, as I noted earlier, in part an effort to weed out those intuitions that derive from tainted sources. But even among those intuitions that seem to derive from sources that we may regard as reliable, there is no a priori guarantee of harmony. There are some areas of morality – for example, the area concerned with causing new people to exist – in which there seem to be deep incompatibilities that do not seem to be the result of any obvious error. In these areas there may be no way of achieving coherence that does not involve a rejection of something that is true. One has to suspect that the richness of moral life and experience will continue indefinitely to resist our efforts to reduce morality to a comprehensively unified system.

Acknowledgment

I am deeply grateful to David Boonin-Vail, Walter Feinberg, and Hugh LaFollette for instructive comments on an earlier draft.

References

Audi, Robert: "Intuitionism, pluralism, and the foundations of ethics," *Moral Knowledge?*, ed. Walter Sinnott-Armstrong and Mark Timmons (New York: Oxford University Press, 1996), pp. 101–36.

Barzun, Jacques: *A Stroll With William James* (New York: Harper & Row, 1983).

Brandt, Richard B.: *A Theory of the Right and the Good* (Oxford: Clarendon Press, 1979).

Brink, David: *Moral Realism and the Foundations of Ethics* (Cambridge: Cambridge University Press).

Brody, Baruch: "Intuitions and objective moral knowledge," *The Monist* ,62 (1979): 446–56.

Daniels, Norman: *Justice and Justification: Reflective Equilibrium in Theory and Practice* (Cambridge: Cambridge University Press, 1996).

DePaul, Michael R.: *Balance and Refinement: Beyond Coherence Methods of Moral Inquiry* (London: Routledge, 1993).

Gaus, Gerald: *Justificatory Liberalism: An Essay on Epistemology and Political Theory* (New York: Oxford University Press, 1996).

Goldman, Alan H.: *Moral Knowledge* (London: Routledge, 1988).

Griffin, James: *Value Judgement: Improving Our Ethical Beliefs* (Oxford: Clarendon Press, 1996).

Hare, R. M.: "Abortion and the golden rule," *Philosophy and Public Affairs*, 4 (1975): 201– 22.

Johnston, Mark: "Dispositional theories of value," *Proceedings of the Aristotelian Society*, supplementary volume, 63 (1989): 139–74.

Lewis, David: "Dispositional theories of value," *Proceedings of the Aristotelian Society*, supplementary volume, 63 (1989): 113–37.

McDowell, John: "Values and secondary qualities," *Morality and Objectivity; A Tribute to J. L. Mackie*, ed. Ted Honderich (London: Routledge, 1985), pp. 110–29.

——: "Projection and truth in ethics," *Moral Discourse and Practice*, ed. Stephen Darwall et al. (New York: Oxford University Press, 1997), pp. 215–25.

McGinn, Colin: "In and out of the mind," *London Review of Books* (2 December 1993): 30–1.

Rachels, James: *The End of Life: Euthanasia and Morality* (Oxford: Oxford University Press, 1986).

Rawls, John: *A Theory of Justice* (Oxford: Clarendon Press, 1972).

Ross, W. D.: *The Right and the Good* (Oxford: Clarendon Press, 1930).

Sayre-McCord, Geoffrey: "Coherentist epistemology and moral theory," *Moral Knowledge?*, ed. Walter Sinnott-Armstrong and Mark Timmons (New York: Oxford University Press, 1996), pp. 137–89.

Sidgwick, Henry: *The Methods of Ethics*, seventh edition (London: Macmillan, 1907).

Singer, Peter: "Sidgwick and reflective equilibrium," *The Monist*, 58 (1974): 490–517.

——: *Practical Ethics*, second edition (Cambridge: Cambridge University Press, 1993).

Timmons, Mark: "Foundationalism and the structure of ethical justification," *Ethics*, 97 (1987): 595–609.

Unger, Peter: *Living High and Letting Die: Our Illusion of Innocence* (New York: Oxford University Press, 1996).

Wiggins, David: *Needs, Values, Truth*, second edition (Oxford: Blackwell, 1991).

Wright, Crispin: "Moral values, projection, and secondary qualities," *Proceedings of the Aristotelian Society*, supplementary volume, 62 (1988): 1–26.

Chapter 6

The End of Ethics

John D. Caputo

Introduction

The end of ethics does not mean that all hell has broken loose. It does not mean that the philosophers have decided to lend their voice to the general anarchy, to unchecked greed, the free flow of drugs, and widespread violence. The end of ethics does not mean that "anything goes," which can now be taken to be official, because even the philosophers concur. The end of ethics means instead that for certain philosophers – for this is a philosophical position, with all the usual complexities and perplexities that accompany such thinking – the business as usual of ethics has given out and the ethical verities that we all like to think are true, the beliefs and practices we all cherish, are now seen to be in a more difficult spot than we liked to think. The end of ethics is thus a moment of unvarnished honesty in which we are forced to concede that in ethics we are more likely to begin with the conclusions, with the "ends" or triumphant ethical finales we had in mind all along, and worry about the premises later. Waiting for firm theoretical premises to bolster and back up our ethical beliefs is a little like waiting for a proof of the veracity of perception before dodging out of the way of a projectile barreling at our head.

The end of ethics means that the premises invoked in ethical theory always come too late, after the fact. To this way of thinking, ethicians appear rather like the crowd that gathers around the scene of an accident to see what has just happened. An accident, of course, is something that no one saw (*theorein*) coming, although afterwards everyone has something to say about it, up to and including insisting that the proper authorities should have seen that this would happen. So if there are "cases" in the end of ethics, the cases are casualties, "falls" (*casus*), stumbling over unforeseen difficulties and obstacles, the "accidents" that strikes at us in daily life, that sometimes strike us down.

If anyone were courageous or foolish enough to produce a "guide to ethical theory" and wanted to give this view a place in an ethics book, then we might want to call it "accidentalism." An accident is something that happens to us beyond our control and outside the horizon of foreseeability. Our theories and principles, whose whole aim and purpose is to prepare us for and foresee what is coming, were still in bed at this early hour of the day. The singular situations of daily life fly too close to the ground to be detected by the radar of ethical theory. Ethical life is a series of such accidents and casualties, against which ethical theory can provide little insurance. At least not when life gets interesting. Guides to ethical theory work best, if they work at all, for the more routinized, everyday, foreseeable decisions that do not demand much of us, decisions that are more or less programmable and decidable, decisions that so much resemble the past and are so stale that they have actually made it into the ethics handbooks, the "manuals." But as soon as something *new* or *different* happens ethical theory is struck dumb, the crowd gathers around the scene, and everyone starts buzzing, until finally it is agreed that we should all have seen this coming.

It is thus arguable that the discourse on the end of ethics has no place whatever in a "guide to ethical theory." For in such a discourse all our efforts are concentrated on what Kierkegaard liked to call the "existing individual." Now one might think that Kierkegaard's expression was redundant, that the adjective "existing" is unnecessary, but Kierkegaard realized that in doing "theory" existence is the first thing to go. So the only guide for ethical life that thinking at the end of ethics can give to the existing individual is to shout "heads up," rather like the shout of "incoming" in the trenches, for you never know what is coming. The end of ethics does not mean the end of concrete, "factical" life, as Heidegger liked to call it, of making ethical decisions – on the contrary, it is trying to recall us precisely to the difficulty of such choices – but the end of "ethical theory," of "guides to ethical theory," in any strong, hard, virile sense, which pretends to show the way to the perplexed. For the end of ethics, we always proceed in the blind, of the sure guidance theoretical seeing pretends to lend in advance as we negotiate the ups and down of existence. In short, the end of ethics would have to be a bit of a black sheep in any guide to ethical theory, given its reluctance to be a guide, its recalcitrance about ethics, and its resistance to theory.

In the end of ethics, ethical judgments, decisions about what to do in concrete or "factical" life, are buffeted and beset by two difficulties. (1) They are not derived from a theoretical premise upon which they depend for their "justification." It is not as if, were the theoretical premise challenged or refuted, the existing individual would have to be sent home, thoroughly disheartened and disillusioned, knowing now that the ethical life and practice is over, refuted, shown to be a sham. Among other things, that would leave the existing individual with the further or intensified embarrassment of still having to live. (2) Ethical judgments occur in the singular, in the unprecedented and unrepeatable situations of individual lives. That means that we can never say a law or a principle is just, for that would be too sweeping and pretentious, the manifestations of its injustice being just around the corner, and certainly not that a human being at large is just—the more just the individual the less likely he or she is to make such a claim. At most, we might say, with fear and trembling, that a singular event was carried out with justice. But we would want to underline the "fear and trembling," lest the ethician standing in the crowd watching the proceedings rush out and phone his editor with the latest "principle," which will soon enough prove to be too sweeping. Such a principle will make good copy for the next guide to ethical theory, which will be published any day now, revised and updated, taking into account everything that has happened recently. It will of course fail to note what has not happened yet, which will be treated in the next revised and updated edition. That at least makes for a profitable business for the authors and publishers of such guides.

The Wholly Other

But why then does all hell *not* break loose? Have we not been painted into a corner, forced into the most erratic decisionism, compelled to lurch from decision to decision with no idea of what we are doing, or why, or what to do next? How are we to proceed if there is no one to show the way or serve as a guide? The way out of this seeming impasse is to stress what is positive or affirmative about what we are calling, not without a certain devilishness and love of giving scandal, the end of ethics. For thinking at the end of ethics is "affirmative" but without being "positive." That is to say, it is through and through the affirmation of something it dearly loves, yet without setting out a positive position, a positive, rule-governed program about what to do and what not to do, about which such position takers are all too positive. The end of ethics means that the business of ethics is to be conducted with a little more fear and trembling than philosophers have been wont to show. To a certain extent, the end of ethics is a little bit like the death of God for people who still believe in God: it clears away the idols and allows a more divine God to break out. In just the same way, the end of ethics clears the way for a more ethical ethics, allowing the very ethicalness of ethics to break out, while insisting that most of what passes itself off as ethics is an idol. The end of ethics is also like the end of metaphysics for those of us who still believe in philosophy: it clears away the speculative brush in order to let the little sprouts and saplings of concrete factical life get some sun.

On the view that I am defending here[1] everything turns on a certain affirmation, beyond any positivity or positionality, of the "other," the affirmation of – to borrow the language of Kierkegaard and Levinas,[2] which was later on taken up by Derrida[3] – the "wholly other," *tout autre*. As an affirmation of the wholly other, this view originates not in a *no* but a *yes,* not in a refusal but a welcome to the wholly other, opening our home to the stranger who knocks at our door. Strictly speaking the expression "wholly other" would mean something absolutely unthinkable, something so utterly alien to us that we would just have no relationship to it at all, something that we love and affirm, the wholly other would just pass us by like a ship in the night. That would reduce the "wholly other" to a simple irrelevancy or even to a logical impossibility or contradiction in terms. So the expression "wholly other" obviously is a term of art for thinking at the end of ethics, and it can have several senses.

In one sense, which is very futural, the wholly other means something that takes us by surprise in a radical way, something that in some important way we did not see coming. The wholly other refers to something importantly unforeseen, unanticipated, unexpected, for which we are unprepared, something that exceeds our horizon of expectation. Seen from the point of view of a classical ethics of virtue, this sort of thinking at the end of ethics cultivates the virtue, the excellence and *arete*, of openness to the other, the slightly paradoxical frame of mind of a radical hospitality in which one is ready to be surprised, ready to be overtaken by that for which one cannot prepare or be ready.

The way to think about the wholly other is to differentiate it from the relatively other, something that is, we might say "merely new," which is what Lyotard calls a new move in an old game (Lyotard and Thébaud 1985). In the merely new there is nothing really or radically new going on, but only some sort of new example or new instance of a form that is already familiar or in place, a new maneuver or strategy within an already agreed upon and familiar set of rules. A college basketball coach may design a new defense that completely confounds the opponents while yet abiding by all the current NCAA rules. An artist might make a new contribution, produce a new work of art, that remains within an existing art form while representing a new piece, a new example of the genre that exemplifies everything that the existing form stands for, or even takes it to a new height. Suppose, e.g., that we found hidden away in some library basement archives a hitherto unpublished and unknown novel by Anthony Trollope, which was truly wonderful, and which included all the usual Trollopian gestures, the conflicts that arise when a member of one class wants to marry another, the unfair position in which young women are placed who are forced to secure their futures by way of marriage, the tensions between the partisans of high and low Anglicanism, etc. Or suppose we find a hitherto unknown Rogers and Hammerstein musical. Or a old Beatles recording that was lost and utterly forgotten. We would then encounter one more twist, one more novel innovation within the form or genre, which would deepen our understanding of the genre but would not force us to imagine some wholly different genre in order to understand it. Or suppose that in her dissertation, a young Ph.D. student in astrophysics supplied data and argumentation that demonstrated still one more implication of the Big Bang theory, in which she would show with some finesse and elegance that she certainly understands how this theory works, but without changing basic assumptions about the theory as a whole.

But things get really interesting when something radically new, or absolutely new, happens, which is what we mean by the wholly other. For that would represent, to use Lyotard's formulation, not a new move in an old game, but the invention of a new game altogether. Then we are sent back to the drawing boards, forced to reexamine basic assumptions, a little bit stunned, shocked, amazed, and confused. When Marcel Duchamp takes a urinal, signs it and places it solemnly upon a pedestal, and by so doing declares it a work of art, the critics are confounded and, rocked by the oddity and novelty of it all, they wander out of the gallery asking, "but is it art?" It is only when we are driven to the extreme of asking but is this art, or is this literature, or is this physics, that something wholly other is happening. For then the horizon of expectation and foreseeability is shattered and the basic assumptions that are shared by everyone who understood the old form have been shaken to their roots. When an artistic genre or a scientific paradigm is in place, that means that a "community" of practitioners has formed around it, a group bound together by their common understanding of the rules which the existing form obeys and the criteria by which new productions within the genre are to be judged. The works that are produced in the old form already have a preexisting audience and standards of judgment. But when something wholly new happens, the shared assumptions and the agreements about criteria are broken up, the preexisting audience is dispersed and this work is on its own. Then the new production will simply die of its oddity, perish by its strangeness, or "catch on," which means that a *new* community and a *new* audience will begin to conceptualize and formulate what has happened. By the time *that* has happened, the new work or production will been imitated and assimilated, *new* criteria will have been formulated, the crowd of critics and commentators who have gathered around the scene to see what just happened, will have regained their composure. The owl of Minerva, as Hegel said, that is, the new-found wisdom and composure of the critics, commentators, and dissertation directors, manages to spread its wings only at the dusk of this long day. Only then can they explain to us all what this is and why, really, given he rules of art, science, or basketball, it was inevitable that such a thing would happen, and indeed, though this is strictly between us, they themselves, privately, knew all along that it was bound to happen. Just about then something *else* happens, which utterly confounds them.

The end of ethics is very much oriented toward these surprises, these anomalous, unexpected, horizon-breaking events that leave us asking, what is this? What is going on? What is happening to us? What is going to happen next? Is this ethical? Is this humane? The affirmation that moves and inspires thinking at the end of ethics is the affirmation of something to come, something deeply futural, that we cannot foresee (Derrida 1989: 25–65). It does not merely brace itself for it but desires it, welcomes and affirms what is to come, because it always thinks the present is an enclosure that needs to be shaken loose and opened up so as to permit the emergence of the new and novel. It treats the rules that define the present situation with a certain provisionalness, as regulations temporarily in place, temporary shelter taken before something else comes along that takes us by surprise.

The unforeseeability of the wholly other represents a kind of nemesis to the present which keeps the present off balance and prevents it from acquiring too much prestige. The affirmation of the wholly other is the affirmation that justice – since we are talking about ethics, justice is the issue – is always to come, that the present order can never be called just. Or that *democracy*, since politics should always be very ethical, is not to be found in the empirical democracies all around us, but is more deeply a democracy to come. The most unjust and undemocratic thing we can say today is that justice or democracy, at least in principle and in broad outline, is here, today, now, and we need only fill in the dots, while not getting too impatient about all the injustice and undemocratic oppression that surrounds us. This distancing of ourselves from the present is not just an empirical decision, not just a factual conclusion drawn from the observation of the many injustices around us, although it is also that.[4] Injustice, like the poor, we always have with us, and we can always count on the fact there will be more than enough examples of injustice to assure us that the present cannot lay claim to justice. The notion of the wholly other is the affirmation that justice is always to come, is always *structurally* to come, so that there will always be a structural gap between the present and justice. The alternative is to say that justice is an idea that we more or less understand, the ideal end of inquiry, as in pragmatism, an ideal that we have made much progress in implementing, and that the present is an imperfect approximation of justice. The danger of that way of thinking is that it tends to promote "good conscience" about the progress we have made in reaching this ideal against which we measure the present, leading us to conclude that we are not doing badly at all. For thinkers at the end of ethics, that sort of thinking leads to a complacency with the present, a high level of tolerance for injustice, which can always be written off as a certain empirical shortfall, a temporary setback, over and against the ideal which is being implemented here and now, among us, we the chosen ones of historical progress. It is not much consolation to anyone to be told that the broken lives, the ruined futures, the children disabled from the womb, the ones being left out from these ideal visions, are so much empirical shortfall on the way to the ideal.

To be sure, the ever present press of injustice might produce despair and dejection, for the poor will be with us no matter we do. That is why we insist on taking an affirmative tone, on an affirmation that proceeds from a love and desire for justice, from the affirmation of the least among us, of their needs and wants. Hence by insisting that justice is always to come, our aim is to expose the present to the white light of an absolute scrutiny which has zero tolerance for injustice, for injustice is all around us. What is to come is urgently needed now. On this telling, we can never have a "good conscience," which would be very complacent state of mind, but rather we have installed bad conscience as a kind of structural feature of ethical life. Citing a story from Blanchot, Jacques Derrida speaks of the notion of a Messiah who is never actually going to show up, a Messiah whose very meaning or structure is never to be here, now, in the present, so that the Messiah is always, structurally, *to come* (1997b: 46 n. 14). In this story, when someone identifies the Messiah one day, dressed in rags, on the outskirts of the city, he approaches the Messiah and asks, "when will you come?" For the meaning of the Messiah is always that, to be the horizon of hope and expectation, and we should never confuse the coming of the Messiah, his *venue*, with actual *presence*. If the Messiah ever appeared in the flesh, that would ruin everything, for what we have left to hope for and expect? How could we ever have time and a future? Even in Christianity, where the faithful believe the Messiah did come and take flesh, they concluded that the world was over, that it was ending any day now, and that there was no more future. When it did not end, they set about asking and praying, when will you come *again?* For this "when will you come?" is the key to having a future. The Messiah, or justice, or democracy – something – must always be to come, and the present is always to be pried open with hope and expectation, for the present is most certainly not the messianic time. To live in time is to hope in what is to come. Always.

I am not saying that we have no idea at all of justice, in which we case we would not recognize injustice when we saw it. Justice always has to do with the wholly other, with the affirmation of the coming of the wholly other, with the promotion of the life of the wholly other, above all of those who suffer from their alterity, who are the victims of the "same." But the singularity of the situations in which justice is to be realized, in which the wholly other is found, makes the prospects for justice, the prospective forms that justice will assume, unforeseeable, and forces us to stay open to the multiplicity of its possible forms. The multiplicity of justice, says Lyotard, is the justice of multiplicity (1985: 100). If we put it in Kantian terms, Lyotard says, then the "concept" of justice is less like a category and more like an unrepresentable sublime.

The unforeseeable, unforegraspable character of the wholly other keeps us on our toes about the unfathomable difficulty that the future poses to ethical judgment. I have in mind in particular the difficulties that arise from rapidly advancing medical technologies that make it possible, to choose among many examples, for infertile couples and lesbian women to have children, technologies that force us to distinguish between birth mothers and other sorts of motherhood and throw us into confusion about who or what a mother is. The classical patriarchal anxiety used to lie in finding ways for men to make sure that they were the fathers of the children of their wives, there being no question at all as to who the mothers are. Even if with some sanguininity we say that those patriarchal days are numbered now, still each day greets us with some new surprise about what is technologically possible which raises the question of how to open to the future, to affirm what is to come, without doing more harm than good, while knowing that we cannot just resort to rules, for the rules were made for the old game, and that medical technologies change with such swiftness that the old games grow obsolete almost daily. Today, the latest challenge is the prospect of human cloning, something you will not see discussed in the ethics books of even a decade ago, which raises difficulties of unexplored complexity. Gregor Mendel himself, carefully working his little pea-garden, would not have been able to imagine the human genome project. Thinking at the end of ethics means that the most serious reflection is conducted at the frontiers, in the passage beyond the present borders, limits or ends, where we are forced to think anew, to confront what we didn't see coming, to cross over into foreign lands, to rethink what we thought we knew in the light of what now imposes itself upon us and impresses upon us how little we really did know.

Singularities

The wholly other takes still another twist that is captured in a famous phrase by Derrida which is trickier in French than English, *tout autre est tout autre*, "every other is wholly other" (1995a, ch. 4). That is a way of signaling the unfathomableness of the singular, of singularities, if we may pluralize the singular. The singular, we recall, is not a specimen of a species, a case that falls under a general rule, a particular subsumed under a universal, an individual member of a class. It is rather marked by its idiosyncrasy, its idiomaticity, its uniqueness, its anomaly, its unclassifiability. It is unprecedented, which is why it poses a problem for Anglo-Saxon law, which loves precedents, and it is unrepeatable, so it will not give rise to general rules which the theoreticians and authors of manuals can rush to record and organize into a general system. The singular is something for which one can not make a substitution: I can pay you to do a lot of things for me, to mow my lawn or plough the snow off my driveway, and I can get a machine to substitute for my labor. But I can not ask someone else to bear my responsibility to you (not "ethically," anyway, although we get away with that sort of thing all the time). Or to die for me, which would only temporarily defer my own death, which I am not in the end going to outrun. The idiosyncrasy of the singular is resistant to all the resources we have to get hold of things, to get them within our grasp, to "conceptualize" them, if that means to grasp them round about, to seize hold of them, to get them within our sights, to seize them, know them, master them. When I am in a singular situation, faced with something singular, I do not have it, but rather it has me.

Of course, in some sense, we need concepts, and I have been conceptualizing all along in these pages. So we need to make our way by means of special "concepts," ones that do not grasp or pretend to dominate or totalize, which is why Lyotard prefers the "sublime" to "categories." The best sort of concepts are those which are internally structured to point to their own inadequacy, concepts whose very meaning is to say that what we are here signifying exceeds our grasp. The most famous such idea was Anselm's idea of God as that than which no greater (*majus*) or better (*melius*) can be conceived, or, as that which is greater and better than anything that can be conceived at all. That is a concept which says that whatever conceptual understanding you may reach of God, God is greater or better than that. God is infinite by de-finition. The "concepts" of singularity or of the wholly other are also like that: they point to the excess of difference beyond the concept of what they signify. (Indeed, perhaps, if one is resourceful enough with evolutionary theory, one could even make the "concept" of the human "species" and human "specimens" dance.)

In the ethical situation, it is the singularity of the "other" which I encounter here, the utter singularity, the wholly other character of what faces me here and now, that I must settle into. The singularity of this situation makes demands upon me to which I must respond, elicits a choice from me for which I do not have the comforting recourse of universal rules. I must respond, be responsible, in a deep and radical way. If all I had to do would be to invoke a rule, pull the lever of a universal principle, it would be much easier – it would not take much agonizing, much fear and trembling – and it would be far less "responsible." If things turned out badly I could always blame the rule, the universal. "I would like to help you," injustice says, "but rules are rules." "I understand your situation," injustice says, "but it is the principle of the thing that prevents me." "Don't blame me, I do not make the rules. I just work here. I am just doing my job." Seen thus, the singular is always the exception, the excess, that which exceeds and excepts itself from the sweep of universality, from the horizon of predictability and foreseeability.

Among the ancient Greeks Aristotle was the most sensitive to singularity, at least in his ethics, since as a biologist and a metaphysician he loved species and substantial form and unchanging being as much as the next Greek. At the beginning of his ethics Aristotle warned that if you love precision you will hate ethics and you should try mathematics, because in ethics we have to do with singular situations that defy precise prescriptions. The best we can offer, he said, is a general schema, one that it will be up to you to put into practice, to learn how to put it into practice, which is what he called *phronesis*.[5] *Phronesis* means having the wit to cope with the shifting circumstances of singularity that call for different things at different times. It is usually translated as practical wisdom, the wisdom to make practical judgments, and in the middle ages it was translated as *prudentia*. *Phronesis* is not just a matter of "application," of taking a universal and applying it, of accommodating an ideal to the imperfect circumstances in which it is to be realized, which is not *phronesis* but *techne*. In a technical judgment or application, I start with a perfect model or exemplar and try to realize it in imperfect materials. No existing circular object, try as hard as we might, can be made absolutely, perfectly, mathematically circular. No engineer ever succeeds in erecting a building as perfect as the one in the architect's blueprints. So in *techne* the passage from the ideal to the real, the universal to the singular, is a movement of loss of formal perfection, although we are glad enough to have the real material building and we cannot live in blueprints. The builder does the best he can and then he throws his tools on the truck and heads home.

But in *phronesis* the movement into the concrete represents an improvement, for the universal with which we begin in ethics is just a schema, a vague and general outline, and the movement into concrete practice (*praxis*) is an enhancement, a filling out, giving flesh and blood and detail to what was in the beginning only a vague or general idea. So Aristotle would tell you that courage as a schema is a matter of dealing with an approaching danger in a manner that is not too rash and not too timid. On the one hand, courage is practical wisdom not practical stupidity: it is not courage but foolishness to stand in front of a bus that is out of control in order to prevent it from crashing into a crowd of people. But neither is it courage to just take off and head for shelter without taking a certain measured risk in warning others of the danger and helping them seek safety. But just how much is enough and not too much? Well, that is where the *phronesis* comes in; that is where you will have to use your judgment, which you should have been practicing or exercising before now, in order to know how to decide what to do here and now, which depends upon the circumstances. Aristotle cannot decide that for you. He cannot stand in your shoes, make your decisions. You are the one who is responsible, not Aristotle. Aristotle has his own responsibilities. When you make your decision, if it is a wise one, you will have taken a more or less empty schema and made it dance, rather than to have taken some perfect ideal and adapted it to limiting circumstances.

But even Aristotle, who is a very sage commentator on these matters standing at the beginning of ethics and an antecedent figure for the thinkers at the end of ethics, is not enough. That is because Aristotle has a more settled view of things than they do. Aristotle thought the main problem facing ethical judgment lay in the movement from the general schema to the concrete situation, but he did not think there was a crisis in the schemata themselves. The general schemata are the beliefs and practices we have grown up with, that we have grown up in, that have shaped and formed and nourished us and made us to be what we are. So the main thing we have to do is to assimilate them, to make them our own, so that we can keep them going, and keep ourselves going, in a living and innovative way, so that we will be able to judge wisely in the shifting sands of singular reality. Aristotle was looking for new moves in traditional games.

Furthermore, his *polis* tended to be a homogeneous, top down, aristocratic, rigidly closed little world in which barbarians took their orders from Greeks, slaves from free men, women from men, and craftsmen from the best and the brightest. The latter, Aristotle's *phronemoi*, are the well bred, well educated, proud and noble, good looking men of practical wit and wisdom. They are the leisured set who get into the best schools and set the standards for everyone else, something like a very honorable English "gentleman," over whom a munificent nature beams with pride, and upon whom every one else was to keep their eye, with an eye to imitating them. ("Upstairs, Downstairs," the famous BBC *Masterpiece Theater* series, gives us a very nice little glimpse of the sort of stratifications and gentlemanly ideal of the Greek *polis*.)

That is a bit too much for thinkers at the end of ethics, who would point to widespread and radical disagreement about the schemata, who affirm a radical plurivocity and heterogeneity of ways to live, who are radically egalitarian about matters involving men and women, rich and poor, upstairs and downstairs, etc. For them, the problem posed by the singularity of judgment is not just a matter of moving from the universal to the particular but of assessing radically singular situations where the general schemata are in doubt. In the multi-cultural, multi-racial, multi-lingual world that is sometimes called postmodern, where immigrants legal and illegal move freely about, where gay and lesbian rights are regularly defended, where medical advances throw us into confusion about who is the parent of whom, where human cloning is foreseeable, things are not so simple. Even Aristotle, smart as he was, would have a tough time telling us who the *phronimos* is today whom we are supposed to follow, for there are many prudent men, and quite a few prudent women too, straight and gay, white and black and in between, well to do and indigent, and they don't all agree. What we require now is a kind of *metaphronesis*, the wit to move about in a world where there is no agreement about *the* good life, where there are many competing good lives, too many to count and tabulate, a world where there is no agreement about *the* person of practical wisdom, or *the* schemata. We must be more radically fixed upon the demands made upon us by the singular situation which is filled with surprises that upset the received or common wisdom, that resist schematization. We are required to keep our eye on the idiosyncratic demands that here and now are made upon us, which in a way demands everything of us, not moderation.

Gifts

That brings us to still another way that the singularity of the wholly other leads us away from the Aristotelian model. Aristotle defended a very sensible idea of moderation, of setting out measured or mean states for ethical judgment to aim at, like a target that we do not want to overshoot (excess, hyperbole) or fall short of (defect). For thinking at the end of ethics, that is too tame and moderate, too sensible, middle range and calculating a way of going about things. In short, it is not *affirmative* enough, for remember that the thinkers at the end of ethics have not come to denounce and deny things, but to affirm them, to affirm the other, the wholly other. Aristotle thought in terms of rules or schemata whose median mark we must somehow hit, like a very sensible archer aiming at the center of the target. But this discourse at the end of ethics would rather have us think in terms of the *gift* and *giving*, which would favor the model of excess, of hyperbolic overflow.[6] This is more like an archer shooting arrows at the moon, a slightly mad archer – a divine madness, to be sure, as Plato would say – who would tell us that the point of archery lies not in hitting finite targets but in seeing how far into the air one may send one's shots.

Let us return to our notion of the special sort of "quasi-concepts" this discourse requires, concepts into which the idea of excess, rather than of moderation, has been built, concepts that are defeated by admitting into them the notion of a limit, like Anselm's very beautiful idea of God. God's measure is to be without measure. God is the sheer excess of never containable or comprehensible excess, Who is always more than anything you say or think. Thinkers at the end of ethics want to import this notion of unending excess into our relationships with one another, while lamenting the limits and measures that ethics is always seeking.

What better example of such a concept than love? Thus, far from letting all hell break loose, the excess that those who think at the end of ethics have in mind has more to do with letting love break out, with letting loose the excess of the good beyond ethics, with letting the good out of ethics. If someone asks us whether we love them, and, after a long pause, considerable deliberation, and a nervous shuffling of feet, we respond, "well, yes, up to a point, in certain respects," then, whatever it is we feel, it is not love, for love is unqualified, unconditional. The measure of love is love without measure. The condition under which love is possible is that love be given without conditions, unconditionally. Love is that of which we can never have enough. We may ruefully conclude that our love was misguided and misdirected, but there is never too much love. Love is something we "give" and we give it without return, without expectation of a reward. To love someone is to love them for themselves, not for ourselves or for what may come our way as a result of this, for then we would not love them but ourselves. Some men love God, Meister Eckhart said, the way they love their cow: for its milk. Love is not an economic exchange in which I invest my love in someone with the expectation of gain or profit, of being compensated later on, at the point when my love will be rewarded. I was not in it for the reward but for the love, which is "without why," as Meister Eckhart said. Love does not transpire in an "economic" time, in which I think the time now spent loving is well spent because it will come back later on in the form of numerous remunerations.

This notion of giving and loving has the interesting effect of making a certain amount of difficulty for the idea of "duty," which is the basic stock and trade of ethics. My duty is what I ought or should do, what I "have to" do, must do, not with a physical necessity, to be sure, but a "moral" one, so that if I do not do it, I am guilty or in the wrong. That means that if you help me because you are always dutiful in meeting your obligations, you are helping me because you have to, because you must or should or ought to help me, which is better than being guilty or in the wrong, which is most unpleasant. But you do not help me because there is anything about me or my situation in itself that prompts or motivates or calls upon you to help me. Well, frankly, in that case, if it is all that disagreeable to you, I would rather that you not bother. Kant thought he could improve the idea of duty by distinguishing between (a) doing things that are merely "according to" duty – I might, e.g., serve others (do my duty) because I enjoy the sense of dependence upon me that this produces in them – from (b) doing things that are done "for the sake of duty," doing it because I ought to and only for that reason. While that distinction is useful for showing that when it comes to duty we should not be out for self-gratification, and that we should have pure intentions, not selfish ones, it ends up making things worse. For on Kant's telling, it would actually be easier to be ethical, and certainly easier to tell if someone were being dutiful, if they had a positive, physiological dislike for their duty. Once again I would rather you not bother. On this point, the Aristotelian idea of an ethics of virtues, of *arete*, however aristocratic and snooty, has it all over Kant's "deontology," which was however very democratic.

My idea is to make this whole idea of duty tremble. That of course leaves the ethicians gasping for breath, their pupils dilated, their fingers pointed in disbelief and horror at such an unholy suggestion. But I pray you, before the execution is carried out, allow me an explanation.

What is good and salutary about a duty is what I will call its "heteronomic" component, that it comes from without and overtakes me, that it shocks and rocks the circle of the "same" (me) with something coming from without, from the outside, from the other side, so that I am no longer locked up inside the imprisoning walls of the self and am called upon to respond to the other. What I like about the idea of duty is the check it puts upon the "I," and "me" and "mine," those formidable pronouns so much loved and favored by Narcissus. What I like about duty is what is called the "call of duty," for when duty calls, that is the call of the other calling me beyond myself, so that I am no longer confined to the very sphere of I and me and mine. (After a while, all that solitude becomes very boring.) But what is not so good, not all that salutary, not all that wonderful about duty is – apart from the fact that duties tend to come as rules that bind us to universals while that blinding us to singularity, about which I have already complained long and loudly enough – is the way a duty blocks a *gift*. To "give" someone what is their "due" is to do my duty, and not truly to give a gift. When I pay my loan back to the bank, they send me a letter that says thank you, but everybody understands that if I did not pay my loan back the next letter I would get would be from their lawyers, so there should be no illusions about getting or giving gifts from bankers, especially if you read the fine print on their "offers." Lawyers try to do things *pro bono*, for the good of it, and that is to their credit. Of course, if we give them too much credit, then they get a return, and it turns out to be a prudent thing (good for business) for law firms to encourage their lawyers to do, especially the young junior associates who want to become partners. Then it is not *pro bono*, not really, or *pro deo*, but mostly *pro meo*.

To give a gift (like love) is to do precisely what I do not have to do or to do something for which I do not expect a payback. That, it is turning out, is hard to do. So, far from being a license for an "anything goes" anarchy, the end of ethics is asking for something very difficult and rare. To give a gift is to do *more* than duty requires or self-interest permits. The whole idea of a gift is to go beyond what I have or must or ought to do. That means that the idea of a gift is parasitic on the idea of duties, for without duties there would be nothing to exceed. Hence, if ethics is concerned with duties then I am "against ethics." I think that we should put an end to ethics, not in the sense of calling it off and ending it, or of putting an end to the ethicians, but in the sense of de-limiting it, of setting off its limits or ends, and showing that things only start to get interesting when you get past duty. You have to have duties and laws, in order to protect the weak against the strong. Laws and duties have to have force, teeth, a bite, because we cannot run a railroad, or the banks, on gifts alone. We cannot depend on gifts in a world as violent as ours. We cannot depend upon the love of giving gifts to motivate bankers, stockholders, or the chief executives of tobacco companies. We need the law and we need a salutary fear of the law. We might here invoke an old distinction that St. Augustine made between a *timor servilis* and *timor castus*. A "servile fear" is the fear of being punished for wrongdoing. In Augustine it is the fear of being banished from God, the fear of going to hell, with which the Jesuits filled young Stephen Dedalus in that unforgettable retreat that Stephen took in *Portrait of an Artist as a Young Man*. The fear of being punished is not bad (so long as it is not pathological!); it keeps a lot of bankers and lawyers honest. But it is far from the best. A "chaste" fear, on the other hand, is the salutary and affirmative fear of offending God. In Levinasian terms, we might say a servile fear is the fear of suffering violence, while a chaste fear is the fear of our own violence, the fear we have of using others for our own ends, of doing everything for our own good and not the good of others, the fear we have that in the end everything will come back to the I and me and mine.

To be sure, there is no way to extinguish the love of self, which would not necessarily be an entirely salutary thing to do in the first place. The idea is, as far as possible, to check the way the self tries to insinuate itself into even our best intentions, to find a way of getting a return out of even the most disinterested gestures. What better way to prove oneself the finest of fellows than to give disinterestedly to the other! Such inner self-congratulation, such silent, heightened self-esteem, is no less a return upon our funds than a testimonial dinner in one's honor, full of fine speeches about our generosity. The best we can do is, as Derrida once said, to concede that there are only degrees of narcissism, ranging from the meanest and most self-interested up to the most open and hospitable, which is where the gift, "if there is one" (*s'il y en a*), is to be found (1995b: 199).

Laws and duties, as opposed to gifts, are lower level, structurally blind, coercive structures that we might think of as like training wheels on a bicycle: every cyclist begins with them but they are ludicrous beyond a certain point and every freewheeling cyclist has long ago thrown them off. Accordingly what I am after is a *non-coercive heteronomy*, a call coming from the other that does not boil down to a rule or a coercion but rather, let us say, a call or solicitation, an address – the call coming from the other – to which I respond. Then I can be responsible beyond or without duty, and duties will prove to be actually get in the way of genuine responsibility, the ability to respond, to answer, in the form of the gift, without coercion, since an uncoerced response is better that a coerced one. So laws and duties are not enough. I agree that things will not work without laws and duties, but what interests me is how much of an obstacle and blockage laws and duties are to good workings and the free flow of our lives. Beyond laws and duties we need gifts. Gifts are necessary. So what I am arguing is slightly paradoxical: gifts are necessary, even though the idea of a gift is the idea of what is not necessitated, of what we did not need to do. When we receive a gift, one of the things we say is "you didn't have to do that!" That is very true. The gift is what we did not have to do, but if we do not do them, things will fall apart. The gift obeys the paradoxical logic of the supplement: the gift is something extra, something you do not have to do, but we need them, and if you don't have them then something important is missing, something you need. The supplement comes as something extra but all the same you need it.

Let me give you two examples: marriage and the schools.

Consider a marriage in which the partners were strictly guided by their mutual duties to each other. They would each perform their marital duties, dutifully do what each is required to do, nothing less but nothing more. They would undoubtedly have made a prenuptial agreement (contract) about how to protect their separate interests were they later to separate and divorce (which in this case we could all have predicted!) When one could use a little extra help, the other would decline on the grounds that he or she was not duty bound to do it. The marriage would turn on a balance of payments, of settling disputes on the basis of whose rights were being violated. Neither of them would put themselves in the wrong for the sake of the love. Their lives would not be punctuated by the multiple acts of loving generosity and gift giving that make marriage sweet (when it is sweet), that fill the air of the marriage with love. For a marriage requires what is not required; what it needs is for each to do for the other what neither needed to do, again and again.

Now one might object that this is a loaded example, for a marriage is a community of love and not (just) of law, to begin with. We need laws to protect marriage partners, particularly to protect women in a patriarchal world, but nobody would say that laws are enough to turn the wheels of a marriage. True enough. But the delimitation of law and duty that I am advocating goes beyond communities of love, like marriages and families, and applies to institutions, which nobody is likely to confuse with a community of love. To see this, I turn to my second example, the schools. When public school teachers are sufficiently aggravated by their school boards, when their negotiations for the next contract reach a stalemate, they will sometimes threaten to "work the contract." That means that they will do their duty, nothing less and nothing more, precisely what is called for in the contract. The law, the contract will be all in all, and everything they do will be contracted to the contract. That means that they will not direct "*extra*-curricular activities," will not get to school a little bit earlier to help a student out, or stay a little later, or make a call to a parent that evening, or make a little *extra* effort with a student who needs a little *extra* attention, or in general do any of the myriad of micro-acts of generosity that lubricate the system and make it work. You cannot have a purely economic order devoid of gifts, or if you do, it will be hell, a nightmare, like a world in which the lawyers run everything, in which nobody does anything without compensation and unless it is mandated by law. So the gift on the part of the teachers is necessary; it is the little extras, the things that teachers do not have or need to do, that we really need and make a difference. The school boards, who represent the taxpayers, on the other hand, are no less bound by the gift, by the need to do what they do not need to do. The schools, the children, represent the future that they will not live to see, so what they are doing cannot be confined to economic time. They cannot exchange the present expenditures for a future return, for they will not live to see the future in which this investment will return a profit. If the schools are an investment in the future, it is not a future they will inhabit. So the taxpayers can either do what they have to do, meeting the requirements to keep the schools open and functioning, while keeping as much money in their pockets as they can get away with, and that is all, or they can give without the expectation of a return to a future that they will not live to see.

What is true of the schools is true of any institution, commercial or governmental, national or international. The workplace, *any* workplace – from factories to universities to law firms – is hell to live and work in precisely to the extent that it is driven entirely by law, contracted to the demands of the contract. The laws are needed, and who would deny this, to get us past the sweat shops and dusty mines which ground the lives and health of workers into the ground. But laws are not enough. When workers will not do anything they are not required to do, when they will not make an extra effort to do something well, when they will not spend an extra moment that is not mandated by the clock, then the work will not be done well and they will be miserable on the job. When employers are not generous with employees, when they will not do anything more than is spelled out in the contract, they will turn the place into a living hell. When a nation's leaders and the electorate that elected them treat the nation's weakest and most defenseless citizens in the most rigorous and parsimonious way, and tell them that the rest of us are not responsible for them, that they are on their own to raise their fatherless children, to get off drugs, to get a job and to climb out of poverty, they will turn the nation into hell. When nations erect walls of law around themselves, subjecting refugees and immigrants, legal and illegal, to the most rigorous immigration laws, demanding application fees that such people above all cannot afford, when they offer the others, the *tout autre*, of other nations the minimum of hospitality, the minimum that international law requires, they turn the earth itself, which on a more generous reading, belongs to us all, into hell.

Conclusion

The end of ethics does not mean that all hell has broken loose. Far from it. It is precisely hell that we seek to avoid by this slightly insolent talk about bringing ethics to an end. It is a question not of leveling the laws but of loosening them up, not of demolishing the rule of law but of opening the law to the singularity of the singular individual, which is all there is, after all. *Sola individua existent.* In raising hell with ethics and with guides to ethical theory, we are not taking sides with hell itself. On the contrary, we make a certain contact with the kingdom of God. Man is not made for the Sabbath, Jesus said, but the Sabbath for man. His attitude toward rules and law bought Jesus a lot of trouble in his day. For Jesus, too, on my telling, belongs to the tradition of those who called for the end of ethics, who thought the individual who strayed (the singular) is more important than the hundred (the universal), who counted every single and singular tear and every hair on our head, who flaunted the Sabbath laws, who dined with sinners, and took the side of the outcast and the stranger. He also had a powerful notion of "forgiveness" – a particularly potent form of "giving" – which is a little shocking and even gives scandal to those who are intent on seeing injustice "compensated," on seeing the debt of "guilt" paid off, who in general are not inclined to let sinners take a walk, a streak that is not absent from those who claim to follow Jesus. It should be added that Jesus was not picking a fight with the Jews in all this but rather, as himself a Jew, picking up on a Jewish prophetic tradition that took the side of the "widow, the orphan, and the stranger" against the powers that be. This streak surfaces today in the work of Levinas, who has made his way into the forefront of contemporary continental philosophy and into the pen of writers like Lyotard and Derrida, who are not, by any conventional standard, very "religious." But that is as it should be among thinkers who are not impressed with boundaries, limits, and confining definitions, or with contracting contracts. The followers of philosophers like Derrida and Lyotard love to sing the praises of the "other of philosophy," but they turn pale and grim, and then grow red in the face, if ever it is suggested that religion, too, is the other of philosophy, for when they said "other" it was literature, Nietzsche, and the death of God that they had in mind and it never occurred to them that somebody would try to resurrect the dead God on them. They did not see that coming. Had we time enough and space, it would repay our efforts to follow up this biblical streak in what we are saying, for it is not Aristotle or Kant or Nietzsche who can show the way here.

In sum, the discourse on the end of ethics means setting off the ends, limits and boundaries of ethics. It means to insist upon the provisionalness of ethical rules, the inaccessibility of the singular to ethical universals, the unforeseeability of the future to ethical mandates, and the excess of the gift beyond ethical moderation and duty. This discourse proceeds on the belief that ethics ends where singularity begins, which means where existence begins, since singulars are the sole existents. When the sea of singularity gets rough, when the winds of existence blow, ethics generally goes below. When things get difficult and the way is blocked, ethics is no where to be found. Just when we need ethics the most, we find that ethics has tipped its hat, politely made its excuses, and quietly slipped out the back door, leaving the rest of us to face the worst.

Notes

1 In Caputo (1993), I have developed the views expressed here in book length. In my forthcoming book (1997) I have put a more affirmative and slightly (ir)religious spin on these views.
2 The best introduction to Levinas's ethics is a series of interviews published (1985), while the best place to find his ethics of the "absolutely other" is in 1969.
3 I am drawing upon several of Derrida's works here, especially 1992. For an introduction to Derrida see his 1997a.
4 Jacques Derrida (1994) develops this sort of argument against the euphoria over the new world order to be found in Francis Fukuyama's best seller (1992).
5 I have elaborated upon the way this Aristotelian ethic makes its way into contemporary ethical thought in Caputo 1987.
6 For more on the gift, see Derrida 1991 (chs 3–4 and 1997a, ch. 5).

References

Caputo, J.: *The Prayers and Tears of Jacques Derrida: Religion without Religion* (Bloomington, IN: Indiana University Press, 1997).
——: *Against Ethics* (Bloomington: Indiana University Press, 1993).
——: *Radical Hermeneutics* (Bloomington, IN: Indiana University Press, 1987).
Derrida, J.: *Deconstruction in a Nutshell: A Conversation with Jacques Derrida* (ed. with a commentary, by J. Caputo) (New York: Fordham University Press, 1997a).
——: *Politics of Friendship* (trans. George Collins) (New York: Verso, 1997b).
——: *The Gift of Death* (trans. David Wills) (Chicago: University of Chicago Press, 1995a).
——: *Points . . . Interviews, 1974–94* (ed. Elisabeth Weber, trans. Peggy Kamuf and others)

(Stanford: Stanford University Press, 1995b).

——: *Specters of Marx: The State of the Debt, the Work of Mourning, and the New International* (trans. Peggy Kamuf) (New York: Routledge, 1994).

——: "The Force of Law": "The Mystical Foundation of Authority" (trans. Mary Quaitance). In *Deconstruction and the Possibility of Justice* (ed. Drucilla Cornell et al.) (New York: Routledge, 1992).

——: *Given Time, I: Counterfeit Money* (trans. Peggy Kamuf) (Chicago: University of Chicago Press, 1991).

——: "Psyche: Inventions of the Other" (trans. Catherine Porter). In *Reading de Man Reading* (eds. Lindsay Waters and Wlad Godzich) (Minneapolis: University of Minnesota Press, 1989).

Fukuyama, F.: *The End of History and the Last Man* (New York: Avon Books, 1992).

Levinas: *Ethics and Infinity* (trans. Richard Cohen) (Pittsburgh: Duquesne University Press, 1985).

——: *Totality and Infinity* (trans. Alphonso Lingis) (Pittsburgh: Duquesne University Press, 1969).

Lyotard, J. and J. Thébaud: *Just Gaming* (trans. Wlad Godzich) (Minneapolis: University of Minnesota Press, 1985).

Chapter 7

Psychological Egoism

Elliott Sober

Psychological egoism is a theory about motivation that claims that all of our ultimate desires are self-directed. Whenever we want others to do well (or ill), we have these other-directed desires only instrumentally; we care about others only because we think that the welfare of others will have ramifications for our own welfare. As stated, egoism is a descriptive, not a normative, claim. It aims to characterize what motivates human beings in fact; the theory does not say whether it is good or bad that people are so motivated.

Egoism has exerted a powerful influence in the social sciences and has made large inroads in the thinking of ordinary people. Economists typically think of human beings as being moved by "rational self-interest," where this excludes any irreducible concern for the welfare of others. And ordinary folks often claim that people help others only because this makes them feel good about themselves, or because they seek the approval of third parties.

It is easy to invent egoistic explanations for even the most harrowing acts of self-sacrifice. The soldier in a foxhole who throws himself on a grenade to save the lives of his comrades is a fixture in the literature on egoism. How could this act be a product of self-interest if the soldier knows that it will end his life? The egoist may answer that the soldier realizes in an instant that he would rather die than suffer the guilt feelings that would haunt him if he saved himself and allowed his friends to perish. The soldier prefers to die and then have no sensations at all rather than live and suffer the torments of the damned. This reply may sound forced, but it remains to be seen what grounds we have for regarding it as false.

The criticisms that have been leveled against psychological egoism can be divided into three categories. First, there is the claim that it is not a genuine theory at all. Second, there is the allegation that it is a theory that is refuted by what we observe in human behavior. Third, there is the idea that, although egoism is a theory that is consistent with what we observe, there are other, extra-evidential considerations that suggest that it should be rejected in favor of an alternative theory, motivational pluralism, according to which human beings have both egoistic and altruistic ultimate desires. All three types of criticism will be considered in what follows, but first we need to state the theory more carefully.

1   Clarifying Egoism

When egoism claims that all our ultimate desires are self-directed, what do "ultimate" and "self-directed" mean?

There are some things that we want for their own sakes; other things we want only because we think they will get us something else. The familiar means/end relation that links one desire to another also allows desires to be chained together – Sarah may want to drive her car because she wants to get to the bakery, she may want to go to the bakery because she wants to buy bread, etc. The crucial relation that we need to define is this:

> S wants m solely as a means to acquiring e if and only if S wants m, S wants e, and S wants m only because she believes that obtaining m will help her obtain e.

An ultimate desire is simply a desire that someone has for reasons that go beyond its ability to contribute instrumentally to the attainment of something else. Consider pain. The most obvious reason that people want to avoid pain is simply that they dislike experiencing it. Avoiding pain is one of our ultimate goals. However, many people realize that being in pain reduces their ability to concentrate, so they may sometimes take an aspirin in part because they want to remove a source of distraction. This shows that the things we want as ends in themselves we also may want for instrumental reasons.

When psychological egoism seeks to explain why one person helped another, it isn't enough to show that *one* of the reasons for helping was self-benefit; this is quite consistent with there being another, purely altruistic, reason that the individual had for helping. Symmetrically, to refute egoism, one need not cite examples of helping in which only other-directed motives play a role. If people sometimes help for both egoistic and altruistic ultimate reasons, then psychological egoism is false.

Egoism and altruism both require the distinction between self-directed and other-directed desires. This distinction is to be understood in terms of a desire's propositional content. If Adam wants the apple, this is elliptical for saying that Adam wants it to be the case that *he has the apple*. This desire is purely self-directed, since its propositional content mentions Adam, but no other agent; I assume that Adam does not regard the apple as an agent. In contrast, when Eve wants *Adam to have the apple*, this desire is purely other-directed; its propositional content mentions another person, Adam, but not Eve herself. Egoism claims that all of our ultimate desires are self-directed; altruism, that some are other-directed. The fact that Eve has an other- directed desire is not enough to refute egoism; one must ask *why* Eve wants Adam to have the apple.

A special version of egoism is psychological hedonism. The hedonist says that the only ultimate desires that people have are attaining pleasure and avoiding pain. Hedonism is sometimes criticized for holding that pleasure is a single type of sensation – that the pleasure we get from the taste of a peach and the pleasure we get from seeing those we love prosper somehow boil down to the same thing (LaFollette 1988). However, this criticism does not apply to hedonism as I have described it. The salient fact about this theory is its claim that people are motivational solipsists; the only things they care about ultimately are states of their own consciousness. Egoists need not be hedonists. If people desire their own survival as an end in itself, they may be egoists, but they are not hedonists.

There are desires that are neither purely self-directed nor purely other-directed. If Phyllis wants to be famous, this means that she wants others to know who she is. This desire's propositional content involves a relation between self and others. If Phyllis seeks fame solely because she thinks this will be pleasurable or profitable, then she may be an egoist (depending on what her other ultimate desires happen to be). But what if she wants to be famous as an end in itself? There is no reason to cram this possibility within egoism or altruism; to include some ultimate relational desires, but not others, within egoism, runs the risk of making the theory appear ad hoc or unclear (Kavka 1986); the same point also applies to altruism. So let us recognize *relationism* as a possibility distinct from both.

A fourth possibility involves desires that mention neither self nor other. The desire that some general moral principle be upheld falls into this category. When a utilitarian desires the greatest good for the greatest number, the desire is impersonal; the desire covers all sentient beings, presumably including the desirer himself, but the desire's content singles out neither self nor specific others. For this reason, I suggest that it is neither altruistic nor egoistic. Just as was true with respect to relational desires, the defender of psychological egoism can grant that there are desires concerning general moral principles that are not self-directed; the question is whether we have these desires instrumentally or as ends in themselves.

With egoism characterized in the way I have suggested, it obviously is not entailed by the truism that people act on the basis of their own desires, nor by the truism that they seek to have their desires satisfied. The fact that Joe acts on the basis of Joe's desires, not on the basis of Jim's, tells us whose desires are doing the work; it says nothing about whether the ultimate desires in Joe's head are purely self-directed. And the fact that Joe wants his desires to be satisfied means merely that he wants their propositional contents to come true; Joe's desire that it rain tomorrow is satisfied if and only if it rains tomorrow (Stampe 1994). If there is rain, the desire is satisfied, whether or not Joe knows that it is. To want one's desires satisfied is not the same as wanting the feeling of satisfaction that sometimes accompanies a satisfied desire.

Egoism is sometimes criticized for attributing too much calculation to spontaneous acts of helping. People who help in emergency situations often report doing so "without thinking" (Clark and Word 1974). However, it is hard to take such reports literally when the acts involve a precise series of complicated actions that are well-suited to an apparent end. A lifeguard who rescues a struggling swimmer is properly viewed as having a goal and as selecting actions that advance that goal. The fact that she engaged in no ponderous and self-conscious calculation does not show that no means/end reasoning occurred. In any case, actions that really do occur without the mediation of beliefs and desires fall outside the scope of both egoism and altruism. People jerk their legs when their knees are tapped with hammers, but that refutes neither theory.

A related criticism is that egoism assumes that people are more rational than they really are. However, recall that egoism is simply a claim about the ultimate desires that people have. As such, it says nothing about how people decide what to do on the basis of their beliefs and desires. Theorists who assume that egoism is true also often assume that people are rational calculators; however, theories are not convicted by a principle of guilt by association. The assumption of rationality is no more a part of psychological egoism than it is part of motivational pluralism.

If egoism holds that all ultimate desires are self-directed, what are we to say of someone whose ultimate goal is his own destruction? And if altruism holds that some of our ultimate desires are other-directed, what are we to make of Iago, who has the ultimate goal of destroying Othello? It is jarring to say that a depressed person bent on suicide is an egoist, or that Iago is an altruist. What we need to add to both theories is the idea of what is good (or apparently good). Egoists seek their own benefit; altruists want others to do well. Although these additions to the theories bring them more in line with ordinary usage of the terms "egoism" and "altruism," they do not materially affect the substantive task of determining which theory is true. The crux of the problem is to tell whether all ultimate desires are self-directed.

It may strike some readers that the problem is easy. Individuals can merely gaze within their own minds and determine by introspection what their ultimate motives are. Perhaps advocates of egoism are right about themselves and advocates of motivational pluralism are right about themselves; both sides err only when they generalize beyond their own cases. An implicit assumption, in both philosophical and psychological explorations of this topic, is that people are basically the same. If egoism is false, it is false for practically everyone (sociopaths, perhaps, excepted). And if it is true, it is true because it characterizes a basic feature of human nature.

However, the fact that earlier work in psychology and philosophy often ignored the possibility of individual variation is no reason to build this into our understanding of the problem. Why, then, should we not say that advocates of egoism know their own hearts and that defenders of altruism know theirs? The reason is that there is no independent reason to think that the testimony of introspection is to be trusted in this instance. Introspection is misleading or incomplete in what it tells us about other facets of the mind; no one has shown why the mind must be an open book with respect to this question about ultimate motives. The problem, if it can be solved, must be solved in some other way.

2 Is Egoism Empirically Testable?

One standard philosophical objection to egoism is that it is not a testable hypothesis. As the example of the soldier in the foxhole suggests, it seems that egoism can accommodate any behavior whatever. Whether people are nasty or nice to each other, the theory can explain why. This claim about the flexibility of egoism is then linked to a Popperian criterion concerning what it takes for a statement to be scientific, with the conclusion drawn that egoism is not a genuine scientific theory at all. It is, despite appearances, empirically vacuous.

This argument is flawed in two ways. The first pertains to its sanguine confidence that no observation could ever disconfirm egoism. The fact that the theory can accommodate the soldier in the foxhole and other behaviors that have been considered by philosophers hardly suffices to justify this global claim. As it happens, the experimental work in social psychology on altruism and egoism shows that the relevant observational evidence extends beyond the existence of instances of helping behavior (Batson 1991; Schroeder et al. 1995). In addition, the Duhemian point that theories are testable only in conjunction with background assumptions should lead us to draw back from the charge of untestability. If two theories make the same predictions against one background framework, they may make different predictions against another. How do we know that new background theories will never be developed that allow egoism to be put to the test? The charge of untestability presupposes that we have an omniscient grasp of the future of science.

The second defect in this argument is that it neglects to notice that the charge of untestability is a two-edged sword. The argument is advanced as a reason for rejecting egoism. What, then, are we to accept as a positive account of motivation? Presumably, motivational pluralism is supposed to be the acceptable alternative. However, this cannot be where the argument leads. If egoism is untestable, then so is motivational pluralism. As flexible as egoism is in its ability to accommodate observations, pluralism is more flexible still. After all, pluralism deploys all the variables that egoism invokes, and then some. The two theories are related to each other in the same way that "$y = f(x)$" and "$y = g(x,w)$" are related.

The reason egoism appears to be untestable is that it is an *ism*. It does not provide *specific* explanations for behaviors, but merely indicates the *kind* of explanation that all behaviors will have. This is why it is possible for egoism to be retained even when specific egoistic explanations are found wanting. Why did George donate all that money to charity? A defender of egoism might suggest that George did so because he wanted to improve his business contacts by impressing others. However, suppose one then learns that George donated the money anonymously. This refutes the specific egoistic explanation just described, but it isn't hard to invent another. George made the donation because it made him feel good and because he knew that if he did not, he would experience pangs of guilt. The pattern here is typical – hedonism is the position to which egoists standardly retreat. If external benefits don't suffice to explain, one invokes internal, psychological benefits instead.

That egoism is a claim about a *type* of explanation, and therefore is distinct from the *specific explanations* that are of the type required, is a pattern that arises in many debates about *ism*s. Consider adaptationism in evolutionary biology. Adaptationists emphasize the importance of natural selection in explaining the observed traits of organisms. Because this *ism*, by itself, does not provide a specific explanation for any trait, it remains possible for a biologist to continue to be an adaptationist even after a specific adaptationist explanation is found wanting. Why did wings evolve in insects? The hypothesis that wings evolved as an adaptation for flying is thrown in doubt by the fact that very small wing buds provide no lift whatever; although 5 percent of an eye can still function as a light sensor, 5 percent of a wing does nothing to get an organism off the ground. However, wing buds are found in some flightless insect species; they function as thermo-regulators. This suggests an alternative adaptationist hypothesis – that insect wings started to evolve because they initially promoted thermo-regulation and then continued to evolve because they then facilitated flight. And if this hypothesis is challenged, the adaptationist can cast about for a third alternative. It is no good to reject adaptationism because it has this sort of flexibility; the alternative *ism*, evolutionary pluralism, claims that natural selection is one among several important causes of evolution. As flexible as adaptationism is, pluralism is more flexible still.

3   Butler's Stone

As noted above, even though hedonism is a special version of egoism, hedonistic explanations are often what egoists invoke when a nonhedonistic explanation is found wanting. If George didn't donate money to charity to make business contacts, perhaps he did so for the warm glow of satisfaction that the donation provided. For this reason, arguments that attempt to refute hedonism have a special location in the dialectical landscape. Although refuting hedonism is not sufficient to refute egoism, it would make an important contribution to that larger enterprise.

Many philosophers have thought that Joseph Butler (1692–1752) refuted hedonism once and for all (Broad 1965; Feinberg 1984; Nagel 1970) in the following passage:

> That all particular appetites and passions are towards *external things themselves*, distinct from the *pleasure arising from them*, is manifested from hence; that there could not be this pleasure, were it not for that prior suitableness between the object and the passion: there could be no enjoyment or delight from one thing more than another, from eating food more than from swallowing a stone, if there were not an affection or appetite to one thing more than another. (Butler 1965 [1726]: 227)

I'll call this argument *Butler's stone*. Although Butler does not explicitly say in this passage that hedonism is false, let us construe the argument with this as its conclusion:

1   People sometimes experience pleasure.
2   When people experience pleasure, this is because they had a desire for some external thing, and that desire was satisfied.

Hedonism is false.

I don't propose to challenge the first premiss. However, I think the second premiss is false and that the conclusion does not follow from the premisses.

The second premiss is over-stated; although some pleasures are the result of a desire's being satisfied, others are not (Broad 1965: 66). One can enjoy the smell of violets without having formed the desire to smell a flower, or something sweet. Since desires are propositional attitude, forming a desire is a cognitive achievement. Pleasure and pain, on the other hand, are sometimes cognitively mediated, but sometimes they are not. Notice that this defect in the argument can be repaired; Butler does not need to say that desire satisfaction is the one and only road to pleasure.

The transition from premisses to conclusion is where the argument really goes wrong. Consider the causal chain from a *desire* (the desire for food, say), to an *action* (eating), to a *result* – pleasure. Because the pleasure traces back to an antecedently existing desire, it will be false that the resulting pleasure caused the desire (on the assumption that cause must precede effect). However, this does not settle how two *desires* – the *desire for food* and the *desire for pleasure* – are related. In particular, it leaves entirely open what caused the desire for food. Hedonism says that people desire food *because* they want pleasure (and think that food will bring them pleasure). Butler's stone concludes that this causal claim is false, but for no good reason. The crucial mistake in the argument comes from confusing two quite different items – the *pleasure* that results from a desire's being satisfied and the *desire for pleasure*. Even if the occurrence of pleasure presupposed that the agent desired something besides pleasure, nothing follows about the relationship between the *desire for pleasure* and the desire for something else (Sober 1992; Stewart 1992; Sober and Wilson 1998). Hedonism does not deny that people desire external things; rather, the theory tries to explain why that is so.

It is curious that this argument has been interpreted so widely as refuting hedonism. At the end of the sermon in which the stone passage occurs, Butler says this: "Let it be allowed, though virtue or moral rectitude does indeed consist in affection to and pursuit of what is right and good, as such; yet, that when we sit down in a cool hour, we can neither justify to ourselves this or any other pursuit, till we are convinced that it will be for our happiness, or at least not contrary to it" (Butler 1965 [1726]: 240). And if we return to the language of the stone argument itself, we see that Butler is making a claim about the content of "particular appetites and passions." Read narrowly, the argument says merely that if people desire pleasure, their desires do not fall under that rubric; the argument does not say that people never desire pleasure nor does it say that the desire for pleasure is never ultimate. Did Butler fail to refute hedonism in the stone argument because he wasn't even trying to do so?

4 The "Paradox" of Hedonism and its "Irrationality"

Individuals who focus exclusively on attaining pleasure or happiness inevitably fail to get what they want. They are like stockbrokers who think only that they should buy low and sell high. People who have an end in view but never consider what means they should use to pursue their goal surely will fail to get what they want. This has led some philosophers to claim that pleasure and happiness are attainable only as byproducts of becoming absorbed in specific activities. They also have suggested that this fact about pleasure and happiness constitutes a paradox for hedonism – the word "paradox" indicating that we are supposed to find here a flaw in hedonism as a psychological theory (Butler 1965 [1726]; Feinberg 1984).

The obvious reply to this criticism is that there is nothing in hedonism that says that people must be monomaniacs. Hedonism says that people have attaining pleasure and avoiding pain as their only *ultimate* goals; it does not say that attaining pleasure and avoiding pain are the only goals (ultimate *or* proximate) that people ever have. Hedonists reflect on which activities are most apt to bring pleasure and prevent pain, and decide what to do on that basis (Sidgwick 1922 [1907]). Furthermore, if hedonistic monomaniacs always fail to get what they want, what follows from this? Even if this entailed that people *should* not be hedonists, it does not show that people are not hedonists *in fact*. Recall that hedonism is a descriptive, not a normative, theory.

The normative/descriptive distinction also is needed to evaluate the claim that egoism is irrational. Nagel (1970) defends this claim by contending that when egoists consider their own interests in deliberation, but not those of others, they neglect the fact that there is no property that they have and others lack that could justify this asymmetry. To evaluate whether egoists are irrational, we need to decide whether rationality should be understood "instrumentally" or "substantively." Instrumental rationality just means the ability to choose efficient means to achieve whatever ends one might have. The substantive notion means, not just that efficient means have been secured, but that the ends are praiseworthy, or at least are morally unobjectionable (Gibbard 1990). Efficient serial killers might be instrumentally rational, but they are not substantively rational. Regardless of which notion captures what the word "rational" means, the fact remains that this line of argument cannot show that people really have or are capable of having altruistic ultimate motives. If rationality just means instrumental rationality, then rationality does not entail altruism (or its possibility); and if rationality means substantive rationality, then even if rationality entails altruism, it needs to be shown that people really are substantively rational. Perhaps we *ought* to be rational and maybe we *ought* to be altruistic as well. This does not show that egoism is false as a descriptive thesis.

5   The Experience Machine

In the science fiction movie *Total Recall*, people centuries from now use their computer technology to go on "virtual vacations." Instead of going on a real vacation, they plug into a computer that provides a thoroughly convincing simulation of a real vacation. The movie quite plausibly suggests that people in the future often might choose to "vacation" in this way, especially if real trips to exotic locales are expensive and dangerous, while "virtual vacations" are cheap and completely convincing from an experiential point of view.

Robert Nozick wrote *Anarchy, State, and Utopia* considerably before *Total Recall* appeared. He there uses the idea of an "experience machine" to construct an argument that seems to show that hedonism is false (Nozick 1974: 42–5). Nozick's machine can be programmed to provide thoroughly convincing simulations of any real-life experience one might choose. Suppose you were offered the chance to plug into the experience machine for the rest of your life. The machine would be programmed to make you instantly forget that you had chosen to plug in and then would provide whatever sequence of experiences you would find maximally pleasurable and minimally painful. Of course, your beliefs about the type of life you are leading will be false. If you choose to plug into the experience machine, you will live your life strapped to a laboratory table with tubes and electrodes sticking into your body. You'll never *do* anything; however, the level of pleasure you'll experience, thanks to the machine, will be extraordinary.

If you were offered the chance to plug into the experience machine for the rest of your life, what would you do? Your first reaction might be to doubt that the machine will perform as promised; certainly no machine now on the market can deliver what this machine is said to be able to do, and this will remain true at least for the foreseeable future. However, for the sake of argument, try to set this hesitation to one side. Imagine yourself being offered the chance to plug in, and suppose that the machine will work as described. My guess is that many people, perhaps including yourself, would decline the opportunity of plugging in.

This fact about people seems to refute hedonism. Apparently, many people prefer to have a real life over a simulated one, even if real life brings less pleasure and more pain than the life they'd have if they plugged into the machine. It seems that people care irreducibly about how they are related to the world outside their own minds; it is false that the only things they care about as ends in themselves are pleasant states of consciousness.

Can hedonism explain why many people would decline the offer to plug into the machine? To see whether this is possible, we need to map out the sequence of events that will comprise your life if you choose to plug into the experience machine and the sequence of events that will occur if you do not. In both cases, the process begins with deliberation, which terminates in a decision. If you decide to plug in, there is a time lag between your decision and your actually being connected to the machine. The two time lines we need to consider are detailed in figure 7.1.

Figure 7.1

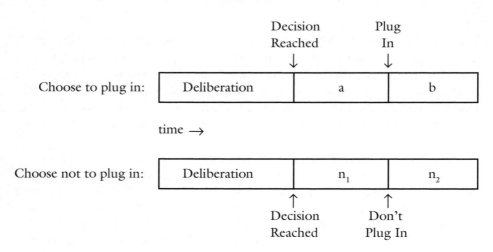

The four letters in these two time lines represent how pleasant your experiences will be during different temporal periods, depending on what you decide. If you choose to plug into the machine, you'll have an immense level of *bliss* (b) after you plug in. This will dwarf the amount of pleasure you'll experience in the same period of time if you decide not to plug in and to lead a normal life instead; $b > n_2$. If this were the only consideration involved, the hedonist would have to predict that people will choose to plug into the machine. How can hedonism explain the fact that many people make the opposite decision?

The hedonist's strategy is to look at earlier events. If you decided to plug into the machine, how would you feel before you were actually connected? Presumably, you would experience a great deal of *anxiety* (a). You'd realize that you were about to stop leading a real life. You will never again see the people you love; all of your projects and plans are about to be terminated. It is clear that you would have less pleasure during this period of time than you would if you rejected the option of plugging into the machine and continued with your real life instead; $a < n_2$.

If hedonists are to explain why people choose not to plug into the experience machine, and are to do this by considering just the pleasure and pain that subjects expect to come their way *after* they decide what to do, the claim must be that $a + b < n_1 + n_2$. Since b is far greater than n_2, this inequality will be true only if a is far far smaller than n_1. That is, hedonists seem compelled to argue that people reject the option of plugging in because the amount of pain they would experience between deciding to plug in and actually being connected to the machine is *gigantic* – so large that it dwarfs the pleasure they'd experience after they are connected.

This suggestion is not plausible. The period of time between deciding to plug in and actually doing so can be made very brief, compared with the long stretch of years you'll spend attached to the machine and enjoying a maximally pleasurable ensemble of experiences. I grant that people who decide to connect to the machine will experience sadness and anxiety during the brief interval between deciding to plug in and actually plugging in. But the idea that this negative experience swamps all subsequent pleasures just isn't credible.

To see why, let's consider a second thought experiment, suggested to me by William Talbott. Suppose you were offered $5,000 if you went through 10 seconds of a certain experience. The experience is believing that you had just decided to spend the rest of your life plugged into an experience machine. After your 10 second jolt of this experience, you will return to your normal life and will realize that you just had a "nightmare"; you then will receive the money as promised. I expect that many people would choose the 10 seconds just described because it will earn them $5,000. This shows that hedonism is mistaken if it claims that the experience of believing you will be plugged into an experience machine for the rest of your life is so horrible that no one would ever choose a life that included it.

The hedonist still has not been able to explain why many people would choose a normal life over a life plugged into the experience machine. The reason is that a hedonistic calculation seems to lead inevitably to the conclusion that $a + b > n_1 + n_2$. Does this mean that the hedonist must concede defeat? I think that the hedonist has a way out. Quite apart from the amount of pleasure and pain that accrues to subjects *after* they decide what to do, there is the level of pleasure and pain arising in the deliberation process itself. The hedonist can maintain that *deciding* to plug into the machine is so aversive that people almost always make the other choice. When people deliberate about the alternatives, they feel bad when they think of the life they'll lead if they plug into the machine; they feel much better when they consider the life they'll lead in the real world if they decline to plug in. The *idea* of life attached to the machine is painful, even though such a life would be quite pleasurable; the *idea* of real life is pleasurable, even though real life often includes pain. This hedonistic explanation of why people refuse to plug in exploits the distinction that Schlick (1939) drew between the pleasant idea of a state and the idea of a pleasant state.

To see what is involved in this suggestion, let's consider in more detail what goes through people's minds as they deliberate. They realize that plugging in will mean abandoning the projects and attachments they hold dear; plugging into the machine resembles suicide in terms of the utter separation it effects with the real world. The difference is that suicide means an end to consciousness, whereas the experience machine delivers (literally) escapist pleasures. Hedonism is not betraying its own principles when it claims that many people would feel great contempt for the idea of plugging in and would regard the temptation to do so as loathsome. People who decline the chance to plug in are repelled by the idea of narcissistic escape and find pleasure in the idea of choosing a real life.

One virtue of this hedonistic explanation is that it explains the results obtained in both the thought experiments described. It explains why people often *decline* to plug into the experience machine for the rest of their lives; it also explains why people offered $5,000 often *agree* to have ten seconds of the experience of believing that they have just decided to plug into the machine for the rest of their lives. In both cases, deliberation is guided, not so much by beliefs about which actions will bring *future* pleasure, but by the pleasure and pain that accompany certain thoughts *during the deliberation process itself.*

The problem of the experience machine resembles the problem of the soldier in the foxhole, discussed earlier. How can hedonism explain this act of suicidal self-sacrifice, if the soldier believes that he will not experience anything after he dies? The hedonist can suggest that there is a self-directed benefit that accrues *before* the act of self-sacrifice is performed. It is no violation of hedonism to maintain that the soldier decides to sacrifice his life because that decision is less painful than the decision to let his friends die. The problem of suicidal self-sacrifice and the problem posed by the experience machine can be addressed in the same way.

6   Burden of Proof

Philosophers sometimes maintain that a common sense idea should be regarded as innocent until proven guilty. That is, if a question is raised about whether some common sense proposition is true, and no argument can be produced that justifies or refutes it, then the sensible thing to do is to keep on believing the proposition. Put differently, the idea is that the burden of proof lies with those who challenge common sense.

This general attitude sometimes surfaces in discussion of egoism and altruism. The claim is advanced that the egoism hypothesis goes contrary to common sense. The common sense picture of human motivation is said to be pluralistic – people care about themselves, but also care about others, not just as means, but as ends in themselves. The conclusion is then drawn that if philosophical and scientific argumentation for and against egoism is indecisive, then we should reject egoism and continue to accept pluralism.

One objection to this proposed tie-breaker is that it is far from obvious that "common sense" is on the side of motivational pluralism rather than egoism. What is common sense? Isn't it just what people commonly believe? If so, it is arguable that egoism has made large inroads; it now seems to be a view that is endorsed by large numbers of people. Philosophers need to be careful not to confuse common sense with what they themselves happen to find obvious. As far as I know, no empirical survey has determined whether a pluralistic theory of motivation is more popular than psychological egoism.

Regardless of what people commonly believe about psychological egoism and motivational pluralism, I reject the idea that conformity with common sense is a tie-breaker in this debate. It does not have this status in physics or biology, and I see no reason why it should do so when the question happens to be philosophical or psychological in character. In fact, it is arguable that our intuitions in this domain are especially prone to error. People have a picture of their own motives and the motives of others. If certain types of self-deception – either regarding one's own motives or those of others – were advantageous, then evolution might have enshrined these falsehoods in the set of "obvious" propositions we call common sense. A philosophy informed by an evolutionary perspective has no business taking common sense at face value.

7   Parsimony

I so far have argued that hedonism and has not been refuted by philosophical arguments or by observed behavior; if this is right, then egoism has not been refuted either. This does not mean that egoism is true; after all, motivational pluralism has not been refuted either. In the light of this impasse, it is worth noting that social scientists often implicitly assume that if a behavior *can* be explained in egoistic terms, then it *ought* to be so explained. The fact that they have no direct argument in favor of this position seems not to be relevant. And the fact that the behavior also can be explained in terms of motivational pluralism also seems not to be relevant. However, why should egoism be the default hypothesis that we should assume is true unless we are forced to abandon it?

One answer to consider is that egoism is more parsimonious – it postulates only one type of ultimate motive, whereas pluralism postulates two (Hume 1970 [1751]; Batson 1991). Even if we assume that parsimony marks not just an aesthetic difference between theories, but a reason for finding some theories more plausible than others, there still is a defect in this defense of egoism. The problem is that egoism is *less* parsimonious than pluralism when we consider how many causal beliefs the two theories postulate. When Sally wants Otto to do well, the defender of egoism counts this as an instrumental desire while the proponent of motivational pluralism may hold that Sally has this other-directed desire as an end in itself. But notice that the egoistic explanation attributes to Sally a causal belief – *that she stands to receive a benefit from Otto's doing well*. Motivational pluralism is not committed to saying that Sally has this belief. An egoist has a shorter list of ultimate desires than a pluralist, but the egoist has a longer list of causal beliefs. For this reason, it is quite unclear why psychological egoism should be regarded as the more parsimonious theory (Sober and Wilson 1998).

8   An Evolutionary Approach

Psychological motives are proximate mechanisms in the sense of that term used in evolutionary biology. When a sunflower turns towards the sun, there must be some mechanism inside the sunflower that causes it to do so. Hence, if phototropism is an adaptation that evolved because it provided organisms with certain benefits, then a proximate mechanism that causes that behavior also must have evolved. Similarly, if certain forms of helping behavior in human beings are evolutionary adaptations, then the motives that cause those behaviors in individual human beings also must have evolved. Perhaps a general perspective on the evolution of proximate mechanisms will throw light on the specific problem of whether egoism or motivational pluralism was more likely to have evolved.

Pursuing this evolutionary approach does not presuppose that every detail of human behavior, or every act of helping, can be completely explained by the hypothesis of evolution by natural selection. Doubtless there are many facts about behavior and many instances of helping for which natural selection is not a relevant explanation. However, I want to consider a single fact about human behavior, and my claim is that selection is relevant to explaining it. The phenomenon of interest is that human parents take care of their children; the average amount of parental care provided by human beings is strikingly greater than that provided by parents in many other species. I will assume that natural selection is at least part of the explanation of why parental care evolved in our lineage. This is not to deny that human parents vary; some parents take better care of their children than others, and some even abuse and kill their offspring. Another striking fact about individual variation is that mothers, on average, expend more time and effort on parental care than fathers. Perhaps there are evolutionary explanations for these individual differences as well; the question I want to address here, however, makes no assumption as to whether this is true.

To tease out some general principles that govern how one might predict the proximate mechanism that will evolve to cause a particular behavior, I'll switch examples to a hypothetical mindless organism whose problem is to select items from its environment to eat. Some particles that float by in the liquid medium in which the organism lives contain protein; others contain poison. The organism has evolved a particular behavior – it tends to eat protein and avoid poison. What proximate mechanism might have evolved that allows it to do so?

First let's survey the range of possible design solutions that we need to consider. The most obvious design solution to this problem is for the organism to have a detector that distinguishes protein from poison. It captures a morsel that floats by, puts the particle in its detector, and then has the output of this detector wired to a behavior; the organism either eats the morsel, or spits it out. I'll call this the *direct* solution to the design problem; the organism needs to discriminate between protein and poison and this solution accomplishes that end by using a detector that detects that very contrast in properties.

It isn't hard to imagine other solutions to the design problem that are less direct. Suppose that protein tends to be red and that poison tends to be green in the organism's environment. If so, the organism could use a color detector to make the requisite discrimination. This design solution is *indirect*; the organism needs to distinguish protein from poison and accomplishes this by discriminating between two other properties that happen to be correlated with the target contrast. In general, there may be many indirect design solutions that the organism might exploit; there are as many indirect solutions as there are correlations between the protein/

poison distinction and other properties found in the environment. Finally, we may add to our list the idea that there can be pluralistic solutions to a design problem. In addition to the monistic solution of having a protein detector and the monistic solution of having a color detector, an organism might deploy both a protein detector *and* a color detector.

Given this multitude of possibilities, how might one predict which of them will evolve? Three principles are relevant here – *availability*, *reliability*, and *efficiency* (Sober 1994; Sober and Wilson 1998).

Natural selection acts only on the range of variation that exists ancestrally. A protein detector might be a good thing for the organism to have, but if that device was never present as an ancestral variant, then natural selection cannot cause that trait to evolve. So the first sort of information we'd like to have concerns which proximate mechanisms were *available* ancestrally.

Let's suppose for the sake of argument that both a protein detector and a color detector are available ancestrally. Which of them is more likely to evolve? Here we need to address the issue of *reliability*. Which device does the more reliable job of indicating which particles in the environment are good to eat? Without further information, not much can be said. A color detector may have any degree of reliability, and the same is true of a protein detector. There is no *a priori* reason why the direct strategy should be more or less reliable than the indirect strategy. However, there is a special circumstance in which they will differ. It is illustrated by figure 7.2.

The double arrows indicate correlation; gaining nutrition is correlated with an organism's fitness, and a particle's being red rather than green is correlated with its nutritional content (figure 7.2). In the diagram, there is no arrow from fitness to color except the one that passes through nutrition. This means that an organism's fitness is correlated with the color of the particles that it eats. There is no *a priori* reason that color should be relevant to fitness only by virtue of indicating nutritional content. For example, if eating red particles attracted predators more than

Figure 7.2

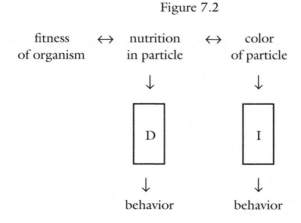

143

eating green ones does, then color would have two sorts of relevance for fitness. However, if nutrition "screens off" fitness from color in the way indicated, we can state the following principle about the reliability of the direct device D and the indirect device I:

(D/I)   If nutrition and color are less than perfectly correlated, and if D detects nutrition at least as well as I detects color, then D will be more reliable than I.

This is the Direct/Indirect Asymmetry Principle. Direct solutions to a design problem aren't always more reliable, but they are more reliable in this circumstance.

A second principle about reliability also can be extracted from this diagram. Just as scientists do a better job discriminating between hypotheses if they have more evidence rather than less, so it will be true that organisms make more reliable discriminations if they have two sources of information about what to eat rather than just one:

(TBO)   If nutrition and color are less than perfectly correlated, and if D and I are each reliable, though fallible, detectors of fitness, then D and I working together will be more reliable than either of them working alone.

This is the Two-is-Better-than-One Principle. It requires an assumption – that the two devices do not interfere with each other when they are both present in an organism; they function fairly independently.

The D/I Asymmetry and the TBO Principle pertain to the issue of reliability. Let us now turn to the third consideration that is relevant to predicting which proximate mechanism will evolve, namely *efficiency*. Even if a nutrition detector and a color detector are both available, and even if the nutrition detector is more reliable, it doesn't follow that natural selection will favor the nutrition detector. It may be that a nutrition detector requires more energy to build and maintain than a color detector. Organisms run on energy no less than automobiles do. Efficiency is relevant to a trait's overall fitness just as much as its reliability is.

With these three considerations in hand, let's return to the problem of predicting which motivational mechanism for providing parental care is likely to have evolved in the lineage leading to human beings. The three motivational mechanisms we need to consider correspond to three different rules for selecting a behavior in the light of what one believes:

(HED)   Provide parental care if and only if doing so will maximize pleasure and minimize pain.

(ALT)   Provide parental care if and only if doing so will advance the welfare of one's children.

(PLUR)   Provide parental care if and only if doing so will either maximize pleasure and minimize pain, or will advance the welfare of one's children.

(ALT) is a relatively direct, and (HED) a relatively indirect, solution to the design problem of getting an organism to take care of its offspring. Just as an organism can find nutrition by detecting color, so it is possible in principle for a hedonistic organism to be built in such a way that it will provide parental care; what is required is that the organism be so constituted that providing parental care is the thing that maximizes its pleasure and minimizes its pain (or that the organism at least believes that this is so).

Let's consider how reliable these three mechanisms will be in a certain situation. Suppose that a parent learns that its child is in danger. Imagine that your neighbor tells you that your child has just fallen through the ice on a frozen lake. Figure 7.3 shows how (HED) and (ALT) will do their work.

Figure 7.3

child needs help → parent believes child needs help → parent feels anxiety and fear

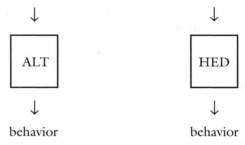

The altruistic parent will be moved to action just by virtue of believing that its child needs help. The hedonistic parent will not; rather, what moves the hedonistic parent to action is the feelings of anxiety and fear that are caused by the news, or the parent's belief that such negative feelings will continue unless the child's situation is improved. It should be clear from figure 7.3 that the (D/I) Asymmetry Principle applies. In the circumstance specified, (ALT) will be more reliable than (HED). And by the (TBO) Principle, (PLUR) will do better than both. In this example, hedonism comes in last in the three-way competition, at least as far as reliability is concerned.

The important thing about this example is that the feelings that the parent has are *belief mediated*. The only reason the parent feels anxiety and fear is that the parent *believes* that its child is in trouble. This is true of many of the situations that egoism and hedonism are called upon to explain, but it is not true of all of them. For example, consider the following situation in which pain is a direct effect, and belief a relatively indirect effect, of bodily injury (figure 7.4).

Figure 7.4

fingers are burned → pain → belief that one's fingers have been injured

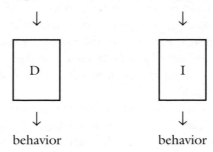

Now hedonism is a direct solution to the design problem; it would be silly to build the organism so that it is unresponsive to pain and withdraws its fingers from the flame only after it forms a belief about bodily injury. In this situation, *belief is pain-mediated* and the (D/I) Asymmetry Principle explains why a hedonistic focus on pain makes sense. However, the same principle indicates what is misguided about hedonism as a design solution when pain is belief-mediated, which is what occurs so often in the context of parental care.

If hedonism is less reliable than either pure altruism or motivational pluralism, how do these three mechanisms compare when we consider the issues of evolutionary availability and efficiency? With respect to availability, I want to make this claim: *if hedonism was available ancestrally as a design solution, so was altruism.* The reason is that the two motivational mechanisms differ in only a very minor way. Both require a belief/desire psychology. And both the hedonistic and the altruistic parent want their children to do well; the only difference is that the hedonist has this propositional content as an instrumental desire while the altruist has it as an ultimate desire. If altruism and pluralism did not evolve, this was not because they were unavailable as variants for selection to act upon.

What about the question of efficiency? Does it cost more calories to build and maintain an altruistic or a pluralistic organism than it does to build and maintain a hedonist? I don't see why. What requires energy is building the hardware that implements a belief/desire psychology. However, it is hard to see why having one ultimate desire rather than two should make an energetic difference; nor is it easy to see why having the ultimate desire that your children to do well should require more calories than having the ultimate desire to avoid pain and attain pleasure. People with more beliefs apparently don't need to eat more than people with fewer. The same point seems to apply to the issue of how many, or which, ultimate desires one has.

In summary, hedonism is a less reliable mechanism than pure altruism or pluralism as a device for delivering parental care. And, with respect to the issues of availability and efficiency, we found no difference among these three motivational mechanisms. This suggests that natural selection is more likely to have made us motivational pluralists than to have made us hedonists.

From an evolutionary point of view, hedonism is a very bizarre motivational mechanism. What matters in the process of natural selection is an organism's ability to survive and be reproductively successful. Reproductive success involves not just the production of offspring, but the survival of those offspring to reproductive age. So what matters is the survival of one's own body and the bodies of one's children. Hedonism, on the other hand, says that organisms care ultimately about the states of their own consciousness, and about that alone. Why would natural selection have led organisms to care about something that is peripheral to fitness, rather than have them set their eyes on the prize? If organisms were unable to conceptualize propositions about their own bodies and the bodies of their offspring, that might be a reason. After all, it can make sense for an organism to exploit the indirect strategy of deciding what to eat on the basis of color rather than on the basis of nutritional value, if the organism has no epistemic access to nutritional content. But if an organism is smart enough to form representations about itself and its offspring, this justification of the indirect strategy will not be plausible. The fact that we evolved from ancestors who were cognitively less sophisticated makes it unsurprising that avoiding pain and attaining pleasure are two of our ultimate goals. But the fact that human beings are able to form representations with so many different propositional contents suggests that evolution supplemented this list of what we care about as ends in themselves.

9   Concluding Comments

I have argued that past philosophical and psychological attempts to resolve the debate between egoism and motivational pluralism have not succeeded. It would be astonishing if this dispute about an apparently empirical matter could be resolved by arguments *a priori*. And, unfortunately, the observations that people casually make in ordinary life and that scientists make in the laboratory have not been decisive either; although some simple versions of egoism are refuted by what we observe, other versions of egoism can be constructed that seem to fit the available observations. Perhaps more sophisticated experiments and observations of behavior will answer the question. But for now, the situation in philosophy and psychology is one of stalemate.

Can evolutionary considerations break through this impasse? The argument of the previous section aims to establish that a purely egoistic set of motives is less likely to have evolved than a set of motives that includes both egoistic and altruistic ultimate desires. I do not suggest that this argument *proves* that people are motivational pluralists; there is much that remains unknown about the mind and how it evolved, and there is no guarantee that further details will not substantially alter the picture I have tried to develop. However, I do think that the argument suffices to show that egoism does not deserve to be regarded as the default hypothesis that we should accept as long as it is consistent with what we observe. In my opinion, the weight of evidence favors pluralism, if only to a small degree.

References

Batson, C. D.: *The Altruism Question: Toward A Social-Psychological Answer* (Hillsdale, NJ: Lawrence Erlbaum Associates, 1991).

Broad, C. D.: *Five Types of Ethical Theory* (Totowa, NJ: Littlefield, Adams, 1965).

Butler, J.: Fifteen Sermons upon Human Nature (1726); Reprinted in L. A. Selby-Bigge (ed.), *British Moralists: Being Selections From Writers Principally of the Eighteenth Century*, volume 1 (New York: Dover Books, 1965), pp. 180–241.

Clark, R. D. and Word, L. E. "Where is the apathetic bystander? Situational characteristics of the emergency," *Journal of Personality and Social Psychology*, 29 (1974): 279–87.

Feinberg, J.: "Psychological egoism," in S. Cahn, P. Kitcher, and G. Sher (eds.), *Reason at Work* (San Diego, CA: Harcourt Brace and Jovanovich, 1984), pp. 25–35.

Gibbard, A.: *Wise Choices, Apt Feelings* (Cambridge: Harvard University Press, 1990).

Hume, D. "On self love," in *An Enquiry Concerning the Principles of Morals* (1751); (Indianapolis: Hackett, 1970).

Kavka, G.: *Hobbesian Moral and Political Theory* (Princeton, NJ: Princeton University Press, 1986).

LaFollette, H.: "The truth in psychological egoism," in J. Feinberg (ed.), *Reason and Responsibility*, 7th edn. (Belmont, CA: Wadsworth, 1988), pp. 500–7.

Nagel, T.: *The Possibility of Altruism* (Oxford: Oxford University Press, 1970).

Nozick, R.: *Anarchy, State, and Utopia* (New York: Basic Books, 1974).

Schlick, M.: *Problems of Ethics* (New York: Prentice Hall, 1939).

Schroeder, D., Penner, L., Dovidio, J. and Piliavin, J.: *The Psychology of Helping and Altruism* (New York: McGraw Hill, 1995).

Sidgwick, H.: *The Methods of Ethics* (1907) 7th edn. (London: Macmillan, 1922).

Sober, E.: "Hedonism and Butler's stone," *Ethics* 103 (1992): 97–103.

——: "Did evolution make us psychological egoists?" In *From a Biological Point of View: Essays in Evolutionary Philosophy* (New York: Cambridge University Press, 1994), pp. 8–27.

—— and Wilson, D.S.: *Unto Others – the Evolution and Psychology of Unselfish Behavior* (Cambridge, MA: Harvard University Press, 1998).

Stampe, D.: "Desire," in S. Guttenplan (ed.), *A Companion to the Philosophy of Mind* (Cambridge, MA: Basil Blackwell, 1994), pp. 244–50.

Stewart, R. M.: "Butler's argument against psychological hedonism," *Canadian Journal of Philosophy* 22 (1992): 211–21.

Chapter 8

Moral Psychology

Laurence Thomas

If it is obvious that human beings are quintessential social creatures, what exactly this means is far less so. The writings of the philosopher Jean-Jacques Rousseau are very instructive in this regard. He writes:

> The benefits that accrue to man in civil society more than makes up for whatever advantages that he possessed in the state of nature. His faculties are exercised and developed, his intellectual horizon expands, his sentiments are enriched. Indeed, his very soul is entirely elevated. (*The Social Contract*, Bk 1, ch. viii)

And the great theorist of the moral sentiments, Adam Smith, had this to say:

> Were it possible that a human creature could grow up in some solitary place without any communication with his own species, he could no more think of his character, of the propriety or demit of his own sentiments and conduct, of the beauty or deformity of his mind, than of the beauty of his own face. . . . Bring him into society, and he is immediately provided with the mirror which he wanted before. (*A Theory of Moral Sentiments*, III.i.3)

For both of these thinkers, a fully developed human being is impossible in the absence of interaction with other fellow human beings; and, what is more, each held that a fully developed human being is necessarily one whose moral sensibilities are richly developed.

That is, Rousseau and Smith advanced a view that might seem to be quite at odds with the facts, namely that there is very strong congruence between being psychologically healthy and embracing an altruistic conception of morality. Determining to what extent and in what ways this is so is the fundamental task of moral psychology.

I   In the Beginning

Nothing more fully bestows a sense of worth upon persons than parental love. As infants, children are born into the world without a sense of self and so without a sense of value. And it is parental love, and nothing else, that makes it possible for children to have to have a proper sense of self. Parents love their children regardless of the talents and physical features of their children. Or, at any rate, so it is ideally.

Anything other than love will invariably miss the mark, because anything else will be tied in some way to either the performances or appearances of the child. Thus, it is in virtue of being the unmistakable object of manifest parental love that children come to have a sense of intrinsic self-worth, that children come to value themselves as human beings. So while there is no denying that morality is an intrinsic good, it is not first among intrinsic goods nor the most basic. Parental love – precisely because it is parental love, and not morality – bestows a sense of intrinsic worth that is absolutely fundamental to the psychological well-being of persons. Observe that parents who treated their children morally but did not love them, supposing that this were a possibility, would unquestionably fail as parents. It is one sublime feature of the parental–child relationship that parental love simultaneously contributes to both the moral and the psychological well-being of the child, that these two aspects of well-being take place in tandem.

The idea behind parental love, of course, is not that parents do not make demands upon their children, moral and otherwise. Good parents make many such demands. Rather, it is that the child's performance is not a condition of its being loved by its parents. Most profoundly, parents at their best are able to make the appropriate moral and social demands of the child without the child ever coming to feel, at least not in any sustained way, that its performance is a condition of being loved by its parents. This, too, is a most sublime feature of the parent–child relationship.

It is most significant that insofar as children have the stable conviction that they are loved by their parents, this is because they *experience* this love from their parents. Arguments and all sorts of eloquent utterances are inadequate here unless they take place against the backdrop of the child's having the experience of being loved. This, of course, should come as no surprise, because the experience of being loved is important to the well-being of the child long before its linguistic skills enable it to comprehend and appreciate eloquent words and sophisticated arguments to the effect that it is loved.

A complete account of the experience of being loved would invariably have to be adjusted for cultural differences, even down to something so seemingly mundane as differences between hugs and kisses. *La bise*, the kiss on each cheek, remains an important part of French culture as one of the ways in which parents and family members express affection to children. Not so in America. Accordingly, a child raised in the United States would not expect such routine behavior from its parents and family members, and its absence would not be interpreted by her or him as a lack of love. A general account, though, of the experience of being loved would be that displays of affection must be manifested across an exceedingly wide spectrum of behavior on the child's part. From time to time, displays of affection are very much needed, not only when a child's behavior is stellar, but in the face of grave disappointment – nay, outright disapproval. For even in the context of punishment or severe chastisement, parents can make it unmistakably clear that they very much love their child. Chastisement followed by a hug is not just a wonderful gesture, it is indispensable to the child's having the realization that parental love is not tied to performance.

The considerations in the preceding two paragraphs speak in a most phenomenal way to the richness of non-verbal behavior among human beings and the congruence between such behavior and our actual beliefs. What seems impossible from a practical point of view is that a child should have the experience of being richly loved by its parents, when in fact they actually detest him. Rousseau had observed that parenting is so demanding that if it were not for parental love, there would be nothing to recommend the endeavor. Can the sentiment of parental love be feigned for a brief period of time? Absolutely. Can it be routinely feigned over time in the context of both foreseen and, especially, unforeseen demands, where there is near constant interaction? Absolutely not! We can momentarily hide what we detest; we cannot continuously do so.

One naturally asks whether it is possible for a child who has unquestionably been the object of parental love to fail to have the secure conviction of being loved by its parents. The answer: this is possible. For in the face of unquestionable parental love, things can still go wrong. A child could have a most horrendous experience about which its parents are unaware or about which they came to be aware too late, for instance, being sexually molested by a non-family member. The child thinks that the parents know; the parents do not. The result is that the child's feeling of being loved by its parents falls considerably short of being as secure as it should be. Consider a different question. Is it possible for a child to fail to become a competent speaker of the language of its parents and the society in which the family lives? Again, the answer has to be that this is possible. But as with the case of parental love, something would have to go wrong. A most traumatic psychological experience might have this effect. Suppose, for instance, that a 4-year old were to witness the killing of both parents as he or she were nestled between them in bed. A macabre moment such as this would be utterly devastating for any child. Things can go dramatically wrong even when parents are doing their part in every respect. When that does not happen, however, the child will come to have the secure conviction that it is loved by its parents, just as the child will come to be a competent speaker of the language of its parents and the society in which the family lives.

Now, it is perhaps tempting to suppose that a child who is the object of parental love comes to be a very self-interested individual. For it might be thought that an inevitable consequence of a child's being the object of parental love is that the child comes to believe that the concerns of others do not matter. Not so, however. As a purely conceptual point, the belief that one's life has value and the belief that one's life is the only life that has value are two fundamentally different beliefs; and, of course, there is no inconsistency whatsoever in having the first, but not the second, belief. What is more, precisely what is involved in bringing it about that a child has a sense of intrinsic self-worth is having the experience of being treated in the appropriate way by those who themselves have worth, and so have regard for themselves.

From the moral point of view, the intrinsic self-worth that parental love bestows upon the child is what underwrites the child's sense of how she or he should be treated by others. To be sure, children learn to avoid bodily pain as a natural evolutionary reaction. But much of what comprises proper moral treatment is not tied to the absence of bodily pain as such. The child who has a sense of intrinsic self-worth does not want to be betrayed or exploited or mislead or the object of base ingratitude. Although none of these are about bodily pain, there is no question about the fundamental importance of not being treated in these ways. Parental love generates in the child the sense that it should not be treated in these ways.

I have maintained that parental love engenders in the child a sense of intrinsic self-worth. This language is obviously Kantian in its inspiration, reflecting the idea that individuals rightly hold themselves to be deserving of being treated in the morally right way by any other person regardless of their moral performances or their social accomplishments or their physical appearances or their intellectual abilities. Parental love at its best loves the child regardless of any claim that the child might have to excelling in any of these areas. The sense of affirmation that comes with parental love thus characterized is the precursor of intrinsic self-worth. For at the outset, surely, the child does not have a sense of itself as a moral being, a being who both can wrong others and be wronged by others. The sense of worth that is bestowed upon a child by parental love girds the sense of intrinsic self-worth that persons should have from the moral point of view. Parental love takes a creature, namely an infant human, which has no sense of itself as having value and bestows upon it the sense that it has value in the eyes of its parents, where this value is not tied to its performance. Intrinsic self-worth is just the moral analogue to the sense of self that parental love secures.

So far the argument has been that there is a congruence between parental love, a child's being psychologically healthy, and a person's coming to having the sense that she or he deserves to be treated properly by others. In view of the doctrine known as psychological egoism, which is that people are naturally inclined to promote their own interests, some might discount the significance of what has been argued thus far. As a brief response, it should simply be pointed out that self-deprecatory behavior is a reality among human beings, as the very idea of the Uncle Tom makes abundantly clear. So a proponent of psychological egoism cannot maintain that, come what may, people advance their self-interests or view themselves as morally meritorious in the eyes of others. That, alas, is demonstrably false.

In any case, while parental love and intrinsic self-worth may very well suffice to explain why a person does not want to be wronged by others, without appealing to an egoistic conception of things, we need, now, to make the case that such a person is not inclined to wrong others. I proceed to this task in the next section.

II   The Golden Rule

The Golden Rule reads:

Do unto others as you would have them to do unto you.

This is easily one of the most familiar and morally inspiring precepts of western culture. But what exactly are the presuppositions of this rule regarding how human beings are motivated to behave towards others? Is it that human beings are motivated to behave morally toward others only because they are concerned with being treated morally in return? On this view, a person who had no desire to be treated morally would have little reason to behave morally toward others. But, of course, it is the very rare person, indeed, who does not want to be treated morally, who does not mind being lied to, robbed, or otherwise harmed. On the other hand, there are many who suppose that they can get away with acting immorally. If, in the spirit of Thrasymachus about whom we read in Plato's *Republic*, a person could enjoy a reputation for being moral while nonetheless living immorally, then it would seem that he would have no motivation to act morally. Or so it is, any rate, if the only motivation a person has for behaving morally towards others is that he wants to be treated morally in return. What is more, on this view of moral motivation the Golden Rule turns out to be very uninspiring.

A far more noble reading of the Golden Rule, as it pertains to moral motivation, certainly a reading suggested by Bishop Joseph Butler, would be as follows: Human beings should find the thought of wronging another sufficiently repulsive that they would thereby be motivated to refrain from doing so. The problem would seem to be that this rendering of the Golden Rule is just a little too noble, flying squarely in the face of human reality.

Perhaps. But any question of human moral motivation has to take into account the matter of moral climate. What persons might be motivated to do in one moral climate, they might not be motivated to do in another. Thus, how a single person might behave were she permanently isolated on desert island tells us very little about how she might behave were she among other human beings. Plato, to be sure, insisted that the truly moral person would act morally regardless of how evil a moral climate she found herself in, because morality would always have an inexorable hold upon her. It seems that one could reject this strong Platonic view while being true to the spirit of Butler's reading of the Golden Rule. Butler most certainly did not comment upon the Golden Rule with an evil moral climate in mind.

Essentially, Butler thought that the motivational structure of human beings was such that persons would not, under ordinary circumstances, be moved to wrong others, precisely because they would find doing so repugnant as revealed by their own desire not to be wronged by others. There would be the proper appreciation of the facts of the matter which, in turn, would motivate a person to behave in the morally right way. With the proper appreciation, a person has an effective will with respect to doing what is right. Naturally, a detailed account of Butler's view would undoubtedly make reference to the moral sentiment of sympathy. Still, something has to be said about how things are perceived, because sympathy that is warranted requires a certain conception of things. Sympathy for a person is most inappropriate, even incomprehensible, if that individual is believed to have just won the Nobel Prize or to have just committed a cold-blooded murder. Thus, without denying the role of sympathy in Butler's view, I focus upon having the proper appreciation. At this point, a somewhat unusual example, when talking about the Golden Rule, will prove very instructive with respect to the first part of the thesis, namely having the proper appreciation.

Suppose that Azouma has been the object of an extraordinary act of beneficence – say, Jones risked her life in order to save his. She jumped into freezing water risking hypothermia and death. She gave Azouma mouth-to-mouth resuscitation in order to revive him, and stayed with him until medical care arrived. Upon complete recovery, Azouma learns how it happens that he is still alive, namely that Jones saved him at enormous risk to herself. Needless to say, there should be a groundswell of gratitude in his bosom toward her. But suppose, instead, that Azouma is utterly oblivious to what Jones did on his behalf. He would not be grateful to her. If we presume he knew of her heroics. Then we would not merely regard Azouma's reaction as most unusual and, of course, terribly inappropriate, but we would also think that "there is something wrong with him."

And one reason why we would think this is precisely that we could not imagine that Azouma could behave in a like manner on behalf of anyone without feeling that the beneficiary of his actions owed him a considerable measure of gratitude. This gets us to the very heart of Butler's view. For if we bear in mind that the expectation of gratitude does not presuppose an egoistic conception of the self, then the very same psychological structure that would make it natural for Azouma to feel that he was owed gratitude should likewise make it natural for Azouma to display gratitude toward Jones. This is because Azouma's belief that he is owed gratitude would not be tied to the view that he is special, but to the view that it is appropriate for a person to acknowledge that he has benefited from the sacrifices that anyone has made on his behalf.

Wronging others can be seen as the flip-side of gratitude. We expect a person to find being wronged by others very distasteful. But likewise, this expectation does not presuppose an egoistic conception of the self. Instead, it presupposes nothing more than an adequate appreciation of the self and, a particular assessment of the wrong-doer, namely that in so acting this person displays an indifference to the other's life. It is a person's own sense of intrinsic self-worth that gives his person a purchase on how the other might feel if she is wronged.

In this regard, the example of gratitude proves to be most illuminating, precisely because not showing gratitude, certainly in a case that is as dramatic as the one that I described, constitutes a kind of wrongful behavior. This is easily missed because we typically think of wrongful behavior as involving (a threat that would result in) the diminution of an individual's well-being or deception or the denial of a material good the entitlement to which he had come to have by just means. Ingratitude is none of these. It constitutes a wrong because it stands as an affront to the sacrifice which an individual made on another's behalf. Anyone person who has experienced profound ingratitude is aware of just this fact; any person who is aware of just this fact has all that she or he needs to appreciate the significance and wrong of not displaying gratitude toward another. And Butler's position would be that just as, and precisely because, no reasonable person would, or even could, want to experience the former, such a person would be moved to display gratitude toward another.

I have said that wrong-doing does not presuppose an egoistic conception of the self. A word about this point is in order.

Although wrongs can involve a setback to a person's interests, a wrong can prove to be what I would call a fortuitous misfortune. Yet, even in such instances people typically do not want to be wronged. Here are two examples. Although a victim of injustice, such as a wrongful dismissal, may lead someone to go into private business, thereby achieving a good and a success that she would not have achieved otherwise, it is very unlikely that she will be grateful for having been wronged. In the beginnings of a romantic relationship, a discovered betrayal may result in the wronged partner leaving the relationship and forming romantic ties with another, with the result being that she ends up being in one of the most admired and remarkable marriages imaginable. All the same, she may remember the betrayal with great pain. If in either case the woman were to discount entirely the wrong done to her by exclaiming "Look at how well-off I am now," something would surely be amiss here. There would be a failure to attach the proper significance to something very important, namely that the wrong-doer showed an utter disregard for her as a moral being. Wrong-doing, then, does not cease to be that just because it turns out that a person is better off on account of that wrong-doing; and no one views the matter that way. Accordingly, even when a wrong does involve a setback in interests, without any fortuitous gain, it is a mistake to think that this setback in interests must exhaust the explanation for why we have a wrong in such instances.

Significantly, the awareness that one would not be better off, but for the occurrence of such-and-such wrongful outcome does not entail that one must, at some level or the other, be grateful for the occurrence that outcome. A 14-year-old who is aware that but for the death of his loving parents he would not have been adopted by the wealthy and ever so loving family will surely not be grateful for the death of his parents, even though he is acutely aware of the reality that but for the death of his parents he would not be enjoying the opportunities that he now enjoys with the wealthy family. Many, though perhaps not all, fortuitous misfortunes are such that one can be deeply pained by the circumstances that gave rise to them, while appreciating the benefits that now accrue to one. A full account of fortuitous misfortunes is beyond the purview of this essay.

Now, it is important to underscore the fact that the proper appreciation of which I have spoken in regard to gratitude or wrong-doing is, in both cases, tied to the notion of intrinsic self-worth. To be psychologically healthy is to have a proper appreciation of the facts as they bear upon the life of human beings. Fire burns human flesh. Guns fired either harm or kill. And so forth. No psychologically healthy person could fail to have an appreciation of these facts. Likewise, certain modes of behavior reveal an indifference to the good of another's life, whereas others reflect a concern, to the point of making a sacrifice, for the good of another's life. In the wake of moral maturity, the child moves from the judgment that a hostile act hurts her to the rich judgment that a hostile act constitutes a moral wrong against her. In all of these instances, our full appreciation is tied the sense of what it is to be a moral self – a sense which is inextricably tied the development of intrinsic self-worth in our own life.

We tend to overlook the parallel here because physical harm is just that – physical. However, to appreciate the wrong of killing a human being requires more than grasping that guns fired either harm or kill and that fire burns human flesh. One must also grasp that human beings are of a certain moral kind – creatures who possess intrinsic self-worth. In the maturing that marks the transition from childhood to adulthood, what is grasped at is not that fire burns human flesh and that fired guns harm or kill, but the gravity of doing these things. And this maturing is ineluctably tied to a greater appreciation of what it is to be a moral self, and so the significance of having intrinsic self-worth. It is not tied to having witnessed or experienced painfully many wrongs. Without ever having been threatened or perhaps even witnessing a murder, no psychologically healthy person could fail to grasp the significance of killing a human being. Our moral judgment that both American Slavery and the Holocaust are wrong cannot possibly be extricated from this view.

So far so good. But having the proper appreciation is only part of the thesis before us in our attempt to understand the Golden Rule. The psychologically healthy person must be moved to act in the morally right way. And the problem with this aspect of the thesis is that it seems patently false. Not only that, theories of punishment and blame typically take it as a theoretical given that it is possible for a psychologically healthy person to have the proper appreciation and yet fail to act in the morally right way. In view of these considerations, the connection between being moral and being psychologically healthy suddenly looks very tenuous. However, we must proceed cautiously here, because things are not always what they appear to be.

Consider the case of Rusal. While watching a typical television sitcom one day, Rusal came to have the desire to want to kill a few people just for having the experience of it; and in fact he did just that. However, this cannot be not be attributed to any of the usual forms of motivation such as greed or revenge or anger or jealousy. Rusal went out, killed a few people at random, came home satisfied with the experience, and then watched another sitcom.

The first thing to which I want to draw attention is that if we start with the assumption that Rusal is a psychologically healthy person who, in virtue of being such, has the proper appreciation of human life, then this case is extremely difficult to imagine. No such person would simply take to killing individuals. Indeed, no such person would simply come to have the desire to want to kill a few people. And surely we want just such a view of the psychologically healthy person. At the very least, the psychologically healthy individual would not kill another human being without having some motive or the other; and merely wanting to have the experience of killing, allowing that we can make sense of this possibility, would not suffice as a sufficient motivation for a psychologically healthy individual to kill anyone.

Suppose, however, that we allow that greed or revenge or some other vicious motive was at play. Notice how much easier it becomes to imagine Rusal's act of killing (without denying either that he is psychologically healthy or that he has the proper appreciation of human life). Though let me quickly point out that if we can attribute a motive to Rusal's killings, then a small modification will be in order at least in most instances, namely that the killings cannot have been entirely at random. And notice, too, how grave a deed a vicious motive suddenly renders plausible: the murdering of a human being by someone who is psychologically healthy and so has the proper appreciation of human life.

The example of Rusal is extremely instructive in many respects. Up to a point, at any rate, neither the motive of revenge nor jealousy nor greed nor anger suffices to make a person psychologically unhealthy. On the other hand, however, these motives, and their corresponding sentiments, may be a formidable impediment to the proper appreciation of the facts becoming the person's effective will with respect to doing what is morally right. We might say that greed or jealousy or anger or revenge is to a person's effective will with respect to doing what is right what alcohol inebriation is to truth in matters of risky behavior. The inebriated person does not stop knowing the truth that driving at 120 miles an hour is exceedingly dangerous. It is just that this truth no longer has the effect on his will that it would have were he sober.

So the view, then, concerning the congruence between being moral and being psychologically healthy can perhaps be put as follows. The psychologically healthy person has a proper appreciation of the facts of the matter and this appreciation motivates the person to act in the morally right way, provided that there are no impediments to this appreciation becoming a person's effective will with respect to doing what is morally right. Most important, this view does not require us to say that an individual is psychologically unhealthy merely in virtue of there being impediments of this sort; accordingly, it does not requires us to say that persons who commit immoral behavior are, on that account alone, psychologically unhealthy.

Significantly, we can on this account allow that immoral people are psychologically healthy even as we privilege the connection between being moral and being psychologically healthy. Of importance is the idea of impediments to a person's having an effective will with respect to doing what is morally right does not turn out to be vacuous or lacking in sufficient explanatory power. On the one hand, the case of Rusal would suggest that the idea will not be vacuous. On the other, there is the question of what other things might be an impediment to an appreciation becoming a person's effective will with respect to doing what is morally right. Fear? Utter destitution? Either of these, perhaps, strike us as more like greed or anger or jealousy or revenge. But what about the desire for power or control? What about lust?

And if we should get a complete, or sufficiently rich, account of things that can be an impediment to an appreciation becoming a person's effective will, shall it turn out that all immoral behavior can be reduced to the existence of one or more impediments in a person's life? Consider, for example, the person who sexually abuses children. Is it that this person lacks a proper appreciation of his moral behavior or is there some impediment that gets in the way of his doing what is right? A similar question can be asked concerning the rapist.

At this point, though, the account might prove instructive in a rather surprising way. Psychological health is certainly not an all-or-nothing matter. And while there are no doubt paradigmatic cases on either side, there is certainly no simple line to be drawn between the psychologically healthy and the psychologically unhealthy. All the same, it is clear that a person's psychological health may not be optimal. In ordinary language, we speak of people having psychological problems without holding that they are psychologically unhealthy. When an individual's psychological health is not optimal, then it may be easier for his will to do what is right to be impeded, which could be true in two (non-mutually exclusive) ways: (i) a motive or sentiment that would normally be an impediment becomes an impediment much more readily in the absence or optimal psychological health; (ii) the set of things that would be an impediment expands.

At any event, it remains a most significant fact that on a very reasonable and defensible conception of what it means to be psychologically healthy, the vicious motives may be a part of the life of the psychologically healthy person. What does this mean? That greed and jealousy, for example, are natural responses to certain circumstances? And if so, then why is it expected that we should nonetheless be able to prevent them from being an impediment to the effective will to do what is right? To some extent, I address this issue in the section which follows.

III Conceptions of the Moral Self

None of the great moral theorists addressed the notion of psychological health as we understand it today. In one sense, this should come as no surprise since it was not until the late 1800s, with the work of William James, that the field of psychology was acknowledged as a discipline, whereas today child psychology is a well-defined sub-discipline in the field of psychology. Still, it is not clear that the great moral theorists even anticipated the richness of the field of psychology. In particular, none spoke of how important the parent–child relationship was to the child becoming a psychologically healthy adult. Aristotle and Kant both addressed the topic of moral training and education. But neither of these two great thinkers specifically addressed the topic just mentioned. Rousseau, in *Émile*, comes closest to anticipating the psychological issues of the parent–child relationship that we address nowadays.

When the great moral theorists wrote, they may very well have presupposed what we may call a robust conception of the moral self. Roughly, the robust conception is the idea that, in the absence of being insane, a person is sufficiently able to grasp what is morally appropriate and act accordingly.

In contrast to what I have called the robust conception of the moral self, there is what we may call the fragile conception of the moral self. On this view, the quality of the parent–child relationship has a dramatic impact upon the wherewithal of persons, in their adult life, to grasp sufficiently what is morally appropriate and to act accordingly. Here are three instances in which this is thought to be so. (1) A child who has been the systematic object of parental love is less likely to engage in hostile behavior toward others than is a child who has been the object of considerable physical abuse. Instead, such a child is much more likely to exercise the virtue of self-command, to borrow Adam Smith's expression. (2) A child who has been the systematic object of parental love is far more likely to engage in healthy trusting relationships than is a child who has been the object of considerable physical abuse. (3) There is a greater chance that an adult male will abuse his female spouse if, as a child, this male routinely witnessed his father engaging in such behavior toward the person who is both the father's wife and the child's mother.

The virtue and attractiveness of the robust conception of the moral self is that when it comes to attributing blame for wrong-doing, this conception is very agent-centered, in that the blame falls squarely upon the agent who commits the wrong-doing. The robust conception does not deny that things go wrong in the parent–child relationship, it merely insists that the problems there generally do not suffice to shift the blame away from the agent who commits a wrong-doing. The virtue and attractiveness of the fragile conception, obviously, is that it gives weight to the quality of an aspect of our lives that is surely important, namely the parent–child relationship. Is there a way to reconcile these two views? The answer may lie in one word: knowledge.

Suppose that an individual knows that he has a genetic pre-disposition for alcoholism, then it is surely incumbent upon him to take preventive measures. In a like manner, if persons are aware of the severe shortcomings of their childhood, then it may be incumbent upon them to take the appropriate measures to prevents these shortcomings from being an impediment with respect to doing what is morally right. And just as a person with a genetic pre-disposition for alcohol or the recovered alcoholic must always refrain from consuming alcoholic beverages, it could turn out that a person who has endured severe childhood shortcomings must forever take certain precautionary measures.

Likewise, if a person knows that she is given to greed or jealousy or envy or anger, then there could be special steps that she could take to prevent the untoward expression of these sentiments. A person would take responsibility for her anger or greed not just by willing it away.

But does this solution not raise, at one level removed, the specter of the robust conception of the moral self? After all, how can it be reasonable to expect persons to always take the necessary steps to prevent certain shortcomings in their life from having an adverse effect upon their moral behavior unless, in the first place, it is reasonable to assume that persons have the wherewithal to so conduct their lives?

The answer, perhaps surprisingly, may turn upon one's view of what it means to be psychologically healthy. Is the psychologically healthy person simply one who is capable of practical reasoning as understood in terms of means-end deliberation? Or, is he one who can be primarily characterized as a person who experiences the appropriate sentiments in the light of what he knows? The arguments of this essay favor the second view. The mentally insane are not devoid of the capacity for practical reasoning. The Son of Sam thought that he had been called by a divine spirit to kill people. He did not attempt to do this with a feather or a shoe string. No, he employed a gun instead – a very effective means for killing people. And Jeffrey Dahmer, who molested children and devoured some of their body parts, knew very well that he had to be shrewd in attracting young boys and that he should take measures to keep this a secret. Regrettably, he was successful to a considerable extent on both accounts. As with the Son of Sam, Dahmer's problem was not that he lacked the ability to engage in practical reasoning. Neither could they have committed the horrors they committed had that been the case.

If this is right, then from the standpoint of practical reasoning, it may be reasonable to expect persons to take certain steps in order to ensure that certain things are not an impediment to their experiencing the proper moral sentiments. This could require anything from taking certain forms of medication to avoiding certain environments. The mistake of social institutions, then, could be in pretending that the robust model holds in pure form. Without a doubt, moral blame for moral-wrong-doing is proper. Just so, things could be terribly misguided if we ignore shortcomings of the self which individuals could take steps to repair if only there were proper channels for acknowledging these shortcomings in the first place.

Moral reasoning, while it certainly does involve practical reasoning, cannot be simply regarded as an instance of practical reasoning. The conception of psychological health presented presupposes this view of things.

IV   Moral Motivation and Others

One of the most inspiring and extraordinary claims about the moral person that is found on record was made by Socrates in Plato's *Republic*. Socrates claimed that the truly just person is one who would (continue to) behave morally, although the person is systematically treated immorally by all the world. The intuitive idea here is very straightforward. Living morally should be sufficiently attractive in and of itself; and surely there can be no better evidence that a person finds living morally that attractive than that the individual so live even though she is systematically treated immorally by all the world.

Although this Socratic idea that living morally should be sufficiently attractive in and of itself strikes a most responsive chord in our hearts, the problem seems to be that the view places such enormous weight upon morality being its own source of motivation as to render far too irrelevant the importance which others rightly seem to play in our leading a moral life. It is not just that we are often inspired by others to do what is morally right; but, I dare say, a world without such inspiration would be a much less rich world morally speaking. In recalling and reflecting upon the life of a Mother Teresa or a Martin Luther King or a Raul Wallenberg, who could not be inspired, if only momentarily, to live a better moral life? And it seems most counterintuitive to say that individuals are not as morally upright as they could be just because they would not have behaved in certain moral ways but for the inspiration that they found in the life of another.

Without aiming here to determine what Socrates might have had in mind, it is very useful to distinguish between the thesis that (a) living morally is sufficiently attractive in and of itself and the thesis that (b) living morally is inspired by certain forms of behavior. Now, suppose that we understand thesis (a) to mean that a moral person is one who does what is right without regard to obtaining any further benefit or satisfying any further goal. Although thesis (a) is compatible with the strong view that a moral person is one who would act morally though all the world treats him immorally, thesis (a) does not entail this strong view. And while thesis (b) may be incompatible with the strong view, there is no question but that theses (a) and (b) are compatible.

Aristotle wrote:

> But he who is unable to live in society, or who has no need because he is sufficient himself, must be either a beast or a god. (*Politics* 1.2)

Aristotle's observation seems to accord well with the views of Smith and Rousseau articulated centuries later, which were presented at the beginning of this essay. What is more, the observation reflects masterfully the initial claim of this essay that human beings are quintessential social creatures.

We are inclined to say that the person who is not moved by the innocence of an infant is not just different, but someone whose moral sentiments are amiss in some fundamental way. Are we not inclined to make a similar claim about the person who fails to find inspiring the life of a Mother Teresa or Martin Luther King or Raul Wallenberg? If so, then bearing in mind that both psychological health and morality admit of degrees, there is perhaps a deeper connection between morality and psychological health than many of us have been inclined to suppose. Because we are human beings, rather than gods or beasts, the quality of the moral lives of those around us would seem to bear upon the quality of the moral life that we live.

References

Audi, Robert: *Moral Knowledge and Ethical Character* (New York: Oxford University Press, 1997).

Baier, Annette: *Moral Prejudices* (Cambridge, MA: Harvard University Press, 1994).

Benhabib, Seyla: *Situating the Self* (New York: Routledge, 1992).

Brink, David: *Moral Realism and the Foundation of Ethics* (New York: Cambridge University Press, 1989).

Canto-Sperber, Monique: *La philosophie morale britannique* (Paris: Presses Universitaires de France, 1994).

Card, Claudia: *The Unnatural Lottery: Character and Moral Luck* (Philadelphia, PA: Temple University Press, 1996).

Coles, Robert: *The Moral Life of Children* (New York: Houghton Mifflin, 1986).

Deigh, John: *The Sources of Moral Agency* (New York: Cambridge University Press, 1996).

Eisenstadt, S. N.: "Cultural Tradition, Historical Experience, and Social Change: The Limits of Convergence," in Grethe B. Peterson (ed.), *The Tanner Lectures on Human Values* XI (Salt Lake City: The University of Utah Press, 1990), pp. 441–504.

Flanagan, Owen: *The Varieties of Moral Personality* (Cambridge, MA: Harvard University Press, 1994).

—— and Amélie Oksenberg Rorty: *Identity, Character, and Morality: Essays in Moral Psychology* (Cambridge, MA: MIT Press, 1990).

Gilligan, Carol: *In A Different Voice* (Cambridge, MA: Harvard University Press, 1982).

Greenspan, Patricia S.: *Emotions and Reasons* (New York: Routledge, 1988).

Kohlberg, Lawrence: *The Philosophy of Moral Development* (New York: Harper and Row, 1981).

Moody-Adams, Michele: *Fieldwork in Familiar Places* (Cambridge, MA: Harvard University Press, 1998).

Nussbaum, Martha C.: *The Fragility of Goodness* (New York: Cambridge University Press, 1986).

Rorty, Amélie Oksenberg: *Mind in Action* (Boston, MA: Beacon Press, 1988).

——: *Philosophers on Education* (New York: Routledge, 1998).

Rosenthal, Abigail L.: *A Good Look at Evil* (Philadelphia, PA: Temple University Press, 1987).

Ruwen, Ogien: *Le Réalisme Moral* (Paris: Presses Universitaires de France, 1998).

Sherman, Nancy: *The Fabric of Character* (New York: Oxford University Press, 1989).

Solomon, Robert C.: *The Passions* (New York: Doubleday, 1976).

Stocker, Michael, with Elizabeth Hegamen: *Valuing Emotions* (New York: Cambridge University Press, 1994).

Strawson, P. F.: "Freedom and Resentment," *Proceedings of the British Academy*, 48 (1962).

Thomas, Laurence: "Moral Psychology," *Encyclopedia of Ethics* (1990).

——: "Morality and Psychological Development," in Peter Singer (ed.), *A Companion to Ethics* (Boston: MA Basil Blackwell, 1990), pp. 464–75.

Watson, Gary: "Responsibility and the Limits of Evil: Variations on a Strawsonian Theme," Ferdinand Schoeman (ed.), *Responsibility, Character, and the Emotions: New Essays in Moral Psychology* (New York: Cambridge University Press, 1987).

Wilson, James Q.: *The Moral Sense* (New York: The Free Press, 1993).

Wolf, Susan: *Freedom Within Reason* (New York: Oxford University Press, 1990).

Part II

Normative Ethics

Chapter 9

Act-Utilitarianism

R. G. Frey

So much has been written about act-utilitarianism in recent years, both by way of criticism and response, that it is not possible in the compass of a single essay even to begin to do justice to the many sides of the various debates that, collectively, comprise contemporary discussion of the theory. What I have done, in order to give an overview of the present state of play with regard to the theory, therefore, is to focus upon what I take to be the most important development in that theory today.

For simplicity's sake, I shall take act-utilitarianism to be the view that an act is right if its consequences are at least as good as those of any alternative. As given, this view is consequentialist, welfarist, aggregative, maximizing, and impersonal, and the principle of utility that it endorses sets up what I shall call the utilitarian goal.

The view is consequentialist, in that it holds that acts are right or wrong solely in virtue of the goodness or badness of their actual consequences. This view may be called act-consequentialism, or, here, for reasons of brevity, simply consequentialism. It is matters to do with consequentialism, and the conflicts that consequentialist thinking is supposed to engender with ordinary morality, that will be the focus of this essay. The view is welfarist, in that rightness is made a function of goodness, and goodness is understood as referring to human welfare.[1] (I leave aside here questions to do with the inclusion of animals within the scope of the theory, though in my view the "higher" animals are to be included.) The view is impersonal and aggregative, in that rightness is determined by considering, impersonally, the increases and diminutions in well-being of all those affected by the act and summing those increases and diminutions across persons.[2] The view is a maximizing one: one concrete formulation of the principle of utility, framed in the light of welfarist considerations, is "Always maximize net desire-satisfaction."[3]

The act-utilitarian goal, understood in the light of the above characterization, then, is to maximize human welfare. The crucial question to which this goal gives rise is how best to go about achieving it, and it has for some time now been thought by act-utilitarians, especially since R. M. Hare's *Moral Thinking* (1981), that the best way of going about maximizing human welfare overall may be to forego trying to maximize it on each occasion. It is this insight, in some form or other, that has spurred the most important developments in act-utilitarian theory today.

I

What has driven and continues to drive much of the opposition to act-utiliarianism, including virtually all the different versions of rule-utilitarianism, has been the thought that some alternative view can better account for a number of our moral intuitions. Our moral intuitions, it is said, frown upon murdering or torturing someone, upon enslaving people or using them as means, upon acting in certain contexts and so using people in certain ways for mere marginal increases in utility, all of which act-utilitarianism is supposed to (be able to) license. It is supposed to license these things because of its constituent consequentialism: if such acts were to have better actual consequences than the actual consequences of any alternative act, then the act-utilitarian would be compelled to call such acts right. And this, allegedly, con-flicts with our moral intuitions or ordinary moral convictions or what some people think of as commonsense morality. Even most of the *contemporary* examples of problems with act-utilitarianism take this form; thus, act-utilitarianism is said by some to produce clashes with our moral intuitions over the rightness of our show-ing partiality to our own projects and concerns and to members of our family with-out incurring the accusation of bias or selfishness or over regarding people as separate and so not treating a benefit to one person as compensation for loss to another.

(Interestingly, those who use this manner of argument against act-utilitarianism generally never mention cases and instances where our moral intuitions and consequentialism coincide. The relative absence of such cases is very often explained by the fact that the opposing theorist already has settled intuitions about a case and has convinced himself that there is a way of making those intuitions fall out of or be compatible with his theory of the right. This yields (at least) two possible positions, on one of which rightness has nothing whatever to do with an act's consequences and on the other of which the rightness of certain acts has nothing whatever to do with an act's consequences. A third position, that the rightness of an act is a function of its consequences plus something else, e.g., the intention and/or motive with which it was performed, is possible but, strictly speaking, not anti-consequentialist.)

This is familiar territory in past debates over utilitarianism generally, though it is no more settled for all that, and it raises directly the question of whether our moral intuitions have probative force in ethics. This is an important issue in its own right, separate from the fate of any form of utilitarianism, but far too broad and complex an issue to be gone into in any detail here. But a few words on it are necessary, because the assumption of its truth has driven the urge to modify act-utilitarianism.

For those inclined to the view that moral intuitions do have probative force in ethics, the trick, as it were, has been to make it appear that certain of our intuitions are more secure than others, so secure, in fact, that we believe them to be more "correct" or "true" than any normative ethical theory. Obviously, those who adopt this line need to identify which these crucial intuitions are, and various ways of doing this have been suggested. Today, reflective equilibrium methodologies, both thick and thin, are perhaps the preferred way, though some relatively straightforward, old-fashioned intuitionists still survive.

Even with the back and forth movement between intuition and principle that reflective equilibrium methodologies involve, however, it is clear that some intuitions survive and remain intact. Thus, in *A Theory of Justice* (1971), Rawls appears to think that, if a moral/political theory gave the result that slavery was justified, that would be enough to demand from us amendment and/or abandonment of the theory. His intuition on this score needs no revision. Other writers privilege other of their moral intuitions either about particular acts or classes of acts. Of course, the more we find people, whether in our own or another culture, differing over these crucial intuitions, the more difficulty we encounter in selecting just which the crucial ones are. Thus, reflective equilibrium methodologists on the one hand and straightforward intuitionists on the other seek ways to discount the variation in these crucial intuitions, or, at the very least, to reduce the scope and depth of variations.

(Plainly, fashion changes where moral intuitions are concerned. Whereas promising and truth-telling fell into the favored class earlier, my impression today is that they do not, or, at least, that often the favored intuitions are found elsewhere. For example, today, they seem in part to turn upon political orientation. Thus, someone who is politically conservative not uncommonly puts the wrongness of abortion into the favored class, whereas political liberals are very unlikely to agree.)

Whatever the scope and depth of variations, the assumption that certain intuitions survive critical scrutiny has been the springboard from which assaults upon act-utilitarianism have nearly always begun. Equally, it has been the spur for developments in the theory, as numerous act-utilitarians have responded by trying to find ever more sophisticated ways of building into the theory, on act-utilitarian grounds, all kinds of devices that permit them to obtain results in particular cases much more in line with what are thought to be the crucial intuitions selected by critics as those which survive critical scrutiny. Even some of the patron saints of act-utilitarianism have led adherents of the theory to think along these lines. Thus, in Book IV of *The Methods of Ethics* (1874), Sidgwick is at pains to impress upon his readers that act-utilitarianism, far from being a wholly destructive force in normative ethics, can often be used to provide support for parts of commonsense morality. Of course, it will not support all parts and to every last detail, and Sidgwick himself seeks the reform of much of it. But neither, Sidgwick implies, is act-utilitarianism going to be allowed to sweep aside just any part of commonsense morality. His view appears to be, certainly with regard, e.g., to justice, that sometimes the theory must give way.

The point here is not which amendments to the theory Sidgwick favored but that he thought amending the theory an appropriate response to at least certain clashes between the application of the theory in particular cases and certain of the views that are taken to constitute commonsense morality. Implicitly, therefore, Sidgwick rejects the hard line on this issue adopted by J. J. C. Smart (Smart and Williams 1973). Sidgwick, no more than anyone else, had a way of indicating just how he knew which were the privileged bits of commonsense morality, but the effect of his position was to encourage act-utilitarians to search for ways of bringing the results of their theory, in its application to particular cases, in line with the dominant moral intuitions on those cases. One result of this search was to erode what were widely thought of by act-utilitarians as strengths of their theory, namely, its simplicity and ease of operation. But this erosion was thought necessary, if the theory was to avoid rejection for failing to account for those moral intuitions that were held by critics to be "just too secure" to be mistaken.

I take the failed experiment with (the different forms of) rule-utilitarianism to have been in part driven by the search for this complication in utilitarian thinking. Rule-utilitarianism, at least in all its varieties with which I am familiar, has long been known to suffer from certain types of instabilities that seem irreducibly part of the theory, but what lured utilitarians to give it a try was in no small measure the thought, played up by rule-utilitarians, that it could better account for just those moral intuitions that were held (by critics) to be the crucial ones that survived critical scrutiny. To this extent, rule-utilitarians implicitly supported using the accommodation of these moral intuitions as the test of adequacy of a normative ethical theory, though usually without any articulated defense of that test. And this in part proved their undoing. For once one begins to use certain of one's moral intuitions in this way, the question is bound to arise of why we should try to accommodate these privileged intuitions within a utilitarian structure at all. Squeezed by David Lyons' extensional equivalence argument for the collapse of rule- into act-utilitarianism on the one side (1965), and by the privileged moral intuitions on the other, with the possibility, if not actuality, that they could be better accommodated within altogether non-utilitarian positions, the various forms of rule-utilitarianism failed to bite.

II

The search for complication to act-utilitarianism, in order to bring the results of the application of the theory in particular cases in line with favored moral intuitions with regard to those cases, has led almost universally among act-utilitarians to an indirect, split-level account of the theory, of the sort to be found in Hare's *Moral Thinking*. I take Hare as the exemplar of indirect consequentialism/act-utilitarianism because *Moral Thinking* remains perhaps the best-known statement of the view, but the shift to an indirect consequentialism has been the major response by act-utilitarians to accommodate parts, including deontological parts of ordinary morality. I think there is something both right and wrong about this tactic by act-utilitarians.[4]

The crucial move in an indirect consequentialism/act-utilitarianism is to distinguish the level of theory from the level of practice. Hare, for example, distinguishes two levels of moral thinking, critical and intuitive: he adopts act-utilitarianism at the critical level and then uses it in order to select those guides at the intuitive or practical level by which to conduct one's life. The guides selected will be those, according to Hare, whose general acceptance will maximize utility. Given that these guides have been selected with an eye to the situations that we are likely to find ourselves in (so that fantastic examples cease to tell against a theory), then action in accordance with them, Hare claims, is likely to give us the best chance of doing the right thing, i.e., of performing that act whose overall consequences are at least as good as those of any alternative.

The main effect of this distinction of levels is, at the level of practice, to make Hare's theory only indirectly consequentialist, since it bars any extensive appeal to an act's consequences at the intuitive level. In turn, the effect of this indirect consequentialism is to remove entirely the picture of act-utilitarianism at the intuitive level being applied on a case-by-case basis, which is the source of the difficulty over particular cases, so far as disagreement with ordinary morality is concerned. Direct consequentialist thinking produces clashes that indirect consequentialist thinking does not.

Moreover, since we do not consult consequentialist thinking on a case-by-case basis at the intuitive level, Hare's indirect consequentialism avoids other problems that such a basis of application is supposed to produce. For example, it deals with the problem, obvious for some time now, that, in seeking to maximize human well-being on each and every occasion, we may fail to maximize human well-being overall; we may do better overall not to try to maximize well-being on each occasion. The indirect move addresses this problem. Again, since in principle there is no reason why, in Hare's hands, act-utilitarian thinking at the critical level might not yield as guides for life at the intuitive level precisely those patterns of rules or strict moral duties or schemes of full-fledged moral rights that deontologists advocate, his theory can accommodate the kinds of claims about rules, duties, and rights that might be held to be a vital part of deontological morality.

As I say, all this has been well known for some time now, and work on act-utilitarianism by theorists today nearly always begins with the move to an indirect consequentialism. This is why the continuing criticism of act-utilitarianism of the direct kind, whether by rule-utilitarians, various types of deontologists, or editors of ethics textbooks for undergraduates, falls wide of the mark. Equally, however, it is why the striking results of act-utilitarian thinking in particular cases, of the sort Smart used to describe, are no longer characteristic of the theory. For what one does at the level of practice for Hare is to follow the simple, general rules for living that act-utilitarian thinking at the critical level has selected as those which give us the best chance of maximizing human well-being. This is not to say that one may never engage in direct consequentialist thinking; but, as we shall see, Hare thinks that various forms of human shortcomings typically get in the way of assessing acts' consequences, especially as they affect our own situations, thereby making such assessments less likely to serve as reliable guides to get us to the utilitarian goal of maximizing well-being.

It is clear, then, what Hare has done. Direct consequentialist thinking at the intuitive level can produce clashes with ordinary morality: the act which has best consequences on this occasion may not be the act held by privileged moral intuitions on the case to be the right one. A shift to indirect consequentialist thinking does not give this result; it has the act-utilitarian acting in accordance with the general rules, duties, and rights – all of which can bar direct appeal to consequences in order to determine rightness – selected by act-utilitarian thinking as giving us the best chance overall of maximizing human well-being. So, if clashes with some (privileged subset of) ordinary moral intuitions on particular cases is the issue, Hare has a way of disposing of them. Because his theory is indirectly consequentialist, we do not do our moral thinking at the intuitive or practical level in the way, stereotypically, act-utilitarians have been portrayed, deciding what to do on each and every occasion, on a case-by-case basis, by trying to determine which of the alternative acts available to us has the best consequences.[5] Rather, at the intuitive level, we are to think in terms of the general rules (or whatever) that act-utilitarian thinking at the critical level has selected for us.

Foundationally, the resultant theory remains act-utilitarian: rules and other deontological considerations figure, as it were, in the superstructure of the theory. Accordingly, it is always open to an opposing theorist to object that the rules or rights embedded in the theory are not embedded foundationally, that this is what really matters so far as the views of ordinary morality is concerned, and that this is precisely what indirect strategies of consequentialist thinking still do not give us. This is unlikely to impress Hare. After all, if by appeal to rules and rights he can show that, e.g., acts for mere marginal increases of utility are no longer deemed right by the act-utilitarian, why does it matter that, foundationally, rules and rights are not embedded in the theory in the way they are in rule-theories or rights-theories?

Which rules we have at the intuitive level is a function of their acceptance-utility, and Hare includes under this the cost versus the benefits of making the rules part of our character. We need simple rules that do not grow too complicated and so are easy to formulate, teach, and learn. The rules so selected can permit few exceptions, none of which, in the examples Hare gives in *Moral Thinking*, involve acting for mere marginal increases in utility. Thus, Hare clearly endorses the view that following the rules selected by act-utilitarian thinking as giving us the best chance of doing the right or optimific thing can lead to sub-optimal outcomes, something else that is at odds with the usual stereotype of the act-utilitarian.

Finally, the rules selected for use at the intuitive level are not sacrosanct, and Hare gives an account of when it is appropriate to turn to critical level thinking and reflect upon the set of rules we presently have. We do this when there appear to be conflicts between several of the rules or when there appear to be large utility losses beginning to be systematically incurred or when a sort of case arises which none of our simple, general rules cover. And he appends cautions about and constraints upon how this sort of critical thinking is to be conducted.

An obvious problem with a two-level account of moral thinking is that of seepage between the levels. If and when seepage occurs, then the set of rules selected for use at the intuitive level will be directly exposed to consequentialist thinking, so that breaking a rule for a marginal increase in utility may come back into the picture. Something like the seepage point is made by Bernard Williams (1973) in a way that I find problematic and which enables us to see another significant feature of Hare's account of moral thinking.

Williams urges that, even though we have time to do critical thinking in a particular case, we cannot expose rules appropriate to the intuitive level to (the demands of) act-utilitarian thinking at the critical level. The reason is that there is an inherent conflict between the vantage point of the intuitive morality one accepts and the vantage point of the critical morality one accepts. One is not a consequentialist at the intuitive level but at the critical level. Williams' point, then, is presumably that, if seepage occurs, then the kind of thinking appropriate to the critical level may come to affect the kind of thinking appropriate to the intuitive level. If this is the case, if as a result of seepage one may expose the rules selected for use at the intuitive level to further act-utilitarian thinking, then it remains distinctly possible that a rule will be broken for a marginal increase in utility. In short, if seepage occurs, rule-breaking for marginal increases may occur.

So, what is to prevent seepage or the damage that seepage may cause? Hare's answer involves character and dispositions: one inculcates the guides into oneself thoroughly. One tries to make one's character of a certain sort, one containing dispositions acting upon which gives one the best chance of doing the right or optimific thing. Even motives and whole lives are treated this way by Hare. What one will have done is to have made oneself into a person whose intuitive morality is at odds with rule-breaking for marginal increases in utility. Put differently, the act-utilitarian is not constantly yearning at the intuitive level for direct consequentialist thinking, in order to mount a case for rule-breaking. For not only has the indirect strategy confined that thinking to the critical level but also, even if seepage occurs, the act-utilitarian has built deeply into his character the traits and dispositions that give him the best chance of doing the optimific thing. Obviously, the indirect strategy has many advantages for the act-utilitarian.

III

Hare's central motive for the move to an indirect theory is that he thinks we are more likely to do the right, i.e., optimific thing if we forego act-utilitarian thinking on a case-by-case basis. He thinks this for a number of factors, such as our lack of time in which to calculate an act's consequences, our inclination to bias and temptation, our weakness in the face of various pressures, our inability to be detached and clear-headed, our lack of factual information about situations, our tendency to emphasize self-interest and self-importance and to exaggerate the effects of acts upon ourselves, and so on. We might think of these as human shortcomings, and, unquestionably, they plague us, if not always, then at least a good deal of the time. If we are concerned with what to do, then we have good reason to avoid the kind of thinking, namely, direct consequentialist thinking, that is likely to give these factors free, or more free, reign.

Of course, in addition to these human shortcomings, there are epistemological problems about where an act's consequences begin and end. Once again, these militate against our reliance upon direct consequentialist thinking at the intuitive level and in favor of reliance upon, say, some simple, general rules.

The indirect strategy, then, has a number of advantages for the act-utilitarian, and it seems right that any plausible account of the theory must adopt such a strategy. In Hare's hands, the strategy is put in an unusual light: he claims that he does not take our moral intuitions to have probative force in ethics, but in the end the main reason we are given for endorsing the indirect strategy is that it reduces conflicts with ordinary morality. There are two issues masked here, one concerned with giving an account of the right, the other concerned with giving an account of how we are to think morally about what to do. Hare runs these together, as the very title of his book indicates, and it would not be too much of an exaggeration to say that consequentialism is for Hare both an account of the right and an account of how we are to think morally. He seems to be trying to save consequentialism as an account of how we do our moral thinking by showing why, based in consequentialist reasoning, we are not to do our moral thinking at the intuitive level in consequentialist terms.

Yet, in principle at least, another option is available: we could separate our account of moral thinking from our account of the right. In fact, this can seem the natural upshot of the indirect strategy. Indeed, this seems the natural consequence of Hare's position, in that human shortcomings and epistemological problems generally get in the way of doing the assessment of consequences in the case of particular acts. The result is that we do not do our moral thinking at the level of deciding what to do on the basis of case-by-case consequentialist reasoning but rather on the basis of guides selected by that reasoning at the critical level as likely to give us the best chance of doing the right, i.e., optimific thing. So it is not so much that Hare adopts an indirect strategy for reasons of conformity with certain privileged moral intuitions about particular cases or kinds of cases, but rather because human shortcomings and epistemological difficulties in assessing where consequences begin and end make the indirect strategy a more likely way of achieving the utilitarian goal of maximizing well-being.

In fact, a split-level position is quite compatible with rejecting consequentialism as the model for our moral thinking about what to do. For the net effect of the split-level account of moral thinking is to retain consequentialism as an account of the right but to provide excellent reasons for not doing our moral thinking at the intuitive level in consequentialist terms. In Hare's hands at least, the most distinctive feature of the agent that Hare envisages us as becoming is precisely that we do not do our moral thinking at the intuitive level in consequentialist terms.

Since it is effectively non-consequentialist at the intuitive or practical level, the indirect strategy is compatible with quite severe deontological constraints. For it is perfectly possible that act-utilitarian thinking at the critical level will select guides for behavior at the intuitive level that, except at the level of utility-catastrophes or conflicts of guides, bar direct appeals to consequentialism. This in turn means that such thinking at the critical level may well yield the result at the intuitive level of injecting (i) person-relative principles into a theory that is person-neutral, (ii) some incommensurable values into a theory of trade-offs, (iii) devices that limit or bar utilitarian sacrifice and such trade-offs into a theory that has traditionally been portrayed as permitting these very things, and so on. In short, on the split-level strategy, deontological devices can make their way into act-utilitarianism because at the practical level one is effectively not thinking as a consequentialist.

To critics, of course, putting deontological devices into act-utilitarianism in this way will not still their disquiet. For the theory used at the critical level will be seen as pulling in one direction and the constraints at the practical level as pulling in another, and unless the constraints are strong enough, unless they bar appeals to consequentialist thinking altogether at the practical level, except at the level of ca-tastrophe,[6] the theory used at the critical level may reassert itself and license utilitarian sacrifice, etc. I take this way of putting the point to be the analog of Bernard Williams' idea that the split-level position combines two thoughts – roughly, consequentialism and deontological constraints – that are incompatible. But they do not seem incompatible at all, at least if one continues to distinguish between levels of moral thinking. One does know that consequentialist thinking is going on at the critical level and that, as we have seen, that there are (comparatively rare) circumstances in which direct consequentialist thinking may be engaged in at the practical level, but this *per se* does not strike a blow at deontological constraints, any more than a view of rights as trumps is struck down by the thought that there can arise (comparatively rare) circumstances in which a right can be set aside. The thought that I would probably stand a better chance of maximizing human welfare if I rigorously adhered to the terms of contracts I make is not *incompatible* with consequentialist/utilitarian thinking. Of course, as noted earlier, to the extent that the two levels of moral thinking cannot be kept apart, then the deontological con-straints incorporated into act-utilitarianism will be exposed to direct consequentialist thinking, not in comparatively rare circumstances, but all the time. This is why the point about seepage, and the inculcation of certain traits and dispositions into our character, is so important.

If, however, the deontological devices built into act-utilitarianism are strong enough effectively to make a person-neutral theory person-relative at the practical level, then what, it may be asked, is the cash value of being an act-utilitarian? The answer, of course, is in terms of the utilitarian goal of maximizing human welfare, but that is not to the point here. Rather, the point is that the split-level strategy is quite compatible with hybrid theories, ones that are act-utilitarian at the critical level but that (can) feature all kinds of deontological devices that bar consequentialist thinking (except at the level of catastrophe) at the practical level. Such devices may not be built into act-utilitarianism in the manner that a deontologist may desire, but clashes in ordinary morality that all too frequently feature consequentialist thinking riding roughshod over deontological restrictions will have very much diminished. Importantly, these clashes will have diminished, not because we take certain moral intuitions to be privileged and developed the theory to account for them, but because in our best judgment acting in certain ways will give us the best chance of maximizing human well-being.

The problem of seepage is important, then, because it could have the effect of undermining the incorporation of deontological restrictions into act-utilitarianism, an effect that results typically from trying to do consequentialist thinking at the practical level. What hybrid theories do, then, is to permit consequentialism to flourish as an account of moral thinking at the critical level but to bar consequentialism as an account of moral thinking at the intuitive level, with the result that hybrid theories typically do not allow the agent at the level of deciding what to do to think as a consequentialist. Nor is this result undone by the claim that sometimes we simply have to act on the basis of the consequences available to us and decide what to do; for, excepting the level of catastrophe, hybrid theories will still have the agent deciding what to do in the light of the deonotological restrictions featured at the practical level. For these remain as part of the strategy we endorse as likely to give us the best chance of maximizing human well-being.

The label "act-utilitarianism", then, is misleading for three reasons. First, it can connote that consequentialism will be employed on a case-by-case basis for deciding what to do; second, it can suggest that consequentialism specifies the kind of thinking we should employ in deciding what to do; and third, it can suggest that acts are the central focus around which we should attempt to construct an account of moral thinking about what to do. The indirect strategy involves the rejection of the first, hybrid theories involve the rejection of the second, and something along the lines of Hare's account of character traits and dispositions in effect, as we shall see, involves the rejection of the third. For what the third point is about is turning ourselves into people whose actions flow from an account of character in which the traits and dispositions that comprise character are inculcated in us overseen by the utilitarian goal of maximizing human welfare. Coincidentally, this has the result that clashes with certain privileged moral intuitions are much diminished, but that result does not require that we treat those intuitions as having probative force. Some might think the move to a hybrid theory is motivated by an attempt better to account for certain of our moral intuitions, but that is not the case. The theory incorporates the indirect strategy and deontological restrictions in pursuit of the utilitarian goal.

IV

Consequentialism is an account of what makes right acts right, not a methodology for deciding what to do at the practical level. It cannot be refuted, therefore, by showing at the practical level that consequentialist thinking can be at odds with certain privileged moral intuitions, since hybrid theories do not have us thinking as consequentialists at that level.

We may not be able to determine on any particular occasion which act is right, consequentially; but that in no way shows that acts are not right in virtue of their consequences. Once one realizes this, that consequentialism can be true as an account of what makes right acts right even if we cannot determine (for reasons given) which act is right, then one can see that the real opponent of consequentialism is other accounts of what makes right acts right, such as the traditional Catholic view that some acts are right or wrong independently of their consequences, in themselves, by their very nature. Accordingly, consequentialism as an account of the right is not refuted by showing that its use in conducting our moral thinking about what to do may engender some conflicts with ordinary morality. Samuel Scheffler (1982); David Brink (1989); and Peter Railton (1988) all note the point.

In thinking about how we determine the adequacy of any account of the right, however, do not moral intuitions creep back into the picture here? Everything depends upon how they creep back in. If all reliance upon moral intuitions about particular cases is to be given up, then how are we to determine adequacy? But it need not be true that "all" reliance upon moral intuitions about cases is to be given up; for one can sever the claim that they have probative force from the claim that they indicate a very rough path to which an account of rightness must loosely cohere. The thought would be that, if an account of rightness gives repeated instances of clashes with the intuitions of ordinary morality, if it would repeatedly call right acts or classes of acts that ordinary morality calls wrong, then this information is at least relevant to the determination of adequacy. But it is not clear that consequentialism is in this situation. It tells us what makes right acts right, it does not tell us which acts are right. The old-style intuitionist would claim to know which classes of acts these were, but I take it that no consequentialist would want to make such a claim.

The whole way of thinking here about intuitions strikes me as confused. The thought seems to be, if moral intuitions are to figure in the test of adequacy of an account of the right, that they give us insight into a kind of moral reality that is external to us and also fixed and binding. With access to this moral reality, we can "see" what is right and wrong and then use that "seeing" as a kind of moral arbiter of adequacy. But quite independently of whose "sight" of this moral reality is the "accurate" or "correct" one, it is far from obvious that there is any such reality in the first place. Certain claims about moral realism in meta-ethics notwithstanding, we need some reason to believe that people's moral intuitions penetrate to an external reality of fixed, abiding moral *principles* that determine completely whether classes of acts are right or wrong. To get at an account of rightness by claiming that it fails to call right certain classes of acts is to treat one's moral intuitions as if they gave us an independent check – independent of any theory – on moral reality. But there is no reason to think they provide such an independent check, not because people differ over the relevant classes of acts (though this is often true), but because this whole way of thinking is misguided. The only way our moral intuitions could serve as a check on an independently existing moral reality is if there really was such a reality and our intuitions could penetrate to it, and nothing in the usual cases presented against consequentialism has even come close to establishing such an external reality. To use one's moral intuitions as arbiters is what I find objectionable. I do not object to using them as rough guides to what is likely to give us the best chance of doing the right, i.e., optimific thing.

Again, there is no inherent reason to think that an account of what makes right acts right needs to be practiced, in order to be adequate. Such an account is not an action-guide, and it is a mistake for us to have thought that it was. This still leaves the question, it might be thought, of how widely our account of the right and our intuitions about what it would be right to do in this case can diverge, but this is still to misconstrue what consequentialism is about, as if it were something other than an account of the right. Rule-utilitarians have in the main been guilty of this confusion, since the main spur for development of the various forms of rule-utilitarianism was better to account for certain of our intuitions about which acts are right, as if consequentialism was inadequate because it formed the basis of our moral thinking about what to do and did not conform with the relevant intuitions in certain particular cases.

V

If the adequacy of an account of the right is not really the central issue here, then what is? This is the issue of how we are to conduct our moral thinking about what to do. If we are not to employ consequentialism as an action-guide, then how are we to think morally about what to do? Railton marks the distinction between consequentialism as an account of the right and as a decision procedure and seeks to orient his discussion about how we are to think morally about what to do in terms of character. Hare, I think, at least if we see his split-level strategy as coming to involve him with a hybrid theory, is in the same line of work. Whether he actually thought of his position in this light, or whether he thought that the split-level strategy was the most viable way for him to try to remain a consequentialist in practice, is not to the point. It is quite clear that a hybrid theory, in the way discussed earlier, is precisely one that marks the distinction between rightness and procedure for deciding what to do.

In Hare, as well as Railton, how we are to think morally about what to do involves appeal to the traits and dispositions of character and trying to make ourselves into persons with characters of a certain kind. We are to turn ourselves into people whose actions flow from a character in which the traits and dispositions that comprise character are inculcated in us overseen by the utilitarian goal of maximizing human welfare. Hare urges that we build deep into our characters dispositions and, through these, principles that seem likely to foster human well-being. With such inculcation, we should typically come to feel a great reluctance to depart from the way these dispositions and principles would lead us to behave and so come to feel guilt and remorse when we do depart from them. Moreover, if these dispositions and principles are embedded sufficiently deeply in us, they come to supply motives for us. Thus, if the appropriate disposition or trait has been embedded deeply enough, we come to want to tell the truth, not because of consequentialist considerations, but because truth-telling has become motive for our action. This is a Harean rendition of the deontological thought that we ought to want to come to tell the truth for its own sake. Moreover, if our character comes to reflect these deeply embedded dispositions and principles, then it will reinforce the prevention of seepage between the two levels of moral thinking. We have so deeply embedded certain dispositions into our character that we are very reluctant to behave differently and feel guilt and remorse when we do. In fact, we have brought ourselves to be persons the dispositions of whose character have come to motivate us to behave in certain ways. Any reversion to direct consequentialist thinking is thereby even more remote.

But do we not use results in particular cases to determine which traits and dispositions to inculcate? We try to see which most assist the maximization of human welfare. But how are we to determine which traits and dispositions these are, if not by seeing in particular cases what someone acting out of one of those traits and dispositions produces in the world? This is not giving probative force to our moral intuitions about those particular cases but merely trying to determine what the world would look like if trait A as opposed to B were displayed or acted upon. One compares past and probable results produced by acting upon A and B and decides accordingly which has the better chance of maximizing human welfare. One is not using one's moral intuitions about cases to decide rightness, but using past and probable results with respect to effect upon human welfare in order to decide which trait would likely give us a better chance to maximize human welfare. It is true that we look at the results of particular cases in order to conduct this assessment of effect upon human welfare, but we do not look at those results as having probative force with respect to rightness. I can attempt to assess past and probable results with regard to human welfare quite separately from any thought that those results must conform with certain views of ordinary morality.

The emphasis in all this is upon making ourselves into people of a certain kind. It often has been true – it was initially true of act-utilitarianism – that the focus of how we are to think morally about what to do has been to conform our thinking to some external standard, which ordinary morality codified and which our moral intuitions gave us access to. It seems to me that this emphasis is misplaced, that the central issue is an internal one, about what sort of person we make ourselves into, with our actions flowing out of our character so described. And the problem is that the decision of what sort of person to make ourselves is not a decision for which an external set of procedures or steps can be given; it is not as if making oneself into a certain sort of person, one whose actions flow out of traits and dispositions that have been inculcated in us overseen by the utilitarian goal of maximizing human welfare, can be reduced to a decision procedure. We all think about what is required in order to make ourselves into, say, good parents; but it is not as if there are three things that, if done, makes one a good parent. Rather, good parenting seems more likely achieved through instilling in someone certain character traits, in getting them to do certain things out of dispositions to behave that way, in getting them to behave habitually to look after the child's welfare, etc. The focus is not on external conformity to something, but on the internal issue of making oneself into a certain sort of person.

The analogy of good parenting is interesting for another reason as well. It must be remembered that we inculcate into ourselves certain dispositions overseen by the utilitarian goal of maximizing human welfare, and this means that we have to be able to have our dispositions to behave in particular ways sensitive to circumstances. Thus, for good parenting, our disposition to look after the welfare of our child has to be sensitive to circumstances: in one setting, we may think we best do this by denying the child what he wants, in another by giving the child what he wants. It is not as if there is a fixed set of rules and procedures that could be given one that fixed indefinitely how one was to behave to one's child, in order to be a good parent.

With the focus upon internal development of character traits and dispositions, not conformity to external standards, moral thinking about how to act takes on a different appearance. It is much more intimately connected with making oneself into the sort of creature who behaves out of certain dispositions than into the sort of creature who acts only out of consequentialist concerns. There is a single-mindedness about the latter, a kind of blindness, that gets in the way; it is as if the consequentialist had reified a consequentialist account of moral thinking about what to do into an external standard and saw himself as condemned to conform to that standard. Being a good parent, being a good man does not look like this, and it was a mistake to think otherwise.

A great deal more would have to be said on the issue of character even to begin to flesh out this sketch of a view of how we are to think morally about what to do, certainly, if we are to think in terms of specific character traits and dispositions to inculcate into ourselves and conceptions of lives that we might envisage ourselves as living. But even this much indicates why Bernard Williams' claim that act-utilitarianism combines two thoughts that are incompatible, one consequentialist, the other not, falls wide of the mark. For it does not combine them in ways that have the different thoughts working on the same level, that of doing our moral thinking about what to do, and the emphasis upon character and habitual action out of certain dispositions is designed to prevent seepage between levels of moral thinking from occurring. If asked for an ironclad guarantee that seepage will not occur, none can be given; but an account of character traits and dispositions can be given that make it extremely unlikely direct consequentialist thinking will revert to being a decision procedure for the act-utilitarian.

In the end, then, the label "act-utilitarianism" can be misleading, not only because it can connote that consequentialism will be employed on a case-by-case basis for deciding what to do and because consequentialism, therefore, will be taken to form the kind of thinking in which we should engage in deciding morally what to do, but also because it can lead one to think that individual acts are the focus around which we should attempt to construct our account of moral thinking about what to do. Plainly, this last is not the case. Nor, if one thinks of good parenting as the analogy, would anyone think differently; for there is no specified series of acts that must be done in order to be a good parent, as if we could list those acts and tick off whether or not one had done them.

VI

Nonconsequentialists might insist that the distinction between an account of the right and an account of how we are to think morally inserts into consequentialism certain deontological considerations that affect how we are to act, considerations which our deontological intuitions about the relevant cases have already told us apply. But this also is not the case: the aim is not to encumber consequentialism with deontological restrictions, but to make clear that issues to do with our moral thinking are concerned here with trying to find out which character traits and dispositions give us the best chance of maximizing human welfare.

Suppose a police officer has apprehended a drug-pusher whom he knows to be connected with the central figures in the illegal drug traffic in this country and from whom, therefore, the names and whereabouts of these women may be had. Under interrogation, the man has steadfastly refused to talk: frustrated, the officer has begun to consider the possibility of torturing the man, even though, as he confesses, his moral upbringing, his professional ethics, and the "ordinary moral convictions" of people within his society all repudiate torture as a means of extracting information. Perplexed and troubled, the officer approaches us for advice: we are act-utilitarians.

This sort of scenario, beloved of all nonconsequentialists (one thinks of the fat man in the mouth of the cave, the trolley problem, the survival lottery, and masses of other examples), where the good consequences of torturing the man can obviously be made to outweigh the bad consequences of inflicting the torture, is not one, if I am right, that befits the discussion of act-utilitarianism at all. For on the view of act-utilitarianism that I have been discussing, the ingredients that go to make up a good character are no different for the policeman as for anyone else, and what we have to ponder are which character traits and dispositions are those that we think likely, if realized among us, will give us the best chance of maximizing human welfare. Notice, then, that what nonconsequentialists want from this and the other examples – dramatic clashes between act-utilitarianism and deontological convictions about how we are to behave in such situations - is not really forthcoming. What will be right is whatever course of action turns out to be optimific; how the policeman is to think morally about the situation is quite different, in accordance with his moral upbringing, his professional ethics, and the traits and dispositions of character inculcated in him on act-utilitarian grounds. Being a good policeman is like being a good parent, more at matter of making oneself into a certain sort of person.

One reason that cases like the above are beloved of nonconsequentialists is that, if they can eliminate further appeals to additional sets of consequences on the part of the consequentialist, they think they can force the consequentialist to choose to behave in precisely the way that their deontological convictions will antecedently tell them is wrong. This is why so much work goes into thinking away other sets of consequences, of the effects of acts in the public domain, of others learning about what was done and fear, etc., setting in as a result, and so on. With the examples denuded, the choice is left stark, with the path the consequentialist is to follow all too clearly indicated. Thus, in the survival lottery, suppose *ex hypothesi* there are no additional consequences to consider of any sort, no indirect effects to take account, no publicity of acts to worry about, and so on; suppose, then, that one person may be seized, their organs transplanted into five individuals, and that all five will turn out to have lives as high in quality as the life seized: is not the consequentialist to take the life in question? The problem is the same as before: the example assumes that consequentialism is not merely an account of the right but also an account of how we are to do our moral thinking. But if we bear in mind the problems involved in determining optimificity, we encounter another ploy by the nonconsequentialist: assume for the sake of argument that seizing the individual and transplanting his organs is optimific. Now surely the consequentialist will take the life? There are two points to notice in this regard.

First, the assumption that we know what is optimific overcomes the epistemological hurdles that normally plague us, and in a way that will not be available to us on very many occasions. But this really does not matter here, since a much deeper point is at issue.

Second, the act-utilitarian is a consequentialist about rightness but not about how he does his moral thinking about what to do, and his reason for this distinction is not simply because he takes there to be serious epistemological difficulties in the way of determining optimificity. That is, the account of how we are to do our thinking about how to act is not in terms of character because we find it difficult to ascertain optimificity; rather, it is in terms of character because what it is to be a good person, as well as a good parent or good policeman, is not in terms of individual acts or external rules but in terms of character traits and dispositions. Being a good person is a matter of making oneself into a certain sort of person, a person whose character has been made into a particular kind and who acts out of that character. So the assumption that we know what is optimific in some circumstance does not affect the general point, that the account of rightness is in terms of optimificity, the account of how we do our moral thinking is in terms of character development and making ourselves into persons of a particular kind.

There is here, of course, a question that can be asked, namely, that of how far apart can our account of rightness and our account of how we are to do our moral thinking can grow. If we have a consequentialist account of rightness, can we have a nonconsequentialist account of how we are to think morally about what to do? Why not? So long as our internal development of character traits and dispositions is overseen by the utilitarian goal of maximizing human welfare, the account of how we are to think morally about what to do retains its link with act-utilitarianism.

Notes

1 I shall not here pursue important issues in value theory. Thus, if it is welfare or well-being around which the act-utilitarian's value theory orients, is well-being to be understood subjectively or objectively? Is it to be understood in terms of states of mind or desires/preferences? If the latter, which desires/preferences are at issue, actual, future, or fully-informed ones? If the last, which fully-informed desires/preferences, if satisfied, count as constitutive of our well-being? Are full-informational accounts of well-being really defensible? Should we move on to what are sometimes called "objective list" views of well-being, thereby effectively making something part of a person's well-being independently of how it strikes them from within the life being lived? And does the notion of well-being actually capture what we take to be of central importance about our lives from the inside?

2 There are issues here that I shall not discuss. I shall not go into the distinction between agent-neutral and agent-relative values and the claim, increasingly heard, that values, the values of agents, are agent-relative. Again, is the act-utilitarian to focus upon the greatest total or the greatest average welfare? If the former, then the charge of failing to recognize the separateness of persons is advanced (and, arguably, has been answered), whereas if the latter is emphasized, problems to do with Derek Parfit's "repugnant conclusion" are thought to arise. The former option is the one usually endorsed. Another charge that arises here (and to which various answers have been given) is that an aggregative act-utilitarianism severs one from one's integrity by severing one from one's projects and concerns, since the impersonal aggregation of the increases and diminutions in well-being of all those affected by what one proposes to do may require one not to act in aid of one's own projects and concerns. Here, a further charge is sometimes laid: adopting an impersonal point of view from which to aggregate well-being can precisely fail to show partiality to those, e.g., one's spouse or child, to whom one can seem bound by special moral ties.

3 I shall not consider whether something other than maximizing, such as satisficing, might be selected instead around which to orient the principle of utility, and I shall not inquire into whether it is always rational to maximize. Moreover, I shall not canvas the rather extensive literature on whether interpersonal comparisons of well-being or utility are possible or whether, if they are not, act-utilitarians will simply be left with judgments of Paretian optimality. Nor shall I bother to inquire whether it is really the case, as act-utilitarians usually assume, that judgments of intrapersonal comparisons are relatively unproblematic.

4 What is wrong with the tactic is, expressed baldly, that it still does not embrace the view that consequentialism must be rejected as an account of how we are to think morally about what to do.

5 I shall not here go into the question of how exactly we determine what the alternatives available to us at any moment are.

6 There is nothing unique about consequentialism/act-utilitarianism here in containing a

catastrophe exemption. Thus, rights-theorists with a conception of rights as trumps allow for a catastrophe exemption as well. Of course, to the act-utilitarian the exemption will apply to utility-catastrophes whereas to rights-theorists the exemption will apply to rights-catastrophes. The extent to which rights-catastrophes in effect amount to utility-catastrophes I shall not discuss here.

References

Brink, D. O.: *Moral Realism and The Foundations of Ethics* (Cambridge: Cambridge University Press, 1989).

Frey, R. G. (ed.): *Utility and Rights* (Oxford: Basil Blackwell, 1984).

Griffin, J. : *Well-Being* (Oxford: Clarendon Press, 1986).

Hare, R. M.: *Moral Thinking: Its Levels, Method and Point* (Oxford: Clarendon Press, 1981).

Kagan, S.: *The Limits of Morality* (Oxford: Clarendon Press, 1989).

Lyons, D.: *Forms and Limits of Utilitarianism* (Oxford: Clarendon Press, 1965).

Mackie, J. L.: *Ethics: Inventing Right and Wrong* (Harmondsworth: Penguin, 1977).

Parfit, D.: *Reasons and Persons* (Oxford: Clarendon Press, 1984).

Railton, P.: "Alienation, Consequentialism, and the Demands of Morality," *Philosophy and Public Affairs*, 13 (1984): 134–71.

——: "How Thinking about Character and Utilitarianism Might Lead to Rethinking the Character of Utilitarianism," *Midwest Studies in Philosophy*, vol. XIII (1988): 398–416.

Rawls, J.: *A Theory of Justice* (Cambridge: Harvard University Press, 1971).

Scheffler, S.: *The Rejection of Consequentialism* (Oxford: Clarendon Press, 1982).

Sidgwick, H.: *Methods of Ethics*, 7th edn. (London: Macmillan, 1907), 1st edn., 1874.

Slote, M.: *Commonsense Morality and Consequentialism* (London: Routledge and Kegan Paul, 1985).

Smart, J. J. C.: "An Outline of a System of Utilitarian Ethics," in J. J. C. Smart, Bernard Williams, *Utilitarianism: For and Against* (Cambridge: Cambridge University Press, 1973).

Sumner, L. W. : *The Moral Foundations of Rights* (Oxford: Clarendon Press, 1987).

Williams, B.: "A Critique of Utilitarianism," in J. J. C. Smart, Bernard Williams, *Utilitarianism: For and Against* (Cambridge: Cambridge University Press, 1973).

——: "Persons, Character, and Morality," in Bernard Williams, *Moral Luck* (Cambridge: Cambridge University Press, 1981).

Chapter 10

Rule-Consequentialism

Brad Hooker

1 Introduction

Just what is the connection between moral rightness and consequences? For nearly half a century now, consequentialists have divided themselves into different camps with respect to this question. Act-consequentialists believe that the moral rightness of an act depends entirely on whether the act's consequences are at least as good as that of any alternative act. Rule-consequentialists believe that the rightness of an act depends not on its own consequences, but rather on the consequences of a code of rules. (For prominent presentations of rule-consequentialism, see Berkeley 1712; Austin 1832; Urmson 1953; Rawls 1955; Brandt 1959, 1967, 1979, 1988, 1989, 1996; and Harsanyi 1982.) This essay explores the prospects for rule-consequentialism.

2 What Constitutes Benefit?

Rule-consequentialism holds that any code of rules is to be evaluated in terms of how much *good* could reasonably be expected to result from the code. By "good' here I mean whatever has non-instrumental value. What has non-instrumental value?

Utilitarians, who have been the most prominent kind of consequentialists, believe that the only thing with non-instrumental value is utility. All utilitarians have held that pleasure and the absence of pain are at least a large part of utility. Indeed, utilitarianism is often said to maintain that pleasure and the absence of pain are the *only* things that matter non-instrumentally. Certainly, this was the official view of the classic utilitarians Jeremy Bentham (1789), J. S. Mill (1861), and Henry Sidgwick (1874) – though in Sidgwick's case, equality seems to have independent weight as a tie breaker (Sidgwick 1907 [1874]: 417).

Perhaps more common over the last thirty years has been the view that utility is constituted by the fulfillment of people's desires, even if these desires are for things other than pleasure. Many people, even when fully informed and thinking carefully, persistently want things in addition to pleasure. They care, for example, about knowing important truths, about achieving valuable goals, about having deep personal relationships, about living their lives in broad accordance with their own choices rather than always in accordance with someone else's (Griffin 1986, pt. 1; Crisp 1997, chs 2, 3). The pleasure these things can bring is of course important. Still, human beings can care about these things in themselves, i.e., in addition to whatever pleasure they bring.

This view, however, can be challenged. Some desires seem to be about things too unconnected with you for them to play a direct role in determining your good. Would your desiring that a stranger recovers fully from her illness make her recovery good for you, even if you never see or hear from her again (Parfit 1984: 494)? Naturally, the fulfillment of such a desire would *indirectly* benefit you *if* it brought you pleasure or peace of mind. But this is not to say that the fulfillment of your desire that the stranger recovers herself constitutes a benefit to you. Rather if you get pleasure or peace of mind from the fulfillment of this desire, this pleasure or peace of mind constitutes a benefit to you (since you doubtless also desire pleasure and peace of mind for yourself).

The view that the fulfillment of your desires itself *constitutes* a benefit to you – if this view is to be at all plausible – will have to limit the desires in question. The only desires the fulfillment of which constitutes a benefit to you are your desires for states of affairs in which you are an essential constituent (Overvold 1980, 1982; Hooker 1991). You are not an essential constituent of the state of affairs in which this stranger recovers. So her recovery doesn't itself constitute a benefit to you.

There seem to be reasons for further restrictions on the desires directly relevant to personal good. Think how bizarre desires can be. When we encounter particularly bizarre ones, we might begin to wonder whether the things are good simply because they are desired. Would my desiring to count all the blades of grass in the lawns on the street make this good for me (Rawls 1971: 432; cf. Parfit 1984: 500; Crisp 1997: 56ff)? Whatever *pleasure* I get from the activity would be good for me. But it seems that the *desire-fulfillment as such* is worthless in this case. Intuitively, the fulfillment of my desires constitutes a benefit to me only if these desires are for the right things (Finnis 1980, 1983; Parfit 1984, Appendix I; Hurka 1987, 1993; Brink 1989: 221–36; Scanlon 1993; Griffin 1996, ch. 2; Crisp 1997, ch. 3). Indeed, some things seem to be desired because they are perceived as valuable, not valuable merely because desired or pleasant (Brink 1989: 230–1, especially fn. 9).

Views holding that something benefits a person if and only if it increases the person's pleasure or desire-fulfillment are in a sense "subjectivist' theories of personal good. For these theories make something's status as a benefit depend always on the person's subjective mental states. "Objectivist" theories claim that the contribution to personal good made by such things as important knowledge, important achievement, friendship, and autonomy is not exhausted by the extent to which these things bring people pleasure or fulfil their desires. These things can constitute benefits even when they don't increase pleasure. Likewise, they can constitute benefits even when they are not the objects of desire. Objectivist theories will typically add that pleasure is of course an objective good. These theories will also hold that ignorance, failure, friendlessness, servitude, and pain constitute harms.

For the most part, I will be neutral in this essay about which theory of personal good is best. *Usually* what gives people pleasure or enjoyment is also what satisfies their desires and involves the objective goods that could plausibly be listed. So usually we don't need to decide as among these theories of personal good.

But not always. Suppose the ruling elite believed that quantity of pleasure were all that matters. Then (to take a familiar leaf from *Nineteen Eighty-Four*) they might feel justified in manipulating the people and even giving them drugs that induce contentment but drain ambition and curiosity, if they thought such practices would maximize aggregate pleasure. Or suppose the ruling elite believed that the fulfillment of desire were all that matters. Again, the ruling elite might feel justified in manipulating the formation of preferences and development of desires such that these are easily satisfied. Now we can accept that – to some extent – our desires should be modified so that there is some reasonable hope of fulfilling them. But this could be pushed too far either in the name of maximizing pleasure or in the name of maximizing desire-fulfillment. A life could be maximally pleasurable, have maximum desire-fulfillment, and still be empty – if it lacked desires for friendship, achievement, knowledge, and autonomy.

3   Distribution

The term "rule-utilitarianism" is usually used to refer to theories that evaluate acts in terms of rules selected for their utility – i.e., for their effects on social well-being. The term "rule-consequentialism" is usually used to refer to a broader class of theories of which rule-utilitarian theories are a subclass. Rule-consequentialist theories evaluate acts in terms of rules selected for their good consequences. Non-utilitarian versions of rule-consequentialism say the consequences that matter are not limited to net effects on overall well-being. Most prominently, some versions of rule-consequentialism say that what matters are not only how much well-being results but also how it is distributed, in particular the fairness of alternative distributions.[1] Table 10.1 might prove helpful.

Which version of rule-consequentialism is best? The problem with rule-utilitarianism is that it has the potential to be unfairly inegalitarian. (For discussion of some utilitarian replies to this objection about distribution, see Hooker 1995: 30.) Consider a set of rules which leaves each member of a smaller group very badly off, and each member of a much larger group very well off (table 10.2).

Table 10.1

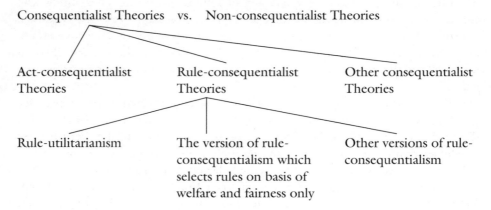

Consequentialist Theories   vs.   Non-consequentialist Theories

Act-consequentialist Theories

Rule-consequentialist Theories

Other consequentialist Theories

Rule-utilitarianism

The version of rule-consequentialism which selects rules on basis of welfare and fairness only

Other versions of rule-consequentialism

Table 10.2

Well-being

First Code:	per person	per group	for both groups
10,000 people in group A	1	10,000	
100,000 people in group B	10	1,000,000	
			1,010,000

Now if no alternative rule would provide greater net aggregate benefit, then utilitarians would endorse this code. Yet suppose the next best rule *from the point of view of utility* would be one with the results set out in table 10.3.

Table 10.3

Well-being

Second Code:	per person	per group	for both groups
10,000 people in group A	8	80,000	
100,000 people in group B	9	900,000	
			980,000

Let us assume that the first code leaves the people in group A less well off for some reason other than that these people opted to work less hard or imprudently took bad risks. In that case, the second code seems morally superior to, because fairer than, the first code. This is why we should reject rule-utilitarianism in favor of a distribution-sensitive rule-consequentialism that considers fairness as well as well-being.

What are the relative weights given to well-being and fairness by this distribution-sensitive rule-consequentialism? Clearly, well-being does not have overriding weight. For there can be cases in which the amount of aggregate net benefit produced would not justify rules that were unfair to some group. That was what my schematic example above was meant to show.

Does fairness have overriding weight? This is particularly unsettled territory, since even what constitutes fairness is unclear. Nevertheless, we cannot rule out the possibility that some unfair practice so greatly increases overall well-being that the practice is justified. But it is certainly unclear where the threshold is for fairness to trump well-being. Perhaps the best we can say is that, in the choice between codes, judgement will be needed in balancing fairness against well-being. By evaluating rules in terms of two values (well-being and fairness) instead of one (well-being), distribution-sensitive rule-consequentialism is messier than rule-utilitarianism. Still, this seems to be a case where the more plausible theory is the messier one.

4   Criteria of Rightness versus Decision Procedures

Rule-consequentialism is often portrayed as merely part of a broader consequentialist theory. This broader theory evaluates *all things* by their consequences. So it evaluates the desirability of acts by their consequences, the desirability of rules by their consequences, etc. The standard point to make along these lines is that, even if the rightness of an act depends on its consequences, better consequences will result if people do *not* try always to decide what to do by calculating consequences than if they try always to decide in this way. In other words, consequentialists can and should deny that

> On every occasion, an agent should decide which act to do by ascertaining which act has the greatest expected good.

Consequentialists agree that our *decision procedure* for day-to-day moral thinking should instead be as follows:

> At least normally, an agent should decide how to act by referring to tried and true rules, such as "Don't harm others", "Don't steal", "Keep your promises", "Tell the truth", etc.

Why? First, we frequently lack information about the probable consequences of various acts we might do. Where we cannot even estimate the consequences, we can hardly choose on the basis of maximizing the good. Second, we often do not have the time to collect this information. Third, human limitations and biases are such that we are not accurate calculators of the expected overall consequences of our alternatives. For example, most of us are biased in such a way that we tend to underestimate the harm to others of acts that would benefit us.

Now if there will be greater overall good where people are largely disposed to focus and act on non-consequentialist considerations, then consequentialism itself endorses such dispositions.[2] So consequentialists advocate firm dispositions to follow certain rules, including firm dispositions not to harm others, not to steal, not to break promises, etc. Different consequentialists thus by and large agree about how people should do their day-to-day moral thinking.

What different kinds of consequentialists disagree about is what makes an act morally permissible, i.e., about the criterion for moral rightness.

Act-consequentialism claims that an act is morally right (both permissible and required) if and only if the actual (or expected) good produced by *that particular act* would be at least as great as that of any other act open to the agent.

In contrast,

Rule-consequentialism claims that an act is permissible if and only if it is allowed by a code that could reasonably be expected to result in as much good as could reasonably be expected to result from any other identifiable code.[3]

The distinction between act-consequentialism's criterion of rightness and the dispositions it favors is important in many ways. It is important if we want to know what act-consequentialism wants from us. It is also important if act-consequentialism had better not conflict too sharply with our intuitive moral reactions. For if act-consequentialism claimed that we should always be focused on and motivated by calculations of what would maximize the good impartially conceived, many philosophers have thought it would be ridiculous. But the idea that act-consequentialism must make this ridiculous prescription is undermined by the distinction between act-consequentialism's criterion of rightness and the decision procedures it favors.

Nevertheless, the distinction is powerless to protect act-consequentialism from other objections. True, act-consequentialism's implications *about focus and motivation* are not as counter-intuitive as might initially be thought. But this is irrelevant to objections about act-consequentialism's criterion of rightness.

5   Formulations of Rule-Consequentialism

We need to augment our formulation of rule-consequentialism. All recognizable forms of rule-consequentialism make moral rightness depend on rules which are evaluated in terms of their consequences. But different forms of rule-consequentialism disagree about the conditions under which rules are to be evaluated. For instance, one version of rule-consequentialism is formulated in terms of the rules the *compliance with which* would be optimific. Another version is formulated in terms of rules the *acceptance of which* would produce the most good. Should rule-consequentialism be formulated in terms of compliance or in terms of acceptance?

Although compliance with the right rules is the first priority, it isn't the only thing of importance. We also care about people's having *moral concerns*. So we had better consider the costs of securing not only compliance but also adequate moral motivation. From a rule-consequentialist point of view, "moral motivation" means acceptance of moral rules. By "acceptance of moral rules", I mean a disposition to comply with them, dispositions to feel guilt when one breaks them and to resent others' breaking them, and a belief that the rules and these dispositions are justified (Brandt 1967 §8 [1992: 120–1], 1979: 164–76, 1996: 67, 69, 145, 156, 201, 266–8, 289).

The focus on *acceptance of rules*, i.e., *dispositions*, is crucial because the acceptance of a rule – or perhaps at this point it would be better to say the *internalization* of a rule – can have consequences over and above compliance with the rule (Lyons 1965: 137ff; Williams 1973: 119–20, 122, 129–30; Adams 1976, especially p. 470; Blackburn 1985: 21 n. 12).

The most obvious example of this involves rules that deter perfectly. Suppose you accept a rule prescribing that you retaliate against attackers. Suppose also that you are totally transparent, in the sense that people can see exactly what your dispositions are. So everyone knows about your disposition to retaliate, and therefore *never* attacks you. Thus, your accepting that rule is so successful at deterring attack that you *never* have an opportunity to comply with the rule. Your accepting the rule thus obviously has important consequences that simply *cannot* come from your acting on the rule, since you in fact never do (Kavka 1978).

Now suppose everyone internalized rules such as "Don't kill except when killing will maximize the aggregate good," "Don't steal except when stealing will maximize the aggregate good," "Don't break your promises except when breaking them will maximize the good," etc. Presumably, if everyone had internalized these rules, sooner or later awareness of this would become widespread. And people's becoming aware of this would undermine their ability to rely confidently on others to behave in agreed-upon ways. Trust would break down. The consequences would be terrible. And these terrible consequences would result, not from individual acts of complying with these rules, but from public awareness that the rules's exception clauses – the ones prescribing killing, stealing, and so on when such acts would maximize the good – were too available (Brandt 1979: 271–7; Harsanyi 1982: 56–61, 1993: 116–18; Johnson 1991, especially chs 3, 4, 9).

I am aware that there has been some controversy over the argument just outlined. But there is another way in which a cost-benefit analysis of *internalization* is richer than a cost-benefit analysis of compliance. Getting one code of rules internalized might involve greater costs than getting another code internalized. These costs are immensely important. For example, one possible objection to a code might be that it is so complicated or calls for so much self-sacrifice that too much of humanity's resources would have to be devoted to getting it widely internalized. The internalization costs would be so high that internalizing this code would not, on balance, be optimal. When this is the case, rule-consequentialists hold that the code isn't justified, and complying with it isn't required.

These points about internalization costs beg to be deployed at a number of places in the discussion of rule-consequentialism. One such place I explore in the next section.

6　Collapse

If we formulate rule-consequentialism in terms of *compliance*, we risk having rule-consequentialism collapse into act-consequentialism. The objection that rule-consequentialism collapses into extensional equivalence with act-consequentialism assumes rules are to be evaluated in terms of only the effects of compliance. While compliance can be one effect of internalizing rules, we have seen that there are also other effects. We must consider not only the benefits of compliance but also the other effects of rule internalization. With these effects factored into the evaluation of rules, the cost-benefit analysis will not favor rules extensionally equivalent to act-consequentialism.

One version of the objection that rule-consequentialism collapses into act-consequentialism claims that rule-consequentialism must favor just the one simple rule that one must always do what will maximize the good (Smart 1973: 11–12). The objection assumes that, if each person successfully complies with a rule requiring the maximization of the good, then the good would be maximized. That the good would be maximized under these conditions has been challenged (see Hodgson 1967, ch. 2; Regan 1980, ch. 5). But whether or not everyone's *complying* with the act-consequentialist principle would maximize the good, we should again consider the wider costs and benefits of rule *internalization*. The impartial good would not in fact be maximized by the internalization of just this one act-consequentialist rule. To internalize just the one act-consequentialist rule is to have just one moral disposition, the disposition to try to comply with act-consequentialism. To have just this one moral disposition is to have act-consequentialism as one's moral decision procedure. But we've already seen why act-consequentialism is not a good decision procedure.

In addition, the costs of getting a disposition to try to comply with act-consequentialism internalized would be extremely high. For getting that one rule internalized amounts to getting people to be disposed always to do what would be impartially best. Such a disposition would have to overcome people's immensely powerful natural biases towards themselves and their loved ones. To be sure, there are great benefits to be gained from getting people to care about others, and to be willing to make sacrifices for strangers. But think how much time, energy, attention, and psychological conflict that would be required to get people to internalize an overriding completely impartial altruism (if this is even possible at all). The costs of trying to make humans into saints would be too great.

That may seem like a paradoxical thing to assert. Wouldn't a world full of people each with an overriding disposition to maximize the impartial good be so ideal as to be worth any costs of getting from here to there? I think not. Bear in mind that the costs would hardly be a once-and-for-all-time sacrifice. Rather, getting this overriding impartiality internalized would have to be done for every new generation. We are contemplating here a radical reshaping of something deep in human nature. It is not as if the impartiality internalized by one generation will be reflected in the genes of their children. Rather, there will be the high cost of getting the overriding impartiality internalized in their children, just as there was when the parents were children themselves. (I am ignoring here the possibility of genetic engineering to create more altruistic humans.) The internalization costs will be incurred for each new generation of humans.

I have been arguing as if getting overriding impartiality internalized by the vast majority is a serious possibility, though one with prohibitive transition costs. It may not, however, be a serious possibility. In any case, the only *realistic* way to make humans totally and always impartial would be to reduce their special concern for themselves and those with whom they have special attachments. What would be left might be merely a life of insipid impartiality, devoid of deep personal attachments and inimical to great enthusiasm and joy. Strong concern and commitment focused on particular projects and individuals play an ineliminable role in a rewarding human life. But these features would have to be eliminated if human beings are to internalize an overriding motivation to maximize the impartial good. (This paragraph borrows heavily from Sidgwick 1907: 434; Williams 1973: 129–31; Adams 1976; Parfit 1984: 27–8, 30, 32–5; Dworkin 1986: 215; Griffin 1986, chs 2, 4, 1996: 77, 104; Crisp 1997: 106.)

So in the light of the transition and permanent costs of getting internalized an overriding impartiality, I hold that there must be some point short of this where the costs of going further outweigh the benefits. Remember why this matters here. Getting internalized an overriding impartiality would be part of getting internalized an overriding disposition to do what will maximize the impartial good. So if there is a compelling rule-consequentialist reason against getting internalized an overriding impartiality, there is a compelling rule-consequentialist reason against getting internalized an overriding disposition to do what will maximize the impartial good. I have just argued that there is a compelling rule-consequentialist reason against getting internalized an overriding impartiality. Such a disposition would *not* find favor with rule-consequentialism. So there is a compelling rule-consequentialist reason against getting internalized an overriding disposition to do what will maximize the impartial good. This kills the first way of developing the collapse objection.

The other way of developing the collapse objection starts by admitting that internalization of just the one act-consequentialist rule would lead to bad consequences. But this way of developing the collapse objection maintains that utility could be gained from the provision of specific exception clauses to moral rules against harming others, breaking promises, etc. If this is right, then rule-consequentialists are forced by their own criterion for rule selection to embrace rules with these exception clauses. The same sort of reasoning will militate in favor of adding specific exceptions aimed at each situation in which following some rule would not bring about the best consequences. Once all the exception clauses are added, rule-consequentialism will have the same implications for action that act-consequentialism has. This would be a fatal collapse.

To this way of developing the collapse objection, rule-consequentialists will reply by returning to the points about trust and expectations that I alluded to earlier. How much confidence would you have in others if you knew they accepted such highly qualified rules? How much mutual trust would there be in a society of agents who accepted endless exceptions to rules against harming others, breaking promises, lying, etc.?

Furthermore, the point about internalization costs is again relevant. The more plentiful and more complicated the rules to be learned, the higher the costs of learning them would be. At some point the costs of having to learn more rules, or more complications, would outweigh the benefits. Hence, the rules whose teaching and internalization would have the best results are limited in number and complexity. These limitations will keep the code from being extensionally equivalent with act-consequentialism. So this kind of rule-consequentialism does *not* collapse into act-consequentialism.

7 Rule-consequentialism and the Distribution of Acceptance

A relatively simple form of rule consequentialism selects rules by their consequences given internalization of them by 100 percent of the population. But I think the theory should be formulated in terms of internalization by less than 100 percent of the population. Rule-consequentialism needs to be formulated this way in order to make room for rules about what to do when others have no moral conscience at all. Let us refer to such people as unmitigated amoralists.

Suppose we assume internalization of the rules by 100 percent of the population. We might still need rules for dealing with non-compliance, since *internalization* by 100 percent of the people does not guarantee 100 percent *compliance*. Some people might fully accept the best rules and yet sometimes, seduced by temptation, act wrongly. Thus there is need for rules dealing with non-compliance. These rules might specify, for example, what penalties apply for what crimes. They might also specify what to do when those around you accept that they should be helping to save others but aren't.

Contrast what is needed to deter or rehabilitate someone with a moral conscience too weak to ensure good behavior in some circumstances, with what is needed to deal with unmitigated amoralists (people who have no moral conscience at all). If we imagine a world with acceptance of the best code by 100 percent of the population, we have simply imagined unmitigated amoralists out of existence. Hence, we have imagined out of existence any rule-consequentialist rationale for having rules for deterring and dealing with unmitigated amoralists.

Here is why. On the rule-consequentialist view, there is always at least some cost associated with every additional rule added to the code. Every additional rule takes at least a little time to learn and at least a little memory to store. Then the question is whether there is some benefit from internalization of the rule that outweighs the cost. We can of course frame rules applying to non-existent situations. For example, "be kind to any rational non-humans living on the moon." But, if the situation envisaged really is non-existent, where is the benefit of including such a rule in the code to be internalized? Presumably there are no benefits from such never-to-be-applied rules. These rules, which have *some* costs and *no* benefits, fail a cost-benefit analysis.

The reasoning seems to me to generate the following important conclusion. Rule-consequentialism cannot generate or justify rules about how to deter murder, rape, robbery, fraud, etc. *by unmitigated amoralists*, unless rule-consequentialism picks its rules with reference to an imagined world where there is internalization of the envisaged rules by less than 100 percent of the population. So rule-consequentialism should evaluate rules in terms of internalization by less than 100 percent of the population.

But should we assume internalization by 99, or 90, or 80 percent, or even less?[4] Any precise number will of course be somewhat arbitrary, but we do have some relevant factors to consider. On one hand, we want a percentage close enough to 100 percent to hold on to the idea that moral rules are for acceptance *by the whole society of human beings*. On the other hand, we want a percentage far enough short of 100 percent to *make salient the problems about non-compliance* – such problems should not be thought of as incidental. Acknowledging that any one percentage will nevertheless be somewhat arbitrary, I propose we take internalization by 90 percent of people in each future generation as the condition under which rules have to be optimal. Let me just add that this distinction between the 90 percent who are moral and the 10 percent who are amoral is supposed to cut across all other distinctions, such as distinctions in nationality and financial status.

8   Arguments for Rule-Consequentialism

One argument for rule-consequentialism is that general internalization of rule-consequentialism would actually maximize the impartial good. The idea is that *from a purely consequentialist point of view* rule-consequentialism seems better than act-consequentialism and all other theories.

Many act-consequentialists reply by invoking their distinction between their criterion of rightness and the decision procedure for day-to-day moral decisions. They admit act-consequentialism is not a good procedure for agents to use when deciding what to do. But they think this does not invalidate act-consequentialism's criterion of rightness. They would add that, even if rule-consequentialism is an optimal decision procedure, this would not entail that rule-consequentialism correctly identifies what makes right acts right and wrong acts wrong.

Let us turn, then, to arguments for rule-consequentialism other than the one that internalizing rule-consequentialism would maximize the good.[5] Consider the moral code whose acceptance by society would be best, i.e., would maximize net good, impartially calculated. Shouldn't we try to follow that code? Isn't the code best for general adoption by the group of which we are members the one we should try to follow? These general thoughts about morality seem intuitively attractive and broadly rule-consequentialist.

And consider the related question "What if everyone felt free to do what you're doing?" This question may in the end prove to be an inadequate test of moral rightness. But there is no denying its initial appeal. And there is no denying that rule-consequentialism is an (at least initially) appealing interpretation of the test.

Rule-consequentialism thus taps into and develops familiar and intuitively plausible ideas about morality. Morality is to be understood as a social code, a collective enterprise, something people are to pursue together. And the elements of this code are to be evaluated in terms of both fairness and the overall effects on the well-being of individuals, impartially considered.

But rule-consequentialism's leading rivals all likewise emerge from attractive general ideas about morality. For example, act-utilitarianism can be seen as emerging from the idea that all that ultimately matters from the moral point of view is whether individuals are benefitted or harmed, that everything else is only instrumentally important (Scanlon 1982: 108). And act-consequentialism, the broader theory than act-utilitarianism, can be seen as emerging from the intuition that it can't be wrong to do what produces the most good (Foot 1985).

Now consider moral contractualism, the theory that an act is right if and only if allowed by rules which could not be reasonably rejected by anyone motivated to find rules that no one with this same motivation could reject. Contractualism develops from the idea that morality consists of rules to which everyone would consent under appropriate conditions. This seems a very appealing general idea – moral rules grounded in reasonable agreement.

Consider yet another theory. The moral particularism of Jonathan Dancy (1981, 1983, 1993) builds on the idea that moral truth is found not in cold inflexible principles but rather through a finely tuned sensitivity to particular cases in all their rich complexity. Actually, to be distinct, moral particularism must go beyond the claim that there are some conflicts between competing moral considerations which are so difficult that agents would have to have fine moral sensitivity and judgement to resolve them correctly. To be distinct, moral particularism must be the view that what counts as a consideration at all can be decided only on a case by case basis. This is just how Dancy frames his theory: the very same consideration can count morally in favor of doing an action in one case, and against in another, and there are few if any considerations that must always count on the same side morally. (Dancy points out that such properties as moral rightness itself do *always* count morally in favor of an act.)

Finally, as I understand what has come to be called virtue ethics, this approach grows from the thought that right and wrong actions can be understood only in terms of choices that a fully virtuous person would make. This thought then suggests that we take the nature of and rationale for the virtues as the primary focal points for our moral philosophy.

Thus all these moral theories – rule-consequentialism, act-utilitarianism, act-consequentialism, contractualism, particularism, virtue ethics – tap into familiar and intuitively attractive general ideas about morality, though different ones. So no one could claim that any one theory is the only one with this feature. The conclusion to draw from this is simple. The fact that a theory arises from and develops attractive general ideas about morality is hardly enough to show that it is superior to all its rivals.

Now among the questions we can go on to ask about competing moral theories are (1) whether they are coherent and develop from initially attractive ideas about morality, and (2) whether the claims they end up making about right and wrong in various circumstances are intuitively plausible.[6] I have already argued that rule-consequentialism develops from attractive ideas about morality. But I shall not fully discuss here the objection that rule-consequentialism *incoherently* claims that maximizing the good is the overarching goal and then that following certain rules can be right even when breaking them would produce more good.[7] I admit that if we start from an overarching commitment to maximize overall good, then our rule-consequentialism might be an incoherent account of moral rightness. But I propose our route to rule-consequentialism starts elsewhere: we don't start from, and indeed don't have, an overarching commitment to maximize overall good. If I am right about that, then this objection falls apart (Hooker 1995: 27–9; and 1996: 538–9).

What other route to rule-consequentialism might there be? In the next few sections, I will show that rule-consequentialism's implications about what is right or wrong in particular circumstances match our confident moral convictions quite well. But let me immediately address the familiar challenge to the idea that moral theories are to be tested by their match with intuitions. The familiar challenge is that moral convictions are merely inherited prejudices and as such cannot provide good reason for anything.

In reply to this challenge, let me say I of course recognize that people from different cultures have different moral intuitions, as do people even from the same culture. We must always be willing to reconsider our moral intuitions. They are scarcely infallible.

But, while they are not infallible, they can be crucial. Suppose we have two moral theories which are each coherent developments of appealing general ideas about morality. Suppose one of these theories has implications that match our convictions quite closely, and the other has implications that conflict with many of our most confidently held moral convictions. In this case, I cannot see what could reasonably keep us from thinking better of the theory with the more intuitively plausible implications. Indeed, it seems to me that we are at least as confident about what is right in *some* specific kinds of situation as we are about any of the general ideas about morality that get developed into different moral theories such as Aristotelianism, Kantianism, contractualism, and act-consequentialism. This is why almost all moral philosophers are unable to resist "testing" these theories by comparing the judgments that follow from them with our confident convictions about right and wrong in various kinds of situations.

Let me take stock. I've suggested three different ways of arguing for rule-consequentialism.

One is that rule-consequentialism is, from a purely consequentialist point of view, best. I myself am not relying on this argument.

The second is that rule-consequentialism develops from some very attractive general ideas about morality. Though this is an important feature of rule-consequentialism, I acknowledge rule-consequentialism is hardly the only theory that plugs into or develops from attractive general ideas about morality. So the fact that a theory is a coherent development of some initially very attractive ideas is not enough to make it superior to all its rivals.

The third argument for rule-consequentialism is that we can reach a reflective equilibrium between rule-consequentialism and our confident moral convictions. At least *some* moral convictions seem more secure than any theory that could oppose them. If this is right, then appeal to reflective equilibrium between abstract theory and moral conviction must be part of the defense of rule-consequentialism.

9   Rule-Consequentialism on Prohibitions

Whatever act-consequentialism says about day-to-day moral thinking, act-consequentialism's criterion of moral rightness entails that *whenever* killing an innocent person, or stealing, or breaking a promise, etc., would maximize the good, such acts would be morally right. W. D. Ross put forward the following example (table 10.4) to illustrate that keeping one's promises can be right even when this would produce *slightly* less good (Ross 1930: 34–5):

Table 10.4

Numbers below represent units of good

	Effects on person A	Effects on person B	Total good
Keeping promise to A	1000	0	1,000
Breaking promise to A	0	1,001	1,001

Most of us would agree with Ross that keeping the promise would be morally right in this case. Act-consequentialism, of course, favors breaking the promise in this case, since that is the alternative with the most good. So, if we agree with Ross about this case, we must reject act-consequentialism.

Most of us also believe (as Ross went on to observe) that, if breaking the promise would produce *much greater* good than keeping it, breaking the promise could be right. We believe parallel things about inflicting harm on innocent people, stealing, lying, etc. Thus most of us reject what is sometimes called "absolutism" in ethics. Absolutists hold that certain acts (e.g., physical attack on the innocent, promise-breaking, stealing, lying) are *always* wrong, even when they would prevent the most extreme *disasters*.

Absolutism and act-consequentialism are, we might say, two ends of a spectrum. Whereas absolutism never permits certain kinds of act, even when necessary to prevent extreme disaster, act-consequentialism insists such act are right not only when a great disaster is at stake but also when a *marginal* gain in net good is in the offing. Act-consequentialists seem mistaken about these cases of marginal gain, just as absolutists seem mistaken about the disaster cases. Thus, absolutism seems to go too far in one direction, act-consequentialism in the other.

Rule-consequentialism, on the other hand, concurs with our beliefs both about when we can, and when we cannot, do normally forbidden acts for the sake of the overall good. It claims that individual acts of murder, torture, promise-breaking, and so on, can be wrong even when they result in somewhat more good than not doing them would. The rule-consequentialist reason for this is that the general internalization of a code prohibiting murder, torture, promise-breaking, and so on would clearly result in more good than general internalization of a code with no prohibitions on such acts.

Another rule whose general internalization would be optimal is a rule telling us to do what is necessary to prevent disasters. This rule is relevant when the only way to prevent a disaster is to break a promise or do some other normally prohibited act. In such cases, rule-consequentialism holds that the normally prohibited act should be done. I mention this rule about preventing disaster because its existence undermines the objection that rule-consequentialism would, in a counterintuitive way, prescribe sticking to rules even when this would result in disaster.

10 Doing Good for Others

Morality paradigmatically requires us to be willing to make sacrifices for others. Yet act-consequentialism is widely accused of going too far here too. Utility, impartially calculated, would be maximized if I gave away most of my material goods to the appropriate charities. Giving away most of my material goods is therefore required of me by (most versions of) act-consequentialism. I should probably even change to some more lucrative employment so that I would then have more money to give to charity (Unger 1996: 151). I could make much more money as a corporate lawyer, banker, stockbroker, accountant, gossip-columnist, or bounty-hunter than as an employee of a philosophy department. If people should be willing to make any sacrifices that are smaller than the benefits thereby secured for others, then I should move to the better paying job so that I will have a bigger salary to contribute to the needy. With a bigger salary, I would then have to give an even larger percentage of my earnings to aid agencies. The result would be a life of devoted money-making – only then to deny myself virtually all the rewards I could buy for myself with the money. After all, from an act-consequentialist perspective, my own enjoyment is insignificant compared to the very lives of those who would be saved by my additional contributions. Such reflections give special poignancy to Shelly Kagan's remark: "Given the parameters of the actual world, there is no question that [maximally] promoting the good would require a life of hardship, self-denial, and austerity" (1989: 360).

But many of us may on reflection think that it would be *morally unreasonable* to demand this level of self-sacrifice for the sake of others.[8] However praiseworthy such self-sacrifice may be, most of us are quite confident that perpetual self-impoverishment for the sake of strangers is above and beyond what morality *requires* of us.[9]

I have been discussing the objection that act-consequentialism requires us to make *huge* sacrifices in order to maximize our contribution to famine relief. Act-consequentialism also requires self-sacrifice even when the benefit to the other person is only *slightly* larger than the cost to the agent. Consider, for example, the corner office in our building. Offices are allotted on the basis of seniority. Suppose you are the most senior person who might want this corner office. But if you do not take it, it will go to an acquaintance who spends ten percent more time in her office than you do in yours. Suppose we therefore reasonably guess that she would benefit a bit more from moving into this office than you would. This is not a life and death matter. Nor will she be so depressed by not getting the corner office that her work or domestic life will be seriously compromised. Nevertheless, she would get a bit more enjoyment out of the better office than you would. But you still take it for yourself. No one would think you unreasonable or immoral for doing so. Except in special circumstances, morality does not, we think, really *require* you to sacrifice your own good for the sake of slightly larger gains to others.

I have offered two objections about the demands of act-consequentialism. (1) Act-consequentialism requires *huge* sacrifices from you. (2) Act-consequentialism requires you to sacrifice your own good even when the aggregate good will be only *slightly* increased by the your sacrifice. In both ways, act-consequentialism is *unreasonably demanding*.

In contrast, rule-consequentialism would *not* require you to pass up the corner office and let your colleague have it. You are certainly permitted to do that if you want, but rule-consequentialism would not *require* such impartiality in your decisions about what to do with your own time, energy, money, or place in line. The rules the internalization of which could reasonably be thought to produce the most good would *allow* each person considerable partiality towards self (and even *require* partiality towards friends and family – see Brandt 1989: fn. 22.). For, as I noted earlier, the costs of getting a complete impartiality internalized by each new generation would be prohibitive.

Likewise, whereas act-consequentialism requires huge sacrifices for the sake of maximizing the good, rule-consequentialism seems not to require more than a reasonable amount of sacrifice for this purpose. Why? A rule-consequentialist might point out that, if everyone relatively well off in the world were to contribute quite modest amounts to the best aid agencies, the worst elements of poverty could be overcome.

The World Bank has been calling for contributions from the rich countries of 0.7 percent of GDP, the current average being less than half that. Much of this aid does not go to the most needy, but instead to countries that offer business for, or military alliances with, the donor country. The UN estimates that if merely 60 percent of the aid that the rich countries now give (i.e., 60 percent of about $57 billion) were intelligently spent on providing basic health services and clean water and on eliminating illiteracy, these problems could be fixed (*The Economist*, June 22, 1996: 64).

A rule-consequentialist will be interested in redistribution beyond what is required to secure the very basic necessities. But even after including these other potential benefits in the cost-benefit analysis, we might well conclude that the amount the world's relatively well off would each be required to give would not be unreasonably severe. (For challenges to this view, see Carson 1991; Mulgan 1994 and 1997.)

Consider the following example. Walking along a deserted road on your way to the airport for a flight to the other side of the world, you see a child drowning in a shallow pool beside the road. You could easily save the child, at no risk to yourself. But if you do save the child, you will miss your flight and lose the cost of the nonrefundable ticket.[10]

Everyone agrees you are obligated to save the child. This is true even if you are not terribly rich. Suppose the ticket costs as much as a tenth of your annual income. You would still be morally wrong not to make the sacrifice and save the child. And even if the probability of the child's drowning without your rescue is less than 100 percent – suppose, for example, it is 80 percent – you are obligated to sacrifice your ticket to save the child.

Now consider a variant of the example (Singer 1972: 233; Kagan 1991: 924–5; and Murphy 1993: 291. See also Hooker 1995: 25–6). You and I are walking to the airport when we see two small children drowning in a lake. You and I could each easily save the children, at no risk to ourselves. The two children are positioned in the lake in such a way that you and I could each save one and still get to our flights. But if one of us saves both children, he will miss his flight. Suppose you save one child, but I do nothing. Surely, you should now save the other.

Yet, were rule-consequentialism framed in terms of 100 percent compliance, how could it tell you to save the other? With 100 percent compliance, there would be no need for you to save the second child. With 100 percent compliance, once you'd done your share, you'd have done all that was needed. The rule that would be best given 100 percent compliance would presumably not require you to sacrifice more than you would have to sacrifice if everyone did their part. But if this rule is applied to our case, where I am in fact not coming to the rescue, you are *not* obligated to save this child. This is clearly an implausible implication.

But I argued that rule-consequentialism should be framed in terms of less that 100 percent compliance. If rule-consequentialism is framed in terms of 90 percent compliance, we can envisage that there is a need for rules about how to act when others around you aren't doing their part. The rule might be, "When you happen to be surrounded by others who are not helping, then prevent disaster even if this involves doing more than you would have to do if the others helped." This rule *would* require you to save the second child from the shallow pond.

But if the world we live in – the real world – is one where partial compliance is ubiquitous, then a rule requiring you to make up for the non-compliance of others could become unreasonably demanding. Just how much would rule-consequentialism require you to make up for non-compliance by other people in a position to help? In earlier work, I assumed that rule-consequentialism would formulate a rule about aiding the needy in terms of a *fairly precise* level of contribution or sacrifice to the reduction of world poverty.

I now think this approach is hopeless. Consider a concrete moral code that could reasonably be expected to produce at least as much good as any other we can identify. It would contain rules requiring us not to injure others physically, not to steal, not to break promises, not to lie, etc. These rules might have *some* exceptions built into them (though not a general break-the-rule-whenever-you-could-thereby-produce-more-good exception, nor an unlimited set of much more specific exceptions). Nonetheless, there is pressure to have *fairly general* rules that can be applied to a wide array of situations. Oxfam's petitioning the rich to help the very poor is hardly the only situation where some people have an opportunity to help others at relatively little cost to themselves. There will be situations where the rich can help other rich, situations where poor can help other poor, even situations where the poor can help the rich. And there will be situations where the help needs to be in the form of physical effort, other situations where the help needs to be in the form of money or time.

Given all this, perhaps the optimific rule for such a world would not be "the rich should give the very needy at least precisely n percent of their annual income", but rather "people should help others in great need when they can do so at modest to themselves, cost being assessed aggregatively, not iteratively" (Cullity 1995: 293-5). Such a rule would apply in a wide array of situations – indeed, whenever some person can help another in great need. It is not limited to what the rich should do nor to what should be done concerning world poverty.

But because cost to the agent is to be assessed aggregatively rather than iteratively, the rule does not require one to help another in great need whenever the cost of helping *on that particular occasion* is modest. Having to help others whenever doing so *on that occasion* involves modest cost could easily be very costly. For each of us faces an indefinitely long string of such occasions, because any day on which we could give money to UNICEF or Oxfam counts as such an occasion. But many small sacrifices added together can amount to a huge sacrifice. The end of that road is self-impoverishment. If I am right, rule-consequentialism instead endorses a rule requiring sacrifices over the course of your life that add up to something significant. It allows but does not require personal sacrifice beyond this point.

I propose that this rule *would* have good consequences even in possible worlds that are either much poorer or much richer than ours. I don't have space here to argue either that rule-consequentialism would indeed end up with this rule in *all* possible worlds, or that this rule *always* has intuitively acceptable consequences. I mention this rule only in order to sketch one way in which a defense of rule-consequentialism might go (cf. Hooker 1998).

11 Conclusion

Rule-consequentialism has an uncertain future. It needs to be carefully formulated if it is to avoid being a sitting target. In this essay, I have tried to improve its defenses by fine-tuning its formulation. I have also argued here that the theory develops from appealing general beliefs about morality, that it does not collapse into act-consequentialism, and that it coheres well with our intuitions about moral prohibitions and permissible partiality. As I see things, the theory is healthy now. But it is hardly invulnerable. Like someone walking through a dangerous city who has so far managed to fight off muggers emerging from behind every corner, the theory might meet an attack it cannot survive. I am curious to see whether that happens.[11]

Notes

1   The use of "consequentialism" and "utilitarianism" so that consequentialism allows for a concern for distribution in a way that utilitarianism does not is very common. For some examples, see Mackie 1977: 129, 149; Scanlon 1978, especially sect. 2; Scheffler 1982: 26–34, 70–9; Parfit 1984: 26; Griffin 1992: 126; 1996: 165. Examples of writers including distributive considerations *within* utilitarianism include Brandt 1959: 404, 426, 429–31; Raphael 1994: 47; Skorupski 1995: 54; and arguably Mill 1861.

2   See Mill 1861, ch. II; Sidgwick 1907: 405–6, 413, 489–90; Moore 1903: 162–4; Bales 1971; Hare 1981; Railton 1984: 140–6, 152–3; Parfit 1984: 24–9; Brink 1989: 216, 256–61. For criticism of the mileage some have tried to get from this, see Johnson 1989; Griffin 1992: 123–4; 1996: 104–5. See also Williams 1973: 123.

3   I have taken the liberty here of formulating the theory in what seems to me the most attractive relatively succinct way. I shall have to add complications to this formulation later.

4 Earlier rule-consequentialists have addressed this question. See, e.g., Brandt: 1967 §8; and 1988 [1992: 149–54].

5 I am grateful to Dale Miller for pressing me to provide the argument developed in the rest of this section.

6 There are other questions to ask as well. For a discussion of the importance of questions about helpfulness and about parsimony at the level of first principles, see Hooker 1996.

7 See Lyons 1965, ch. IV; Williams 1972: 99–102, 105–8; Slote 1992: 59; Raphael 1994: 52; Scarre 1996: 125–6. Relatedly, Regan (1980: 209) complains that rule-consequentialists "are only half-hearted consequentialists".

8 See Crisp 1992; and Quinn 1993: 171: "We think there is something morally amiss when people are forced to be farmers or flute players just because the balance of social needs tips in that direction. Barring great emergencies, we think people's lives must be theirs to lead."

9 Even Kagan, whose book goes on to defend act-consequentialism for 400 pages, starts by acknowledging that it "strikes us as outrageously extreme in its demands" (1989: 2.).

10 This example has been central to the contemporary philosophical debate about beneficence. The example and the debate owe their prominence to Singer 1972 (see his restatement in ch. 8 of his 1993). Some important contributions to this discussion are Fishkin 1982; Scheffler 1982; Kagan 1989, especially pp. 3–4, 231–2; Nagel 1991; Murphy 1993; Cullity 1994; and Unger, 1996.

11 I have had help with this essay from Roger Crisp, Jonathan Dancy, Max de Gaynesford, Hanjo Glock, Hugh LaFollette, Andrew Mason, Elinor Mason, Dale Miller, David Oderberg, and Derek Parfit, and the audience at the 1997 International Society for Utilitarian Studies Conference.

References

Adams, R. M.: "Motive Utilitarianism," *The Journal of Philosophy*, 73 (1976): 467–81.
Austin, J.: *The Province of Jurisprudence Determined* (1832).
Bales, R. E.: "Act-utilitarianism: Account of Right-making Characteristics or Decision-making Procedure?" *American Philosophical Quarterly*, 8 (1971): 257–65.
Bentham, Jeremy: *An Introduction to the Principles of Morals and Legislation* (1789).
Berkeley, G.: *Passive Obedience, or the Christian Doctrine of Not Resisting the Supreme Power, Proved and Vindicated upon the Principles of the Law of Nature* (1712).
Blackburn, Simon: "Errors and the Phenomenology of Value," *Morality and Objectivity, A Tribute to J. L. Mackie*, ed. T. Honderich (London: Routledge and Kegan Paul, 1985).
Brandt, R. B.: *Ethical Theory* (Englewood Cliffs, NJ: Prentice-Hall, 1959).
——: "Some Merits of One Form of Rule-utilitarianism," *University of Colorado Studies in Philosophy*, 3 (1967): 39–65. Reprinted in Brandt 1992, pp. 111–36.
——: *A Theory of the Good and the Right* (Oxford: Clarendon Press, 1979).
——: "Fairness to Indirect Optimific Theories in Ethics," *Ethics*, 98 (1988): 341–60. Reprinted in Brandt 1992, pp. 137–57.
——: "Morality and its Critics," *American Philosophical Quarterly*, 26 (1989): 89–100. Reprinted in Brandt 1992, pp. 73–92.
——: *Morality, Utilitarianism, and Rights* (New York: Cambridge University Press, 1992).
——: *Facts, Values, and Morality* (New York: Cambridge University Press, 1996).

Brink, David O.: *Moral Realism and the Foundations of Ethics* (New York: Cambridge University Press, 1989).

Carson, Thomas: "A Note on Hooker's Rule Consequentialism," *Mind*, 100 (1991): 117–21.

Crisp, Roger: "Utilitarianism and the Life of Virtue," *Philosophical Quarterly*, 42 (1992): 139–60.

——: *Mill on Utilitarianism* (London: Routledge, 1997).

Cullity, Garrett: "International Aid and the Scope of Kindness," *Ethics*, 105 (1994): 99–127.

——: "Moral Character and the Iteration Problem," *Utilitas*, 7 (1995): 289–99.

Dancy, Jonathan: "On Moral Properties," *Mind*, 90 (1981): 367–85.

——: "Ethical Particularism and Morally Relevant Properties," *Mind*, 92 (1983): 530–47.

——: *Moral Reasons* (Oxford: Blackwell, 1993).

Dworkin, Ronald: *Law's Empire* (Cambridge, MA: Harvard University Press, 1986).

Finnis, John: *Natural Law and Natural Rights* (Oxford: Clarendon Press, 1980).

——: *Fundamentals of Ethics* (New York: Oxford University Press, 1983).

Fishkin, James: *The Limits of Obligation* (New Haven: Yale University Press, 1982).

Foot, Philippa: "Utilitarianism and the Virtues," *Mind*, 94 (1985): 196–209.

Griffin, James: *Well-Being: Its Meaning, Method and Moral Importance* (Oxford: Clarendon Press, 1986).

——: "The Human Good and the Ambitions of Consequentialism," *Social Philosophy and Policy*, 9 (1992): 118–32.

——: *Value Judgement: Improving Our Ethical Beliefs* (Oxford: Clarendon Press, 1996).

Hare, R. M.: *Moral Think: Its Method, Levels, and Point* (Oxford: Clarendon Press, 1981).

Harsanyi, John: "Morality and the Theory of Rational Behavior," *Utilitarianism and Beyond*, eds., A. Sen and B. Williams (Cambridge: Cambridge University Press, 1982), pp. 39–62. Reprinted from *Social Research*, 44 (1977).

——: "Expectation Effects, Individual Utilities, and Rational Desires," *Rationality, Rules, and Utility: New Essays on the Moral Philosophy of Richard Brandt*, ed. B. Hooker (Boulder: Westview Press, 1993) pp. 115–26.

Hodgson, D. H.: *Consequences of Utilitarianism* (Oxford: Clarendon Press, 1967).

Hooker, Brad: "Mark Overvold's Contribution to Philosophy," *Journal of Philosophical Research*, 26 (1991): 333–44.

——: "Rule-consequentialism, Incoherence, Fairness," *Proceedings of the Aristotelian Society*, 95 (1995): 19–35.

——: "Ross-style Pluralism Versus Rule-consequentialism," *Mind*, 105 (1996): 531–52.

——: "Rule-consequentialism and Obligations Toward the Needy," *Pacific Philosophical Quarterly*, 79 (1998): 19–33.

Hurka, Thomas: "The Well-rounded Life," *Journal of Philosophy*, 84 (1987): 707–26.

——: *Perfectionism* (New York: Oxford University Press, 1993).

Johnson, Conrad: "Character Traits and Objectively Right Action," *Social Theory and Practice*, 15 (1989): 67–88.

——: *Moral Legislation* (New York: Cambridge University Press, 1991).

Kagan, Shelly: *The Limits of Morality* (Oxford: Clarendon Press, 1989).

——: "Replies to My Critics," *Philosophy and Phenomenological Research*, 51 (1991): 924–5.

Kavka, Gregory: "Some Paradoxes of Deterrence," *Journal of Philosophy*, 75 (1978): 285–302.

Lyons, David: *Forms and Limits of Utilitarianism* (Oxford: Clarendon Press, 1965).

Mackie, J. L.: *Ethics: Inventing Right and Wrong* (Hammondsworth: Penguin, 1977).

Mill, J. S.: *Utilitarianism* (1861).

Moore, G. E.: *Principia Ethica* (Cambridge: Cambridge University Press, 1903).

Mulgan, T.: "Rule Consequentialism and Famine," *Analysis*, 54 (1994): 187–92.

——: "One False Virtue of Rule Consequentialism and One New Vice," *Pacific Philosophical Quarterly*, 77 (1997): 362–73.

Murphy, Liam: "The Demands of Beneficence," *Philosophy and Public Affairs*, 22 (1993): 267–92.

——: "A Relatively Plausible Principle of Benevolence: A Reply to Mulgan," *Philosophy and Public Affairs*, 26 (1997): 80–6.

Nagel, Thomas: *Equality and Partiality* (New York: Oxford University Press, 1991).

Overvold, Mark: "Self-interest and the Concept of Self-sacrifice," *Canadian Journal of Philosophy*, 10 (1980): 105–18.

——: "Self-interest and Getting What You Want," *The Limits of Utilitarianism*, eds. H. B. Miller and W. H. Williams (Minneapolis: University of Minnesota Press, 1982), pp. 186–94.

Parfit, Derek: *Reasons and Persons* (Oxford: Clarendon Press, 1984).

Quinn, Warren: *Morality and Action* (New York: Cambridge University Press, 1993).

Railton, Peter: "Alienation, Consequentialism, and the Demands of Morality," *Philosophy and Public Affairs*, 13 (1984): 174–31.

Raphael, D. D.: *Moral Philosophy*, 2nd edn. (Oxford: Oxford University Press, 1994).

Rawls, John: "Two Concepts of Rules," *Philosophical Review*, 64 (1955): 3–32

——: *A Theory of Justice* (Cambridge, MA: Harvard University Press, 1971).

Regan, D.: *Utilitarianism and Co-operation* (Oxford: Clarendon Press, 1980).

Ross, W. D.: *The Right and the Good* (Oxford: Clarendon Press, 1930).

Scanlon, T. M.: "Rights, Goals and Fairness," *Public and Private Morality*, ed. S. Hampshire (Cambridge, UK: Cambridge University Press, 1978) pp. 93–111.

——: "Contractualism and Utilitarianism," *Utilitarianism and Beyond*, eds. A. Sen and B. Williams (Cambridge: Cambridge University Press, 1982), pp. 103–28.

——: "Value, Desire, and Quality of Life," *The Quality of Life*, eds. M. Nussbaum and A. Sen (Oxford: Clarendon Press, 1993), pp. 185–200.

Scarre, Geoffrey: *Utilitarianism* (London: Routledge, 1996).

Scheffler, S.: *The Rejection of Consequentialism* (Oxford: Clarendon Press, 1982).

Sidgwick, Henry: *Methods of Ethics*, seventh edn. (London: Macmillan, 1907), first edn., 1874.

Singer, Peter: "Famine, Affluence, and Morality," *Philosophy and Public Affairs*, 1 (1972): 229–43.

——: *Practical Ethics*, second edn. (Cambridge, UK: Cambridge University Press, 1993).

Skorupski, John: "Agent-Neutrality, Consequentialism, Utilitarianism . . . A Terminological Note," *Utilitas*, 7 (1995): 49–54.

Slote, Michael: *From Morality to Virtue* (New York: Oxford University Press, 1992).

Smart, J. J. C.: "Outline of a System of Utilitarian Ethics," *Utilitarianism: For & Against*, eds. J. J. C. Smart and Bernard Williams (Cambridge: Cambridge University Press, 1973), pp. 3–74.

Unger, Peter: *Living High and Letting Die: Our Illusion of Innocence* (New York: Oxford University Press, 1996).

Urmson, J. O.: "The Interpretation of the Philosophy of J. S. Mill," *Philosophical Quarterly*, 3 (1953): 33–9.

Williams, Bernard: *Morality: An Introduction to Ethics* (New York: Harper and Row, 1972).

——: "A Critique of Utilitarianism," *Utilitarianism: For & Against*, eds. J. J. C. Smart and B. Williams (Cambridge, UK: Cambridge University Press, 1973) pp. 77–150.

Chapter 11

Nonconsequentialism

F. M. Kamm

I Introduction

Nonconsequentialism is a normative ethical theory which denies that the rightness or wrongness of our conduct is determined solely by the goodness or badness of the consequences of our acts or the rules to which those acts conform. It does not deny that consequences can be a factor in determining the rightness of an act. It does insist that even when the consequences of two acts or act-types are the same, one might be wrong and the other right. This theory denies both act and rule consequentialism, understood as holding that the right act or system of rules is the one that maximizes or satisfices good consequences as determined by an impartial calculation of goods and evils. This calculation requires that we have a theory of what is good; it may be extremely liberal, holding that killings are bad or that autonomy is good, but we are still required to maximize the good.

Despite the name "consequentialism," many consequentialists think that we always ought to maximize the goodness of states of affairs where this includes the act itself and its consequences. Nonconsequentialists also deny this. Because of the possibility of this alternative contrast, consequentialism is sometimes referred to as teleology and nonconsequentialism as deontology.

Contemporary nonconsequentialism finds its spiritual roots in the work of Immanuel Kant and W. D. Ross. Nonconsequentialists are drawn to Kant's formulation of the Categorical Imperative which specifies that we should always treat rational humanity in oneself and in others as an end in itself and never merely as a means, and to his distinction between perfect and imperfect duties. Ends-in-themselves are said to have unconditional value, value independent of serving anyone's personal ends and independent of being in a particular context. Merely counting each person's interests in the way consequentialists do is not enough to express the fact that each person is an end-in-itself. Rather, if I am an end-in-myself, then this constrains conduct that would maximize overall good.

Some nonconsequentialists suggest that we divide the imperative into two components: (a) treat persons as ends in themselves, and (b) do not treat them as mere means. If we treat people as mere means, we do not treat them as ends-in-themselves, because we are interested in them only as causally efficacious tools to some goal not serving their ends. Nonetheless, we might fail to treat people as ends-in-themselves, even though we do not treat them as mere means. For example, if we harm someone as a *foreseen* effect of failing to constrain our conduct.

The second element of the Kantian legacy is his distinction between perfect and imperfect duties. He is thought of as an absolutist because he held that though we have some moral "leeway" in how or when we fulfill imperfect duties, the perfect duties must always be done. Thus, on his view, I may not kill one person to save others. Contemporary nonconsequentialists often deny the absolutist conception of perfect duties, but do accept that the class of negative duties (e.g., not to harm) are more stringent than the positive duties (e.g., to aid).

W. D. Ross was the second inspiration for contemporary nonconsequentialism. Although Ross thought there was a prima facie duty of beneficence, there are numerous other prima facie duties, for example, a duty not to harm, a duty of gratitude, a duty to do justice. If these prima facie duties conflict, as he thought they might, we have no single scale on which to weigh them or rule by which to order them so as to determine our actual duty. Some contemporary nonconsequentialists have tried to strengthen Ross's view by more precisely determining the relative weights or ordering of prima facie duties, or at least by more precisely characterizing them. This might require stating duties so that they specify their own limits, or finding more basic duties than Ross described that are not as easily outweighed.

II   Contemporary Nonconsequentialism Outlined

Nonconsequentialism is now typically thought to include prerogatives not to maximize the good and constraints on producing the good. The prerogative merely denies that agents must maximize good consequences. It suggests the possibility that some acts are supererogatory, because while they are not morally required, they are morally valuable in virtue of producing better consequences. Constraints limit what we may do in pursuit of our own or even impartial good. Partial nonconsequentialists might advocate prerogatives but no constraints (Scheffler 1982) or constraints but no prerogatives (Kagan 1989).

The most commonly proposed constraints are a strong duty not to harm (contrasted with a weaker duty to aid) and/or a prohibition against intending harm (contrasted with a weaker duty not to cause or allow harm that is *merely* foreseen.)

However, this characterization ignores important moral complexities. Consider the Trolley case: a runaway trolley will kill five people if a bystander does not divert it onto another track, where, he foresees, it will kill one person. Nonconsequentialists typically think the bystander may divert the trolley – killing one to save the five (or even two) – although in other cases they oppose killing one person to save five

(Foot 1978b). An appropriately complex constraint must capture nonconsequentialist judgments of all cases. If it does, it will capture the precise way in which an individual is thought to be inviolable, that is, protected by a negative right not to be harmed even if the harm would maximize good.

Some say these internally complex constraints are absolute; others insist that no constraints are absolute. We may permissibly infringe them to produce a sufficiently great good.

Finally, most nonconsequentialists employ a distinctive methodology. They test and develop theories or principles by intuitive judgments on cases. They compare the implications which proposed principles have for hypothetical cases (such as the Trolley case) with their considered judgments about what we can permissibly do in such cases. If the implications of the principles and the judgments conflict, we may develop alternative principles or theories. If implications of principles and judgments are compatible, the nonconsequentialist must still offer a theory identifying the fundamental, morally significant factors that underlie the principles in order for them to be fully justified.

Nonconsequentialism is not merely concerned with prerogatives and constraints, although they have been the focus of contemporary discussion. For example, the nonconsequentialist may also propose that there are distinctive ways of aiding people that do not merely try to maximize the good. In the remainder of this essay, I shall explore these points in more detail.

III   Prerogatives

Moral prerogatives permit an agent (1) to act in ways that do not maximize the impartial good, and (2) to act for reasons that stem from his personal perspective, rather than from the perspective of an impartial judge. But how should we make these prerogatives more precise? Suppose we assign a constant by which each agent can multiply the weight of his personal concerns, so that they can outweigh an impartial good. The result would sometimes conflict with our intuition. For example, no matter how great the noninfinite factor, we can envision some disaster whose aversion would seem to require the agent to sacrifice his most significant projects, even though, intuitively, we do not think he is morally obligated to do so. Yet it seems morally ludicrous for agents to multiply their insignificant projects by this same factor so that they often outweigh vital needs of others. It seems more reasonable for the multiplicative factor to depend on the relative importance of the project to the agent, and even to permit agents to give fundamental projects lexical priority relative to the impartial good. Even this seems an imperfect characterization, since a true prerogative gives the agent the option to care *less* for himself than for others, and this does not seem to be captured by a multiplicative factor greater than one.

Some people justify prerogatives by claiming that humans are psychologically predisposed to be most concerned about their own projects. Hence, if they are morally permitted to pursue their nonoptimific projects for personal reasons, we will not alienate them from their fundamental natures (Scheffler 1982). I find this justification problematic. First, it does not limit others' moral permission to interfere with someone in their quest to maximize the good; it only says someone need not always act of his own accord for impartial good for impartial reasons. Second, this justification suggests agents should be permitted to control that about which they care most. However, I should not be able to control someone else's life, merely because that is what I care about most. Hence, a theory of prerogatives must specify from an impartial perspective what we are entitled to control from a partial perspective, uncoerced by others. This connects prerogatives with constraints as part of a theory of individual rights.

Others justify prerogatives by claiming that consequentialist morality is too demanding, for it could require an agent to sacrifice everything to maximize the impartial good. This justification, though, is troublesome since nonconsequentialism can be very demanding: we may have to make enormous sacrifices in respecting constraints. Why should agents have to sacrifice projects to avoid violating constraints, but not to promote impartial good? To explain this, I believe, we also need a theory of what individuals are entitled to.

Still others ground prerogatives in the idea that people are ends-in-themselves. Since we should not view people as mere means of promoting the greater good, each of us can sometimes justifiably pursue non-optimific goals. On this view, also, prerogatives imply the idea of personal sovereignty and entitlements. Even more fundamentally, prerogatives are a byproduct of the fact that moral obligation is not about producing as much good as possible. It is about respect for persons and doing only the good which that requires.

IV Constraints

(A) Harming versus not-aiding

I have argued that the theory of prerogatives should be connected to a theory of constraints and negative rights. By understanding constraints, we will better understand why we morally must suffer greater losses to avoid violating constraints than to maximize the good. Nonconsequentialists claim there is a strong moral constraint against harming people. Consequentialists argue that there is no intrinsic moral difference between harming and not-aiding (call this the Equivalence Thesis). Hence we may generally harm to aid. Consequentialists sometimes employ the methodology of intuitive judgments about cases to support the Equivalence Thesis. They identify seemingly comparable cases of harming and not-aiding, that is, cases where contextual factors such as intention, foresight, consequences, motive, effort, etc. are equal. They claim that in such cases we judge that harming and not-aiding are morally equivalent. However, to prove a universal claim like the Equivalence

Thesis, one set of comparable cases will not suffice. For it may be that in some equalized contexts, a harming and a not-aiding will be judged equally wrong, yet in other equalized contexts they will not be. If we can find even one set of comparable cases in which a harming is morally worse than a not-aiding, we rebut the Equivalence Thesis.

For example, James Rachels uses the Bathtub Cases to prove the Equivalence Thesis: (1) Smith will inherit a fortune if his little cousin dies. One evening while the child is taking his bath, Smith drowns him. (2) Jones will inherit a fortune if his little cousin dies. As Jones enters the bathroom, the child slips and falls face down in the water. Although Jones could easily save the child, he does nothing, intending that the child die (1975). Rachels, and others following him, claim that here a killing and a letting die are morally equivalent and this shows that killing and letting die are morally equivalent per se. But is even the first claim true? Would it be permissible to impose the same losses on Jones and Smith, if these losses would bring their victim back to life? I don t think so. Although it might be permissible to kill Smith, it would not be permissible to kill Jones. So perhaps there really is a moral difference between the killing and the letting die, even when they are both morally wrong.

The same point can be made if we ask how much effort an agent must expend to avoid killing someone and to save someone, even in cases where death is equally foreseen or intended. Here is a set of Road Cases: (1) We know that if we drive down one road, we will kill someone who cannot move out of the way. The only alternative is to go down a side road, where we risk hurting ourselves. (2) We know that to save someone from drowning, we must go down a side road, where we risk hurting ourselves. I think an agent is obligated to face a larger personal risk to avoid killing than to avoid letting die. If this is right, there is a fundamental moral difference between killing and letting die.

These cases suggest killing and letting die are morally different per se, but they do not tell us *why* they differ. We might be able to determine why if we focus on differences that remain in *these cases*, after equalizing contexts: (1) in killing we introduce a threat that was not previously present; in letting die, we do not interfere with a currently present threat; (2) in killing we act, in letting die we fail to act; (3) in killing we cause someone to lose life that would have been caused independently of our efforts at that time; in letting die, someone loses life that would have been caused only with our help at that time; and (4) in killing we interfere first with the victim; in letting die, we avoid being interfered with (by having to aid) first. These differences might explain the fundamental moral difference between killing and letting die if they are essential (or conceptual) differences between killing and letting die, not just differences in some cases.

Are they? Suppose we actively terminate (e.g., pull a plug on) lifesaving assistance we are providing to save Michael from a threat we did not produce, to avoid the substantial effort involved in continuing aid. We foresee that Michael will die. In this case (Terminate Aid), I believe, we let Michael die even though we *act* to stop the aid (not merely omit to provide it). The letting die is as acceptable as not starting the aid to begin with. Moreover, we are partial *causes* of Michael's death; after all, it resulted because we acted. Hence, we cannot distinguish between killing and letting die simply by saying that the latter involves no action and causes no death.

Still, in Terminate Aid, we do not introduce a cause which induces death. If we did, we would kill. That is, only killings can have this property, although perhaps some killings do not. Moreover, in the letting die case, we stop our being interfered with first and the "victim" loses only what he would be caused to have because of our aid now. I suggest that these are essential properties of letting die, but not of killing and, hence, are essential differences between the two.

We must be careful in speaking of essential properties, for there are two types: (a) those that are essentially true of either killing or letting die per se and also necessarily excluded from cases involving the other; (b) those that are essentially true of one of the dyad, and not necessarily excluded from cases involving the other. The first create the most obvious differences; but the latter still create vital differences even though the properties are "exportable" to an instance of the contrasting behavior. Thus, some *cases* of killing (though not killing *per se*) could contain what is an essential property only of letting die and vice versa. Nonetheless, these exportable properties could still explain the moral difference between killing and letting die per se. Indeed, rather than compare equalized cases of killing and letting die, we could compare two similar cases of killing in which only the second case has an essential exported property of letting die. As an example, killing someone who is independent of our aid is compared with killing someone who is receiving life-saving aid from us. If the action in the second case is less morally problematic than the action in the first, then we have strong evidence that this essential property of letting die is morally significant.

If the property functions in the same way on its home ground (i.e., in letting die) and killing has no essential property which can also improve behavior, then letting die would have at least one more morally improving essential property than killing, and hence be morally better per se in virtue of that property. Exportable properties could explain one way defenders of the Equivalence Thesis might find cases in which a killing and a letting die were morally equivalent: they could find examples of killing and letting die in which essential properties of one of the behaviors were exported to the case involving the other. Then, as long as other morally relevant properties were equivalent, we would have identified a killing and a letting die that were morally equivalent. But that would not show that killing and letting die *per se* were morally equivalent.

I have argued that letting die essentially has properties which make acts morally more permissible. These properties are (1) that the "victim" loses only what would have been caused with the agent's help at that time, and (2) that the agent prevents his being imposed on first. But these properties could be morally important only if we have a stronger claim to what we are caused to have independently of the current aid of others than they have, and this applies both to our life and to the efforts we could make on behalf of others. The moral distinction between killing and letting die captures this view of separate persons.

We must exert great effort to avoid imposing first on others, especially on what they are caused independently of our current aid. We can legitimately make fewer efforts to prevent someone from not having what he would have only by our being imposed on first. We can now see that making great efforts not to kill others, at least when the case does not share certain essential properties of letting die, is consistent with a prerogative not to maximize good. However, if we explain the moral distinction between killing and letting die as I have, we must do more work to explain why killing in the Trolley Case to save five is permissible.

Finally, there are certain things we should remember in applying our conclusions about killing and letting die to the general moral distinction between harming (or making someone worse off) and not aiding. (1) When we kill or let someone die, we might reasonably think that she has some right to her life. But when we harm or do not aid someone, what they lose – or fail to get – may be something to which they have no right. (2) Generally when someone kills, they interfere with another's body in ways they do not do when they let die. However, if we harm someone, we may not necessarily interfere with her body any more than if we do not aid. Suppose we combine these two factors and construct harming and not-aiding cases: (a) Imagine that some money that does not belong to anyone is accidentally transferred to my bank account, but you make me worse off by computer transferring it out. (b) You fail to transfer some unowned money into my account. There may be no great moral difference between these cases, though in the first, someone is made worse off while in the second we fail to improve his condition.

(B) Intending versus foreseeing harm

The Doctrine of Double Effect (DDE) is historically the most important formulation of the supposed moral distinction between intending and foreseeing harm. The doctrine states that we may not intend evil, even when the evil will be a means to a greater good. Nonetheless, we are permitted to employ neutral or good means to promote a greater good, even though we foresee evil side effects if (a) the good is proportionate to the evil and (b) there is no better way to achieve this good. Thus, it is said to be impermissible to end a war by intentionally killing ten civilians (Terror Bombing), but permissible to end the war by intentionally bombing munitions factories, even foreseeing that twenty civilians will certainly die as an unintended side effect (Strategic Bombing).

The moral distinction between intending and foreseeing bad effects applies to omissions as well as actions and is independent of the harming/not-aiding distinction. Some nonconsequentialists embrace only one of these distinctions; others embrace both. Moreover, some nonconsequentialists wish to revise the DDE so that it is a nonabsolute constraint. For example, so that it does not apply at all in situations of self-defense, and in other situations it only implies that we must tolerate worse consequences before intending bad effects than we have to tolerate before acting in ways in which bad effects are merely foreseen.

Many object to the DDE because we can typically describe behavior it supposedly rules out so that the agent does not strictly intend any evil. For example, the Terror Bomber might intend only that the civilians appear dead until peace is declared. Of course, he foresees with certainty that civilians will die since the only way to make them appear dead until the war ends also leads to their death. But the Strategic Bomber also foresees with certainty the deaths of civilians (Bennett 1981). We might try to recapture the moral distinction between these two cases by revising the DDE. The revised version would prohibit intending even minor intrusions on (Kamm), or involvement of, persons (Quinn 1993), when the agent foresees that these others will suffer significant harm to which they did not consent. This is a significant revision to the doctrine. The original DDE barred agents from aiming at evil as a means. The revision prohibits agents from treating persons as tools whenever the results would be foreseeably bad for them, even though there is no intention that evil occur as a means.

The traditional DDE is also too weak to undergird a proper moral constraint because it permits us to always produce a lesser good by means that have bad side effects. As Philippa Foot notes, it permits us to use a gas to save five people even knowing the gas will seep next door, killing one person. It would also permit us to rush to the hospital to save five, foreseeing (but not intending) that we thereby kill one (1978b, 1984). Yet, Foot claims, intuitively we think it is impermissible to do these things.

The DDE is also too strong. It seems to rule out intentionally harming someone to promote that person's overall good (the *intra*personal case), and it rules out intentionally harming someone to help others even when that person is no worse off than he would have been otherwise.

Two further complexities. The DDE suggests that the *greater* good against which the bad side effect is compared must be *intended*. But can it not be a mere foreseen side effect of what was intended? For example, a strategic bomber targets one portion of a munitions factory. He intends to bring about this small good but foresees two side effects: (1) killing ten innocent civilians and (2) stopping a massacre of twenty different civilians. (1) is too large an evil to be outweighed by the small intended good. (2) is a great enough good to outweigh (1), but it is not intended since its occurrence is not necessary to the war effort. Hence, if the DDE is a necessary condition for moral permissibility, it might block the attack on the factory.

If the bomber in this case proceeds only *because* (2) will occur, this need not imply that he intended to produce that good. This suggests that the Counterfactual Test for detecting intention (rather than mere foresight) is flawed. That test states that if we would not proceed with our act had a particular effect *not* occurred – assuming everything else is held constant – then in acting we intend that effect, as a means or as an end. However, as the previous example suggests, in some cases we might proceed only because an effect will occur, yet still not intend its occurrence. This distinction between doing something *because* an effect will occur and doing it in order that it occur suggests that there is a third type of case between the Strategic and the Terror Bomber: Suppose it is militarily valuable to bomb a munitions factory only if it is not immediately rebuilt. The factory will be rebuilt unless the population is grieving as a consequence of the death of civilians in the bombing. Hence, we bomb the factory only if we are convinced civilians will die, even though we do not intend that they die (Munitions Grief Case). I believe it is permissible to bomb in this case, even if Terror bombing is impermissible. Because of this third type of relation to effects – because they will recur – it might be better to speak of the *Doctrine of Triple Effect.*

V   Complications on the Simple Constraints

As I noted earlier, many contemporary nonconsequentialists want to develop W. D. Ross's conception of prima facie duties. Ross thought that when the duties conflict, we have no rule or principle ranking them. So some nonconsequentialists have tried to develop more complex and less frequently overrideable duties. For example, the Trolley Case suggests how we might more precisely characterize the relative moral importance of not harming and aiding. We are looking for a principle that explains why it is permissible to help some by redirecting a fatal threat so that it kills someone else, yet it would be impermissible to kill one person to harvest his organs to save others (Transplant Case). The principle must also explain why some things we could do to stop the trolley (e.g., pushing an innocent bystander into its path) are as impermissible as harvesting someone's organs.

Philosophers have offered many ways of explaining these intuitive judgments. Among them are: (1) When (a) we redirect the trolley, we merely foresee the death of the one, when (b) we harvest the organs for transplant, we intend the death, and when (c) we push the bystander into the trolley, we intend his involvement and foresee his death. Hence, (a) is permissible and (b) and (c) are not. However, this DDE-inspired explanation suggests we could legitimately detonate a bomb to stop the trolley, even though we foresee, but do not intend, that the bomb will involve and kill a bystander. However, I believe, this is impermissible. (2) In Trolley, we do not initiate a new threat. We merely redistribute a preexisting threat so that a greater number are saved. But this, even in combination with (1), cannot be a sufficient condition for acting permissibly. If a trolley is headed toward one person, we may not redirect it foreseeing it will kill five, even if we do this because the redirection also moves a rock that saves twenty people from another threat. Neither is (2) a necessary condition for acting permissibly. Suppose a trolley is headed toward five people seated on a large swivel table. Although we physically cannot redirect the Trolley, we can turn the table and save the five. However, we thereby start a rock slide which will kill one innocent bystander (Lazy Susan Case). Here we start a new threat which kills someone. Nonetheless, I believe it is permissible to act. The problem is explaining why.

I propose the Principle of Permissible Harm (PPH). The basic idea is that it is permissible for (i) greater good and (ii) means that have greater good as their noncausal flip side to cause lesser evil, but not permissible to (iii) intend lesser evil as a means to greater good or to (iv) intend means that cause lesser evil as a foreseen side effect and have greater good as a mere causal effect unmediated by (ii). By "noncausal flip side," I mean that the greater good occurring is, in essence, another way of describing the situation in which the means occur. This principle denies that we may never harm to aid. For example, when harm is an effect of achieving a greater good, we may permissibly do what harms. Suppose by directing gas into a room we can save five people. However, their breathing normally – the greater good – alters the air flow in the room, redirecting germs, killing an innocent person. In this case, it is permissible to use the gas to save five people, because it is the greater good itself which causes the death.

The PPH explains why we may permissibly turn the trolley. The trolley moving away, which kills the one, is a means to saving the five and this greater good is its *noncausal* flip side. That is, given the moving away occurs in a context where no other fatal threat faces the five, the five's being saved just is the trolley moving away. Further, our act of turning the trolley, which ultimately leads to harm, is permissible by (iv) because it produces the harm only by producing a means (the moving trolley) that has greater good as its noncausal flip side. By contrast, a bomb that kills a bystander saves the five as a mere causal effect of its moving the trolley away from them, so the act that sets the bomb off is impermissible according to the PPH.

In the Loop case a trolley is headed toward the five and it can be redirected onto another track where one person sits. However, the track loops back towards the five (Thomson 1985). The trolley will kill the five immediately, or, if we redirect it, it would kill the five after it loops were it not that it grinds into the one person and is stopped. I believe it is permissible to turn the trolley in this case. Yet, grinding into the one is a causal link to saving the five; it is not merely a foreseen side effect. Does this mean that if we turn the trolley, we intend the grinding of the one? Presumably we would refuse to turn the trolley unless this happened to the person, for if the trolley did not grind into him, five people would die anyway and we would also risk its harming him on its way to the five. In short, we turn the trolley *because* he will be crushed. But, as I noted earlier in discussing the Counterfactual Test, that does not imply that we intend to crush him. Consequently, our judgment in the Loop Case is consistent with a revised version of DDE being a necessary condition of permissibility. It also shows that a rational agent can pursue a goal that he knows is achievable only by a certain causal route, without intending that route.

Does the Loop Case undermine the PPH? For if the crushing of the one is causally necessary to save the five, how can the greater good, or means which have greater good as their noncausal flip side, produce the lesser evil? This requires that we revise the PPH. When the trolley heads away from the five, we are left with a *structurally equivalent component* of the greater good, that is, what would be the greater good if it could be sustained. This is so because the only threat the five still face – the trolley coming at them from another direction – arises only because we removed the initial threat. The structural equivalent of the greater good or means that have it as its noncausal flipside produces a new threat as well as the means for eliminating it (the crushing of the person) and this makes turning the trolley permissible. So the PPH should be revised to allow that a structural equivalent of the greater good or means that have it as a noncausal flipside may produce lesser evil, even when this is necessary to sustain the greater good.

What morally significant ideas might justify the PPH? It seems to give expression to the view that persons are ends-in-themselves. For instance, we may not intend their use when this makes them worse off overall. More surprisingly, we see this status revealed in the requirement that only another end-in-itself, for example, a greater good consisting of the well-being of other people (or what is noncausally related to it) may lead to lesser harm.

VI   Inviolability

The PPH implies that persons have rights not to be treated in certain ways simply to save more lives. These rights protect persons against some ways of maximizing the good; it gives them some inviolability. The inviolability is not absolute. It is limited *qualitatively*. (That is, the PPH permits some ways of harming.) It may also be limited *quantitatively*. (For example, the PPH might be overridden to save a million people.). The former limitation accords with the PPH; the latter is a restriction on it.

Are people so inviolable that agents may also not violate the PPH restrictions on harming one, even if that is the only way of minimizing violations of the PPH itself? The claim that we may not violate someone's rights to minimize violations of comparable rights is sometimes called the "paradox of deontology." Some claim that if we really *care* about rights, we should minimize their violation, even if this requires us to violate comparable rights. Those who agree with this, say they cannot see how one person's right could stand in the way of minimizing the violation of comparable rights. If they nevertheless think we should not violate the restrictions of the PPH, it is because they are concerned with the agent who would act, not with the rights of the potential victim per se. This model derives the constraints on violating rights to minimize rights violations from "inside (the agent) out (to the victim)" rather than from "outside the agent (in the victim's right) in (to the agent)" (Anderson 1993; Darwall 1982). Does the agent-focused approach explain the constraint?

The agent-focused explanation of the constraint on minimizing rights violations has frequently employed the idea of agent relativity. On this view, each of us has duties that are fundamentally relative to the particular agent we are. Some argue that both consequentialist and nonconsequentialist theories can embrace agent-relativity. For example, Sen argues that, although each agent has the same, agent-neutral, duty to produce the best state of affairs, from each agent's perspective, the state of affairs in which he kills one person is worse than one in which another agent kills more people (1982). Hence, each individual has a duty to avoid his killing.

This is an agent-relative consequentialist system since there are multiple agent-relative best outcomes, not just one agent-neutral best outcome that different people are in different positions to forward. But how can this approach explain a constraint (which I believe does exist) on my killing one person in order to save a greater number of people whose rights I either have or will *myself* endanger? If I do not kill the single person, the consequences will be a world in which I am the killer of a greater number of people, and this seems like the worse world from my perspective. So if, according to this approach, I must produce the best world, I should kill the one. This, I believe, is the wrong conclusion.

A nonconsequentialist agent-relativist might argue that we have special responsibilities to our victim (who is the person we will kill, not the ones we let die), even if killing him would promote better agent-neutral consequences. That is, our victim's interests are magnified from our perspective (Fried 1978; Nagel 1986). However, if the only way to save a greater number whose rights we ourselves have endangered or will endanger is by killing the one, why should our responsibility to our many victims not dictate that we kill the one? Yet, this is the wrong conclusion.

In order to avoid these problems, both consequentialist and nonconsequentialist agent-relativists might give special weight to an agent's present acts. They might claim that we should be especially responsible for what we do and what we produce *now*, by contrast with our past and future acts. But, why should our current actions and consequences take moral precedence over our past or future ones? Why should *we, now* be so important?

There are, I believe, agent-focused views that are not essentially agent-relative. While they focus on the quality of an agent's act or state of mind, rather than on a victim's right, they do not take note of the "agent's mark" on the act, victim or outcome. For example, the quality of the act or state of mind in which an agent must engage if he kills the one person is found repellant. The act would be the agent's if he did it, but it is not essentially its being *his* rather than what it is in itself that repels him (Nagel 1986; Williams 1981). Advocates of this view might claim it explains why someone should not kill one person to save a greater number of people even from her *own* future bad acts. The explanatory structure of this duty-based constraint is essentially the same as a rights-based constraint. In both, one instance of either an act-type or right-type stands in the way of minimizing misconduct involving many instances of the same act-type or right-type. If the logic of concern for the duty does not require that we minimize its violation but simply not violate it, why does the logic of the concern for the right require that we minimize its violation?

Now consider the Art Works Case: If someone loves beauty, he will be disposed to preserve and not destroy art works. What should this person do if he must destroy one artwork to preserve several equally good ones? Presumably it is permissible for him to destroy one to save the five. This suggests that the constraint on harming persons is not derived from inside the agent out, but from *outside* her in, since the constraint reflects the kind of entity she would act on – a person, not a work of art.

Consequently, I advocate a victim-focused, rights-based account of constraints. Are there any problems this approach cannot explain? Suppose the only way we can prevent five people from being killed in violation of the PPH is to kill one person, A, in violation of the PPH. Does it make sense to express concern for the inviolability of the five by treating A as *violable* for their sakes? But then morality would say that sometimes it is permissible to treat people inconsistently with PPH restrictions, and this just means that people are less inviolable than they would be if it were impermissible to do this. It is true that if we do not kill A, more people will be seriously violated. But this does not mean that their *inviolability* is less. Inviolability is a status. It defines what we can permissibly do to people rather than what actually happens to them. If the five are killed because A is not killed, morality does not endorse (make permissible) their being killed. By contrast, if it were permissible to kill A to save the five, the *inviolability* of all six would be lower. After all, to permit the killing of A implies we may kill any one else in similar circumstances and that morality *endorses* killing people in this way.

The explanation I have offered for why it is impermissible to kill A to save others from being killed *puts emphasis on what it is permissible to do to people rather than on what happens to them. Unlike the agent-relative account, it does not focus on what I do rather than what others do.* The fact that if I kill someone, *I* would be acting now and the victim would be mine does not play a pivotal role in explaining *why* I must not kill him. We explain *that* by focusing on each person's inviolability. His right, not my agency, constitutes the moral constraint. The fact that the other five have this same right does not diminish the constraint against violating the one's rights.

Thus, my account highlights an *agent-neutral value*: the high inviolability of persons. Each agent must respect this value and does so in being constrained by the rights of the first person he encounters, even though the identity of this person will differ for each agent. This agent-neutral value is not a consequentialist value we bring about through action or omission. The value already resides *in* persons.

If a person has a high degree of inviolability, she will have a strong right protecting her. Hence, another way to put the argument I have given for not killing the one is that the importance of persons can be expressed by rights being strong, rather than by their being weaker so that we may minimize violations of them by transgressing them. It would be *self-defeating* for it to be permissible to violate a strong right which itself claims that someone should not be used in order to stop rights violations, in order to stop rights violations.

If people are morally inviolable in a certain way, then, I believe, they have a *higher* – and not merely a different – status. It might be argued that a creature has a higher status if we must harm one of them to prevent harm to many. But we must remember that if the one person may be sacrificed, then those others may, in the appropriate circumstances, also be sacrificed and this lowers their status.

The form of this argument, which focuses on status, might be extended to explain why other rights may not be transgressed. For example, if it were permissible to transgress a right to free speech in order to prevent emotional harm to people, this would imply that even those people who benefit by not being harmed have a weaker right to free speech. But one's status may be higher if one's ability to speak freely is more worthy of protection than one's emotions, because one should have the capacity to deal with these as an individual. In a sense, even the victim benefits by the right not being limited.

Suppose people have a right not to be harmed even to minimize violation of comparable rights of *others*. From behind a veil of ignorance (the *ex ante* perspective), no one knows whether she would be the single person sacrificed or one of the many whose rights would be protected. However, everyone would know that her chances of being one of the many who would be saved is greater than of being the one sacrificed. Why would it not be rational for each to agree to forego a right not to be sacrificed for others; after all, this would reduce the chances that one's own right would be violated?

Moral theories seeking to maximize each person's *ex ante* probability of some good would justify killing in many cases. Suppose a community considers purchasing an ambulance. They know they will save more lives if they have one, but they also foresee that in speeding through town, the ambulance will kill a few people. Now, imagine that we can save still more lives by attaching a device to the ambulance which prevents the driver from swerving to miss a pedestrian whenever swerving would decrease the number of people who live. Using this device would maximize the *ex ante* probability of survival of each person (Ambulance Case). Nonetheless, I believe an agreement to use the device would not make its use legitimate. In general, we cannot permissibly "bargain away" our moral status not to be treated in certain ways to increase our life prospects or minimize rights violations. Our moral status is inalienable. (Although we may permissibly waive our rights supererogatorily and sacrifice ourselves when we want to save others.)

VII   Nonabsoluteness of Constraints

Even internally complex constraints might not be absolute. Although nonconsequentialists must explain when they may be overridden, I shall not attempt to do that here. The point I wish to emphasize is that even if the constraints might be legitimately overridden to achieve some greater goods, this need not imply that they may permissibly be overridden in pursuit of personal goals – not even if the pursuit of those same personal goals legitimates failing to pursue that greater good. The relationship here seems intransitive. Suppose "G" stands for "greater good;" "P", for "personal interests and goals;" "C", for "duty to respect a constraint," and ">" means "may permissibly override." "P > G" and "G > C" may both be true, and yet (P > C) may not be. Suppose someone insisted on transitivity. Then she would need to deny that P > G (i.e., deny prerogatives) or hold that constraints are absolute to avoid P > C.

To defend the intransitivity thesis, we shall assume our discussion of prerogatives explains why P > G and try to show that sometimes G > C. Ordinarily promises morally constrain us. Yet it might sometimes be permissible to break even an important promise (e.g., a bodyguard's promise to protect her employer's life) to save thousands of people. We might permissibly break the promise even if saving the thousands is supererogatory because the sacrifice required to save them is great. This supports the claim that G > C, even if P > G. Nevertheless, we might be required to suffer grave personal loss to respect the constraint (e.g., the bodyguard might have to endanger his life to keep his promise). Hence, −(P > C). So the intransitivity is true. We now see that there are two ways to measure the moral significance of acts: (1) how great a personal loss we are required to suffer to perform them; and (2) the capacity of one act to take precedence over another. Maximizing the good may be more important by measure (2), but not by measure (1); abiding by constraints may be more important by measure (1) and not by (2).

How to explain the intransitivity and the conflicts between these two measures? Constraints are minimum standards we must all meet. We may be required to sacrifice our personal goals to meet these standards, but not to go beyond them. That explains P > G even if -(P > C). Someone might suggest that G > C if the loss *to* the agent of not achieving G exceeds the amount she would have to sacrifice to respect C. But someone might violate C for G even though she cares more about C than G. The evidence for this is that she would suffer a greater personal loss to abide by C than to bring about G. In short, the proper solution is not to "personalize" the loss of G. Rather, the agent understands that promoting the greater good is, from an impartial perspective, morally more important than respecting the constraint.

In essence, my account explains the intransitivity in the relation among prerogatives, constraints, and the pursuit of the greater good in a nonconsequentialist theory by noting that the precedence relation in each premise is based on a different factor: P > G reflects the entitlement of each individual as an end-in-herself not to sacrifice for the greater good; G > C reflects the impartial weight of the good, while −(P > C) reflects the moral importance of minimal standards in relation to personal interests. We should not expect transitivity if different factors account for precedence relations. (Even if the same factors explain the precedence relation in the first two premises, intransitivity may still arise from what I call the Principle of Contextual Interaction: the interaction of P and C could produce a new factor not present when P and G and G and C interact.)

VIII   Nonconsequentialist Principles for Aiding and Aggregating

Nonconsequentialism should not only tell us when there is a duty to aid; it very likely offers distinctive principles of *how* to aid that may conflict with the goal of maximizing the good. It also may provide distinctive reasons for maximizing the good. In this section, I shall consider these principles and reasons.

Suppose we cannot help everyone in need because each needs some scarce resource. Different principles exist for different situations: (a) there may be true scarcity so that more of the resource will not appear; (b) there may be temporary scarcity, so we can eventually help everyone; (c) we may be uncertain whether we are in (a) or (b). I shall focus on (a).

Suppose we are dealing with two-way conflict cases between potential recipients. When there are an equal number of people in conflict who stand to lose the same if not aided and gain the same if aided (and all other morally relevant factors are the same), fairness dictates giving each side an equal chance for the resource by using a random decision procedure. But there may be a conflict situation in which *different* numbers of relevantly similar people are on either side and they stand to lose and gain the same thing. This raises the question of whether nonconsequentialism requires us to give each person an equal chance to be helped, or permits us to aggregate and help the greater number of people.

Some have argued that in conflicts like this, it is worse for the greater number if they die, but better for the lesser number, and there is no impartial point of view from which to judge that it is worse if more die. However, the following Aggregative Argument suggests, this view is flawed: (1) Using Pareto Optimality, we see that it is worse for both B and C to die than for only B to die – even though it is not worse for B. (2) It is worse to a still greater degree, if B, C, and D die. Our judgment that the world is worse to a greater degree, although it is also only worse for one additional person, by comparison to what is true if B and C die, is made from a point of view outside that of any person (this goes beyond Pareto Optimality). (3) A world in which A dies and B survives is just as bad as a world in which B dies and A survives. This is true, from an impartial point of view, even though the worlds are not equally preferred by A and B. (4) Given (3), we can substitute A for B on one side of the moral equation in (1) and get that it is worse if B and C die than if A dies. Nonconsequentialists, as well as consequentialists, can evaluate states of affairs from an impartial point of view.

Although it would be worse that B and C die than that A dies, that does not necessarily mean that it is right for us to save B and C rather than A. As nonconsequentialists, we cannot automatically assume it is morally permissible to maximize the good, for this may violate justice or fairness. Some might claim that if we save B and C on the basis of (4), we abandon A to save the greater number without giving her a chance and this is unfair. They might object that we could generate an intransitivity, where ">" means "clearly ought to be saved", B + C > B quite strictly, A = B quite strictly, but $-(B + C > A)$, because it could be unfair to deprive someone of his chance.

But is it really wrong to produce the best outcome in this case? Here are two arguments against its being wrong. The Consistency Argument *in*directly shows that in saving the greater number, we need not be overriding fairness or justice: In many other cases, nonconsequentialists will not violate justice to save the greater number. For example, they will not kill one to save five. Moreover, they would not deprive a janitor of a chance for an organ transplant simply because a doctor who can save the life of a third party also needs the organ. The fact that nonconsequentialists will often not sacrifice fairness to save an additional life, but they will, in conflicts, save five rather than one, suggests that fairness is not overridden in this latter case. Hence, fairness does not require that we give A a chance.

Second, the Balancing Argument claims that in a conflict, justice demands that each person on one side should have her interests balanced against those of one person on the opposing side; those that are not balanced out in the larger group help determine that the larger group should be saved. If we instead toss a coin between one person and any number on the other side, giving each person an equal chance, we would behave no differently than if it were a contest between one and one. If the presence of each additional person would make no difference, this seems to deny the equal significance of each person. Thus, justice does not conflict with producing the best outcome. (Some might suggest we should give chances in proportion to the numbers of people in each group, but I think this is a mistake.) Hence, aggregation might be required, but for distinctly nonconsequentialist reasons.

How might we extend the nonconsequentialist principles to conflicts when the individuals are not equally needy? Consider a case where the interests of two people conflict with the interests of one. The potential loss of the one (n1) is equal to the potential loss of one of the tandem (n2). The potential loss of the second of the pair (x) is less than the loss of n1 or n2. A consequentialist claims we must maximize good and therefore choose $n_2 + x$. A contractarian arguing behind the veil of ignorance might agree if she is trying to maximize the ex ante expected good of each person. Must a nonconsequentialist, committed to balancing equals, do the same? No, at least not always. Suppose x needs a cure of a sore throat and n is having his life extended ten years. To preclude n1's chance to live in order to gain a small utility to x fails to show adequate respect for n1, since from her partial point of view she is not indifferent between her survival and n2's. In short, we have another intransitivity: although $n_2 + x$ is better than helping only n_2, and helping n_1 is as good as helping n_2, helping $n_2 + x$ is not necessarily better than helping n_1.

This form of reasoning gives equal consideration to each individual's partial point of view from an impartial point of view, so it combines subjective and objective perspectives. Hence, I call it *Sobjectivity*. It implies that certain extra goods (like the throat cure) can be morally irrelevant; I call this the Principle of Irrelevant Goods. Whether a good is irrelevant is context-dependent. Curing a sore throat is morally irrelevant when others' lives are at stake, but not when others ear aches are. The Sore Throat Case shows we must refine the claim that what we owe each person is to balance her interests against the equal interests of an opposing person and let the remainder help determine the outcome.

We might explain this conclusion by saying that any loss or gain (X) that is significantly less than N, and so could not be a contestant on its own against N, cannot legitimately determine any distribution in combination with other losses or gains. I call this Sobjectivity 1. But suppose X is saving someone's leg? We should save one person's life rather than someone else's leg when these are the only morally relevant considerations. Perhaps, though, it is better to save one person's life and a second person's leg than to give a third person an equal chance at having his life saved. If so, we might embrace Sobjectivity 2, which is based on the following reasoning. According to the nonconsequentialist each of us has a duty to suffer at least a relatively minimal loss (e.g., a sore throat) to save another person's life, and if it matters to each person that his be the life saved, each should suffer a minimal loss to give someone a chance at life. Further, so long as the small loss is a duty any given person has to suffer, *no number of them can aggregate*, even when combined with another's life. Where the loss X is greater than the required loss (e.g., losing a leg), then we should prevent N2 + X rather than N1. By contrast, according to a consequentialist, what an individual has a duty to do has nothing to do with what may or may not be aggregated, and an aggregate of losses can weigh against a greater individual loss.

How about the following cases? Even if, according to a nonconsequentialist, no one has a duty to lose three fingers to save a life, from an impartial point of view, we might still think that giving one person a chance at life is more important than saving another's three fingers, even given that we will save a third person's life, too. Then, we would reject Sobjectivity 2 for Sobjectivity 3, which insists that it is from a view outside that of any of the party's duties that we decide matters. A further characterization of the relevant and irrelevant goods might be as follows: a certain good would be relevant in a choice between two lives in the sense of making the side to which it is added deserve a greater proportional chance of winning, even though it had no weight on its own in one individual when counted against saving a life, if the aggregation of many instances of it alone could have proportional weight against saving a life. An extra good could be determinative of our choice when it is conjoined with one life against another life, if that good on its own merits a proportional chance against a life when the choice is about whom to aid.

Notice that approaches like Sobjectivity 2 and 3, which allow balancing and aggregation of contestants and noncontestants, seem to stand as a critique of contractualist theories (Scanlon, 1985), which claim that to raise an objection to a proposed policy, an individual must do so in virtue of the effects of the policy on him alone. But in Sobjectivity 2, a person complains that since there is someone on his side whose life is at stake, his leg should matter, even if it would not matter alone against someone's life.

It is possible that we should restrict Sobjectivity 3 to choosing whom to aid "here and now" (e.g., in an emergency room) and adopt Sobjectivity 4 to make *macro* decisions, for example, whether to invest in research to cure a disease that will kill a few people or in research to cure a disease that will only wither an arm in many. Unlike Sobjectivity 3, Subjectivity 4 permits aggregation of significant (not insignificant) losses to many people to outweigh even greater losses to a few, even when no individual person in the larger group will lose as much as each individual in the smaller group will lose. Thus, Sobjectivity 4, but not 3, is in conflict with common components of contractualist theories. These are helping the worse off first and pairwise comparison (which requires that the side we help must have at least as many people who will suffer as great a loss individually as those on the other side).

Sobjectivity 4 does not imply that many arms are the *equivalent* of a life they can outweigh, in the way that one life is the equivalent of another life. Rather, Sobjectivity 4 implies that we will not bear the *cost* of many arms to save a life. This is supported by the fact that Sobjectivity 4 (unlike Sobjectivity 3) should not be used to decide whom to *harm* in order to aid others. For example, if a threat were headed toward any number of people who would each lose an arm, it would be wrong to turn the threat toward the one person who would be killed. This contrasts with the permissibility of turning a threat away from two people who would be killed and toward one who will be killed. Nor should Sobjectivity 4 be defended by arguing that just as it would be rational for each individual to bear a small risk of death (e.g., from taking a medicine) in order to have a good quality of life, so when there is a high probability of losing an arm (since many peope will lose arms), we may accept a low probability of dying (since only a few will die) in order to save arms. In the multiperson, but not the single person, scenario, we know that someone will die and this is a morally significant difference.

A nonconsequentialist theory of the distribution of scarce resources should also deal with situations involving two candidates for a scarce resource when only one can be helped, seeing if certain characteristics that one candidate has to a greater degree than another are morally relevant to deciding who gets the resource. I call this the problem of interpersonal allocation when there is *intra*personal aggregation, because one candidate has everything the other has and more. Principles I described that apply when the additional goods on one side are distributed over several people can be revised so as to apply when additional goods are concentrated in one person rather than another.

A system I suggest for evaluating candidates for a resource starts off with only three factors – need, urgency, and outcome – but it could add other factors later. Urgency is defined as how badly off someone will be if he is not helped. Need is how badly someone's life *will have gone* if he is not helped. Outcome is defined as the difference in expected outcome produced by the resource relative to the expected outcome if one is not helped.

The neediest may not be the most urgent. Suppose A will die in a month at age 65 unless helped now and B will die in a year at age 20 unless helped now. I suggest that B is less urgent but needier, since one's life will have gone worse (other things equal) if one dies at 20 rather than at 65. To consider how much weight to give to need, we hold the two other factors constant and imagine two candidates who differ only in neediness. A consequentialist argument for taking differential need into account in cases where life is at stake could be that there is something like diminishing marginal utility of life (i.e., a better outcome is provided if we give a unit of life to those who have had less). I do not think this is necessarily true.

One nonconsequentialist argument for taking differential need into account is fairness: give to those who, if not helped, will have had less of the good (e.g., life) that our resource can provide before giving to those who will have had more even if they are not helped. Fairness is a value that depends on comparisons between people. But even if we do not compare candidates, it can simply be of greater moral value to give a certain unit of life to a person who has had less of life (McKerlie 1997).

But need will matter more the more absolutely and comparatively needy a candidate is, and some differences in need may be governed by a Principle of Irrelevant Need. This is especially so when each candidate is absolutely needy, a big gain for each is at stake, and if the needier person is helped he will wind up having more of the good (e.g., a longer life) than the person who was originally less needy than he.

Suppose there is conflict between helping the neediest and helping the most urgent (where outcomes are the same). I claim that when there is true scarcity, it can be more important to help the neediest than the urgent, but if scarcity is only temporary, the urgent should be helped first, since the neediest will be helped eventually anyway.

Still there are constraints on the relevance of need in a nonconsequentialist theory of distribution. Giving a resource to the person who will have had less overall of the good it can provide may be impermissible if it fails to respect the rights of each person. For example, consider another context: If two people have a human right to free speech, how long someone's right has already been respected may be irrelevant in deciding whom to help retain free speech. If having health or life for a number of years were a human right, it might not be appropriate to ration resources on the basis of the degree to which people's rights have already been met.

Now we come to outcome. A consequentialist might consider all effects of a resource. I suggest that for nonconsequentialists (1) effects on third parties whom a resource helps only indirectly (e.g., a patient lives because his doctor gets the resource) should be given less weight than its direct effects, and (2) some differences in outcome between candidates may be irrelevant because achieving them is not the goal of the particular "sphere" which controls the resource (e.g., that one potential recipient in the health care sphere will write a novel if he receives a scarce drug should not count in favor of his getting it). Other differences in expected outcome between candidates may be covered by the Principle of Irrelevant Good, even if they are relevant to the sphere. For example, relative to the fact that each person stands to avoid death and live for ten years, that one person can get a somewhat better quality of life or an additional year of life should not determine who is helped, given that each wants what she can get. One explanation for this is that what both are capable of achieving (ten years) is the part of the outcome about which each cares most in the context, and each wants to be the one to survive. The extra good is frosting on the cake. The fact that someone might accept an additional risk of death (as in surgery) to achieve the "cake plus frosting" for himself does not mean that he would want to accept an additional risk of death so that another person who stands to get the greater good has a greater chance to live. For these reasons, Sobjectivity requires that we ignore the extra good in allocating, even though consequentialism and ex ante maximization of individual expected good would do otherwise.

However, in life and death decisions, any *significant* difference between two people in expected life years may play a role in selecting whom to help. This result follows from Sobjectivity 3. Still, because the large additional benefit would be concentrated in the same person who would already be benefited by having her life saved for at least the same period as the other candidate, it should count for less in determining who gets the resource than if the additional benefit were distributed to a third person. This is on account of fairness and the diminishing moral value of providing an additional benefit to someone who would already be greatly benefited. Large differences in expected quality of life among candidates for a resource should count in situations where improving quality of life is the point of the resource.

What if taking care of the neediest or most urgent conflicts with producing the best difference in outcome? Rather than always favoring the worst off, we might assign multiplicative factors in accord with need and urgency by which we multiply the expected outcome of the neediest and urgent. These factors represent the greater moral significance of a given outcome going to the neediest (or most urgent), but the nonneediest could still get a resource if her expected differential outcome was very large.

We can summarize these views quantitatively in what I call an *outcome modification procedure for allocation*. If we first assign points for each candidate's differential expected outcome, we then assign multiplicative factors for need and urgency in accordance with their importance relative to each other and to outcome. We multiply the outcome points by these factors. The candidate with the highest points gets the resource.

Sometimes the conflict between helping different people can be reduced because it is possible to help everyone to some extent, even though not completely. For example, imagine the following case where each stands to lose and gain the same thing and we can either (a) certainly save five lives on one island, or (b) certainly save one life on another island, or (c) reduce the chances of saving the five in such a way that all six now share the same reduced chance of being saved together. I argued above that a nonconsequentialist should prefer (a) to (b), but it is still possible for her to prefer (c) to both, at least (the suggestion is) so long as we reduce the chance of saving the majority by no more than the proportional weight (1/6) of the minority. There is a preference for (c) over (a), even though the expected utility of these two outcomes is the same, because all will now have a chance to share the same fate.

Finally, we should be aware that many real-life cases in which we can help everyone to some degree are even more complicated. A nonconsequentialist theory must deal with dividing resources among individuals who stand to lose and gain to different degrees, where the probability of satisfying the needs is different, and where the number of people who fall into different need/gain categories differs.

References

Anderson, E.: *Ethics and Economics* (Cambridge, MA: Harvard University Press, 1993).
Bennett, J.: "Morality and Consequences," *The Tanner Lectures on Human Values* (Salt Lake City: University of Utah Press, 1981).

Darwall, S.: "Agent-Centered Restrictions from the Inside Out," *Philosophical Studies* (1982).

Foot, P.: "Killing and Letting Die," in J. Garfield and P. Hennessey, eds., *Abortion: Moral and Legal Perspectives* (Amherst, MA.: University of Massachusetts Press, 1984).

——: "Utilitarianism and the Virtues," *Proceedings of the American Philosophical Association* (1983).

——: "Euthanasia." In her *Vices and Virtues* (Berkeley: University of California Press, 1978a).

——: "The Problem of Abortion and the Doctrine of Double Effect." In her *Vices and Virtues* (1978b).

Fried, C.: *Right and Wrong* (Cambridge, MA.: Harvard University Press, 1978).

Kamm, F. M.: *Morality, Mortality II* (New York: Oxford University Press, 1996).

——: *Morality, Mortality I* (New York: Oxford University Press, 1993).

——: "Harming Some to Aid Others," *Philosophical Studies* (1989).

——: "Nonconsequentialism, the Person as End-in-Itself, and the Significance of Status," *Philosophy and Public Affairs* (1992).

Kant, I.: *Groundwork of the Metaphysic of Morals*, trans. and ed. Paton, H. J. (New York: Harper & Row, 1964).

Kagan, S.: *The Limits of Morality* (New York: Oxford University Press, 1989).

McKerlie, D.: "Priority and Time." *Canadian Journal of Philosophy* (1997).

Nagel, T.: *The View from Nowhere* (New York: Oxford University Press, 1986).

Quinn, W.: "Actions, Intentions, and Consequences: The Doctrine of Double Effect." In his *Morality and Action* (Cambridge: Cambridge University Press, 1993).

Rachels, J.: "Active and Passive Euthanasia," *The New England Journal of Medicine* (1975).

Ross, W. D.: *The Right and the Good* (Oxford: Oxford University Press, 1930).

Scanlon, T.: "Contractualism and Utilitarianism," in A. Sen and B. Williams, *Utilitarianism and Beyond* (Cambridge: Cambridge University Press, 1985).

Scheffler, S.: *The Rejection of Consequentialism* (New York: Oxford University Press, 1982).

Sen, A.: "Rights and Agency," *Philosophy & Public Affairs* (1982).

Thomson, J.: "The Trolley Problem," *The Yale Law Journal* (1985).

Williams, B.: "Utilitarianism and Moral Self-Indulgence," in his *Moral Luck* (Berkeley: University of California Press, 1981).

Chapter 12

Kantianism

Thomas E. Hill, Jr.

Among the most basic ideas in Kant's moral philosophy are these: that moral philosophers must use an *a priori* method, that moral duties are categorical imperatives, and that moral agency presupposes autonomy of the will. In the second section of his *Groundwork of the Metaphysics of Morals* Kant develops each of these ideas in an argument for his central thesis that the idea that we have moral duties presupposes that we are rational agents with autonomy (Kant 1964; abbreviated as G, with citations to the standard Prussian Academy edition, volume IV, by bracketed numbers). The conclusion and each step of the argument remain controversial. Kant's admirers usually see here a great advance in moral theory, but critics often find Kant's contentions obscure and implausible.

When a philosopher inspires such extremes of admiration and disdain as Kant does in his ethical writings, we may well ask ourselves whether Kant's friends and his critics are focusing their attention on the same ideas. Elementary misunderstandings of Kant's ethics are common, and serious Kant scholars often disagree about interpretations. Insightful core ideas may be dismissed or ignored because they are conflated with more radical, controversial ideas. My aim, then, is to do some much needed sorting among the doctrines attributed to Kant. What is central, and what is peripheral? What is commonplace, and what is radical? Which assertions are preliminary starting points, and which are the more remote conclusions? Considering these questions is necessary for a balanced assessment of the strengths and weaknesses of Kant's ethics.

In my remarks below I comment in turn on each of the major themes mentioned above, trying to separate the more widely appealing core points from the more controversial. The modest version of each basic theme, I suggest, leads naturally to the next. Together the steps reflect a Kantian line of reflection for his contention that analysis reveals that the idea that we have moral duties presupposes the idea that we are rational agents with autonomy. To preview, my main suggestions will be these:

(1) Kant's insistence on an *a priori* method, in its modest version, stems in large

part from his belief that moral theory should begin with an analysis of the idea of a moral requirement (duty). Despite his strong rhetoric about setting aside everything empirical, Kant's main point was that empirical methods are unsuitable for analysis of moral concepts and defense of basic principles of rational choice. The reason that Kant insisted on an *a priori* method was not that he believed in rational intuition of moral truths, opposed naturalistic explanations, assumed that duties are imposed by noumenal will, or thought that empirical facts are irrelevant to moral decisions.

(2) Kant thought that analysis of the ordinary idea of duty showed that we regard duties as categorical imperatives. That is, when we suppose that we have a duty we are thereby supposing that we have sufficient (overriding) reason to act accordingly and not just because doing so furthers our (desire based) personal ends. The modest point here is not that duties must always be experienced as unwelcome demands that must be fulfilled from a sense of constraint. Kant's point is also independent of his dubious view that substantive principles regarding lying, obedience to law, sexual purity, etc., are exceptionless and applicable in the same way across all times and places.

(3) The analysis of duty is for Kant merely a step on the way to the conclusion that in thinking of ourselves as having moral duties we must think of ourselves as rational agents with autonomy of the will. The basic point is that in order to be a moral agent, with duties, one must be able to understand and be moved by the sort of reasons that categorical imperatives claim we have. Categorical imperatives are addressed to deliberating rational agents presumed able to follow reasons independent of their concern for happiness and personal ends. To think that we can guide our decisions by such non-instrumental reasons, we must conceive ourselves as agents that implicitly acknowledge and respect the noninstrumental rational standards presupposed by categorical imperatives. As moral agents we might not always live up to the standards that we acknowledge, but our capacity to follow them presupposes that we accept them as rational grounds for our decisions and judgments. More controversially, in regarding our duties as categorical imperatives we presuppose that our disposition to judge our conduct by these basic standards is a constitutive feature of being moral agents, and not something we do because of a prior commitment to following external authorities, tradition, or common sentiments. In a sense, then, particular duties can be understood as requirements that rational agents impose on themselves, and following them is a way of being self-governing.

I   The *A Priori* Method in Moral Philosophy

Kant repeatedly emphasizes in the *Groundwork*, and elsewhere, that we cannot find answers to the fundamental questions of moral philosophy by empirical methods (G 74–80 [406–12], 92–4 [425–7].). To gain a theoretical understanding of nature we must rely on experience. We must use empirical concepts as well as some basic categories of thought. Ordinary, common sense knowledge of what there is, how things work, and what is needed to achieve our goals must also rely on experience. But moral philosophy, Kant insists, is not an empirical science, and its conclusions are not simply inferences from observations of human behavior, emotional responses, and social practices. Rather, to address the basic questions of moral philosophy, according to Kant, we must use an *a priori* method that does not base its conclusions on what we learn from experience. Kant rejects many of the prominent moral theories of his day (e.g. British "moral sense" theories) because they treat moral questions as if they were empirical questions. He rejects, for example, Frances Hutcheson's view that moral goodness is a natural property of actions that causes human beings to feel approbation (Schneewind 1990: 503–24). On this view, the answer to "Which acts are morally good?" would be discoverable by observing what sorts of acts human beings tend to approve? Kant criticizes other theories for mixing empirical and *a priori* arguments in discussions of basic issues that, he thinks, should be approached in a purely *a priori* manner. For example, Kant strongly disapproves of moral philosophies that argue that helping those in need is right and reasonable *because* experience shows that charitable people tend to be happier than uncharitable people.

Why begin moral philosophy by an *a priori* investigation instead of empirical studies? The explanation, I think, concerns Kant's understanding of what the basic questions of ethics are. In the *Groundwork*, he describes his task as seeking out and establishing the supreme principle of morality (G 60 [392]). Judging by how Kant then proceeds to argue, it seems that "seeking out" the supreme principle is a matter of articulating an abstract, basic and comprehensive principle that can be shown to be a deep presupposition in ordinary moral thinking. "Establishing" the principle, I take it, is the further task of showing that the principle is rational to accept and follow. In addressing the first task Kant begins, provisionally, by assuming some very general moral ideas that he takes to be widely accepted, in fact, part of ordinary rational knowledge of morality. These assumptions include the special value of a good will and the idea of duty as more than prudence and efficiency in pursuing one's ends. That these are only assumed provisionally is shown by the fact that, even at the end of second section, Kant forcefully reminds us that his "analytic" mode of argument has not proved we really have moral duties (G 112 [444–5], 107–8 [440–1, 114–15 [446–7]). Instead, it only serves to reveal presuppositions of the common moral idea that we have duties. For all we know at this point, morality might be an illusion. Despite this disclaimer, the results that Kant claims to reach by the analytic method are significant: common moral belief presupposes that the several formulas of the Categorical Imperative are morally fundamental, that rationality is not exclusively instrumental, and that moral agents are to be seen as legislators of moral laws as well as subject to them. These particular conclusions, however, are supposed *results* of the *a priori* method of analysis, not assumptions used to justify the method. Other philosophers might radically disagree with Kant's results but still see the value of his analytic approach.

Kant's main idea is simple and familiar in philosophy. We make use of moral concepts, some of which seem pervasive and essential features of our moral thinking and discourse, even when we disagree in our particular judgments. By reflecting on the meaning, implications, and presuppositions of these concepts, we may be able to understand them, and ourselves, better. To say that the process of reflection is *a priori* is not to imply that it could be done by hypothetical persons with no empirical concepts or experience of life. It is just to say that we are examining our ideas in a rational reflective way, looking for their structure and presuppositions. The aim here is not to explain the causes or effects of behavior that seems to be guided by moral ideas but only to gain a clearer grasp of the content and implications of those ideas themselves. Experiments, surveys, and comparative studies of different cultures can be valuable for many purposes, but they do not serve the philosophical purpose that Kant's analytical method was meant to address.

There was another important reason why Kant wanted moral philosophy to begin with an *a priori* method. This stems from his conviction that believing that we are under moral obligation entails believing that we are subject to a rational requirement of a special sort (a "command of reason"). This conviction was embedded in a long tradition, and Kant thought that it was part of ordinary understanding of morality. The problem is that we can question whether the *apparent* rationality of moral demands is an illusion. In fact reading the British moralists Hutcheson, Hume, and others would naturally raise doubts in those (like Kant) who were deeply influenced by the natural law tradition. Such doubts, Kant thought, call for a response, an effort to vindicate the apparent (and commonly believed) assumption that moral principles express requirements that we would be irrational to disregard (G 114–31 [446–63].) A positive response to the doubts would be to supplement (and build on) the analytical argument mentioned above with further argument that we really have reason-based duties, or at least that it is necessary to presuppose this for practical purposes. To do so would be to show that morality is not a mere illusion. Like the task of analysis, this task, which Kant undertakes in the notoriously difficult third section of the *Groundwork*, is again not one that could be accomplished by empirical investigations. The problem is to establish that guiding one's life by certain principles is *rationally necessary*, that one always has *sufficient reason* to do so.

Even if (contrary to Kant) there are only prudential reasons for following moral principles, to show that following them is always rational is not *simply* a matter of collecting empirical data on the effects of various behavior patterns. One would also need to argue that we always have *sufficient reason* to do what most effectively promotes the effects deemed "prudent," and this is a contested philosophical thesis that is not itself subject to empirical proof (as even most non-Kantians would agree). But the inadequacy of using an empirical method alone becomes even more evident for those who grant Kant's thesis that morality imposes categorical imperatives (G 82–8 [414–20]). According to this, moral principles are rationally necessary to follow, but their rational necessity is not merely prudential or based on hypothetical imperatives. This means (at least) that the reason for following moral principles cannot be simply that doing so serves to promote one's happiness or individual ends. Thus, the rationality of following moral principles could not be established by showing empirically that they are good guides to happiness or means that serve well our particular purposes. For not only is the idea of rationality a normative one (the previous point), but also the sort of sufficient reason that needs to be defended is more than the (empirically discernible) efficacy of our actions in achieving our ends.

This is not the place to review and assess Kant's actual argument in defense of his idea that moral requirements are *rationally necessary* to follow and even *categorically* so. And this assessment, fortunately, is not necessary for present purposes. The need that Kant saw for an *a priori* method, at least in parts of ethics, can be seen in the *problems* he posed, independently of his particular solutions. The essential point is that *if* we understand moral demands as saying to us that it is *unreasonable* not to do what is demanded, then we want some explanation and defense, especially once the seeds of philosophical doubt have been raised. All the more, if we understand moral demands as purporting to tell us what is *categorically* rational to do, then we may question whether morality's claim to be categorically rational is defensible. If, like most contemporary philosophers, we understand that claims about what is *reasonable*, *rational*, supported by *reasons,* etc., are irreducibly evaluative, practical, claims, then it becomes clear that the problems cannot be resolved by empirical investigation alone. The problems may prove to be irresolvable, or perhaps even pseudo-problems (as Humeans think), but at least we can understand why Kant and others believe that any search for resolutions must start with rational, *a priori* reflection.

Now that we have uncovered Kant's rationale for thinking that we must employ an *a priori* method, we can respond to some common objections and clarify certain misconceptions about the method.

(1) One misunderstanding that might lead readers to be skeptical of Kant's methodology stems from the thought that the alternative to empirical methods in moral theory is appeal to rational intuition or rationalistic theological arguments. Hume's famous objections to deriving "moral distinctions" from "reason" seem primarily aimed at views of this type. If turned against Kant, however, objections to rational intuition and theological ethics would miss their mark, for Kant agrees with Hume in rejecting rational intuitionism and theology as the basis of ethics. Like Hume, Kant holds that the traditional *a priori* arguments for the existence of God are inadequate, that morality cannot be based in theology, and that reason is not an intuitive power that "sees" independent moral facts. (Kant does not deny that there is "knowledge" of moral principles and that there are "objective" moral values, but moral validity is determined by, and so not independent of, what rational agents with autonomy could or would accept.)

(2) Some moral theorists, past and present, see their main task as explaining moral phenomena as a part of the natural world. It seems obvious that we raise moral questions, praise and blame in moral terms, experience moral feelings (e.g. guilt, indignation), and are sometimes moved by our moral beliefs. Many philosophers committed to understanding the world, so far as possible, in naturalistic terms

accept the challenge of trying to explain moral phenomena (behavior, feelings, etc.) without appeal to occult, theological, or other "nonnatural" entities. The methodology needed for this project, it seems widely agreed, is empirical, at least in a broad sense. When we turn to Kant's moral philosophy we find that not only does he use terminology (e.g. the will, autonomy, intelligible world) that is outside what most naturalists consider their domain, he even insists that these moral terms cannot be understood entirely in naturalistic terms. Clearly his moral theory is not a successful fulfillment of the naturalists' project, and may even seem to reflect contempt for such a project. Thus an objection to Kant's *a priori* method might be grounded in the thought that it is a method that cannot successfully carry out the project that naturalists consider most important and may even show contempt for it.

It is true, of course, that Kant's moral philosophy is not an attempt to contribute to the naturalists' project, but this does not mean that he would regard it as an unfruitful or unimportant task for empirically oriented scientists and philosophers to undertake. Although Kant insists that the *a priori* tasks in moral theory must be undertaken first, he often refers to "practical anthropology" as empirical work that should follow and supplement basic moral theory (G 55–6 [387–8]; Kant 1997). What he had in mind (and attempted rather casually and unsystematically) was not the full naturalists' project, but his theory of knowledge is friendly to that project, at least if no more is claimed for its results than can be validly inferred from experience. Kant is committed to the position (which in fact he believed that he had proved) that all phenomena are in principle explicable by empirical, natural laws. So, although he thought that for practical purposes we must employ normative ideas that are not reducible to empirical propositions, anything that can count as observable phenomena associated with moral practices must (in principle) be amenable to empirical study and understanding. And, although he denied that empirical science can establish moral truths or vindicate their rational claim on us, his theory of knowledge allows (indeed insists) that all the *observable facts* associated with moral and immoral acts can be studied and (in principle) comprehended from an empirical perspective. This is distinct from the practical perspective we must take up when we deliberate and evaluate acts (see Allison 1991). Each perspective has its legitimate and necessary use, and limits. So, although Kant thinks the basic questions of moral philosophy cannot be answered by empirical methods, he should happily encourage naturalists' ambition to understand the phenomena associated with moral activity *so far as possible* in naturalistic terms through empirical investigations.

(3) Again, some critics familiar with Kant's philosophy as a whole may suppose that Kant's insistence on an *a priori* method is based on his controversial idea that we must think of moral agents not only in empirical terms but also under the idea of free rational agency. This involves thinking of them as belonging to an "intelligible world" that cannot be understood in the terms of empirical science (G 118–21 [450–3]). Hence one might suspect that Kant thought an *a priori* method of investigation in ethics is necessary because moral agents, as such, are not beings that we can comprehend empirically. But I think that this is a mistake, and in fact it gets the order of Kant's thought backwards. As we have seen, there are simpler and less

controversial explanations for Kant's insistence on the *a priori* method. In fact he introduces the perspective of an intelligible world into ethics not as an initial assumption but rather as a point to which he believes his analysis of common moral knowledge finally drives him. Analysis of the idea of duty shows that it presupposes the idea of rational agents with autonomy, and this idea, he argues, can be squared with his earlier conclusions about empirical knowledge only if we think of these agents as "intelligible" or noumenal beings.[1] Many philosophers who find Kant convincing at the earlier stages dissent from this last stage of the argument. There is no doubt that Kant thought it an important part of his systematic moral theory, but it is not a beginning assumption used to justify his methodology. Rather, it is a final theoretical point to which (Kant thought) his particular *a priori* argument (not the method itself) drives us. In short, his controversial views about the ultimate "Idea" of moral agents to which philosophical reflection forces us is not presupposed in the modest methodological procedures with which he begins.

(4) Finally, there is a persistent objection that, I suspect, rests partly on misunderstanding but partly on Kant's tendency to overstate his insights. The objection proceeds as follows. First we note that the reasons we give for thinking that acts are right or wrong are typically empirical facts, e.g. "That will kill him," "You intentionally deceived him," "She saved your life and needs help now," "No society could survive if it tolerated that." Then we also note that most morally sensitive persons realize that the acts picked out by simple descriptions (e.g. "killing", "deceiving") may be wrong in one situation but right in another, depending on the empirical facts of the case. So a method that excluded empirical information, it seems, will not even consider facts that are crucial to determining what is right and what is wrong. Moral decisions must be made in a complex and richly diverse world, and so it seems foolish to suppose that we can discern what is right without knowing accurately and in detail (and so empirically) what this world is like and where we stand in it at the moment.

The objection would be appropriate and (I think) devastating if directed against a moral theorist who claimed that pure reason alone can discern what we ought to do in each situation. But few, if any, today make such a claim, and certainly Kant did not. Those who agree with Kant that some fundamental moral principles can be vindicated through the use of reason are well aware that we need empirical knowledge to apply these principles to our current circumstances. We need to judge whether and how moral principles are relevant, and this requires understanding based on experience. For example, that we should treat all persons with respect, Kant thought, is an ideal norm, not something empirical science or ordinary experience can establish; but, of course, respect and disrespect are expressed in a wide variety of ways that we learn only with experience in different cultural contexts (Kant 1996: 209–13 [462–8]). Kant does not deny that we (rightly) cite facts in explaining the reasons why some particular act is morally required or forbidden; he merely agrees with Hume that empirical facts *alone* do not establish any "ought" claim. Kant was indeed extremely rigoristic by not allowing that familiar moral principles (e.g. about lying) need to be qualified, but his rigidity on these matters cannot be blamed on his rejection of empirical methods for the basic issues in moral theory. Notoriously, Kant endorses some principles in an absolute, unqualified form, and most of us will agree that inflexible adherence to such rules is an over-simple response to complex moral problems. His extreme stand on lying, revolution, and sexual practices, however, does not follow from his thesis that moral philosophy should *begin* with *a priori* methods, e.g. of analysis (Kant 1996: 176–7 [422–3], 96–7 [320], 178–7 [424–5]; Kant 1949). The problem, rather, lies in his thinking that rigid opposition to lying (etc.) is required by the Categorical Imperative.

There remains serious controversy, however, on two related points. *First*, many philosophers would deny that an *a priori* use of reason can establish even one basic moral principle. This objection comes not only from those who think that empirical methods can establish moral principles, but also from those who think that moral principles cannot be established by any method because they have no objective standing. This is a perennial controversy, but it is about the *results* that can be established by an *a priori* method rather than about the value of the method in general. *Second*, even those who side with Kant on the first point may reasonably worry that Kant himself tries to make *too much* of ethics independent of empirical knowledge. It is one thing, they may say, to suppose that some quite abstract, formal principles can be discovered and defended by an *a priori* method, but quite another (and more dubious) thing to exclude empirical facts when taking up other tasks of moral philosophy. For example, if moral philosophers, following Kant and Alan Donagan, want to try to work out a system of universally valid moral principles about substantive matters (such as lying, obedience to law, punishment, charity), then it seems only reasonable to expect that the construction must take into account our (limited) empirical knowledge about the human condition in general and about the diversity of contexts to which putative universal principles must be applied. It is still a matter of dispute how much empirical information Kant intended to exclude when he took up this project in *The Metaphysics of Morals*. His arguments often presuppose facts that could only be known empirically, but they also often raise the suspicion that his determination not to rely on empirical evidence has led to unwarranted rigidity and over-generalization. These worries and controversies cannot be lightly dismissed, but they do not call into question Kant's main reasons for adopting an *a priori* method for the basic issues in moral philosophy.

II Categorical and Hypothetical Imperatives

The vocabulary and tone of Kant's writing about morality is disturbing to many readers, especially when they contrast this with the ethical works of Hume and Aristotle. A good example is Kant's contention that there are *categorical imperatives* of morality. Kant focuses attention on what we morally *must* do, what is *necessary*, a *command* of reason, a *constraint* rather than an aid in the pursuit of happiness (G 82–8 [414–21]). We are easily reminded of angry parents who tell us, in stern imperative tones, "Do it at once, whether you want to or not." So viewed, morality can seem to be dictatorial, not intrinsically appealing or personally fulfilling. Moreover, since Kant tells us that categorical imperatives are unconditional, absolute, apodictic as opposed to mere prudential "counsels," it is natural to assume that this means that moral rules are inflexible and admit of no exceptions. This assumption may seem confirmed when we read Kant's vigorous denial that we may tell a lie to save a friend from murder and his insistence that we must obey the law even if it is imposed by a tyrant (Kant 1949; Kant 1996: 127–33 [316–23] and 176 [371]). Categorical imperatives then seem like demands that we must obey with the attitude of a dutiful soldier following orders, respecting the authority of law without regard to anything else.

Kant's moral theory no doubt contains features with which many ordinary readers, as well as opposing moral theorists, will disagree, but making some distinctions helps us to identify some possible misunderstandings and to sort the more controversial from the less controversial Kantian themes. There may remain disputes both about interpretation and plausibility, but I think that some core ideas that are manifestly at least part of Kant's thought are also quite widely accepted. Three questions, in particular, need to be considered: (1) Are categorical imperatives to be seen as disagreeable orders from an alien power with whom we cannot identify, mere pressures that we see no good reason to follow apart from possible rewards and punishments? (2) Are moral principles, as categorical imperatives, necessarily inflexible and exceptionless? (3) Is a motivating respect for principles that are categorical imperatives necessarily a sense of constraint rather than concern for the good of others?

Despite what one might initially suppose, Kant's basic position on each of these questions, I think, is quite compatible with common opinion (among philosophers and non-philosophers alike). This is not to deny, however, that Kant accepts some further related ideas that remain more controversial. Let us begin with what I take to be the core idea that moral duties are categorical imperatives, and then we can return to the three questions just mentioned.

Kant's remarks about categorical imperatives can be confusing because although he explicitly says that there can only be one categorical imperative he repeatedly writes as though there are many. Kant lists several "formulas" of the Categorical Imperative, which he says are "at bottom the same," but he also refers to more specific principles, such as "Don't lie" and "Punish all and only the guilty" as categorical imperatives (G 88–104 [420–37]; Kant 1996: 14 [221] and 105 [331]). No doubt he had in mind a primary (or strict) sense of the term when he was writing as if there is only one categorical imperative, but he then helped himself to a secondary (or less strict) sense of the term when writing about further principles that (he believed) were warranted by "the Categorical Imperative" (in the strict sense). On this hypothesis, the discrepancy (from singular to plural) becomes harmless, even though there remain questions in various contexts about which sense he had in mind.

Categorical imperatives (in both senses) are *imperatives*, which Kant calls "commands of reason." All imperatives express the idea that something ought to be done, either because it is good in itself or because it is good as a means to an end that is in some way valuable. Through the idea of "ought" they express a relation ("necessitation") between what is rational to do (an "objective principle") and the not so perfectly rational choosers ("imperfect wills") that can do what is rational but might not (G 81–4 [412–17] and G 69n [401]). So, in other words, imperatives say (truly) that we have good reason to do something even while acknowledging (implicitly) that we might in fact not do it. This applies to "hypothetical imperatives," e.g. "one ought to exercise if one aims to be strong," as well as to "categorical imperatives," e.g. "one ought to treat human beings with respect."

What, then, makes an imperative *categorical*? For both the primary and secondary senses, the core idea is that the reasons for following a "categorical imperative" are not merely that doing so will promote the ends that one happens to have, such as becoming rich or (more generally) being happy. Following categorical imperatives may often promote our personal ends, but it may not always do so. Making us happy and helping us get what we want is not what makes moral principles *categorical* imperatives; they are rational to follow, even if doing so does not make us happy or promote our personal ends. They express the idea that it is good and rational to act as they prescribe, but, unlike hypothetical imperatives, they do not simply say what is good to do as a means to getting or achieving what we want.

Furthermore, as Kant uses the term, categorical imperatives do not merely say that we have to have *some* reason to do what they prescribe. They assert that we have sufficient reason, *overriding* other considerations.[2] We always ought to follow categorical imperatives, even if they conflict with what we otherwise would have reason to do based on self-interest and our personal projects. So categorical imperatives do not simply give us "some" reason to act; they give us sufficient reasons, all things considered, reasons that override other considerations. This point, however, should not be confused with the idea that moral rules are always specific, simple, and inflexible, allowing no exceptions or variation for extraordinary circumstances. Kant himself did insist on *some* moral principles (e.g. against lying) in this rigid form, but nothing in the core idea of categorical imperatives prevents them from being vastly complex and justifiably filled with qualifications ("unless", "so long as," "but only if"). Moreover, as Kant says, some ethical principles only say that we ought to adopt certain indeterminate ends (e. g. the happiness of others), without specifying exactly what, or how much, one must do to promote the ends (Kant 1996: 147–56 [382–94]). These too are supposed to be categorical imperatives, for they say we must, for overriding reasons, adopt the prescribed ends, whether or not doing so promotes our happiness and personal projects. So categorical imperatives do not have to be inflexible, rigoristic rules of conduct. In labeling an "ought" judgment as a "categorical imperative" we express the belief that it is an all-things-considered, overriding moral requirement, backed by reasons not entirely dependent on what serves to promote the ends we happen to have. The requirement could be simple and sweepingly general (as Kant regarded "Never lie"), but it could be vastly complex and qualified. We should not confuse issues about the scope and complexity of moral principles with issues about the sort of reason we have to follow them. Kant's claim that we are under categorical imperatives is addressed to the latter.

Beyond these core ideas, Kant held that the one "Categorical Imperative" (in the strict sense) that he formulated (in several ways) is an unconditional and unqualified requirement of reason, applicable in all human conditions and implicitly acknowledged in common moral judgments. Unlike the principle behind instrumental reasons, which we call "the Hypothetical Imperative", it does not simply prescribe taking the necessary means to desired ends. It can be established as rationally necessary, Kant thought, without reliance on empirical studies of human nature, and we can and should be motivated by respect for it apart from any other interests that might be served. It expresses what our own reason, independently of inclination, requires of us, and so we cannot help but acknowledge its authority (even when we fail to meet its requirements). Kant seems at times also to believe that more specific principles (e.g. about lying, obeying the law, and sexual practices) are derivative categorical imperatives, shown by the basic Categorical Imperative to be unconditionally required in *all human conditions*, without exception.[3] These ideas are understandably more controversial than the basic points we have been discussing.

The core idea, however, remains just that moral duties impose categorical imperatives in the sense that we have sufficient, overriding reason to fulfill our moral duties, independently of whether doing so will promote our own happiness or serve our individual ends. Even this core idea is rejected by those philosophers who insist that practical rationality is always nothing but taking efficient means to desired ends, but Kant's view, I suspect, is closer than theirs to ordinary moral opinion and most of Western tradition in moral theory.[4] We think, for example, that Hitler was wrong and *unreasonable* to kill millions of European Jews and this was not just because it was a poor means for him to get what he most wanted. The moral prohibition on murdering people, it is commonly thought, should override personal ambitions; so Hitler had sufficient reason not to do the killing, even though he wanted to.

Now let us return to our earlier questions. (1) It should be clear that categorical imperatives are not to be viewed as orders from an alleged alien authority. Unlike commands from parents, military superiors, and legal authorities, they are conceived as expressing "objective principles," that is principles that anyone in the context would follow if sufficiently guided by reason. They are supposed to tell us what is good in itself to do, not what someone demands that we do.[5] As discussed more fully in the next section of this essay, a key Kantian doctrine is that that basic moral requirements are laws we legislate to ourselves as rational persons with autonomy. We are not morally bound by any alleged requirement unless it is backed by principles that we can recognize as what we ourselves, as a rational, self-governing persons, will for ourselves and others. There are various ways of understanding this, but all clearly rule out the idea that categorical imperatives are imposed by alien authorities and give us reasons only by threats of punishment or promise of rewards. The authority of moral principles is, as it were, the authority of our own reason, our best judgments, all things considered, as to what we ought to do. Moral reasons are *our* reasons; they guide us, rather goad us (Falk 1986). What they require need not be unpleasant or disagreeable at all; but even when it is, we cannot pursue other projects in disregard of them without going against our own best judgment, suffering conflict of will, and inviting self-contempt. These implications of Kant's idea of moral autonomy may be doubted, but at least they make clear that Kantian categorical imperatives would be grossly misunderstood if they were seen as commands of some alleged "authority" independent of our own reason.

(2) It should also be clear that substantive categorical imperatives need not be simple, exceptionless rules, like "Never lie." As noted above, Kant himself believed that there are such absolute rules, but this dubious belief does not follow from the concept of a categorical imperative. What follows is that, no matter how richly complex and filled with "unless" and "so long as" clauses, a categorical imperative should always be respected, not subordinated to other considerations. To call a specified requirement a "categorical imperative" is to make a summary judgment, saying that, all things considered, reason requires a certain course of action. If we believe that a principle states merely a morally relevant consideration, then it should not be called a categorical imperative; for that label is appropriate only when all relevant factors have been taken into account and an all-things-considered conclusion on a particular act or act type has been reached. We can say, trivially, "categorical imperatives must be obeyed, no matter what" because the claim is implicit in what is meant by a categorical imperative. Again, however, nothing follows about the complexity and scope of the principles that summarize our reasonable all-things-considered moral judgments about lying, revolution, sex, promises, etc., i.e. the principles we might take to be categorical imperatives. In short, we should not confuse two distinct questions: (a) How much (if at all) should moral principles about lying, killing, obeying the law, etc., be qualified by explicit or implicit exceptions? and (b) Are moral principles *categorical imperatives*? The core issue for the second question is whether moral principles, no matter how many or few qualifications they contain, are overridingly rational to follow and not simply because doing so promotes the personal ends of the agent.

(3) Finally, a categorical imperative is not something we must follow from a sense of constraint. We do not need to grit our teeth and focus on the requirement as a "command," to which we are "bound" and "subject." We can often, and should, fulfill our moral responsibilities with our mind focused on the good we can do, rather than our own goodness or need to submit to authoritative commands. This requires some explanation.

To be sure, Kant does imply that in general we are not only authors of moral laws but *subject* to them (G 98–102 [431–4]). As *imperatives* they express a relation of *necessitation* between our imperfect wills and objective principles, i.e. the principles that we would follow invariably if we acted in a fully rational way (G 80–1 [413]). Moreover, Kant says that conforming to duty has "moral worth" only if done "from duty" (G 65–7 [397–9]). But none of this, I think, implies that we are *always or typically* averse to doing what we should or that we need to feel "constrained" in order to do it. If we are in fact reluctant to do what we should, then the thought that doing so is an *imperative* to which we are *subject* may serve to move us (or not); but the thought is not essential, I think, to the idea of governing ourselves by principles that are categorical imperatives. Kant did tend to suppose that self-interest is such a strong motive that recognition of the moral law inevitably causes in us feelings of "respect," and he describes this respect as a partly painful feeling, akin to fear, a sense of our "self-conceit" being humbled by recognition that what is morally required is not always what we most want to do (Kant 1997: 62–75 [71–89]). This dark, and perhaps overly pessimistic, view of human psychology, however, is not an implication of the core idea that moral requirements are categorical imperatives. That idea is about the sort of reasons that favor acting as we morally should, leaving open whether on particular occasions acting for those reasons will be experienced as being constrained or obedient to authority. An important point to note here is that all "imperatives" have two sides, as it were. They express "objective principles," or rational principles that even a "holy will" would follow, and yet they do so in a form ("ought") that also conveys the idea that imperfect wills, i.e. those who do not automatically follow them with God-like regularity, are *bound* to obey them, *must* do so, and feel *constrained* when tempted to do otherwise.[6] When we consider our thoughts and feelings in fulfilling our various duties, then, there are several possibilities.

First, we might desire to do something incompatible with what we ought to do but nevertheless understand and respect the reasons behind the moral principle. Here it seems natural to suppose that we are moved both by the moral reasons and by a sense of being under appropriate constraints. Suppose, for example, you are asked to testify in a legal case and telling the truth will prove embarrassing to you and your friend, but you recognize and respect the moral reasons for obeying the law and testifying truthfully and you conclude that, all things considered, this is your duty. If you tell the truth, you do so because you respect the good reasons for doing so but also with a sense of being constrained to do so contrary to your wishes. Or, better, you have had to *constrain yourself* to act on principle rather than inclination. This is the sort of case, I think, that Kant most often highlights.

Second, we might desire to do something incompatible with what we accept as duty but without understanding or even considering the good reasons for accepting it as duty. We might have just relied on common opinion or the authority of another person. Here we would fulfill the duty with a sense of constraint but not from respect for the reasons behind it. Insofar as we have really accepted the opinion that we have the moral duty, then by Kant's analysis we must suppose that *there are* sufficient, overriding reasons but we are not aware of them and so cannot be moved by them. An example might be a person who restrains sexual impulses according to commonly accepted opinions about what is permissible, but who never considers why those restraints are required.

Third, now that we see that the elements of Kant's paradigm case (i.e., the first case above) are separable, we can consider another possibility. That is, we might recognize and respect the reasons for a particular moral requirement but have no inclination or reason to act otherwise. The suggestion is not that we *never* think of duty, but just that in the case at hand there is no need for constraint because nothing even prompts the thought of not doing the right thing. Suppose, for example, your child is badly cut from a fall and needs hospital treatment immediately. In fact, as you would agree if asked, it is your duty to take the child to the hospital, but the constraints and imperatives of moral duty are not at all what is on your mind. Nor are you thinking "The child is *mine* and so I must help." Your love draws your attention to the need of Ken or Leah, the individual person in front of you perceived concretely.[7] The life and interests of *this* child are so clear and vivid that abstract thoughts about all human beings' reasons for helping other human beings are not what is on your mind. But, still, what primarily moves you in the particular context are features of it that would give anyone reason to act similarly in relevantly similar cases. It is not that the child is named "Ken" or "Leah," or anything else in particular. It is not primarily, certainly not only, that the child shares your genes or has lived with you for several years. You are moved by a direct concern for the life and vital interests of the real person, and these are the very sort of reasons about which moral principles speak in more general terms. Your reasons, I would say, are moral reasons insofar as they manifest in the particular case the sort of attitude that the more abstract principles of humanity and beneficence call for. The motivation does not fail to show respect for moral reasons just because it was not the result of a deduction from abstract moral generalizations to particular cases. It seems, then, that we can be moved by the relevant moral reasons without experiencing them as constraints and without even thinking of them in the form of abstract generalizations. If so, even imperfect moral agents, like us, who often experience moral requirements as constraints, need not always do so. In at least some circumstances we can act as categorical imperatives prescribe, responding directly to the reasons behind them, without experiencing them as constraints or even thinking of them abstractly as duties.

Would Kant count these acts as "from duty" and so "morally worthy"? The answer is not entirely clear because the idea of duty includes the two elements (moral reasons and constraint) that can work separately in ways that Kant did not discuss. Even if Kant assumed that the sense of being (self-) constrained is an essential part of acting "from duty," a reasonable extension of Kant's view would, I think, grant that the crucial feature of morally worthy acts is that they manifest responsiveness to the sort of basic reasons that underlie moral principles.

III Autonomy of Moral Agents

Kant argued, still by an analytical method, that there can be only one Categorical Imperative, which he expressed initially in his famous formula of universal law (G 88 [420–1]). In a complex and controversial course of argument, he contended that this formula expresses essentially the same basic moral idea as his later formulas, including the formula of autonomy (G 88–100, 104–108 [420–40]). According to this formula, we must act under the idea that moral agents legislate or will for themselves universal laws, as rational beings, independently of their particular desires as sensuous human beings. Thinking of ourselves as under the Categorical Imperative, then, requires thinking of ourselves as rational agents with what Kant calls autonomy of the will. Thus, assuming Kant's analysis of the idea of moral duty as the idea of being subject to categorical imperatives and so bound by the Categorical Imperative, then believing that we have duties commits us to a conception of ourselves as rational agents with autonomy. Now there is much in this whole argument that for present purposes we can bypass. The core point is Kant's thought that we must attribute at least a modest sort of autonomy to moral agents because we think of them as having the capacities and dispositions to guide their decisions by categorical imperatives. Kant also affirms a more robust, and controversial, conception of autonomy, in line with his stronger claims about the Categorical Imperative, but let us begin with the more modest idea.

What sort of agents could be subject to categorical imperatives? All imperatives are rational requirements addressed to those who can fulfill them but might not, and so the agents must be able to follow the rational requirements, recognized as such. That is, they must be disposed to acknowledge and follow them because they are requirements that express good reasons or are based on good reasons. Since being under an imperative implies the possibility of acting against reason, agents subject to categorical imperatives may in fact fail to follow them, and may even act against them; but insofar as we suppose the agents *ought* to follow the imperatives, we must assume that they *can*. Already it is clear, then, that agents subject to categorical imperatives cannot be complete slaves to the impulses and desires of the moment, for that implies inability to regulate conduct by rational reflection, even about future consequences to oneself. At a minimum the agents must be able to act for reasons, reflecting on facts and interests over time. This much is implicit even in the idea that they can follow hypothetical imperatives. Since, however, categorical imperatives are defined as principles rational to follow independently of how well they serve our happiness and particular personal ends, agents subject to them must also be able and disposed to recognize reasons to act beyond those of instrumental rationality. Their deliberations are not restricted to considering what will satisfy their immediate desires, what will make them most happy in the long run, and what will achieve their desires for others. Apart from these considerations, they also acknowledge reasons of another kind, considerations that also other agents, so far as they are rational, accept as reasons and not just because their desires as individuals would be served. Agents subject to categorical imperatives, then, cannot take the fact that they can satisfy a particular desire or interest as sufficient, by itself, to give them a reason to act; for they realize that further reflection, on rational considerations not so tied to their personal concerns, may give them reason to disregard, suppress, or even try to eliminate that desire or interest. Furthermore, if they judge that, all things considered, these reasons are sufficient to constitute duty, understood as a categorical imperative, they regard them as overriding reasons – determining what they ought to do, despite any inclination not to.

Agents conceived in this way have the main elements of a modest Kantian idea of autonomy (for more detail see my 1992).

In thinking of agents as having desires but able to reflect to determine whether those desires, all things considered, provide good reasons, we are already attributing to them a necessary condition of autonomy. To follow categorical imperatives, however, agents must also be able to acknowledge and act on reasons that are more than requirements to take the means to satisfy their desire-based ends. This is a further feature of Kant's idea of autonomy. When we add that, to follow categorical imperatives, they must respect these special reasons as overriding their desire-based reasons, we have a fuller, but still modest, idea of Kantian autonomy. Some philosophers deny that moral agents must have autonomy even in this limited sense, but the ideas regarding autonomy that draw the most controversy go beyond the basic points mentioned so far.

First, Kant held that moral agents, in a sense, impose moral requirements on themselves. They are *authors* of moral laws as well as *subject* to them. They can be compared to autonomous states, bound to no higher authority, with a power to govern themselves in accord with their own constitution, without needing the approval of any further authority. These metaphorical descriptions may be understood in several ways, but some basic points seem clear. Rational agents with autonomy identify with the perspective from which moral judgments are made so that that they see moral requirements not as externally imposed, for example, by cultural norms or divine commands. They cannot, then, knowingly act contrary to their moral beliefs without inner conflict and self-disapproval. When they act from moral principle, they are governing themselves by their own standards; and when they act immorally, they are in conflict with deep commitments essential to them as moral agents. Also, in conceiving of moral agents as "authors" of moral laws, Kant implicitly contrasts his idea of rational autonomy with rational intuitionism. That is, reason does not simply "perceive" moral facts as things that exist independently of the use of reason by moral agents; rather moral agents determine particular moral requirements through reasoning from a basic moral perspective (as if legislating according to values inherent in their constitution).

Second, Kant apparently thought that virtually all sane, competent adult human beings have the characteristics of autonomy that his analysis revealed as essential to moral agency. This, however, is a point of faith beyond what his analytical argument aims to establish. That argument, at best, shows that the idea of a moral agent who acknowledges duties presupposes that such agents are rational and have autonomy. But whether all, or even most, functional adult human beings are moral agents in this sense cannot be settled by conceptual analysis, and Kant, of course, did not undertake any empirical investigations to give evidence for his assumption. In our times, after the Holocaust, it is harder to share Kant's faith that a moral point of view is universally acknowledged as authoritative. Kant tries to make sense of moral life by offering an abstract model of moral agents with certain essential features; but whether that model fits this or that person, i.e. whether they are moral agents in his sense, depends on what we find when we try to employ it. Merely finding examples of sociopaths that fail to be moral agents in Kant's sense, however, does not show that Kant's argument was incorrect or his model valueless. Instead, it would confirm doubts about the common 18th century faith, which Kant shared, that all minimally rational human beings implicitly acknowledge moral standards. Some Kantians will defend Kant on the point; and some critics may argue that Kant's model does not even fit ordinary moral agents. Controversy here is not easily resolved.

Third, Kant held that rational agents with autonomy act from pure practical reason alone. When they act from respect for overriding moral reasons, then, they are not to be understood simply as acting on good (morally approved) *sentiments* as opposed to other desires and inclinations. It is a familiar Kantian theme that they act on principle, where the governing maxim is not of the form "I will do X because, as it happens, X promotes Y, which I want" but, rather, "I will do X, regardless of its effect on what I desire." The claim that we can act from pure practical reason, however, goes beyond these familiar Kantian themes. A sophisticated Humean, for example, might accept those themes but insist that the agent's underlying motive for adopting the maxim of duty is a strong, but "calm," sentiment in favor of so acting. The feelings that move us are not always reflected in the maxims we use to guide and explain our conduct. Even Kant conceded this when he repeatedly insisted that we do not know for sure what moves us to act even when we take ourselves to be acting for the best moral reasons. It is clear, however, that Kant meant to deny the Humean thesis that all motivation must stem from sentiments. Insofar as we take ourselves to be moral agents, Kant argues, we must conceive ourselves as *capable* of being moved by practical reason alone. Sometimes we may be moved by mere sentiment when we think we are guided by reason alone, but we must suppose that we can do what reason requires even if we lack any feeling prompting us to do so. Here Kant goes beyond claims we have explicitly discussed previously, and Kant's view is widely disputed.

There is, however, a way of understanding Kant's point that is less radical than what is usually attributed to him. Kant denies that all action must be motivated by sentiment, feeling, inclination, or sensuous desire, but these terms can be interpreted broadly or narrowly. Similarly, when Kant insists that we can act from reason alone, we can think of "reason" in more or less radical metaphysical ways. If we interpret desires and sentiments narrowly as felt internal pushes and pulls, then Kant's denial that these must be present as motivating causes of all action is more plausible. If, however, we interpret "desire" broadly as just a given disposition to act, then Kant does not deny that we "desire" to follow moral principles. In fact he insists that all moral agents have, inescapably, a predisposition to morality, even though he attributes it to our rational nature rather than our sensuous nature. Again, if "reason" is given a narrow Humean interpretation, it cannot motivate any act because it is merely an "inert" power to discover natural facts and relations of ideas. But Kant agrees with Hume that reason, so construed (as "theoretical reason"), is not by itself a source of motivation. To have practical reason, according to Kant, is (among other things) to be disposed to acknowledge certain procedural norms for choice, and so in the broad sense it is a kind of "desire" that can figure in practical explanations of why agents choose to act as they do. Humeans question whether these normative commitments are special in ways that warrant attributing them to our nature as *rational*, as opposed to sensuous, beings. Kant, and followers, think that there are good reasons for the attribution. This is a dispute that needs more work on both sides; but it is rarely discussed in a fruitful way. This, I think, is largely because Kant's normative position tends to be conflated with his widely rejected appeal to the distinction between noumena and phenomena, to which I turn next.

Fourth, the core ideas of autonomy suggested here also fall short of the most controversial ideas that Kant introduces when he tries to reconcile his ethics with the conclusions he reached in his *Critique of Pure Reason*. In the third section of the *Groundwork*, and other writings, Kant argues that to attribute to moral agents the sort of freedom of will that morality requires we must think of them as belonging to an "intelligible world" as well as the "sensible world." The idea of responsible choice employed in practical discussions cannot be reduced to or fully explained by empirical phenomena: a fact that is marked by saying that wills are *noumenal*, in contrast with what is known through experience (the *phenomenal*). Autonomous wills cannot be known as substances in space and time, subject to empirical causal laws. We can "think" but not "comprehend" their existence as "causes" of a nonempirical kind. These are features of Kant's thought that have led many to reject his ethical theory altogether. It is significant, however, that Kant does not start with them as the elements from which to build his ethical theory, even though the views were largely reflected in his earlier *Critique of Pure Reason*. Rather Kant argues first from (supposedly) common moral thought to general normative principles, and only then develops the extreme metaphysical picture (or nonpicture) to square his ethics with the rest of his philosophy. Less radical contemporary interpretations of this aspect of Kant's thought regard it as only an attempt to distinguish two perspectives on human action, the *theoretical/empirical perspective* appropriate to natural science and the *practical/evaluative perspective* when we think about reasons for acting, obligation, and responsibility. This interpretative strategy is to admit that the practical perspective is committed to irreducibly normative ideas, but deny that it is inseparably committed to a faith in mysterious entities outside of space and time. It is not supposed to be a denial of the conclusions of science but another way of thinking and talking about the same human conduct that psychologists study from the empirical perspective. Even this two perspectives approach is, of course, unconvincing to many critics, and obviously much depends on how in particular the less radical account of the practical conception is spelled out.

Notes

1   Note, for example, that although Kant is committed to the possibility of noumenal "causation" in the *Critique of Pure Reason*, his argument for beginning ethics with an *a priori* investigation precedes his conclusion that our conception of morality requires us to think

of moral agents from a nonempirical standpoint (G 74–81 [406–14] and 118–23 [450–5]).

2   For example, if it is a categorical imperative not to give false witness, then the (moral) reasons not to give false witness override or defeat the consideration that you might make some money by doing so. In other words, all things considered, you should not bear false witness. The question naturally arises, what should one do if two different categorical imperatives conflict? Kant's response was that this is a conceptual impossibility. There cannot be genuine conflicts of duty, only competing grounds or considerations relevant to determining what one's duty is. Thus, if two alleged categorical imperatives give contradictory directions, then we must regard one of them as mistaken, or only valid in a more qualified form. I discuss this problem in more detail in 1996: 167–98. For a somewhat different view, see Donagan (1993: 7–21).

3   I use capital letters to indicate the basic principle, the Categorical Imperative, and small case letters for the derivative principles, categorical imperatives.

4   Aristotle and most other ancient moral philosophers, I think, do not accept that we have reason to be moral only as a means to some desired end independent of it. The Aristotelian view, for example, is apparently that virtue is a constituent part of "happiness," not a mere means to it. We cannot say, either, that he sees moral requirements as "independent" of what promotes our happiness, but it is important that "happiness" for Aristotle is not merely a subjective state or merely an end that we inevitably desire (Annas 1993; Hill 1999).

5   In later writings, trying to reconcile his moral philosophy with some minimal religious beliefs, Kant says that, once we determine through reason what our duties are, we can and should think of them as if commands of God (exemplifying pure practical reason). But this does not alter the main point. Duties are not derived from personal orders, should not be followed from fear of punishment or hope of reward, and are binding only because rationality requires them.

6   "Holy will" is Kant's term for the will of any being that conceived (as God often is) as necessarily willing what is rational, without temptations or the possibility of willing in an irrational way (G 81 [414]). Such a will is perfectly guided by rational principles (regarding what is good) but these principles do not impose imperatives or duties on a holy will. Such a will would be a member of the "kingdom of ends" as a "completely independent being," one whose will (along with the rational will of all members) legislates the moral laws but without being "subject" to the laws as authoritative constraints (G 100–1 [433–4]).

7   Kant thought that acts that express a moral attitude (e.g. a commendable regard for persons as ends) are not acts "from inclinations", such as "pathological love" (i.e. a feeling distinct from commitments of will made for good reasons). So in the case imagined here I am supposing that the love is not so blind and detached from your general commitments and moral attitudes. It is also not a driving force, as conceived on a mechanical model, although it alerts you to concrete needs and you may act *with* love (lovingly). My claim now is not that Kant's statements about acts "from duty" are compatible with his acknowledging that our imagined case is a "morally worthy" act, but only that it is a case of acting for the reasons behind recognizing the aid is a "duty," and so should have been counted as morally worthy.

References

Allison, H.: *Kant's Theory of Freedom* (Cambridge: Cambridge University Press, 1991).

Annas, J.: *The Morality of Happiness* (Oxford: Oxford University Press, 1993).

Donagan, A.: "Moral Dilemmas, Genuine and Spurious: A Comparative Anatomy," *Ethics*, 104 (1993).

Falk, D.: "Guiding and Goading." In his *Ought, Reasons, and Morality* (Ithaca: Cornell University Press, 1986).

Hill, T.: "Happiness and Human Flourishing in Kant's Ethics," *Social Philosophy and Policy* (1999).

——: "Moral Dilemmas, Gaps, and Residues," in *Moral Dilemmas and Moral Theory*, ed. H. E.) (New York and Oxford: Oxford University Press, 1996).

——: "The Kantian Conception of Autonomy." In my *Dignity and Practical Reason in Kant's Moral Theory* (Ithaca, NY: Cornell University Press, 1992).

Kant I.: *Anthropology from a Pragmatic Point of View*, trans. Mary J. Gregor (The Hague: Martinus Nijhoff, 1997a).

——: *The Metaphysics of Morals*, trans. Mary Gregor (Cambridge: Cambridge University Press, 1996).

——: *Critique of Practical Reason*, trans. Mary Gregor (Cambridge: Cambridge University Press, 1997b).

——: *Groundwork of the Metaphysic of Morals*, trans. and ed. H. J. Paton (New York: Harper & Row, 1964).

——: "On a Supposed Right to Lie out of Benevolent Motives." In *Kant's Critique of Practical Reason and Other Writings on Moral Philosophy*, trans. L. W. Beck (Chicago: University of Chicago Press, 1949).

Schneewind, J. B.: *Moral Philosophy from Montaigne to Kant*, vol. II (Oxford: Oxford University Press, 1990).

——————— Chapter 13 ———————

Contractarianism

Geoffrey Sayre-McCord

Introduction

Contractarianism, as a general approach to moral and political thought, has had a long and distinguished history – its roots are easily traced as far back as Plato's *Republic*, where Glaucon advanced it as a view of justice, and its influential representatives include Pufendorf, Hobbes, Locke, Rousseau, Hume, and Kant. In various ways, to various purposes, and against the background of various assumptions, each of these philosophers offered contractarian arguments for the views they defended. What binds the tradition together, in the face of this variety, is the conviction that moral norms or political institutions find legitimacy, when they do, in their ability to secure (under the appropriate conditions) the agreement of those to whom they apply.

As long as the tradition is, it seemed, until recently, to have quietly faded into the past. Several things were responsible for contractarianism's decline. The first was the unsettling realization that even evidently legitimate governments had never actually secured the consent of those governed, which pushed contractarianism to an appeal to the hypothetical consent of hypothetical people under hypothetical circumstances. The second was the rise of utilitarianism and, later, Marxism, as substantive alternatives that advanced their own positive views of political legitimacy along with their own criticisms of contractarianism. And the third was the influence of positivist criticisms of moral and political theory that seemed to undermine all attempts to develop a rationally defensible normative theory.

Recently, however, contractarianism has enjoyed a dramatic resurgence in popularity. This striking renewal of interest is due not only to the eventual rejection of positivism but, in part, to developments in formal decision and game theory (developments that promise a clarity and rigor of formulation all too rare in moral theory), in part, to an increasing dissatisfaction with traditional arguments for utilitarianism and its competitors, and, in part, to the sense that individuals deserve a pre-eminent place in any plausible account of moral and political obligation.

The variety of views that count themselves contractarian is daunting. Some hark back to Hobbes (and his emphasis on a preoccupation with one's own advantage), others to Kant (and his emphasis on a respect for others as ends-in-themselves). Some restrict themselves to subjective theories of value and maximizing conceptions of rationality, others embrace objective theories of value and more elaborate accounts of practical reason. Some give a prominent role to game theory and principles of bargaining, others emphasize consensus and conciliation. And some defend familiar forms of utilitarianism (albeit with new foundations), while others defend theories that give a prominent role to rights.

In what follows I hope both to place the contemporary work into historical perspective and to set out some distinctions and contrasts that might help organize, and explain the shape of, contemporary work. The historical perspective I offer, however, is not scrupulously historical. I smooth over a good deal of the twists and turns that due care to the historical record would sanction, and I leave out of account almost completely the various social and political forces that induced not just the twists and turns but the main line of development I identify. For the sake of making clear the positions that emerged as contractarianism developed, and the philosophical considerations that recommended them, the historical picture offered here is more than a little contrived. While the views described emerged (for the most part) in the order suggested and (I believe) for the reasons offered, the succession of views was not nearly so clean as my description implies. Indeed, because each view won devotees long after others saw reasons for change, a number of the positions characterized here as long superceded kept a grip on life even as their off-spring thrived and attempted patricide. So, while I describe one view as giving way to another in the face of its perceived weaknesses, I force on the history of contractarian thought an air of inevitable development that is only partially born out by what actually happened. Still, I hope, this bit of sanitized analytical history will provide a way of thinking about contractarianism that sheds some light on why it developed as it did.

The Background

Contractarianism came into its own in the seventeenth and eighteenth centuries, primarily as a political theory. It developed directly as a response to concerns about the legitimacy of government and the grounds of political obligation. As faith in the divine right of kings evaporated, and the assurance that some were by nature born to rule waned, people came to see political authority as a reflection of human convention. The question arose: what could possibly justify the state and explain our obligation to it? "Man was born free; and everywhere he is in chains" Rousseau (1978: 46) famously noted, "What can make [this change] legitimate?" Social contract theories offered an appealing answer that traced the grounds of political legitimacy and obligation not to God or to nature, but to the wills of the people who were affected. In the process, it promised to articulate the origins of, obligations to, and limits on, legitimate government.

Viewing government either as a conventionally established arrangement among people, or between a people and their sovereign, the social contract was called on in three capacities. First, at least initially, it was offered as an explanation of how governments actually arose. As the explanation would have it, governments emerged in a pre-political context – the "state of nature" – as conventional solutions to the problems that inevitably arise among people in the absence of a state. Second, the social contract was offered as an account of why people have an obligation of allegiance to their government. The idea was that people have such an obligation because either they had consented, or they had good reason to consent, to the government's authority (as a way to avoid the hardships threatened by the "state of nature"). And third, the social contract was advanced as a justification for limiting the powers of government. The suggestion was that a government's powers are properly limited to those necessary for solving the problems that give rise to government in the first place, since more extensive powers would go beyond what people would have reason to consent to were they in a "state of nature".

Contractarianism provided, as a result, a normative framework that might be used to defend or to attack the legitimacy of particular governments. As it happened, contractarian arguments were in fact relied upon both to foment and to resist revolutionary pressures. Thus Rousseau's *The Social Contract* came to the fore as a natural source for the condemnation of virtually all existing governments while Hobbes' *Leviathan* was, in its implications and intention, conservative in the extreme. When the point was to attack the legitimacy of some particular government, contractarians would argue that the relevant people had no reason to recognize its authority because the life they could realistically expect to face without it would be better. When the point was to defend the legitimacy of some government, contractarians would argue that the relevant people had reason to recognize the authority of some government because the life they could realistically expect to face without the government would be palpably worse.

Originally, and especially while natural law theory still held sway, the contractarian arguments played out against two substantive assumptions: that real consent had (sometimes) actually been given and that people had a moral obligation to keep the agreements they had made. The first assumption legitimated the sovereign's power, since the relevant people were supposed to have given their permission for its exercise. The second established the political obligations of those party to the agreement, since they were seen as having undertaken, by way of the agreement, certain specific moral obligations.

Just what constituted giving consent, however, became a ticklish and difficult issue for those who thought it required. Instances of explicit consent seemed rarely on offer. So tacit consent, given (say) by the acceptance of benefits or participation in certain conventional practices, emerged as the only sort of consent that might actually be given on a regular basis. Yet tacit consent, if characterized in a way that allowed it to be often enough secured, was so easily given (especially under conditions where no viable options existed) as to be of little use in justifying political authority and obligation. To the extent those too poor to move accepted the benefits of the state, for instance, their tacit consent seemed not so much a reflection of their wills as the inevitable up-shot of their situation. Virtually unavoidable, tacit consent seemed insufficient grounds for distinguishing legitimate from illegitimate government.

Questions arose as well about the need for real consent, explicit or otherwise. For it appeared, on the one hand, that particular legitimate governments had never received consent of any kind, and, on the other hand, that whatever might justify a person's moral obligation to keep agreements would serve as well to justify a political obligation (even in the absence of actual agreement). (Hume 1985) Whatever did legitimize government eventually seemed not to depend on the government's consensual pedigree.

Thus actual consent looked to be neither sufficient nor necessary for legitimate government and political obligation. Nonetheless, the idea that people would, with good reason, willingly give their consent, seemed to offer a compelling endorsement of whatever they would agree to – even if they hadn't actually given their consent. Conversely, the idea that people would, with good reason, not willingly offer their consent, seemed a powerful condemnation – even if their consent had in fact been given either for bad reasons or unwillingly.

As a result, appeals to actual consent, along with the fanciful histories that accompanied early attempts to identify when it had been given, were replaced by appeals to hypothetical consent – appeals to what people would agree to, if only they were rational, and not to what they had agreed to. But this raised difficulties of its own, for while real agreement might establish real obligations, hypothetical consent, which was no consent at all, apparently established no obligations whatsoever. Still, that people would have given consent, if they were given the chance and were rational, does seem to establish something: that they had reason to support what they would have consented to. So, leaving behind the suggestion that consent (of any sort) was the source of the obligation, contractarians shifted to the claim that what mattered was that people had reason to give their consent if it were needed either to establish or to maintain the government in question. The reasons for giving consent, not the consent itself, were taken as establishing obligation. The authority of some government, in turn, was seen to depend on people having reason to recognize it as authoritative, not on their actually having given that recognition (via consent or contract, or indeed in any other way).

The switch to hypothetical consent (which plays a role in Hobbes and is clear in both Rousseau and Kant) allowed contractarians to avoid explicit consent's implausible histories and tacit consent's excessively lenient account of commitment, as well as their shared reliance on the assumption that people have a moral obligation to keep their agreements. Appeals to hypothetical consent emphasized instead the reasons agents had for reaching agreement in the first place. And they allowed the theories to rely not on what people might actually have done (perhaps for bad reasons or unwillingly) but on what they had good reason to do.

The reasons people were seen as having were not, importantly, provided by some independently specifiable theory of what constituted legitimate government. The argument was not that people had reason to give their consent because the government was legitimate, but that it was legitimate because they had reason to give their consent. The reasons people (supposedly) had needed to be found, therefore, in considerations that did not presuppose an account of legitimacy. The considerations offered were, in a straightforward sense, standardly practical, in that they emphasized the advantages to each that would come from the state.

Of course the details of the theory shifted substantially as different accounts of the pre-political state of nature were offered, since those accounts influenced significantly what people might reasonably have agreed to and so what powers they might have recognized as necessary or desirable. Hobbes, for instance, saw the state of nature as so threatening that it called for an absolute sovereign limited only by an inability to demand that citizens willingly submit to death. Whereas Locke, convinced that a pre-political state of nature would be a tolerably harmonious community suffering primarily from the undesirable effects of people trying to enforce individually what they each regard as their rights, saw the government's legitimate role as really quite limited.

In any case, and whatever the description of the pre-political state of nature, contractarians offered the description as a realistic characterization of how things would actually be without government. The contractarian approach asked people to consider seriously what life would really be like without government. In an age of revolutions, this was not a call to imaginative flights of fancy, it was the pressing of a seemingly realistic possibility. To the extent the prospect of life without government was palpably worse than life with government, people could see themselves as more than willing to consent to some government or other, rather than face the alternative.

Crucial to these contractarian arguments, of course, was their effectiveness in advancing a credible view of how life would be in the absence of government. Those who saw themselves as facing the prospect described saw as well that they had reason to give their consent, if it were required, to some political authority. Against the background of a compelling description of state of nature, the contractarian argument had a great deal of appeal.

As long as the state of nature represents a genuine threat, and as long as staying out of that situation requires mutual cooperation in support of government conventionally established, the real people facing the threat will each find they have reason to recognize the authority of the state. It won't be actual consent that carries the burden so much as there being compelling grounds for giving it if asked – grounds provided by the thought that without the government life would be much worse. So while the proof of acceptability was originally thought to be found in actual acceptance, via real consent, that proof came to seem securable, and sufficient, in the absence of consent.

To admit that having some particular government is better than having none, however, is not yet to hold that any government whatsoever is acceptable. Some governments might still be so terrible that people would reasonably prefer no government. Moreover, those governments that do improve on the state of nature will not do so in the same way, and if people faced a choice they might well prefer one of these to the others. No doubt, for any given government, some people falling under it would prefer a different government even if not the state of nature. Yet the question people faced wasn't just which government (or form of government) would they prefer to a "state of nature" nor was it which would they most prefer given their particular convictions, tastes, skills, weakness....It was, instead, which government (or form of government) would they prefer from among those that might also secure the support and agreement of the others who are to establish and maintain it. The question became: what form of government would properly (and plausibly) secure the agreement of each in light of the fact that no acceptable government would be establishable without the consent of all (or at least most). Indeed, at the core of contractarianism is the insistence that the arrangements must prove acceptable to all who would fall under them.

To this point, the argument for being willing to give consent was not merely addressed to real people, it was put to them in terms they were supposed to see as accurately characterizing a choice they might in fact have. It was hypothetical consent theory in the face of a possibly real choice. And the reasons people were seen as having were reasons they supposedly actually had in their circumstances.

Unfortunately, while people might willingly consent to (maybe almost any) government rather than face the state of nature, that willingness could well reflect aspects of their actual situation that are morally suspect. That a person has reason to give consent to enslavement rather than face the (perhaps quite real) prospect of painful death at the hands of the would-be master does nothing to establish the legitimacy of the enslavement. Real reasons, under coercive circumstances, may legitimize giving consent, but they won't legitimize others acting on that consent. Thus, in order to justify the authority of some government, hypothetical consent needed to emerge in situations reasonably viewed as morally untainted.

The pressure to purify the circumstances of agreement naturally led the hypothetical consent contractarians to advance as well idealized circumstances for that consent. Those who resisted an appeal to idealized circumstances did so for either of two reasons. On the one hand, some thought the actual circumstances, and thus the "state of nature," are appropriately untainted even if life is less good than it might be. On the other hand, some thought that whatever reasons a person might have for making an agreement under idealized conditions, those reasons would be irrelevant to real agents unless those reasons were likewise reasons they would have under suitably realistic conditions – in which case there was no point in appealing to the idealization. Still, most contractarians were moved by considerations of fairness to hold that the relevant choice situation was one made under idealized conditions.

Similar considerations worked to recommend too that the people whose consent mattered were not people as they actually are – sometimes irrational and often ignorant – but those people as they would be were they (for instance) perfectly rational and appropriately informed. That a person, when irrational or ignorant, would or even does give consent under certain (perhaps non-coercive) circumstances to some arrangement, does nothing to establish that he has reason to give that consent. Consent under non-coercive circumstances may legitimize others acting on that consent, but it won't legitimize thinking the person has reason to consent.

All the while recognizing that the question is whether real people have reason to endorse the government whose legitimacy is at issue, contractarians began to distinguish these real people and their actual circumstances from the (suitably idealized) people who are supposed to reach agreement and the (appropriately idealized) circumstances under which their agreement was supposed to be secured. That suitably idealized people would, under appropriately fair circumstances, willingly agree to some (form of) government, came to seem the plausible standard of legitimacy. What grounds could there possibly be, one is inclined to ask, for objecting to such a government?

A natural worry, however, is that the rhetorical force of this question was bought at the expense of vacuousness. For it began to look as if all the interesting justificatory work would be done in specifying who might count as suitable parties to the agreement, and what would count as appropriately fair circumstances. The contractarian test came to seem empty without the addition of some non-contractarian theory that would identify not only who counts as suitably rational, and what circumstances are appropriately non-coercive, but also what reasons there are for consenting under those circumstances. Such a theory would presumably support its own substantive account of political legitimacy. Whereas, initially, contractarianism appealed to real people in their actual circumstances facing a real choice, it now was so removed from the real world, and so normatively laden in its assumptions, that the contractarian framework seemed at best a useful heuristic for discovering some independently specifiable criterion that must be defended on some other, non-contractarian, grounds.

A number of theories emerged as candidates for the role. The most influential, early on, was utilitarianism, which held, in effect, that what rational people would agree to (under actual as well as idealized circumstances) is precisely whichever government would maximize over-all welfare. The legitimacy of a government turned, utilitarians argued, on how well the government advanced the interests of everyone concerned. And the reason any particular person had for recognizing the legitimacy of the government – and so for consenting to its authority – was traceable not (for instance) to how that person would fare, but to how people in general would. Of course this theory didn't require the contractarian framework for its articulation or deployment. Yet if one asked whether, on the utilitarian view, all rational people could, under appropriately fair conditions, willingly give their consent to the (form of) government it endorsed, the answer was an easy "yes".

Other theories, such as natural rights theories and (on some interpretations) Marxism, also stepped into the breach and offered accounts of what might constitute fair conditions of, and good reasons for, agreement. Each of them, though, was in a position to side-step an appeal to the contractarian framework even as it had the resources to say that all (really) rational people would, in the appropriate circumstances, willingly agree to the (form of) government the theory legitimized. To the extent these theories didn't co-opt the rhetorical force of the contractarian framework, they were used instead to undermine it on the grounds (for instance) that the framework illegitimately valorized the individual or ignored the value of community or substituted market relations for moral ones (see Pateman 1988, Sandel 1982).

Once contractarianism stepped away from reliance on the real consent of real people, and once it moved on to embrace as relevant only the hypothetical consent of idealized people in idealized circumstances, it not only invited non-contractarian additions, it seemed to need them. And once the additions were at hand, they didn't just add to contractarianism, they displaced it.

Recent Contractarianism

That is pretty much where things stood until the middle of the twentieth century. Although, in the first half of this century things got even worse, thanks to the influence of logical positivism. For according to the positivists grand attempts at moral theory and political justification are, despite pretensions to the contrary, actually only elaborate devices for bringing others onto one's own side.

The relatively recent revival of contractarianism has depended upon an emerging conviction that, contra positivism, there must be room for reasoned argument about normative matters. But the revival has required two other things as well: first, a growing dissatisfaction with the theories that had displaced contractarianism, and, second, the prospect that recognizably contractarian considerations might after all contribute non-trivially to moral theory.

Moreover, just as political contractarianism emerged as a response to the recognition that political legitimacy and obligation could not be traced to God or nature, moral contractarianism's appeal has grown substantially with the sense that moral constraints must in some way be a reflection of human reason or social convention, not of God or (non-human) nature. Contractarianism holds out the seductive prospect of a theory that demystifies morality's status and shows it to be a compelling expression of humanity's nature. For if morality finds its source and authority in our capacity to embrace its demands, then understanding morality will ultimately require appealing to what we would need in any case to explain our own capacities and practices. Nothing occult or mysterious or supernatural need be implicated (Mackie 1977; Milo 1995).

The contractarian framework, with its appeal to what people would agree to under appropriate circumstances, has found a natural home in two very different approaches that take their inspiration (though frequently little else) from Kant and Hobbes. The Kantian approach begins with our natural concern with morality and uses the contractarian framework to specify and draw out the implications of that concern. Contractarianism, in this case, is advanced as a way to articulate the content of morality. The Hobbesian approach, in contrast, acknowledges our concern with morality but sees that concern itself as properly called into question and uses the contractarian framework to show why and to what extent we have (non-moral) reason to embrace morality. Contractarianism, in this case, is advanced as a way to justify a concern for morality's content and demands. On either approach, contractarianism's distinctive commitment to seeing legitimacy as grounded in what people might willingly agree to under the appropriate circumstances finds a central role.

Kantian Contractarianism

The Kantian approach has famously been pursued by John Rawls, who introduces the contractarian framework to articulate morality's impartiality. In the process, he hopes to take "seriously the distinction between persons" in a way that other attempts to capture impartiality do not (1971: 187).

That moral demands are impartial is, of course, acknowledged by virtually all moral theories. Yet the nature of that impartiality and its implications for morality's authority and content are quite controversial.

One familiar way to capture morality's impartiality is to suppose that moral demands flow from a source equally concerned for all who fall under them. Thus many religious views portray morality's demands as reflecting God's equal love for all, while Ideal Observer theories treat the demands as an expression of what an equi-sympathetic observer would approve of, and utilitarian views see the demands as giving equal weight to the welfare of all. This way of capturing impartiality leads naturally (although not inevitably) to moral principles that are decidedly utilitarian in their implications.

Another way of capturing morality's impartiality, however, is to see its principles as those we would each, individually, choose to govern everyone's behavior if our choice was made in ignorance of how we, as we actually are, might benefit or suffer as a result (Harsanyi 1953; Rawls 1971). With this in mind, Rawls describes the appropriate circumstances of agreement – the relevant "state of nature" – as including a "veil of ignorance" that shields from view all information concerning the particular talents, tastes, history and situation of those seeking agreement. Impartiality is achieved by eliminating all the information that would engage partial concern. Collective and partial choice under circumstances of radical ignorance is substituted for individual choice under circumstances of extraordinary impartiality and knowledge. And with the substitution comes the appeal to contractarianism. For now the legitimacy of certain principles, and their standing as distinctively moral, appropriately impartial, principles, turns on whether people would – under the relevant circumstances (in this case, circumstances of ignorance that neutralize partiality) – choose the principles. Hypothetical choice, under hypothetical circumstances, sets the standard for moral legitimacy, on this view, because such choice embodies impartiality.

One apparently significant advantage of the contractarian approach to impartiality is that it need appeal neither to interpersonal utility comparisons nor to any general method of balancing the interests or welfare of people. In contrast, when impartiality is embodied in equal love, or sympathy, or concern for other's welfare, an appeal to interpersonal utility comparisons and an over-all balance of advantages seems inevitable. Many see this difference as grounds for thinking that the contractarian embodiment of impartiality captures especially well the moral significance of the individual and the idea that one person's loss cannot always be morally compensated by another's gain (Rawls 1971, but see Harsanyi 1953).

Impartiality is only one aspect of morality that invites contractarian elaboration. Rather than starting from the conviction that moral demands are impartial or fair, some versions of contemporary contractarianism focus instead on the idea that moral reasons are public and shared – they provide reasons for all. These approaches shift attention away from conflicting interests that call for impartial arbitration towards a collective concern to accept principles all can embrace as reasonable. Contractarianism's appeal to mutual agreement (under appropriate circumstances) strikes many as doing a uniquely satisfying job of articulating the sense in which morality's demands can lay claim to the allegiance of all. Indeed, by treating moral norms as just those everyone has reason to accept, contractarianism not only articulates the connection between morality and mutual acceptability but takes that connection as definitive. A concern to act morally, on this view, is a concern to act in light of principles that everyone might reasonably embrace. To determine what these principles are we need to ask the distinctively contractarian question: to what could people, under the appropriate circumstances, reasonably agree? This time, though, the appropriate circumstances are conceived not as involving radical ignorance but instead as being occupied by participants who offer considerations for and against various principles in a context where all are supposed to be both reasonable and concerned to settle on principles all the participants can accept. (See Scanlon 1998; Habermas 1990.)

While impartiality and mutual acceptability have both played crucial roles in making contemporary contractarianism attractive, they themselves find support in a third aspect of morality – the evident importance of equal concern and respect. Many hold that the moral significance of individuals is best captured by a view that treats morality's demands as themselves a reflection of what each person, uncoerced and conceived of as a full participant in the process, could rationally embrace. To treat a people with equal concern and respect, on this view, is to see them, no less than oneself, as having a legitimate say in the principles that should govern your interactions. By governing oneself by principles others could endorse, one thereby gives expression to the equal concern and respect that is distinctive of morality.

As I have suggested, contractarians disagree among themselves as to which, if any, of these various considerations ought to be given primacy. Even among those who agree on that, there is significant disagreement as to how impartiality, or mutual acceptability, or equal concern and respect, might find their best expression. Despite the disagreement, however, there is consensus among those taking this approach, that the relevance of the contractarian framework is found in its capacity to articulate crucial and distinctive features of morality. Thought of in these terms, contractarianism addresses those who are already concerned to do as morality demands but are trying to figure out what, precisely, that might be. Contractarianism is offered as a way of specifying those demands and is defended as appropriate by appeal to its capacity to articulate and embody crucial features of morality.

The Kantian approach to contractarianism faces two related problems. One concerns whether, in the end, any real work is being done by the appeal to the agreement of people, properly situated. The more successful an account is in eliminating the influence of individual differences on choice, in the name of impartiality, the less room there seems to be for the idea that the choices of distinct individuals matter to the outcome. When it comes to choices behind a veil of ignorance, for instance, asking what all might agree to under that circumstance appears functionally equivalent to asking what any one person might agree to, since the veil hides from the scene all the features of a person that might distinguish one person from others. Do the notions of collective choice or mutual agreement really have any substantive place in such theories? It is not at all clear. In any case, a second familiar problem emerges when one asks on what basis the people are to reach a collective choice or mutual agreement, supposing they do. Any grounds people who are "properly situated" might have for settling on one choice or agreement rather than others threaten to stand independently of any choice or agreement at all. Even hypothetical agreement among people seems to drop out of the picture. The concern underlying both of these problems is that the contractarian appeal to what people – in the plural – might agree to, under whatever circumstances, seems not to be playing anything other than a heuristic role.

This is a serious concern. If it is not met, the contractarian framework will stand as mere window dressing, a decorative over-lay that might have evocative advantages but that contributes not at all to the substance of a theory or the justification of the principles it endorses. The central challenge is to find a role for the distinctively contractarian idea that morality's demands reflect, in some non-trivial way, what people might reasonably agree to under the appropriate circumstances. Of course, a range of obviously non-contractarian theories can end up saying that the principles they advance might be chosen by reasonable people properly situated. When they do say this, however, the appeal to what the people might agree to (or choose) swings off the side as a fifth wheel rolling along with the theory but driving no part of it. The content of the principles advanced is wholly unaffected by consideration of what people might reasonably agree to – all the influence goes the other direction.

In order to meet the central challenge a contractarian theory has to show that the appeal to what people might agree to is sensitive in some way either (i) to the variety of people participating in the choice, or (ii) to the variety of people to be governed by what is chosen, or (iii) to the variety of people being addressed by the argument. Only then will the idea that morality turns on what distinct individuals might agree to have a significant role. If, alternatively, the key choice or agreement in play might as well be made by and for a single individual, talk of what people (as opposed to a person) might agree to will have no substantive impact on the nature of the principles that are supported by the argument and the contractarian framework will be making no significant contribution to the theory. As it happens, all three of these options have been explored, exploited, and defended.

Thus some contractarians argue that the appropriate circumstances of choice leave intact, in the way a veil of ignorance might not, the key fact that those who are seeking to reach agreement differ from one another in ways that influence which principles might be genuine candidates for mutual agreement. This sort of argument usually characterizes the relevant agreement as being a result of bargaining or some kind of balanced accommodation, the particular content of which reflects differences among the participants. By leaving intact individual differences and allowing those differences to have some impact on the nature of the principles that are supported by the argument, such views make genuine room for the contractarian thought that the legitimacy of certain principles depends non-trivially on what people collectively might agree to.

Other contractarians argue that the outcome of the choice in question is shaped substantially by the fact that what is being chosen (a set of principles to govern interactions among individuals, or a set of basic institutions to structure society, or whatever) is chosen for a potentially diverse group of people who differ in talents, values, personality, etc. This sort of argument turns our attention to the ways in which the choice problem is shaped by the prospect of the results applying to different people. Even if, in the appropriate circumstances, one chooser is as good as another and more than one is no real addition (as might be the case behind a veil of ignorance), it may be that what such a chooser would select is influenced by the fact that those for whom she is choosing are different in ways that need to be accommodated, from the start, by the choice she makes.

Still other contractarians argue that the whole choice situation – the circumstances under which it is to be made and the nature of those who are to make it – is answerable, in a non-trivial way, to the fact that the over-all contractarian argument is being offered not to a single person but to people insofar as they see themselves as together trying to settle on acceptable principles for interacting with each other. This sort of argument focuses on the situation of the actual people to whom the arguments are addressed and maintains that their differences have an impact on just how the choice situation is to be described. A crucial feature of our actual situation, it seems, is that we can expect reasonable people to disagree fundamentally about central philosophical and moral issues in ways that mean there is no real prospect of reaching an across the board consensus. Nonetheless, there may be room for all reasonable people to agree (for their different reasons) that there are reasons to regulate our interactions by norms that are mutually acceptable by all who are reasonable and we may see the original contract situation as articulating the common ground shared by all those who are reasonable (Rawls 1993).

All three lines of argument have more than a little plausibility. At the very least, they suggest there might be room to defend the view that the contractarian framework, in some guise or other, can play more than a heuristic role in a theory. Still, those who offer some version of contractarianism as the best articulation of moral concerns we are assumed to share face two additional worries.

The first is that the variety of contractarian theories itself testifies to the fact that people's prior understandings of morality differ significantly, even when it comes to thinking through what impartiality, say, consists in. And this raises a problem since, in the face of a range of different contractarian theories, the question naturally arises: which, if any, of these articulations of our prior concern captures accurately the object of that concern? Asking what people, appropriately situated, might agree to seems to provide no purchase whatsoever on that question, since all the different versions of contractarianism will travel with their own preferred description of the circumstances of choice and of the grounds on which the people so situated will reach agreement. Whatever counts as good grounds for settling on one (contractarian) characterization of our moral concern rather than another, it seems it won't be grounds that turn in any interesting sense on what people would agree to, if they were properly situated. The fundamental argument for one view rather than another looks as if it will have to be decidedly non-contractarian.

The second worry arises even if a particular characterization of the contractarian framework settles out as successfully capturing our moral concerns. It centers on the question: what reason is there to embrace that moral concern? Even those who are concerned to act as morality requires might, on reflection, wonder whether they have any good reason to retain or act on that concern, especially in situations where morality quite clearly requires sacrifice. Why not think of the concern as merely a reflection of socialization that one would do better to be without? Insofar as contractarianism is offered solely as a way to articulate a concern for morality that we are assumed to share, it will in effect ignore the issue. But it is an issue, many think, that should not be put to one side casually, not least of all because so often peoples' actual concerns reflect ignorance, superstition, and prejudice. Morality of course presents itself as legitimately commanding allegiance and sacrifice. But do we really have reason to offer the allegiance and make the sacrifices, when called for?

The Hobbesian approach to contractarianism takes this challenge seriously and sees the contractarian framework as offering a uniquely compelling answer to it. Before turning to this approach, though, I should mention one tempting answer that is available to the Kantian contractarian. As this answer would have it, those who acknowledge that some course of action is morally right or required, but wonder whether they have reason to act accordingly, are failing to appreciate something that follows directly from what they have acknowledged: that they have (moral) reason to act as required. Acknowledging a moral demand, it seems reasonable to think, carries in its wake recognition of a moral reason to act accordingly. But this observation just pushes the problem back a step, since now the question is whether one has any good reason to give weight to moral reasons in one's deliberations. One might insist at this point that moral reasons are necessarily weighty so that once we admit there are moral reasons there's no good sense to be given to wondering about the weight of those reasons. Yet it is not hard to sympathize with those who would feel cheated by such an answer – cheated of a non-question-begging defense of the importance of morality.

Hobbesian contractarianism

The Hobbesian approach to contractarianism offers such a defense. Those who take this approach argue that we have non-moral reasons to embrace morality. The distinctively contractarian element in this approach comes with explaining the way in which the reasons we each have for embracing morality are reasons that reflect the interdependence of our interests and the opportunities we have for mutual benefit. Speaking in broad terms, the Hobbesian approach views morality as constituted by a set of principles the adoption of which is advantageous for everyone in a way that means each person would have (non-moral) reason to adopt the principles as long as others did as well. And it sees the legitimacy of morality's demands as turning on our having (non-moral) reason to support them.

One of the earliest versions of contractarianism, advanced in Plato's *Republic*, contained the core elements of the Hobbesian strand of contemporary moral contractarianism. Put in Glaucon's mouth, this version of contractarianism is pleasingly direct. According to the view he sets out, the rules of justice are conventional and represent a compromise. On the one hand, people would prefer to have their wills unchecked by others. On the other hand, they would prefer not to suffer the unchecked wills of others. Recognizing that they can't enjoy the first without suffering the second, and rightly fearing the second, they band together to establish and enforce mutually agreeable limits on each other's wills. These limits, Glaucon suggests, simply are the rules of justice. Thus, as Glaucon tells the story, the constraints justice imposes are a reflection of convention, yet the reflection of a convention we each have (non-moral) reason to encourage and embrace (given the human condition). The convention that constitutes morality, while a compromise of sorts, is nonetheless a reasonable one that redounds to our mutual advantage. (Gauthier 1986, Buchanan 1975, and Harman 1978 all offer contemporary defenses of this sort of view).

Game theory provides resources for representing perspicuously the underlying structure of social interactions that give point, in the way Glaucon suggests, to moral principles. In the process it has made possible a sophisticated investigation of the various different ways in which the reasons any particular person might have to act in one way or another depend upon what others have reason to do. Perhaps most influential on this front has been the Prisoners Dilemma which models a situation where the options and available benefits are such that, if each person directly maximizes her expected utility, they will together predictably end up worse off than they would have been had they cooperatively forgone immediately available benefits.[1] But various other notions from game theory and economics have played crucial roles in recent discussions of contractarianism. Especially important on this front have been developments concerning the understanding of Free Riders (who enjoy a benefit thanks to the efforts of others without themselves participating in producing that benefit), externalities (which are costs imposed by decisions that are shifted to those who have had no say in their production), and assurance problems (where a potentially available benefit for all will be beyond reach unless all have assurance that others will do their parts). In each of these cases, it looks as if a successfully established and internalized set of principles requiring certain sorts of acts, demanding the consideration of others, and underwriting confidence that others will act in concert, would alleviate problems we would all otherwise face. Reciprocal constraints, intelligently selected, lead to mutual advantage.

The hope held out by Hobbesian contractarianism is that, at least to some extent, moral principles might ultimately be justified by showing the extent to which we all benefit from living in a community of people who constrain their pursuit of interest by those principles. At the same time, though, the hope must be balanced by the recognition that in many ways the Hobbesian approach will likely support principles that match commonsense at best only imperfectly.

On the Hobbesian view, for instance, the advantages we each enjoy from morality come primarily from others embracing moral principles and secondarily from our avoiding the burdens we would suffer were others to punish us for violating those principles. In particular situations, the balance of advantages may fall in favor of violating particular principles, especially if one can do so undetected (and so unpunished) by others. As a result, even where there might be mutual advantage in establishing recognizably moral principles to govern our interactions, there may in certain cases be no advantage from – and so no reason, on this view, for – compliance. And even when there is an advantage to be gained, the motive for so complying appears to be distinctly non-moral. Thus at most the Hobbesian approach seems to underwrite acting morally for non-moral, indeed apparently selfish, reasons. To the extent a full justification of being moral involved justifying doing as morality requires *because* morality requires it, the Hobbesian might seem incapable of providing the justification (but see Gauthier 1986 and Sayre-McCord 1989).

Moreover, on this view, the principles that would be mutually advantageous overlap only contingently, and then pretty clearly only partially, with those we currently recognize as moral principles. After all, to the extent the principles we have reason to embrace turn on what others too have (non-moral) reason to embrace the principles will almost surely reflect the differential power, wealth, and general situation of those party to the arrangement. Similarly, when it comes to those whose protection brings no advantage to others (e.g., the weak and infirm) the principles the adoption of which would bring mutual benefit would presumably not offer them protection, since such protection would bring no advantage to others. In both cases, the resulting – mutually advantageous – principles will presumably differ from those recommended by commonsense morality.

The tension between commonsense morality and the principles that would be recommended by Hobbesian contractarian is due in no small part to holding that principles are legitimate only if they can be shown to be advantageous to real people in their actual circumstances. For, almost inevitably, morally suspect differences among people will then influence the content of the principles that will qualify as legitimate (because genuinely advantageous). Yet the more one corrects for these morally suspect differences by focusing not on actual advantages people can expect but on the advantages that would be secured under hypothetical circumstances, the less one can claim real people have (non-moral) reason to care. If I have been born to comfort and wealth or have secured such a life through force or fraud or cunning, any subsequent agreements I might make would no doubt be distorted by my initial advantages. Of course someone might, on grounds of fairness, say, insist on disallowing the influence of these advantages, but then the prospect of mutual advantage plummets as the real benefits to me disappear. The moral appeal of the resulting principles seems to be inversely proportional to their claim on actually being advantageous to all. Be that as it may, if one takes seriously the idea that people should act as they have reason to, and if one thinks what one has reason to do is whatever is personally advantageous, then a mismatch between advantage and commonsense morality would be all the worse for commonsense.

Fortunately, Hobbesian contractarians can and usually do admit that people's interests and preferences may be other-regarding, sympathetically directed, and broadly sensitive in ways that mean a true appraisal of how their interests are intertwined with other's will reveal, after all, an argument from mutual advantage to principles that are recognizably moral. Their appeal to interest and advantage in defending moral principles does not have to be an appeal solely to self-interest and private advantage. By taking honest account of human nature, and the extent to which we can be engaged by the welfare of others (to a greater or lesser degree, in response to both nature and nurture), it is at least plausible to think real advantage for all may be secured by the adoption of moral principles already securely established in commonsense.

No doubt any defense of morality that needs to appeal, in this way, to our fellow feeling leaves moral principles contingent in two ways that may be disturbing. First of all, the content of the principles is, on such a view, contingent upon the existence and shape of our concern for others. Second of all, the force of the argument offered for giving allegiance to the principles will be contingent as well on the actual concerns of those addressed. Although, unlike Kantian contractarianism, the Hobbesian variety need not suppose that the people addressed by the argument already possess a distinctively moral concern.

Significantly, the Kantian and Hobbesian approaches may compliment rather than compete with each other. For it may well be that the concern we have non-moral reason to embrace (as the Hobbesian would argue) is a distinctly moral concern the content of which calls for contractarian elaboration (as the Kantian would maintain).

Conclusion

There is a third version of contractarianism, inspired by Hume, that takes for granted neither a concern for morality nor any particular account of what people have reason to do or accept (Hume 1978). It sets out to explain why evaluative concepts and commitments would naturally emerge among beings with our capacities, concerns, strengths and weaknesses. The distinctly contractarian elements in the evolutionary story revolve around the evaluative concepts and commitments themselves being conventional solutions to problems people would otherwise face. In setting out to explain our evaluative concepts without presupposing others the Humean contractarianism is more ambitious than either the Kantian or the Hobbesian approaches. Yet the ambition is mitigated by the fact that the Humean approach is concerned neither to establish any particular substantive moral view nor to argue that people have reason, of any particular sort, to be moral. Instead, it hopes to account for the evaluative concepts we actually possess (contractarian in content or not, rationally embraced or not) by appealing initially only to non-evaluative features of our situation and the de facto advantages that come with the capacity to think in evaluative terms.

Once evaluative concepts are up and running, and have a life of their own, the Humean – no less than others – will rely on them in justifying or criticizing not only particular actions and institutions but also, in some cases, the conventions that give shape to the concepts themselves. As a result, the Humean contractarian might well end up defending a particular evaluative stance concerning morality and practical reasons more broadly. So she may embrace the Kantian view that we possess a moral concern that is best articulated by appeal to the contractarian framework, or she may share the Hobbesian view that a proper understanding of what people have reason to do shows that their reasons are essentially bound up with their own advantage. Or she may reject both views. Her commitment is to seeing the evaluative concepts she relies on as being grounded in, and shaped by, a distinctive set of conventions. Just as moves in a game of chess make sense only in the context defined by the rules of the game, so too, the Humean maintains, evaluative judgments make sense only in the context defined by the conventional rules governing the concepts that are deployed in those judgments. Our capacity to think in moral terms and to talk of reasons depends, on this view, upon resources that are available only once certain conventions and practices have been established.

Significantly, Humeanism offers an account of the conventions that give place and point to distinctively evaluative concepts, not (or at least not merely) an account of fellow feeling or altruism or cooperative dispositions. Thus it hopes to explain our capacity to make evaluative judgments and not (merely) our capacity to get along or respond emotionally. Presumably the conventions that define our evaluative concepts require the presence of various affective reactions and dispositions. But the Humean's focus is on those conventions themselves and the way in which they serve to constitute our evaluative concepts by setting standards for their correct application.

The Humean approach resembles the Hobbesian, in that the introduction of evaluative concepts (and the principles or standards that specify their content) is seen as an advantageous solution to a problem people collectively would otherwise face. Yet there are some crucial differences. In particular, on the Humean view, while the concepts do have this benefit they are not seen as deliberately introduced on the basis of reasons people recognize (since, by hypothesis, there is no substantive concept of reason yet in play and so no sense to be made of people actually recognizing reasons). Thus, in the first instance, the concepts are seen as arising in an explicable way, given the situations in which people would find themselves, but not as rational solutions to a problem of collective choice. Of course, once the relevant concepts are in place, it is possible to reflect back on the introduction and evolution of the evaluative concepts. And on reflection, the Humean approach assumes, one will discover there are good grounds for being glad something like the original concepts were introduced and for endorsing what they have become as they have evolved. However, at this point, the grounds for approving of the evaluative concepts we share will go beyond the austere resources of an appeal to self-interest and will implicate substantive considerations of fairness, justice, and value in ways that a Hobbesian excludes from consideration. (See Sayre-McCord 1994.)

Of course, reflecting on the origin and nature of our evaluative principles may well reveal deep problems with our current understanding of our evaluative concepts. But then the grounds for criticism and the justifications offered for altering our understanding of what justice, say, requires, will of necessity invoke evaluative concepts we have and can understand. The original, mutually advantageous, conventions will be providing, in these cases, both the resources and the reasons for reflectively correcting the conventions as they stand. The process of reflective adaptation that is then in play is a crucial element in making sense of an otherwise puzzling and anyway distinctive feature of evaluative concepts – their essential contestability.

The process of reflective adaptation plays an important role in addressing two worries. The first worry is that Humean conventionalism is committed to an objectionable form of relativism since the concepts that may emerge in one community might well differ substantially from those in another community. The second worry is that by giving a central role to mutual advantage the approach will inevitably underwrite moral principles that are arbitrarily parochial in their focus and implications. After all, the concepts that do emerge in a particular society, it seems, will be shaped by the interests of those in the community without regard to others. Both considerations raise serious worries, of course, but only insofar as the relativism involved is objectionable and the parochialism arbitrary. There is no doubt that some versions of relativism are objectionable and that parochial concerns are often arbitrary. Still, that different communities may develop different evaluative concepts to answer to their particular situations seems not only something that obviously happens but also unobjectionable (as long as the concepts in questions are unobjectionable). Similarly, that the concepts that develop within a community answer to that community's needs and interests seems not at all arbitrary. Nor does it seem disturbing on other grounds once we notice that the content of the concepts we have an interest in having may well, and in fact do, bring within their scope the interests of others. To the extent there are reasons to expand the scope of our principled concern or adjusting our understanding of our commitment's implications, those reasons are articulated using our current concepts. And these are concepts the currency of which finds an explanation in the Humean story of their social role. Our capacity reasonably to criticize principles and practices cannot outstrip the conceptual resources we have for identifying and articulating the supposed difficulties and what the Humean view offers is an explanation – a metaphysically and epistemically modest explanation – of those resources. Barring the discovery that our evaluative concepts carry the seeds of their own destruction, Humean contractarianism is well placed to accommodate and even embrace whatever substantive considerations might be mobilized for thinking there is reason re-evaluate our evaluative commitments.

This very capacity to accommodate and adapt to new considerations calls into question the value of Humean contractarianism, to the extent one hopes to use contractarianism to identify and defend some particular (and fixed) set of evaluative principles. It is important to recognize that this approach cannot offer, and does not pretend to offer, such a defense. Instead, the aim of Humean contractarianism is to explain the origin and nature of our evaluative concepts in a way that shows them to find their source in human nature. At the same time, though, the hope is to show that in discovering the origin and nature of evaluative principles we simultaneously show them, thereby, to have a claim on our allegiance. In playing the role they do in social interaction, in serving as the medium (so to speak) through which people can coordinate actions and recommendations and resolve conflicts, our evaluative concepts at least in part earn their own endorsement.

Whether and how the Humean approach might mesh with the Kantian and Hobbesian approaches to contractarianism is unsettled. Those tempted by Humean contractarianism, myself included, suspect that it can offer a philosophically satisfying account of (i) when the Kantian appeal to what people might find mutually agreeable under fair conditions is relevant to determining moral demands (and when it is not) and (ii) why the Hobbesian appeal to our non-moral interest in resolving conflict and coordinating behavior is relevant to morality's demands (but why it does not ultimately limit their scope).

Whether and how contractarianism of any sort might ultimately be defended is also unsettled. However, those tempted by contractarianism suspect that a proper understanding of morality must see morality as a reflection of what those subject to its demands might reasonably accept.[2]

Notes

1   See Luce and Raiffa (1957) for the classic description of the dilemma. Here is the dilemma. Imagine two prisoners find themselves facing the following offer. If neither con-

fesses to the crime they are being charged with, they will both be convicted of some lesser crime (that carries a penalty, let's say, of a year in prison). If they both confess, then both will be convicted of the more serious crime but will receive some leniency for having confessed (so they will each, say, serve five years). But if one confesses and the other doesn't, the person who confesses will get off free with no penalty and the other will serve the maximum sentence (of, say, ten years). Assuming the various years in prison represent costs to the individuals in proportion as they add up, the prisoners face a kind of dilemma: each sees that whether the other person confesses or not she does better to confess, since if the other person confesses she can, by confessing herself, spend only five years, rather than 10, in prison and if the other person doesn't confess she can, by confessing herself, spend no time at all in prison rather than a year. But if each acts according to this reasoning, they will together confess themselves into five years of jail each rather than the one that they would have been sentenced had they both kept quiet. Yet as soon as one has reason to think the other will not confess she finds herself again with compelling reason to confess. . . . The structure of the dilemma remains even if the costs and benefits at stake are radically different and regardless of whether they represent the selfish concern of the criminal simply to stay out of jail or the selfless preoccupation with worries about the welfare of her children. Moreover, assuming the pay-offs have the Prisoners' Dilemma structure, prior promises to remain silent leave the dilemma in place. What is needed to solve it is either something that will change the pay-offs so as to eliminate the dilemma or grounds for reasoning in some way that breaks free from simply maximizing expected utility.

2   Thanks are due to Robert Goodin, Philip Pettit, Michael Ridge, and Michael Smith for comments on an earlier draft of this essay.

References

Buchanan, James: *The Limits of Liberty* (Chicago: University of Chicago Press, 1975).

Gauthier, David: *Morals By Agreement* (Oxford: Clarendon Press, 1986).

——: "Why Contractarianism?" in P. Vallentyne (ed.), *Contractarianism and Rational Choice* (New York: Cambridge University Press, 1991), pp. 5–30.

Gough, J. W.: *The Social Contract*, 2nd edn. (Oxford: Clarendon Press, 1957).

Habermas, Jürgen: "Discourse Ethics: Notes on a Program of Philosophical Justification," in Christian Lenhardt and Shierry Weber Nicholasen (trans.), *Moral Consciousness and Communicative Action* (Cambridge: MIT Press, 1990).

Harman, Gilbert: "Relativistic Ethics: Morality as Politics," *Midwest Studies in Philosophy*, III (1978): 109–21.

Hume, David : *A Treatise of Human Nature* (Oxford: Oxford University Press, 1978).

——: "Of the Original Contract," in Eugene Miller (ed.), *Essays: Moral, Political and Literary* (Indianapolis: Liberty Classics, 1985), pp. 465–87.

Harsanyi, John: "Cardinal Utility in Welfare Economics and the Theory of Risk-Taking," *Journal of Political Economy*, 61 (1953): 309–21.

——: *Essays on Ethics, Social Behavior, and Scientific Explanation* (Dordrecht: D. Reidel, 1976).

Kant, Immanuel: *Groundwork of the Metaphysic of Morals*, H. J. Paton (trans.) (New York: Harper & Row, 1964).

——: "On the Common Saying: 'This May be True in Theory, But It Doesn't Apply In Practice," in *Kant's Political Writings*, ed. Hans Reiss (Cambridge: Cambridge University Press, 1970).

Lessnoff, Michael: *Social Contract* (New York: Macmillan, 1986).

Luce, R. D. and Howard Raiffa: *Games and Decisions* (New York: John Wiley and Sons, 1957).

Mackie, J. L.: *Ethics: Inventing Right and Wrong* (Harmondsworth: Penguin Books, 1977).

Milo, Ronald: "Contractarian Constructivism," *Journal of Philosophy*, 92 (1995): 181–204.

Pateman, Carole: *The Sexual Contract* (Stanford: Stanford University Press, 1988).

Plato: *The Republic*, G. M. A. Grube (trans.) with revisions by C. D. C. Reeve (Indianapolis: Hackett Publishing Company, 1992).

Rawls, John: *A Theory of Justice* (Cambridge, MA: Harvard University Press, 1971).

——: *Political Liberalism* (New York: Columbia University Press, 1993).

Rousseau, Jean-Jacques: *On the Social Contract*, Roger and Judith Masters (trans.) (New York: St. Martin's Press, 1978).

Sandel, Michael: *Liberalism and the Limits of Justice* (Cambridge: Cambridge University Press, 1982).

Sayre-McCord, Geoffrey: "Deception and Reasons to Be Moral," *American Philosophical Quarterly*, 26 (1989): 113–22.

——: "On Why Hume's 'General Point of View' Isn't Ideal – and Shouldn't Be," *Social Philosophy & Policy*, 11, (1994): 202–28.

Scanlon, Thomas: "Contractualism and Utilitarianism," in Amartya Sen and Bernard Williams (eds.), *Utilitarianism and Beyond* (Cambridge: Cambridge University Press, 1982), pp. 103–28.

——: *What We Owe to Each Other* (Cambridge, MA: Harvard University Press, 1998).

Skyrms, Brian: *Evolution of the Social Contract* (New York: Cambridge University Press, 1996).

Vallentyne, Peter (ed.): *Contractarianism and Rational Choice* (New York: Cambridge University Press, 1991).

Chapter 14

Intuitionism

David McNaughton

Two Kinds of Moral Theory

What makes an action morally right? Different moral theories give different answers to this question. The simplest answer would be that just one consideration was relevant to the rightness of an action. *Consequentialism* is a popular and influential theory which claims just that. According to consequentialism, the only consideration relevant to determining the rightness of an action is the effect that action will have on the amount of value in the world. Any action of any significance will affect value. In many cases, it will have some good effects and some bad ones. From the moral point of view, the more your actions can bring about good things and avoid or remove bad things the better. So the only consideration relevant to the rightness of an action is the balance of good consequences over bad. What matters, with respect to the rightness of what you do, is the extent to which your action makes things go better (or less badly) than they would have done if you had not acted (or acted in some other way). Thus, from the moral point of view, the right action is the one with the best results. Agents act rightly just if there was no other act they could do which would have made things go even better.

Consequentialism is not so much one theory as a group or family of theories, all of which share the basic premise that when we judge things from the moral point of view, we must do so by reference to the value of the consequences they produce. The view sketched in the first paragraph is the simplest and most popular version, which we might call maximizing act-consequentialism. It is a *maximizing* version of consequentialism, because it tells us that the right action is the one that produces the *most* good. Other versions, sometimes called *satisficing* consequentialism, make the weaker claim that an action is right if it produces enough or sufficient in the way of good consequences. It is an *act*-consequentialist theory, because its primary focus is on how we should judge acts rather than motives or moral rules.

Act-consequentialist theories can be further divided into those that give either a *monist* or a *pluralist* account of goodness. Monists hold that there is just one kind of thing that is intrinsically good. Thus classical utilitarians, such as Bentham and Mill, asserted that pleasure alone was good. Pluralists maintain that there are a number of distinct kinds of good thing. One might think, for example, that not only the amount of pleasure, but also the way in which it was distributed was morally important. If that is so, then fairness in the distribution of benefits and burdens would be a separate good. If there were two worlds in which there was equal pleasure, but in one the pleasures were more fairly distributed than in the other, then the fairer world would also be the better world. Some other candidates for intrinsic goods are knowledge, beauty, achievement, and self-esteem.

Although act-consequentialists may be either monist or pluralist about the *good*, they are all monists about the *right*. As we have seen, they agree that only one consideration, namely the goodness of the consequences, is relevant to whether an action is right. By contrast, *deontological* theories either deny that the goodness of the consequences of an act bears directly on its rightness, or deny that the value of the consequences is the *sole* criterion of rightness. Most, though perhaps not all, adopt a pluralist account of rightness, in that they hold that a number of distinct considerations are directly relevant to determining the rightness of an act. That one has made a promise, for example, or that one's act would involve lying, or directly harming some innocent person, are all factors that have been held to carry independent weight in determining which action would be the right one. Thus the classical way of drawing the distinction between consequentialism and deontology contrasts their different accounts of the relation between the right and the good. Act-consequentialism holds that the right is wholly determined by the good; the rightness of any action depends solely on the amount of value it will produce compared with other actions. Deontology claims, by contrast, that the right is independent of the good. The rightness of an action is not, or not simply, a function of the amount of value produced by it; other factors are relevant. Indeed, it may often be right to produce less good than one could.

1.1   Intuitionism

Intuitionism is one species of deontological theory. Like other deontological theories, it holds that there are a number of distinct considerations that bear on the rightness of any act or, as we might put it for brevity, that there are a number of distinct moral principles or duties. What chiefly distinguishes it from other deontological theories is the claim that some of these duties are fundamental or underivative. They are not grounded in, or derived from, some more general theory. When we reflect on our moral experience, we come to realize that we have such duties as a duty to keep promises, a duty not to harm, or a duty to make amends for wrongs we have done. Each of these duties is distinct from the others and distinct from any duty we may have to make the world a better place. If we ask how we know that these are our duties, the reply is that they are *self-evident*. In a rather outdated terminology (which we find, for example, in Sidgwick) such fundamental self-evident moral principles are known as Intuitions, hence the name of the theory.

Other deontological theories, while agreeing with the intuitionist that there are a number of distinct duties, reject the claim that they are self-evident. Rather, they seek to provide a theoretical underpinning for them by showing how they can be generated by some plausible account of human nature or of the nature of rational agency. Thus Kantianism starts from claims about the nature of practical reasons, and from this derives a test which any maxim, or principle, upon which an agent might act must pass if it is to be acceptable. Our various duties are then generated by seeing which maxims pass and which fail that test. Libertarianism starts from a general theory about the nature of persons from which it derives rights to self-determination and the ownership of property. Intuitionism offers no such theoretical backing for what it takes to be our most fundamental duties. They have to stand on their own feet, to be self-supporting.

The term "intuitionism" is misleading and unfortunate. It encourages various popular misconceptions, such as the view that intuitionists believe in a mysterious faculty or "moral sense," unknown to science, by which we detect moral properties. Confusion may also be caused by a change in philosophical usage. The term "moral intuitions" is now used to pick out, not ultimate self-evident principles, but rather the judgments we are inclined to make about what we ought to do in particular cases. To avoid confusion I will use the phrase "moral intuition" only in its contemporary sense.

Intuitionism flourished in England between the World Wars, although its roots go far back into eighteenth century moral philosophy and beyond. After the Second World War, it became unfashionable, and remained so until very recently. Few people bothered to read its proponents – Prichard, Ross, Broad and Ewing – carefully or sympathetically and consequently it was often caricatured. In the immediate aftermath of the Second World War that neglect was unsurprising, since the prevailing orthodoxy rejected the idea that there could be objective moral truths and moral knowledge. Even after 1970, while interest in objectivist moral theories like Kantianism revived, intuitionism continued to be regarded as a "non-starter." No doubt the over-hasty dismissal of the theory stems in part from the failure to study the classic intuitionist texts carefully, but that failure itself needs explanation.

2   Objections to Intuitionism

Intuitionism has been, I think, often prejudged to be not worth studying because it is taken to be fundamentally non-explanatory. Here's why. We begin moral theorizing by reflecting on our everyday moral thought and experience. Armed with only a rather disparate collection of moral principles culled from various sources, we find ourselves in a variety of morally perplexing situations. Faced with these difficulties we might hope a moral theory would deliver four things. First, that it would reveal some systematic structure in our moral thought. Second, that it would tell us how to deal with moral conflicts, where competing considerations pull us in different directions. Third, it should offer a plausible account of how moral knowledge is possible (if it is). Fourth, a moral theory should say something about why morality matters.

Intuitionism has been accused of failing to deliver the goods in all four respects. First, critics claims intuitionism is unsystematic: an unconnected heap of duties with no underlying rationale. Second, intuitionism is held to have nothing helpful to say about the resolution of moral conflict. Third, intuitionism is held to be unable to explain moral knowledge. Critics say that, in response to the question "How do we know an action is right?", the intuitionist can only answer: "by intuition". But this might be seen as "not really an answer at all, but a confession of bewilderment got up to look like an answer" (Warnock 1967: 7). Fourth, critics claim intuitionism cannot explain why we *care* about morality. Even if we could know moral truths "by intuition", why should such knowledge play any role in motivating our conduct?

To its critics, intuitionism stops just at the point where the real philosophical work should start. While it is conceded that it gives a pretty accurate sketch of much of our everyday moral thought,

> the theory, appraised as a contribution to philosophy, seems deliberately, almost perversely, to answer no questions, to throw no light on any problem. One might almost say that the doctrine actually consists in a protracted denial that there is anything of the slightest interest to be said. (Warnock 1967: 12–13)

In short, it looks as if intuitionism should scarcely be dignified with the title of theory at all.

3   Defending Intuitionism

These criticisms can all be met. In many cases, they rest on misunderstanding. All that is needed to rebut these charges is a clear exposition of the resources that intuitionism has at its disposal. It will emerge that intuitionism is a great deal more systematic and explanatory than its critics admit. Nevertheless, there is an element of truth in the claim that intuitionism is anti-theoretical. Intuitionists characteristically believe that many philosophers have had unrealistic expectations about what moral theory can deliver. Some people hoped moral theory could supply definitive answers to at least some of the many disputed, troubling and puzzling moral problems that face us. Intuitionists are sceptical about the power of abstract moral theory to answer all moral questions. They typically hold, with Aristotle, that we cannot expect more precision in ethics than the subject is capable of. It is a mistake to suppose that difficult moral issues can be definitively resolved with a high degree of certainty. Thus, the failure of intuitionism to supply a theory which will help us resolve our moral quandaries stems not from a perverse refusal to answer sensible questions, but from a principled scepticism about the pretensions of moral theory to perform such a task.

I shall attempt to make good some of these defensive claims in what follows. If this defense is successful then intuitionism will be in good shape as a moral theory. We have seen that even its critics concede that intuitionism does a good job of delineating the outlines of our ordinary moral thinking. This is certainly a strong point in its favor, since many concede that a crucial test for an adequate moral theory is that it does not deliver moral verdicts too far out of line with everyday moral judgments. If the four objections just sketched can be rebutted then it will have been shown that it fulfils the other criteria for a good moral theory: it is systematic, it offers a plausible account of moral knowledge, and it can explain why we care about morality. Although I cannot argue the point here, it could be claimed that intuitionism does at least as well as its rivals in all these crucial respects.

4 How Systematic is Intuitionism?

Of all the different versions of intuitionism, by far the most systematic and best-known account is that of W. D. Ross, which I will use as the starting point for discussion. As we have seen, intuitionism adopts a pluralist stance about the right. There are, it claims, a number of distinct and fundamental moral considerations which bear upon whether an act is right. That immediately raises the question of what happens when there is a conflict between such considerations. What determines whether the act is right or not? Ross's answer to this question is justly famous, but since it is often misunderstood, we need to look at it in some detail.

4.1 Ross's conception of "a prima facie duty"

Any theory that holds that there is more than one moral principle has to offer an analysis of what happens in cases of moral conflict; cases where, whatever we do, we shall breach a moral principle. It would be unfortunate, to say the least, if the theory maintained that, in every such case, one could not avoid acting wrongly. Some writers do indeed make the controversial claim that there can be tragic dilemmas in which, whatever the agent does, she will have acted wrongly. Tragic dilemmas, if they are possible at all, are by their very nature exceptional. So even if we admit their possibility, a pluralist deontology has to tell us what we should do when two duties conflict. Some deontological theories try to resolve the problem by claiming that some duties are absolute or exceptionless, and thus take precedence over all others. (Of course, if there is more than one absolute duty, then the theory must be constructed so that the absolute duties cannot conflict, on pain of the problem reappearing.) Another possible solution would be to place all duties in a lexical order, as we order words in a dictionary, so that the highest always took precedence over the next highest, and so on. The difficulty with this suggestion is that it plainly runs counter to our moral intuitions. On one occasion, for example, we may think our duty to keep a promise should take precedence over our duty to help others, yet in a different situation we will judge the opposite – it all depends on how serious the promise, how great the good to be achieved, and the context in which the conflict occurs. No principle or duty systematically trumps another, though some may be thought to be particularly weighty.

Ross characteristically maintains that our ordinary moral thought is to be respected, here as elsewhere. He holds that each moral consideration is relevant to determining the rightness (or wrongness) of an action, but the presence of any one consideration cannot, in the case of conflict, guarantee that the act will be right, because it may be outweighed by competing moral considerations which count the other way. Which one wins out in any one instance depends upon the particular details of the case. He expressed this thought, not entirely happily as we shall see, by saying that our various duties – to keep promises, to help others etc. – are *prima facie duties.*

It is important to note that though one prima facie duty might be *outweighed* by another duty, the defeated prima facie duty is not thereby removed or canceled. If, for example, I ought to break my promise to take my son to the circus in order to visit my mother who is ill, the fact that I have made a promise remains morally relevant, and can still affect what I ought subsequently to do. I should do something to make amends to my son, even though I was justified in breaking my promise to him. A defeated consideration can linger, bringing its influence to bear on later decisions.

Ross was understandably unhappy about his own terminology, which he regarded as doubly misleading. To say that, *prima facie*, something has a certain characteristic suggests that it appears, at first sight, to have that characteristic but that subsequent investigation might show the appearances to be misleading. But this is not what Ross means. As we have seen, Ross needs a term which suggests that certain characteristics always count in favor of an action's being right, even when the action, because of other facts about it, turns out to be the wrong thing to do. The term "*pro tanto*," first suggested by Broad (1930: 282) better conveys the thought. To say that showing gratitude to someone is *pro tanto* right, is to say that, in virtue of the fact that an act expresses gratitude, it is right, *so far as that goes,* which carries the implication that other things not yet taken into account may yet make that act not the right one. An alternative, suggested by Ross in *The Foundations of Ethics* (1939: 85), is to abandon the term duty, which he also thinks of as misleading, and speak instead of responsibilities.

Why did Ross think that the term "duty" was misleading? Because he holds that, strictly speaking, only a particular act can be my duty; the term is misapplied in describing a type of action, such as the general duty to keep promises. My duty is that act which, when we have taken all morally relevant considerations into account, is the one we ought to do. Talk of *prima facie* duties unfortunately suggests that "what we are speaking of is a certain kind of duty, whereas it is in fact not a duty, but something related in a special way to duty" (1930: 20). I think we use the word "duty" perfectly properly in both ways. To avoid confusion, I shall restrict my use of the term to general duties, such as the duty to keep promises. Instead of saying that a particular action is my duty, I shall talk instead of it being the right action or the one I ought to do.[1]

What exactly is the relation, then, between the *prima facie* or *pro tanto* duties and an action's being right (or wrong)? Philip Stratton-Lake (1999) has suggested that we should think of the contrast as one between evidence and verdict. A prima facie duty is best seen as a fundamental evidential consideration, which must always be taken into account in reaching the final verdict on the rightness or wrongness of the act. This is true, as far as it goes, but the relation is closer than the terms evidence and verdict suggest. Something can count as evidence for a thing's having a certain property without its being what makes the thing have that property. What *makes* an action right, however, are the characteristics which count in its favor, that it is the keeping of a promise, or the bringing about of some good thing, etc. The relationship appears metaphysical rather than epistemic. The action is right *in virtue* of these considerations; they are reasons *for the act's being right*. They are not merely reasons for *reaching the verdict* that the action is right. Of course, only the features on the winning side make the act right. Where an action is right, any features that count against its being right, cannot be what makes it right. Nevertheless, as we saw, a defeated consideration can remain relevant to what I ought subsequently to do.

Ross is not, in his doctrine of *prima facie* duties, yet offering us an account of *how* we decide which way any particular conflict is to be resolved. He is simply spelling out how we are to understand moral conflicts, and how it can be that a moral consideration can bear on the rightness of an act without necessarily determining it.

4.2   Imposing order on our moral intuitions

I turn now to the charge that intuitionism is unsystematic because it does not impose any order or structure on the plethora of moral precepts which permeate moral thought. There are, no doubt, a number of ways in which a theory might seek to impose structure. One familiar model is provided by act-consequentialism. It tries to show that the multitude of considerations which appear to bear on the rightness of an action can be reduced to one – the production of good consequences. This does not, however, leave the other moral principles which we espouse with no role. No consequentialist thinks that we should, on each occasion, decide what to do by weighing up the total value of all the consequences of all the possible courses of action open to us, if for no other reason than that it would not be productive of the greatest good to spend so much time calculating and so little time acting. So we must appeal to secondary principles to guide our day to day choices. The choice of these derivative principles is, of course, determined by the overriding aim to maximize the good.

It is not commonly realized that Ross's Intuitionism is systematic in much the way that consequentialism is. The disagreement between the two theories concerns primarily the number of basic or underivative moral considerations there are. Consequentialism holds there is just one. Ross thinks this an over-simplification; there is a small number of fundamental moral considerations which cannot be reduced any further. All other moral principles are derived from these basic ones.

In *The Right and the Good* (1930: 21) Ross famously offers the following division of *prima facie* duties, while noting that it may need further refinement. It is a first shot at a list of fundamental and underived duties, which can be summarized as follows.

1 Duties resting on a previous act of my own. These in turn divide into two main categories:
   (a) duties of *fidelity*; these result from my having made a promise or something like a promise
   (b) duties of *reparation*; these stem from my having done something wrong so that I am now required to make amends.
2 Duties resting on previous acts of others; these are duties of *gratitude*, which I owe to those who have helped me.
3 Duties to prevent (or overturn) a distribution of benefits and burdens which is not in accordance with the merit of the persons concerned; these are duties of *justice*.
4 Duties which rest on the fact that there are other people in the world whose condition we could make better; these are duties of *beneficence*.
5 Duties which rest on the fact that I could better myself; these are duties of *self-improvement*.
6 Duties of not injuring others; these are duties of *non-maleficence*.

To offer such a list of fundamental morally relevant considerations is only, of course, to make a start on a systematic intuitionist theory. To complete it we need a principled method for determining what should be on the list and an account that explains how other duties are derived from these fundamental ones. The solution to the second issue will enable us to tackle the first. Unfortunately, Ross is not as explicit about the relation between the fundamental and the derived duties as he might be, and the skeleton of his theory has to be pieced together from scattered remarks. After reviewing and revising his list, he writes (1930: 27), "These seem to be, in principle, all the ways in which *prima facie* duties arise. In actual experience they are compounded together in highly complex ways." What these ways might be we have to work out from various examples he discusses. The duty to obey the laws of one's country, Ross suggests, "arises from" three basic duties: gratitude, fidelity and beneficence. Standardly, we owe a debt of gratitude to our country for benefits received; we have made an implicit promise to obey by living in it; and we should be law-abiding because things go better for society if we are. Similarly, there are two fundamental principles that count against lying: non-maleficence and fidelity. Lying normally inflicts an injury on the person lied to, and undermines an implicit undertaking, underlying day-to-day communication, to tell the truth (1930: 54–5).

In these examples, the duty that is not basic may be said to arise from or rest on one or more basic duties in the following sense. An action which we have a derivative duty to perform (e.g., not lying) will normally be an action which falls under one or more fundamental duties (in this case, fidelity and non-maleficence). It is because lying is standardly harmful and a breach of an implicit undertaking that it is wrong. However, Ross makes it clear, in discussing these examples, that there can be special circumstances in which one or more of the fundamental considerations which count against acting in these ways do not obtain. In such cases, the force or bindingness of the derivative duty may be weakened. Ross holds, for example, that the implicit undertaking to tell the truth cannot hold where I am an utter stranger to a society, and have had no chance to reach agreements, implicit or otherwise, with its members. Since he holds that a large part of our duty not to lie stems from the supposed implicit promise, its absence greatly weakens our duty not to lie.

Although Ross does not discuss this point, it seems perfectly possible that there might be cases where *none* of the considerations which normally tell against lying or law-breaking apply. A government may be so oppressive and unjust that neither gratitude nor beneficence dictate that its citizens should obey. And if, like the old Soviet Union, it refuses to let dissidents emigrate, then any argument from tacit consent to the government also lapses. In these non-standard circumstances, the fact that an act is illegal would not count *at all*, from the moral point of view, against doing that act. If that is right, then these kinds of duty are derivative, and not fundamental, because the characteristics by which they are picked out are not ones that are themselves *always* relevant to the rightness of acts. The *mere* fact that an act is illegal, or a lie, does not count against doing that act.

Being underivative, in the sense just defined, is not, however, sufficient for inclusion in Ross's list of basic duties, for he is also striving for as high a level of generality as possible. If one duty is just a specific instance of a more general kind of duty, then it will not be basic. Thus it is plausible to hold that we can only be in debt if we have borrowed money on the understanding (explicit or implicit) that we will repay. So the duty to repay debts is just a specific instance of the more general duty of fidelity, the duty to keep our undertakings. If that is right, then the duty to repay our debts is not derivative in the way that the duty to obey the law is, since the fact that an act will be the repaying of a debt *always* counts in its favor. Debt repayment does not get into the list of basic duties, not because it is not itself always morally relevant, but because it is insufficiently general.

I am not here concerned to defend Ross's analysis of any of these duties; I mention them because they illustrate the structure of his theory. With the two distinctions between derivative and underivative duties and between more and less general underivative duties in place, we can now see that Ross offers a systematic structure into which every possible duty can be assigned a place. Challenges to Ross's particular list can come from one of two directions. It may be claimed either that the list needs shortening because it contains a duty that is not really basic, or that it needs lengthening because it leaves out a basic duty.

In fact Ross himself thinks that he can shorten his original list. He holds that both self-improvement and justice may be seen as more specific instances of the duty of beneficence. Ross is a pluralist about the good, as well as a pluralist about the right. There are three kinds of good for Ross: virtue, knowledge, and pleasure (at least where it is merited). His original reason for distinguishing self-improvement from beneficence is that, while we have a duty to give pleasure to others we tend to think that we have no such duty towards ourselves. But our inclination to believe that we have no such duty may arise merely from the fact that it seems redundant to require us to do what we are already so strongly motivated to do. If that is so then self-improvement is merely a species of beneficence.[2] Similarly, Ross thinks that justice, as he understands it, can be shown to be a specific kind of beneficence, for the distribution of benefits and burdens in accordance with merit is itself a specific kind of good.[3]

4.3 Critical reflections on the structure of Ross's list

It is possible to raise questions both about the structure of Ross's list of fundamental duties and about particular items on it. Let me begin with a structural issue. We have seen that some of the original items on Ross's list – justice and self-improvement – got subsumed under the duty of beneficence. We might wonder what prevents the other duties being thus subsumed, and the whole theory collapsing back into consequentialism. Of the four other types of duty which remain on Ross's pared down list, the first three, fidelity, reparation and gratitude, are what are sometimes called "duties of special relationship". In each case the duty rests on some previous act either of my own or of others. It is because something morally significant has already occurred in the relationship between us that the other person has a claim on me. The other is not just an instance of someone whom I could benefit; he has a claim in virtue of our prior relationship to a benefit, and often to a very specific benefit, arising from the nature of my promise, or the sort of kindness he did me, or the wrong I did him. Others who don't stand in these relationships do not have these claims. As Ross says:

> The essential defect of the "ideal utilitarian" theory [i.e., consequentialism] is that it ignores, or at least does not do full justice to, the highly personal character of duty. If the only duty is to produce the maximum of good, the question who is to have the good – whether it is myself, or my benefactor, or a person to whom I have made a promise to confer that good on him, or a mere fellow man to whom I stand in no such special relation – should make no difference to my having a duty to produce that good. But we are all in fact sure that it makes a vast difference. (p. 22)

The consequentialist cannot capture this thought by pointing out that, if promise keeping, gratitude and reparation are such good things then consequentialism will certainly endorse our encouraging and promoting such acts. For as well as the general duty I may have to encourage widespread promise keeping, I also have a specific duty to benefit *you*, because it is to you that I made the promise. And it is precisely the personal nature of this claim which consequentialism cannot allow to be intrinsically morally significant. The consequentialist will indeed claim that I should adopt a policy of keeping my promises, but that is only because such a policy will tend to promote the general good. But this distorts the way we think about promising as a personal tie. In virtue of having promised you some good thing, I (rather than someone else) have a moral reason to give you (rather than someone else) the promised benefit. That this obligation is distinct from any general duty to promote the good can be seen by reflecting on the following example. Suppose I have made a promise to you to help you to move house, and suppose that a neighbor has made a similar promise to a friend of his. Assuming that the benefits are roughly proportional, then I would be at fault if I were to neglect my promise to you in order to help my neighbor fulfil his.

What about the duty not to harm? Is this a duty which consequentialism could accommodate? It depends on how we understand that duty, and here Ross is not as clear as he might be. He claims that it is wrong to inflict a certain level of harm on someone in order to produce a similar, or slightly larger, benefit for someone else. But this might be because bringing about a harm of a certain sort produces more disvalue than failing to give a benefit of a similar sort. Generally speaking, taking away something someone already has seems far worse than failing to give them that thing when they lack it. If that is so, then consequentialism can accommodate the thought by simply recognizing the greater disvalue in depriving someone of an existing good.

But there seems to be more to the duty not to harm than this. We tend to think it wrong to inflict a harm directly on some (innocent) person, even to prevent a similar harm being perpetrated against another innocent person. This suggests, though the issue is disputed, that the fact that the act would involve *my* directly harming another person is a reason for me not to do it, even if the disvalue would be the same whatever I do (since if I refrain from harming, someone else will be harmed). There are things we owe it to others not to do to them, even to prevent other people doing similar awful things. Clearly the consequentialist could not allow the thought that it would be *I*, rather than someone else, doing the harming to be a morally significant reason. There is nothing, of course, to prevent a consequentialist claiming, as before, that a policy of trying to avoid harming people oneself might have beneficial long term consequences. And, as before, this appears to fail to capture the intuition that somehow I owe it directly to my potential victim not to harm him.[4]

Ross is opposed to consequentialism insofar as he believes that there are duties of reparation, gratitude, fidelity, and non-maleficence, which sometimes require us not to bring about as much good as we can. But in another respect Ross agrees with consequentialism, for he construes the duty of beneficence as requiring us to make everyone's lives go as well as possible. And that leaves him open to some of the criticisms which have been leveled against consequentialism. First, it means that good deeds are always obligatory and never supererogatory. We typically think that there are saintly or heroic actions which go well beyond the call of duty and for which people receive especial praise. But on the view of beneficence which Ross and the consequentialist share the duty to do good has no upper limits. Second, it means that every choice is a moral choice. There is always the opportunity to do good, so there can never be morally indifferent choices. Ross's uncritical acceptance of the consequentialist conception of beneficence leads him into uncharacteristic conflict with normal reflective ethical thought.

We appear to operate with a more limited conception of beneficence, but capturing that conception is tricky and defending it difficult. We seem to think that each of us has the right to devote some time and resources to our own personal projects, even if we could do more good elsewhere, and that it is proper to allow personal preference a role in deciding which good causes to endorse. Articulating such an account in a perspicuous and defensible way is an important task for an intuitionism which respects our moral intuitions.[5]

I have said that Ross's account of beneficence makes every choice a morally significant one. One might object that Ross over-moralizes our choices in another way, by apparently insisting that the only thing that can outweigh a prima facie duty is another prima facie duty. There are two worries here. First, one might hold that there can on occasion be good and pressing reasons for not fulfilling a *prima facie* duty which are not themselves reasons of duty. I promised to mark this student's essay by tomorrow. I'm very tired and nothing disastrous will happen if I am a day late. So I go to bed, and with good reason. But that reason is not one on Ross's list of duties. Second, any moral reason in favor of an act, however slight, becomes a duty unless overridden by a more pressing moral demand. But there are surely cases where I have some moral reason to act in which the reason has not got the kind of strength which constitutes duty. I have reason to be grateful to you for a minor favor. It would be good to show my appreciation. But do I have a duty to do so, unless some other obligation trumps it? That seems too strong.

These are genuine worries about Ross's system, but easily accommodated. We could construe Ross's list as a list of morally relevant reasons without supposing either that only a moral reason can trump a moral reason, or that every moral reason will lead to one's having a duty unless a stronger moral reason can be found on the other side.

5 Intuitionist Epistemology

5.1 *Methodology*

How are we to determine if a particular moral consideration meets the criteria for being a distinct, fundamental and underivative *prima facie* duty? Ross's answer, which is implicit in the previous discussion, is that we should appeal to our reflective judgments about carefully constructed cases involving the duty or duties whose status as fundamental is in dispute. We should devise specific moral examples in which we attempt to isolate the influence of the supposedly fundamental moral consideration. Thus, as we have seen, we determine whether fidelity is independent of beneficence by thinking about a case where I can produce equal amounts of good either by keeping or by breaking a promise. We will judge, so he claims, that we have a duty to keep the promise (see Ross 1930: 18). Similarly, were someone to suggest that our duty to be truthful is fundamental rather than derivative, the test would be to construct a case where lying was insulated from its usual accompanying wrong-making features. Such a case might be playing a game of Cheat with my children, where lying did no harm and was not in breach of any tacit agreement or understanding. We then have to judge whether, in this case, the fact that the game involves lying counts against playing it.

This answer is in keeping with his general methodology (Ross 1930: 39–41). For Ross, the material from which we build any moral theory is the reflective judgment of thoughtful people. If the deliverances of a theory conflict with those judgments, then so much the worse for the theory. This does not mean, Ross hastens to add, that theoretical reflections can never influence our moral judgments. Where, however, theory tells us that some consideration cannot be morally relevant, but reflective scrutiny of crucial cases leaves us convinced that it is relevant, then it is the theory that must be rejected. If, for example, consequentialism tells us that

> we should give up our view that there is a special obligatoriness attaching to the keeping of promises because it is self-evident that the only duty is to produce as much good as possible, we have to ask ourselves whether we really, when we reflect, *are* convinced that this is self-evident, and whether we really *can* get rid of our view that promise-keeping has a bindingness independent of productiveness of maximum good. (p. 40)

Ross claims we cannot perform this feat. If theory requires that we abandon our reflective moral judgments, then what theory demands is unreasonable.

> [T]o ask us to give up at the bidding of a theory our actual apprehension of what is right and what is wrong seems like asking people to repudiate their actual experience of beauty, at the bidding of a theory which says "only that which satisfies such and such conditions can be beautiful". (p. 40)

We should not abandon our moral beliefs in the face of theoretical objections because, on Ross's view, we have direct insight as to what is morally relevant in the particular case. Further reflection or experience can lead us to change our minds. But in ethics, as in aesthetics, the crucial test of a theory is whether reflection on it changes our apprehension of the particular case.

So what is the nature of this direct insight, and in what cases can we have moral knowledge?

5.2 Certainty and probable opinion

It is often supposed that intuitionists think that there is a special, utterly mysterious, and possibly infallible, moral sense (intuition) by which we detect the presence of moral properties. This is pure invention on the part of intuitionism's opponents.[6] To the best of my knowledge, no intuitionist has ever postulated such an occult moral faculty. Insofar as we can know moral truths, we know them in ways that are familiar from our knowledge of other truths.

Nor should we conclude that, for an intuitionist, all moral truths are obvious. There are many of which we cannot be sure, and about which we should be diffident. Ross draws a sharp distinction between "our apprehension of the *prima facie* rightness of certain types" (1930: 29) and our judgment about the overall rightness or wrongness of particular acts. Claims about *prima facie* rightness (or wrongness) are self-evident. That an act is, for example, *prima facie* right in virtue of being the keeping of a promise, is something that we can know a priori, by reflection. It cannot be proved, but it requires no proof. It is something of which we can be certain. By contrast, judgments about what we should actually do in some particular case lack this certainty. For we cannot be certain in any case where there are conflicting moral considerations on each side. Even where we can only see considerations supporting one conclusion, we cannot be certain that there are not things to be said on the other side.

5.3 Self-evidence

The fundamental *prima facie* principles are, however, known with certainty. Ross does not suppose that moral agents are aware of them from the moment they first make a moral judgment. We can come to know them by a process of *intuitive induction*. Particular moral truths come first in the order of judging. We take some act to be right in virtue of being, say, an act of promise-keeping. After reflecting on a number of acts involving promise-keeping, we come to the conclusion that promise-keeping is a right-making characteristic. If this were simply an inductive inference, then its strength would depend on the number and variety of cases I had considered. But, Ross holds, having formed the principle, we can then come to have direct insight into its truth (see Ross 1939: 168–73). It is a necessary truth, knowable *a priori* because self-evident and thus requiring no proof. A truth is self-evident if understanding it is sufficient for being justified in believing it. One knows the proposition provided one believes it on the *basis* of understanding it (see Audi 1996: 114).

Such truths are self-evident, but that does not mean that they are *obvious*. They are evident to those with sufficient mental abilities and experience who have reflected properly about them. Ross's analogy here is with our knowledge of mathematical axioms and forms of inference. It may not be immediately obvious that some basic form of inference is valid, but reflection leads us to see that it is. We may go through several examples of reasoning using this pattern of inference before we come to see that it is a universally valid pattern. When we do grasp its validity, however, it is by thinking about the pattern of inference itself. We do not hold it on the basis of an inference from some premises external to it. These self-evident axioms and principles are not *analytic*; that is, they are not true in virtue of the meanings of the terms employed in them. Ross is thus committed to there being synthetic propositions which can be known *a priori*. The possibility of synthetic *a priori* knowledge is disputed but – and this is the important point in defending intuitionism against its detractors – Ross is not claiming that moral principles are known by some special and mysterious faculty. The only faculty involved is reason itself. Ross is here placing himself squarely in a mainstream philosophical tradition which holds that there are substantial claims whose truth we can know by direct rational insight.

5.4   Does Ross claim more than he need?

Robert Audi suggests that Ross sometimes expresses himself in ways that make his claim sound stronger, and thus less plausible, than it need be. It is not, for example, necessary in order to apprehend the truth of a proposition that is self-evident, that one apprehends its self-evidence (Audi 1996: 106). So Ross need not, and perhaps does not, hold that we have intuitive knowledge that the fundamental moral principles are self-evident. What we do have intuitive knowledge of is the moral principles themselves. Nor should we be misled by Ross's claiming that we can be certain of the general principles of duty into thinking that we could not be mistaken about them. By "certain" Ross means "self-evident" (1930: 30) and one can certainly be mistaken about a self-evident proposition. Moore was certainly right when he said that by calling some propositions intuitions he means

> *merely* to assert that they are incapable of proof. . . . [I do not] imply . . . that any proposition whatever is true, *because* we cognize it in a particular way. . . . I hold, on the contrary, that in every way in which it is possible to cognize a true proposition it is also possible to cognize a false one. (Quoted in Audi 1996: 108)

Further reflection can lead one to change one's mind, as Ross changed his on the question of whether we have a *prima facie* duty to give pleasure to ourselves.

As Audi further points out (1996: 117) Ross also makes a stronger claim than he needs (perhaps under the influence of the analogy with simple logical and mathematical axioms) when he says not only that these self-evident principles need no proof, but also that they cannot be proved. Though we can know them without evidence, that does not mean that there can be no further evidence for them. The intuitionist does not think that the principles are in need of additional evidence, so will not think they require extra support in order to be credible. But the fact that further support is not needed does not mean that it cannot be provided. While I think that this is a theoretical possibility, I am more skeptical than Audi about the possibility of any other theory providing independent support for a list of duties of Ross's kind. Kantianism, for example, appears to hold that some principles are exceptionless, and not *prima facie*.

If we could appeal to the confirmatory support of another theory, however, that might strengthen intuitionism in other ways. Take, for example, the worry some have that intuitionism lacks the unity desirable in a theory because the basic duties which Ross arrives at are not connected to each other: they are simply distinct and none is derivable from any other. If we could find a theory under which we could see them all as, for example, expressions of some common recognizably moral attitude, then such a connection would have been made. In Kantianism, we find, perhaps, such a unifying motif. What underlies all moral principles is respect for persons, and the Rossian duties might all be seen as various expressions of that overarching respect.

6 Believing and Caring

I turn now to the fourth objection raised against intuitionism. Moral beliefs have practical import: they should and do make a difference to how we live. But how, it was often said, can intuitionism explain this? It claims that we can know certain moral facts, but why is such knowledge of practical and not just of theoretical importance? Why might not someone simply notice these moral facts and carry on regardless?

This hoary old objection to intuitionism is a complete non-starter. Facts can, in appropriate contexts, supply us with reasons, either reasons to believe something or reasons to do something. That a large lorry is hurtling towards you is a reason to move out of its path. That she is honest and reliable is a reason to believe what she says. We can, of course, recognize that some fact obtains without recognizing that it gives us a reason to act. In such a case, of course, we are not going to be moved to act by our recognition of that fact. But we often realize not only that a fact obtains, but that its obtaining gives us a reason to do something. That realization will, at least in normal circumstances, motivate us to act. Indeed, it would be surprising if it did not. The intuitionist claims that we are able to recognize that certain kinds of fact, such as that I have made a promise, or that this person needs help, provide us with reason to act. So the objection now becomes: the intuitionist cannot explain why my belief that I have reason to act moves me to act. But one might reasonably wonder what the force of this complaint is. I surely have explained why someone is motivated to act if I explain that they believed there were good reasons to act. And if a mystery does remain, it is surely not a problem for intuitionism alone, but for any account of reasons for action (or belief) which takes them to be facts.[7]

7   The Place of Moral Principles: Generalism or Particularism?

There has been considerable discussion of late about the codifiability of our moral judgments. Some moral philosophers have held that the task of moral thinking is to refine and qualify our moral principles to the extent that the decision about what to do in any particular case can be "read off" from the principles. Critics of this view doubt not only whether such a degree of codification is feasible, given the complexity of our moral thought, but also whether it is desirable. Such an approach, they maintain, seriously distorts the nature of moral thinking, by downplaying the central role of judgment and imagination in the morally sensitive person's evaluation of all but the most straightforward situation. In each case, you need to discern, firstly, which features are relevant and, secondly, how they interact with each other and what weight is to be given to each in the light of the others. Finally, one needs sensitivity in deciding just what response is appropriate. Appeal to general principle is of little help in determining, for example, whether this is an occasion for tact or plain speaking, or a combination. Nor will it help you recognize just what would be the most tactful way of making the point, where tact is required.

This is a debate about the *extent* of codifiability; there is as yet no suggestion that moral principles have no place in moral thinking, only that they may have a limited role. In that debate, Ross sides with those who think their role is very limited. Firstly, Ross's principles are remarkably general and, with some of them at least, judgment is clearly required in deciding whether some action falls under them. The most striking example is the duty of non-maleficence. Deontologists have spilled much ink trying to provide a watertight account of when one is in violation of the duty not to harm. Ross appears to have almost no interest in providing such an account, indeed he gives the impression that little more can be done, at a general level, to make the harm principle more precise. Secondly, very little general guidance can be given for resolving conflicts of duty. Ross offers some very general remarks about the comparative stringency of the *prima facie* duties – that fidelity is more pressing than beneficence, for example – but that is all. For the rest, Ross says, citing Aristotle, the decision rests with perception.

> This sense of our particular duty in particular circumstances, preceded and informed by the fullest reflection we can bestow on the act in all its bearings, is highly fallible, but it is the only guide we have to our duty. (1930: 42)

Many have seen intuitionism's insistence that nothing more can be said about how to resolve moral conflict as a weakness, but I see it as a strength. There is no suggestion that the task is easy, or that one should just plump for whichever solution seems most attractive. There is hard thinking to be done, but it is (nearly) all by thinking about the particular case and comparing it with others.

As we have seen, Ross is skeptical about the weight we should give in moral thinking to abstract theoretical considerations. Moral reflection can continue perfectly well in its own space. We are able to recognize which features of action are morally relevant without the aid of abstract theory, and where theory conflicts with intuitive insight it is theory that should give way. Could, and should, an intuitionist be even more radical in his rejection of theory? Ross retains one, albeit minimal, theoretical commitment. He assumes that underivative moral considerations carry the same valency wherever they occur. So, if fidelity is a basic duty, that I have promised to do something should always count in favor of my doing it. We might doubt whether this is true. Does a promise to do a wicked deed give me *any* reason to do it? Other principles might be open to similar doubt. If my benefactor helped me only by perpetrating some horrendous crime, do I owe her any duty of gratitude?

There are two possible responses to these doubts. Those who think there must be general moral truths insist that the principle has not yet been fully captured. It must be further refined, in the way Ross apparently eschews, until we find a version of the principle which holds in all cases. The moral particularist denies that there must be a general principle backing our judgments in any particular case.[8] She gives up the search for exceptionless principles. What motivates that search is an atomistic rather than a holistic conception of reasons. For the atomist, if a consideration counts as a basic or underivative reason for something in one place it must so count everywhere. Its status as a reason does not depend on what other factors may be present in this particular case; it is context-independent. On the holistic conception, whether a consideration is a reason depends not only on what other features are present in a particular case but on the way they are interrelated. So there is no expectation that we will necessarily uncover a moral reason that always counts in the same way in every situation.

If we abandon Ross's generalism, won't we greatly weaken the case for intuitionism? The defense against the charge of being unsystematic rested on Ross's claim to supply a method for uncovering the fundamental moral principles from which all others were derived. Drop that claim and you abandon the defense. Should this worry the particularist? Only if the only way a moral outlook can be coherent and structured is by resting on a few general moral principles. But why suppose that? That the judgments someone makes in different cases can have a shape, hang together, and be consistent only if they are underpinned by general principles is itself a generalist prejudice. Many things can have a coherent structure. Not only mathematical and logical systems, but also narratives, works of art, and human lives. To suppose that moral thought must be modeled on the former rather than the latter is to be in the grip of the wrong picture.

As Ross rightly saw, moral thought begins with the recognition that certain features are salient in particular situations. He thought that we were then able, by intuitive induction, to come to apprehend that certain of these features were morally relevant in all cases. But these general principles do no epistemic work in normal fully reflective moral judgment. We do not need to infer from general principles the presence of the right- or wrong-making features in any particular case, because we can become aware of them directly. The role of the general principle is metaphysical rather than epistemic. The existence of general principles underpinning our thought is there to provide a guarantee of underlying consistency as we move from one individual judgment to another. The particularist denies the need for such a guarantee.

I have tried to show that ethical intuitionism can, in a slightly modified version of Ross's account, satisfactorily meet objections, especially the claim that it is not really a theory at all. So far as that goes, I think it the best moral theory around. But I am also inclined to believe that it does not go far enough in rejecting a conception of moral theory as a search for general moral principles and I have suggested how a more radical particularist intuitionism might look.[9]

Notes

1 For a contrary view, see Stratton-Lake (1997).
2 In *The Foundations of Ethics*, Ross reverted to his original view. Indeed, he goes so far as to describe the fact that "we have a duty to produce pleasure for others, and have not a duty to produce it for ourselves" as "one of the most certain facts in morals" (1939: 75).
3 Some of the material in this section is drawn from McNaughton (1996).
4 Both duties of special relationship and the constraint against harming are held by some to be agent-relative. For discussion see Nagel (1986, ch. 9) and McNaughton and Rawling (1991).
5 For a recent discussion see Wiggins, Dancy and Darwall in *Utilitas*, 1998.
6 Perhaps the best-known and most influential account on these lines is found in Mackie (1977, ch. 1). Audi (1996) cites other examples.
7 For recent discussion, see Stratton-Lake (1999).
8 For advocacy of particularism, see Dancy (1983) and (1993), chs 10–12; Little (1995); McDowell (1979), and McNaughton (1988), ch. 13.
9 I am grateful to Eve Garrard and Hugh LaFollette for detailed comments on earlier drafts and to Jonathan Dancy and Philip Stratton-Lake for many discussions of these topics.

References

Audi, R: "Intuitionism, Pluralism, and the Foundations of Ethics," in W. Sinnott-Armstrong and M. Timmons (eds.), *Moral Knowledge: New Readings in Moral Epistemology* (Oxford: Oxford University Press, 1996), pp. 101–36.

Broad, C. D.: *Five Types of Ethical Theory* (London: Routledge, 1930), ch. 7.

Dancy, J.: "Ethical Particularism and Morally Relevant Properties," *Mind*, 92 (1930): 530–47.

——: *Moral Reasons* (Oxford: Blackwell, 1993), chs. 10–12.

——: "An Ethic of *Prima Facie* Duties," in Singer, P. (ed.) *A Companion to Ethics* (Oxford: Blackwell, 1993), pp. 230–40.

——: "Wiggins and Ross," *Utilitas*, 10 (1998): 281–5.

Darwall, S.: "Under Moore's Spell," *Utilitas*, 10, 286–91.

Ewing, A.C.: *The Definition of Good* (London: Routledge and Kegan Paul, 1998), chs. 4–6.

——: (1953) *Ethics*. London: English Universities Press.

Little, M.: "Seeing and Caring: The Role of Affect in Feminist Moral Epistemology, *Hypatia*, 10, no. 3 (1995): 117–37.

Mackie, J. L.: *Ethics: Inventing Right and Wrong* (Harmondsworth: Penguin Books, 1977), ch. 1.

McDowell, J.: "Virtue and Reason," *The Monist*, 62 (1979): 331–50.

McNaughton, D.: *Moral Vision* (Oxford: Blackwell, 1988), chs. 11, 13.

——, and Rawling, P.: "Agent-Relativity and the Doing-Happening Distinction," *Philosophical Studies*, 63 (1991): 167–85.

——: "An Unconnected Heap of Duties?," *Philosophical Quarterly*, 46 (1996): 433–47.

Nagel, T.: *The View from Nowhere* (Oxford: Oxford University Press, 1986), ch. 9.

Prichard, H. A.: *Moral Obligation: Essays and Lectures*, ed. J. O. Urmson (Oxford: Clarendon Press, 1968).

Ross, W. D.: *The Right and the Good* (Oxford: Clarendon Press, 1930).

——: *The Foundations of Ethics* (Oxford: Clarendon Press, 1939).

Stratton-Lake, P.: "Why Externalism is not a Problem for Ethical Intuitionists," Proceedings of the Aristotelian Society, 99 (1999): 77–90.

——: "Can Hooker's Rule-consequentialist Principle Justify Rossian Prima Facie Duties?," *Mind*, 106 (1997): 751–8.

Warnock, G. J.: *Contemporary Moral Philosophy* (New York: St. Martin's Press, 1967).

Wiggins, D.: "*The Right and the Good* and W. D. Ross's Criticism of Consequentialism," *Utilitas*, 10 (1998): 261–80.

Chapter 15

Rights

L. W. Sumner

Of all the moral concepts, rights seem most in tune with the temper of our time. At their best they evoke images of heroic struggles against oppression and discrimination. At their worst they furnish the material for lurid tabloid stories of litigious former spouses and lovers. Whatever the use to which they are put, they are ubiquitous, the global currency of moral/political argument at the end of the millennium. Liberal societies in particular seem replete with conflicts of rights: young against old, ethnic minority against majority, natives against foreigners, rich against poor, women against men, believers against non-believers, children against parents, gays against straights, employees against employers, consumers against producers, students against teachers, cyclists against drivers, pedestrians against cyclists, citizens against the police, and everyone against the state.

Love them or hate them, rights are unavoidable and no modern ethical theory seems complete without taking some account of them. It is therefore important to understand them: what they are, what their distinctive function is in our moral/political thinking, how we might distinguish reasonable from unreasonable claims of rights, and how rights might fit into the larger framework of an ethical theory. The aim of this essay is to help promote this understanding.

We can begin by trying to identify the distinctive kind of normative work rights are best equipped to do. Let us say that one part of our moral thinking has to do with the promotion of collective social goals which we deem to be valuable for their own sake: the general welfare, equality of opportunity, the eradication of poverty, bettering the lot of the worst off, or whatever. It is this part of our thinking which is well captured by the broad family of consequentialist ethical theories. On the other hand, we also tend to think that some means societies might use in order to achieve these goals are unjustifiable because they exploit or victimize particular individuals or groups. One way of expressing this thought is to say that these parties have rights which constrain or limit the pursuit of social goals, rights which must (at least sometimes) be respected even though a valuable goal would be better promoted by ignoring or infringing them. Rights then function morally as safeguards for the position of individuals or particular groups in the face of social endeavors; in the image made famous by Ronald Dworkin (1977: xi), they can be invoked as trumps against the pursuit of collective goals. It is this part of our moral thinking which is well captured by deontological theories, and rights therefore seem most at home in such theories.

Rights impose constraints on the pursuit of collective goals. This very general characterization serves to identify in a preliminary way the moral/political function of rights, and also begins to explain their perennial appeal. But it is not yet sufficient to show how rights are distinctive or unique. Duties and obligations impose similar constraints: if I have an obligation to pay my income tax then that is what I must do even though more good would result from my donating the money to Oxfam. So what is the particular way in which rights limit our promotion of valuable states of affairs? And what exactly is the relationship between rights and duties? We need to look more closely at the anatomy of rights.

How Rights Work

A simple example will serve to get us started. Suppose that Bernard has borrowed Alice's laptop computer with the promise to return it by Tuesday, and Tuesday has arrived. Alice now has the right to have her computer returned by Bernard. Note to begin with that there are three distinct elements to this right. First, it has a *subject*: the holder or bearer of the right (in this case, Alice). Second, it has an *object*: the person against whom the right is held (in this case, Bernard). Third, it has a *content*: what it is the right to do or to have done (in this case, to have the computer re-turned). Every right has these three elements, though they may not always be spelled out fully in the specification of the right. The paradigm subjects of rights are per-sons, though nothing so far prevents them from being attributed as well to other beings, such as children, animals, corporations, collectivities, and so on. The object of a right must be an agent capable of having duties or obligations, since Alice's right that Bernard return her computer on Tuesday correlates with Bernard's obli-gation to return the computer on Tuesday. Since rights can be held only against agents, the class of objects of rights may be much narrower than the class of sub-jects. The object of Alice's right is a specific assignable person, since it is Bernard who has borrowed her computer and who is duty-bound to return it. However, the objects of a right may also be an unassignable group; some rights, such as the right not to be assaulted or killed, may hold against everyone in general.

Finally, the content of a right is always some action on the part of either the subject or the object of the right. This fact is obscured by the shorthand way in which we refer to many rights, where it may appear that the content of the right is a thing or state of affairs. We may speak, for instance, of the right to an education or to health care or to life itself. But in all such cases the full specification of the right will reveal the actions which constitute its content: that the state provide subsidized public education or health care, or that others not act in such a way as to endanger life, or whatever. The contents of many rights are intricate and complex actions on the part of (assignable or unassignable) others, which must be fully spelled out before we know exactly what the right amounts to. In the case of Alice's right the action in question is simple and specific: having her computer returned by Tuesday. Alice therefore has the right that something be done (by the person against whom her right is held). This kind of normative advantage on Alice's part is usually described as a *claim*: Alice has a claim *against Bernard* that he return her computer, which is equivalent to Bernard's duty *to Alice* to return her computer. In general, A's claim against B that B do X is logically equivalent to B's duty toward A to do X: claims and duties are in this way correlative. Claims are always of the form that something be done: the actions which make up their content must be those of another, never those of the right-holder herself. Since the content of Alice's right against Bernard has the form of a claim, we may call it a *claim-right*. Claim-rights constitute one important class of rights, exemplified primarily by contractual rights (held against assignable parties) and by rights to security of the person (held against everyone in general).

However, not all rights are claim-rights. Another example will make this clear. Alice owns her computer, which implies (among other things) that she has the right to use it (when she wants to). This right has the same subject (Alice) as her claim-right, but a different content and a different object. Its content is once again an action, but this time an action on the part of the right-holder rather than someone else: it is a right *to do* rather than a right *to have done*. The content of the right therefore does not have the form of a claim; it is common instead to refer to it as a *liberty*. To say that Alice has the liberty to use her computer is to say that she is under no obligation not to use it, or that her use of it is permissible. Actually, it is implicitly to say more than this, since Alice's right to use her computer (when she wants to) includes her right not to use it (when she doesn't want to). Alice therefore has two distinct liberties: to use the computer (which means that she has no duty not to use it) and not to use it (which means that she has no duty to use it). We normally treat these as the two sides of one (complex) liberty: to use or not to use the computer, as she wishes. In general, A's liberty to do X (or not) is logically equivalent to the absence both of A's duty to do X and A's duty not to do X. Alice's ownership right over the computer therefore entails her freedom to choose whether or not to use the computer; how this is to go is up to her. Since the content of her right has the form of a liberty, we may call it a *liberty-right*. Liberty-rights constitute another important class of rights, exemplified primarily by property rights and by rights to various freedoms (of thought, belief, conscience, expression, etc.).

So far we have located a subject and a content for Alice's liberty-right, but not an object. Against whom is this right held? In the case of claim-rights the answer to this question is straightforward: whoever bears the duty which is equivalent to the claim. Because claim-rights specify obligations, and because these obligations are assigned to particular parties (or to everyone in general), claim-rights enable us to easily locate their objects. But Alice's liberty-right to use her computer involves on the face of it no claim (or duty); the liberty in question just consists in the absence of duties on Alice's part. It is therefore not so obviously held *against* anyone. And indeed if we restrict ourselves just to its stipulated content, that is true: it is a right which imposes no duties. However, we know that property rights are typically protected by duties imposed on others: for instance, duties not to interfere with the use or enjoyment of the property in question. By virtue of her property right Alice has more than just the bare unprotected liberty to use (or not use) her computer as she pleases; this liberty is safeguarded by what H. L. A. Hart (1982: 171–3) has usefully called a "protective perimeter" of duties imposed on others. Bernard therefore (and everyone else) has the duty not to interfere with Alice's use of her computer (by stealing it, damaging it, using it without permission, etc.). We learn therefore the lesson that liberty-rights are not as simple as they seem: they involve a complex bundle of liberties (held by the subject) and duties (imposed on others). The others who bear these duties are the (implicit) objects of the right.

Even claim-rights are not as simple as they seem. Let us return to Alice's right that Bernard return her computer by Tuesday. Alice's claim against Bernard is, as we have seen, logically equivalent to Bernard's duty toward Alice. But suppose that Bernard needs the computer for an additional day and asks to return it on Wednesday instead. Alice can, of course, refuse the request and insist on the performance of Bernard's duty. But she can also agree to it, in which case she waives her right to have the computer returned by Tuesday and releases Bernard from his original obligation. She now has a new right (to have the computer returned by Wednesday) and Bernard has a new correlative obligation. In waiving her original right Alice has exercised a *power* which enables her to alter Bernard's obligation. Indeed, in entering into the agreement about the computer in the first place, both Alice and Bernard have exercised powers which result in the creation of Alice's claim-right against Bernard and Bernard's liberty-right to use Alice's computer. Contractual rights, which constitute one important class of claim-rights, therefore involve more than just claims; they also involve powers (and liberties to exercise those powers, and duties imposed on others not to interfere with those liberties, and immunities against being deprived of the powers, and so on). Even relatively simple-seeming claim-rights are therefore typically quite complex bundles of different elements. The core of the right is still a claim, but this core is surrounded by a periphery made up of other elements (claims, liberties, powers, etc.). This periphery may be quite different for different claim-rights. Contractual rights typically confer on their subjects considerable discretion about the exercise of the right, including the power to waive it or to annul it entirely. Other claim-rights, such as the right not to be harmed or killed, may impose more limits on the subject's liberty (or power) to waive or annul the right. The full specification of a claim-right, including all of its periphery, can therefore be a very complex matter.

The same complexity, and the same relation of core to periphery, can be found in the case of liberty-rights. Alice's liberty-right to use her computer (or not, as she pleases) is not accompanied only by a protective perimeter of duties imposed on others. It also includes her power to annul her liberty to use the computer, either temporarily (by lending the computer to Bernard) or permanently (by selling it), plus her liberty to exercise this power, plus further duties imposed on others not to interfere with her exercise of this power, plus. . . . Like claim-rights, liberty-rights are typically complex bundles of different elements. The core of the right (what it is a right to) is still a liberty, but it too is surrounded by a periphery made up of other elements (claims, liberties, powers, etc.)

A full exploration of the intricate anatomy of rights can be a complicated affair (see, for instance, Wellman 1985, ch. 2; Sumner 1987, ch. 2). Fortunately, we have revealed enough of this anatomy to be able to answer some of our questions about the distinctive normative function of rights. First, the relationship between rights and duties. Although these two deontological concepts are clearly connected, the connections between them are more complex than they first appear. There is a simple relationship between claims and their correlative duties: A's claim against B that B do X is logically equivalent to B's duty toward A to do X. Exclusive attention to claim-rights might lead one to think that rights are just duties seen, as it were, from the perspective of the patient rather than the agent. But this is not the case. In the first place, not all duties are relational in the sense of being owed to assignable persons. Bernard's duty to return Alice's computer has an obvious object (Alice) but my duty to pay my income tax does not: it is not clear to whom (if anyone) this duty is owed. If there are non-relational duties then they do not correlate with any rights. More importantly, there is more to a right, even a claim-right, than just a claim against some correlative duty-bearer. Claim-rights, like liberty-rights, are typically complex clusters of different kinds of elements (duties, liberties, powers, immunities, etc.). Every such right will include some duties, either in its core or in its periphery (or both). But no right of either kind can just be reduced to a duty, or a set of duties. Rights also contain elements which are not duties, and are not definable in terms of duties. Furthermore, they have a structure, an internal logic, which is distinctively different from that of duties.

This brings us to our other question: how is it that rights impose constraints on our pursuit of goals? The complex structure of rights reveals two answers to this question. First, by containing duties imposed on their objects, rights limit the freedom of others to pursue valuable collective goals; they must (at least sometimes) fulfil their duty even when a worthwhile goal would be better promoted by not doing so. Second, by containing liberties conferred on their subjects, rights secure the freedom of right-holders not to pursue valuable collective goals; they may (at least sometimes) choose to exercise their right even when a worthwhile goal would be better promoted by not doing so. Rights therefore impose restrictions on others (who must not promote the collectively best outcome) and confer prerogatives on their holders (who need not do so). By these means rights define protected spaces in which individuals are able to pursue their own personal projects or have their personal interests safeguarded, free from the demands of larger collective enterprises.

The qualifiers "at least sometimes" in the preceding paragraph deserve some brief attention. They signal that neither the duties which rights impose on others nor the liberties they confer on their holders need be absolute. And this brings us to a fourth dimension of a right (besides its subject, object, and content), namely its *strength*. The strength of a right is its level of resistance to rival normative considerations, such as the promotion of worthwhile goals. A right will insulate its holder to some extent against the necessity of taking these considerations into account, but it will also typically have a threshold above which they dominate or override the right. Should it turn out, for instance, that Bernard needs Alice's computer in order to arrange relief for a large-scale disaster in Africa then his duty to return it on time (and her claim that it be returned) may be overridden even if she wants the computer back. Likewise, the same degree of urgency may override her liberty-right to use the computer when she pleases. Rights raise thresholds against considerations of social utility but these thresholds are seldom insurmountable. Some particularly important rights (against torture, perhaps, or slavery, or genocide) may be absolute, but most are not.

Why Theories Need Rights

Since the normative role rights are equipped to play seems useful, even necessary, it is not surprising that most ethical theories make some effort to accommodate them. Given the currency of rights talk in moral/political argument, any theory that either ignored or rejected rights completely would risk dismissal as being hopelessly out of step with our ordinary moral thinking. Not all theories, however, are equally comfortable with rights and not all find it equally easy to take them seriously. Rather than make a positive case for a rights-friendly theory, we will proceed by examining three challenges to rights emanating from three different theoretical orientations. If these challenges can be successfully met then we will have better reason for thinking that only an ethical theory which makes room for rights will be worthy of our allegiance.

The first challenge comes from a surprising direction. At the beginning of this essay I noted that rights seem most at home in deontological theories. We should therefore be able to assume that any deontological theory will provide a hospitable environment for rights. But this is not necessarily so. Some such theories, especially those affiliating with the Kantian or the Thomistic natural law traditions, have a decided preference for the language of duties over that of rights (see, for instance, Finnis 1980, ch. 8). Within such theories there is a tendency to treat rights as mere shadows cast by duties, so that any separate treatment of them is redundant. Now we already have the materials at hand for a response to this disparagement of rights, since we know that rights are not reducible to duties. It is true of claims that they are just (relational) duties looked at from the point of view of the patient rather than the agent, but rights are not just claims (even claim-rights are not just claims). So a theory which treats rights as just shadows cast by duties fails to understand their nature.

However, the redundancy thesis espoused by some deontological theories deserves a little more attention than this, since it enables us to say a little more about the distinctive normative role and contribution of rights. Thus far we have said that rights are complex bundles or packages of simpler constituent elements and shown how they function to constrain the pursuit of goals. But we do not yet have an adequate picture of the internal logic or rationale which unifies these diverse elements. For this we need (what we may call) a conception of the nature of rights. Two such conceptions have dominated the literature on rights. The interest (or benefit) conception holds that the point of rights is to protect the interests or welfare of their holders; it is this purpose which unifies the various elements making up a particular right and which explains why those elements are included and not others. Central to the interest conception is the idea of the right-holder as the beneficiary of duties imposed on others, or as the one whose interest provides the justification for imposing such duties (MacCormick 1982, ch. 8; Raz 1986, ch. 7; Lyons 1994, ch.1) By contrast, the choice (or will) conception holds that rights function so as to protect the freedom or autonomy of their holders. Central to this conception is the idea of the right-holder having the freedom to choose among a set of options, and of this freedom being protected by a set of duties imposed on others (Hart 1982, ch. 7; Wellman 1985, ch. 4; Sumner 1987, ch. 2; Steiner 1994, ch. 3). The main difference between the two conceptions lies in the emphasis which the choice conception places on the right-holder's power to alter, waive, annul, or otherwise control the duties imposed by the right. It is the ability to exercise this power which gives the right-holder control over the normative relations involved in the right. On the choice conception, but not on the interest conception, every right must involve some such means of control. (The distinction between these two conceptions must not be confused with the distinction between the two basic categories of rights: claim-rights and liberty-rights. Both conceptions can make sense of both kinds of rights.)

Each of these conceptions attempts to explain what rights are fundamentally *for* and each purports to apply across the full range of the kinds of rights we typically take ourselves (and other subjects of rights) to have. As comprehensive accounts of the nature of rights, each has its problems; fortunately, however, we need not decide which to accept. Either will suffice to show why rights are not redundant, even in a theory rich in duties. That rights have a distinctive normative function is clearest on the choice conception, for we have no other concept similarly dedicated to the protection of the freedom or autonomy of agents. We must be careful not to mistake the issue here. It is not whether the concept of a right might be eliminable in principle in favor of other concepts. Since rights are reducible to packages of claims, liberties, powers, etc., we could in principle substitute these simpler concepts for the more complex concept of a right. But the result would not merely be impossibly clumsy; it would also obscure the point or rationale which binds these packages together. The idea of rights as protected choices illuminates that rationale and reveals why the concept of a right has a role to play for which we have no reasonable substitute. The choice conception also makes short work of the redundancy thesis, since it requires that every right include some discretionary powers on the part of the right-holder, which means in turn that rights are not reducible to duties (not even the kinds of relational duties which are equivalent to claims).

Rights might seem in greater danger of redundancy on the interest conception, since they can function to protect interests while conferring no room for discretion or choice on the right-holder. On this conception, therefore, unlike the choice conception, a right could consist in just a claim, which is in turn logically equivalent to a (relational) duty. However, even here it would be a mistake to think that rights could simply be deleted from a theory of duties without loss. For the interest conception also provides an account of the point or rationale of certain kinds of duties – namely, that the justification for their imposition is to be found in a feature not of the agent or duty-bearer but of the patients whom the duty protects. Duties can have different grounds, which may focus primarily either on agent or on patient. The interest conception singles out duties whose rationale consists in protecting the interests of patients. Again it assigns to rights a point which would be lost in a theory which spoke only the language of duties.

Rights therefore can be safeguarded against redundancy in deontological theories. A challenge from the opposite end of the theoretical spectrum focuses on the function of rights as constraints on the pursuit of collective goals. Consequentialist theories see the whole point of morality as consisting in the pursuit of a very abstract goal: bringing about the best overall state of affairs or making the world go as well as possible. Rights, as we have seen, are impediments to achieving this goal, since they both permit their subjects to choose non-optimizing actions and require their objects to do so. We should not be surprised then to find that rights have been regarded with suspicion or even outright hostility by some consequentialists (Frey 1984). The consequentialist camp is internally divided on the issue of whether to make room for moral rights, some consequentialists being friendlier to this project than others (John Stuart Mill, for instance, was much more rights-friendly than Jeremy Bentham). Toward the end of this essay I will explore a consequentialist strategy for not only accommodating rights but providing a foundation for them. Meanwhile, it will suffice to say that we have identified a normative role for rights – as protections of individual interests or autonomy against the demands of collective goals – which seems very appealing and whose absolute exclusion from an ethical theory threatens to condemn that theory to irrelevancy. Most impartial observers, if asked to choose between the unfettered promotion of the impersonally best consequences, on the one hand, and its constraint in order to safeguard individual welfare or freedom, on the other, are likely to opt for the latter. Consequentialists may still choose to take the high road (though I will suggest later that they are mistaken to do so), but few are likely to follow them.

The third challenge to the inclusion of rights in an ethical theory is much more interesting than either of the other two. It emanates from relatively recent developments in feminist ethical theory (see, for example, Hardwig 1990; Sherwin 1992). Feminists have tended to be critical of approaches to ethical issues which are formulated primarily or exclusively in terms of rights. They see the discourse of rights as locking us into a legalistic form of moral thinking in which justice becomes the pre-eminent virtue. Justice may be appropriate in the public sphere, where individuals confront one another as strangers or as fellow citizens, but it is out of place in other contexts, especially in close personal relationships which thrive on values such as trust and loyalty. Rights, in their view, are adapted to a social ontology of isolated individuals indifferent or hostile to one another who need the protection of fenced off private domains – the world of business or politics, perhaps, but not that of family or friendship. Feminists are also suspicious of the kind of autonomy whose protection is the centerpiece of the choice conception of rights and which seems to promote a very masculine ideal of the rugged, self-reliant, self-defining individual with no roots and no intimate ties to others.

There are a number of important themes in this critique which we will do well to distinguish. Consider first the alleged individualism of rights. It is true that persons are usually assumed to be the paradigm holders of rights (we have operated with that assumption so far in this essay). However, there is nothing in the logic of rights which restricts them to individuals. Some rights, such as the right not to be as-saulted or killed, belong to individuals simply as such, but others, such as the right to religious holidays or to services in one's native language, can be held by individu-als only as members of an ethno-cultural group. Even individual rights, therefore, need not define their holders as abstractions isolated from their social contexts. Furthermore, nothing seems to prevent us from taking a further step and attribut-ing some rights (of self-determination or cultural survival, for example) to ethno-cultural groups as wholes, where the right cannot be decomposed into the separate rights of the several members of the group. What is necessary in order to qualify as a potential right-holder is the possession of some value (interests on the interest conception, autonomy on the choice conception) which the right can function to protect. It is at the very least arguable that groups united by a common culture, language, history, or religion could satisfy the requirement of having either a collec-tive interest or the capacity for collective choice. If so, then such groups could be the subjects of rights which will safeguard their liberties or restrict the ways in which they may be legitimately treated. Furthermore, if groups are capable of collective agency they will also be capable of serving as the objects of rights (the bearers of the duties entailed by the right). Many rights (both claim- and liberty-rights) are held against the world at large, which still standardly means each individual member of that world considered separately. But rights can, in principle at least, also be held against groups considered collectively, and some rights (of exit from the group, for instance) appear to have this form. Therefore, if the point of the individualism critique is that rights can belong only to individuals or be held only against indi-viduals, it is misconceived.

Neither does it appear to be true that rights presuppose a certain picture of the nature society or of social relationships. Rights are versatile normative instruments which can be put to many different political uses. It is true that they can serve libertarians well, who dream of a suburban society of self-reliant burghers, sur-rounded by picket fences of liberty-rights, who have only negative duties of noninterference toward one another. But they are just as adaptable to the purposes of communitarians, socialists, egalitarians, or – dare one say it – feminists. Rights can be invoked to support a cutthroat competitive marketplace, but they can also promote an ideal of social solidarity by making it a requirement of justice that resources be allocated for the support of the needy and disadvantaged, or that discrimination on the basis of race, gender, or sexual orientation be eliminated, or that the vulnerable be protected against exploitation and oppression. Since women have historically been more likely than men to suffer from these social evils, appeals to rights and justice have been the main rhetorical weapons which they have used to better their lot (it is difficult to imagine the pro-choice movement, for instance, without such weapons). Availing themselves of the language of rights has not transformed women into isolated, rugged, masculine individuals; on the contrary, the reproductive rights which they have claimed have been deeply rooted in their identities as sole childbearers and primary childrearers.

The feminist critique, however, has another aspect to it which is more faithful to the social ideology of rights. Rights, as we have seen, impose duties and duties are normative constraints on the freedom of others, constraints whose justification lies in the protection they afford the rights-holder. The language of rights does therefore presuppose a social landscape in which interests tend to conflict and in which these conflicts must be managed in a principled way. Members of a world free of conflict might have no need for the protections afforded by rights. Since the public sphere is manifestly not free of conflict, rights may be conceded an appropriate, though regrettable, role in it, though even here a fixation on rights may lead us to exaggerate conflict and competition and to overlook possibilities for cooperation and reconciliation. But what place could there be for rights in the more intimate setting of a family or friendship? If personal relationships are viewed through a sufficiently romantic gauze then they might come to appear frictionless. However, this utopian ideal is not a good fit for the daily lives of most friends, lovers, spouses, parents, and children who must also learn to manage conflicts in their personal attachments. It was a great moral and political step forward when the parties to such relationships began to be conceived as distinct individuals with a standing of their own (a process still incomplete for children, who are too often considered even now to be the property of their parents), rather than as subordinates whose interests were submerged in those of the male head of household. To consider that these parties have rights against one another (not to be verbally, physically, sexually, or emotionally abused, for instance) is to establish certain basic expectations that every relationship should be expected to meet. The participants in any healthy, functional relationship will routinely treat one another in ways which greatly exceed this basic minimum. But that is no reason to deny that they do have such rights, and that the relationship can sink to such depths that the rights of one or more of the parties to it are being violated. Friendship may mean giving your friend more than she has a right to, but it also means not giving her less.

The valuable lesson we learn from the feminist critique is that rights do not occupy the entire moral landscape. They are specialized normative devices with a particular function, one to which they are very well adapted, but they cannot take the place of other equally important values such as loyalty, trust, and care. Nor are they a substitute for other means by which we judge personal character. If rights protect personal prerogatives, then they also protect the prerogative to behave badly – that is, in ways which, while they do not actually violate any duties or rights, are nonetheless mean-minded and selfish (Waldron 1993). Our moral vocabulary needs the resources to describe deficiencies of character which are compatible with the most punctilious respect for rights. Anyone who believes that human interactions require nothing more than minimal regard for the rights of others would make a very unattractive friend or spouse or neighbor – or business associate for that matter. But it is no fault of rights that the indolent or small-minded might find it convenient to think that they exhaust the requirements of virtue, and it is no solution to this problem to expel rights entirely from our moral thinking. Rights have an important, indeed indispensable, job to do within any complete and comprehensive moral theory. What the feminist critique does well to remind us is that they do not and should not stand alone.

Why Rights Need a Theory

We began by noting the extent to which rights have become the common currency of moral/political discourse and we have seen how that currency can be defended against various kinds of theoretical challenge. Ironically, however, the greatest threat to the integrity of rights discourse stems from its very popularity. It is the agility of rights, their talent for turning up on both (or all) sides of every issue, that is simultaneously their most impressive and their most troubling feature. Rival interest groups which converge on little else agree that rights are indispensable weapons in the political arena. To claim a right to something is not just to say that it would be nice to have it or generous of others to provide it: rather, one is entitled to expect or demand it, others are obliged to provide it, it would be unjust of them to deny or withhold it. Once a right has been invoked on one side of an issue it must therefore be countered by a weapon of similar potency on the other. But then if one interest group has built its case on an appeal to rights none of its competitors can afford not to respond in kind. Like any other weapons, once they have appeared in the public arena rights claims will tend to proliferate and to escalate.

In an arms race it can be better for each side to increase its stock even though the resulting escalation will be worse for all sides. Where military weapons are concerned the increased threat is that of mutual annihilation. Where rhetorical weapons are concerned, what all sides must fear is a backlash of skepticism or cynicism. An argumentative device capable of justifying anything is capable of justifying nothing. When rights claims have once been deployed on all sides of all public issues they may no longer be taken seriously as means of resolving any of those issues. Indeed, the danger is that they will no longer be taken seriously at all. Just as fiscal inflation reduces the real value of money, the inflation of rights rhetoric threatens to debase the currency.

If we once pause to reflect on the bewildering array of rights invoked in both personal and political morality then we cannot avoid asking ourselves some hard questions. Do all of these rights deserve to be taken seriously? If not, which are genuine and which are spurious? And in cases in which genuine rights conflict, which ones deserve to be taken more seriously? In order to answer questions like these we need a verification procedure for rights claims, or a criterion of authenticity for rights. As we saw earlier, the full specification of any right includes four dimensions: its subject(s), its content, its object(s), and its strength. Ideally, then, we want a criterion capable of confirming or disconfirming each of these elements in any rights claim. Non-ideally, we at least need some resources to sort reasonable from unreasonable claims. But where are we to find them?

This sounds like a job for philosophers. However, not everyone working within the rights paradigm is equally helpful. Some philosophers go about their business by simply assuming a certain set of basic rights and then working out their implications for social and political arrangements. Robert Nozick, for instance, opens his most famous book with the claim that "Individuals have rights, and there are things no person or group may do to them (without violating their rights)" (Nozick 1974: ix). The rights Nozick has in mind here are (nearly absolute) property rights which stand as ethical impediments to social programs employed by the welfare state in pursuit of such goals as equalizing resources or meeting the needs of the disadvantaged. Working from this premise, Nozick devotes much ingenious argumentation to the project of working out just how much more than the bare nightwatchman state might be compatible with respect for individual rights. However, the premise itself – the assumption that individuals have just these rights and no others – is given much less attention. A more recent example of this kind of "top-down" argumentation, also within the libertarian political camp, may be found in the work of Hillel Steiner (1994). Following out the moral/political implications of libertarian premisses about rights can be an illuminating process, especially when libertarians themselves disagree about these implications. It can also serve to remind those of us of more egalitarian or social-democratic persuasion what the costs would be of failing to defend a more generous set of fundamental rights. However, ultimately a top-down methodology invites the response that it is persuasive only to the already converted, serving for the rest of us merely as a theoretically interesting exercise: yes, you have shown us where we can (and cannot) get to from here, but why should we start from *here*? If we want some means of testing the authenticity of rights claims, then we want this to apply as well to the starting points of moral/political argument, which will determine the destinations we can reach.

Other philosophers have a different way of proceeding with rights which we might call intuitionist or casuistical. The most accomplished and influential practitioner of this methodology has been Judith Jarvis Thomson (1990). Unlike those who elect to work from an assumed set of basic rights, Thomson's aim is to determine which kinds of rights we have. Furthermore, she thinks that there are some general principles which lie behind the kinds of rights we tend to attribute to ourselves and others, and she wants to determine what those principles are (1990: 1). So we seem here much closer to the ideal of a test or criterion of authenticity for rights: some alleged rights will presumably fare well in terms of these principles (whatever they turn out to be), while others will fare badly. The question then becomes one of discovering or revealing these principles. This is where Thomson's intuitionist methodology comes into play. She rests claims about the kinds of rights we have on appeals to our considered moral judgments, appeals of the sort "But surely A ought to do such and such" or "Plainly it would be wrong for B to do so and so." Because she expects general agreement with these judgments, she makes no attempt to show that they are true. Furthermore, as she herself says (1990: 4), she rests argumentative weight on them, by using them to draw conclusions about people's rights. She therefore takes for granted much of the content of our ordinary morality and offers no means of confirming (or disconfirming) it. Her strategy is to argue from some (hopefully uncontroversial) fixed points in our moral thinking to implications for rights which may not (without some careful argument) seem to follow from them. All moral theorizing, she tells us (1990: 33), begins with a body of data, and her data are moral judgments which she expects her readers to accept as moral truths.

What Thomson's procedure shares with the top-down methodology of Nozick and Steiner is that certain things get taken for granted and used to support arguments for other things. However, whereas Nozick and Steiner assume some very general principles about the kinds of rights we have, the judgments Thomson takes for granted are about particular cases. Furthermore, they are not about rights but about what someone ought or ought not to do, or what it would be right or wrong to do; any claims about rights appear only as the conclusions of arguments from such judgments. Her methodology is therefore more "bottom-up" or particularist. It also more closely resembles common-law judicial reasoning which tries to work from relatively fixed points in the law to conclusions about new cases. It is particularly well suited to a certain picture about morality in general, and the territory of rights in particular, which Thomson professes to share (1990: 33): that it does not form a system governed by a small set of very general principles. In her view, therefore, it is impossible to argue to rights from any such set of principles. Rather, again like the common law, the principles must be uncovered through the process of arguing to, and about, rights.

The results which Thomson reaches by means of her intuitionist methodology are very impressive. She is particularly good at trying to work out rigorously what we mean casually when we say such things as that a right can be overridden or forfeited. Furthermore, the kinds of rights she takes to be genuine are, for the most part, familiar features of our (liberal) moral discourse: claims against harm or invasion by others, protected liberties, and so on. However, the argumentative structure she erects is clearly only as secure as its foundations, and those foundations consist of particular moral judgments whose truth is taken for granted. What happens if some of those judgments are disputable, or disputed? Thomson says (1990: 4, 33) that a mistake on her part about any of these judgments would be just as serious as a mistake in her reasoning from them. Are any of them mistaken? This question we could not settle without working through Thomson's arguments in detail, a task which is inappropriate for this essay. However, just as a matter of autobiography, I will say that my intuitions about the cases Thomson constructs do not always coincide with hers. Wherever that is true then the further course of her argument once again becomes merely an interesting exercise for me, on a par with the arguments of Nozick and Steiner. Furthermore, as is common in analytic ethics, many of Thomson's examples are very schematic and stripped of all social and political context. Very often my response is not so much that I agree or disagree with Thomson's assumption about the case in question, but that I want to know more, often much more, before making up my mind either way. But then many of Thomson's "data" remain question marks for me, not so much mistaken as indeterminate.

The intuitionist methodology which Thomson uses to generate a criterion of authenticity for rights is very common in analytic ethics, where appeals are constantly made to "what we believe" or "what we would say" about particular cases. In a certain respect, it is unexceptionable. Since not everything can be called into question at once, we have to assume something in order to be able to argue to any conclusions. The question is: what to assume? Thomson's implicit contention seems to be that our judgments about particular cases are more secure than any general moral principles; they therefore make safer starting points for moral argument. She makes no attempt to argue for this contention, and I can think of no way of proving (or disproving) it. She may well be right, but other methodological possibilities are equally worth exploring. So far we have considered only two: arguments from general principles about rights and arguments to rights from particular moral judgments. It is time to introduce a third: that a criterion of authenticity for rights needs the resources of a general ethical theory.

By an ethical theory I mean a relatively small, coherent set of fundamental normative principles general enough to cover the whole of our moral thinking. Since some, but not all, of that thinking involves rights, the territory of rights will form a particular subdomain in the overall landscape of a theory. The idea then is that the ultimate resource to which we appeal in order to develop a criterion of authenticity for rights is the set of basic principles in a theory. But what kind of theory? Since the options here are virtually infinite, we need to simplify the problem by focussing on a few basic types of theory. Let us assume that every moral theory has a structure or hierarchy of principles, some of which are basic (serving, in effect, as axioms) while others are derivable from them (theorems). Assume further that every such principle gives justificatory priority to a particular category of moral concepts: duties, rights, virtues, the good, etc. Then in general a theory is X-based if its basic principles give priority to concepts from category X. In this way we can classify theories as duty-based, rights-based, virtue-based, and so on. Now let us ask the question which of these types of (foundationalist) theory is most likely to generate an operational criterion for authenticating rights.

Two kinds of theory can, I think, be excluded at the outset. On the face of it, duty-based theories might seem a hospitable environment for rights, since they are deontological right down to their foundations. However, as we noted earlier, duties form a wider category than rights and need not be patient-centered in the way that is characteristic of rights. The most basic principles in a duty-based theory – the ones which tell us what our most general duties are – may therefore refer not to some feature of moral patients (such as their welfare or autonomy) but to some feature of moral agents (such as their rationality or autonomy). Any duty-based theory with this ultimate derivation of our duties will have difficulty accommodating rights in the full sense in which they have a distinctive and ineliminable normative function. Virtue-based theories, which also tend to be agent-centered, may be excluded for the same reason. If a theory derives rights from principles about the virtues (or about the virtue of justice in particular), and if it grounds these principles in turn on an account of the good of the moral agent, then it too will lack the focus on moral patients that is the peculiar contribution of rights.

The most obvious kind of theory to provide a criterion of authenticity for rights is one which is rights-based. I will pass over the problem of how comprehensive or complete such a theory could be. After all, we know that rights define only one domain of the moral territory and are out of place in others. We might wonder, for instance, how adequate a picture of personal relationships, and of the many values which such relationships can exemplify, a purely rights-based theory could ever generate. I will also pass over the question of what the basic principles of rights in a rights-based theory might look like or how they themselves might be validated. There is a problem with the very idea of a rights-based theory which runs much deeper.

In our earlier exploration of the anatomy of rights we found their constituent elements to be such things as liberties, duties, powers, and immunities. All of these elements share one important characteristic: they are the creatures of rule systems. The parallel cases of liberties and powers will suffice to make (or remind us of) the point. A liberty defines what is normatively permissible for an agent – what she may (is allowed to) do. A power defines what is normatively possible for an agent – what she can (is able to) do (by way of altering her own or others' normative relationships). Liberties presuppose a rule system with the triad of deontic modal concepts (required/permitted/prohibited), while powers presuppose a rule system with the triad of alethic modal concepts (necessary/possible/impossible). A rule system with deontic concepts alone is capable of generating rights on the interest conception, while a system with both sets of concepts is necessary for rights on the choice conception. A legal system is the best example of a rule system with both kinds of resources, which is why it is capable of conferring rights on those subject to its jurisdiction. Those rights have legal force as long as the rules which define them, and the system itself, satisfy whatever requirements are deemed to be necessary for legal validity.

But we want a theory to support not legal rights, not any sort of merely conventional rights, but moral rights – the kinds of rights we use to criticize or justify a system of conventional rights. Legal rights presuppose a system of legal rules, so presumably moral rights must presuppose a system of moral rules. In the case of legal rules we can explain the existence of the rule system in terms of some source (a legislature or a court, for instance) which has the authority to make law. But what are the conditions for the existence of a system of moral rules (or laws)? What makes these rules moral, as opposed to conventional, is precisely the fact that they issue from no authority. But then how can we make sense of their existence? By virtue of what are they rules? And what is the source of their authority over us?

A moral theory can, I think, provide intelligible answers to these important questions. But a theory which takes rights (or, for that matter, duties) as basic labors under a special disability since it must provide existence conditions for moral rules without recourse to any deeper principles. It is vulnerable to the accusation of hypothesizing some ghostly moral realm, the analogue of a legal system, in which moral rules somehow exist with no moral legislator. We are asked to assume that these rules are capable of imposing requirements and prohibitions, and conferring abilities and disabilities, without any of the substructure which supports the existence of a legal system. Rights and duties are of course legalistic concepts, imported into ethics from the law. Whenever such borrowing occurs the question may be raised whether the concepts make sense in the absence of the framework within which they originally developed. Now we know that sense can be made of the concept of a moral right, but only if we presuppose the background of a system of moral rules. The issue is whether a theory which treats rights as basic can make any sense of such a rule system. I cannot prove the impossibility of its doing so, but the story it would need to tell about the origin and authority of the system remain deeply mysterious.

Whether or not the foregoing considerations suffice to exclude rights-based theories as the appropriate theoretical setting for rights, there is another option worth exploring. Consequentialist theories utilize the concept of the good as their basic moral category and combine particular instances of the good into an overall goal to be pursued (or optimized). On the face of it, a goal-based ethical theory would seem to be the least likely home for moral rights, since (as we have seen) rights serve as normative constraints on the pursuit of goals. However, appearances here may be deceiving (Sumner 1987, ch. 6). A goal may be pursued in either of two ways: directly, by just aiming at it in every instance, or indirectly, by employing some more complex motivational strategy. While some goals are best pursued directly, others are not. The goal of personal happiness will serve as an example of the latter sort. If everything you do is directly and consciously motivated by the desire to maximize your own happiness, then you will almost certainly frustrate your own aim. Your goal will be much more efficiently pursued by sometimes aiming at other things (personal relationships, for instance) which require some suppression of your self-centered fixation.

Now suppose we are talking about a very abstract moral goal such as the general welfare or equality of resources. Would such a goal be best pursued directly or indirectly? If the former, then there will indeed be no room for taking rights seriously, since they must be acknowledged as obstacles to the pursuit of the goal. But there are good reasons for thinking that, like personal happiness, moral goals are best pursued indirectly. These reasons have principally to do with the cognitive and motivational limitations of moral decision-makers, whether they be individuals or social agencies. Left with no guidance save the general exhortation to promote some abstract moral goal, most decision-makers are likely to choose counterproductive means, as the result either of deficient information or of a natural human tendency to interpret situations in one's own favor. If this hypothesis is correct, then the kinds of goals advocated by most consequentialist theories will be best pursued by accepting and internalizing a set of constraints on their direct pursuit. Since rights serve as just such constraints, then respect for (a suitably contoured set of) rights might be required by a goal-based theory. If so, then there will be room within such a theory for rights to play their characteristic normative role, while the theory's basic goal will serve as the criterion for authenticating rights. A right will count as genuine on this view just in case its recognition within some conventional rule system (formal or informal) is (or would be) morally justified, where the standard of justification is promotion of the theory's basic goal.

A goal-based theory imposes an external control on the proliferation of rights: the purpose of rights is to promote some independently defined value such as welfare or autonomy, and rights are to be recognized as legitimate only to the extent that they serve this purpose. The same basic aim will therefore also serve to demarcate the subdomain of rights, by identifying those areas of private or public life where thinking in terms of rights is inappropriate or counterproductive. A goal-based theory also has no problem accounting for the rule system necessary for making sense of rights, since the only rules it requires (or acknowledges) are ordinary conventional ones (legal and nonlegal, institutional and non-institutional, formal and informal). A moral right on this account is a right whose recognition in some such rule system is (or would be) morally justified – no Platonic heaven is necessary of moral rules with no moral legislator.

The most familiar form of consequentialism is of course utilitarianism, which is distinctive by virtue of its welfarist theory of the good and its aggregative procedure for combining individual welfare into a sum to be maximized. But consequentialist theories come in many different shapes with different theories of the good (both monistic and pluralistic) and different procedures (both aggregative and distributive) for defining a collective goal. For our present purposes it matters not which particular form of consequentialism we have in mind, for their common property is the priority they attach to promotion of their favored goal. Trying to fit rights into this kind of collectivist framework may seem a little like trying to square the circle, but once the air of paradox is dispelled the idea has considerable attraction. It is also the working paradigm in much judicial reasoning about rights, which often takes the form of trying to locate the appropriate balance between conflicting rights. If each of the rights in conflict (for instance, freedom of political expression versus equal respect for minorities) is intended to secure some important social goal, then striking the appropriate balance between them means drawing their boundaries in whatever way will promote the optimal tradeoff between these goals. Any such approach is basically consequentialist, since it treats rights as devices for the pursuit of social goals. But it is compatible with, indeed requires, taking (the appropriate set of) rights seriously.

Other kinds of theories, such as some forms of contractualism, may share with consequentialism the virtue of controlling rights externally rather than internally. My aim here has not been to provide an exhaustive inventory of the possible theoretical settings for rights, but rather to make two tentative suggestions. The first is that the strategy of situating rights within a general ethical theory is worth exploring thoroughly before we settle for the more modest methodology of particularist intuitionism. The second is that among such theories those that are goal – rather than rights – based have a better chance both of making sense of rights and of controlling the inflation of rights claims. I have not been able to give either suggestion more than a very cursory defense, but both merit further development.

References

Dworkin, R.: *Taking Rights Seriously* (Cambridge, MA: Harvard University Press, 1977).

Finnis, J.: *Natural Law and Natural Rights* (Oxford: Clarendon Press, 1980).

Freeden, M.: *Rights* (Minneapolis: University of Minnesota Press, 1991).

Frey, R. G.: "Act-Utilitarianism, Consequentialism, and Moral Rights," *Utility and Rights,* ed. R. G. Frey (Minneapolis: University of Minnesota Press, 1984), pp. 61–85.

Hardwig, J.: "Should Women Think in Terms of Rights?," *Feminism and Political Theory,* ed. C. Sunstein (Chicago: University of Chicago Press, 1990), pp. 53–67.

Hart, H. L. A.: *Essays on Bentham: Studies in Jurisprudence and Political Theory* (Oxford: Clarendon Press, 1982).

Jones, P.: *Rights* (Basingstoke: Macmillan, 1994).

Lomasky, L. E.: *Persons, Rights, and the Moral Community* (New York and Oxford: Oxford University Press, 1987).

Lyons, D.: *Rights, Welfare, and Mill's Moral Theory* (New York and Oxford: Oxford University Press, 1994).

MacCormick, N.: *Legal Right and Social Democracy: Essays in Legal and Political Philosophy* (Oxford: Clarendon Press, 1982).

Nozick, R.: *Anarchy, State, and Utopia* (New York: Basic Books, 1974).

Raz, J.: *The Morality of Freedom* (Oxford: Clarendon Press, 1986).

Sherwin, S.: *No Longer Patient: Feminist Ethics and Health Care* (Philadelphia: Temple University Press, 1992).

Steiner, H.: *An Essay on Rights* (Oxford: Blackwell, 1994).

Sumner, L. W.: *The Moral Foundation of Rights* (Oxford: Clarendon Press, 1987).

Thomson, J. J.: *The Realm of Rights* (Cambridge, MA and London: Harvard University Press, 1990).

Waldron, J.: *Liberal Rights: Collected Papers, 1981–1991* (Cambridge and New York: Cambridge University Press, 1993).

Wellman, C.: *A Theory of Rights: Persons Under Laws, Institutions, and Morals* (Totawa, NJ: Rowman and Allanheld, 1985).

Chapter 16

Libertarianism

Jan Narveson

The Theory in General

What is libertarianism

Libertarianism is the view that we all have one single, general, fundamental right – the right to liberty. Rights imply duties, of course: for a certain agent, A, to have a right is for A to have a status such that other people are required to behave in certain ways towards A in the respects implied by the specific content of that right. For A to have the right to do x is for A to be such that some other person or persons is or are obligated to act in certain ways in relation to A's x-ing. So one can, substantively speaking, equivalently express the libertarian view as a *general prohibition on aggression*. An important further matter: What about the enforcement of this requirement? The libertarian principle prohibits *aggression* – not, flatly, all use or threat of force; it merely restricts it to defensive purposes.

Beyond that, we may distinguish two senses of "rights.". It is plausible to say, with Mill, that *all* moral duties are enforceable, "if not by law, by the opinion of his fellow-creatures; if not by opinion, by the reproaches of his own conscience"[1]– by the tendency to disdain or enthuse, and so on. But let us distinguish rights of the kind that may be enforced *by using force* against others, and those that may not, but where we are confined to remonstrations, lookings-askance, and the like. The Libertarian principle concerns the former. In saying that we have a general and fundamental right to liberty, it holds that the use of force against innocent persons is wrong. Whether it also addresses, or can be made to address, the latter as well is an interesting question. Later in this essay I will suggest that it can.

But is the libertarian saying that aggression against innocents is wrong *in all conceivable circumstances*? Perhaps no theory should be held to such a standard of unqualified statement. Libertarianism is often regarded as a flat-out, uncompromising theory. Whether it permits adjustments for catastrophic situations may depend on foundational questions concerning the fundamental rationale of the theory.

Certainly it is not *pacifist*. The question is whether absolutely all justified use of force is nonaggressive in the precise sense of the theory. In catastrophic circumstances, defending ourselves may be impossible without doing violence to innocents. If the libertarian right is based on considerations of self-preservation or the like, then it surely allows us to prefer preventing the heavens falling to what some consider "strict justice". Why not say, simply, that justice cannot require us to let the heavens fall?

A moral theory – not an ethical theory

Meanwhile, since nonaggression is its *only* tenet, libertarianism is apparently a very narrow view. On the face of it, it says nothing about a large range of topics that have historically fallen within the range of ethical inquiry. Most generally, there is the question, How shall I live? What is the good life? Libertarianism, we might say, is inherently committed to *not* answering that. Within the limits set by its stricture against aggression, it holds that we are free to choose among possible lives. The lives of the aesthete, the pleasure-seeker, the hard-driving businessperson, the teacher, the mountain-climber, the saint, are all acceptable, so far as it goes, to the libertarian. We may have our views about which lives are better, but they remain, so far as others are concerned, in the realm of advice and suggestion, not of prescriptive requirement. Whether the libertarian has anything to offer even in the way of "advice and suggestion" is a good question – which will be answered, in the affirmative, below.

Liberalism and libertarianism

Libertarianism comes on as ultra-tolerant. Indeed, it is right to regard libertarianism as an extreme form of *liberalism*, which is, I suggest, the view that the source of all relevant moral values is the individuals who are subject to its rules. Each, ultimately, is to be ruled by himself. If such a view is interpreted as a philosophy of *life*, it will seem totally crazy, or totally vapid – telling us to choose, but without giving us any means of choosing. But the reply to this is simply that that is not what the theory is about. Alternatively, it could be said that the means of choosing is the individual's own inner resources: you do what *you* most prefer, all things considered. But what *do* you prefer? That is quite strictly *your* question; it is impossible for anyone else to make your decisions: you may turn to another for advice, but it is you who must decide which others, and whether to take it when offered.

Libertarianism is, then, a view about one major aspect of morality in its social sense. Of course, that aspect has always been a prominent feature of moral inquiry as well. It is reasonable to identify morality, as distinct from ethics in general, as *the set of interpersonally authoritative rules*, for people in society, in groups. The widest possible group of moral agents is the group of all the agents there are, and many moral philosophers, such as Kant, have proposed theories of that scope. Libertarianism is such a theory, holding that the rule against aggression holds for all people, no matter what society they live in. That is a very ambitious claim; the libertarian bites off quite a lot, theoretically speaking.

Libertarianism as familiar

Philosophical moral theories, in this narrower sense in which such theories are proposed sets of general rules for society, have invariably been elaborations, purifications, or more precise explications of more or less inchoate customs of the societies known to their authors. Libertarianism certainly falls within that tradition. Informal rules against killing, inflicting serious physical injuries, theft of recognized items of property, and lying are familiar from virtually all cultures, albeit with much variation in detail. In proposing as the one very general rule of interpersonal behavior that all are to refrain from aggression, whatever else, it invokes a rule that will look familiar to everyone, at least as applied to fellow members of the tribe. But, typically as philosophical moral theories go, libertarianism is in intention universal. The fact that someone is from the tribe over the hill, or the nation across the sea, is held to make no fundamental difference: we owe it to all, and they owe it to us, that our interests not be pursued by aggressive means. In the main, that prohibition itself is no great surprise; only in its refusal to accept anything except countering aggression as justifying the use of interpersonal force is it unique.

Persons and self-ownership

Aggression is acting *against persons*, and thus the vague idea that individuals are to be held "inviolate" or "sacrosanct" is readily identified with the libertarian idea – though we must be careful not to impute a religious connotation if we so characterize it. But a more general and precise analysis is certainly required. One important thrust in that direction consists in identifying the fundamental libertarian status as that of *self-ownership* – a characterization which, in borrowing a term from commerce, may raise eyebrows. But the reason for it is readily discerned. To say that someone owns something is to say that he has authority over it, that he decides about its use or disposition, that he may do as he chooses with it. If x is mine, then you can only use it with my permission – you can't just do as you like with it; I, on the other hand, may indeed do just that. To say, then, that a person "owns himself" is to say that it is he who decides what is to be done with that self – it is "his" to do with or to it, or to allow or forbid others from doing to or with it, whatever can be done with or to it by that self's "owner" or others.

In saying that, we raise what is surely the main interpretive problem for this view. We may do as we like with what is ours – but, this being a universal, social doctrine, only up to the point where what we do collides with the identical rights of others.

Now those rights in their turn will all devolve from the other person's authoritative relation to *his* person. But obviously it is possible for A to do what would preclude some actions that B, in turn, might want to do. In general, anyone's desire to do anything is potentially in conflict with someone else's desired course of action. Your combing your hair is incompatible with my shaving it all off; my going to the opera is incompatible with your burning down the opera house; and so on. Libertarianism wants to allow everyone the completest possible freedom of action compatible with the same fundamental freedom for all others, and the question is whether that idea, as such, can generate any clear and coherent rules at all.

The idea of self-ownership helps supply the answer. Selves – persons – consist of bodies and psychologies. (Whether the latter can somehow be analyzed in terms of the former is a metaphysical question to which libertarianism need have no special answers.) Central to the human being, for purposes of ethical theory, is our command-and-control center, our "faculty of practical reason." Each person is taken to have a set of interests, desires, and presumably values (which may or may not be somehow identified with the former), which add up to a more or less coherent stock of preferences capable of feeding into practical decisions; each person has, in addition, a stock of powers – bodily, emotional, and intellectual – which are what are immediately put in action when decisions are made; and finally, each person comes equipped with a reasoning facility and a chooser or decider, which puts into action the results of deliberations in the light of his interests and his repertoire of unilaterally actualizable capabilities. The body, being a quite well-defined physical object, especially lends itself to territorial delineation: we are to refrain both from *damaging* others' bodies and also from simply *using* them, in whatever ways it is possible for one person to use another, without the latter's consent. Minds are less easy to specify in such terms, but one person may attempt to pre-empt another's decision-making powers, by bullying, harassing, intimidating, and so on. But ownership of one's body – putting a moral imprimatur on the de facto power of a given mind over its associated body – is a useful starting point.

The provision *without his consent* is crucial. Jones is to be the master of Jones's being. If he wants to injure himself, that is his right; if he wants to interact with Smith in some way that Smith agrees to engage in – say, sexually, or as fellow rower in a boat race, or opponent in a wrestling match – that again is his right. A's morally certified liberty is to be as nearly as possible complete, so long as A's's actions are confined to this initial "domain" of A's person, and thus it extends, in principle, to suicide or euthanasia as well. Those who would maintain the inviolability of selves above and beyond the preferences of those selves regarding themselves abandon libertarianism for some other theory.

Libertarianism and property rights

Many human disputes concern the use, not of our own bodies as such, but of things outside anyone's bodies: pools of oil under the surface of the earth, trees, rivers, mountainsides. Some of those things are natural, existing prior to human effort, others are modified by human activity, often beyond recognition – microcomputers do not grow on trees, and scarcely resemble anything in nature. The term "libertarianism" has recently solidified in the direction of the view that objects outside of human bodies can also be owned by individual persons. The right of private property is taken by libertarians to be a straight implication of the general liberty principle, and to be very strong indeed. With Locke, who held in the seventeenth century that a person's property cannot rightly be taken without his consent, either by private persons or by governments, the modern libertarian holds that property rights are so strong as to preclude anyone else's using what belongs to any person, for whatever purposes, not only in the case where the would-be taker's purposes are evil but also where they are as good as you like. Taking must be approved by the person taken from.

A brief explanation of this view is needed, though the subject could take us far afield. This brief explanation is as follows. Libertarianism holds that we are to be allowed to do as we wish. Only people have basic rights, and libertarians hold that they have only one basic right. Having that, what about the case in which people act in ways that happen to utilize external objects? They find things that they then use, either by simply contemplating them, as with the sunset, or as a setting for exercise, as when we walk in a forest, or by bending them to such human purposes as the satisfaction of hunger or the provision of shelter or assorted kinds of pleasure. These being things we may do, provided that we do not thereby injure others, what, then, constitutes "injury" of the relevant kind?

Here there are really only two distinctive views to consider. One is the case where somebody else is already using the item in question for his purposes. It is clear that a theory forbidding interference with others' activities generally, forbids it in the special case where that other is already using a thing. Property is rightful possession; but libertarianism says that *all* activities are, so far as they go, rightful just by being activities that their agents want to engage in, provided no others are thereby injured.

The other view holds, as most contemporary writers apparently do, that when we take possession of some hitherto unused thing, we injure others by depriving them of the opportunity for future use of that item. If that were so, it is very difficult to say what the implications would be, though it is quite clear that they would not be anything like so simple as those who infer a ground for some kind of general tax seem to think (Steiner 1994). But we needn't worry about the potential incoherence of the idea, for it is wrong anyway. We can interfere only with what someone is doing, not with what he isn't; deprive someone only of something he *has*, not of something he *hasn't* – however much he might like to have it. Interference, disruption, despoliation, invasion, are real relations between actual people, not phantoms of philosophical imagination. Libertarianism allows you to dream, of course, but it certainly doesn't give you the right that other people make your dreams come true. We must do that ourselves, and in doing so, must respect others, not expect them to stand back as you help yourself to the benefits of what they have already done, or compel them to provide you with benefits you have done nothing for.

In short, the idea that there is a restriction of the kind widely quoted from Locke, that we may take from the "state of nature" so long as there is "enough and as good left for others," is a straight misreading of the liberty principle, which in Locke's version as well as mine is a pure negative principle: "no one ought to harm another in his Life, Health, Liberty or Possessions" (para. 6). We do not do this when we take what no one has as yet used or even laid eyes on.

It is also true that virtually all property is *made*, in a more robust sense than merely being discovered. Humans create, remaking the world to a degree unrecognizable to Cro-Magnon man. And we spend our lives, in considerable part, in activities of exchanging. What we exchange when we exchange, we should realize, are, *always, services*. Those services often consist in realigning rights over things: I give you my right over this item in exchange for your letting me have the right to that ten-dollar bill. This Peruvian slum-dweller agrees to dig in this mound for a dollar a day; that movie star acts in this film, produced by this company, in exchange for a million dollars; and so on. Every person in these scenarios undertakes to improve his or her situation relative to his status quo ex ante, and typically succeeds in that undertaking. Insofar as the exchanges are agreed to by those party to them, who are in turn not acting fraudulently or under compulsion by any other persons, they are accepted by the liberty principle as legitimate activities.

Almost all theorists these days seem to think that there is something inherently wrong with a society of which the above descriptions would hold. Don't the high-rollers *owe* the poor something more than mere recognition of the latter's liberty? Or isn't the "liberty" of the slum-dweller so far from what we had in mind in setting out to defend liberty as to be a caricature? The libertarian resolutely answer both in the negative. The descriptions above show people relating to each other, trying to make the best lives they can manage; as such we have no business picking on them, threatening them with jail if they don't hand over sums to pay for universities, slum-clearance projects or whatever; nor should we be herding the poor into the offices of bureaucrats or imposing restrictions preventing them from engaging in peaceful activities that would better their situations if they were allowed to engage in them. But to go farther on these matters would take us beyond the confines of a short article. Suffice to say that it is not difficult to see the connection between the liberty principle and the familiar relations of "market society." Attempts to use it to support the panoply of highly interventionist programs we encounter from contemporary governments seem bound to fail.

Owning property is having the right to do whatever you want to that can be done with it, within the limits presented by other peoples' property rights (in themselves and in other things). This is a unitary matter; property need not be dissected into different modes or incidents, as many seem to think. In particular, there is no relevant, morally basic distinction between capitalist-type rights and primary use-type rights: initial acquirers may use their property by ploughing it up, renting it, selling or bartering, subdividing, establish stocks in it, and so on, limited only by their imaginations and the interests of others.

Refinements and Queries

Fairness and equity

Almost all theorists insist that there is a general requirement of fairness, especially in economic matters, that upsets the preceding conclusions about liberty. But libertarians can reply that considerations of fairness are relevant only when those concerned have claims, and these claims must stem from the roles they play in voluntary activities. Of course it is fair that if B has contributed x to productive activities, then his share of the gains that were the point of the activities in the first place should be proportionate to x's marginal contribution to those gains. Even there, the "should" is weak; for wages are arranged by agreement. What people have freely settled on is, basically, what they are entitled to, whether that conforms to someone's idea of their "just due" or not. But society as a whole isn't a productive enterprise in the relevant sense. If it can be said to be for the "production" of anything in particular, it is peace. And there fairness tells us that peace is to be repaid with peace, not war; to impose forcibly on some, in order to give others what they are not entitled to, hardly rates as "fair." Similarly, since people are not equal, and rarely contribute equally to production, to give each, nevertheless, an equal share in society's product would be inequitable, not equitable. For liberty to be equal – fairly distributed – is for each to supply it equally to each other in return for each getting it for himself: the equality is in the amount of forcible interference by each with anyone else: *none*.

Relation to political philosophy

There is a general impression that libertarianism is exclusively a political theory. The impression is understandable, but wrong – clearly, the prohibition against using other people and their property is intended to apply to everyone, whether acting privately or publicly. What makes it understandable is that the libertarian view as applied to the private relations of persons is so widely accepted, at least in substance, that it is taken to be obvious and, like the air around us, becomes part of the environment. Ordinary people understand that they are not to steal from anyone – though they sometimes do, anyway. The poor person does not think that he may just go ahead and help himself to the wealthy person's car or golf clubs or house, nor does the wealthy person think himself entitled to invade the shacks of the poor.

Yet there is a remarkable divergence between libertarians and others in regard to the application of these moral truisms to the actions of governments. The libertarian, uniquely, holds that it is just as wrong for governments to take people's money or expropriate their lands as for privately acting individuals or gangs to do so. Indeed, libertarians tend to regards governments as equivalent to gangs of thieves. We may think that some such gangs are more morally praiseworthy than others: some aim at and some even achieve good results, after all, and the libertarian may even agree with others about which results are to be considered "good" and which not, so far as they go. Nevertheless, he insists, to achieve these results *by those means* is wrong, just as it would be in the case of any individual. If I am collecting money to support the Harvard graduate school, I may not do so by staging a holdup, no matter how admirable we may think that institution's activities. Why, then, may the government do that? It purports to be acting on the part of the public, to be sure; but that is always false; you will never find all of those taxed supporting any government venture to the precise extent that the amount exacted from them is what they would wish to spend on that particular cause if they had their choice. And the fact that 90 percent of your fellow men want to spend your money that way doesn't make it right, any more than, to borrow from Mill again, the fact that 99 percent of your fellows disagree with you on some point of philosophy or aesthetics justifies them in suppressing your opinion (Mill, ch. 4).

As libertarians see it, their position is a simple matter of consistency with principles we all accept at the person-to-person level. Extending this to the most general level has one major implication: the right moral model for groups large or small is the *association*, the *voluntary* group. Associations are formed of people who share its purposes, and are willing to work with each other in the ways more or less specified or understood by the structure of the association at the time of joining. The hallmark of the free association is that if they don't like it, they can leave. Associations are typified by clubs, businesses – including their customers, who buy voluntarily – study groups, churches, and indefinitely many others. Within the association, there will often be a governing structure, to which members are likely to pay attention because they organize the activities that are the point of the association. That structure may or may not be democratic, but the individual's option to leave preserves his liberty: if he finds the association's governing body going wrong, he votes with his feet, whether or not he has a ballot.

Custom and community

Communities and societies are not, as such, voluntary associations; their members were simply born there, or moved there with parents, or are there for other accidental reasons. The individual may be able to leave a community, but the costs of doing so are typically high. This raises a serious question, from the libertarian point of view, what to say about the rules of such groups. Does custom have, as Aquinas claimed, the force of law?

Here's an example. In the movie, Zorba the Greek, a woman has an affair with the hero, and is stoned to death as an adulterer by community members. From the libertarian point of view, *prima facie*, this woman has been intolerably wronged: for engaging in a purely consensual activity with another consenting individual, she suffers the penalty of death. Has she been relevantly harmed? We are given to understand that the woman in question did not question the mores; she accepted her penalty stoically, as did the hero. What are we to think? A libertarian will surely disapprove of such customs, and will think that such communities need improvement and instruction. And so, most likely, would most people of broadly liberal persuasion today – which is to say, nearly everybody. Nevertheless, it is fascinating that in typical communities around the world, their members do not see their rules as highly oppressive, or perhaps as oppressive at all. And the libertarian can and should say that those people have the right to accept such rules. The people in those communities will also, most likely, join with their fellows in teaching those customs to their children, perpetuating what we outsiders will think of as oppression. Who is right here? Or is there a right and wrong at all on such matters?

To this we can respond that aggressive interference in such communities by outsiders is not justified, but perhaps voluntary intervention, in the way of discussion and education by persons who take on the responsibility of sympathetically involving themselves, learning the group's language and customs and not setting themselves up as superiors, can do some good.

But this is a good point at which to make some important distinctions.

Negative and positive rights

First, we need to emphasize a distinction that is absolutely basic to the libertarian point of view. This is the distinction between what have come to be called "negative" and "positive" rights. That terminology has been applied, notably by Sir Isaiah Berlin, in ways that confuse the issue as much as they illuminate it, but there is in fact a straightforward, relatively simple, and familiar distinction here. A *negative* right is one which entails duties to *refrain* from certain actions, namely actions that would interfere with, impede, or render impossible the action by the rightholder to which he is being said to have a right. A *positive* right, by contrast, entails not only those duties, but also duties to *assist* the rightholder in doing those things, if it should happen that that person is unable to do those things on his own, or with the purely voluntary assistance of others. In short, the distinction is between non-hindrance and help. The distinction is readily illustrated in the case of the idea of a right to life. A murderer violates the right to life of his victim, period: the right to life is at least the negative right that others not forcibly deprive us of our lives, and the murderer does precisely that. But consider the victim in the ditch, as in the New Testament parable of the Good Samaritan. Others walk by, eyes averted; but the Good Samaritan intervenes by positive action to prevent death, tending to the victim's wounds, and/or -in an updated version – driving him to the hospital or arranging an ambulance, etc. Now, if the victim had a positive right to life against all and sundry, then all who walk by would violate that right, even though they did not violate the negative version; its violator was only the evil person who set upon the victim in the first place. The Good Samaritan provides the help that a positive right would *require* him to do. In the Libertarian's view, he goes further than he morally must.

The libertarian view, then, is that our fundamental right of liberty is negative, not positive. The reasoning behind that is straightforward. A positive right, by definition, cuts further into our liberty than the corresponding negative one: if you are *forced* to help others in need, then you do not have your choice whether to help them. Yet your not helping them does not cut into the liberty of the victims: it does not disenable them from doing whatever they can do anyway – which, to be sure, is not much. But it does not worsen their situations as compared with what they are at the time when action could take place. Instead, it merely leaves them no better off.

Some have regarded the positive/negative distinction as defective, even "bogus," (Shue 1985) and in any case as fundamentally insignificant. Police, for example, cost money to maintain, and yet the libertarian calls upon police to uphold people's negative rights, does he not? But in fact, that is a misunderstanding. Whether we *also* have a positive right to police assistance is a distinct issue from the issue of whether we have a negative right to life and property. We can have the latter without government-maintained police, or even, logically, with no police at all. At any rate, the libertarian can certainly hold that we should do without government-monopolized police, as well as without government postal services and the rest of it. Conceptually, the distinction is clear.

The second claim was made famous by James Rachels, who describes cases in which the difference between killing and letting-die is all but indiscernible. But whether it is nevertheless morally insignificant is, again, a separate issue, even in his paradigm case: the uncle who fails to lift the child's head above the water, thereby not preventing its likely death, nevertheless does not *murder* the child; the one who shoves it under in order to make sure that it dies, does murder it. And, of course, in virtually all cases, the two are sharply different. You, for example, are at this very moment failing to save the lives of millions of people, any of whose lives you conceivably might be able to save – yet you aren't *killing* anyone at all, never have and (I trust) never will. The thought that perhaps you deserve a jail sentence for all those omissions would be regarded by almost anyone as too absurd to bear mention.

Now: do we have a positive right, even to life? To take this really seriously would be to assert that those who walk by are guilty of murder, as much so as the original criminal. Very, very few people can take such a view seriously. What most of us surely think, and act on in daily life, is that helping others in severe need is a good thing to do, something we surely *ought* to be willing to do, and ought actually to do, at least when we can do it without great trouble or danger. We think that those who do go to great trouble and risk to do such things have gone beyond the call of duty, or at least that if we are to say that they have "only" done that – as they might, modestly, themselves – then it is in a sense of "duty" quite different from that in which we all have the duty to refrain from murder and theft and the rest of it in the first place. As observed above, it seems that most people, in short, are essentially libertarians in their day-to-day dealing with others.

Duties and virtues: charity, in particular

The other distinction we need to make here is that between moral *requirements* of the strong type that the libertarian wants to hold us all to in regard to non-aggression, and moral *virtues*, in regard to what goes beyond those requirements, but in a good direction. These might be called either "duties of charity," understanding that phrase to imply that charity may not be forcibly exacted from us, or "works of supererogation." In any case, we may apply the familiar notion of virtue here. Of course justice is a virtue, and a very important one – in a clear sense the fundamental and cardinal one. But there are other dispositions besides justice which can and should come in for specifically moral attention. Possession of quick reflexes is a virtue in a basketball player, but has no particular connection with morals. Charity, by contrast, is a specifically moral virtue. What makes it so? Later in this essay, I will discuss the subject of the foundations of morality, in particular as it applies to the libertarian view; but we can recognize right away why a community would do well to commend those who volunteer to assist people in need, and in general to do good works for others. Now, many good things, such as excellence in basketball-playing, are not, as such, community pursuits – though hockey comes very close to being so in Canada. But everyone has a body that can be in better or worse condition, and which it is in the interest of its possessor, *prima facie*, that it be better rather than worse. The disposition to help it along with assorted ministrations is plainly one we all stand to benefit from if everyone has it (and if the ministrations are competently performed.) It deserves, therefore, the encouragement and support of anyone. That is what singles it out as a "moral" virtue, and there is no reason at all why the libertarian cannot join with others in such recognition.

In general, then, the libertarian can perfectly well recognize that works of charity are to be commended, praised, and rewarded by people generally. Still, says the libertarian, such positive acts of doing good to others are not basically required of us in the way that forbearances from inflicting evils are required. We may properly be compelled to refrain from doing evil to others. But for not doing good, or not enough good, we may be at most criticized, perhaps shunned – but no more. In particular, says the libertarian, we may not be *taxed*; that is a compulsory extraction of what is ours.

Are there specifically libertarian virtues – virtues that libertarians especially would and should support as such? Yes: the relief of people from oppression, for example, would seem to be a specialty of the house for anyone interested in human liberty. And being interested in human liberty, generally speaking, is a specialty of the libertarian house – though by no means a monopoly of theirs. We must, of course, be very careful to distinguish *group* "liberation" from the liberalizing that the libertarian is anxious to promote. That a large group of people, living within the same boundaries on some map, should be under the thumb of one set of leaders rather than some other set is not obviously something for the libertarian to get excited about. Whether a given movement of national independence enables its citizens to be freer than before is an open question, as it stands; it will depend on conditions specific to the case, and opinions will reasonably differ.

Where libertarian opinions cannot differ, however, is on the matter of what our basic duties are. The libertarian denies that there is an enforceable duty to liberate others from oppression. That is something we perhaps should get into, if our talents lie that way – as they usually do not. But it is clearly not something that the libertarian can coherently hold to be an enforceable duty. Here the libertarian parts company with his counterpart in the supposedly liberal community: proponents of government measures to promote literacy, health, income, and other aspects of welfare, often talk as if such measures were required by respect for liberty. Not so. Respect for liberty requires that we *not aggress* against others, not intervene to deprive them of what is theirs, to stymie their activities, whatever they may be. It does not, by contrast, require Beethoven to forego the frivolous activity of creating works of art that will be appreciated by a comparative fraction of the bourgeoisie and instead help free someone from the throes of oppression. If we want to do things like that, well and good – indeed, if done right, *morally* well and good, as we have seen above. But the libertarian principle calls upon us to refrain from "invading and despoiling" *any* non-aggressive person, be they currently healthy or sick, rich or poor, foreigners or next-door neighbors, and whether or not doing so might result in somebody's being freer from oppression by some other persons than he otherwise might be. The libertarian principle discerns a gulf between worsening and not-bettering, and insists that our fundamental requirement is to refrain from the former, whether or not we advance beyond the latter.

The Duty of Mutual Aid

Is this understating our moral responsibilities? Suppose there is a disaster in your community: rivers rise, leaving people homeless, their livelihoods imperilled. Doesn't duty call? Shouldn't we get out there and do our bit to help people out? Of course, we should. As, indeed, we do: in every emergency, people spring to the assistance of their imperilled fellows. This is, one might add, especially true, as a matter of document, in such individualistic, "capitalist" places as America and Canada, where the levels of mutual assistance in time of need are positively awesome.

I suggest that the libertarian need have no qualms about classifying mutual aid as a duty. But is it an *enforceable* duty? May we clap in jail those who don't join the line-up to build the sandbag dikes? Certainly not; and in saying this, I am sure that I say what almost all ordinary people will agree with, especially in practice. It is a point of pride and honor to devote effort to making one's community a good place to live, and helping out when help is desperately needed is an elementary point in such efforts. But to make them compulsory is wrong. And demeaning as well. How is honor due to him who toils for his neighbor, if he toils because the police await him if he does not?

When something is both a duty and yet a *nonenforceable* one, what is meant? We need to make a distinction, for as noted at the outset, we can agree with Mill that all morality is in some sense "enforceable". But let us now use a term, "reinforceable", designed to be more general than "enforceable". We *reinforce* what we think to be right by remonstrances, by excluding what we think to be offenders from our company, or by withholding certain kinds of good services from them. We *enforce* when we literally curtail the other person's capacity or power to do something. Incarceration and execution, and threats of same, count in this way. These are all things that the liberty principle forbids except in the specific case of violation of others' libertarian rights. But when we talk of virtues, or of supererogatory duties, we are beyond "rights" talk, and the reinforcement we apply to those we think deficient in such respects must stay within the bounds of the liberty principle. There is still considerable scope within those bounds, however. Mill's life was made uncomfortable by his friends and acquaintances because of his long-standing, uncustomarily public friendship with Helen Taylor. But on his own principles, those friends had the right to do those things, even though he thought, plausibly, that it was wrong of them to disapprove. It is in this sense that people may be said, on the libertarian (or anybody's?) view to "have a right to do wrong." Adding, as I have here, a whole category of morals on top of rights may, perhaps, redraw the territory customarily thought to be occupied by libertarian ideas. But I think not. Instead, one should think of this as clarifying its commitments. Some have understood libertarianism to be so austere a doctrine as to preclude all criticism of any and all behavior that does not, in itself, curtail the liberty of others. But that is to assimilate all criticism to that of the judge at his bench, where the sole topic for deliberation is whether the person before him is or is not to be fined, imprisoned, or hanged. But those are hardly the only moral decisions we need to make.

Children – a special case

From the point of view of the long-run survival of communities and, for that matter, of the human race, no one institution is more important than the family. Families generally produce and, with occasional exceptions, raise to maturity the new persons who must continually come on the scene if there are to be people in future. Those new people begin life about as helpless as one can readily imagine, and continue, though steadily maturing, to be dependent on parents, or others, for a decade or two. In early stages of childhood, human organisms are not equipped with the kind of capacities that lend themselves to sophisticated talk of rights and duties. Young children, perforce, will do more or less as they are told.

If it is less, though, then what? The libertarian, especially, has a problem about children, and from two opposite directions. On the one hand, there is a temptation to suppose that the libertarian principle should be applied to absolutely all humans, down to newborns. On the other, if it is pointed out, as is only reasonable, that children do not have the kind of facilities we had in mind in talking of a *right to liberty*, are they, then, left in the dark? For example, should we simply declare newborns to be the property of their parents, just as we declare the newly created painting of an artist to belong to its maker?

In this short exposition, my purpose is more nearly to raise than to try to resolve such issues. But a few things will be reasonably clear, at least. In the first place, the libertarian cannot accept that there is a *duty to procreate*, since that would clearly be a positive duty of the type he basically denies. Libertarianism, of course, allows them to pursue careers, or take same-sex partners or none, instead of raising families. But this still leaves us with the question of what those adults who do have children owe to them, and more generally what we all owe to all children. The situation is complicated by the fact that most people love their children and are disposed to treat them well if they can. They need no imposed duties to do that. Still, that dodges the issue. Are libertarians to claim that even small children have only the rights of noninterference that they proclaim so strongly on behalf of adults?

If we take that view, we are faced with an embarrassing consequence. For libertarianism denies that we owe assistance to anyone, as a fundamental duty, however admirable it may be to render it. But do we want to say this of parents in relation to their children? May they let them starve? But if it says they owe them more, what does that stem from? Not, certainly, from a negotiated agreement between the parents and the children – the standard way in which adults come to be bound to each other. It might be suggested that the sexual acts from which children typically result somehow carry with them the obligation to support any resulting children. But just how does this act, logically disparate from the parental duty thus allegedly engendered, manage to engender it, then?

The libertarian does have some resources for staking out a credible view on this matter – much aided by the fact that for very few parents is there any issue at all, since parents, as noted, normally come equipped with intense motivation to do well by their children. We can say, first, that while parents do, in a sense, "make" their children, they certainly don't do so in the same sense in which they make dinner, or microchips. Thus, claims to property rights in those children are rather more tenuous than in the usual cases. Second, the children in question, whatever they may be like while children, grow up to become adults, with the usual capabilities, including the capability to make things miserable for others. In the same way that people have a responsibility not to allow their property to create nuisance or danger to others, so too they have a responsibility not to bring up their children in ways that will make them a nuisance or danger to others. And thirdly, we could agree that if parents really don't want their infant children, they don't have to take them on. But suppose that other members of the community are all ready to do so? May we not insist, in self-defense and pursuance of relevant interests, that they at least allow those others to take them, rather than, say, stuffing them in the garbage?

It can be allowed that parents have the right to instruct and, within limits, to discipline their children. Modern experience suggests that the ancient method of discipline by the rod is a terrible mistake, and we may suggest that persons interested in child-rearing should, and do, make an effort to circulate such knowledge. And we may surmise that the propensity to snatch misbehaving children from their parents and put them into group homes and other institutions is a mistake, and at some point a violation of the rights of both parents and children. All such options and suggestions, certainly, need to be carefully explored – libertarianism is not a completed book. Nor should the problem about children be thought uniquely embarrassing to the libertarian; no one else has better answers here, unless your criterion of a "good answer" is merely that you happen to like it.

Micro-liberty

Liberal communities specialize in tolerance. Within their capacious walls, we can expect people of all sorts to gather and, we hope, flourish. Among them will be groups identifying with each other from tribal or religious or other ethnic back-grounds, and sometimes by common ideology. Characteristically, or perhaps al-ways and by definition, groups of the latter kind will have customs, moral views, imposing strong duties on their members. Recall the example early on from Zorba the Greek. If such a community were to emigrate to North America, the practice of stoning adulteresses would quickly come under severe scrutiny. Would it still, if the surrounding community were not merely rather liberal, but outrightly libertarian? No doubt it would, at least in the sense that outsiders would be quick to spread the word that women in such communities could, if they wanted to, opt out.

But what should we say, for example, about people who marry and then take lovers outside the marriage? Should we insist that the natural right of liberty allows people to do just that, so that their complaining spouses in fact have nothing to complain of? Or, alternatively, that promises are sacred and so this must be im-moral? Again, we must remember that the libertarian idea is not a theory of life, but only a theory about the proper principles for relations among people in general. Couples are not just "people in general": they have understandings, implicit and explicit, and those understandings matter a great deal to them. A liberty principle does not undermine these understandings; but it does put them in perspective. New worlds await the adventurous; but people are entitled to remain in the old ones if they so prefer.

Foundations: Why Liberty?

Now that we have a fair idea of what the libertarian advocates, we are in better position to tackle the question of why we should advocate it. What is the appeal of this position – so popular, as we have seen, with people in their everyday relations, and so unpopular with governments and contemporary theorists? To raise this ques-tion is to call for exploration of the foundations of morals. There have been many views about that matter, and it may seem hubris to broach it in the few remaining pages of a medium-size essay. But there is no alternative.

The very notion of "foundations" of morals is out of philosophical fashion today. That, I think, is largely because of what we can argue to be a misguided assimilation of moral theory to general epistemology and metaphysics. The latter are familiarly held to be without any particular foundations, and for plausible reasons. But morals has nothing to do with the question of the reality of the external world or whether mind is irreducible to matter. Morals takes place in a limited and wholly familiar field, the world of everyday experience. That there are some general features of people and their environments that make it sensible to accept some kinds of general rules for our mutual relations rather than others or none, is all that need be meant by the idea of foundations, in the moral area. And those who believe that there is literally no reason why we should think it wrong to kill each other, or right to help those in need, may perhaps be talking in the misleading way of skeptics about the existence of the material world. As Hume observes, the moment the latter leave their studies, they are comfortably familiar with the ways of such material objects as their automobiles or the trees across the street, and manage to get on quite well in relating to them. We should not seek "foundations" of morals in any fancier sense than that in which we have foundations for the view that it would be nice to be able to eat this evening.

That said, let us acknowledge that philosophers tend to seek extraordinary bases for ordinary things, such as the rules of morals. Especially pertinent here are supposed "basic moral rules," basic in the sense that they cannot be derived from or based on anything else at all. Such was the idea of Intuitionism, which held that there are moral truths that one simply "sees," that are just "there." Now, it is surely true that many people will scratch their heads if you ask them why they believe that murder is wrong, or what they suppose they mean by the word "wrong" anyway. But to infer from this that there are no reasons for these homely beliefs is to point to a problem inherent in any form of moral intuitionism: the Emperor's New Clothes. People can genuinely come to wonder why murder is wrong, or even to doubt that it is. Cloaking murder with an "intuition of wrongness" won't answer them. And if intuitionism has no more than this to say to us, the thought crosses the mind that perhaps what it says is really nothing at all.

Another tendency in moral philosophy is to suppose, to put it in terms of the distinction made at the outset, that we can, as it were, go straight from Ethics to Morals. We will claim, perhaps, that the meaning of life is Self-realization and that the reason we ought to respect other people's lives is that self-realization is a terribly important thing. Or that there is really nothing like the life of the philosopher, and in order to be one we must all make the world safe for philosophy . . . Again, we do not *answer* the question why murder is wrong in terms such as that.

Let us review the general features of social life relevant to our problem. People have preferences of great variety; among them, often, will be some ideals, and certainly some strongly held values. When they act, they attempt to bring about the objects of those preferences, as best they can. Were there only one individual in the world, there would be no problem of morals, though certainly he would be faced with the questions of general ethics – of trying to decide what he should devote his life to; but basically, that person's problem is just to do the best he could in the face of a not very helpful natural environment, and that would be that. But of course, we aren't in that situation. We live in a social world, encountering many others in daily life. Those people, unlike trees or rocks, have minds of their own, making decisions and choices, pursuing their various values. Some of those values will be similar to ones we have, but even the similar ones have an important potential for bringing us into conflict. And they have another important potential – to help promote projects we do value. Rationally, we want to avoid the former and promote the latter.

Why do we care about our own liberty? The obvious reason is that liberty, in social terms, is the absence of acts by others preventing us from doing what we are interested in doing – as any of them could do. Given liberty, we are on our own steam, at least; lacking it, we can't get where we want to go.

Then there is the potential for help at the hands of others. This potential, in principle, can be harnessed in two ways. One is by using force – enslaving, coercing them into providing us with the desired benefits. The other is by co-operative methods. These are the relations to others wherein both the other and the agent benefit as a result. A does something for B, B does something for A. Co-operative relations have many nice properties. Most important is that they are good for us both – by definition. A close second is that they reduce the other person's motivation to make life miserable for his partner. If you benefit yourself from benefitting me, you have reason to continue, rather than to turn to assault and domination.

But it is pretty easy for people, even when in potentially cooperative relation to each other, to be tempted instead to take advantage of each other. When A's back is turned, perhaps B should attack, thus gaining the benefits already got from A, while eliminating the onerous need to do his share. This, it is thought, is how *egoists* would behave. Yet if both made a habit of it, there would be problems – to put it mildly. Two persons disposed to take advantage of each other at every opportunity are not two winners, but two losers. Devoting our time to fighting, or in suspicious efforts to cover ourselves, build defenses, and so on, is not going to get a great deal done.

When we consider one-on-one relations with others, it is not difficult to realize the potential value of rules calling for cooperation and forbidding tendencies to try to dominate and extort. And if we broaden the net a bit, another large factor comes into prominent view: the differing abilities and interests of people are conducive to specialization of many sorts, increasing the likelihood that any given person will be able to find others who will cater to his peculiar interests. Moreover, some among those many will be brilliant, ingenious, creative, industrious, enterprising, and so on. Such people will, if not prevented, come up with useful ideas about how to do things that might very well improve our lives.

The short of it – there is no room for the "long" – is that cooperation fits very well into anyone's profile as a person. Almost all of us have considerable abilities that we can, if allowed, bring into play to realize what we want in life, almost whatever it may be. All of us differ at least somewhat, and many a lot. How do we do best insofar as general rules of conduct can affect the issue?

The "rule" that *others* are to devote themselves to *our* welfare has an initial appeal, but one that withers under even fairly superficial analysis. First, and especially: why should they do so? That is to say, why *would* they do so, in view of the fact that they do not carry in their genes any special affection for us? But even that is misleading. For many of them do carry in their genes general affection for us, enough that, on a decent day, they are quite likely to be helpful where help is relatively easy to render and can do a lot of good. But what nonlibertarians propose is a rule of the heavy-weapons type: we should stand ready to enforce the rule of helping others with the threat of jail and the like. Such a rule, for this purpose, has two major disadvantages. For one thing, its administrative costs are high: maintaining jails is expensive, not to mention the legal and other apparatus that goes with them. By contrast, voluntary cooperation carries its own fuel: it is largely self-enforcing, as each has motivation to participate so long as the other does, and both realize that cooperation doesn't end sharply at noon but goes on the next day and the day after. When each is motivated to cooperation by interests he or she actually has, there is little or no need for outsiders to participate. Coercive methods, on the other hand, are necessarily inefficient. Why go for relations in which some gain only at the expense of others, when instead we can have relations in which one person gains only when at least some others do too?

But further: we don't want the help of others to be a matter of sheer happenstance. It is in everyone's interest that everyone have a sense of duty toward others, to help when they easily can. The ideal compromise is to make this a matter of noncompulsive obligation, as discussed before. We will praise those who are helpful, and will downrate those who are not when they readily could be. The libertarian's objection to compulsion holds here as well; but after all, the point of morality is to enable all to live well, and in a limited but important class of cases, the help of our fellows when in urgent need may be essential to our doing so. All are to be *allowed* to live as they please; but all are to be *encouraged* to charity and good service to their fellows.

It is obvious why each of us wants to be free of real interference, so far as we can. It does not follow directly that we would do well to make it a right. But the cost of accepting a general right of liberty, in which each is allowed to do as he prefers, with the minimal constraint compatible with everyone's being able to exercise this right, is low. Positive rights would add to the burden, without providing compensating advantages for all: not only are we to desist from invading and despoiling, but we *also* have to devote some or a good deal of our energies to helping to realize the aims of others, even when we don't share those aims – as we typically don't. Why would we do that? Not for the sake of the gains it enables us to have – for if we all could gain, we would not require anyone to stand over us with the power to jail us for nonassistance. And if only most of us could gain, why wouldn't we form an association of like-minded persons, who would commit themselves to help fellow members without imposing extra burdens on others outside it? Why would those potentially outside it accept a general rule imposing those pointless and irksome burdens, as they surely are from their point of view?

The liberty principle accords quite well with the core of ordinary morality as practiced by most people most of the time. But that, as such, is not what recommends it. Instead, what recommends it is the same thing that recommends it to those ordinary people themselves: it is the principle that can be most expected, among possible principles, to enable each of us to live the better lives that we envisage to be achievable, given our various interests. There are reasons explaining why few societies have, nevertheless, looked very much like libertarian societies, despite the general acceptance of the liberty principle among people in their daily lives. Those reasons are based on the logic of coalitions – of ganging up on people to exact short-term gains. In the longer run, though, we all suffer at the hands of such systems. But that is a subject for another discussion.

Note

1 J. S. Mill, *Utilitarianism*, ch. 5. For example, "We do not call anything wrong, unless we mean to imply that a person ought to be punished in some way or other for doing it; if not by law, by the opinion of his fellow-creatures; if not by opinion, by the reproaches of his own conscience. This seems the real turning point of the distinction between morality and simple expediency. It is a part of the notion of Duty in every one of its forms, that a person may rightfully be compelled to fulfil it."

References

Locke, J. Locke: *Second Treatise of Civil Government.*
Mill, J.: *On Liberty.*
Rachels, R.: "Active and Passive Euthanasia," *New England Journal of Medicine*, vol. 292, (1975): 78–80. Widely reprinted, in J. Narveson, *Moral Issues* (Toronto/New York: Oxford University Press, 1975).
Shue, H.: "The Bogus Distinction – 'Negative' and 'Positive' Rights," in N. Bowie, *Making Ethical Decisions* (New York: McGraw-Hill, 1985), pp. 223–31.
Steiner, H.: "Compossibility and Domains" in his *A Theory of Rights.*
——: *An Essay on Rights* (Oxford: Blackwell, 1994).

Chapter 17

Virtue Ethics

Michael Slote

1 The Revival of Virtue Ethics

Most ethical theories in the ancient world were forms of virtue ethics, but in the modern era there have, until recently, been few virtue ethicists. Most modern moral theories treat rightness as a matter of producing good results or conforming to moral rules or principles, but virtue ethics specifies what is moral in relation to such inner factors as character and motive, and unlike most modern views, it treats *aretaic* notions like "admirable" and "excellent" – rather than deontic concepts like "ought," "right," and "obligatory" – as fundamental to the enterprise of ethics.

In recent years, and largely due to dissatisfaction with the reigning forms of moral theory, the ethics of virtue has undergone a considerable revival. This revival dates from the publication of G. E. M. Anscombe's "Modern Moral Philosophy" (Anscombe 1958), and it would seem that virtue ethics has now taken a place among the main approaches to substantive ethical theorizing. It is important to say something about how virtue ethics has developed since the publication of Anscombe's article and about its present directions and prospects, and in doing so, I shall assume, as indicated above, that a view counts as a form of virtue ethics if and only if it treats aretaic terms as fundamental (and deontic notions as either derivative or dispensable) and it focuses mainly on inner character and/or motive rather than on rules for or consequences of actions. This characterization is fairly rough, but it has the virtue of being broad enough to help us understand the sheer variety of the possible forms virtue ethics may take. It also allows us to rule out certain sorts of views that someone might initially mistake for forms of virtue ethics.

Many philosophers have spoken about virtue and the virtues, without, in the contemporary sense, counting as virtue ethicists. For example, Kant (1964) has a "doctrine of virtue," an account of moral virtue that flows out of what he has to say about right and wrong action, and Rawls, too, in *A Theory of Justice* (Rawls 1971) has an account of moral worth or virtue that likewise supplements or complements what he has to say about justice and right action. But any view that treats virtue as simply one part of a moral theory doesn't count as virtue ethics. Virtue ethics seeks an account of virtue that is self-standing and central, rather than derivative or merely complementary, and we might then say (slightly altering a suggestion of Roger Crisp's) that Kant and Rawls have *theories of virtue*, but are not necessarily proponents of any form of *virtue ethics*.

2   The Variety of Virtue Ethics

The above characterization of virtue ethics is also significant for what it *doesn't* contain. In the ancient world, every form of virtue ethics was eudaimonistic. That is, such views treated the question of the agent's long-term well-being or *eudaimonia* as, in Julia Annas's words, the "entry point" for ethical theory, and they all assumed that nothing could count as a virtue unless it contributed to the well-being of the virtuous individual (Annas 1993). But (perhaps as a result of the influence of Christianity) some modern views treat the inner life as the foundation for all morality – James Martineau (1891) is one example, and David Hume (1958/1739) is at least a near-example – *without* assuming that virtue necessarily pays (in this world). Such approaches are naturally regarded as forms of virtue ethics, and our above rough characterization includes them as such.

The above description of virtue ethics also allows for the possibility of types of virtue ethics that not only focus on how people should *be*, rather than on how they should *act*, but *have nothing to say* about the moral evaluation of actions (see, e.g., Stephen 1882; Pincoffs 1986). But the majority of virtue ethicists regard it as one of their main tasks to say something substantial about how people should act or live, and under this assumption the task of virtue ethics includes giving a *distinctively virtue-ethical account* of the rightness or wrongness, goodness or badness, of human actions.

However, among those who have accepted or admitted this task, there is a division between those who believe virtue ethics should be *theoretical* and those who think it should not. Aristotle treats knowledge of right and wrong as a matter of being sensitive to and perceptive about what a given situation calls for in the way of action, and in Aristotle's philosophy the idea that the virtuous person sees what is noble or ignoble, right or wrong, in any given situation replaces the familiar assumption that right action is a matter of obeying preexisting moral *rules*. Aristotle thinks rules inadequate to capturing the widely varying requirements of different situations and relies, instead, on the sensitivity – some have likened it to connoisseurship – of the virtuous individual to moral distinctions and nuance. But if rules are not the basis for morality, then morality lacks a certain kind of *generality*, and theory, to the extent it seeks generalizations and general explanations, may well be out of place in moral philosophy. And indeed several recent virtue ethicists –

e.g., John McDowell (1979) and Martha Nussbaum (1986) – have taken something like this line about the undesirability of the kind of moral theory offered by Kant, contract theorists, and consequentialists. For all these theories treat principles or rules of action as lying at the heart of morality and the justifications moral philosophy offers.

But other virtue ethicists have held that virtue ethics should have a general form or structure and should allow of general rules and explanations, and these thinkers have more or less explicitly *advocated* moral theory and deplored the tendency of some recent virtue ethicists to scorn the task of theorizing. Those virtue ethicists who advocate theory have the burden, of course, of explaining how one or another of their preferred theories differs from the kinds of theories offered by consequentialists, Kantians, and others and, also, of justifying the particular theory they prefer. But a number of recent virtue ethicists have not shied from these tasks, and in what follows I shall say something about the different kinds of virtue-ethical theory that have been offered in recent years. All these theories have roots in earlier forms of virtue ethics – some ancient, some modern – and indeed most of the most important differences among contemporary theories are traceable to differences among their historic sources. In particular, and as I noted above, the virtue ethics of ancient times and of the earlier modern era have tended to differ in regard to the assumption of eudaimonism, and it is important to see that this distinction represents a fundamental divide among the virtue theories that have recently been developed or developing.

3 Aristotle and Rosalind Hursthouse's Virtue Theory

Thus one of the most notable of the explicitly theoretical forms of virtue ethics that have appeared in recent years is the eudaimonistic view advocated by Rosalind Hursthouse (1991a). Hursthouse treats ethics as having, roughly, the following structure: acts are right or wrong depending on whether the virtuous individual would choose them; an individual counts as virtuous if s/he has and exercises all the virtues; and virtues are qualities of character that an agent needs in order to attain *eudaimonia*, overall well-being or a good life. Such a view treats our understanding of the good life as grounding what we have to say in other realms of the ethical (though this is not the only way one can be a eudaimonist); and Hursthouse also makes it clear that she thinks of Aristotle's own ethics as having the above *theoretical* structure. Most significantly, she holds and thinks Aristotle holds that acts count as right *because a virtuous person would choose them*.

But this is not the only way one can interpret Aristotle. We saw earlier that Aristotle speaks of the virtuous individual as perceiving (Aristotle also says *seeing*) what is morally admirable, required, or noble in any given situation, and it makes most sense to talk of perceiving when what is perceived is at least somewhat independent of the perceiver. As a result, Aristotle is frequently interpreted as a moral intuitionist who regards the moral quality of actions as largely independent of the moral character of the agent – that is how he can say, for example, that one becomes just by performing just actions. In that case, Aristotle's statement that the virtuous individual is the measure of what is right or noble doesn't have to entail Hursthouse's claim that acts are right or noble *because* a virtuous person would have performed them. It can amount, instead, to the *epistemological thesis* that virtuous individuals are perfect judges of what is right and what is wrong; and if we interpret Aristotle in this intuitionist fashion, then we must say that if individuals count as virtuous, that is *because* they reliably see, and seamlessly act on their view of, what is (independently) noble or right in various situations.

Thus on Hursthouse's interpretation of Aristotle, the ethical character of individuals explains that of actions, but, if anything, just the reverse is true for the interpretation we have just offered. And without speaking now to the merits of these interpretations as interpretations of Aristotle, it is worth noting how differently they see the structure of ethics. For Hursthouse, evaluations of agents and/or their inner lives are *prior* to evaluations of their actions, whereas on the view I have been talking about act-evaluations are *not* derivative from agent-evaluations, but rather are independent of and in some sense prior to the latter. However, for Hursthouse and Hursthouse's Aristotle, aretaic evaluations of agents are not the end of ethical explanation, but are themselves ultimately *based* in claims about what traits are necessary to the good life, to eudaimonia. By contrast, on the alternative interpretation I have been describing, we needn't ground our assessments of actions in further or prior evaluations of any sort. Those assessments can be basic and, together perhaps with evaluations of desires and emotions, serve to ground judgments about who is a virtuous person. Claims about eudaimonia, rather than serving as the foundation of other judgments, will be based in independently grounded ideas about virtuous activity and the virtuousness of individuals; but such an interpretation accords well with Aristotle's well-known view that the good life by and large consists in acting virtuously.

On pain of circularity, Hursthouse's Aristotle cannot make this last claim and has to understand the good life as specifiable *independently* of our account of what is virtuous, and indeed there is a longstanding way of understanding Aristotle that lends itself to such a view of the good life. For Aristotle is typically regarded as a *teleological* ethicist, as one who sees the virtues as ways of achieving the good life, and if we say such things we presumably are thinking of the good life as something specified independently of virtue, rather than, as under the other interpretation, as *consisting largely* of virtuous activity. Truth is, there is no interpretation of Aristotle that sits well with everything it seems plausible to say about Aristotle; but in any case the two interpretations I have been working with are of more than historical interest: they represent possible ways of pursuing virtue ethics today, and that is perhaps what is most important about them. For the moment, however, we shall leave aside the question which of these ways of doing virtue ethics has more contemporary promise, for we have not yet canvassed all the possibilities that lie before virtue ethics as a living enterprise. There are *more radical* forms of virtue ethics that

I believe are promising in today's circumstances, and we need to understand them and contrast them with the kinds of approaches we have so far been talking about.

4   Agent-Based Virtue Ethics

Hursthouse's view treats agent-evaluation as prior to act-evaluation, but (claims about) eudaimonia as grounding both; but it is also possible to treat agent-evaluation as in no need of justification in terms of eudaimonia, but rather as *basic*. Such a view or theory will then derive its ethical assessments of actions from what it has to say about (the motives and/or character traits of) agents, and judgments about eudaimonia, in turn, will be either independent of or derived from claims about virtue and right actions. Any view with this overall structure we can call *agent-based*; and agent-based views clearly contrast with the *agent-prior, eudaimonia-based* form of virtue ethics Hursthouse defends, as well as with the kind of *intuitionist* view that treats act-evaluation as independent of agent-evaluation and as derived from no other more ultimate form of evaluation.

But are agent-based views in the least bit plausible? Certain motives, to be sure, seem admirable and noble independently of whether they actually lead to human happiness: e.g., strength of purpose and even benevolence. But if we treat motives like benevolence as basically admirable and derive our evaluations of actions from those actions' relation to such motives, we end up with a theory that (to simplify matters) says that acts are right or wrong depending on whether they reflect or express benevolence or an absence of benevolence; and such a view seems, for one thing, to go against the maxim "'ought' implies 'can'." Motives are not within our immediate control, so if we make the rightness of actions dependent solely on the motive they express, we seem to be taking right action and the fulfillment of obligations out of the situational control of the moral agent.

But this conclusion in fact doesn't follow from agent-basing. A person may be malicious, but, if we assume that free will and determinism are compatible, he may still have it within his power to perform actions that *don't reflect that malice*. Presented with an opportunity to hurt someone, he can *refrain*; and were he to refrain, he would not be acting wrongly according to the kind of agent-based view mentioned above. Even so, one wonders whether anything can be said positively in favor of agent-basing, because, for one thing, there appears to be only one clear-cut example of an agent-based virtue ethics in the entire history of philosophy: James Martineau's view in *Types of Ethical Theory* (1891). Martineau held that motives could be hierarchically ranked on an intuitive basis – with reverence for God, followed by compassion at the top, and malice at the bottom – and that whether an act was right or wrong depended on whether it exhibited the highest motive operating in the context in which the act occurred. Such a view is pretty clearly agent-based; but in fact there seems to be no other example of agent-basing in the history of ethics. Kant, Hume, Hutcheson, Abelard, Leslie Stephen, Augustine, and

Schopenhauer all offer varying forms of resistance to being interpreted as agent-basers, and even Plato, who says in Book IV of the *Republic* that acts are right to the extent they sustain the virtue of the soul, treats appreciation of the value inherent in the Form of the Good as prior to our understanding of virtue in souls. Plato's view may, like Hursthouse's, be agent-prior; but it is arguably not agent-based.

5 Morality as Universal Benevolence

Interestingly enough, Henry Sidgwick (1907) took the idea of agent-basing seriously enough to devote a chapter of *The Methods of Ethics* to examining Martineau's views. But Sidgwick concluded that Martineau's rigid hierarchy of motives was implausible: if ambition sometimes outranks the love of ease, surely there are other times, when one has been ambitious enough for long enough, when the love of ease ought to take precedence over (lingering or incessant) ambition. Martineau doesn't allow for such flexibility, and taking advantage of this defect, Sidgwick argues that the principle of utility ought to be the criterion of whether and when ambition overrides love of ease, and indeed ought to be the criterion of all moral evaluation of motives and actions.

But in assuming this, Sidgwick ignores another possibility for agent-basing. Instead of judging the relative merits of motives in terms of how well they or acting on them serves human or sentient happiness, we might instead judge them in terms of *how well they approximate to the motive of universal or impartial benevolence that utilitarianism itself so often invokes*. This would leave us with a form of agent-basing, with a monistic view far from Martineau's hierarchical conception, but also very different from any form of utilitarianism. The utilitarian judges both motives and actions in terms of how well they actually or expectably serve human well-being, but an agent-based *morality as universal benevolence* will regard universal or impartial benevolence as in itself the highest and best of motives and will evaluate actions solely in terms of *how close their motives are to universal benevolence*. Such a view can answer the objections Sidgwick makes to Martineau's hierarchy, but, more importantly, it appeals to some of the same ideas and intuitions that underlie utilitarianism itself.

The idea that universal benevolence is in itself and without considering its consequences the morally best of motives is advocated by Francis Hutcheson (1738), who also promulgated an early (though perhaps not the historically earliest) version of the principle of utility. Hutcheson, that is, evaluated motives "in themselves," but by and large evaluated actions in terms of their consequences. Utilitarianism as a mature theory eventually developed out of the moral sentimentalism of Hutcheson, Hume, and others; and utilitarianism certainly results if one begins with the "hybrid" theory of Hutcheson and alters it so that motives as well as actions end up being evaluated in terms of their consequences. But it is also possible to alter the hybrid commitments of Hutcheson's ethics in just the opposite direction. If, like

Hutcheson, one evaluates motives intrinsically and independently of their consequences, one can also start evaluating actions in terms of their inherent motivation
rather than by reference to their consequences, and this yields precisely the agent-
based virtue-ethical view I have called morality as universal benevolence.

Such a view evaluates actions differently from act-utilitarianism, because it places
a lower moral evaluation than the latter does on actions that (expectably) maximize
human happiness but whose agents are motivationally indifferent to or opposed to
such happiness (imagine a case, for example, where someone does the happiness-
maximizing act only because it hurts someone he dislikes). As a result, morality as
universal benevolence also conforms better than utilitarianism does to our intuitive
feeling that a person cannot be said to have acted morally wrongly just because an
act of hers actually resulted in terrible consequences. If the agent's motives were
good enough, e.g., were deeply and genuinely benevolent, then the agent will have
done all she could to determine the facts relevant to her choice of action, and if
through no fault of her own the action has bad results (perhaps because something
is distorting her cognitive functioning, perhaps because there are relevant facts no
one *could* in her circumstances learn), then we arguably have no reason to accuse
her of having, in moral terms, acted wrongly. This intuition favors morality as universal benevolence over utilitarianism, yet it is an intuition that places a fundamental importance, even value, on a motive, universal benevolence, that utilitarianism
itself makes considerable use of. So we here have at least one kind of agent-based
virtue ethics that is plausible enough, at least, to give utilitarianism a run for its
money.

There is more to be said later on this particular topic, but at this point I think it
would further help us to see the promise of agent-basing, if we considered a criticism that could be lodged against morality as universal benevolence *from within the
perspective of agent-basing*. For even if we are committed to evaluating motives by
reference only to their intrinsic character and intentionality as motives, it is still
possible to ask whether universal benevolence is really the best of motives and whether
actions reflecting such benevolence are always right or best. Defenders of partialism
in ethics would, I think, want to say, to the contrary, that loving and caring more
for individuals who are close to one is morally more acceptable and more admirable
than treating everyone, in a fundamental sense, equally. And this criticism yields the
possibility of a form of agent-based view that treats as the morally best pattern of
motivation some combination of special concern about near and dear with lesser
(though still substantial) concern for human beings generally.

If there is something familiar about this kind of view, that is because it approaches
what has recently been said by advocates of a morality of *caring*. Carol Gilligan
(1982) and Nel Noddings (1984) have spoken of a morality or ethic of caring as
quintessentially feminine and thus as opposed to traditional (masculine) approaches
to morality that stress rights, justice, or quantified utility. And though defenders of
a morality of caring haven't explicitly spoken to the issue of agent-basing and sometimes say things that seem somewhat out of keeping with an agent-based approach,
it is well worth considering whether a morality of caring is most consistently and

powerfully deployed as an agent-based virtue ethics. After all, caring is a practical motive, and in calling something a morality of caring, one really invites the conclusion that that motive is the basis for morality as a whole and, most particularly, for the evaluation of human actions. And I believe that a morality of caring is most plausibly understood in just this way.

If one does so, it is necessary to say more about caring about or concern for distant others than Noddings, for example, has said, but I in fact believe that an agent-based ethic of caring is the most promising form of contemporary virtue ethics. However, before I say more about why I think so, I would like to mention some criticisms of utilitarianism, Kantianism, and contact theory. The reader has just seen something of the richness and variety of contemporary forms of virtue ethics, but what also favors virtue ethics are the defects of other theories of morality, and these will be the subject of discussion in the next section.

6   Virtue Ethics vs. Kantian Ethics

As I mentioned earlier, deficiencies noted in or attributed to the forms of ethics that have recently been dominant have served to motivate the revival of virtue ethics over the past few years. At present, I think it is fairly clear that Kantian approaches to ethics occupy center stage in the field of ethics, and so I would like to begin this section by discussing some of what I take to be the problems of Kantianism. Thereafter, we shall, in turn, consider criticisms of consequentialism and of recent contractarianism.

It is often claimed that Kant provides us with a legal or legislative model of the moral life that is entirely antithetical to virtue ethics. But in fact the idea of universal or universalizable law implicit in the Categorical Imperative ultimately rests for Kant on a strongly held conception of what it is for an act to have moral worth, and moral worth is an aretaic, not a deontic, concept. Kant holds, I believe, that the ultimate criterion for distinguishing right from wrong must allow moral worth or merit to attach to morally required actions done from a sense of duty (from a "good will"); and he also thinks that when our morality is determined ("heteronomously") by some "material" end like our own or others' happiness, conscientious action will *lack* such worth. Only if we are responsive to and guided by the *form* of morality, the universality or universalizability implicit in any genuine moral or rational principle, does he think our acting from duty will have moral worth. And the familiar "Universal Law" formulation of the Categorical Imperative – according to which one acts permissibly only when one's maxim, the personal rule of conduct one is following in performing a given act, is consistently willable as a law for all human beings – represents an attempt to treat the distinction between right and wrong in precisely such formal terms.

So Kant's defense of the Categorical Imperative (CI) arguably appeals to foundational aretaic judgments. But, of course, those judgments would be disputed by agent-based and other virtue ethicists. If Kant holds that (acting from) concern for others has moral worth only if it derives from a sense of duty defined by the CI, the virtue ethicist will insist, to the contrary, that (acting from) intrinsic concern for the good of others has moral merit or worth in its own right. Indeed, the typical virtue ethicist will want to go further and claim, again contrary to Kant, that a self-conscious application of the moral dictates of concern for others can in some cases be morally *less* meritorious than a spontaneous act of compassion or friendship (see Stocker 1976, and further discussion below).

To the extent Kantian ethics rests on fundamental, though disputable judgments about when actions have or lack moral merit, it comes close to being – perhaps even is – a form of (non-agent-based) virtue ethics. But the differences in particular judgments from what usually goes under the name of virtue ethics are fairly clear as well, and they seem to favor the latter over Kantianism. More significantly, perhaps, not only virtue ethicists but philosophers of many other ethical persuasions have questioned the capacity of (one or another version of the) the CI to function as a general criterion of right and wrong (apart from questions about moral worth or merit).

The Formula of Universal Law has difficulty, for example, in accounting for the *permissibility* of certain kinds of morally accepted human activity. For the maxim of someone who simply wants *tout court* to be a postman or to win an Olympic medal or to marry a particular person is arguably not universalizable in the way Kant says permissible maxims must be, and even recent defenders of a Kantian approach have tended to recognize this implication as a weakness in the Formula of Universal Law as a criterion of permissible or right action.

However, if we switch to other versions of the CI, other problems arise. The Formula of Humanity version of the CI says, roughly, that we must treat people (including ourselves) as ends-in-themselves and never solely as means (because, unlike everything else in the world, humans can *set ends for themselves* and thus have a dignity that is beyond the mere "price" that attaches to things that can be ends of action but cannot *set* ends). But the force of the argument from the fact we uniquely set ends to the conclusion that people are and ought to be ends-in-themselves is far from obvious, and the conclusion itself is not clear in its meaning and implications.

For example, how does it follow from the fact that we should treat others as ends-in-themselves that, as Kantians claim, it is always wrong to make trade-offs in human lives: e.g., to kill (or maim?) one innocent person in order to prevent a catastrophe to a whole country or to humanity as a whole? The refusal to kill even one innocent person has been said by Kantians and certain other deontologists to be an expression of our respect for human dignity, a way of acknowledging and showing the supreme value we place on human beings and human lives. But critics have responded that the willingness to sacrifice one person in order to *preserve a greater number of human lives* is just as good, and perhaps even better, as a way of acknowledging the dignity and importance of human beings.

Moreover, the mere fact that one has *sacrificed* one person for the sake of others in no way obviously shows that one is treating that person *solely* as a means. For even if a person's well-being is in itself important to one, saving a whole *group* of people might be more important: one might feel morally impelled to sacrifice one person whom one views as an end – and this could be *either* oneself *or* some other person – in order to preserve some *larger* group of people one thinks of in the same way. Kantians want to be able to show that consequentialist views that in certain circumstances favor the killing, say, of one person to prevent a catastrophe involving others (as well perhaps as the person being killed) are mistaken. But it is difficult to see how an argument to that effect making use of the Formula of Humanity can be successfully brought to fruition. And this failure of Kantianism to show clearly how the intuitive moral judgments it wishes to defend can be justified in its own terms is one reason why we should now be considering the merits and prospects of virtue ethics.

7   Virtue Ethics vs. Consequentialism and Contract Theory

Consequentialism also has a difficult time justifying our ordinary deontological intuitions (some utilitarians, like Bentham, have actually thought this was an *advantage* of such approaches to morality), and, as we have already noted, it has the further problem of making moral evaluations dependent entirely on consequences. This is implausible enough with regard to actions, but it is very implausible or at least anti-commonsensical in relation to the evaluation of motives. Bentham (1982) and other (mainly utilitarian) consequentialists have held that a motive like (universal) benevolence can be morally bad if (unbeknownst to those who have it) it does more harm than good (advocates of trickle-down economics in effect seem to want to say that it in fact *does* do more harm than good). But if, unbeknownst to everyone, including economists, ruthless capitalistic competitiveness produces a higher level of well-being than would be forthcoming if people were more benevolent toward one another and, in particular, more compassionate toward the poor, it nonetheless seems unintuitive to suppose that capitalistic ruthlessness is a morally better motive than kindness and compassion. To be sure, if we knew such facts about a given society, we might (though we might *not*) say that it is good, since it is for the best, that people are so ruthless. But it can be good that a certain motive occurs even when that motive is morally shameful; that is, it is readily conceivable that good results in a given set of circumstances require there to be someone or someones with morally horrendous motives. But that is precisely how the situation *should* be described, whereas the motive utilitarian must say, counterintuitively, that because of the good results, the motives in question turn out to be morally good and morally better, say, than any more benevolent or conscientious attitude. It is for reasons of this kind that virtue ethics, and agent-based virtue ethics more particularly, can seem more attractive than consequentialism. (I shall not dwell on the criticism that utilitarianism and consequentialism generally are "too demanding," since I believe those criticisms can be answered (Slote 1992).)

Contract theory (contractarianism) suffers from a somewhat different set of disadvantages. For apart from questions about whether Rawls (1971), Gauthier (1986), or Scanlon (1982, 1995) actually succeeds in deriving certain moral/political principles or claims from the description of certain idealized circumstances of bargaining and/or contract, there is an important issue about the *scope* of such approaches. None of the above figures seems to want to deny that there are parts of morality/ ethics that lie outside and unaccounted for by the (or his) contract model of justification, and in effect contract theory seems to handle questions about obligation better than questions about supererogatory or good action and, in addition, to be more capable of giving a rounded picture of political values than of ethical/moral values generally. A criticism of incompleteness can also, perhaps, be directed at virtue ethics (though not so easily at consequentialism and Kantian ethics); but we shall later on see that virtue ethics is likely to be able to answer the objection from incompleteness, whereas contractarianism seems to its own proponents incapable, in principle, of doing so. Once again, we are given reason to look more closely at virtue ethics.

But it would be unfair to suggest that all the problems and deficiencies lie on the side of theories other than virtue ethics. Certainly, there are well-known criticisms of virtue ethics and its potential as a general approach to ethics that we have not yet (closely) considered. But I propose that we do this in the context of defending a particular form of virtue ethics, and so I would like at this point to say more about why I consider an agent-based (understanding of the) ethic of caring to be the most promising contemporary form of virtue ethics.

8   Problems with Aristotle and Anti-Theory

Most recent advocates of virtue ethics have focused on Aristotle and used him as a model for reviving that approach. But one problem with doing so is that Aristotelian ethics seems unable to address, much less resolve, certain crucial issues of contemporary moral philosophy. Here, I am not mainly referring to difficulties in Aristotle's doctrine of "the mean," his idea that all virtuous action lies in a mean between two related extremes of vice, though such a view has well-known problems dealing with the moral grounds of truth-telling, promise-keeping, and loyalty. Rather, I am referring to the absence, in Aristotle, of any commitment to generalized humanitarianism. Recent ethics has been very much concerned with whether making (large) personal sacrifices for the greater good of needy, but distant others is morally obligatory or merely supererogatory, but because Aristotle never specifically defends the idea of *general* concern for the well-being of others and because he leaves no room, in addition, for supererogatory degrees of moral excellence, his philosophy appears to be largely irrelevant to this important issue. For purposes of contemporary relevance, therefore, I think we need a form of virtue ethics that bears on this issue, and I believe that an ethic of caring can help us here.

But before I say more about such an ethic, I would like to address a criticism of it that comes from within virtue ethics itself. As noted earlier, one major problem for recent virtue ethics has been the question of its (or the) proper attitude to the choice between theory and anti-theory. Those who advocate the avoidance of theory typically hold that our sense and understanding of ethical phenomena are too rich and complex to be captured by any generalizing theory; and why, they might ask, should we suppose that ethics has to be like science? Why should it not be thought of as more like history writing or art connoisseurship, where sensitivity, experience, and judgment seem to make general theories unnecessary?

These questions and criticisms are relevant to an ethic of caring, because a philosophically developed form of that approach of the sort to be sketched here seems to be an instance of moral theory, not of anti-theory. But those who argue in the above way against moral theory suppose that our ethical intuitions, and the judgments and decisions to which they give rise, are all right as they stand. What if they are not?

The problem of moral luck, for example, indicates an area of our ethical thought where intuitions *clash, internally, with one another.* Notoriously, if someone is driving down a deserted road and not paying attention, we don't treat her as particularly blameworthy if in fact no car is coming in the opposite direction. But if we imagine the same circumstances from the point of view of the agent but alter the assumption that there is no car coming in the opposite direction and no resulting crash, we see things very differently, are inclined to assign considerable blame. Yet our sense of morality tells us that there cannot be such a thing as moral luck of this kind, that someone's (degree of) blameworthiness cannot depend on factors of luck that are outside her ken or control.

So our morality is inconsistent in this area, and moral intuitions cannot all just be accepted for their richness and variety. Some intuitions have to be abandoned if we are to achieve consistency in our ethical/moral thought and we need theory to tell us which intuitions are best, most plausibly, abandoned. The situation is similar to that in set theory and in confirmation theory, where initial attempts to proceed in an entirely intuitive manner were stymied by the discovery that intuitions in these areas are mutually inconsistent. We need theory in ethics for much the same sort of reason.

But there is an additional reason to prefer virtue theory to virtue anti-theory. Kantianism, contractarianism, and consequentialism are all prime examples of theorizing, and given the importance of such approaches in contemporary ethics, it is highly unlikely that any anti-theory can or will be regarded as a serious alternative to, or competitor with, them. Virtue ethics is taken increasingly seriously nowadays, I think, in part because it is showing, or beginning to show, itself capable of producing theories with sufficient structure and sufficiently clear implications to allow of a critical comparison with other prevalent forms of ethics. And such comparison might ultimately redound to the advantage of virtue ethics if (some form or version of) it can accomplish what a systematic approach to ethics must try to accomplish and do so more plausibly or coherently than Kantian, consequentialist, or contractarian ethics proves capable of doing. This is precisely what I hope and believe an ethic of caring can do for us.

9 Developing an Ethic of Caring

As I mentioned earlier, any philosophically acceptable version of a caring ethic must not only discuss how we should treat those we know or are close to, but also consider (in a way that Noddings does not) our obligations to distant or unknown others. We must, that is, distinguish caring about intimates from humanitarian caring about people generally, and the real question that faces an ethic of caring is how to combine (in a theory that prescribes for individuals and also in the individuals themselves) these two kinds of morally worthy concern. (For simplicity's sake I shall not consider gradations of concern *between* these two categories.)

In order to deal with this issue, I think we need a better understanding of (the commitments of) human love. An (agent-based) ethic of caring seems to me superior to our earlier-discussed morality as universal benevolence, because it accommodates and indeed mandates a greater concern for people near and dear to one than for people generally. This has intuitive force with most of us, but the real challenge then is finding an appropriate level or floor of humane or humanitarian concern for people we don't know. For obvious reasons, this is (relatively) easy for an impartialist morality of universal benevolence to accomplish – so if agent-based virtue ethics is to move in the direction of an ethic of caring, the latter needs to say something plausible about humanitarianism. Interestingly enough, I think it becomes easier to specify a morally reasonable level of general humanitarianism, if one gets clearer about what is involved in loving two or more people. If a parent has two children and loves them (equally), the concern s/he feels for the one and the concern s/he feels for the other do not naturally amalgamate into some overall larger concern for their aggregate well-being. Instead, those concerns in some sense remain separate from one another, and by that I mean that a loving parent will not always seek to do what is best or good *on the whole* for his or her two (or more) children. Let me illustrate this.

Imagine that a parent – say, a father – has two children aged in their twenties, one bright and ambitious, the other handicapped. Imagine further that there is little he can do for the better-off child, but a great deal that he can do for the worse-off, so that, in fact, at every turn he can accomplish more good for the handicapped child than he could be acting to help the successful one. In such a situation both Rawlsian and utilitarian-consequentialist considerations of justice favor always helping the worse-off child, and the case can certainly be made that, from an impersonal or objective standpoint, it would be (a) better (thing) if the handicapped child always received the father's attention or help. Still, given what it is to love (children equally), a loving parent *won't* in fact (always) do what promotes the greater overall or aggregate good of his (or her) two (or more) children. Rather, the parent will naturally (want to) "show the flag" of concern for each child.

In fact, a loving father with two children invariably *strikes some sort of balance* between the concern or love he has for the one and that which he has for the other, and that means that he will often help or pay attention to a much-better-off child, even though that time could be spend doing more good for the other and producing more total or aggregate good (for them) as well. In saying this, however, I am not supposing that such a parent is guided by moral rules or principles that dictate such behavior. Anyone who needs such props in order to act in a "balanced" way toward his children can be suspected of an unloving, or at least of a less than equally loving, attitude toward the children – I am saying that (equal) love naturally (and unself-consciously) tends toward some sort of balance, so that no/neither child receives, over time, most of a parent's attention or efforts.

Love, then, seems to rule out a purely aggregative concern for people, but the latter sort of attitude *is* morally appropriate in other contexts. A person may, for example, wish the people of Bangladesh well and even make charitable donations toward their well-being without knowing, much less loving, any particular Bangladeshi. And such a humanitarian motive of caring tends to embody aggregative thinking of the sort love rules out. The moral concern one feels for an unknown Bangladeshi whose name one may have happened to hear is fungible, so to speak, within the larger humane concern one feels toward for the Bangladeshi people as a whole, and indeed that larger concern seems appropriately subsumable, in turn, under the even larger concern that a moral humanitarian has for (unknown) people generally. When concerns are thus fungible within some larger concern(s), considerations of overall utility or good govern them, and this means that when one acts out of a sense of shared humanity, one doesn't, as with love, feel the need to help any individual or group at some *cost* to considerations of or concern for overall good.

The view I would like to defend allows for and mandates both non-fungible intimate concern about certain individuals and fungible humane concern for people generally, but the question arises how these two forms of concern are to be integrated within a single moral scheme or psychology, and the answer I want to propose is that the non-fungible balanced caring that is so characteristic of loving concern for more than one individual should also govern the relations between the two large categories we can call intimate caring and humanitarian caring. Over time, the morally good individual will show concern both for (the group of) those near and dear to her and for humanity in general, and neither concern will dwarf the other. But this view has some important and possibly controversial implications about how people ought best to act in response to world hunger, disease, and poverty.

It is tempting for a partialist to think that we should be less concerned with people the more distant they are from us in social/psychological terms, and even allowing a floor of substantial concern for all human beings, however distant, this "inverse care" law seems to suggest that in deciding what to do, say, about world hunger, we should add up everyone's interests, using a (possibly variable) multiplier to give more weight to the interests or well-being of those near and dear to us. Such an aggregative though partialistic approach might very well tell us that we should spend all or most of our time and money helping people we don't (yet) know – rather than those near and dear to us. It will all depend on whether the numbers and the emergency elsewhere are sufficient great.

However, a caring morality that advocates *balance* as between one's intimate and one's humanitarian concerns for other people doesn't have this implication. Just as someone who loves two children won't simply aggregate in regard to them, a person who loves *everyone in a given group* will be very reluctant to allow the interests of those people entirely to yield to sheer numbers of needy others, in the way that an aggregatively employed inverse care law can easily recommend. Rather, it will seem morally appropriate to (and for) such a person to *balance* concern for humanity against concern for (the group of) those s/he loves or cares most deeply about; and this means spending substantial time, efforts, and money in both directions, rather than "specializing" in either. So on the view of caring I think most plausible, an appropriately caring person will expend considerable time, money, and effort on behalf of (the class of) those near and dear to her, even if she can or could do a great deal more good helping people she isn't (yet) acquainted with, just as we are supposed and in fact do want to spend a good deal of time with and for a less needy child, even when our other child could (always) benefit more from our attentions.

But if intimate caring is to be *balanced against* the humanitarian, then we also cannot neglect the interests of people we don't know. So a morality of the kind I am sketching and defending here is far from privatistic or narrow – it demands a good deal of personal sacrifice, for it tells us we cannot allow ourselves to spend most of our time helping those we most naturally want to help, those near and dear to us. Such a morality indeed demands more of us than what most of us in fact do for (unknown or distant) other people, but, of course, because it involves a principle of balancing rather than of partial or impartial aggregation, it is also less demanding than utilitarianism is generally thought to be.

However, it is high time I said a bit about where or how self-concern fits into the above picture. Assuming that we can think of self-concern as a third moral category alongside intimate caring and humanitarian caring, there are (at least) two possible views of it that seem compatible with the rest of what we have said. Either we treat self-concern as *permissibly* balanced against both the other forms of concern or caring, but regard a lesser degree of self-concern as yielding opportunities for supererogation. Or else we say that self-concern not only may but ideally *should* be balanced against the other two, so that someone who is lacking in self-concern is regarded not as morally praiseworthy, but as morally deficient (perhaps because he is considered lacking in self-esteem). Either view, as I say, is compatible with what has gone before, and at this point I am not sure which one to favor. So we should move on to other issues.

10   Clarifications and Criticisms

Perhaps the most pressing of these issues, given our previous discussion, concerns whether an ethic of caring is really best conceived in agent-based terms. Many advocates of caring (e.g., Noddings 1984) have said that caring is morally good or required because it is a necessary ingredient or element in desirable personal relationships, like that between a mother and a child. But this argument, though it certainly moves us away from agent-basing, seems to me to be weak. If playing a role in a desirable relationship is what makes caring admirable, why don't we equally admire being cared for, which is also a necessary element in what a mother and child have together? Surely we think caring more morally praiseworthy than being (or letting oneself be) cared for, and the difference seems, in the end, to have to do with a fundamental moral difference between those two attitudes or activities, just as an agent-based version of a caring ethic tells us.

However, an agent-based virtue ethics also needs to take a stand about deontology, and at first blush it may seem that our expanded ethic of caring and morality as universal benevolence would both have a difficult time justifying our common-sense deontological intuitions about the wrongness of killing one innocent to save a number of others. Morality as universal benevolence seems like utilitarianism turned outside in, and if universal benevolence seeks good or the best consequences overall for human happiness, it will presumably, like utilitarianism, allow sacrifices of certain individuals in the name of such overall happiness. And even an agent-based morality of caring might seem to entail such consequences. How, for example, can caring about the well-being of one's family *preclude* the permissibility and advisability of killing one family member (or a stranger) to save the rest (in the kinds of dire circumstances that are the stuff of Greek tragedy)? But in what follows I would like to sketch some reasons for thinking that a morality of caring (and perhaps even morality as universal benevolence) does allow for a substantial kind of deontology.

I believe that a person who loves or really cares about another person will be reluctant and often unwilling to kill or hurt them for the sake of saving a somewhat large number of others whom they love or care about, but the typical believer in deontology will presumably want to reply that that reluctance and/or unwillingness comes from an independent commitment to certain moral rules or principles rather than arising with or out of motives or emotions. If that were so, then deontology as such would remain unavailable to any agent-based view that wished to *remain* agent-based, but I think the matter is far less clear than the above reply assumes, and this may become clearer if we look at some different, even opposed, motives/emotions, e.g., at hatred.

Imagine an uncle who for some reason hates his three nephews. All three want to go to medical school, and (given that their parents are dead and other relatives unavailable) all three are living with a friendly neighbor, but hoping to get the money for medical school from their uncle. The uncle has reason to believe that the neighbor is willing to help the boys through medical school, but won't save money to that end, if he believes the uncle is willing to do so. So the uncle figures that if he helps the oldest of the boys, the neighbor will spend his extra money elsewhere and won't have anything for the other two when, at spaced intervals, they are ready for medical school. If, then, he doesn't help the first nephew, the other two will be helped, but if he does help him, he can prevent the other two from being helped. However, there is something galling to him about this last option; the idea of doing something that will make his first nephew *grateful* to him simply sticks in his craw, and so it is hatred that leads him to deny the first nephew help and thus do something that on the whole is less bad for those he hates.

But if a negative emotion can understandably lead someone to produce results that are overall less bad, then why shouldn't positive feelings like caring or love lead someone to do what produces results that are on the whole less good? And the point of bringing in a negative emotion like hatred is that someone who acts from hatred is far less open to the suspicion that they are basing their actions on independent moral considerations than is someone who acts from love. When someone who loves another refuses to kill that person in order to save others she loves, it can be suspected that that refusal is less a matter of love itself and more a matter of the fact that someone who loves will also wish to fulfill her independently given moral obligations toward those she loves. (Such a view is to be found in Rawls 1971: 485–90.) But there is presumably no such thing as the morality or deontology of hatred, so when the uncle acts as I am assuming he does, what he does comes from and is understandable in terms of his motives/feelings.

Something similar also naturally arises in connection with (less intense) negative attitudes towards groups (rather than specific known individuals). Consider an Englishman who really dislikes the French and who finds himself in a position where he can prevent others from helping a number of French people by himself helping a single Frenchman. Couldn't such a person naturally say/think: "I'm not going to help any frog, no matter what others may stupidly want to do"? But if negative emotions both toward particular individuals and toward groups can yield a refusal to bring about overall worst results, what good reason do we have to deny the opposite possibility to positive attitudes toward groups and individuals of the kind an ethic of caring praises?

If we lack such a reason, then we can understand deontology as growing out of or along with emotions/motives like caring and love, rather than as presupposing independent moral standards or rules. And that is good for the morality of caring. For if this weren't possible, it would be difficult to see how such a morality could deny the permissibility of killing a stranger (or two) to save a person one loves, given its own emphasis on caring more for certain people than for others. This would then go against both common-sense deontology *and* consequentialism. But I think that in fact we can understand deontology in the above-sketched agent-based terms and avoid the implausible implications of views that emphasize the permissibility of partiality without allowing for deontology. (See Scheffler 1994; Kagan 1984.)

Another potential criticism of virtue ethics and of the ethic of caring in particular concerns their treatment of human good and of the good life. Utilitarians have a very definite conception of such good: they are, or tend to be, hedonists; and although hedonism has seemed a somewhat constrictive view to many ethicists, there is still something appealing in the notion that nothing really *benefits* us unless it adds to our happiness or the overall pleasantness of our lives. Some of Kant's views also tend toward a hedonistic conception of human well-being, but some forms of virtue ethics seem to go entirely in the opposite direction from hedonism by making it difficult to understand how pleasure can benefit us at all. Both the Stoics and Aristotle regard happiness or the good life as primarily a matter of being virtuous or exercising virtue and have to rely on ad hoc devices to find a place for pleasure and the absence of pain in making human lives better.

Of course, the Epicureans were both virtue ethicists *and* hedonists, and there is actually nothing about virtue ethics per se that requires one to deny the importance of pleasure/pain in determining human well-offness. In fact, the agent-based virtue ethicist James Martineau (1891) also seems to have been inclined in the direction of hedonism, and current-day virtue ethics seems to have a whole host of options in attempting to determine what makes for human well-being or a good life. My own inclination, in fact, is to think that an agent-based virtue ethics of caring should reject all hedonistic conceptions of human good in favor of some modified version of the Aristotelian/Stoic tendency to locate our good in living virtuously. Even if the good life doesn't simply *consist* in being virtuous, it can be argued that every basic human good involves or includes one or another important virtue (Slote 1997), and it is possible on such a basis to hope that the notion of a good life can ultimately be understood in a distinctively virtue-ethical fashion. But at this point Kantian ethics and utilitarianism have more determinate or better worked-out views of human good or well-being, and that may count in their favor.

Virtue ethics is also frequently criticized for being incapable of guiding action, of telling us what we should do. In part, this charge derives from the mistaken and confused assumption that a virtue ethics cannot tell us what to do but only how to *be*. But if virtue ethics *is* capable of being applied to practical moral questions, it should be possible to say how, and this is a task most virtue ethicists have shunned. Rosalind Hursthouse (1991a) has usefully and insightfully addressed this task, but her agent-prior account of moral judgment itself invites some difficult questions about the possibility of applying virtue ethics to practical moral problems. Both on agent-prior and on agent-based theories, the rightness or wrongness of an action depends on what it reflects about the character and/or motives of the person who performs it, but it seems out of place to refer to or examine one's own motives, *rather than facts about people and the world*, in order to solve a perplexing moral problem. And yet this is exactly what Hursthouse tells us, and any agent-based theory seems to tell us, to do.

Thus consider a case where the solely relevant virtue is kindness, one where a daughter has to decide whether to allow or oppose the taking of heroic measures to keep her aged, dying, suffering mother alive. If the daughter *doesn't know* whether to advocate or oppose such measures, surely looking inward at or for motives won't help to solve her moral problem, and so where we most need moral guidance, it would seem that agent-based and agent-prior forms of virtue ethics are not only irrelevant but make it impossible to find a solution to one's moral difficulties. But these criticisms can in fact be answered.

Consider, to add detail to the above example, the case of someone who hears that her aged mother has suddenly been taken to the hospital and who flies from a distant city to be with her. And imagine that when she arrives at the hospital, she, as her mother's sole living relation, is immediately faced with the practical issue of whether, morally speaking, it would be right or wrong for her to advocate, or allow, the taking of heroic measures to preserve her mother's life. Agent-based and agent-prior virtue ethics don't offer the woman a ready answer to this question, but it is worth noting that if we assume that the daughter is at that point ignorant of her mother's particular condition and prospects, there is no reason for *most moral theories* to offer a ready answer to that question.

However, a reasonable agent-prior or agent-based virtue ethics *can* offer her an answer to the (different) question of what (morally) she should do when she gets to the hospital. It will tell her she should (would be wrong not to) *find out more* about her mother's condition and prospects, as regards quality and duration of life and certainly as regards future suffering and incapacity. And it will tell her this by reference to her actual motives, because if she doesn't find out more and decides what to do or to advocate about her mother solely on the basis of her present relative ignorance, she will demonstrate callousness or indifference, rather than kindness and a caring attitude, toward her mother.

Then, once the facts and probabilities have emerged and assuming they fairly clearly point to horrendously painful and debilitating prospects for her mother, the woman's decision is, once again, derivable from a plausible form of agent-prior or agent-based virtue ethics. At that point, it would be callous, indifferent, or cruel of her to insist on heroic measures and benevolent, kind, caring, or loving of her not to do so and, indeed, to insist that heroic measures *not* be taken, and so it would seem that in such an evolving moral situation, the right decisions can be reached by agent-based or agent-prior considerations.

Of course, a loving, caring daughter could also justify the decision, e.g., not to advocate heroic measures by reference to facts about the bad prospects of her mother. But because a deeply caring person is of necessity concerned to find out relevant facts about the prospects of someone she cares about, she can also properly justify her decision by saying: it would be (have been) callous (or uncaring or unloving) of me to try to keep her alive, given her prospects. So agent-based and agent-prior views and an ethic of caring in particular really can be used to determine how one ought to act in certain situations and thus to decide (applied) moral issues. Such approaches are not, in that respect, at any sort of disadvantage vis-a-vis other theoretical approaches to ethics.

That having been said, however, it is also worth noting that an ideally benevolent or caring person will not make use of any moral theory in deciding how to act. A truly caring or benevolent person is absorbed in seeking the good of others, and there is no reason why such a person should (have to) be occupied with questions about the rightness or wrongness of her own actions or with the truth or falsity of one or another moral theory. Indeed, worrying about the moral character of one's own actions seems to detract from the strength or genuineness of concern for (the welfare of) other people – a point made both by Hutcheson (1738) and Noddings (1984); and to that extent agent-based conceptions stand diametrically opposed to the Kantian view that conscientious attention to the rightness of one's actions is always called for and praiseworthy. Thus agent-based virtue theories are genuinely theories; but they are also self-effacing: they hold that attention to and use of moral principles/theories (to solve moral problems) tends to get in the way of what is morally highest and best – namely, (certain kinds of) absorption in and dedication to people's well-being. So agent-based theories *can* be applied, but ideally they *won't be*.

11 Virtue Politics

However, everything we have just been saying holds only at the level of individual decision-making and doesn't (yet) tell us how any virtue ethics can plausibly deal with questions of social justice. This is no small problem for virtue ethics, because none of the forms of virtue ethics that flourished in the ancient world advocated an egalitarian or democratic conception of justice, and so any contemporary virtue ethics whose treatment of political questions is inspired, say, by Aristotle runs the risk of appearing hopelessly retrograde and outmoded from the standpoint of contemporary political values. On the other hand, if virtue ethics decides *not* to offer any account of social justice, it will seem truncated and inadequate by comparison with theories like Kantianism and utilitarianism/consequentialism that are ready-made for treating issues both of individual and of social morality.

In recent years, virtue ethicists have been seeking a way out of this dilemma. Stoicism was more friendly to democratic ideals than either Aristotle or Plato was, and lately there have been some proposals – e.g., Nussbaum 1992 – for turning Stoic ethics in the direction of modern-day democratic theory. However, some virtue ethicists have (also) wanted to say that a proper understanding of Aristotle (taken together with contemporary empirical/ethical assumptions about racial and gender equality) can in fact help us to defend democracy.

Thus although Alasdair MacIntyre (1981) makes use of Aristotle to argue for an anti-liberal conception of political morality, Martha Nussbaum (1990) has recently pointed out that Aristotle's *Politics* proposes a rather democratic and egalitarian ideal of social cooperation *except for the conditions it attaches to citizenship*. In that case, she holds, if Aristotle was mistaken about the moral capacities of women, manual laborers, and others he excluded from citizenship, his own (other) ideas might actually help us to justify present-day ideals and institutions.

Rosalind Hursthouse (1991b) also defends the contemporary relevance of Aristotle's political philosophy, though her line of argument is quite different from Nussbaum's. Aristotle held virtuous living to be the main component of eudaimonia and regarded states or societies as just to the extent they enable their citizens to achieve eudaimonia. And Hursthouse believes that we can and should *derive* most or all modern-day political and civil rights from this Aristotelian conception of justice rather than treating such rights as the *basis* for understanding justice. This way of proceeding is rather reminiscent of utilitarian attempts to ground rights in considerations of social utility (Hursthouse invokes Hume almost as often as she does Aristotle), but that fact hardly counts against her Aristotelian defense of democratic rights. We are granting that (utilitarian) consequentialism can deal with political questions in a systematic way and has a reasonable chance of justifying egalitarian and democratic political ideals in its own terms. If Hursthouse's Aristotle has similarly good prospects, then virtue ethics, and in particular virtue ethics as inspired by Aristotle, has, or may end up having, no reason to apologize for what it has to say on political questions.

But the comparison with utilitarianism and with Hume may also remind us that virtue ethics needn't take its inspiration from Aristotle, but may prefer to make an ultimate appeal to ideals like benevolence and caring that have little if any role in Aristotelian ethics. The forms of agent-based virtue ethics we discussed earlier have no reason to shy from questions of social morality, and in the light of their relative *disconnection* from Aristotelianism, they may actually have an easier time accounting for modern-day political values than any Neo-Aristotelian conception of ethics like Nussbaum's or Hursthouse's.

Thus given the degree to which morality as universal benevolence "internalizes" act-utilitarianism, it is hardly surprising that that form of agent-basing has a capacity for justifying egalitarian and democratic ideals that is comparable to that of utilitarianism. Of course, the order of moral explanation is very different in the two approaches, and in fact there are some differences in what they tell us about justice and injustice. But, as far as I can tell, the differences tend to favor the agent-based view over utilitarianism.

The latter allows, for example, that widespread, ruthlessly competitive capitalistic motivation might conceivably (via trickle-down economics) produce greater social benefits than would communal altruism and good will and would in that case be *required for social justice*. By contrast, the political philosophy most naturally associated with morality as universal benevolence would regard societies as just when (enough of) their inhabitants possess morally good (enough) motivation vis-a-vis one another (exactly as an agent counts as moral when *her* overall motivation is good enough); and since ruthlessness is a far cry from universalistic benevolence, the society just described, despite its "efficiency," would plausibly count as lacking in justice, according to an agent-based social morality based in universal benevolence.

However, we also saw earlier that this kind of agent-basing is open to the criticism that it places insufficient moral value on the sort of differential personal concern that is distinctive of love and friendship. An agent-based morality of caring – whether or not we want to think of it as especially "feminine" – gives a high moral priority to such differential attitudes, but when it also mandates a ground floor of humane concern for all one's fellow humans, it may give rise to a distinctive conception of social justice as well, and that conception, like that associated with morality as universal benevolence, might well enable us to give a defense of democratic ideals. If love and intimate caring are ideal motives in connection with those near and dear to us and substantial humane concern is ideal in relation to people we are not acquainted with, then perhaps concern for the good of (the people of) one's own country is the best attitude one can have (whether as an elected official or as a voting citizen) in relation to specifically *political* choices that affect or primarily affect one's own country. (Concern for other countries and for smaller units within one's own country could easily enter into the picture in other cases, but I shall simplify here.)

The just society, then, might be one whose public institutions and laws reflect or express an appropriate concern, on the part of its citizens or inhabitants, for the good of the country, for the public good; and also one whose citizens in their non-political choices and institutions exhibit the ideal pattern of motivation advocated by agent-based morality as caring. (Such a view is defended in my "The Justice of Caring" (1998).)

It would appear, then, that virtue ethics needn't be regarded as a truncated or partial approach to ethics. Whether we favor an ethic of caring or prefer some other approach, an ethics of virtue has its own distinctive ways of dealing with the full gamut of the moral and political questions that any systematic or self-standing view must ultimately address, and in this respect, therefore, and given the problems other approaches clearly face, virtue ethics can at this point claim to have taken a place alongside contract theory, Kantianism, and consequentialism as one of the major options in contemporary ethical theory.

References

Anscombe, G. E. M.: "Modern moral philosophy," *Philosophy*, 33 (1958): 1–19.

Annas, Julia: *The Morality of Happiness* (Oxford: Oxford University Press, 1993).

Baier, Annette: "What do women want in a moral theory?," *Nous*, XIX (1985): 53–63.

Bentham, Jeremy: *An Introduction to the Principles of Morals and Legislation* (London: Methuen, 1982).

Gauthier, David: *Morals by Agreement* (Oxford: Oxford University Press, 1986).

Gilligan, Carol: *In a Different Voice: Psychological Theory and Women's Development* (Cambridge, MA: Harvard University Press, 1982).

Hume, David: *A Treatise of Human Nature,* 1739.

Hursthouse, Rosalind: "Virtue theory and abortion," *Philosophy and Public Affairs,* 20 (1991a): 223–46.

——: "After Hume's justice," *The Aristotelian Society,* XCI (1991b): 229–45.

Hutcheson, Francis: *An Inquiry Concerning the Original of Our Ideas of Beauty and Virtue,* fourth edn., 1738.

Kagan, Shelly: "Does consequentialism demand too much?," *Philosophy and Public Affairs,* 13 (1984): 239–54.

Kant, Immanuel: *Doctrine of Virtue* (New York: Harper, 1964).

MacIntyre, Alasdair: *After Virtue* (Notre Dame: University of Notre Dame Press, 1981).

Martineau, James: *Types of Ethical Theory,* 1891.

McDowell, John: "Virtue and reason," *The Monist,* 62 (1979): 331–50.

Noddings, Nel: *Caring: a Feminine Approach to Ethics and Moral Education* (University of California Press, 1984).

Nussbaum, Martha: *The Fragility of Goodness* (Cambridge: Cambridge University Press, 1986).

——: "Aristotelian social democracy," *Liberalism and the Good*, ed. R. B. Douglass, G. Mara, and H. Richardson (London: Routledge, 1990).

——: "Human functioning and social justice," *Political Theory*, 20 (1992): 202–46.

Pincoffs, Edmund: *Quandaries and Virtues* (University Press of Kansas, 1986).

Rawls, John: *A Theory of Justice* (Cambridge, MA: Harvard University Press, 1971).

Scanlon, Thomas: "Contractualism and utilitarianism," *Utilitarianism and Beyond*, ed. A. Sen and B. Williams (Cambridge: Cambridge University Press, 1982).

Scanlon, Thomas: "Moral theory: understanding and disagreement," *Philosophy and Phenomenological Research*, LV (1995): 343–56.

Scheffler, Samuel: *The Rejection of Consequentialism* (revised edn., New York: Oxford, 1994).

Sidgwick, H.: *Methods of Ethics*, 7th edn. (London: Maacmillan, 1907), 1st edn., 1874.

Slote, Michael: *From Morality to Virtue* (New York: Oxford University Press, 1992).

——: "The virtue in self-interest," *Social Philosophy and Policy*, 14 (1997).

——: "The justice of caring," *Social Philosophy and Policy*, 15 (1998).

Stephen, Leslie: *The Science of Ethics* (New York: G. P. Putnam's Sons, 1882).

Stocker, Michael: "The schizophrenia of modern ethical theories," *Journal of Philosophy*, 73 (1976): 453–66.

Chapter 18

Feminist Ethics

Alison M. Jaggar

Throughout the history of western ethics, the moral status of women has been a persistent though rarely central topic of debate. A few isolated voices have contended that women are men's moral equals but most of the dominant figures in the tradition have offered ingenious arguments to justify women's subordination to men. Despite the long history of this controversy, the expression "feminist ethics" was coined only in the 1980s, after feminism's "second wave" had swept into the academies of North America – and, to a lesser extent, western Europe – a critical mass of philosophers for whom the status of women was an important ethical concern. The appearance of this expression not only signaled a perception that attention to women and gender was indispensable to adequately understanding many issues in practical ethics; it also reflected a new belief that women's subordination had far-reaching, though hitherto unnoticed, consequences for ethical theory.

Feminist ethical theory is distinguished by its exploration of the ways in which cultural devaluation of women and the feminine may be reflected and rationalized in the central concepts and methods of moral philosophy. Not all feminist philosophers are convinced that western ethical theory is deeply flawed by such devaluation; on the contrary, some propose that one or another existing theory – perhaps with a little fine tuning – is entirely adequate to address feminist ethical concerns. However, many feminist philosophers contend that western ethical theory is deeply male biased. Although they sometimes disagree with each other regarding the nature of this alleged bias and/or in their prescriptions of an alternative to it, their work is characterized by attention to certain recurrent themes. The present essay traces the evolution of those themes and in so doing offers a critical reconstruction of the development of western feminist ethical theory.

I   Including Women in Ethical Theory

Most of the great western philosophers assigned a higher ethical priority to men's interests than to women's, contending that women's proper role was to support men in men's undertakings. One theme continuing from ancient to modern times is that women's primary responsibility is to produce children for their husbands and the state, while providing their husbands with physical and emotional care. Aristotle, for example, asserts that a wife must obey and serve her husband because he has bought her with a great price; Aquinas writes that woman was made to be a helper to man, "not indeed, as a helpmate in other works, as some say, since man can be more efficiently helped by another man in other works; but as a helper in the work of generation," and Rousseau argues that "woman is intended to please man." Feminist philosophers have revealed what Susan Okin calls "functionalist" treatments of women by, among others, Plato, Aristotle, Aquinas, Hobbes, Locke, Rousseau, Kant, Hegel, Nietzsche, and Rawls (Okin 1979, 1989; Clarke and Lange 1979).

Even though western philosophers generally treated women's interests as instrumental to men's, they regarded this treatment as standing in need of justification; their justifications typically took the form of arguing that women were in some important sense less fully or perfectly human than men. Some held that women were incapable of the same moral perfection as men: for instance, Aristotle says that women's temperance, courage and justice are of a different – and lesser – kind than men's; Rousseau asserts that women's merit consists in such "feminine" virtues as obedience, silence, and faithfulness; Kant writes, "The virtue of a woman is a *beautiful virtue*. That of the male sex should be a *noble virtue*." Many philosophers argued that women's capacity for reason was also different from and inferior to men's; major figures developing such arguments included Aristotle, Aquinas, Rousseau, Kant, Hegel, Nietzsche and Sartre. Since the western tradition typically regards rationality as the essential human characteristic, often defining moral agency in terms of the capacity for reason, arguments that women's reason is inferior to men's are deeply damaging to women's aspirations for equality. They suggest that women may be less morally valuable than men because their supposedly lesser rationality places them closer to animals and further from God; moreover, by entailing that women have less moral authority than men, they provide a strong rationale for placing women under men's political authority.

1   Including women equally as objects of ethical concern

At the turn of the twenty-first century, when a commitment to women's equality is enshrined in United Nations declarations of human rights as well as in many national constitutions, it may seem hardly controversial to claim that women's interests should weigh equally with men's. Yet despite the lip service paid almost universally to the idea that persons should receive equal moral consideration regardless of their sex, feminists note that in practice public policies often accord less weight to women's interests than to men's. Sometimes this inequality of consideration may be attributed to faulty applications of ethical theory but sometimes feminists trace it to bias endemic in the theory itself.

(a) Utilizing "gender" in ethical analyses

One reason for public policy's frequent bias against women is that equality of consideration is often assumed to require treating men and women indistinguishably. Deliberately ignoring distinctions of sex often has the consequence that ethical analyses fail to take account of morally salient differences between men and women.

Feminist research has revealed that many superficially sex-neutral issues in fact affect men and women differently and feminists insist that these differences must be addressed by any public policy that is ethically adequate. Examples of such differences abound; for instance, women often suffer more than men from war, even though men constitute most of the combatants. Over the twentieth century, as the proportion of civilian casualties has multiplied, women's share of the suffering has increased, since women who are not injured or killed directly are often displaced and become refugees; even in times of so-called peace, women suffer disproportionately from the allocation of tax money to military expenditures rather than to social services and benefit least from job opportunities in the military and related industries. Many issues of global justice have significantly different implications for men and women. They include: population policies that target women's rather than men's fertility; economic development policies that invest in men's enterprises while failing to acknowledge the value of women's agricultural and domestic work; foreign investments in industries that exploit women's labor; and the increasing economic prominence of the global tourism industry and its concomitant sex trade.

The above examples illustrate that men and women are differently situated in all known societies; they are subjected to systematically different norms and expectations that govern virtually every aspect of their lives. All known societies assign different work to biological males and females, different family responsibilities, different standards of appropriate sexual behavior, dress and diet, even different norms of physical deportment and patterns of speech. To distinguish these sets of social norms and expectations from biological differences between men and women, western feminists of the late 1960s appropriated the hitherto grammatical term "gender." They contended that, whereas sex differences were socially invariant, gender differences varied both among and within societies; they observed that masculinities and femininities, the social meanings assigned to being male and female, differed both in different societies and also among individuals of different castes, classes and ethnicities in any given society. More recent work in feminist theory has challenged the apparent clarity of the sex/gender distinction, especially the supposed naturalness and immutability of sex, but I shall not pursue that discussion here.

The realization that gender is a variable salient for much ethical practice has convinced some feminists that it is also a category indispensable to ethical theory. Those who hold this view argue that ethical theory cannot remain satisfied with conceptualizing humans on such a high level of abstraction that their inevitable differences, including their gender differences, become invisible. They contend that an adequate ethical theory cannot conceptualize human beings as undifferentiated, ignoring gender and related characteristics such as age, ability, class and race; instead, it requires a more complex conceptual apparatus that reflects the inevitable differences among people.

In opposition to this contention, other feminists object that what is required for more adequate analyses in practical ethics is not that ethical theory be revised but simply that those utilizing the theory take more account of the morally salient differences among individuals. Liberal feminists, in particular, often fear that elevating gender to the status of a concept in ethical theory would abandon feminism's traditional insistence that there exist no morally significant differences between men and women and so play dangerously into anti-feminist hands. These liberals endorse the older feminist position that sex differences should be conceived simply as "accidental" or inessential properties qualifying an underlying – and sex-neutral – human essence; they contend that ethics should address issues of gender on the level of first-order practice rather than second-order theory. Later in the essay, we shall see how this dispute has developed.

(b) Expanding the domain of ethics

Modern, although not ancient, moral philosophy has given little attention to many issues of special concern to women, most notably issues of sexuality and domestic life. This neglect has often been rationalized by a theoretical bifurcation of social life into a public domain, regulated by universal principles of right, and a private domain, in which varying goods may be properly pursued. Even philosophers like Aristotle, Hegel and Marx, who regard the home as having some ethical importance, portray it as an arena in which the most fully human excellences are incapable of being realized.

Inspired by the 1960s slogan, "The personal is political" (and, by extension, ethical), many feminists have challenged not only philosophers' neglect of the gendered aspects of most ethical issues but also their theoretical rationale for excluding some issues altogether. Feminists point out that the public/private dichotomy is covertly gendered, since women traditionally have been excluded from what is conceptualized as the public and restricted to what is defined as the private; the home, for instance, has become symbolically associated with the feminine, despite the fact that heads of households are paradigmatically male. Feminists argue that excluding the domestic realm from the moral domain is not only arbitrary but also covertly promotes masculine interests. For instance, by denying the conceptual resources for raising questions about the justice of the domestic division of labor, it obscures the social necessity and arduousness of women's work in the home; moreover, by relegating intimate relationships to the domain of the personal or subjective, it screens and may even license the domestic abuse of women and girls.

Contemporary feminists have sought to expand the domain of ethics to embrace not only the domestic sphere but also many other aspects of social life. They have raised ethical questions concerning: abortion; sexuality, including compulsory heterosexuality, sexual harassment and rape; representation, including mass media and pornographic portrayals of women; self-presentation, including body image and fashion; and the role of language in reinforcing as well as reflecting women's subordination. Although mainstream ethics has given little attention to these issues until very recently, they all have ethically significant consequences for women's lives and are sometimes matters of life and death.

Although they may sometimes speak of including "women's issues" within the domain of ethics, feminists' use of this language does not imply that they recognize a category of women's ethical issues that is distinct from men's, much less from human, issues. What are often categorized as women's issues are also in practice men's, since men's and women's lives are always enmeshed with each other; for instance, whether or not childcare or abortion is available significantly affects the lives of men as well as women. Men are involved in domestic, sexual and personal relations, just as women are involved in the economy, science and the military, despite the symbolic casting of the former as feminine and the latter as masculine. Most contemporary feminists contend that, if women are more preoccupied with or affected by certain matters than men, this is not natural or inevitable but instead reflects women's culturally assigned confinement to and/or responsibility for some areas of life and their relative exclusion from others.

In order to give due weight to women's interests, many feminists assert that ethical theory must operate with a more complex set of categories and virtually all agree that it must expand its domain.

2 Including women equally as moral subjects

The question of moral rationality and subjectivity is logically independent of the question of moral considerability; there is no logical reason why the interests of children, mentally disabled persons, animals or ecosystems should not count as morally equal to those of rational moral agents. However, western disregard for women's interests has often been justified by denying that women are full moral agents and so it has often been thought necessary to validate women's moral subjectivity in order to demonstrate that women's claims to moral concern are equal with men's. Demonstrating that women should have equal political rights certainly requires establishing that they have equal moral authority.

Efforts to establish that women are full moral subjects long predate the emergence of contemporary feminist ethics. In the *Republic* (written in the fifth century BC, Plato declares that some women are capable of being guardians or rulers; in *The Book of the City of Ladies* (1405), Christine de Pisan argues that women are equal or even superior to men in such virtues as wisdom, courage, prudence, constance and chastity; in *A Vindication of the Rights of Woman* (1792), Mary Wollstonecraft denies the existence of virtues specific to one sex or the other and insists that women are as potentially rational and as fully human as men; in *The Subjection of Women* (1869), John Stuart Mill suggests that women's apparent inferiority in reasoning and principled morality is most likely due to their different socialization; and early in the twentieth century Bertrand Russell argued that women's intelligence and virtue varied in just the same ways as men's.

At the end of the twentieth century, contending that women are moral subjects equally with men may seem as superfluous as arguing that women are entitled to the same moral consideration. But although women now vote in all western democracies, their suffrage was achieved in many of these nations only during the lifetimes of many people living today. British women received the vote after World War I but they did not receive it on the same terms as men until after World War II; French and Italian women received the vote only after World War II; Swiss women were unable to vote in national elections until 1973 and did not have suffrage in all cantons until the 1990s. The dearth of women political leaders suggests that western publics still lack confidence in women's moral authority. Although women's potential for moral subjectivity is rarely disputed directly nowadays by respected authorities, recent moral psychology has claimed that women are less likely than men to actualize that potential and attain the highest levels of moral development (Kohlberg 1981). During the 1980s, however, some theorists altered feminism's traditional response to such claims: instead of continuing to insist that women were capable of reaching men's level of moral development, they began to challenge the standard by which moral rationality and subjectivity were judged. The following sections explore their challenges.

II Is Modern Ethical Theory Male-Biased?

When western feminists criticize modern ethical theory, their usual targets are those liberal theories, rooted in the European Enlightenment, that still dominate contemporary western philosophy. Such theories include Kantianism and its descendants such as some versions of contractarianism and discourse ethics, utilitarianism in its various forms and, sometimes, existentialism. Few feminists whole-heartedly endorse neo-Aristotelian theories such as communitarianism and virtue ethics but their reservations about these theories so far have received less development than their reservations about liberal theory. This may be partly because their criticisms of modern liberal theory share common elements with neo-Aristotelian criticisms.

By setting aside traditional constraints on the realm of the ethical and paying attention to gender differences, some feminists have succeeded in utilizing liberal theory to illuminate a number of practical ethical issues of special concern to women;

for example, Susan Okin uses Rawlsian contractarian theory to show how contemporary marriage practices discriminate against women (Okin 1989). Despite such achievements, many feminists argue that modern ethical theory is so thoroughly infected with masculine bias that it has only limited usefulness for feminism. The present section of this essay elaborates feminist criticisms of modern ethical theory and the next section outlines an influential feminist alternative; in the following section, I offer some critical discussion of that alternative.

1   The values of modern theory as ethically inadequate

Despite their differences, Enlightenment ethical theories have much in common; most fundamentally they share a commitment to the equal moral value of every human individual. In the Kantian tradition, this value is expressed by recognizing the worth of each individual's autonomy; in the utilitarian tradition, it is expressed by assigning equal weight to each individual's happiness. In both traditions, realizing this value requires non-paternalism expressed by non-interference in the lives of others (Baier 1987).

Few feminists reject modern ethical values entirely and some have deployed them to good effect, arguing that women are entitled equally with men to respect and autonomy. However, even when feminists endorse modern values, they often propose that widely accepted interpretations of them should be revised; for instance, some fault common interpretations of Kantian theory for assuming that autonomy is a natural property possessed by all normal adults instead of recognizing that it is a potential realizable only in community.

A more fundamental challenge to modern ethical theory is the charge that it often generates ethical prescriptions that, according to its critics, are morally repellent to many women. These critics do not attribute the alleged incompatibility between ethical theory and women's moral sensibilities to improper application of the theories, still less to deficient sensibilities in women. On the contrary, they assert that liberal values offer an impoverished ethical vision, providing a model of human interaction that is appropriate at best only for a limited domain of life and at worst may rationalize inhumanity to others. For instance, Baier notes that "noninterference can, especially for the relatively powerless, such as the very young, amount to neglect, and even between equals can be isolating and alienating" (Baier 1987: 48–9).

Impartiality is a core value in modern ethical theory but, since about 1980, it has been challenged both by communitarians and by some feminists. Their criticisms overlap but are not identical. The ideal of impartiality requires that each individual receive equal consideration, regardless of an agent's subjective connections or loyalties to particular individuals. Some feminists have argued that this ideal is unrealizable, since it is psychologically impossible for human thinking to be detached from its context of origin or from its motivating passions and commitments (Noddings 1984; Young 1990: 103–5). Others, communitarians as well as feminists, have argued that the ideal of impartiality is morally defective, since it entails readiness to sacrifice those we love to abstract principles and absent strangers. Some argue that treating people as ethically equivalent denies the moral significance of individuality, which appreciates precisely the uniqueness of each person (Sherwin 1987). According to its feminist critics, too much emphasis on impartiality under-rates those personal values that are more fundamental to a good human life.

2 Modern conceptions of the moral subject as unrealistic and repellent

Modern ethical theory typically utilizes a neo-Cartesian conception of the moral subject as an agent that is essentially rational. Although the canonical theorists certainly assumed that moral agents were embodied members of communities, they regarded people's bodies and community memberships as "accidental" or contingent properties irrelevant to their claims to moral subjectivity.

Some feminists have found that the modern conception of the subject is a valuable resource for maintaining that women are full moral agents, disqualified neither by their female bodies nor by their frequently dependent social status. Accepting the modern conception, they insist that women are just as capable as men of transcending the limitations of their bodies and they argue that the western philosophical association of men with mind and women with body has no defensible basis. In their view, this association serves simply to rationalize men's political dominance, as well as social arrangements that assign to women the primary responsibility for taking care of bodily needs.

Other feminists are critical of modern ethical theory's abstract, rationalistic and individualistic conception of the moral subject. These critics often focus on the modern devaluation of the body, charging that it has been an important contributor to what they perceive as the flaws in Enlightenment ethical theory. They argue that devaluing the body in comparison with the mind has encouraged ethical theory to ignore many fundamental aspects of human life and to posit ideals unattainable by human beings. Disparagement of the body, they contend, turns theoretical attention away from bodily-related differences among individuals, such as age, sex and ability, and encourages regarding people as indistinguishable and interchangeable. Ethical reflection on embodiment would reveal that inequality, dependence and interdependence, specificity, social embeddedness and historical community must be recognized as permanent features of human social life and that seeking to transcend these is a waste of time. Instead of devoting so much ethical attention to abstractions such as equality, autonomy, generality, isolated individuals, ideal communities and the universal human condition, many feminists argue that ethical theory should pay more attention to people's bodies. This would enable it to recognize the central ethical issues of vulnerability, development and mortality rather than change-lessness, of temporality and situatedness rather than timelessness and nonlocatedness, of particularity rather than universality and of interdependence and cooperation rather than independence and self-sufficiency.

3 Modern conceptions of moral rationality as unrealizable or pathological

Enlightenment ethical theory regards rationality both as a natural property belonging to all normal human adults and as the only reliable guide to distinguishing right from wrong action. Viewing emotions as contaminants of pure reason, it defines moral rationality in terms of individuals' abilities to consider dispassionately the interests of all those affected in any situation, thus overcoming the supposedly normal human tendency towards self-interested bias. Some feminists dispute both the descriptive and the prescriptive elements of this account. On the descriptive level, they challenge the assumption that people are predominantly self-aggrandizing, an assumption they see as facilitated by liberalism's disregard for human embodiment. Instead, they contend that the social meanings attached to bodily characteristics such as parentage, age or sex result in embodied individuals developing moral identities that are not purely abstract and universal but also defined by the social relations involved in the meanings assigned to various specific bodies. Individuals with relational moral identities are unlikely to make a sharp separation between their own interests and those of others; they are more likely to be moved by considerations of particular attachment than by abstract concern for duty, more by care, more than by respect, and more by responsibility than by right.

For feminist critics of modern ethical theory, people's propensities to care for others and to regard their own interests as linked with those of others are not just weaknesses to be overcome by moral reason. Baier challenges what she calls the rationalism or intellectualism of modern moral theory, a rationalism that assumes that we need not worry what passions persons have, as long as their rational wills can control them.

> This Kantian picture of a controlling reason dictating to possibly unruly passions also tends to seem less useful when we are led to consider what sort of person we need to fill the role of parent, or indeed want in any close relationship. It might be important for father figures to have rational control over their violent urges to beat to death the children whose screams enrage them, but more than control of such nasty passions seems needed in the mother or primary parent, or parent-substitute, by most psychological theories. They need to love their children, not just to control their irritation. (Baier 1987: 55)

We shall see in the next section that not only do some feminists deny that emotions are necessarily subversive of moral reason; they regard them as indispensable to it.

In modern ethical theory, impartiality is not only a substantive ideal; it is also a defining characteristic of moral rationality, providing a necessary and sometimes sufficient condition of right action. We have seen already that some feminists challenge the substance of this ideal; others may accept the ethical intuition at its core but observe that the concept is too indeterminate to guide right action. Modern moral philosophers have offered a variety of recommendations for achieving impartiality, such as disregarding one's own self-interested motivations or adopting others' points of view, but a number of feminist critics have argued that these recommendations are quite unhelpful since they cannot be operationalized in practice. For instance, Marilyn Friedman notes that the limited nature of individuals' experience and of their familiarity with the thinking of others makes it highly unlikely that any real person (as opposed to an archangel) could project herself imaginatively into the standpoint of another, let alone of many others; nor could one who attempted this imaginative feat ever know how far she had been successful. Friedman concludes that available philosophical conceptions of impartiality offer no practical guide to moral justification. She recommends that people who wish to do the right thing should focus instead on partiality, concentrating on eliminating particular nameable biases from their thinking (Friedman 1993: 31).

4 The alleged masculinity of modern ethical theory

Why do some feminists allege that the distinctive values of modern ethical theory, its conception of the moral subject and its conception of moral reason are characteristically masculine? What is specifically masculine about valuing equality, autonomy and respect, understanding human subjects in terms of their minds rather than their bodies, and construing moral reason in terms of dispassionate impartiality? Marxist critics have long argued that modern ethical theory is based on a "possessive individualist" conception of human nature that portrays humans as essentially separate from others, insatiably appetitive and with interests typically in conflict, and they have charged that this conception reflects the adversarial market relations of bourgeois society. Feminists have accepted much of this picture but they have added the claim that men are more likely than women to understand human nature in such adversarial terms (Gilligan 1982). Few feminists attribute this alleged difference in perspective to some innate psychological differences between the sexes; instead, they explain it by reference to the contingently different social situations of men and women. Some draw on neo-Freudian object relations theory, which appeals to gendered patterns of parenting to argue that a preoccupation with separation is distinctively masculine. Others argue that disregard of the body is a luxury available only to those whose bodies are normative and/or who are freed from primary responsibility for bodily maintenance.

Basing ethical theory on a model of human nature that reflects men's distinctive experiences and values is problematic most obviously because it valorizes the ethical perspectives of only one segment of the population. Feminists further contend that the dominant model fails to describe accurately the moral psychology not only of most women but also of many men. Basing ethical theory based on false empirical postulates is likely to result in unrealizable ideals and epistemologies. Moreover, an ethical theory based on a masculine image of human nature devalues the symbolically feminine dimensions of human life; it also neglects more "feminine" ethical visions, promoting an image of the ethical life that many find repellent, especially many women. In addition to advancing an exclusionary, limited, and – to many – repugnant ethical vision, modern ethical theory impugns the moral authority of those who disagree with it by labeling them as morally deviant, immature or irrational (Gilligan 1982). For its feminist critics, modern ethical theory proposes a male-biased ethical vision that justifies itself by an equally male-biased moral epistemology.

Some feminists charge that modern ethical theory is masculine, finally, in projecting its devaluation of women and of feminine experience onto the universe at large. It follows the larger western philosophical tradition that interprets reality through conceptual dichotomies such as culture/nature, transcendence/immanence, permanent/unchanging, universal/particular, mind/body, reason/emotion and public/private. By associating the more highly valued term with masculinity and the less valued with femininity, western ethical theory inscribes cultural hostility for women into its portrayal of ultimate reality.

III Women's Experience as a Paradigm for Ethical Theory

In response to the charge that modern ethical theory assumes masculine experience as normative, some feminist ethics has sought to take women's experience as its paradigm or at least as its point of departure. The best known example of this approach is the ethics of care, which elaborates a moral perspective said to arise from women's characteristic experiences of nurturing particular others, especially their experiences of rearing children (Gilligan 1982; Noddings 1984; Ruddick 1989; Held 1993). Although the project of deriving ethics from women's experience is generally associated with the ethics of care, a few feminists reject care's emphasis on nurturing or mothering and seek to derive ethics from other facets of women's experience; for instance, Sarah Lucia Hoagland aims to derive new value from reflecting on lesbian lives (Hoagland 1989).

Since feminist ethical theory is often identified with the ethics of care, it is worth emphasizing that neither the ethics of care nor the project of basing ethical theory exclusively or primarily on women's experience should be taken as feminist orthodoxy. I have nevertheless chosen to devote considerable space to care ethics because it offers the best known and, many believe, most radical challenge made by feminists to modern ethical theory. It contends that attention to women's moral experience advances values that are ethically superior to those characteristic of modernity and fosters more adequate conceptions of moral subjectivity and moral rationality.

1 Appreciating the values implicit in women's ethical practice

Proponents of care ethics characteristically advocate that ethical priority should be given to the values that they see as central to women's practices of nurturing and especially of mothering; these include the values of emotional sensitivity and responsiveness to the needs of particular others, intimacy and connection, responsibility and trust. Modern ethical theory has always feared that justice would be subverted if too much weight were accorded to these values but it has accepted them in what it has seen as their proper place, namely, within the limited domain of intimate personal relations; on the epistemological level, it has accorded them a similarly minor role as possible motivators to right action. Most care theorists reject this relegation to what Benhabib calls "the margins of ethical theory;" instead, they often propose that the values hitherto associated with the private domain should become more prominent both in ethical theory and in society at large. For instance, Virginia Held considers how to export to wider society the relations suitable for mothering persons and children (Held 1993). Sara Ruddick considers how "maternal thinking" may promote a politics of peace (Ruddick 1989). Joan Tronto argues that care may be a political as well as an ethical ideal, describing "the qualities necessary for democratic citizens to live well together in a pluralistic society" (Tronto 1993: 161–2).

2 "Feminizing" the ethical subject

We have seen that modern ethical theory is dominated by a neo-Cartesian model of the subject as disembodied, asocial, unified, rational and essentially similar to all other selves; we have also seen that some feminists accept this model but that many challenge it. In developing their challenges, feminists have drawn insight from several traditions, such as Marxism, psychoanalysis, communitarianism and postmodernism, but they have been especially influenced by the work of psychologists such as Jean Baker Miller and Carol Gilligan. Gilligan asserted that women and girls tend to see themselves as connected to others and to fear isolation and abandonment, unlike men who are said to see themselves as separated from others and to fear connection and intimacy. She reported that women's conception of their selves as relational gives them different moral preoccupations and encourages them to construe moral dilemmas as conflicts of responsibilities rather than rights, to seek to resolve those dilemmas in ways that will repair and strengthen relationships, to practice positive caretaking rather than respectful nonintervention, and to prioritize the personal values of care, trust, attentiveness and love for particular others above impersonal principles of equality, respect, rights and justice. Many feminist ethical theorists advocate a so-called relational model of the self. They contend that such a model is superior to the Cartesian conception for understanding not only women but also men; contrary to the view of human nature presupposed by modern ethical theory, all human beings in fact are interdependent, constrained and unequal. Thus some feminists argue that a relational conception of moral subjectivity is both more adequate empirically than an atomistic model and also generates a more acceptable ethics (Whitbeck 1984). For these theorists, "masculine" consciousness is false consciousness.

3   Rethinking moral rationality

The "style" of moral reasoning associated with care ethics is often contrasted with that characteristic of justice ethics. Whereas justice thinking focuses primarily on the structure of an ethical situation, deliberately disregarding the specific identities of the individuals involved, care thinking is characterized by a distinctive ethical orientation toward particular persons. This orientation has both affective and cognitive dimensions: caring individuals are both concerned about the other's welfare and perceive insightfully how it is with the other. Contrary to justice thinking, which is portrayed as appealing to universalizable moral principles that guide impartial calculation of who is entitled to what, accounts of care thinking emphasize its responsiveness to particular situations whose morally salient features are perceived with an acuteness thought to be made possible by the carer's emotional posture of empathy, openness and receptiveness (Blum 1992).

Perhaps the most distinctive and controversial feature attributed to care thinking is its particularity; this means not only that it addresses the needs of others in their concrete specificity but that it is unmediated by general principles. Care responds to others as unique, irreplaceable individuals rather than as "generalized" others seen simply as representatives of a common humanity (Benhabib 1992). Such responsiveness requires paying as much attention to the ways in which people differ from each other as to the ways in which they are the same. Another aspect of care's particularity is that its conclusions are nonuniversalizable; that is, they carry no implication that someone else in a similar situation should act similarly. The radical particularism of care thinking challenges a fundamental assumption of modern ethical theory, namely, that appraising particular actions or practices requires appeal to general principles.

Proponents of care ethics resist reducing care to a simple emotional response; they consider it not simply as a motivator to right action, the latter determined through a process of rational calculation, but also as a distinct moral capacity with cognitive dimensions necessary to determining what actions are morally appropriate (Blum 1992). Care is not rational in the senses of being egoistic, dispassionate or deductive, but Nel Noddings asserts that "rationality and reasoning involve more than the identification of principles and their deductive application" (Noddings 1990: 27). Proponents of care thinking regard care as rational in the broad sense of being a distinctively human way of engaging with others; it is both ethically valuable in itself and tends to produce morally appropriate action.

IV   Ethical Theory: Feminine or Feminist?

The ethics of care has revealed some serious gaps and biases in modern ethical theory, many of which are attributable to that theory's exclusion of women's experience and concerns. A more adequate ethical theory must, in my view, develop some means of including the moral perspectives of women, as well the perspectives of other devalued or marginalized groups. Nevertheless, I find that the way the ethics of care so far has developed ethics from the perspective of women is problematic both in methodological principle and ethical practice.

1   Can ethical theory be built on women's experience?

Attempts to derive ethical theory from empirical experience reflect the naturalist conviction that philosophical ideals must be compatible with people's actual moral sensibilities; on this view, apparent divergence between ethical theory and ethical practice may not be dismissed immediately as a failure in practice. Moreover, an ethical theory that is responsive to feminist concerns requires that specific attention be paid to women's ethical experience in order to acknowledge women's hitherto devalued capacities as moral agents.

Although these contentions are, in my view, correct, it is necessary to remember that naturalistic approaches to ethical theory involve characteristic moral dangers. One is conventionalism, which takes accepted values and ways of thinking as self-justifying; linked with conventionalism is relativism, which asserts that what is morally permissible varies for different moral communities. Both conventionalism and relativism are problematic for feminism, because they conflict with its steadfast opposition to all forms of male dominance.

In addition to its moral dangers, ethical naturalism faces considerable methodological problems. One of these is that the term "ethical experience" is so broad that it is unclear how it should be investigated. Another is that what people say about ethics is notoriously unreliable as a guide to their actions. Moreover, it is difficult to find empirical confirmation for generalizations about the moral experience of large and diverse groups, such as women or lesbians, even when these generalizations are made by philosophers who themselves are women or lesbian.

Methodological problems underlie many feminist debates about how women's ethical experience should be characterized and they emerge with special clarity in the ethics of care. We have seen that care theorists assert that culturally feminine experiences such as nurturing provide the basis for an ethical vision quite distinct from that promoted by modern ethical theory. In a complex modern society, however, all unqualified generalizations about men's and women's experiences are *prima facie* dubious; the life situations of both women and men in contemporary western societies vary so widely by class, race/ethnicity and even generation that it seems quite unlikely that all or most women share a moral perspective different from that of all or most men. In fact, investigations into the empirical validity of care theorists' claims have often failed to confirm a link between gender and caring; when subjects are matched for education and occupation, women often achieve almost identical scores with men on justice-oriented tests of moral development, leaving women who work in the home as the main female representatives of the care perspectives. Moreover, many men as well as women have been found to employ care thinking, especially lower-class men and men of color. For these reasons, Marilyn Friedman argues that the ethics of care is feminine in a sense that is more symbolic or normative than empirical; rather than reflecting empirical dispositions in women toward empathy, sensitivity and altruism, she suggests that care expresses the cultural expectation that women be more empathic, sensitive and altruistic than men (Friedman 1993: 123–4).

Recent advocates of an ethics of care acknowledge that some women think in terms of justice and some men in terms of care, but they nevertheless associate caring with women because they regard the care perspective as emerging from forms of socialization and practice that, in contemporary western society, are predominantly feminine; these include raising children, tending to the elderly, maintaining a supportive home environment and nursing. Joan Tronto argues that the ethics of care is associated not only with gender, but also with race and class. She links the ethical perspective of care with the work of maintaining and cleaning the body, tasks that in western history have been relegated primarily to women but not to all women or to women exclusively; such caring work is done not only by women but also by the working classes and especially, in much of the West, by people of color (Tronto 1993). Tronto's analysis of the social genesis of care thinking fits well with Lawrence Blum's argument that justice ethics expresses a juridical-administrative perspective that is indeed masculine but which reflects the concerns not of all men but specifically of those in professional and administrative classes (Blum 1982). Together, Tronto's and Blum's arguments suggest that both the ethics of justice and the ethics of care are not only gendered but simultaneously raced and classed.

2 Is women's moral experience a dependable basis for feminist ethical theory?

In the preceding section, we noted some difficulties in determining just what is women's moral experience. But even if we grant that the ethics of care is in some sense *feminine*, this would not be sufficient to establish it as an ethics that is *feminist*, since feminism is often critical of the feminine. One necessary condition of an ethical theory's being feminist is that it should provide conceptual resources adequate for criticizing all forms of male dominance and some feminists, including myself, doubt that the ethics of care offers such resources.

One concern raised by a number of feminist philosophers is that the ethics of care is insufficiently suspicious of the characteristically feminine moral failing of self sacrifice. Arguing that care for one's abuser, for instance, may be morally pathological rather than virtuous, and noting that Noddings justifies the responsibility to care for oneself only in the instrumental terms of maintaining one's capacity to care for others, some feminists have characterized care as a slave morality (Card 1990).

Other problems result from care's characteristic focus on the specific needs of particular individuals. The morally problematic situations described by care theorists typically involve only a few individuals and typically require the agent to respond to others perceived in their concrete particularity. A number of critics have wondered how this model of moral rationality can avoid partiality to the particular others known to the agent. They have also questioned how care thinking can address large-scale social or global problems involving large numbers of people who could never be known personally by any single agent.

I have worried that care thinking may distort our understanding of some morally problematic situations. Care's narrow focus is valuable in encouraging awareness of moral complexity and individual responsibility in small-scale situations but it may well obscure perception of the macro-situations that provide the context for individual encounters. For instance, it may enable us to discern insensitivity or bullying on the part of particular individuals while diverting moral attention away from the social structures of privilege that legitimate their behavior. Similarly, attending to an individual's immediate needs for food, shelter, comfort or companionship may distract us from moral scrutiny of the structures that create those needs or leave them unfulfilled. Thus care thinking may encourage what are sometimes called band aid or social work approaches to moral problems, rather than encouraging efforts to address them institutionally or even to prevent their occurrence through social reform (Jaggar 1995a).

A final problem that I find in the ethics of care is its lack of guidance in determining which caring responses are ethically appropriate. Most care theorists acknowledge the need to distinguish appropriate from inappropriate caring but they seem to assume that this distinction is self-evident or at least that the carer/cared-for dyad can be relied on to make it. However, such an assumption is evidently unwarranted; examples of morally inappropriate behavior often rationalized as caring by both agents and recipients include over-indulgence or "spoiling," co-dependence, even domestic violence and incest. The care tradition may contain the conceptual resources for distinguishing appropriate from inappropriate caring but so far I have not found a convincing account (Jaggar 1995a).

The ethics of care is often caricatured as a "feel good" situationist ethics that rejects justice and is concerned exclusively with personal relations; in fact most care theorists regard justice as necessary, though not sufficient, for feminist ethics; they also recognize that transforming personal relations requires transforming the larger society. Feminist ethical theory, in turn, is often equated with the ethics of care but in fact the only orthodoxy in feminist ethical theory is its broad commitment to eliminating male bias. In the next section, I indicate how this commitment has encouraged exciting theoretical developments in several ethical fields.

V   Recent Directions in Feminist Ethical Theory

Feminists who perceive modern ethical theory as taking over older western gendered binaries have several responses available to them. They may contend that women are as capable as men of realizing values culturally coded as masculine; they may embrace the hitherto devalued "feminine" pole of the binaries; they may try somehow to combine "masculine" and "feminine" values; they may deny that there is any basis for symbolizing these oppositions in gendered terms; or they may seek to rethink the conceptual dichotomies. Many liberal feminists adopt the first and/or fourth of these strategies, while care theorists tend toward the second and third; my own preferences run to the fourth and fifth. All these strategies have been used by feminists in addressing a wide variety of ethical issues.

1 From practice to theory: the examples of health care, environmental and development ethics

Health care, environmental and development ethics are often construed as fields in practical rather than theoretical ethics; however, feminist work has directly challenged the theoretical concepts that often frame discussions in each of these areas. Over the past twenty-five years, the evolution of feminist health care, environmental and development ethics has followed a trajectory that, not surprisingly, has paralleled the developments described earlier in this essay: attempts at including women's concerns have frequently been followed by charges that the theoretical frameworks are male biased; feminists then have often tried to substitute more "feminine" frameworks, found these also problematic, and moved to various proposals for reconceptualizing each field.

Feminist health care, environmental and development ethics each begin by noting that prevailing social practices have more severely adverse consequences for women than for men. Feminists charge that many health care practices are unjust to women, who often receive less treatment than men for the same illnesses, are allowed less autonomy and are treated more paternalistically; for example, women's "advance directives" are more likely than men's to be disregarded. Feminists have criticized mainstream health care ethics for ignoring such injustices by failing to utilize gender in their analyses, as well as for neglecting many issues of special concern to women – or for seeing women's health issues only in terms of reproduction; they contend that health care ethics must expand its range of topics and utilize the category of gender – mediated, as always, by categories of class, race, disability and so on (Sherwin 1992; Dula and Goering 1994; Wendell 1996). Feminists working in environmental ethics have revealed that environmental degradation often has more serious consequences for women than for men, especially for poor women and mothers, and they have argued that environmental ethics also needs to utilize the category of gender along with such related categories as caste, class, and ethnicity (Warren 1990). Similarly, feminist work in development ethics observes that "development" policies have often discriminated against women by denying them land ownership and credit; some feminists have also noted that women are disproportionately affected by the "structural adjustments" mandated by international lending institutions, which have drastically reduced the welfare functions of states in the developing world. Their conclusion, predictably, is that development ethics must also take gender into account (Moser 1993).

As in so many disciplines, feminist attempts at inclusion led to the discovery that it was impossible simply to "add women and stir" them into these areas of practical ethics; the categories available were often biased against women's experience. In health care ethics, feminists charged that prevailing conceptualizations of the "normal" patient as male – and white – led to inappropriate treatments being given to women, especially women of color, and to construing women's normal bodily experiences, such as menstruation, pregnancy, birth, lactation and menopause, as illnesses. In environmental ethics, feminists asserted that much of environmental ethical theory was masculine: either it advocated the "mastery" of nature or, in the guise of deep ecology, it manifested a frightening disregard for real people.

Feminists have diagnosed male bias not only in development practice but also in both dominant forms of development theory – liberal modernization theory and neo-Marxist dependency theory. Both approaches cast development as a war of the sexes in which the symbolically – and often empirically – masculine must overcome the symbolically feminine – and often real women. One battle in this war is that of the public with the private; the "masculine" public sphere is portrayed as a realm of innovation regulated by universal and formally egalitarian principles, whereas the private sphere of women and the household is portrayed as closer to nature, tradition-bound, particularistic, and stagnant. A second gendered battle is that of the nation to escape engulfment by "primordial" community and tradition and to achieve independence, self-sufficiency and self-reliance; a third battle must be waged to dominate nature and the natural. In these accounts, the nation is always masculine while community, tradition and nature are all construed as feminine. Feminist critics deny that such gendered metaphors are simply stylistic flourishes, a form of "packaging" separable from the literal meaning of development discourse. Instead, they charge that these metaphors posit the modern (male) West as the norm of development and the traditional (female) third world as the aberration. White, bourgeois, western men become the paradigms of maturity and progress while nonwestern women are portrayed as backward, childlike, unreasonable, instinctive, and conservative, incapable of acting as agents of historical change. Man is not just superior to woman but locked in conflict with her (Scott 1996).

As alternatives to male-biased theories in health care, environmental and development ethics, some feminists have proposed more "feminine" alternatives. For instance, they have suggested that conceptions of appropriate health care should place more emphasis on "care" as opposed to "cure;" the ethics of care has been especially influential in nursing ethics. Some ecofeminists have asserted that women have a special connection with nature; they emphasize the ethical importance of people's environmental "homes" and, in the words of one critic, portray women as caring "angels in the ecosystem." Some work in feminist development ethics seems to identify sustainable development with women's unpaid subsistence agriculture (Mies and Shiva 1993). In each of these fields, other feminists have subjected such proposals to severe criticism.

Finally, health care, environmental and developmental ethics have developed new theoretical directions far too numerous and complex to summarize here. They include: rethinking the autonomy/paternalism dilemma in medical decision making and redefining health, normalcy, illness and reproduction in terms that are explicitly social and political as well as biological and medical. In environmental ethics, feminists are challenging ethical frameworks constructed around gendered polarities (Plumwood 1993). In development ethics, they propose to replace a preoccupation with efficiency and even welfare with a concern for women's empowerment (Sen and Grown 1987; Kabeer 1995).

2   Universal or local ethics

Rapid globalization has lent new urgency to the old question of whether ethical standards are universal. The problem has special poignancy for feminists because western feminism has recently been preoccupied with issues of "difference," first differences between women and men, then among women; it has also been shaken by revelations of earlier western feminism's complicity with imperialist projects. Western feminists are seriously troubled, therefore, by the dilemma of respecting cultural difference, on the one hand, while maintaining an unwavering opposition to male dominance, on the other; in classroom discussions of this dilemma, the practice of female genital surgery has become a stock example.

One feminist response relies on the notion of "capabilities." Pioneered initially by Amartya Sen as an alternative to utilitarianism, the concept has been developed by Martha Nussbaum on whose version I focus here. Capabilities are proposed as a universal standard for measuring people's quality of life, which is to be assessed by how well a given society enables them to develop and realize their distinctively human capabilities. Nussbaum lists ten human capabilities to function, together comprising her "thick, vague conception of human nature," which she offers as a guide to development policy. She contends that this conception articulates a cross-cultural and trans-historical consensus on the central and basic human functions, reflecting "the actual self-interpretations and self-evaluations of human beings in history" (Nussbaum 1995: 72–5). However, Nussbaum offers little evidence that her list of capabilities indeed reflects a tacit universal consensus and her writings quickly dismiss disagreement; she advocates "participatory dialogue" about how postulated capabilities might be specified locally but not about which capabilities reach the list or whether list-making is the best approach. My own view is that any ethical vision guiding global development must emerge from extensive and explicit democratic discussion that addresses means along with ends. For this reason, I believe that human rights, properly construed, have better credentials than capabilities as a universal standard of development.

The concept of rights was central to the emergence of western feminism but it is part of the same modern ethical tradition that received so much feminist criticism in the 1980s. Building on Marxist and anti-colonialist critiques, some feminists contend that rights are the discourse of the dominant, so infected by their bourgeois, masculine and western origins that they are incapable of articulating a deep challenge either to local forms of male dominance or to a scandalously inequitable world order. Feminist charges include the following:

- Appeals to rights are often used to rationalize male power over women; for example, the right to privacy obscures domestic violence, the right to freedom of expression justifies misogynist pornography.
- Because women are not similarly situated with men, granting them formally equal rights often produces inequalities of outcome; for instance, the advent of no fault divorce has thrown many ex-wives – but not ex-husbands – into poverty.
- Attempts to avert such outcomes by granting women "special" rights, such as maternity leaves, inevitably backfire in a cultural context that conceptualizes equality as sameness. Special rights stigmatize women as inherently sexually vulnerable or as less reliable workers.
- Legal equality of rights may obscure inequalities of power to exercise them. The procedures associated with claiming and redressing rights are often degrading, intimidating and humiliating for women; this is especially evident in rape and sexual harassment trials.
- Women may harm themselves exercising their rights; for example, millions of women in US alone have been harmed exercising their rights to have cosmetic surgery or to prostitute themselves. A focus on women's rights ignores the ways in which women's social situations often coerce their "choices" to exercise those rights.
- Finally, advocates of the ethics of care contend that rights talk is part of an inherently adversarial morality that disparages the more basic and important human values of interdependence, cooperation and trust.

For all these reasons, feminist critics charge that rights talk may not only be unhelpful to women but may even rationalize inequality.

Other feminists, including myself, believe that the rights tradition has the conceptual resources to address those charges. For instance, rights may be interpreted to take account of morally salient differences among rights holders and they may be assigned to groups as well as individuals. They may also include "positive" as well as "negative" rights; these are "entitlements" rather than liberties and they carry claims not only to noninterference but also to correlative duties on the part of others. Such rights may be thought of as embodying the values of community, mutual aid and social solidarity.

Those who regard rights as indispensable for women's liberation look to the burgeoning global feminist movement inspired by the slogan, "Women's rights are human rights." The theorists of this movement have followed the now-familiar evolution of much feminist ethics; beginning by criticizing abuses of women unrecognized as rights violations, they moved to challenging the covert male norm concealed in traditional conceptions of so-called human rights and to proposing radical reinterpretations. Space does not permit a full account of these feminist proposals but central to them is a recognition that violations of women's human rights are typically carried out by non-state as well as state actors – often by male family members – and that they occur in the private as well as the public sphere. This recognition requires expanding the definition of state sanctioned repression to include acceptance of family forms in which brides are sold and in which fathers and husbands exert strict control over women's sexuality, dress, speech and movement. Slavery must be defined to include forced domestic labor and prostitution. Because some violations of human rights are gender specific, the definitions of war crimes and genocide must be expanded to include systematic rape, sexual torture, female infanticide, the systematic withholding of food, medical care and education from girls, and the battery, starvation, mutilation and even murder of women. Feminists have also highlighted the link between violations of women's civic and political rights and violations of their economic and social rights: economies as well as laws dictate the world wide preference for boys over girls and women's economic vulnerability exposes them to the more blatant abuses (Peters and Wolper 1995).

The male bias and consequent false humanism of older conceptions of human rights should be corrected, perhaps by imagining the normative human as female rather than male. Women, after all, are vastly over-represented among the poor and illiterate of the world and they are certainly those most vulnerable to oppressive systems of power.

The slogan "women's rights as human rights" emerged from a grassroots activist movement. It avoids meta-ethical questions regarding the grounding of rights, a concept that Bentham notoriously characterized as nonsense on stilts. Instead, the slogan indicates a vision that is ethical rather than metaphysical, a vision that has a good claim to expressing the "overlapping consensus" of feminists world wide. As will become evident in the next section, I believe that this is the only justification it needs.

VI   Rethinking Ethical Theory

The term "ethical theory" covers a wide range of intellectual enquiries, all of which share an interest in questions about morality in general rather than in immediately practical ethical concerns. The questions addressed by ethical theory range from the metaphysical, such as whether there exists an objective moral realm, to the epistemological, most notably, how moral claims may be justified, to more directly normative but still general inquiries into such central ethical notions as the good, the right and the just. For much of the twentieth century, western ethics has been dominated by a particular understanding of ethical theory but, as the century has drawn to a close, this model has been increasingly challenged. Some feminists are among its most outspoken challengers.

The idea of ethical theory now brought into question is one that Margaret Walker labels the theoretical-juridical model. Walker traces this conception of ethics back to

Henry Sidgwick, noting that his career as Knightsbridge Professor of Moral Philosophy at Cambridge (1883–1900) marked a decisive shift toward academic specialization and the professionalization of philosophy and other "disciplines" in the universities. According to Sidgwick, the job of Ethics or the philosophical study of morality was not to determine the right or reasonable thing to do in particular situations but rather "to seek systematic and precise general knowledge of what is *right* and what makes judgments *valid*." Sidgwick regarded this project as unlike science in that its task was to formulate regulatory rather than explanatory laws but as scientific in form because it sought systematic, precise and general knowledge through a method guided by disinterested demands of precision, clarity and consistency. Thus Sidgwick defined what Walker calls "the idea of a *pure core of knowledge* at the heart of morality," a core that excluded both empirical contributions from the social sciences and considerations of the historical and cultural placement of "our" moral views (Walker 1997: 35). He fathered the idea of an ethical theory as

> a consistent (and usually very compact) set of law-like moral principles or procedures for decision that is intended to yield by deduction or instantiation (with the support of adequate collateral information) some determinate judgment for an agent in a given situation about what it is right, or at least morally justifiable, to do. (Walker 1997: 36)

In the philosophical tradition stemming from Sidgwick, the aim of Ethics is to discover/construct, test, compare and refine ethical theories and an individual's moral capacity is pictured as a kind of theory within "him." Ethics is juridical both in constructing theories that deliver verdicts on particular practical problems and in adjudicating theories for their (logical and epistemological) adequacy (Walker 1997: 37).

Sidgwick's definition of Ethics makes it clear that he regarded justification as central to ethical theory – though later in his career he changed this view. Sidgwick's successors maintained his epistemological focus but developed a distinct approach to addressing his questions. G. E. Moore's *Principia Ethica*, published in 1903, is credited with initiating the linguistic turn in ethical theory, directing philosophical attention away from explicit consideration of normative issues and refocusing it on the language and logic of ethics. Moore and his heirs construed their project of analyzing ethical language and logic in terms reminiscent of Sidgwick; they pursued systematic and general knowledge of moral concepts through a careful, clear and disinterested inquiry into uses of moral language. Ignoring as irrelevant most social facts, including facts about the social situations of those who used the language they analyzed, they sought to discover universal ethical truths, apparently assuming that the concepts implicit in "our" moral language were transhistorical and transcultural. Although "meta-ethical" analyses were expected to be impartial and dispassionate, many philosophers hoped that they could generate substantive theoretical conclusions. Moore believed that determining the meaning of "good" would reveal what was intrinsically good; R. M. Hare claimed that his analysis of "*The Language of Morals*" (1952) excavated the fundamental principles of right.

Although the term "applied ethics" is still often used to refer to thinking about practical moral questions, the second half of the twentieth century has seen a steady erosion of the idea of ethical theory as a product of (more or less) pure reason to be "applied" to practical issues. The hold of this deductivist model has weakened in even the early work of John Rawls, whom many regard as the twentieth century's ethical theorist *par excellence*. Rawls's concept of reflective equilibrium, reached by weighing general principles and considered moral judgements against each other with an openness to modifying either, exemplifies a model of moral reasoning that does not privilege theory over intuition. In his more recent work, Rawls lowers even further the status of ethical theory by abandoning the ideal of an "Archimedean point" and substituting the notion of a specific community's "overlapping consensus" about justice. Other philosophers have developed additional challenges to the Sidgwickian conception of ethical theory. Walker observes that,

> Code-like theory has provoked criticism from Aristotelians, Humeans, communitarians, contemporary casuists, pragmatists, historicists, Wittegensteinians, and others in the last several decades. So clear is this schism in late-twentieth-century moral philosophy that talk of 'antitheory' in ethics is now familiar. (Walker 1997: 53–4)

One way in which some feminists have challenged this model is by contending, as do some care theorists, that ethical theory is entirely dispensable as guide to right action.

A few feminists have added a moral and political dimension to the increasingly common claim that the codelike conception of ethical theory offers a misleading model of moral justification. Margaret Walker charges that this conception conceals the specific, partial and situated character of views and positions that are put forward "authoritatively as truths about 'human' interest, 'our' intuitions, 'rational' behavior, or 'the' moral agent" (Walker 1997: 54). The cloak of scientific objectivity woven by Sidgwick "signifies the promise and ensuing prestige of scientific accomplishment," while shielding from view "the historical, cultural, and social location of the moral philosopher, and of moral philosophy itself, as a practice of authority sustained by particular institutions and arrangements" (Walker 1997: 56).

The accounts of moral justification predominant in modern ethical theory invoke such ideals as rationality, universality, impersonality, detachment, dispassion, neutrality and transcendence. They aspire to evaluate actions and practices from a postulated "moral point of view" often explicated in metaphorical terms such as a god's eye view, the perspective of an ideal observer or an archangel, an Archimedean point, a view from nowhere or a view from everywhere. These metaphors are paradoxical, of course, since their aim is to designate an imagined perspective that is precisely not a specific point of view.

A number of feminists have argued that philosophers' claims to articulate the moral point of view have often in fact described only the view from their chairs in the gentleman's club; however, the particularity of their views has been concealed by the falsely universal pretensions implicit in their accounts of their methods for justifying them. Elizabeth Anderson contends that G. E. Moore's account of "our" moral intuitions in fact reflected the beliefs of those with the most social power even in Moore's narrow, elite – and overwhelmingly male – circle and she suggests that this biased outcome was not accidental but reflected a tendency endemic to individualist intuitionism (Anderson 1993). Elsewhere I have traced similar feminist challenges to the accounts of justification produced by other prominent twentieth century philosophers (Jaggar, forthcoming). One common theme linking those challenges is feminists' claim that people's perceptions, values and modes of reasoning, their understanding of their own and others' needs and interests, even their constructions of moral situations, vary not only individually but also systematically according to their social experience and locations. For this reason, feminist critics charge, the recommendations characteristic of many modern accounts of justification, recommendations that moral agents should put themselves in the place of others, think from others' perspectives, reverse perspectives with them, and so on, are epistemically incoherent. Although such thought experiments may have rough-and-ready heuristic value, there is no reason to suppose that philosophers' imaginations are more insightful or reliable than anybody else's. Claiming that their imagination enables them to fly up to attain "the moral point of view" is a disingenuous rhetorical device by which some philosophers lend a tone of magisterial authority to their own pronouncements.

By refusing to acknowledge the effects of people's social identities on their moral understandings, the ideal of point-of-viewlessness insulates itself from any critical examination of its own social origins or functions. Specifically, it denies that any philosophical significance attaches to the fact that only a few persons are authorized to define moral knowledge. Yet, as Walker notes, "To have the social, intellectual, or moral authority to perform this feat, one must already be on the advantaged side of practices that distribute power, privilege, and responsibilities in the community in which one does it" (Walker 1997: 271). From "the" moral point of view, the fact that "Western Anglo-European philosophical ethics as a cultural tradition and product has been until just recently almost entirely a product of some men's – and almost no women's – thinking" is a matter of only historical, not philosophical, interest. Some feminist critics charge that traditional conceptions of the moral point of view are more than simply expressions of a juridical-administrative perspective that some have characterized as masculine; nor they have served only as a means of rationalizing practices oppressive to women and members of other subordinated groups; they have even had a function beyond that of invalidating criticism of these practices. Invoking them has been, finally, a means by which philosophers have rationalized their claims to define the criteria of ethical justification and to judge when those criteria have been met.

A number of feminist philosophers, including myself, are working to rethink how moral justification might be more transparent and less covertly elitist and authoritarian. Like Habermas, we see empirical discourse as indispensable to justifying particular claims in particular contexts; however, we find that Habermas's account has only limited usefulness, in part because his ideal of "domination free" discourse imposes such stringent and counterfactual conditions that it seems virtually impossible for it to be achieved in real life. In contrast with the idealizations characteristic of most philosophical accounts, we address directly the inevitabilities of cultural difference and hierarchy among participants in empirical discourses. Although these new feminist understandings of moral justification are less idealized and more naturalistic than traditional accounts in that they operate at a lower level of abstraction, they are not naturalized in the classic Quineian sense of claiming "scientific" or value neutral status. On the contrary, they are still explicitly normative, linking the development of increasing moral objectivity with developing justificatory practices that are increasingly egalitarian, democratic and inclusive (Benhabib 1992; Jaggar 1995b; Walker 1997).

Feminist challenges to mainstream ethical theory have pursued transparency by making visible what Walker calls "the gendered structures of authority that produce and circulate (moral) understandings" (Walker 1997: 73). However, such challenges are far from constituting a wholesale rejection of ethical theory, even modern ethical theory. As Walker observes, feminist demands for transparency are embarrassing precisely because they invoke the familiar modern values of representation, consent, self-determination and respect,. They appeal to values that "are of specifically democratic, participatory, and egalitarian kinds, squarely founded on moral and political ideals of modern Western social thought" (Walker 1997: 73).

Contemporary feminist philosophers continue to do ethical theory in the sense of thinking generally about morality and, like other ethical theorists, we lean heavily on the analysis of language. However, our analyses differ from those of mainstream ethical theory in several respects. For one thing, we examine more than the strictly logical aspects of language: we look at metaphor, symbol and "nonlogical" implications, [Calhoun 1988] including emphases, omissions and silences, and we pay attention to the moral and political significance of these aspects. We often say we are analyzing "discourses" rather than "language," thereby suggesting that we are examining conceptual frameworks that are multiple, contingent and disclose as much about the authors of the discourse as they reveal about the moral realities to which ethical discourses purport to refer. We question the implicit normativity of terms like "we," "our" and "ordinary language." We take as objects of our scrutiny the discourses of philosophy; these include not only the discourses of our colleagues, which construct what is authorized and taught as ethical theory, but also our own discourses, which often construct what is authorized and taught as feminist ethical theory.

Our version of feminist ethical theory thus has several distinguishing features. First, it utilizes the categories of gender and other inseparable categories of social difference and hierarchy on the level of theoretical as well as practical ethics. Second, it enlarges the domain of ethics to include ethics itself: we undertake the ethical analysis of ethical analysis, the ethical theory of ethical theory. We see contemporary ethical theory as a discourse situated in a larger society and we ask who defines it and how their – and its – authority is maintained; we also see ethical theory as a professional practice and so we are led to examine such aspects of that practice as canon formation, prizes, prestigious offices and lectureships. Finally, our work is – or aspires to be – distinguished by its self-reflectiveness: we try to be conscious of the assumptions and implications of our own ethical theorizing, including their practical consequences; we seek to produce ethical theory that we acknowledge to be partial and provisional from our own explicitly situated perspectives.

References

Anderson, Elizabeth: *Value in Ethics and Economics* (Cambridge, MA, and London: Harvard University Press, 1993).

Baier, Annette C.:. "The Need for More than Justice," *Science, Morality and Feminist Theory,* eds. Marsha Hanen and Kai Nielsen (Calgary, Canada: University of Calgary Press, 1987).

Benhabib, Seyla: *Situating the Self: Gender, Community and Postmodernism in Contemporary Ethics* (New York: Routledge, 1992).

Blum, Lawrence A.: "Kant's and Hegel's Moral Rationalism: A Feminist Perspective," *Canadian Journal of Philosophy,* XII (1982): 2, 287–302.

——: "Care," *Encyclopaedia of Ethics,* ed. Lawrence C. Becker (New York: Garland, 1992).

Calhoun, Cheshire: "Justice, Care, Gender Bias," *Journal of Philosophy,* 85 (1988): 9.

Card, Claudia: "Gender and Moral Luck," in *Identity, Character and Morality,* eds. Owen Flanagan and Amelie Rorty (Cambridge, MA: MIT Press, 1990).

Clark, Lorenne M. G. and Lynda Lange, eds.: *The Sexism of Social and Political Theory* (Toronto, Buffalo, London: University of Toronto Press, 1979).

Dula, Annette and Sarah Goering: *It Just Ain't Fair: The Ethics of Health Care for African Americans* (Westport and London: Praeger, 1994).

Friedman, Marilyn: *What Are Friends For? Feminist Perspectives on Personal Relationships and Moral Theory* (Ithaca: Cornell University Press, 1993).

Gilligan, Carol: *In a Different Voice: Psychological Theory and Women's Development* (Cambridge, MA: Harvard University Press, 1982).

Held, Virginia: *Feminist Morality: Transforming Culture, Society, and Politics* (Chicago: University of Chicago Press, 1993).

Hoagland, Sarah Lucia: *Lesbian Ethics; Toward New Value* (Palo Alto, CA: Institute of Lesbian Studies).

Jaggar, Alison M.: "Caring as a Feminist Practice of Moral Reason," in Virginia Held, ed., *Justice and Care: Essential Readings in Feminist Ethics* (Boulder: Westview, 1995a).

—— et al.: *Morality and Social Justice: Point Counterpoint* (Lanham, MD and London, UK: Rowman and Littlefield, 1995b).

——: "Feminism and Moral Justification," in *Feminism in Philosophy,* eds. Miranda Fricker and Jennifer Hornsby (Cambridge University Press Companion Series, forthcoming).

Kabeer, Naila: *Reversed Realities: Gender Hierarchies in Development Thought* (New York: Verso, 1995).

Kohlberg, Lawrence: *The Philosophy of Moral Development: Moral Stages and the Idea of Justice* (San Francisco: Harper and Row, 1981).

Mies, Maria and Vandana Shiva: *Ecofeminism* (London: Zed Press, 1993).

Moser, Carolyn: *Gender, Planning and Development* (London: Routledge, 1993).

Noddings, Nel: *Caring: A Feminine Approach to Ethics and Moral Education* (Berkeley:

University of California Press, 1984).

——: "Feminist Fears in Ethics," *Journal of Social Philosophy*, 21 (1990): 2–3.

Nussbaum, Martha: "Human Capabilities, Female Human Beings," in *Women, Culture and Development*, eds. Martha Nussbaum and Jonathan Glover (Oxford: Clarendon Press, 1995).

Okin, Susan Moller: *Women in Western Political Thought* (Princeton: Princeton University Press, 1979).

——: *Justice, Gender and the Family* (New York: Basic Books, 1989).

Peters, Julie and Andrea Wolper, eds.: *Women's Rights, Human Rights: International Feminist Perspectives* (New York: Routledge, 1995).

Plumwood, Val: *Feminism and the Mastery of Nature* (London: Routledge, 1993).

Ruddick, Sara:. *Maternal Thinking: Towards a Politics of Peace* (New York: Beacon Press, 1989).

Scott, Catherine V.: *Gender and Development: Rethinking Modernization and Dependency Theory* (Boulder: Lynne Rienner, 1996).

Sen, Gita and Caren Grown: *Development, Crises and Alternative Visions: Third World Women's Perspectives* (New York: Monthly Review Press, 1987).

Sherwin, Susan: "A Feminist Approach to Ethics," *Resources for Feminist Research*, 16 (1987): 3.

——: *No Longer Patient: Feminist Ethics and Health Care* (Philadelphia: Temple University Press, 1992).

Tronto, Joan C.: *Moral Boundaries: A Political Argument for an Ethic of Care* (New York: Routledge, 1993).

Walker, Margaret: *Moral Understandings: A Feminist Study in Ethics* (New York: Routledge, 1997).

Warren, K. J.: "The Power and Promise of Ecological Feminism," *Environmental Ethics*, 12 (1990): 2.

Wendell, Susan: *The Rejected Body: Feminist Philosophical Reflections on Disability* (New York: Routledge, 1996).

Whitbeck, Caroline:. "A Different Reality: Feminist Ontology," in *Beyond Domination*, ed. Carol Gould (Totowa, NJ: Rowman and Allanheld, 1984).

Young, Iris Marion: *Justice and the Politics of Difference* (Princeton: Princeton University Press, 1990).

Chapter 19

Continental Ethics

William R. Schroeder

Introduction

This essay will explore some key features of Continental ethics through an examination of several especially creative ethical thinkers in the Continental tradition: Hegel, Nietzsche, Scheler, Sartre, and Levinas. After an introductory discussion of relationships between Continental and Analytic approaches to ethics, I describe some of the major innovations of each of these philosophers. Then I examine some apparent disagreements among them and conclude by describing some of their challenges to mainstream ethical theory. My goal is to provide a sense of the originality and diversity of ethical positions among Continental thinkers.

Three features of Continental ethics can provide benchmarks to establish the contours of the landscape. The first feature is that Continental ethicists have blazed some of the trails that are producing a virtual revolution in current ethical theory in the Analytic tradition. The second feature is a common suspicion among Continental thinkers that seems almost entirely absent from Analytic ethical theory, at least until quite recently, namely, that there is something deeply suspect – even immoral – about morality itself. The third feature is a common project among Continental ethicists that establishes a different tone than that typically found in Analytic ethical theory; this project is finding the conditions that will enable genuine personal flourishing – or ethical radiance – among individuals. Far less emphasis is given to duty and obligation in Continental ethics and far more attention is paid to the cultural, psychological, interpersonal, and emotional conditions of a personal transformation that makes serious ethical achievement possible.

The first feature concerns the many areas of common interest between Continental thinkers and recent Analytic ethicists. In the past thirty years, there has been a two-pronged revolution in Analytic ethics. One prong involves a search for alternatives to the long-reigning hegemony of Kantian deontology and utilitarian consequentialism. In the process a variety of major assumptions that have long-guided ethical thinking are being challenged. Perhaps the most notable emerging alternative is the renewal of virtue ethics, which centers ethical practice on the formation of character dispositions and clarifies the main components of the virtues and the ways they might be cultivated (Slote, McIntyre, Foot, Wallace). I would argue that Nietzsche began this project (in its contemporary form) and that Nicolai Hartmann makes central, if little known, contributions to it. Another important development is a renewed interest in moral realism as a way of restoring some degree of objectivity to ethical aspirations and assessments (Murdoch, McDowell, Boyd). Max Scheler developed an intriguing version of value realism that might offer some useful handholds to help scale this mountain. Relevant too are efforts to recuperate the history of ethics by clarifying goods dominant in previous eras and thus to deepen our responsiveness to their continuing resonance in this era (Taylor). This approach to all fields of philosophy – not just ethics – was pioneered by Hegel who made important contributions. Feminists are challenging the duty-based, rationalist orientation of some ethical theories, suggesting that they ignore the taproot of ethical action – sensitivity and nurturing – and miss a more particularized grasp of lived situations that can navigate through ethical complexities without abstractions or principles (Nussbaum; Noddings). Scheler and Nietzsche made some important contributions to this project as well. Another important development questions whether all positive values are comparable and commensurable and whether they can be integrated into a coherent system (Nagel; Stocker). Nietzsche, Scheler, and Sartre stress this potentially tragic fact about fundamental values.

This diverse array of new experimental directions in Analytic ethics is supplemented by a second, equally important, development – the vigorous growth of applied ethics. Applied ethics attempts to refine commonly accepted moral intuitions to make them more coherent, and to utilize the socially established purposes of specific institutions to provide a rational foundation for normative guidelines for actors within such institutions. Applied ethics takes the basic functions of an institution for granted; it resolves tensions and hard cases by ordering these functions. Such social institutions constitute what Hegel called the ethical substance of a society – established traditions and procedures for achieving commonly valued outcomes. Each institution (e.g., medicine, law, business, engineering, academia) functions as a limited frame within which genuine resolution of major disputes might be achieved. Hegel's *Philosophy of Right* (1821) might be considered the first treatise in applied ethics – first addressing the sphere of the family, then the sphere of civil society, and finally that of the State. He does not so much try to justify the values within these spheres as render them coherent. He searches for the rational elements of those institutions and attempts to discover their most effective realization. My contention is that both prongs of these recent developments in Analytic ethics might benefit from some understanding of Continental contributions. The brief expository sketches in the next section offer some evidence to support this claim. For the moment I have only indicated common directions.

The second feature of Continental ethics sharply distinguishes it from much of current Analytic ethics, namely its ethically motivated suspicion of conventional morality and a skepticism about the value of many commonly accepted moral values. Continental figures find conventional morality deficient, even ethically objectionable. They also regard much traditional moral theory to be misguided and bankrupt. In addition, they are skeptical about the psychology and philosophical anthropology that informs much of everyday morality and ethical theory, and they try to discover alternatives. Nietzsche's tirades against Christian morality and its Enlightenment heirs offer only the most flamboyant example of this line of thought. Additional examples include Hegel's attacks on the emptiness of Kantian ethics, Scheler's attacks on common mistakes of rationalism in philosophical ethics (and their ruinous ethical results), Sartre's reservations about the world of the Good (and its consequent need for Evil), and Levinas's doubts about the interest-seeking character of politics. Analytic thinkers want to believe the house of ethics is basically shipshape, needing only a coat of paint and a good cleaning, but Continental figures think the traditional house has become a prison and new habitats must be created.

The third feature follows from the second. It consists in an entirely different orientation among Continental thinkers. Their primary goal is to determine the conditions of ethical flourishing for various types of individuals, rather than to establish the borders of behavior that must not be transgressed. Since they have no confidence in traditional frameworks and guidelines, they seek to discover new paths that will facilitate radiant ethical achievement. Again, this is perhaps most evident in Nietzsche who spends even more time exploring the psychological, physiological, and cultural conditions of becoming a "greater" person (more enriched, more varied, subtler, and stronger) than he does on his genealogical critiques of modern values. But this is also true of Hegel, who attempts to discern the social institutions that will most support the achievement of individual harmony and recognition. And of Scheler, whose examinations of the diverse strata of value and of the role of feeling and basic moral tenor in ethical response reveal ways to strengthen one's strongest ethical capacities. And of Sartre, who explores an experience he calls "conversion," which he regards as a precondition of personal authenticity. And of Levinas, who believes that a special orientation toward other people is a necessary precondition for ethical life. For Continental figures, one function of ethical theory is to elucidate a transformation of personal existence that enables a more promising kind of ethical practice.

Some Major Figures

G. W. F. Hegel (1770–1831)

Hegel reacted against the formalism (lack of substantive norms) and the abstractness of Kant's ethics. He rejects the idea that one can test ethical maxims on the basis of any single formula (e.g., the categorical imperative), that an action can be genuinely motivated solely by duty, and that individuals can live ethically in isolation from rational social contexts and institutional norms. Hegel shows that the categorical imperative (the demand that maxims be universalizable without contradiction) is ultimately contentless – sanctioning almost any action, depending on how the "maxim" of the action is interpreted and which features of the situation are deemed relevant (Hegel 1977 [1807]: 256–62). He claims that adopting the moral viewpoint may be ethically counterproductive because it forces one to abstract oneself from all the concrete social ties (one's relation to one's family and profession) which give ethics its point and structure (Hegel 1977 [1807]: 365–83). Hegel is profoundly skeptical of the whole project of generating moral precepts *a priori* – on the basis of pure reason alone. Instead, he insists that individual flourishing is encouraged by social institutions, that the direction of individual self-realization is related to the goals of those social institutions that surround them, and that these structures provide the basic normative content of ethics.

In his earliest writings Hegel also reacts against the experience of division and conflict typical of modern social life. Individuals experience sharp conflicts between reason and passions (a division only exacerbated by Kant's uncompromising rigorism about moral motivation); they also often experience themselves opposed to other individuals and to the larger political order. One of Hegel's main aims is to produce a theory that might overcome these divisions. Overcoming this divided and alienated condition is required for achieving genuine freedom, and Hegel takes freedom thus understood to be the defining goal of human life. Such harmonious freedom is a humanly created achievement (as opposed to a naive unity that is easily lost). The right institutions are needed to make this harmony possible. Reason is one important means by which these mediated unities are produced. Hegel realizes that his conception of freedom is not the same as the negative freedom sought throughout the modern world – removing obstacles to doing what one wants. That freedom dominates modern economic life. Hegel does not reject this characteristically modern aspiration, but asserts that the proper social institutions are needed to fulfill other human aspirations and insists that social institutions can enhance as well as limit human choices. Hegelian individuals do not see themselves as isolated from or imprisoned by his ideal social institutions, but instead see themselves expressed and realized in them (Hegel 1967 [1821]: 105–10).

Reciprocal recognition is the way Hegelian freedom is realized in interpersonal life. It involves reciprocal acknowledgment that others one encounters are fully self-conscious like oneself. The process of achieving this acknowledgment also enriches the self-consciousness of each person. Prior to social acknowledgment self-consciousness is only nascent; after the process of acknowledgment the identity of each participant as both living and self-conscious is ratified. In becoming socially recognized one becomes more actual for oneself – more fully self-conscious (Hegel 1977 [1807]: 111–13). Reciprocal recognition transcends a stage of encounter in which individuals violently struggle to prove their superiority. The outcomes of these battles leave at least one party unrecognized and dominated by the other. Though such domination initially seems to achieve the aspirations of self-consciousness; it does not really do so (the slave's recognition of the master is corrupted by the fact that he is a slave, and the slave's labor leaves the master's talents underdeveloped.) (Hegel 1977 [1807]: 115–19). When two persons achieve reciprocal recognition, they experience a deeper harmony; they no longer see each other as alien. Both produce the harmony together, and both are enriched by it. It establishes a genuine community. To be recognized in one's performance of a social role is to achieve social actuality.

Hegel suggests that there are three spheres in which persons can experience themselves as realized/expressed (or, alternatively, as foreign or alienated): in relation to things, to their own willed actions, and to communal life generally. A sense of connection with material goods can be achieved through appropriate property relations; a material thing becomes one's own by becoming one's property. Property is thus essential to individual freedom for Hegel (Hegel 1967 [1821]: 40–4). But property relations cannot be established in isolation. Complex legal understandings and a judicial enforcement mechanism are necessary to sustain property relations. Even at the lowest levels of freedom's realization, an entire institutional system is presupposed. So important is property that Hegel suggests that the rational State will make some modest amount of property available to everyone to insure this modest degree of self-actualization (Hegel, 1967 [1821]: 45, 57–64).

The second sphere is one's own practical activity. Here an action is one's own only if it derives from one's free decision. Hegel accepts Kant's claim that action is not truly one's own if one follows the commands of others or if one unthinkingly conforms to tradition. But he does not go so far as to claim that freedom requires performing the act solely for duty's sake alone. Any practical action expresses one's joy in exercising one's capacities; this can never be purged from action without disabling it altogether. Moreover, reason alone will not supply any substantive goods or duties. These derive from the concrete communities in which one lives – as a member of a family, a profession, and a state (Hegel 1967 [1821]: 105–10). Duties, goods, and norms derive from these concrete relations. They are the substance of ethics, but they will be expressions of oneself as a rational being only if they exhibit a coherent order.

Thus, neither the first nor second spheres of ethical life can stand alone; specific social and institutional relations are necessary to achieve full freedom in them. The state and other social institutions play a central role in Hegel's theory because they make individual freedom possible. If institutions are irrationally organized or inconsistent, then they will undermine the achievement of freedom. Rational institutions are necessary if there is to be any freedom – any sense of social harmony. This is the source of the positive role of the social institutions (including the state) in the self-actualization of individuals. By breathing life into their social roles, individuals make the social order express themselves, and by insuring that these roles are coherent and conducive to self-realization, social institutions enhance the identity of individuals (Hegel 1977 [1807]: 266–78).

But not just any social and political order is rational. A rational social order must satisfy various criteria (Hegel 1967 [1821]: 155–60, 174–6): It must guarantee property relations and ensure that each person owns at least some property. It must facilitate interpersonal recognition and cultivate the capacity for moral reflection and deliberation. It must provide institutional means for mastering a profession (allowing individuals to create their own self-identity) and participating as a citizen. It must regulate the economic sphere in which individuals pursue their own desires, and it must respect the integrity of individuals. It must prevent conflict among professions and mediate disagreements over property and rights. It must also not allow citizens to fall into the illusion of isolated individuality, abdicating their responsibilities to the state and other social institutions. The state (and all the mediating institutions of society, including families and guilds) thus plays an active and essential role in making freedom possible for Hegel, and there are many ways for existing states to fall short of these evaluative criteria. For Hegel, institutions and political organization are essential to ethical life because they provide the proper environment for achieving expressive, integrated lives.

Friedrich Nietzsche (1844–1900)

Nietzsche is probably the most sweeping critic of traditional moral ideals and moral philosophy – far-reaching enough to call himself an "immoralist." Fortunately, he does not only demolish; he also constructs an alternative orientation to, and a different basis for, ethics. Nietzsche's major nemesis is Christianity and its modern offshoots. Among these offshoots he includes many Enlightenment assumptions and ideals (liberty, equality, fraternity). Nietzsche sensed the imminent collapse of religion as a serious intellectual option and correctly predicted a resulting rise of nihilism. He sought above all to avoid the worst effects of this reaction (Nietzsche 1974 [1882], §125). To overcome nihilism humanity must transcend the fantasies of religion and commence a new approach to life. Nietzsche's entire project is to enable the transition to this new way of living. He offers a series of alternative ideals to guide the process and produces a more penetrating human psychology in order to achieve realistic progress. He also describes some cultural changes that may contribute to this transition.

Nietzsche attacks both the moral point of view and traditional moral values, especially Christian values. By "morality" he means a system of duties and obligations ("shalts") that present themselves as universally justified imperatives. He issues two challenges to morality in general: first, a challenge to its direction; and second, a demonstration of its immoral sources. Together these objections establish the need for a new alternative.

Nietzsche offers a number of arguments to show the general misguidedness of morality. First, he clarifies the basic effect of morality on those who try to live up to it. Through guilt morality typically turns people against themselves, undermining their sense of passion, self-esteem, and creativity; often it makes them cower before some external principle or power. It makes people weak, fearful, ashamed of themselves, self-effacing, and dependent (Nietzsche 1982 [1881], §18; 1968 [1887], III §11). It does this in part because it uses fear as its central motivation and in part because it extirpates and eradicates the very foundations of any organism and of life itself: sexuality, self-expression, the exercise of power (Nietzsche 1954 [1888] pp. 486–92). Nietzsche seeks to create a different ambiance: a sense of innocence, of new birth, an experimental light-footed approach to life, a stimulus to continually reach beyond one's current achievements (Nietzsche 1954 [1883–5], I §1, I §22). Though it may take considerable effort to achieve this stance, it embodies Nietzsche's goal of living "beyond good and evil."

Most moral codes are repressive and puritanical; they make impossible demands on people, and the failure to live up to these demands produces people who hate life and themselves (Nietzsche 1954 [1883–5], I §3). Even if one succeeds in being moral, one is rarely a radiant, joyful person. Instead one often seethes with repressed aggression and resentment. Instead, the approach Nietzsche would substitute works to cultivate the basic instincts of life and humanity, to increase humanity's capacity for self-transformation, and to make possible a general affirmation of life (despite its sufferings, accidents, and "amorality"). He tries to educate people to create goals for themselves, to live with buoyancy, grace, and confidence, finding joy in their actual attainments (Nietzsche 1954 [1883–5], IV §13). None of this, he contends, is typically associated with the moral point of view or with being moral.

In addition, morality typically demands automatistic, habituated responses – abiding by tradition (or duty) for tradition's (or duty's) sake (Nietzsche 1982 [1881], §19). Nietzsche thinks this makes serious, supple responses to the complexity of actual situations almost impossible. Nietzsche's formula for this effect is that morality turns people into herd animals, thus inhibiting subtle responses to complex situations. Also, most moralities stress one's duties to other people (vs. self-perfection) and the urge to judge others (or oneself) rather than achieve self-transformation. Finally, morality often arrogates itself to the mantle of the sole hegemonic standard for evaluating people, and thus devalues many other criteria on which they can be assessed: physical, intellectual, emotional, vital, artistic, interpersonal, and political. Moral excellence is only one dimension of human achievement, but morality pretends it is the only important – or at least the most significant – measure of any consequence. Nietzsche simply rejects this; serious personal evaluation would include all these dimensions. Nietzsche himself adds the following tests: health and vigor, the capacity to affirm life, strength and hardness, and the amount of truth one can bear (Nietzsche 1968 [1886], §227). Morality is a minimal standard at best; Nietzsche expects more of people, and advocates self-perfection along many dimensions.

Nietzsche's second general line of attack is a series of points designed to show that morality is rooted in or dependent on upon immoral sources or at least wholly non- moral standpoints. First among these is the claim that the decision to be moral cannot itself be a moral decision and cannot be defended on moral grounds on pain of circularity (Nietzsche 1982 [1881], §97). Also, many motivations for behaving morally are not themselves very admirable, e.g., fear, despair, egoism, habit, fanaticism. Similarly the standpoint from which one must evaluate morality as a cultural-social institution cannot itself derive from the morality being evaluated. Any judge must somehow achieve an extra-moral standpoint – overcoming the biases of years of moral indoctrination to be able to explore the many perspectives needed to provide a fair evaluation of diverse moral codes. Still another point is that moral innovators almost always are called "immoral" by the then dominant morality, and hence the dominant morality subverts efforts to improve the institution as a whole.

An entirely different type of challenge derives from Nietzsche's examination of Christian morality, viz., that many historical moralities to date have been "slave" moralities. Slave moralities develop by undermining and transvaluing "master" moralities (Nietzsche, 1968 [1886], §268). Nietzsche suggests that "master moralities" are those in which flourishing human beings bestow value on the traits that make their flourishing possible. Everything that produces delight, joy, power – everything that affirms this life – is sanctified with the appellation "good." For such moralities "bad" is almost an afterthought – indicating simply a lack of good traits; the bad person is less condemned than unfortunate. However, those who are more impoverished, less advantaged, and less talented resent and hate the success of those who flourish. They seethe with unbounded hatred. To avenge themselves, they create the category of "evil." They substitute for the opposition "good/bad" the more vituperative opposition of "good/evil," and they invert what counts as good (Nietzsche 1968 [1887], I §5–10). How else could meekness, self-effacement, and poverty have become virtues? Thus, for slave moralities "evil" becomes whatever master moralities have called good – whatever has made human flourishing possible. And "good" becomes whatever was previously merely bad – characteristics indicating misfortune, weakness, disability, self-denial, and life-denial. Thus, Nietzsche accuses morality of inverting what is truly valuable and exhorting humanity in the wrong direction. It has transformed what is truly good into something evil, and turned mediocrity into virtue. Thus it inhibits and destroys the best and most promising traits in the human species.

Nietzsche inaugurates a revaluation of values, in which specific values inherited from the past are tested and assessed to determine their overall promise. Nietzsche explores the actual effects of living in accord with specific ideals for specific human types. He investigates a number of types of value (epistemic, aesthetic, moral, religious) as well as important modern values, e.g., equality, happiness, democracy, truth, and many Christian values, e.g., love, compassion, and humility. His method of examination involves interrogating a value from many different points of view (Nietzsche 1954 [1888], Preface): What is the typical result of embodying the value? What are the typical motives for pursuing the value? What is the manner in which the value is typically lived? What alternatives are there to this value? Who typically pursues this ideal and how does it function in practice? By answering these questions Nietzsche is able to challenge a wide variety of traditional values. Often his investigations show how the value might be refurbished or transfigured. His aim is not simply to reject or debunk, but to discover which values still have something to offer the future, life- affirming development of humanity.

For example, Nietzsche is suspicious of Christian ideals like love and pity. Some types of love are expressions of envy of and/or resentment of the higher qualities of the beloved person and are efforts to appropriate these qualities magically. Nietzsche regards both of these as corrupt motivations for love, and he believes that such symbolic efforts to appropriate human excellence are impoverished substitutes for real self-perfection. Thus, love can express something dark and dubious, and its effect can be to inhibit real self-development. Love can also lead to dishonesty and unrealistic demands if one too readily believes one's idealized vision of the lover. Further, love can lead to insensitivity because the power of the emotion can block one's insight into the deeper psychic dynamics of the beloved or because the lover may refuse to look too deeply. Nietzsche sketches a tougher ideal of friendship as an alternative to personal love (Nietzsche 1954 [1883–5], I §14). One's friend may function as an inspiration but not at the cost of one's real self-development. And a true friend is unafraid to challenge one's self-satisfaction and self-deceptions when one's self-development is at stake. The friend is truthful when the lover is silent; the friend challenges the partner to new achievements when the lover celebrates past glories.

Nietzsche's constructive ethic consists of several elements: (1) a general stance; (2) a number of supporting strategies by which that stance is made plausible; and (3) some new values that concretize this stance.

The general stance Nietzsche defends is the enhancement of human capacities – elevating various possibilities of human development to such new heights that contemporary humanity will seem crude and bestial by comparison. This "new" humanity will develop by sublimating the passions of present humanity; indeed Nietzsche's whole enterprise is to harness and organize the actual powers of human beings rather than attempt to define a new "ideal" humanity (Nietzsche 1954 [1883–5], I §5). Thus the most critical task for human types and for individuals is to discover the conditions best suited to their development. This may require restricting oneself to pursuing a single capacity for extended periods until it has become second nature and then gradually introducing additional goals. Such personal development requires both discipline and self-knowledge; it requires a great love for one's own future possibilities and a refusal to allow them to lie fallow. Sometimes one must create ways of making disparate or conflicting passions reinforce, rather than debilitate, one another. Often it involves giving shape and style to one's various capacities; this is Nietzsche's understanding of giving a law to oneself (Nietzsche 1974 [1882], §290). But this differs from finding a basic principle; it is more like finding an overall aim that can integrate many of one's talents and aspirations. Through this process of shaping, cultivating, and pruning one becomes a distinctive personality, rather than an anonymous, faceless person.

Three strategies support this general stance: a naturalistic point of departure, an intuitive appeal to health over decadence, and a call to creativity. Nietzsche's position is naturalistic in the sense that he takes himself less to be defining and recommending a transcendent ideal than to be developing and enhancing the capacities and passions humanity already has. He calls this "remaining true to the earth" (Nietzsche 1954 [1883–5], I §22). He thinks the capacity to see life as it is and celebrate its real possibilities provides an evaluative standard. The error of religion (and much of classical philosophy) has been to create unreal fantasy worlds that discouraged this-worldly human development. This error is complicated by that of traditional morality, which rebelled against life and against the conditions of human flourishing. Nietzsche's naturalism seeks to reverse these disastrous effects and establish a more promising approach to ethical self-development.

The second strategy is an intuitive preference for health over decadence. Health is a basic condition for the flourishing of all human talents and capacities (Nietzsche 1974 [1882], §382). Nietzsche examines its physiological, emotional, and psychic dimensions in both individuals and cultures. A third strategy is to endorse the value of creativity. People are to use their lives to conduct experiments from which future humanity might learn. They should organize the complexity of instincts, drives, and capacities creatively and test particular patterns of such organization. The sheer process of creation has value for Nietzsche. In addition, the most advanced persons bear an additional responsibility: to create new values that can guide the future of human development, that define what "human enhancement" will mean (Nietzsche 1968 [1886], §211).

In addition to health and creativity, other fundamental Nietzschean values are life-affirmation, moral strength (a notion that captures what he means by "power"), and deftness. These characteristics are boundary conditions for living well for Nietzsche in the sense that if one does not embody them one cannot attain one's central defining aspiration or virtue. Also, one would fall outside the wide variety of forms of life that might be promising experiments.

Nietzsche also lauds a variety of particular virtues as plausible beginnings in the task of forging a new humanity. Consider the following list: magnanimity, good-naturedness, gift-giving virtue, justice; then also honesty with oneself, courage, insight, joy, pride, gratitude, reverence, composure, wisdom; and finally, hardness, the willingness to fight for what matters, distance from others, and love of the great possibilities in the future. The first list articulates a way of being with other people purged of all negativity and bad feeling; embodying such virtues would allow one to contribute to other people without abandoning one's life to them. The second list elaborates Nietzsche's notion of "cleanliness" in relation to oneself, an avoidance of negative passions. It solicits one's finest effort at self-perfection while avoiding gloominess and self-inflation. The final group affirms the importance of conflict in producing self-perfection and extols commitment to the future. These specific values concretize Nietzsche's central ethical stance.

Max Scheler (1874–1928)

Scheler's ethics is rooted in a phenomenological study of the emotions and a critical response to previous ethical theories as well as Nietzsche's attacks on Christianity. He seeks to clarify the import of ethical emotions like love and hate, sympathy and resentment, suffering and shame. He thinks such emotions are the conduits through which humans grasp values, much like the senses are the conduits through which we grasp physical objects and thought is the conduit through we grasp concepts and logical truths. Emotions have their own distinctive order, relationships, and objects; their logic cannot be reduced to the logic of perception or of thought (Scheler 1973b: 117–18). Emotions target a specific type of object, values; loving and preferring express an attraction to value. Values motivate all striving or desire. Moreover, Scheler thinks values can be ranked in a hierarchy: sensory, vital, cultural, and spiritual (Scheler 1973a [1913–16]: 104–10). Humanity participates in all four of these dimensions, and different people experience the values within each level to different degrees of urgency. The distinctive subset of values to which a person is most powerfully drawn defines his or her basic moral tenor (Scheler 1973b: 99–111). Scheler's ethics centers on persons, and he regards the realization of a person's basic moral tenor to be among the highest goods.

A close study of the relation of values to human emotions will indicate the flaws in classical ethical theories. Eudaimonism is the view that happiness represents both a natural motive and the highest human flourishing. For Scheler there are four qualitatively different types of happiness (corresponding to the four dimensions of value), but happiness neither defines value, nor is it the typical motivation for action (Scheler 1973a [1913–16]: 328–44). Many eudaimonistic theories identify happiness with pleasure – the lowest form of happiness – because this is the only form of happiness that can be directly sought. Other types of happiness emerge indirectly through realizing certain values. Pursuing sensory pleasures typically compensates for deeper levels of unhappiness (Scheler 1973a [1913–16]: 345–8). Moreover, such pleasures are not always valuable; addictive pleasures exhibit disvalue as do pleasures taken at another's suffering. Scheler grants that bliss, the highest happiness, is a precondition for grasping the best value possibilities of situations, but insists that it cannot be the direct object of an intention. Actions target values themselves, the better one realizes one's basic moral tenor, the more fully one will be attuned to the higher value possibilities of situations.

Scheler also rejects consequentialism, an ethics of goods, and an ethics of duty. Consequences, like goods, are good only because they embody values. Values explain what existing things and future events are good. Goods often develop, but such developments do not determine value; values determine which developments are good. Goods and purposes, like consequences, are bearers of value, not definers thereof (Scheler 1973a [1913–16]: 12–23). In general, Scheler thinks that the moral quality of an agent cannot depend on success in realizing consequences because such success is not entirely in the agent's control. Scheler agrees with Kant that moral tenor defines the moral value of a person, but he disagrees with Kant in thinking that moral tenors are quite diverse, and cannot be reduced to a pure desire to do one's duty. Genuine duties also are logically dependent on values, and typically duties are negative – requiring the non-pursuit of evil, rather than the positive achievement of good (Scheler 1973a [1913–16]: 232–8). Kant's theory suggests that the moral standpoint is impersonal; Scheler disagrees with this, insisting that the realization of one's distinctive personal moral tenor determines moral achievement. Finally, Scheler thinks that reliance on imperatives is necessary only when one is value-blind. With adequate value insight, the bludgeon of duty is unnecessary to motivate action, and utilizing duty to motivate an action is a violation of the person when insight would be sufficient.

Values are distinct from the goods in which they are embodied; they are given differently. A value can be given clearly (justice) while the state of affairs (a just society) that embodies it is given indistinctly, and a good can be given clearly (a work of art) while the value(s) it embodies may be given indistinctly. Values are not destroyed when their bearers are crushed. Thus, values are components of goods, but are not reducible to goods (Scheler 1973a [1913–16]: 12–23). Positive values are given as to be realized, but this "pull" is not always sufficient to motivate action. Persons are good to the extent that they respond to and realize the highest value possibilities in situations (Scheler 1973a [1913–16]: 38–44). The value hierarchy is being continuously clarified both by new personal moral tenors and tenors that exist in diverse cultures and in different eras. All willing and preferring target value realization, not the associated pleasures.

Scheler thinks his ranking of value dimensions (sensory, vital, cultural, spiritual) is intuitively evident, but he suggests properties that support it. Higher values are more enduring, less divisible, provide deeper fulfillment, are the foundation for lower ones, and are more absolute in the sense that transgressing them results in greater guilt (Scheler 1973a [1913–16]: 90–100). To each level of the four-tiered hierarchy there corresponds a characteristic model person (*bon vivant*, hero, genius, saint), and form of social organization (mass, life community, cultural community, and spiritual community) (Scheler 1973a [1913–16]: 109, 585). The sector of the value hierarchy to which one is most attuned is one's basic moral tenor. This tenor organizes one's moral life and determines one's goals. Stepping back from one's moral tenor and evaluating it is difficult because it structures one's perceptions (what kinds of objects one sees, and which dimensions of those objects stand out) and thoughts (Scheler 1973a [1913–16]: 126–42). It can, however, be altered by conversion or expanded through the influence of personal models.

One of Scheler's major contributions is this emphasis on the importance of personal models in ethical development (Scheler 1973a [1913–16]: 572–83). Personal models inspire others to realize their own distinctive moral tenors in addition to expanding their value sensitivity. Usually the influence of models is indirect and unintended; this differentiates them from ordinary leaders. Both persons and cultures can learn from each other's moral tenors, and Scheler thinks personal models are gradually clarifying the value hierarchy in its entirety as well as motivating people to realize their best ethical potential.

Scheler supports his theory of value by clarifying the logic of particular emotions (e.g., love, resentment, and shame). Love, for example, is the state in which the highest possibilities of value of the beloved object emerge; it can be directed toward others or oneself (Scheler 1970 [1913]: 152–61). Self-love is vital to grasping higher levels of value. Personal love of others grasps their basic moral tenor and makes it visible, without intervening to supervise its realization. Resentment results from a sense of impotence characteristic of social groups that lack power and mobility. It inhibits the apprehension of higher values and poisons one's sense of one's own value (Scheler 1961 [1912]: 43–78). Scheler rejects Nietzsche's claim that Christianity is a resentment-based religion, arguing that Christian love flows from the rich sense of self-value and offers itself in the overflowing radiance characteristic of Nietzsche's higher persons. Scheler agrees with Nietzsche that many specifically modern value stances – e.g., humanitarian love, utilitarianism, and relativism – are rooted in resentment. Shame is a natural emotional function that emerges when people suddenly experience a lower dimension of their existence (Scheler 1987: 10–18). It is protective and delays the need to respond to the situation. Shame emerges, for example, when one suddenly becomes aware of one's body when one's spirit or intellect had been the center of attention or when one's particular nature claims attention but only one's stereotypical nature is apprehended. Shame protects the self-value that is being denied or missed though it does not assert it. It encourages the person to withhold response until the purpose of the denial is grasped (Scheler 1987: 27–36). The experience of value is central to each of these emotions. These sketches illustrate why Scheler thinks emotions provide access to values.

Late in his life Scheler also suggested that the most promising ideal to guide human development in the foreseeable future is that of the complete person or whole person, in which all dimensions of human existence are balanced. To achieve this the current era needs to compensate for the overemphasis on reason, will, and asceticism characteristic of modernity. The Apollinian impulse to order must be compensated with the Dionysian impulse to ecstasy; masculine values with feminine ones, and civilized value perspectives with primitive ones (Scheler 1958: 101–15). This view represents a real change for Scheler; no longer does he stress the highest values or even each person's distinctive moral tenor. Instead, he seeks a broad incorporation of value by each person, an intermixing of diverse value perspectives that will sensitize people to the fullest spectrum of values.

Jean-Paul Sartre (1905–80)

Sartre's writings exhibited ethical overtones throughout his career, but he never published a separate treatise on ethics. Indeed, he thought conventional bourgeois morality was bankrupt. Yet he attempted to produce an ethics at many different stages of his career, first in several notebooks and essays written just after the publication of *Being and Nothingness*, then in his biography of Genet, and finally in several unpublished manuscripts written after completing the manuscript for the second volume of his *Critique of Dialectical Reason*. The guiding value in all these works is freedom. Its meaning and presuppositions change as his position evolves, but throughout his career Sartre insisted that freedom is a foundation for all human aims and that persons bear responsibility for their actions and their lives. He grounds the value of freedom in the ontological fact of freedom.

In the early period of *Being and Nothingness* the source of freedom is consciousness itself, which perpetually transcends its situation even as it defines itself within such situations. Every situation allows for several courses of action, and making the choice engenders responsibility for the values the choice embodies. Since nothing determines one's response to a situation, one always chooses that response and bears responsibility for those choices (Sartre 1956 [1943]: 553–6). For Sartre the values one pursues through such choices have no external or rational support. Thus, freedom and responsibility are burdensome, and typically people avoid them through self-deceptive ruses; e.g., presuming that social roles determine obligations, pretending that certain values have objective guarantees, or believing that past actions foreclose present choices (Sartre 1956 [1943]: 55–67). To refuse these self-deceptive ruses, to bear one's responsibility, and to truly author one's long term projects is to live authentically. At this stage Sartre's notion of freedom is formal in the sense that it seems neither to entail nor exclude any particular content.

Sartrean freedom in this early phase is also asocial because the primary effect of other people is to produce a dimension of consciousness over which one has no control, the social self. The Other's look petrifies and summarizes one – fashioning an essential nature, molding a permanent sculpture out of a single amorphous moment (Sartre 1956 [1943]: 259–72). Apart from a brief footnote in *Being and Nothingness*, there is no exit from the struggle among objectifying gazes; either one dominates others by objectifying them, or one is dominated by them by being objectified (Sartre 1956 [1943]: 268–70, 276–8). Even if one attempts continuous domination, one cannot escape the fact of the social self; it always hovers on the horizon ready for reactivation. The inescapable reality of the social self creates a deep self-division which cannot ever be completely healed.

The overall aim of consciousness, on this early view, is to achieve a synthesis of two types of existence – to be already given passivity (matter) and to be self-creating activity (consciousness) – that cannot be synthesized, in effect to become God (Sartre, 1956 [1943]: 85–95). But since such a synthesis is impossible, Sartre declares that human beings are useless passions. Sartrean conversion requires that people abandon this self-deceptive and fruitless project.

In the middle period, when "Existentialism is a Humanism" and *What is Literature?* were published and his *Notebooks for an Ethics* was composed, Sartre extends his basic position on freedom – showing how the invidious conflict among people can be overcome through reciprocity and how authenticity can function as an alternative to the project of becoming God.

He develops the ontological fact of freedom in three ways. First, he accentuates the weight of one's choices by suggesting that one chooses for everyone; in effect, one's actions function as examples for all to follow (Sartre 1956 [1946], 291–2). He thus gives ethical significance to the fact that one's actions have an objective side that is seen and judged by others (Sartre 1956 [1946], p. 293). Second, he suggests that humanity as a whole does not have an essence prior to human action; humanity is something to be made in action both individually and collectively. Historical actions produce the conditions of the lives of present and future generations, and each of one's individual actions reshapes and expresses the fundamental project that informs all of one's future actions. In effect, every action contributes to defining and creating human reality (Sartre, 1956 [1946]: 295–8). Finally, since freedom is the foundation of all action, Sartre claims that freedom must be taken as a basic value guiding one's projects and that one's own freedom requires everyone's freedom. Any act which attempts to deny the value of freedom in effect is denying its own conditions, and thus is self-undermining (Sartre 1956 [1946]: 307–9).

In this period Sartre also grants the possibility of authentic reciprocity, in which people acknowledge and respect each other's freedom. Eventually he will try to show that none can be fully free until all are. One way in which reciprocity can emerge is through common action, in which each person freely adopts the goals of the others (Sartre 1976 [1960]: 351–63). Another way is that one realizes the dependency of the value and ultimate success of one's actions on others because they must choose to maintain a commitment to one's values when one is dead or infirm (Sartre 1949 [1948], 23–42). In addition, Sartre suggests that only through others can one's own pure facticity – one's body and vulnerability – be protected (Sartre 1992 [1983]: 272–94). This is Sartre's version of Hegelian pure recognition. Each protects what is essentially at the mercy of Others. By choosing to protect each other, the alienated social dimension of oneself is recovered and woven into the fabric of freedom, even if the reciprocating other is the weaver. Still another kind of reciprocity is described in Sartre's study of Genet. Often, one group of people defines another (e.g., Jews, Blacks, Gays) as alien (or Evil) by excluding them from humanity, thus solidifying an experience of themselves as all Good (or truly human). Such attempts abdicate freedom by claiming irrevocable Goodness. But the open future threatens any such claim. To the extent that one abides with one's freedom, one must acknowledge the ambiguity that qualifies both oneself and others. This allows one to accept a fundamental identity with others and reduces the urge to exclude and stigmatize them. Sartre further explores the nature of authenticity by clarifying the process of achieving it, which he calls "conversion." Conversion involves learning to fully acknowledge one's freedom and responsibility, instead of escaping them through self-deceptive maneuvers. Conversion is an active correlate of purifying reflection. In purifying reflection one discovers the major Sartrean truths: that human existence is contingent and without support, that values have no external or objective guarantees, that life is a series of freely chosen projects, and that each situation opens new possibilities. This emerges in a flash of recognition. Conversion simply abides with this experience, continuously living in accord with it. Instead of trying to imagine oneself outside history, one lives historically; instead of living oblivious to one's body, one accepts one's embodiment (Sartre 1992 [1983]: 471–514). But one also refuses to be engulfed by the given aspects of life; one refuses to be reduced to one's body, and one responds to the challenges of history. In effect, one lives inauthentically if one allows oneself to become reduced to facticity or if one tries to escape it entirely. One thus commits oneself to specific goals and values, but periodically reviews those commitments. By assuming one's freedom, one lives both within and ahead of history, both within and ahead of one's body, one's past, one's situation, one's social definition, and one's death.

In the later period of *The Critique of Dialectical Reason*, the locus of freedom shifts from consciousness to praxis. Praxis still transcends given situations, but now it is internally shaped by those situations and mediated by a variety of social and material conditions. Thus, Sartre better incorporates the historical weight of situations – the manner in which they make their own demands and bear their own inertia. This inertia derives from the conflicting projects of existing social groups, from the resources and technology handed down by past generations, and from scarcity. In this period Sartre acknowledges that history makes individuals as much as individuals make history. Further, he recognizes that profound social changes are required for most people to be free in the mundane sense of not being dominated by need. In addition, Sartre defines a social process of achieving reciprocal recognition through group action – often revolutionary action. The group-in-fusion emerges when members of a "street action" find themselves aiming at the same goal (often, defending themselves against an attack) and thus searching for an effective means. Here group praxis and individual praxis interpenetrate one another: each member is end and means for the others; each recognizes the other's action as her own; and each directs others only insofar as others also give direction (Sartre 1976 [1960]: 374–83). Sartre also claims that group action typically produces social structures that undermine the spontaneous freedom that a group initially discovers by pursuing collective action. The question thus becomes whether this kind of group reciprocity can be sustained over time. Even if it can, groups never escape an ominous background, e.g., an implicit fear that enforces every members pledge and sustains their brotherhood (Sartre 1976 [1960], pp. 428–44).

Sartre also discovers some other dimensions of alienation in this period. Scarcity produces alienation in that it turns humans against one another in competition. In addition, the current technology embodies the purposes of its creators, and thus current users must conform themselves to these purposes as they use it. To use a car is to live in an entire practical world created by the car, and this shapes the user's own goals and aspirations (Sartre 1976 [1960]: 161–96). Finally, there are the processes by which the group-in-fusion becomes an institution and thus common praxis returns to a condition of social seriality – the condition in which each is other to all the others, and in which only numerical relations exist between them (each is but one of many in a series) (Sartre 1976 [1960]: 664–70). A full overcoming of human alienation would require transforming these conditions. Sartre claims that these conditions make people subhuman. His dialectical ethics clarifies how people can combat the subhumanity in themselves and others.

Sartre's ultimate social aim is clear: a world in which everyone contributes to making history through common group praxis and where each recognizes all the others as history is created. Here each person is free in and through everyone else's freedom (Sartre 1992 [1983]: 468–71). To reach this goal, persons must give their present praxis this historical goal, finding ways to transform the subhumanity of themselves and others. The very condition of praxis foreshadows this aim, just as authenticity is foreshadowed in the dynamic of consciousness. Praxis can flee this implicit goal, however, by maintaining the present inhuman conditions; it does this by adopting and maintaining the values of the dominant order. To transform ourselves from subhuman to truly human, we must alter the historical conditions that create that subhumanity, including scarcity and ossified institutions. Sartre thinks the impetus for this transformation must come from the exploited and suppressed groups and classes, and the potential for such transformation is ever present, but achieving it is never guaranteed. "Ethics" now becomes the effort through which this potential freedom of all is pursued historically. Whether such efforts succeed, are defeated, deviate from their central goal, or undermine themselves depends on human choices and historical conditions. *The Critique* explores the many ways by which historical action can fail. The unpublished dialectical ethics suggests that failure is not inevitable.

Emmanuel Levinas (1906–95)

Levinas offers a new type of ethical theory, one which roots ethics in a fundamental relationship to other people. For Levinas this relationship establishes the fundamental ethical orientation, but the other person remains transcendent, alien, and inassimilable. Buber's I—Thou relationship offers a similar type of theory, but his ethically constitutive interpersonal relation is quite different. Levinas insists on an *asymmetry* between self and other while Buber's I—Thou relation creates sym-metry (both become "Thous" for each other). Levinas insists on the other's absolute transcendence, which prevents symmetry and reciprocity (Levinas 1969 [1961]: 39–40, 51–2). Levinas's other becomes manifest through the human face which both commands one (not to harm) and solicits one's aid; to respond to the other's face is to be responsible to the other and for the other (Levinas 1969 [1961]: 197–200).

Levinas challenges many Greek assumptions in western thought, including the primacy of Being and knowing. In western thought "being" is typically conceived as "what is present" – as the given. And knowing is a matter of assimilating or integrating or possessing Being. One challenge to this analysis of Being was issued by Heidegger, who drew attention to our practical relationship with tools and thus revealed a different kind of knowing (knowing how) and being (tools vs. objects). But Levinas suggests that tools are simply given in a different way and claims that Heidegger's concept of Being never really escapes the orbit of the notion of presence. For Levinas the other's *proximity* is prior to "presence" and makes it possible. The face that makes ethical demands is neither an object that comes to presence nor a tool. The face is a mystery that defies assimilation, and is thus beyond being and knowing in the ordinary sense. Also in knowledge a sovereign subject incorporates what is known, but the Other's command and helplessness shatter one's sovereignty and challenge one's efforts to possess (Levinas 1987 [1947]: 87–90). For these reasons the other is beyond knowledge. Levinas's ethics explores the implications of this mysterious other, which challenges the primacy of both ontology and epistemology. Levinas insists that ethics is first philosophy; it reveals the impossibility of possession, pure presence, and assimilation.

The task then becomes clarifying this fundamental relationship to others. No synthesis with the other is possible; thus no totality (a whole that integrates its parts) can unite self and other. Most interpersonal ideals derive from this notion of totality. For example, Hegelian reciprocal recognition produces a symmetrical harmony that binds the participants together into a new whole. This Hegelian model of unity is completely rejected by Levinas. Instead of inviting such harmony, the Other shatters one's self-possession and self-enclosure, rendering one vulnerable and exposed. To face the other is to answer an already existing summons, demand, and obligation. Others interrogate one; they are the source of one's sense of duty (Levinas 1969 [1961]: 82–4). For Heidegger the fundamental feature of human being is to be at issue; for Levinas the other (not Being or *Dasein's* essence) is the source of this decentering experience. Responding to this challenge is one's first ethical act. One's relationship to the other is like a relationship to infinity, which is perpetually beyond experience (Levinas 1969 [1961]: 48–52). Like time, the other is a dimension in which one is immersed but which one cannot circumscribe, delimit, or define. Like the genuine future, which is forever surprising, the other's face explodes one's own plans and purposes (Levinas 1987 [1947]: 79–81).

Levinas struggles to create appropriate metaphors to clarify this ethical relation to the other and explicate its importance, often using different metaphors in different books. In *Time and the Other* he uses physical pain, death, paternity, and heterosexual desire as useful analogies for this relation. Excruciating pain renders one impotent and shatters one's expectations – emphasizing one's helplessness – but one's response is immediate and pointed (Levinas 1987 [1947]: 68–71). This experience captures the urgency and intrusiveness of the other's call. Death is an ever-present possibility that cannot be assimilated or known, cannot be mastered or escaped. Moreover, it is not similarly threatened; one cannot rebel and dominate death. Facing the ethically fundamental other is like facing death – equally unfathomable, inassimilable, and relentless (Levinas 1987 [1947]: 71–7). In heterosexual erotic love, the other remains a mystery, distinct from oneself yet familiar; by caressing the beloved one yields to this mystery without trying to assimilate it. To caress is not to know or master another, but to meet him or her in an way entirely different from knowledge. In the caress one loses and risks oneself, and this risk is an essential element in ethical response (Levinas 1987 [1947]: 87–90). Finally, in paternity one is related to someone wholly other, but who carries one's legacy. The son offers the father a way to survive death. Fathers are reflected in sons, but sons are wholly distinct from and transcend their fathers (Levinas 1987 [1947]: 87–90). These metaphors help Levinas articulate the relationship to others that grounds ethical responsiveness.

In *Totality and Infinity*, Levinas challenges the concept of totality, replacing it with a relation to infinity. Just as self and other cannot be integrated, politics and ethics cannot be harmonized. Ethics concerns only this fundamental relation to the other; when more than one person is involved, each becomes a third with claims and interests to be weighed. Such weighing of competing interests produces the qualitatively different realm of politics and history. In politics everyone is treated as an object – each equal to the others, but in ethics self and other are never equal. In politics one's obligations to others can be limited, but not in ethics in which the other's command is absolute. One's ethical relation to others is not altered or transformed by history; it is not relative to history; indeed, it can be used to judge historical agents and eras (Levinas 1969 [1961]: 21–6). In this book Levinas develops his central conception of the face of the other. The face is exposed, naked, and defenseless, but it is also upright and commanding. Both higher and lower than oneself; both master and supplicant, the other's primary injunction is not to harm.

In *Otherwise Than Being or Beyond Essence*, these metaphors are reworked, and new ones emerge. Central is a notion of responsibility that involves substituting oneself for the other; Levinas now suggests that one bears the burden not only of one's response to the other, but also of the other's own actions. Thus Levinas moves beyond responsibility as responsiveness to bearing the other's responsibility. One answers for all the others (Levinas 1981 [1974]: 113–18). Such responsibility defines the structure of ethical subjectivity. Levinas realizes this assertion seems excessive, beyond what can be reasonably expected. But ethics is not a matter of reasonable expectations. It develops the implications of one's fundamental relationship with infinity. To assume this excessive responsibility is to leap beyond life and death, to transcend a life that seeks only to sustain itself.

For Levinas, there are no founding values and no basic principles; the core relationship to the other is the basis and source of all ethical obligations. Moreover, there are few arguments. Many of his formulations echo religious metaphors, but he recasts and revitalizes them. He paints conceptual pictures. He tries to show how his apparently abstract notions intersect with a wide diversity of experiences. Other interpretations of such experiences might be possible. But like those of many phenomenologists, his claims embody experiential insights. He is a clever critic of both Hegel and Heidegger, and it clearly the spiritual father of philosophies of dispersion, both in French feminism and in poststructuralism. He attempts to articulate the inexpressible.

Some Implications

In the introduction I indicated some features of Continental ethics that emerge from a contrast with contemporary Analytic ethical theory. I will return to this theme circuitously, first by exploring some apparent contrasts among the Continental ethical theories briefly sketched above, then by indicating some deeper similarities that will develop my earlier remarks and perhaps raise some challenges to the approaches to ethical theory described elsewhere in this book.

Three disagreements among the Continental thinkers seem apparent: (1) some believe that values are in some sense given (Hegel, Scheler, and Levinas) while others believe that they must be created (Nietzsche, Sartre); (2) some seek reciprocity and mutual recognition as their primary social ideal (Hegel, Scheler, Sartre) while others defend the value of a more agonal, asymmetrical relation to others (Nietzsche, Levinas); (3) some take freedom to be the fundamental and most defensible value (Hegel, Sartre) while others question the value of freedom and instead seek to defend a richer set of substantive ideals (Nietzsche, Scheler, Levinas). Each of these apparent oppositions deserves further examination.

The first contrast is less stable than it first appears. The kinds of givenness articulated by these thinkers are quite diverse. Hegel believes that ethics begins with the values of the existing culture; they provide the basic substance of ethical life. Scheler thinks that the emotions provide a window to an independent sphere of values. Levinas thinks the ethically fundamental other transcends, challenges, and calls each person to account. But each of these thinkers believes that the ethical agent must transform or respond to these given elements. Hegel thinks the existing values and institutions of the culture must be rationally interrogated and harmonized, pruned and refined, and above all tested for their contribution to mutual recognition. Scheler thinks that insight into the value hierarchy can always be broadened by moral visionaries (and exposure to alien cultures) and that everyone's creative task is to discover their moral tenors (which are often concealed by others' expectations or their own preoccupations) and to richly embody their distinctive values. Finally, Levinas think the ethical task is finding creative responses to the insistence of the other. The other's call is only a point of departure for serious ethical life; one's response is its core. So each theorist who takes fundamental values to be given also believes that living ethically requires a creative response to the givens, not merely an assimilation of them.

In contrast, the theorists who argue for the importance of value creation also believe this process must be guided by the givens of human existence and historical possibility. Sartre's concept of conversion involves learning to acknowledge the ambiguous reality of the human condition. Then one must commit oneself to values that will take the whole of humanity in promising directions. Sartre's ideal requires finding concrete ways to realize everyone's freedom amidst the cross-currents and inertia of the historical situation. In addition, Nietzsche's hopes for creating perfected human types depends on lucid knowledge of human psychology and cultural dynamics and seeks to find a role for existing virtues that stand the test of his rigorous revaluations. Both thinkers thus defend meta-values or boundary conditions within which new value creation is to occur; they thus indicate promising general directions.

In fact all the theorists acknowledge some dimension of value givenness and some demand for value revision; transformation, or creation. Thus, this initially sharp opposition in fact becomes a difference of degree and emphasis. This suggests the realism/constructivism debate is less clear and coherent than it initially appears. Many have felt that if only values can be given objective guarantees, the work of ethical theory will then be complete. The lesson here is that various kinds of objectivity play significant roles in ethical theory, and that serious ethical thought requires equally penetrating reflection on the individual's uptake of the objective elements. Most Continental ethicists accept both an objective element in and an essential individual contribution to genuine ethical life.

The second opposition concerns the ideal that informs social life: pure recognition vs. asymmetrical challenge. Though both Hegel and Sartre take reciprocal recognition as an ideal, both assert that conflict and struggle are necessary moments on the path to achieving it and that such struggle can make positive contributions to its emergence. Both master and slave learn essential lessons in Hegel's *Phenomenology*, and historical struggles provide the vehicle for the formation of groups that eventually achieve mutual recognition in Sartre's *Critique*. On the other hand, theorists like Nietzsche and Levinas – who extol the value of conflict or challenge in interpersonal life – do not sanction domination or oppression. The conflict produces a mutual enhancement or awakening that does not entail equality (for Nietzsche) or assimilation (for Levinas). Both of these thinkers value the way in which persons unsettle and challenge each other, thereby overcoming ethical stagnation and lassitude. Thus, here too the opposition between the two sides is a matter of degree and nuance. Both groups find an ethically productive role for conflict (negativity), and both acknowledge the virtue of some kind of mutuality or reciprocity as well. Even the seemingly most radically opposed thinkers, Hegel and Levinas, may be miscast. Hegelian recognition does not entail the assimilation of others and transcendence of their distinctiveness or their power to challenge. And despite his insistence on the commanding quality of the other, Levinas embraces a pacific ideal. These reflections show both the importance of intersubjectivity in Continental ethics – especially insofar as personal relations can be a source of ethical transformation – and the radically different ways in which one's ethical relationships with others are conceived (the egoism/altruism opposition is superseded by this conflict-harmony mix; see below).

The third dimension opposes thinkers valuing freedom to those seeking the realization of more substantive ideals. Once their positions are fully explicit, however, the concepts of freedom governing the ethics of both Sartre and Hegel are multifaceted, and – more importantly – rarely stand alone. Hegel expects free persons to breathe life into the their culture's roles and values. Sartre expects people to commit themselves to their own chosen ideals, so long as they remain consistent with the development of social freedom. Also, they both argue that a variety of additional conditions are necessary to achieving freedom. Thus, on closer analysis, they are committed to realizing a broad range of conditions and facets of freedom. On the other side, though Nietzsche is sharply critical of many conceptions of freedom, he values personal coherence and strength and frequently calls them "freedom." Also, while Scheler thinks persons are circumscribed by their basic moral tenors, these tenors nonetheless can be expanded through exposure to distinctive personal models, and he would acknowledge that living in accord with one's basic moral tenor is what many people mean by "freedom." Even Levinas – who generally stresses the demands others impose – accepts the value of a sphere of individual freedom and domesticity that allows people to respond to the other's call effectively. The real issue here concerns less the positive value of freedom or the range of substantive ideals embraced, but the meta-value or boundary-values that govern each think-er's theory (Hegelian recognition, Nietzschean vitality, Schelerian spirit, Sartre's community of ends; Levinas's responsibility to and for other). A kind of freedom finds its place in each theory, as do a variety of substantive ideals. But the meta-values determine the distinctive aspiration and direction of each theory; they indi-cate the real substantive differences among the theorists.

Examining each of these apparent oppositions has provided some clarification of the real issues at stake in Continental Ethics. I shall conclude with a discussion of five features that establish the distinctive conceptual space of Continental ethics. In the process, I will indicate some ways in which Analytic ethics may be misguided. To fully establish the superiority of the Continental "space" of ethical thought would require a separate paper, but at least its outlines can now be sketched.

First, one central assumption motivating ethical theory in the Analytic tradition is that the function of ethics is to combat the inherent egoism or selfishness of indi-viduals. Indeed, many thinkers define the basic goal of morality as "selflessness" or "altruism." Almost immediately this assumption gives ethical theory a policing func-tion, which is one of the reasons many Continental thinkers are skeptical of every-day "morality." For a multitude of reasons – partly because they respect the power of socialization, partly because they believe in a more complex human psychology, partly because they reject the claim that selfishness is always invidious – these think-ers bypass this obsession with selfishness. This does not mean they ignore the ethi-cal significance of interpersonal relations and intersubjectivity; they simply think that the egoism/altruism opposition obscures the function of ethics. For them the goal of ethical theory is awakening people to their higher selves, helping individuals find the inner and outer resources that will enable ethical flourishing. The goal, in effect, is not to police or circumscribe, but to awaken and enliven – to energize people to ethical creativity.

Second, and correlated with this point, Continental ethicists eschew theories of obligation and duty. Scheler expressed one central reason for this. Duties are prima-rily negative and typically dependent on values. Continental thinkers explore the underlying values and articulate the positive motivation for pursuing them. Their task is not to defend a set of regulations that everyone "must" obey – as if people were little children and ethical theorists were schoolmarms. Rather they seek to produce an awakening – as if people all-too-often sleepwalk through their lives. Duties, imperatives, rules, and regulations only deepen this daze (which one might call ethical death), and for that reason they are suspect. This is another reason why I suggested at the outset that Continental thinkers think "morality" narrowly con-strued is itself immoral. Even if such moralities were to succeed, at best they would produce befogged herd people (as Nietzsche suggested). One cannot be inspired by interdictions, but one can be moved by higher values. Finding a way to light this "spark" is one central task of Continental ethical theories.

Third, reason has a different role in Continental ethical theory than in Analytic theories. Initially, "reason" may be defined more broadly (to include, for example, Hegel's dialectical reason), or it may be construed to require a more psychological penetration and subtlety in grasping specific human types and individuals (such as Nietzsche sought with his "genius of the heart"), or it may be reinterpreted entirely as a "logic of the heart" (such as Scheler claimed to discover). But rarely is practical reason a matter of deductive arguments with major and minor premises, nor is it a matter of weighing competing considerations on some commensurable dimension (e.g., happiness or utility), nor is it a matter of providing a indubitable rational justification for some first principle of justice or benevolence. Continental theorists do rationally defend their own *theories*, but one implication of most of their theories is that cognition is only one element of living ethically, and the kind of cognition involved requires subtle analysis. Some might be tempted to claim that these theorists are non-cognitivists, but in fact they are all seeking to articulate a different kind of cognition, one more suited to the real requirements of serious ethical life.

Fourth, Continental ethicists rarely seek or defend a single set of universal values to which everyone is expected to aspire. They do not embrace relativism, and they do not think everyone's "values" are equally good. But they acknowledge that they are different human types, and that different ethos may better realize the highest possibilities of each type. Even Scheler – who was a realist about values – insists that different personalities have distinct basic moral tenors and that these must be respected and enhanced. Hegel might recommend different educational institutions and communal structures for those pursuing very different roles (e.g., political leader, householder, artist, farmer). Nietzsche most assuredly had different guidelines and goals for different human types. They all recognize the value of discovering and defending meta-values or general directions for human aspiration, but at best that is the first step. The serious ethical thinking comes when one examines the manifold ways of pursuing these directions or instantiating these meta-values. Continental theorists above all seek genuine ethical achievement. This is why they examine the many ways in which people get derailed and the conditions that can improve their odds. Contrast this with the central project of Analytic ethics – to produce a rational foundation for a small set of universal principles – and the differences between the traditions become evident.

Fifth, Continental ethical theories nearly always define and respond to the larger cultural stakes of their historical eras. Hegel reacts to the French Revolution, as well as to Kant. Nietzsche responds to the rise of mass culture and to Wagnerian art, as well as to Schopenhauer. Scheler responds to the vicissitudes of the First World War, as well as to Husserl and Brentano. Sartre and Levinas in different ways respond to the horrors of the Second World War, as well as to Heidegger. Their ethical theories do not succeed or fail because of these historical conditions, but these larger cultural developments are never far from their minds. So much of Analytic ethics seems oblivious to the major issues of the larger culture; it almost prides itself on its diffidence toward such developments. Only some of the revolutionary approaches indicated above have registered some awareness of current cultural realities. None of the Continental theories have become outdated because these cultural contexts have receded. Their analysis of the culture's core issues was sufficiently penetrating that most remain alive today. People are not abstract place-holders outside of all time and place; they are historically situated. Explorations of their self-enhancement must take account of this situatedness if they are to be effective.

Finally, the most distinctive feature of Continental ethical theory is that it is not really isolated from metaphysics, philosophical anthropology, philosophical sociology and psychology, or epistemology. One can discuss the ethical elements of Continental theories separately, but they are not really produced independently. They are woven into a systematic treatment of a range of issues, and the confidence one develops in a particular ethical perspective is often connected to one's confidence in the overall system. Analytic philosophy has taken another path. It treats the separate areas of philosophy as distinct specializations, and the issues within each specialty often become detached from any larger systematic vision. Perhaps the reason Continental ethics has attracted so little interest among ethicists in the Analytic tradition is that they find such larger systematic visions alien. But the deeper reason is that the project, perspective, and assumptions informing Continental ethics really are different. Perhaps by clarifying some of these differences, I have created a way to appreciate the force and challenge of Continental ethics. Perhaps I have also raised some questions about the value of Analytic ethics as it is all-too-often pursued.

References

Boyd, R.: "How to be a Moral Realist," Sayre-McCord, G., ed. *Essays on Moral Realism* (Ithaca, NY: Cornell University Press, 1988).

Foot, P.: *Virtues and Vices* (Los Angeles: University of California Press, 1978).

Hegel, G. W. F.: *Phenomenology of Spirit*, trans. A. V. Miller (Oxford: Clarendon Press, 1977) [1807].

——: *The Philosophy of Right*, trans. T. M. Knox (Oxford: Oxford University Press, 1967) [1821].

Levinas, E.: *Otherwise Than Being or Beyond Essence*, trans. Alphonso Lingis (The Hague: Martinus Nijhoff, 1981) [1974].

——: *Time and the Other*, trans. Richard Cohen (Pittsburg: Duquesne University Press, 1987) [1947].

——: *Totality and Infinity*, trans. Alphonso Lingis (Pittsburg: Duquesne University Press, 1969) [1961].

MacIntyre, A.: *After Virtue* (Notre Dame, IN.: University of Notre Dame Press, 1981).

McDowell, J: "Values and Secondary Qualities" in Honderich, T., ed.: *Morality and Objectivity* (London: Routledge & Kegan Paul, 1985).

Murdoch, I: *The Soverignty of the Good* (London: Cambridge University Press, 1970).

Nagel, T.: *Mortal Questions* (New York: Cambridge University Press, 1979).

Nietzsche, F.: *Beyond Good and Evil*, trans. Walter Kaufmann in *Basic Writings of Nietzsche* (New York: Random House, 1968) [1886, 1887].

——: *Daybreak*, trans. R. J. Hollingdale (Cambridge: Cambridge University Press, 1982) [1881].

——: *The Gay Science*, trans. Walter Kaufmann (New York: Random House, 1974) [1882, 1887].

——: *The Genealogy of Morals*, trans. Walter Kaufmann and R. J. Hollingdale in *Basic Writ-

ings of Nietzsche (New York: Random House, 1967) [1887].

——: *Thus Spoke Zarathustra*, trans. Walter Kaufmann (New York: Viking, 1954) [1883–85].

——: *Twilight of Idols*, trans. Walter Kaufmann in *The Portable Nietzsche* (New York: Viking, 1954) [1888].

Noddings, N: *Caring: A Feminist Approach to Ethics and Moral Education* (Berkeley: University of California Press, 1986).

Nussbaum, M.: *Love's Knowledge* (New York: Oxford University Press, 1990).

Sartre, J.-P.: *Being and Nothingness*, trans. Hazel Barnes (New York: Philosophical Library, 1956) [1943].

——: *Critique of Dialectical Reason, Volume 1*, trans. Alan Sheridan-Smith (London: New Left Books, 1976) [1960]

——: "Existentialism is a Humanism," trans. Philip Mairet in *Existentialism from Dostoevsky to Sartre*, ed. Walter Kaufmann (Cleveland, OH: World Publishing, 1956) [1946].

——: *Notebooks for an Ethics*, trans. David Pellauer (Chicago, IL: University of Chicago Press, 1992) [1983].

——: *Saint Genet, Actor and Martyr*, trans. Bernard Frechtman (New York: George Braziller, 1963) [1952].

——: *What is Literature?*, trans. Bernard Frechtman (New York: Philosophical Library, 1949) [1948].

Scheler, M.: *Formalism in Ethics and a Non-Formal Ethic of Values: A New Attempt Toward the Foundation of an Ethical Personalism*, trans. Manfred S. Frings and Roger L. Funk, 5th rev. edn. (Evanston, IL: Northwestern University Press, 1973a) [1913–16].

——: *The Nature of Sympathy*, trans. Peter Heath (Hamden, Connecticut: Archon Books, 1970) [1913].

——: *Person and Self Value: Three Essays*, trans. Manfred Frings (Dordrecht: Martinus Nijhoff, 1987).

——: *Philosophical Perspectives*, trans. Oscar Haac (Boston: Beacon Press, 1958).

——: *Ressentiment*, trans. William Holdheim, ed. Lewis Coser (New York: Free Press, 1961) [1912].

——: *Selected Philosophical Papers*, trans. David Lachterman (Evanston, IL: Northwestern University Press, 1973b).

Slote, M.: *From Morality to Virtue* (New York: Oxford University Press, 1992).

Stocker, M.: *Plural and Conflicting Values* (New York: Oxford University Press, 1990).

Taylor, C.: *Sources of the Self* (Cambridge, MA: Harvard University Press, 1989).

Wallace, J.: *Virtues and Vices* (Ithaca, NY: Cornell University Press, 1978).

Chapter 20

Pragmatic Ethics

Hugh LaFollette

Pragmatism is a philosophical movement developed near the turn of the century in the work of several prominent American philosophers, most notably, Charles Sanders Peirce, William James, and John Dewey. Although many contemporary analytic philosophers never studied American Philosophy in graduate school, analytic philosophy has been significantly shaped by philosophers strongly influenced by that tradition, most especially W. V. Quine, Donald Davidson, Hilary Putnam, and Richard Rorty. Like other philosophical movements, it developed in response to the then-dominant philosophical wisdom. What unified pragmatism was its rejection of certain epistemological assumptions about the nature of truth, objectivity, and rationality. The rejection of these assumptions springs from the pragmatist's belief that practice is primary in philosophy. Meaningful inquiry originates in practice. Theorizing is valuable, for sure, but its value arises from practice, is informed by practice, and, its proper aim is to clarify, coordinate, and inform practice. Theorizing divorced from practice is useless.

Pragmatism is at once both familiar and radical. Familiar in that it often begins with rather ordinary views; radical in that it often sees in those views insights that philosophers and lay people miss or misunderstand. A pragmatic ethic employs criteria without being criterial. It is objective without being absolutist. It acknowledges that ethical judgements are relative, without being relativistic. And it tolerates – indeed, welcomes – some moral differences, without being irresolute. Precisely what each of these means, and why pragmatists hold them, emerges throughout this paper. I begin with the first since it sets the stage for introducing other pivotal pragmatic ideas.

Ethical theorizing begins when we think about how we ought to live. Many people assume that means we must look for moral criteria: some list of rules or principles whereby we can distinguish good from bad and right from wrong, or a list of virtues we try to inculcate. Utilitarians tell us we should promote the greatest happiness of the greatest number. Contractualists tell to look for the criteria emerging from a real or hypothetical agreement. Kantians tell us to treat others as "ends in themselves" and not as mere means. Divine Command theorists tell us to follow the commands of God. So, many will wonder: What are the pragmatists' criteria? How do they distinguish right from wrong? Although pragmatists may employ moral criteria, pragmatism is not criterial.

The Primacy of Habits

When I say that most moral theories are *criterial*, I mean that the theories hold, at least in some attenuated form, that the relevant criteria are (a) logically prior, (b) fixed, (c) complete, and (d) directly applicable. Although many philosophers might deny that their views are criterial on this account, the character of most discussions in ethics suggests this view is still influential if not dominant. Thus, although the principle of utility might be revealed though experience, its truth is thought (a) to be logically prior to experience and (b) to provide a measure for determining what is moral for all people, at all times. Moreover, this principle (c) does not need to be supplemented, and (d) can be directly applied to specific cases. Likewise for deontological theories. Using the model of law, they envision a set of external rules or principles that tell us how we ought to act. To this extent, most deontologists share certain presuppositions with divine command theorists, namely, that *if* morality is to be binding, its source must be independent of those whom it "binds."

Pragmatists disagree. If they speak of criteria at all, they think of them as tools for analysis, as heuristics isolating morally relevant features of action – features people should consider in making moral decisions. Criteria are neither logically prior nor fixed since they can be, and often are, supplanted. They are not complete, since central elements of moral judgement cannot be subsumed under them. And they are not directly applicable since principles cannot give us univocal direction on how we should behave in every circumstance.

The pragmatist's rejection of a criterial view of morality springs from its rejection of the notion of rationality undergirding that view. The belief that morality is primarily conscious adherence to prior and fixed criteria overrationalizes human beings. Many philosophers believe, or speak as if they believe, that everything significant about us involves conscious deliberation. Not so. We could not walk or speak or think the ways we do if we had to consciously determine to take each step, to speak or write the next word, or to add two numbers. Deliberation *is* vital. However, as I explain later, its central role is normally not to *directly* guide action, but to shape, change, and reinforce habits, and therefore to indirectly guide action. This is a significant role since most human activity is habitual. Therefore, before we can understand deliberation's proper role, we must first explore the pragmatist's notion of habit. This notion shows how a pragmatic ethic incorporates common and theoretical ideas of morality, yet uses them in ways that differ from standard uses. My account is strongly influenced by Dewey's ideas, especially the rich notion of habit he developed in *Human Nature and Conduct* (1988 [1922]). Nonetheless, I will not engage in squabbles over textual interpretation. Rather, I loosely employ Dewey's work to explain habit and its role in ethical theory.

The nature of habits

Even those who recognize that conscious deliberation does not play the directing role assigned it by some philosophers might be leery of giving primacy to habits. After all, many of us assume habits are behavioral repetitions, largely beyond our control, and often negative. We tend to construe habits as external forces making us bite our nails, compelling us to drink, and leading us to be lazy, etc. However, habits are not mere repetitions, they are not necessarily bad, and they are not forces compelling us against our wills. At least properly understood they are not.

Habits carry the past into the present. What we learn and experience are not mere flashes on the cosmic stage; they continue in the present, unified and embodied in our habits. Habits, in this robust sense, have four principal elements: (1) They are influenced by our previous interactions with the social environment. (2) They are not simple acts but organized sets of smaller actions. (3) They are typically exhibited in overt behavior in a variety of circumstances, and (4) even when they are not exhibited in standard ways, they are nonetheless operative.

Consider a mundane action: walking. (1) Walking is learned by prior activity within our environment – it takes practice to walk, and still more practice to walk well. (2) Walking is not a single action, but a systemization of "smaller" actions: moving our feet and arms, looking ahead, and varying our paths to avoid obstacles, etc. (3) The habit is present in overt behavior: in the appropriate circumstances, we will walk in the ways we learned how to walk. Finally, (4) the habit is operative, even when not immediately guiding behavior. What makes us walkers is not merely what we do when we walk, but what we do when we are not walking. Walkers think, remember, and imagine differently than non-walkers. This is obviously true of the wheelchair bound. It is equally (but differently) true of people who can walk, but rarely do. A walker might think of her office as "a twenty-minute walk" from home, while a non-walker describes it as a five-minute drive. Walkers will also imagine the future differently than someone who normally travels by auto: their dreams about and plans for a trip to the Alps will differ substantially from those who primarily travel by car.

Thinking is also habitual. (1) Thinking is learned by prior activity – it takes practice to think, and considerably more practice to think well. If we could think effortlessly, we wouldn't need to be educated. Yet, we do need to be educated, and there is ample evidence that some types of education encourage more and better thinking than others. (2) Thinking requires a systemization of discrete intellectual actions. To think well, we must discern the relevant point, remember crucial details, trace the implications of our views, and evaluate those implications. (3) Thinking exhibits itself in overt behavior. When appropriately trained, we will question what we have been told, will engage in heated conversations, etc. Finally (4) thinking is operative, even if not immediately guiding behavior. Thinkers will consider options, entertain ideas, and imagine possibilities, even if there is no one with whom to converse or no way in which the thought leads to immediate overt action. I could give a similar analysis of emotions, etc., but I trust that is unnecessary.

Habits empower and restrict

Habits are two-edged swords: the very features that give us power to act and to think also circumscribe us. Without habits we could not learn from experience; our actions would be haphazard and ineffective. Yet habits also limit us since, while they are operating, we are myopic. You cannot be a scientist if you investigate everything, not even everything within the province of your science. You must look at or for some particular phenomenon. Yet that may lead you to overlook other significant phenomena. Similarly language empowers us, since, without language, we could say nothing; yet it constrains us since we can say only what we can say in that language. As habitual creatures we must walk a fine line between (a) blindly letting habits have their sway, and (b) constantly evaluating them. Neither option is optimal. We can plod through life, mindlessly absorbing the habits of our culture, and never intentionally changing them. Or, we may become so interested "in the delights of reflection; we become afraid of assuming the responsibilities of decisive choice and action . . ." (Dewey 1988 [1922]: 137). Or, as Gadamer puts it, we must both recognize and struggle against our histories (1975). Knowing how to do that is itself a second order habit, developed by practice, over time.

Social nature of habits

Speaking about an *individual's* habits of walking, talking, or thinking might suggest that habits are purely personal possessions. They are not. Since habits are shaped by prior experience, our cultures play a central role in forming our habits, in forming who we are. How we eat, how we talk, what we read, what we believe, and how we think all began in the "instruction" (either formal or by example) we received growing up. Culture is best understood as the social transmission of habits. We inherit (and then refine) habits from our ancestors who inherited (and refined) habits from their ancestors, who . . . , etc. We live in cities rather than caves not because we are more clever than our cave-dwelling ancestors, but because we had "better" ancestors than they did. Ours gave us universities and the Internet; theirs gave them cave paintings. Recognizing this fundamental debt to others, Dewey claims, is the root of all virtue. "It is of grace and not ourselves that we lead civilized lives" (20). Once we recognize that we are who we are and live the lives we live because of our predecessors, then we must recognize that the habits we give our progeny and our peers will likewise shape their worlds, their lives, and their habits.

Habits and will

The fact that social forces shape habits might suggest that individuals cannot choose, and are thus not responsible for, what they do. Far from it. Habits – including our traits, abilities, and character – do carry the marks of our environment. That is the sense in which our habits are ineliminably social. They also embody our previous choices, including our choices to strengthen or alter our habits. That is the sense in which the habits are our own. Habits are the primary vehicles for transmitting our past choices into present action. Thus habits "constitute the self; they are will" (Dewey 1988 [1922]: 21).

Unless we appreciate that social influences and individual choice are wed in habits, then human action and will seem mysterious, the result of decisions by unseen and unexplainable homunculi. Why do some people become writers while others become accountants and others, clerks? Why are some people honest while others are dishonest? Why do some people work hard, while other piddle away their lives? Without habits, which carry past experience and decisions into the present and the future, actions must be created and continuously recreated by brute will. However, that is nothing more than "belief in magic . . . [whereby we hope] to get results without intelligent control of means" (Dewey 1988 [1922]: 22).

Changing habits

We can change the habits we "inherit." But we cannot change them directly and immediately. To believe we could is to believe in mental magic. Too often we think we can close our eyes, tell ourselves to become more honest, more caring, more hardworking, and that, if we just wish hard enough, our dreams will come true. However, believing this will work, as so many self-help books suggest, makes personal change difficult if not impossible. Real change requires hard work, attention to detail, and perseverance. Habits are changed not by private willing, but (a) by identifying and (b) then altering the conditions that make and sustain our habits, and finally, (c) by substituting a more productive habit for the old, detrimental one.

Unfortunately, many of us continue to think (or hope) that we shape our desires and frame our intentions in the recesses of a private mind. However, we do not even form intentions privately. Genuine intentions are themselves habits acquired, developed, and enhanced over time. As a child, I daydreamed of being Superman, of being an astronaut, and of being a soldier. I envisioned myself zipping though the sky "faster than a speeding bullet," rocketing to the moon, and singlehandedly besting an enemy squad. Nonetheless, it would be silly to say that I intended to become an astronaut or solider, or that I desired to be Superman. Daydreams are neither intentions nor desires. They are mental magic. Humans cannot fly unaided. Moreover, although some people are astronauts and others are soldiers, the belief that I could be either merely by dreaming is no less magical than the belief that I could be Superman.

Yet we continue to confuse daydreams with intentions. We assume that if we pleasantly contemplate some goal, then we desire to achieve that goal, and that if we contemplate it often, then we intend to achieve it. Thus, I might assume that I want to quit smoking if I think about quitting. I might assume that I desire to be calm, patient, and less judgmental if I imagine myself doing so. However, passing thoughts are neither desires nor intentions. They are adult daydreams. Daydreams are not necessarily bad; they can provide grist for the intention mill. However, unless we use daydreams to prompt specific plans, then we are reveling in fantasies, not forming desires or intentions.

Someone might contend that I am altering the meaning of common terms. I don't think so. If I am, it is a desirable alteration. Deciding which terms to use has significant practical implications. If we confuse daydreams with intentions and desires, then we are prone to comfort ourselves by saying that we are *really* kind, hardworking, intelligent, honest, and self-directed – no matter how we act. However, if we insist that we have intentions and desires only if we make specific plans (take specific steps) toward that end – then we can judge ourselves and others by what we do, not by inspecting private scenarios dancing before our minds. We can legitimately claim to be kind only if we act kindly, we can legitimately claim to be honest, only if we are regularly honest.

How, then, do we turn daydreams into realities? How do we reshape our habits? None of us designed our initial environments, and none of completely designed our current ones. That is why we do not completely control our habits or our lives (Nussbaum 1986). But we do have some control, and that control depends on our understanding, and then deliberately altering, the conditions which made and sustain our habits. "Social reformers" and "social engineers" alter the environment to prompt changes in others. We can each engineer our own environments to alter our habits. Sometimes we merge these mechanisms: we change the social environment to help us change our personal habits, for instance, by placing high taxes on tobacco or supporting tough laws against drunk driving. Each mechanism relies on the intervening hand of deliberation: purposefully adjusting the environment to diminish, eliminate, or strengthen our (or others') habits. However, deliberation is no mysterious occult property. It is an intellectual habit developed and refined by previous experiences, stimuli, and deliberations. As Mill might say it, "the deliberative and the moral, like the muscular powers, are improved only by being used" (Mill 1985 [1885]).

Multiple habits

However, if we have only one (or a few) narrow habit(s), our chance of changing faulty habits and finding satisfactory substitutes is less likely. We would be like a chess player who knows only one opening or a musician who plays only one tune. If our opponent makes a different first move, or if the only musical composition we know ("Joy to the World") is inappropriate in the circumstances (a funeral), then we do not know how to continue. On the other hand, good chess players know different openings and employ different strategies. Their knowledge and strategies are habits which pave the intellectual roads along which chess-playing deliberation tends to travel. This is essential for being a good chess-player: these habits empower the player to respond appropriately to their opponents' first moves, even moves they have never seen. More generally, multiple habits empower us to be sensitive to wide varieties of situations, thereby making us more responsive to the relevant features of each situation. That is why multiple habits help explain creativity, whether of chess-playing or of life. Creativity is not some inexplicable, mysterious inner power. It arises from a wide set of habits, unified within one person.

The reality of multiple habits not only empowers us to change habits, it also explains the appearance of seemingly uncharacteristic behavior. Suppose Ron is a kindly fellow: generally he responds sympathetically to others in pain. One day, though, he snaps at Belinda who asks him for help. "Why," he says, "are you always bugging me. Go pester someone else." Everyone, even Belinda, recognizes Ron is "out of character." But what does that mean? Does than mean someone other than Ron was snappish with her? No. It just means that being snappish is one of Ron's habits. Normally, it is dominated by more powerful habits. As Ron develops a more unified character, his tendency to snappishness becomes less and less potent; snappish behavior becomes even more uncharacteristic. But it does not disappear. It occasionally rears its ugly head.

Morality is a Habit

I am now able to explain more precisely how understanding the nature of habit illuminates morality. I will first show how moral habits are like other habits, and then show how the notion of habits help explicate central elements of a pragmatic ethic.

Their structure is like other habits

Many people claim that although other actions might be habitual, moral action cannot be. After all, they think that in standard cases moral agents must distinguish right from wrong by consciously applying the appropriate criteria. Of course those embracing this view often disagree about the source and nature of these criteria, and thus offer competing normative theories. However, pragmatists claim that morality, like all significant aspects of life, is not the product of immediate and direct conscious deliberation. If we always (or even often) had to rely on wholly conscious choice to be moral, we would be even less moral than we are. John trips on the sidewalk; Susan reaches down to help him up while Robin walks by. Later Susan has to decide how to handle a dispute between two co-workers; in an adjoining office Robin faces a similar decision. Susan is very sensitive to the way her decision will affect the interests of all involved; Robin is indifferent. What distinguishes Susan from Robin? In the first case Susan saw John and immediately reached out to him. Robin never seriously considered helping; perhaps he didn't even "see" him. In the second case Susan recognized and considered the interests of those involved; Robin likely did not recognize and certainly did not seriously consider his co-worker's interests. The core difference between Susan and Robin is not between their conscious decisions – although those may also differ. The central difference is in what they are habitually disposed (a) to see, (b) to consider relevant, (c) to think about, and (d) to use in guiding their actions.

Like Susan, people who are moral standardly do not *decide* to consider the interests of others, they are the kind of people – they have the appropriate habits – who just consider others' interests. Of course when we are being considerate, we may think about the best ways to help the other. But these deliberations are likewise shaped by our habits (just as the deliberations of philosophers are shaped by their professional habits). The aim of moral education (whether by others or ourselves) is to make us habitually sensitive to the needs and interests of others, and to shape the ways we think about, consider, and promote their interests.

Which habits does morality shape? Since, under special circumstances, virtually any behavior can affect others' interests, then no action and no habit is wholly outside the moral domain. However, just as Dewey warns of the dangers of overrationalization, he also warns about the dangers of overmoralization. So a pragmatist will, except in unusual circumstances, be concerned only with habits that regularly and significantly affect others. These "moral habits" have the same structure as other habits.

(1) They are influenced by prior activity, especially the interaction with our social environment. We may later alter or reject the habits so inculcated, but what we alter or reject is given in prior activity. (2) Moral habits are not simple acts, but an organized array of action. To be benevolent we must interpret our situation as one in which someone needs assistance, we must discern the assistance she needs, and we must provide that assistance. (3) Morals normally exhibit themselves in overt behavior. Someone who is kind will act kindly in a variety of circumstances. Someone who claims to be kind simply because he has kind thoughts is either a liar or has mistaken daydreams for intentions. Finally, (4) even when moral habits are not apparent, they are operative, even if subconsciously. Benevolent people do not always give to others. Sometimes they demand that others help themselves. Even in these cases, however, the benevolent person may worry if she has acted appropriately, may feel regret if she thinks she has not, and may contemplate ways to help others help themselves.

Like other habits, moral habits empower and restrict. They empower because, in embodying previous learning, they permit us to respond quickly and appropriately in morally serious situations. Yet they also restrict, since, when operating, we overlook aspects of our action that may be morally relevant. Hence, we not only need first-order habits making us sensitive to others' interests, we also need second-order habits to evaluate those first-order habits to insure that they are appropriate, especially in changing circumstances. Being fallibilists, pragmatists know that no habit is flawless.

Morality is social

Pragmatists understand why we are inclined to think that morals are personal; after all, individuals are typically the immediate source from which actions proceed. However, this should not lead us to forget that society plays the central role in creating, transmitting, and reshaping our habits. Like Aristotle before him (1985), Dewey recognizes the power of society to make us virtuous or vicious. If we have been well trained, and then taught how to evaluate our habits, then we will be generally be moral. On the other hand, if our moral training has been directed by ignorant, narrowminded folk or selfish oafs, we will likely have seriously flawed moral character.

That is why believing that we are the sole authors of our moral habits is no different from believing that breathing and digestion are wholly private actions. We know that we can breathe only if there is oxygen in the atmosphere, and we can eat only if there is food to ingest. Yet somehow we are tend to think that "honesty, chastity, malice, peevishness, courage, triviality, industry, irresponsibility, are . . . private possessions" (1988 [1922]: 16). Not so. Our habits are essentially social, even if, once they are "ours," we must take responsibility for them. Once we realize the character of social influences, we can avoid either of two intolerable extremes: (a) seeing individuals as mere products of social forces who lack any personal responsibility or (b) conceiving of them as wholly autonomous, free from all social influences.

> There are two schools of social reform. One bases itself upon the notion of a morality which springs from an inner freedom, something mysteriously cooped up within personality. It asserts that the only way to change institutions is for men to purify their own hearts, and that when this has been accomplished, change of institutions will follow of itself. The other school denies the existence of any such inner power, and in some doing, conceives that it has denied all moral freedom. It says that men are made what they are by the forces of their environment, that human nature is purely malleable, and that until institutions are changed, nothing can be done. Clearly this leaves the outcome as hopeless as does an appeal to inner rectitude and benevolence. For it provides no leverage to change the environment . . . There is an alternative . . . We can recognize that all conduct is an *interaction* between elements of human nature and the environment, natural and social. (Dewey 1988 [1922]: 9–10)

Changing habits for moral reasons

Habits are the products of ongoing "natural selection": many habits are tried, but few are chosen. Those "chosen," are "selected" because they are advantageous in the environments in which we live. However, unlike most creatures, we can deliberate and we can alter our own environments. We thereby influence which habits we maintain and which we change. Among other things, we can develop a second order habit of taking responsibility for maintaining or changing or habits, and that (meta-) habit, once acquired, will make us more reflective about our habits of speech, thought, and action. It is not enough to understand the conditions that create, sustain, and alter our habits. We must also have the ability to change our first level habits in light of that understanding. Let me offer an example.

I grew up a bigot, living in a land of bigots. I walked, talked, acted, thought, and imagined like a bigot. I had no acquaintance with blacks, and no experience or habits to prompt me to change my bigoted habits. I enjoyed my (relatively) privileged status, although I did not see my status as privileged – I saw it as reflecting some natural order of things. My upbringing and social norms blinded me to my bigotry. At that point I was unlikely to change my racist ways, since the same conditions which shaped these habits also shaped my deliberative abilities. How could I see my flaws?

Then changes in my social environment spurred personal changes. I watched and listened as blacks challenged their inferior legal and moral status. Their elegant words and courageous deeds clashed with my bigoted habits. At first I "sought" ways to discount these clashes, to find ways of maintaining my current habits. However, the habits that were once so comfortable in my bigoted niche, became ineffective in the early 1960s. I was forced to evolve, although initially not much. I first began to think blacks should be able to drink at the same water fountain with whites. Ethical tokenism, for sure. But a change nonetheless.

The conditions that prompted me to reevaluate my habits did not prompt everyone in my environment to make similar changes. That is not surprising. Since I was younger and my habits were less entrenched than those of my elders, my habits were more susceptible to different experiences. I had relatively few habits which would lead me to discount emerging evidence about the interests and abilities of blacks. Likely I also had beneficial habits of self-reflection. Still, it is vital to recognize that my first changes were prompted by alternations in my external environment. These opened the door for deliberation about and reflection on my racism. Without those external changes, I would likely not have abandoned my bigoted ways.

That is the story of moral evolution: our moral habits change when shifts in the environment force us to move into new moral niches. These initial changes are not brought about by brute force of will. To believe they are is to believe in moral magic, and Dewey repeatedly warned us of the costs of belief in magic: we lose the ability to make real changes. Of course these environmental changes were doubtless spurred by the deliberations and actions of others. But, then, that is exactly what Dewey claims. The route to real change in others and in ourselves is to deliberately change our environments. And that we can do: we are not rudderless ships on a moral sea.

In deliberating about matters moral, we do not – or should not – merely consult some small (moral) segment of our experience. Having a variety of habits is a crucial element of moral deliberation: it increases our ability to think about problems in different ways. We draw on all our experience, on all our habits: our understanding of ourselves, others, biology, economics, and politics. For instance, in deciding whether to be sympathetic to Joe, we not only need to understand what is morally relevant, we must understand Joe's condition and see what is most important to him. Otherwise our efforts may do more harm than good.

So deliberation *is* crucial. But how do we learn to deliberate and to deliberate well? Practice. We must first learn to deliberate badly, before we learn to deliberate well. Bad deliberative habits typically lead to bad results and are pruned by the process of natural selection. Productive deliberative habits tend to lead to success – especially in the right educational environment. We learn how better to think, imagine, and understand. We can develop our moral imagination, understanding, and thought by engaging in sustained and careful discussion of practical ethical quandaries, by talking to people (or reading about people) who have faced significant moral choices, by reading great literature, and by reading philosophical treatises on ethics. Although these deliberative means may lack the immediacy, texture, and depth of actual decisions, they can prepare us to handle real decisions by making us attuned to features and consequences of our actions which, in the press of time, we might overlook. Deliberation amplifies relatively small environmental changes, so that we can evaluate, and perhaps change, our habits *relatively* independently of dramatic external forces. Rather than suffer bad consequences from detrimental changes in environments, we can, as Popper would say, "let hypotheses die in our stead."

Ends and Means

In working to change their habits, people assume they must formulate an end (to change the habit), and then seek the means to that end. However, this ordinary understanding of the relationship between ends and means easily misleads us. Most people think ends are fixed goals motivating activity, and means are the routes to achieving those ends. If Susan says she wants to become a lawyer, then her goal – her desired end point – is to be a lawyer. Given that she has this end, she must now decide how to achieve that end, she must find the means to employ. These means will have no value in themselves; they are merely the route to the desired end.

This is a skewed account of the relation between ends and means, an account that, once incorporated into folk psychology, distorts our understanding of deliberation, human action, and morality. Means and ends are not fundamentally different. Rather they are "two names for the same reality. The terms denote not a division in reality, but a distinction in judgement. . . . The 'end' is merely a series of acts viewed at a removed state; and a means is merely the series viewed at an earlier time . . ." (Dewey 1988 [1922]: 27–8). Initially this claim seems preposterous. Surely there is all the difference in the world between the ends one seeks, and the methods one uses to achieve those ends. Susan's goal is to become a lawyer; so she studies for the LSAT, goes to law school, and works as a waitress in a local restaurant – all are the means for achieving those ends. What is mysterious about that?

Understood as a division in judgement, nothing. But since the division is thought to be fundamental, its standard characterization leads people to misunderstand both ends and means. People come to think of ends as fixed, determinate goals lying somewhere outside activity. The goal provides value and meaning to human action; the only value lies in achieving the remote ends. However, ends are not the source of value nor does "reaching" an "end" complete action. Ends are not really ends to action, but at most a redirection of it. Susan does not stop acting when she becomes a lawyer. Being a lawyer is action.

> Ends arise and function within action. They are not, as current theories too often imply, things lying beyond activity at which that latter is directed. They are not strictly speaking ends or termini of action at all. They are terminals of deliberation, and so turning points *in* activity. (Dewey 1988 [1922]: 154)

Put differently, the end's value does not lie beyond human activity, but it helps organize and focus activity. Susan enjoys doing lawyerly activities, and being a lawyer is the best way to allow her to continue doing those activities. Ends become ways of collectively understanding our efforts and actions. They are like the end of a story. It provides a perspective from which we can understand the story's elements. It is not some element outside the story.

Suppose Francine wants to become educated. The standard view suggests that "being educated" is some fixed, remote end she can achieve by attending university. However, studying, thinking, reading, writing, and reflecting are not mere means to being educated. Rather, they *constitute* becoming educated. The end ("being educated") is just a different way of describing the collective actions one takes at a university. This end is not fixed or final. We can always be more educated than we are. Moreover, can come to better understand what it means to be educated. Or, suppose Bob says he wants to become a good person. On the standard view, "being a good person" is a remote end Bob can achieve by acting in certain ways. However, doing good deeds is no mere means to becoming good; doing good deeds regularly *constitutes* making oneself a good person. There is no end "being a good person" out there that is separable from the activities constituting being a good person. This end is not fixed or final since we can always be better than we are. Moreover, we can come to better understand what it means to be good.

The common view of means suggests that humans are basically passive creatures who would not act unless we are bribed, threatened, or cajoled. This threat or bribe must be some desirable end that motivates us to act. The end infuses the action with meaning: it transforms a distasteful activity (the means) into a tolerable one. This view thereby misconstrues the nature of means: it treats them as *mere* means, actions whose sole value are as a route to the (distant) fixed end. This encourages us to exert only the minimum effort required to achieve the ends. Why should we do more if the end is all the matters? One consequence of thinking that the means do not matter is that we thereby diminish our ability to achieve our ends. We are more likely to achieve our ends if we understand that the means constitute, rather than being a mere route to, those ends.

Acts and consequences / actions and motives

When deliberating we may occasionally employ the distinction between ends and means. That's fine, as long as we understand the distinction does not mark a fundamental cleavage in the moral universe. The same goes for the distinctions between (a) acts and consequences and (b) acts and motives. They may be useful distinctions in deliberation, as long as we do not take them too seriously. The first distinction is thought to sustain the theoretical divide between consequentialists and deontologists; the second, the divide between virtue and deontic theories. But neither distinction is robust enough to sustain the presumed wall separating these theories.

Deontologists claim that right and wrong are determined by the character of action, while consequences are merely the results of action, and hence, not central (and perhaps irrelevant) for determining what is moral. Consequentialists agree with above distinction but reach a different conclusion. They think only consequences matter morally. Acts are merely causally connected with consequences, and hence, not central (and perhaps irrelevant) for determining what is moral. Both views imply acts and consequences are events in narrow slices of time. They just disagree about whether the act or the consequences are morally relevant. Both views err by construing this distinction as marking some deep moral or ontological divide.

Act descriptions embed implicit or explicit reference to consequences, while morally significant descriptions of consequences incorporate unstated act descriptions. Even the strictest deontologist must reject a rigid distinction between acts and their consequences. Suppose I point a loaded gun at Joe's head and pull the trigger. What have I done? Have I twitched my finger? Have I shot a gun? Have I murdered Joe? Have I orphaned his children? Deontologists will presumably claim that the third is the preferred moral description, that the first two insufficiently describe my action, while the fourth describes a "mere" consequence. But why are the first two insufficient? Presumably because they fail to include all the morally relevant features of "what I did." That is a plausible response, however, only because pointing a loaded gun at someone's head and pulling the trigger standardly leads to the other person's death. This "consequence" is so likely that it determines the act description.

Conversely, the consequentialist, as well as the deontologist should be able to distinguish murder from killing. Any adequate consequentialist description of murder will include, either directly or indirectly, not only descriptions of what happened (someone's dying), but also the context: the condition of the "killer" (was she insane, hypnotized, etc.?) and the actions of the "victim" (was she an aggressor?). The consequentialist cannot circumvent this problem by claiming that the consequences were appropriate, excusable, or an instance of self-defense, since these incorporate unstated act descriptions. There may be practical reasons why, in some cases, we want to distinguish acts from consequences; but we should not think they mark any fundamental ontological distinction.

Any attempt to draw a sharp distinction between acts and motives faces the same problem. For although we might find occasions in which the distinction serves a deliberative aim, it does not carve the universe at its moral joints. What makes something a motive (rather than a passing thought) is that it is a disposition to act in certain ways, ways that standardly have certain consequences. Benevolent motives standardly lead to benevolent acts (which standardly lead to good consequences). Of course our best motives occasionally misfire, and the most careful, thoughtful actions occasionally lead to disastrous results. But that is just the point: they *misfire* – there is a story about why the motive did not lead to its normal action or the action did not have its normal results. Conversely, what (a) makes something a benevolent action, rather than a meanspirited one, and (b) leads to good consequences rather than rotten ones, is typically the agent's motives.

This isn't in the least mysterious when we think of other traits. People who regularly say intelligent things in a variety of circumstances are intelligent, and we expect intelligent people to normally say intelligent things. But things occasionally misfire. Bright people can say stupid things and stupid people can say intelligent things. Why should it be mysterious when it comes to morality? Consequently, the decision whether we should call something an act or a consequence, an act or a motive, is best made not by seeking the natural joints of the body moral, but by deciding, for practical reasons, on the best ways to speak and understand our (and others') behavior.

There is a better way of conceptualizing the relationship between acts, motives, and consequences. Actions, motives, and consequences, properly understood, are interrelated concepts each having temporal depth and spatial breadth. Typically (a) actions are what they are because of the motivations of their actors and their expected consequences; (b) motives are what they are because they standardly lead to certain actions and consequences; and (c) consequences are what they because they normally spring from certain motives and actions. None occur in a thin slice of time in one locale. If I lie to you now, I am not just mouthing words, (a) my action springs from my habits (and thus, my motives), (b) I am deceiving you (or at least trying), (c) I am seeking to change your behavior in some way, (d) I am shaping the character of our relationship, and (e) I am strengthening my disposition to lie in the future. If I am myopic, I may think of my action one-dimensionally. But that does not alter its depth or breadth. A "lie" that did not spring from who I am would be a mistake (I did not realize the information I was telling you was false), not a lie. A "lie" that did not deceive (or at least try to deceive) would not be a lie. A "lie" that did not change (or seek to change) your behavior would not be a lie. After all, the aim of the lie is to get you to act – or not act – differently that you would have had I told you the truth, even if the lie is about something trivial (your new sweater). A lie that did not alter our relationship in any degree (by making you distrustful of me if you discovered the lie) would arguably not be a lie. And a lie that does not make me more prone (however slightly) to lie in the future, would arguably have been an accident and not an act. Understanding that each element of this triumvirate is temporally and spatially thick helps focus deliberation. We will primarily think about what we do now since that is most within our control. But in thinking about what we do now, we should realize that our present action springs from who we are and has certain standard consequences.

The Nature of Pragmatic Ethics

Employs criteria, but is not criterial

The previous discussions enable us to say more precisely why pragmatists reject a criterial view of morality. Pragmatism's core contention that practice is primary in philosophy rules out the hope of logically prior criteria. Any meaningful criteria evolve from our attempt to live morally – in deciding what is the best action in the circumstances. Criteria are not discovered by pure reason, and they are not fixed. As ends of action, they are always revisable. As we obtain new evidence about ourselves and our world, and as our worlds changes, we find that what was appropriate for the old environment may not be conducive to survival in the new one. A style of teaching that might have been ideal for one kind of institution (a progressive liberal arts college) at one time (the 60s) may be wholly ineffective in another institution (a regional state university) at another time (the 80s). But that is exactly what we would expect of an evolutionary ethic.

Neither could criteria be complete. The moral world is complex and changeable. No set of criteria could give us univocal answers about how we should behave in all circumstances. If we cannot develop an algorithm for winning at chess, where there are only eighteen first moves, there is no way to develop an algorithm for living, which has a finitely large number of "first moves." Moreover, while the chess environment (the rules) stays constant, our natural and moral environments do not. We must adapt or fail. While there is always one end of chess – the game ends when one player wins – the ends of life change as we grow, and as our environments change. Finally, we cannot resolve practical moral questions simply by applying criteria. We do not make personal or profession decisions by applying fixed, complete criteria. Why should we assume we should make moral decisions that way?

Appropriates insights from other ethical theories

Nonetheless, there is a perfectly good sense in which a pragmatic ethic employs what we might call criteria, but their nature and role dramatically differ from that in a criterial morality (Dewey 1985 [1932]). Pragmatic criteria are not external rules we apply, but are tools we use in making informed judgements. They embody learning from previous action, they express our tentative efforts to isolate morally relevant features of those actions. These emergent criteria can become integrated into our habits, thereby informing the ways that we react to, think about, and imagine our worlds and our relations to others.

This explains why pragmatists think other theories can provide guidance on how to live morally. Standard moral theories err not because they offer silly moral advice, but because they misunderstand that advice. Other moral theories can help us isolate (and habitually focus on) morally relevant features of action. And pragmatists take help wherever they can get it. Utilitarianism does not provide an algorithm for deciding how to act, but it shapes habits to help us "naturally" attend to the ways that our actions impact others. Deontology does not provide a list of general rules to follow, but it cultivates an awareness of the ways our actions might promote or undermine respect for others. Contractarianism does not resolve all moral issues, but it sensitizes us to the need for broad consensus. That is why it is mistaken to suppose that the pragmatist makes specific moral judgements oblivious to rules, principles, virtues, and the collective wisdom of human experience. The pragmatist absorbs these insights into her habits, and thereby shapes how she habitually responds, and how she habitually deliberates when deliberation is required.

This also explains why criterial moralities tend to be minimalistic. They specify minimal sets of rules to follow in order to be moral. Pragmatism, on the other hand, like virtue theories, is more concerned to emphasize exemplary behavior – to use morally relevant features of action to determine the *best* way to behave, not the minimally tolerable way.

Is relative without being relativistic

"Okay," someone might say, "habits are important for morals. But unless we decide what is a good habit and what is not, then how can morals be objective?" The pragmatist claims there is no algorithm nor recipe for deciding which habits are best. But why should we assume there needs to be? There is no recipe for being a good teacher, a good philosopher, a good friend, or deciding whether to take a job. But, we think there are better and worse teachers, philosopher, friends, and decisions. We can give reasons for our evaluations and decisions, and these reasons can be informed by the deliberations of others and by "theories" of friendship, philosophy, pedagogy, and decision-making. It seems sufficient to say:

- Some moral habits are better than others; some are worse than others. We can give reasons for these respective evaluative judgements.
- Because we are fallible, we do not always know which moral habit is best. That is why we allow people considerable latitude in setting their own habits. It permits individuals to choose, and the society an opportunity to witness experi-

ments in moral living. But this does not mean that all habits are equal.

● Because our environments change, a moral habit that is serviceable now may be inappropriate later. But that does not alter that fact that it was once serviceable, and is no longer.

All these claims would be taken as a commonplace were it not for the assumption that moral absolutism and moral relativism are our only options. Absolutists assume relativism is a wolf at the door of ethics: unless we have one unique set of determinable moral principles, then the wolf will enter and devour the hapless progenitor of morality. Relativists agree with absolutists about the status of morality without absolute principles; they just think there are no such principles.

Pragmatism helps us understand why these are not our only options – why the three considerations above reflect our best understanding of the moral life and explain why this provides all the objectivity we need, even if it does not provide the certainty we occasionally want (Bernstein 1983; Dewey 1988 [1922]; Dewey 1970 [1920]; Elgin 1997; Margolis 1996; Margolis 1986; Putnam 1994; Rorty 1989; Rorty 1982; Rorty 1979). The hope that ethics (or science) could provide certainty is itself a symptom of the disease that pragmatism seeks to cure. As Dewey put it:

> in morals a hankering for certainty, born of timidity and nourished by love of authoritative prestige, has led to the idea that absence of immutably fixed and universally applicable ready-made principles is equivalent to moral chaos. (Dewey 1988 [1922]: 164)

Tolerates without being irresolute

Although we acknowledge that some habits are better (or worse) that others, in some circumstances several habits appear to be equally good. In this case, appearances may not be deceiving. Why should we assume that only one set of habits, principles, or ideas can be best? Why not say several of them are objectively better than others, even if we cannot say that one is uniquely best? Pragmatism permits and explains why we should expect and desire some moral disagreements. An evolutionary ethic seeks the optimal behavior within a niche. Since the niches in which people live vary, we should not expect that precisely the same behavior would be optimal in each. Since social norms help compose our environments, then those norms will themselves determine, to some degree, what is genuinely moral. For instance, most societies have norms about appropriate dress at a funeral. But those norms vary. Someone violating those norms (wearing a kilt to a funeral in Houston) will likely not only clash with those norms, they may thereby deeply offend the family of the deceased.

The claim, of course, is not that social norms *determine* what is right and wrong. The pragmatist only claims that social norms are often relevant to how we should behave. There is no algorithm for specifying when and how they are relevant, but as I stated earlier, the pragmatist does not think there are moral algorithms. These are issues about which we can debate, and about which morally minded people might disagree. The pragmatist merely claims that, in cases of such disagreement, the opposing views are best tested in an environment in which open discussion is encouraged (itself a social habit). This increases the likelihood that misguided solutions will be bested in the arena of ideas. And, when some competitors survive, the society will permit and even encourage them to be tested by life (experiments in living). The laboratory of life might reveal that some of them are inadequate. In other cases, the results may be inconclusive. Several may thrive in the same or related environments. That will not disturb the pragmatist. For the pragmatist holds only that some views are better than others. She does not hold that there is always one and only one uniquely good view. Why should she think that?

Consider. Some writing is dense, imprecise, rambling, and boring, while other writing is crisp, lucid, unambiguous, and vigorous. These differences are so pronounced that virtually anyone would spot them in an instant (LaFollette 1991). In that sense, we are objectivists about language. Of course there are borderline cases about which we might genuinely disagree. Moreover, there are some differences which are *just* differences in style and taste. Should an objectivist about language and prose try to squelch these differences? I see no reason why they should, and plenty of reason why they shouldn't. It is hard to see what harm can come from these differences, and it is easy to see how they can be beneficial. Having various linguistic options is more enjoyable: a society in which everyone wrote or spoke in precisely the same way would be a society where fewer people read, and where prose and spoken language would be boring. Moreover, pluralistic writing and speaking styles permit us to say different things in different ways, and hearing a different description of an event may enhance our understanding of the phenomenon.

Likewise, we all recognize that there is no uniquely nutritious or tasty meal, insightful movie, enjoyable music, relaxing vacation, good lecture, etc. What possible reason would the pragmatist have for thinking morality must reveal one and only one appropriate behavior? On the other hand, we all recognize that there are fatty and disgusting meals, pedestrian movies, boring music, tense vacations, and sleep-inducing lectures. What possible reason would the pragmatist have for thinking all moral judgements and behaviors are equally good? Some are good; some are terrible; others are mediocre. Any reflective pragmatist realizes that sloppy or unscrupulous pragmatists (like sloppy and unscrupulous deontologists or consequentialists) may act immorally. Moreover, careful and conscientious pragmatists (like careful and conscientious deontologists or consequentialists) will also occasionally morally botch it because of ignorance or inattention. That is why the careful pragmatist emphasizes our fallibility. We may be mistaken even about those moral judgements about which we seem most confident. Our fallibility does not diminish our need to act. It does, however, give us compelling reason to subject our views to the scrutiny of others. As Mill expresses it:

> The beliefs which we have most warrant for, have no safeguard to rest on, but a standing invitation to the whole world to prove them unfounded. If the challenge is not accepted, or is accepted and the attempt fails, we are far enough from certainty still; but we

have done the best that the existing state of human reason admits of; we have neglected nothing that could give the truth a chance of reaching us. . . . This is the amount of certainty attainable by a fallible being, and this the sole way of attaining it. (Mill 1978)

And the pragmatists say: "Amen."

Redescribes the relationship between theory and practice

So what is a pragmatic ethical *theory*? Pragmatism has no separable ethical theory: meaningful theory cannot exist distinct from practice. Theory without practice (ends without means) becomes an intellectual game only vaguely connected to the phenomena it is supposed to understand and explain. Practice without theory (like means without ends) lacks direction; it becomes little more than a loose amalgam of reactions to specific circumstances. The pragmatist sees theory and practice as two intricately related elements of ethics, properly understood.

Theoriz*ing* is an essential element of inquiry, a tool for understanding, evaluating, modifying, and hopefully improving our moral thought. But theorizing is not prior to or independent of experience, but grows out of and is part of experience. Any theorizing – whether we are theorizing about language, love, life, biology, physics, or ethics – begins from current wisdom, as embodied in our habits. Most of us began theorizing because of clashes between or uncertainty about our habitual reactions to (or intuitions about) a problem we face. Suppose our parents told us not to lie *and* told us not to hurt others – good advice, to be sure. Then one day we find that telling Jo the truth will hurt her. How can we follow our parents' advice? The inability of our habits to cope smoothly with this problem requires us to theorize, to step back from the problem and reflect on it. We might theorize haphazardly and ineffectively or we might do it well. What determines how well we theorize? There is no algorithm. However, we have a better chance of finding a satisfactory solution if we have multiple moral habits. For instance, if we are familiar with a range of practical moral problems, if we read good literature, and if we have a good sense of the ways people reason about practical problems (as captured in various ethical theories), then we will have the resources to find a reasonable solution. But success is never guaranteed.

Embracing a Pragmatist Ethic

A pragmatic ethic is not based on principles, but it is not unprincipled. Deliberation plays a significant role, albeit a different role than that given it on most accounts. Morality does not seek final absolute answers, yet it is not perniciously relativistic. It does recognize that circumstances can be different, and that in different circumstances, different actions may be appropriate. So it does not demand moral uniformity between people and across cultures. Moreover, it understands moral advance as emerging from the crucible of experience, not through the proclamations of something or someone outside us. Just as ideas only prove their superiority in dialogue and in conflict with other ideas, moral insight can likewise prove its superiority in dialogue and conflict with other ideas and experiences. Hence, some range of moral disagreement and some amount of different action will not be, for the pragmatist, something to bemoan. It will be integral to moral advancement, and thus should be permitted and even praised, not lamented. Only someone who thought theory could provide final answers, and answers without the messy task of doing battle on the marketplace of ideas and of life, would find this regrettable.

Acknowledgment

Thanks to Robert Audi, Joan Callahan, Steven Fesmire, John Hardwig, Heather Keith, Larry May, Niall Shanks, John J. Stuhr, and especially Christopher Hookway, Eva LaFollette, Todd Lekan, and Michael Pritchard, for penetrating and helpful comments on earlier versions of this chapter.

References

Aristotle: *Nicomachean Ethics,* trans. T. Irwin (Indianapolis.: Hackett Pub. Co., 1985).

Bernstein, R.: *Beyond Objectivism and Relativism* (Philadelphia: University of Pennsylvania Press, 1983).

Dewey, J.: *Human Nature and Conduct* (Carbondale, IL: Southern Illinois University Press, 1988/1922).

——: *The Later Works, 1925–1953* (vol. 7: 1932) (Carbondale and Edwardsville, IL: Southern Illinois University Press, 1985 / 1932).

——: *Reconstuction in Philosophy* (New York: Henry Holt, 1970/1920).

Elgin, C. Z.: *Between the Absolute and the Arbitrary* (Ithaca, NY: Cornell University Press, 1997).

Gadamer, H. G.: *Truth and Method* (New York: Seabury Press, 1975).

LaFollette, H.: "The Truth in Ethical Relativism," *Journal of Social Philosophy,* 20 (1991): 146–154.

Margolis, J.: *Life Without Principles* (Oxford: Blackwell, 1996).

——: *Pragmatism without Foundations: Reconciling Realism and Relativism* (Oxford, UK; New York, USA: Blackwell, 1986).

Mill, J. S.: *On Liberty* (Indianapolis: Hackett Publishing Company, 1985/1885).

——: *On Liberty* (Indianapolis: Hackett Pub. Co., 1978).

Nussbaum, M. C.: *The Fragility of Goodness: Luck and Ethics in Greek Tragedy and Philosophy* (Cambridge; New York: Cambridge University Press, 1986).

Putnam, H.: *Words and Life* (Cambridge, MA: Harvard University Press, 1994).

Rorty, R.: *Contingency, Irony, and Solidarity* (Cambridge: Cambridge University Press, 1989).

——: *Consequences of Pragmatism* (Minneapolis: University of Minnesota Press, 1982).

——: *Philosophy and the Mirror of Nature* (Princeton: Princeton University Press, 1979).

Chapter 21

Toward Reconciliation in Ethics

James P. Sterba

As the essays in this volume illustrate, there are many conflicting perspectives in contemporary ethical theory. There is a conflict between libertarians who think that the only basic obligation we have is a negative one not to interfere with others and their opponents who think that we also have a positive obligation to help others in need at least to some degree. There is the conflict between utilitarians and their opponents who, while endorsing a positive obligation to help others in need, disagree about the nature, extent, and underlying grounds of this obligation. Cutting across both of these conflicts, there is the conflict between feminists and their opponents concerning what changes need to be made in ethical theory in order to properly take into account the interests and perspectives of women. And there are many more conflicts. In this essay, I will focus on just the three conflicts I mentioned, the conflict between libertarians and their opponents, the conflict between utilitarians and their opponents, and the conflict between feminists and their opponents, and show how these conflicts can be reconciled, with the hope that if conflicts such as these, serious as they are, can be reconciled, the prospect for further reconciliations in ethics should be promising.

I   Libertarians and their Opponents

The libertarian view is nicely set out in this volume by Jan Narveson in his essay "Libertarianism." Libertarians make a strong distinction between harming others and not helping them. They hold that the only basic obligation we have is to not harm others and that we harm others only by interfering with them in inappropriate ways. It follows that the sole basic right people have is a right to noninterference or to liberty. As Narveson puts it,

> Libertarianism is the view that we all have one single, general fundamental right – the right to liberty. . . . [The principle] prohibits aggression . . . it holds that the use of

force against innocent persons is wrong. . . . We may do as we like with what is ours . . . only up to the point where what we do collides with the identical rights of others. . . . Libertarianism wants to allow everyone the completest possible freedom of action compatible with the same fundamental freedom for all others. (Narveson, this volume, pp. 306, 307, 308)

At the Eastern Division American Philosophical Meeting where Narveson defended an earlier version of his paper, opponents vigorously tried to get him to go beyond his theory of negative rights and to endorse a positive obligation to help others in need, but Narveson just as vigorously resisted. Narveson and his opponents reached an impasse here, I believe, because they failed to focus on resources within the libertarian view itself. Rather than try to derive a positive obligation to help others in need from a theory of negative rights itself, Narveson's opponents pressed the case that for an independently grounded positive obligation to help others in need, which Narveson denied. The alternative approach I propose grants libertarians, for the sake of argument, that the only basic obligation we have is a negative one of noninterference and then purports to show that a positive right to help others in need can be derived from this basic negative right of noninterference.

From a basic right of noninterference, libertarians claim to derive a number of more specific requirements, in particular, a right to life, a right to freedom of speech, press and assembly, and a right to property. Here it is important to observe that the libertarian's right to life is not a right to receive from others the goods and resources necessary for preserving one's life; it is simply a right not to be killed unjustly. Correspondingly, the libertarian's right to property is not a right to receive from others the goods and resources necessary for one's welfare, but rather a right to acquire goods and resources either by initial acquisition or by voluntary agreement.

Of course, libertarians would allow that it would be nice of the rich to share their surplus resources with the poor. Nevertheless, according to libertarians, such acts of charity should not be coercively required because there is no basic obligation to help others in need. For this reason, libertarians are opposed to any coercively welfare program.

Now in order to see why libertarians are mistaken about what their basic right of noninterference requires, consider a typical conflict situation between the rich and the poor. In this conflict situation, the rich, of course, have more than enough resources to satisfy their basic needs. By contrast, the poor lack the resources to meet their most basic needs even though they have tried all the means available to them that libertarians regard as legitimate for acquiring such resources. Under circumstances like these, libertarians usually maintain that the rich should have the liberty to use their resources to satisfy their luxury needs if they so wish. Libertarians recognize that this liberty might well be enjoyed at the expense of the satisfaction of the most basic needs of the poor; they just think that liberty always has priority over other political ideals, and since they assume that the liberty of the poor is not at stake in such conflict situations, it is easy for them to conclude that the rich should not be required to sacrifice their liberty so that the basic needs of the poor may be met.

In fact, however, the liberty of the poor is at stake in such conflict situations. What is at stake is the liberty of the poor not to be interfered with in taking from the surplus possessions of the rich what is necessary to satisfy their basic needs. When libertarians are brought to see that this is the case, they are genuinely surprised, one might even say rudely awakened, for they had not previously seen the conflict between the rich and the poor as a conflict of liberties.[1]

Now when the conflict between the rich and the poor is viewed as a conflict of liberties, we can either say that the rich should have the liberty not to be interfered with in using their surplus resources for luxury purposes, or we can say that the poor should have the liberty not to be interfered with in taking from the rich what they require to meet their basic needs. If we choose one liberty, we must reject the other. What needs to be determined, therefore, is which liberty is morally preferable: the liberty of the rich or the liberty of the poor.

I submit that the liberty of the poor, which is the liberty not to be interfered with in taking from the surplus resources of others what is required to meet one's basic needs, is morally preferable to the liberty of the rich, which is the liberty not to be interfered with when using one's surplus resources for luxury purposes. To see that this is the case, we need only appeal to one of the most fundamental principles of morality, one that is common to all political perspectives, namely, the "ought" implies "can" principle. According to this principle, people are not morally required to do what they lack the power to do or what would involve so great a sacrifice that it would be unreasonable to ask, and/or in cases of severe conflict of interest, unreasonable to require them to abide by.

For example, suppose I promised to attend a departmental meeting on Friday, but on Thursday I am involved in a serious car accident which puts me into a coma. Surely it is no longer the case that I ought to attend the meeting now that I lack the power to do so. Or suppose instead that on Thursday I develop a severe case of pneumonia for which I am hospitalized. Surely I could legitimately claim that I cannot attend the meeting on the grounds that the risk to my health involved in attending is a sacrifice that it would be unreasonable to ask me to bear. Or suppose the risk to my health from having pneumonia is not so serious that it would be unreasonable to ask me to attend the meeting (a supererogatory request), it might still be serious enough to be unreasonable to require my attendance at the meeting (a demand that is backed up by blame or coercion).

This "ought" implies "can" principle claims that reason and morality must be linked in an appropriate way, especially if we are going to be able to justifiably use blame or coercion to get people to abide by the requirements of morality. It should be noted, however, that while major figures in the history of philosophy, and most philosophers today, including virtually all libertarian philosophers, accept this linkage between reason and morality, this linkage is not usually conceived to be part of the "ought" implies "can" principle. Nevertheless, I claim that there are good reasons for associating this linkage between reason and morality with the "ought" implies "can" principle, namely, our use of the word "can" as in the example just given, and the natural progression from logical, physical and psychological possibility found in the traditional "ought" implies "can" principle to the notion of moral possibility found in this formulation of the "ought" implies "can" principle. In any case, the acceptability of this formulation of the "ought" implies "can" principle is determined by the virtual universal acceptance of its components and not by the manner in which I have proposed to join those components together.[2]

Now applying the "ought" implies "can" principle to the case at hand, it seems clear that the poor have it within their power willingly to relinquish such an important liberty as the liberty not to be interfered with in taking from the rich what they require to meet their basic needs. Nevertheless, it would be unreasonable to ask or require them to make so great a sacrifice. In the extreme case, it would involve asking or requiring the poor to sit back and starve to death. Of course, the poor may have no real alternative to relinquishing this liberty. To do anything else may involve worse consequences for themselves and their loved ones and may invite a painful death. Accordingly, we may expect that the poor would acquiesce, albeit unwillingly, to a political system that denied them the right to welfare supported by such a liberty, at the same time that we recognize that such a system imposed an unreasonable sacrifice upon the poor – a sacrifice that we could not morally blame the poor for trying to evade (see Sterba 1984). Analogously, we might expect that a woman whose life was threatened would submit to a rapist's demands, at the same time that we recognize the utter unreasonableness of those demands.

By contrast, it would not be unreasonable to ask and require the rich to sacrifice the liberty to meet some of their luxury needs so that the poor can have the liberty to meet their basic needs. Naturally, we might expect that the rich, for reasons of self-interest and past contribution, might be disinclined to make such a sacrifice. We might even suppose that the past contribution of the rich provides a good reason for not sacrificing their liberty to use their surplus for luxury purposes. Yet, unlike the poor, the rich could not claim that relinquishing such a liberty involved so great a sacrifice that it would be unreasonable to ask and require them to make it; unlike the poor, the rich could be morally blameworthy for failing to make such a sacrifice.

Consequently, if we assume that however else we specify the requirements of morality, they cannot violate the "ought" implies "can" principle, it follows that, despite what libertarians claim, the right to liberty endorsed by them actually favors the liberty of the poor over the liberty of the rich.

Yet couldn't libertarians object to this conclusion, claiming that it would be unreasonable to ask the rich to sacrifice the liberty to meet some of their luxury needs so that the poor could have the liberty to meet their basic needs? As I have pointed out, libertarians don't usually see the situation as a conflict of liberties, but suppose they did. How plausible would such an objection be? Not very plausible at all, I think.

For consider: what are libertarians going to say about the poor? Isn't it clearly unreasonable to require the poor to sacrifice the liberty to meet their basic needs so that the rich can have the liberty to meet their luxury needs? Isn't it clearly unreasonable to require the poor to sit back and starve to death? If it is, then, there is no resolution of this conflict that would be reasonable to require both the rich and the poor to accept. But that would mean that libertarians could not be putting forth a moral ideal because a moral ideal resolves severe conflicts of interest in ways that it would be reasonable to ask and require everyone affected to accept. Therefore, as long as libertarians think of themselves as putting forth a moral ideal, they cannot allow that it would be unreasonable in cases of severe conflict of interest *both* to require the rich to sacrifice the liberty to meet some of their luxury needs in order to benefit the poor and to require the poor to sacrifice the liberty to meet their basic needs in order to benefit the rich. But I submit that if one of these requirements is to be judged reasonable, then, by any neutral assessment, it must be the requirement that the rich sacrifice the liberty to meet some of their luxury needs so that the poor can have the liberty to meet their basic needs; there is no other plausible resolution, if libertarians intend to be putting forth a moral ideal.

It should also be noted that this case for restricting the liberty of the rich depends upon the willingness of the poor to take advantage of whatever opportunities are available to them to engage in mutually beneficial work, so that failure of the poor to take advantage of such opportunities would normally cancel, or at least significantly reduce, the obligation of the rich to restrict their own liberty for the benefit of the poor. In addition, the poor would be required to return the equivalent of any surplus possessions they have taken from the rich once they are able to do so and still satisfy their basic needs. Nor would the poor be required to keep the liberty to which they are entitled. They could give up part of it, or all of it, or risk losing it on the chance of gaining a greater share of liberties or other social goods. Consequently, the case for restricting the liberty of the rich for the benefit of the poor is neither unconditional nor inalienable.

Of course, there will be cases in which the poor fail to satisfy their basic needs, not because of any direct restriction of liberty on the part of the rich, but because the poor are in such dire need that they are unable even to attempt to take from the rich what they require to meet their basic needs. In such cases, the rich would not be performing any act of commission that would prevent the poor from taking what they require. Yet, even in such cases, the rich would normally be performing acts of commission that would prevent other persons from taking part of the rich's own surplus possessions and using it to aid the poor. And when assessed from a moral point of view, restricting the liberty of these allies or agents of the poor would not be morally justified for the very same reason that restricting the liberty of the poor to meet their own basic needs would not be morally justified: It would not be reasonable to require all of those affected to accept such a restriction of liberty.

Now it might be objected that the right to welfare which this argument establishes from libertarian premises is not the same as the right to welfare endorsed by welfare liberals and socialists. This is correct. We could mark this difference by referring to the right that this argument establishes as "a negative welfare right" and by referring to the right endorsed by welfare liberals and socialists as "a positive welfare right." The significance of this difference is that a person's negative welfare right can be violated only when other people through acts of commission interfere with its exercise, whereas a person's positive welfare right can be violated not only by such acts of commission but by acts of omission as well. Nonetheless, this difference will have little practical import, for in recognizing the legitimacy of negative welfare rights, libertarians will come to see that virtually any use of their surplus possessions is likely to violate the negative welfare rights of the poor by preventing the poor from rightfully appropriating (some part of) their surplus goods and resources. So, in order to ensure that they will not be engaging in such wrongful actions, it will be incumbent on them to set up institutions guaranteeing adequate positive welfare rights for the poor. Only then will they be able to use legitimately any remaining surplus possessions to meet their own nonbasic needs. Furthermore, in the absence of adequate positive welfare rights, the poor, either acting by themselves or through their allies or agents, would have some discretion in determining when and how to exercise their negative welfare rights. In order not to be subject to that discretion, libertarians will tend to favor the only morally legitimate way of preventing the exercise of such rights: They will set up institutions guaranteeing adequate positive welfare rights that will then take precedence over the exercise of negative welfare rights. For these reasons, recognizing the negative welfare rights of the poor will ultimately lead libertarians to endorse the same sort of welfare institutions favored by welfare liberals and socialists.

In brief, I have argued that a libertarian negative right of noninterference can be seen to support a right to welfare through an application of the "ought" implies "can" principle to conflicts between the rich and the poor. In the interpretation I have used, the principle supports such rights by favoring the liberty of the poor over the liberty of the rich. In another interpretation (developed elsewhere), the principle supports such rights by favoring a conditional right to property over an unconditional right to property (see Sterba 1998, ch. 3). In either interpretation, what is crucial to the derivation of these rights is the claim that it would be unreasonable to require the poor to deny their basic needs and accept anything less than these rights as the condition for their willing cooperation.[3]

II   Utilitarians and their Opponents

The conflict between utilitarians and their opponents is represented in this volume by the contributions of R. G. Frey and Brad Hooker. Drawing on H. M. Hare's work, Frey defends act-utilitarianism by using the standard of maximizing total utility almost exclusively at the critical/theoretical level of moral thinking for the purpose of justifying rules and practices which people will use and accept at the intuitive/practical level of moral thinking. In contrast, Hooker defends a form of rule-consequentialism, which avoids many of the standard critiques of utilitarianism by breaking ranks with utilitarian theories in fundamental ways. For example, Hooker responds to the critique that utilitarianism conflicts with fairness by designating fairness to be one of the consequences his theory takes into account. Similarly, to avoid the critique that if rule consequentialism is justified by its consequences, it will ultimately collapse into act consequentialism, Hooker rejects a consequentialist justification for his rule consequentialism, claiming instead that his view "develops from some very attractive general ideas about morality" and, most importantly that it is in reflective equilibrium with our considered moral judgments. Here I propose to further support Hooker's view by exploring a way of bringing utilitarians and their opponents together.

An attractive way of bringing utilitarians and their opponents together is by appealing to some common ground they share to resolve the differences between them. That common ground is provided by contemporary social contract theory because social contract theory, especially when formulated hypothetically so as not to presuppose an actual contract, has been widely accepted by both utilitarians and their opponents alike, and, as I shall show, it can be used to reasonably resolve the differences between them (see Hare 1999; Harsanyi 1977). In terms of Frey's distinction between critical/theoretical and intuitive/practical levels, this is a discussion that takes place entirely at the critical/theoretical level to determine what sorts of rules and practices should be applied at the intuitive/practical level.

According to one standard formulation of social contract theory, moral principles are those principles people would agree to if they were to discount the knowledge of which particular interests happen to be their own (see Sterba 1980, 1988 which, of course draw on Rawls 1971). Since people obviously know what their own particular interests are, in employing this version of social contract theory, they would just not be taking that knowledge into account when formulating moral requirements. Rather they would be reasoning from their knowledge of all the particular interests that would be affected by their decisions, but not from their knowledge of which particular interests happen to be their own. In employing such a decision procedure, therefore, people, (like members of a jury who heed the judge's instruction to discount certain information in order to reach of fair verdict) would be able to give a fair hearing to everyone's particular interests. And assuming further that people were well-informed of all the particular interests that could be affected by their decisions and that they were fully capable of rationally deliberating with respect to that information, then their deliberations would culminate in a unanimous decision. This is because each of them would be deliberating in a rationally correct manner with respect to the same information and would be using a decision procedure that leads to a uniform evaluation of the alternatives. As a result, each of them would favor the same moral requirements.

But what requirements would people select using this procedure? Would they select requirements that favored utilitarianism or would they select conflicting requirements based, for example, upon generally recognized criteria of justice?

John Harsanyi and others have argued that only requirements that favored utilitarianism would be selected by people using such a decision procedure (Harsanyi 1977). Harsanyi claims that people using such a decision procedure would first assign an equal probability to their occupying each particular position in society and then select the alternative with the highest average expected utility. To determine utility assignments, people using such a decision procedure are said to compare what it would be like to have particular distributive shares in society while possessing the subjective tastes of persons who have those shares. (Similar comparisons are required by R. M. Hare's universalizability criterion, by Hume's impartial spectator and possibly by the Golden Rule.) Harsanyi also assumes that with the knowledge of the appropriate psychological laws and factual information, people using such a decision procedure would arrive at the same comparative utility judgments from which it would then be possible to determine which alternative maximizes their average expected utility.

For example, consider a society with just the three members, X, Y and Z facing the alternatives set out in table 21.1.

Table 21.1

	Alternative A	Alternative C
X	60	30
Y	10	20
Z	10	20

Given these alternatives, Harsanyi thinks that people using this social contract decision procedure would assume that it was equally probable that they would be either X, Y, or Z and, therefore, would select Alternative A as having the higher average expected utility. And if the utility values for two alternatives were as set out in table 21.2, Harsanyi thinks that people using this decision procedure would be indifferent between the alternatives.

Table 21.2

	Alternative B	Alternative C
X	50	30
Y	10	20
Z	10	20

According to Harsanyi, any risk aversion that people using this decision procedure might have in evaluating alternatives would be reflected in a declining marginal utility for money and other social goods. Thus, in our example, we could imagine that a yearly income of $100,000 may be required to provide a utility of 60 while only a yearly income of $5,000 may be needed for a utility of 10. Similarly, a

$40,000 yearly income may be required for a utility of 30 but only a $15,000 yearly income for a utility of 20.

But even if we assume that declining marginal utility of social goods has been taken into account, people using this social contract decision procedure would still have grounds for preferring Alternative C to both Alternative A and Alternative B. This is because there are two factors that people would take into account in reaching decisions when using this decision procedure. One factor is the average utility payoff, and this factor would favor Alternative A. The other factor, however, is the distribution of utility payoffs, and this factor would clearly favor Alternative C. Moreover, given this set of alternatives, it is the second factor that would be decisive for people who are discounting the knowledge of which particular interests happen to be their own.

Of course, if the alternatives were different, people using this decision procedure would choose differently. For example, if the alternatives were as set out in table 21.3, people using this decision procedure would surely prefer Alternative D with its higher average utility payoff to Alternative E with its better distribution. Nevertheless, in at least some cases, the distribution factor would outweigh the average utility factor for people using this decision procedure, and that is what is crucial for an evaluation of the conflicts between utilitarians and their opponents.

Table 21.3

	Alternative D	Alternative E
X	50	40
Y	30	25
Z	20	21

Accordingly, utilitarians who accept such a social contract decision procedure are faced with a difficult choice: either give up their commitment to social contract theory or modify their commitment to social contract theory or modify their commitment to utilitarian goals. Nor can utilitarians easily choose to give up their commitment to social contract theory. For social contract theory is simply an interpretation of a commonly accepted standard of fairness which now has been shown to conflict with, and presumably at least sometimes morally override, the utility of the individual payoffs. Since the acceptability of utilitarianism as traditionally conceived has always depended on showing that such standards of fairness rarely conflict with the utility of the individual payoffs, and that when they do, it is plausible to think that the utility of the individual payoffs is morally overriding, it would seem that unless the above preferences of people using such a decision procedure can be challenged, utilitarians have little choice but to modify their commitment to utilitarian goals.

Needless to say, such a social contract decision procedure could be modified so as to bring the preferences of people using that procedure in line with utilitarianism.

One way to bring this about is to reconstitute the people who are to use this decision procedure so that they would no longer take seriously the distribution factor in their deliberations. Thus, one could conceive of people using this decision procedure as living seriatim the lives or, better, integral parts of the lives of many randomly selected individuals in their society. In this way, each person using this decision procedure would be able to realize, at least approximate the average individual utility payoff in their society. Consequently, they would no longer have any reason to take seriously into account the distribution factor when using this decision procedure.

Yet this proposal for modifying our social contract decision procedure simply exposes the inadequacy of the conception of the nature of persons implicit in utilitarianism. For in order to choose to maximize the average individual utility payoff, people using this decision procedure would have to think of themselves as living seriatim integral parts of the lives of many randomly selected individuals. To make such a choice, therefore, would require that, at least for moral purposes, people begin to think of themselves in a radically different way. In this connection, John Rawls has argued that choosing to maximize the sum of individual utility payoffs also implies an inadequate conception of person because such a choice would be made by a sympathetic spectator who regards everyone's desires and satisfactions as if they were the desires and satisfactions of one person (Rawls 1971). It could be argued, therefore, that both choices fail to pay sufficient attention to the distinction between persons – the choice of the highest sum of individual utility payoffs by requiring that people think of themselves as parts of one "sum person"; the choice of the highest average individual utility payoff by requiring that people think of themselves as parts of what could be called "average persons."

But utilitarians who are attracted to this social contract decision procedure would certainly want to resist these conclusions, for it would mean that, in consistency, they would have to give up either their commitment to social contract theories or their commitment to utilitarianism. Hoping to avoid this result, utilitarians might admit that persons using this social contract decision procedure would prefer Alternative C to Alternatives A and B, but then deny that this would serve to show the inadequacy of utilitarianism on the grounds that these possibilities do not constitute a *realistic* set of alternatives. Thus utilitarians might claim that to demonstrate the inadequacy of utilitarianism, it must be shown that an acceptable distribution with a sufficiently high minimum individual utility payoff would not be the realistic outcome of an alternative that maximizes the utility of the individual payoffs.

Table 21.4

	Alternative A	Alternative C
X	60	30
Y	10	20
Z	10	20

For example, consider again Alternatives A and C (table 21.4). With respect to this set of alternatives, utilitarians might claim that under realistic conditions there would be the possibility of a third alternative, Alternative F, that would both provide at least at high a minimum individual utility payoffs as Alternative C and a higher average individual utility payoff than Alternative A. This third alternative, Alternative F, would be said to result from transferring from X to Y and Z sufficient goods to secure a minimum individual utility payoff that is at least as high as that provided by Alternative C. Such a transfer – assuming uniform declining marginal utility – would be said to provide a greater total individual utility payoff to Y and Z than the same goods provided to X, thus rendering Alternative F preferable to Alternative A on utilitarian grounds.

But is it reasonable to assume that a transfer of goods producing just these results is realistically possible? There are a number of reasons for thinking that this is not the case.

First of all, under realistic conditions might not a significant fraction of the individual utility payoff enjoyed by X derive not directly from the larger share of goods X possesses but rather from the fact that X has considerably more goods than Y or Z? But if under realistic conditions this were the case, then raising the minimum individual utility payoff in Alternative A so as to match that in Alternative C would tend to collapse Alternative A into Alternative C, producing a net loss of utility. Since this would mean that Alternative A would remain the preferred utilitarian alternative, people using our social contract decision procedure would still have reason to select Alternative C.

Secondly, even if under realistic conditions there were an Alternative F that would provide at least as high a minimum individual utility payoffs as Alternative C and a higher average individual utility payoff than Alternative A, might not the only acceptable utilitarian method for transforming Alternative A into Alternative F necessitate a gradual transition so as not to sharply decrease the utility experienced by X who has grown accustomed to his or her preferred status? But if this were the case, people using this social contract decision procedure would have reason to reject, not Alternative F itself, but the acceptable utilitarian method of bringing about such an alternative. For people using our social contract decision procedure would want a sufficiently high minimum individual utility payoff to be secured directly and immediately, regardless of whether a rapid transition would cause a net loss of utility.

Thirdly, how realistic is the assumption of uniform declining marginal utility of goods? While it seems reasonable to grant that everyone experiences some sort of decline in the marginal utility of goods, utilitarians, to approximate an ideal of justice, must go further and assume that the decline occurs uniformly for everyone, either immediately before or at least immediately after his or her basic needs are satisfied (for example, it won't do if the decline occurs only after a yearly income between $35,000 and $50,000 is attained). In defending this assumption, however, utilitarians don't usually claim to know that declining marginal utility occurs uniformly at an early stage in the acquisition of goods. Usually they claim that, given the uncertainties of determining the rates of declining marginal utility for particular individuals, it is best to assume that the decline occurs uniformly for everyone at an early stage in the acquisition of goods. Of course, at this point one might wonder whether those who accept this assumption on such grounds are really basing their normative judgments on utility assessments after all. Yet, even disregarding this point, it is still far from clear that we don't have good evidence in many cases of significant differences in declining marginal utility of goods. Thus increased skill at assessing these differences might well open up the possibility of maximizing utility by distributing a scarce supply of goods primarily to the members of some subgroup within a society (e.g., the X's of the society) instead of making sure that there is an acceptable distribution providing a sufficiently high minimum individual utility payoff to everyone in the society.

Lastly and most importantly, even if it were reasonable to assume that uniform declining marginal utility occurs at an early stage in the acquisition of goods, and even if an alternative that maximizes the average individual utility payoff always provided a relatively high minimum individual utility payoff, and even if a utilitarian transition to such an alternative would be direct and immediate, it still would not be the case that people using our social contract decision procedure would regard as sufficient the minimum individual utility payoff that is so guaranteed. For given the importance of this choice to the life prospects of people choosing in a manner so as to discount which interests happen to be their own, it would be reasonable for them to adopt a somewhat conservative stance and make choices that sacrificed a higher average individual utility payoff for the sake of an even better distribution of utility. This conservative stance would not lead to the choice of the highest possible minimum individual utility payoff, but the risks involved would still lead to the sacrifice of a higher average individual utility payoff for the sake of a better distribution of utility.

On the basis of the above considerations, therefore, people using our social contract decision procedure would have reason to doubt whether a relatively high minimum of utility would be the realistic outcome of an alternative with the highest average individual utility payoff, and even if they were to disregard those doubts, they would still have reason to secure a somewhat better distribution than such an alternative could provide. This is because people using this decision procedure would experience at least some risk aversion to occupying the undesirable distributive positions under an alternative with the highest average individual utility payoff. Hence, it would be rational for people using this decision procedure to favor an alternative which reflected their degree of risk aversion by providing a better distribution of utilities over an alternative which simply maximizes the average individual utility payoff.

Of course, our decision procedure could be reconstructed so that it would straightforwardly lead to utilitarianism. But the only way that this could be done, other than by reconstituting persons using this decision procedure, is by stipulating that people using this decision procedure have no aversion to risk when considering what positions they might occupy. Yet this requirement, unlike that of discounting the knowledge of which particular interests happen to be their own, is not needed to ensure fairness; it is simply a means of ensuring a utilitarian outcome. To introduce the requirement is to beg the question as to the nature of the conflict between fairness and utility. While fairness may be interpreted as requiring us to discount certain knowledge in reaching moral decisions, such a requirement, unless qualified by a restriction ruling out risk aversion, would not lead to the choice of a utilitarian outcome.

Moreover, if we drop the assumption that people in our decision procedure are choosing for realistic conditions, then the contrast between an ideal of fairness and utilitarianism becomes even more striking. For people using our decision procedure would still want to guarantee a sufficiently high minimum of utility for each and every person even if, for example, they assumed that declining marginal utility of social goods did not occur until people acquired a yearly income of well over $100,000. Thus while such an assumption would drastically alter the normative implications of utilitarianism – rendering them even more objectionable – it would leave the requirements of our social contract ideal of fairness relatively unaffected.

Nor is it possible to defend utilitarianism here by using Frey's two level approach to moral thinking. This is because we can imagine the above argument as taking place entirely at the critical/theoretical level of moral thinking which determines what rules and practices will be used and accepted at the intuitive/practical level of moral thinking. At the critical/theoretical level, we are choosing between one set of rules and practices which truly maximizes utility and another set of rules and practices which constrains the pursuit of the maximization of utility with the standard of fairness found in contemporary social contract theory. Only Hooker's incorporation of fairness into the consequences of his theory goes someway toward meeting this objection to utilitarianism.[4]

We have seen, therefore, how it is possible to use contemporary social contract theory to reasonably resolve the differences between utilitarians and their opponents. Since contemporary social contract theory has been widely endorsed by utilitarians and their opponents alike, the constraints it places on the pursuit of utilitarian goals should also be widely endorsed by utilitarians as well as their opponents.

III Feminists and their Opponents

In her contribution to this volume, Alison Jaggar surveys the variety of criticisms that feminists have made of traditional ethics. Jaggar's survey is quite extensive. So I cannot hope to discuss all the critical points she raises, despite the fact that I believe that there are significant possibilities for reconcilating traditional ethics with feminism. In general, I contend that while feminism does conflict with certain interpretations of traditional ethics, there are usually more favorable interpretations available with which it does not conflict. To begin to show this, I will examine in detail at least some of the feminist criticisms of traditional ethics of which Jaggar cites only the conclusions in her contribution to this volume.

One such criticism is that raised by Seyla Benhabib against the hypothetical contractualism of John Rawls. Central to Benhabib's critique of Rawls's hypothetical contractualism is her distinction between the generalized other and the concrete other (Benhabib 1992). According to the standpoint of the generalized other, we are required to view each and every individual as a rational being entitled to the same rights and duties that we would ascribe to ourselves. To assume this standpoint, we abstract from the individuality and concrete identity of the other. We assume that the other, like ourselves, is a being with concrete needs, desires and affects, but that what constitutes his or her moral dignity is not what differentiates us from each other, but rather what all of us, as speaking and acting rational agents, have in common. According to Benhabib, our relation to the other is governed by the norms of formal equality and reciprocity, that is, each is entitled to expect and to assume from us what we can expect and assume from him or her. The norms of our interactions with the other are primarily public and institutionalized ones (Benhabib 1992: 158–9).

By contrast, the standpoint of the concrete other requires us to view each and every rational being as an individual with a concrete history, identity and affective-emotional constitution. To assume this standpoint, we abstract from what constitutes our commonality, and focus on individuality. We seek to comprehend the needs of others, their motivations, what they search for, and what they desire. Our relations to the other are governed by the norms of equity and complementary reciprocity, that is, each is entitled to expect and to assume from the other forms of behavior through which the other feels recognized and confirmed as a concrete, individual being with specific needs, talents and capacities. The norms of our interaction with the other are usually, although not exclusively, private non-institutional ones (Benhabib 1992: 159).

Now the central contention of Benhabib's critique of Rawls's hypothetical contractualism is that his theory is inadequate for ethical decision-making because the veil of ignorance condition imposed on his original position only permits knowledge of others as generalized others and not as concrete others. According to Benhabib, to think of others as simply generalized others is not really to think of others as others at all, since as generalized others, we are not really others, but are all identically the same (Benhabib 1992: 161ff).

By contrast, Benhabib's own feminist ethics permits knowledge of others as both generalized others and concrete others (Benhabib 1992: 164, 169). Thus, unlike Rawls's theory, Benhabib claims that her feminist ethics really does require that we put ourselves in the place of others understood both as generalized and concrete others. Now, according to Rawls, a person in the original position does not know his place in society, his class position or status; nor does he know his fortune in the distribution of natural assets and abilities, his intelligence and strength, and the like. Nor, again, does anyone know his conception of the good, the particulars of his rational plan of life, or even the special features of his psychology such as his aversion to risk or liability to optimism or pessimism (Rawls 1971: 137). From this characterization of persons in the original position, Benhabib concludes that persons in Rawls's original position know others simply as generalized others and not as concrete others, and that this limited knowledge does not suffice for ethical decision-making.

But as far as I can tell, there are at least three interpretations of Rawls's veil of ignorance condition only one of which leads to Benhabib's negative assessment of Rawls's theory. First, we could interpret the veil of ignorance condition, as Benhabib does, to rule out any particular information about others whatsoever, and hence, to rule out any knowledge of concrete others. Second, we could interpret the veil of ignorance condition as simply ruling out knowledge of which particular concrete self one happens to be, but allowing the knowledge of all other characteristics of concrete selves. On this second interpretation, people behind Rawls's veil of ignorance would know the full concreteness of individuals, they simply would not know, or at least would be discounting their knowledge of, which particular concrete selves they happen to be. On this second interpretation, people behind a veil of ignorance would have that knowledge of concrete others that Benhabib thinks is essential for ethical decision-making.

But how essential is this knowledge to ethical decision-making? Do we really need to have this knowledge about others in order to determine what basic rights people should have? It is not clear that we do. To determine that other human beings have the same basic rights to equal political freedom, equal opportunity and an adequate welfare minimum as ourselves, isn't it sufficient to know that they are simply human beings like ourselves? Now, of course, particular characteristics of human beings will determine how these basic rights are to be interpreted. For example, a right to equal opportunity will require something different for a person with disabilities than for a person with normal abilities, and the basic rights of a person who has violated the basic rights of others can be justifiably curtailed. There are also certain rights and responsibilities we have that derive from particular agreements that we have made or particular roles that we have assumed. But to determine what basic rights all human beings have, it would appear to suffice to reflect upon what we have in common (i.e., our general selves). Knowledge of our concrete selves is not needed at this stage of moral reflection, although as I indicated it is needed at other stages.

Now it is possible that interpreters of Rawls's theory may have been misled by the fact that knowledge of concrete selves is not utilized in determining what basic rights people have into concluding that the knowledge of concrete selves isn't available in Rawls's theory at all, and, therefore, not available when it is really needed, e.g., with regard to the application of these basic rights under different concrete conditions. But, as I have argued, this would be a mistaken interpretation of Rawls's theory.

We also need to recognize that sometimes the knowledge of our concrete selves can get in the way of establishing what basic rights people have. Over twenty-five years ago, R. M. Hare argued that all that was needed to secure impartiality in Rawls's original position was an "economical veil of ignorance" (Hare 1973). Hare's economical veil only deprived persons in the original position of the knowledge of each person's particular nature and circumstances (that is, who and where they are) while giving them complete knowledge of the course of history and the present conditions of society, as well as unlimited general information. Actually, Hare's economical veil interpretation of Rawls's veil of ignorance is identical with the second interpretation offered above, which permits the knowledge of concrete selves that Benhabib thinks is so essential for ethical decision-making.

But there is a problem with this interpretation of Rawls's veil of ignorance. People behind Hare's economical veil with their knowledge of the course of history and the present conditions of society could determine when it was possible to secure considerable utility for the overwhelming majority in society by enslaving or denying basic rights to certain minority groups. They could decide that the possibility of their turning up as a member of certain disadvantaged minority groups themselves was an acceptable risk in virtue of the high probability of their belonging to the majority. As a result, it would be in the interest of people behind Hare's economical veil to choose principles that denied the basic needs and desires of certain minorities when this benefited the overwhelming majority in society.

I think that this problem with Hare's interpretation of Rawls's veil of ignorance condition should lead us to favor a third interpretation. According to this interpretation, persons in the original position would have all knowledge of general and concrete others, except that knowledge that would lead to biased choices or stand in the way of an unanimous agreement.[5] This third interpretation of Rawls's veil of ignorance would not be subject to the problem facing Hare's economical veil because it would require us to discount the knowledge of the likelihood of our turning up in advantaged or disadvantaged social positions given that such knowledge would lead to biased choices. This interpretation of the veil of ignorance is also the one that Rawls himself has favored since 1975 when he claimed in his article "Fairness to Goodness" that it superseded earlier interpretations (Rawls 1975). Moreover, given that this interpretation of Rawls's veil of ignorance permits all knowledge of concrete others that would not lead to biased choices or stand in the way of an unanimous agreement, it does not seem to be subject to Benhabib's critique either.[6]

Another aspect of Benhabib's critique of Rawls's hypothetical contractualism which she takes over from Habermas, and which is also endorsed by Iris Young and Marilyn Friedman, is the charge that it represent a monological model of moral decision-making which is, she claims, inferior to the dialogical model of real-life argumentation among a plurality of participants endorsed by communicative ethics (Benhabib 1992: 163; Friedman 1993, ch. 1; Young 1990).[7] Now there is no doubt that ethical decision-making requires real-life argumentation among all the relevant participants to make us aware of the issues and the reasons that support various possible positions. But frequently enough actual arguments among the relevant participants do not end in any agreement. In some cases, the discussion would have to go on much longer before there would be any hope of reaching an agreement from all the relevant participants. In other cases, the immoral obstinacy or hardness of heart of some participants effectively precludes any agreement. In all cases, there remains the question: What should I do? Individuals have to answer this question through their own moral reflection. Obviously, that reflection is immensely aided by informed debate among the relevant participants, but it is rarely settled by such debate, except possibly in those cases in which an informed debate by all the relevant participants reaches a unanimous agreement. In all other cases, we need to reflect on the debate as it has preceded so far, and then decide for ourselves what we think is right. So normally ethical decision-making is both dialogical and monological. It involves an ongoing real-life debate with other relevant participants, and it involves personal reflection on the progress of that debate so far to determine what one thinks is morally right.

But if what one thinks is morally right is to be determined in part by dialogical thinking and in part by monological thinking, is there any role for hypothetical agreements? It should be apparent that hypothetical agreements have an important role to play in monological thinking. When actual agreements are incomplete or defective, determining what people would agree to under more favorable conditions is an important resource for ethical decision-making. In turn, knowledge of the results of morally relevant hypothetical agreements, can have an important impact on what sort of actual agreements people are willing to make. So both before and after attempts at reaching morally informed actual agreements, morally relevant hypothetical agreements have an important role to play in determining what is morally right.

Moreover, just as there are obstacles to arriving at morally informed actual agreements, there are also obstacles to arriving at morally relevant hypothetical agreements. In her book, *Justice, Gender and the Family* (1989), which Jaggar cites in her contribution to this volume, Susan Okin examines the capacity of Rawls's hypothetical contractualism to support a feminist ideal of a gender-free society. Noting Rawls's failure to apply his original position-type thinking to family structures, Okin is skeptical about the possibility of using Rawls's theory to support a feminist ideal. She contends that in a gender-structured society like our own, male philosophers cannot achieve the sympathetic imagination required to see things from the standpoint of women. In a gender-structured society, Okin claims, male philosophers cannot do the original position-type thinking required by Rawls's theory because they lack the ability to put themselves in the position of women. So, according to Okin, original position-type thinking can only really be achieved in a gender-free society.

Yet at the same time that Okin despairs of doing original position-type thinking in an gender-structured society, like our own, she herself purportedly does a considerable amount of just that type of thinking. For example, she claims that Rawls's principles of justice "would seem to require a radical rethinking not only of the division of labor within families but also of all the nonfamily institutions that assume it" (Okin 1989: 104) She also claims that "the abolition of gender seems essential for the fulfillment of Rawls's criterion of political justice"(Okin 1989: 104).

But which is it? Can we or can we not do the original position-type thinking required by Rawls's hypothetical contractualism? I think that Okin's own work, as well the work of others, demonstrates that we can do such thinking and that her reasons for thinking that we cannot are not persuasive. For to do original position-type thinking, it is not necessary that everyone be able to put themselves imaginatively in the position of everyone else. All that is necessary is that some people be able to do so. For some people may not be able to do original position-type thinking because they have been deprived of a proper moral education. Others may be able to do original position-type thinking only after they have been forced to mend their ways and live morally for a period of time.

Moreover, in putting oneself imaginatively in the place of others, one need not completely replicate the experience of others, for example, one need not actually feel what it is like to be a murderer to adequately take into account the murderer's perspective. Original position-type thinking with respect to a particular issue requires only a general appreciation of the benefits and burdens accruing to people affected by that issue. So with respect to a feminist ideal, we need to be able to generally appreciate what women and men stand to gain and lose when moving from a gendered society to a gender-free society.

Of course, even among men and women in our gendered society who are in a broad sense capable of a sense of justice, some may not presently be able to do such original position-type thinking with respect to the proper relationships between men and women; these men and women may only be able to do so after the laws and social practices in our society have significantly shifted toward a more gender-free society. But this inability of some to do original position-type thinking does not render it impossible for others, who have effectively used the opportunities for moral development available to them to achieve the sympathetic imagination necessary for original position-type thinking with respect to the proper relationships between men and women. Accordingly, Okin has not provided any compelling reason to think that Rawls's hypothetical contractualism cannot support the feminist ideal of a gender-free society.

Still another objection to Rawls's hypothetical contractualism, which is informed by Habermas's and Benhabib's work, has been recently raised by Allison Jaggar herself. Jaggar grants that "the theoretical device of hypothetical consent initially may be attractive to feminists working in practical ethics" (Jaggar 1993). But she then goes on to argue that "hypothetical consent is [in fact] an inappropriate conceptual tool for this sort of feminist ethical work" (Jaggar 1993: 69–70). Her main objection here to arguing from hypothetical consent comes "from the fact that this reasoning is about ideal rather than actual societies" (Jaggar 1993: 79). On this account, Jaggar recommends that feminists who work in practical ethics "refrain from speculations about hypothetical consent and devote their energy instead to reflecting on and indeed actively pursuing real life moral consensus" (Jaggar 1993: 81–2).

Unfortunately, the idea that reasoning from hypothetical consent is about ideal rather than nonideal or actual societies derives from Rawls's self-imposed limit on the type of hypothetical consent theory he chose to develop. Since Rawls only sought to construct principles of justice for ideal conditions for which it was assumed that everyone would strictly comply with the chosen principles of justice, many have thought that the device of hypothetical consent can only be usefully applied in ideal conditions. Yet there is no reason why a hypothetical consent account of fairness cannot be extended to nonideal conditions as well. In fact, I have done just that in some of my earlier work where I have developed a hypothetical consent theory of punishment by assuming behind a veil of ignorance that one might be a criminal, a victim of crime or a member of the general public and then deriving principles of punishment (Sterba 1977, 1979, 1984, 1990). So, in general, there seems to be no problem with the application of a hypothetical consent theory of fairness to nonideal conditions.

Yet perhaps what is really troubling Jaggar is not the possibility of developing a hypothetical consent theory that applies to nonideal conditions, but rather the realization that under nonideal conditions, quoting Jaggar:

> we must deal with people constituted through institutions of domination such as gender, race and class. Such people, and they include ourselves, are not only unequal in knowledge and power but often also prejudiced, confused – even brutal or sadistic. (Jaggar 1993: 79)

Here the problem is that such individuals may not be able to achieve the sympathetic imagination required by a morally defensible hypothetical consent theory. Of particular relevance to a feminist ideal is that such individuals may not be able to imaginatively put themselves in the place of women. But this is the same problem raised by Okin that we discussed earlier, and the solution remains the same: We must recognize that in an unjust society only some people will be capable of doing original position type thinking. Others, either through improper moral education or their own fault, may simply not have the ability. Notice also that under nonideal conditions, the possibility of achieving an actual consensus that is morally acceptable and the ability of individuals to do original position-type thinking go hand in hand; for only when a considerable number or people in a society have achieved the sympathetic imagination necessary to put themselves in the position of others will the actual consensus that emerges under real life conditions be morally acceptable. So feminists can't really follow Jaggar's advice and "refrain from speculations about hypothetical consent and devote their energy instead to reflecting on and indeed actively pursuing real life moral consensus" because speculations about hypothetical consent and real life moral consensus are intimately connected.

Another way of putting this point is to claim that the monological thinking that characterizes morally relevant hypothetical agreements and the dialogical thinking that leads to morally informed actual agreements are interdependent such that it is impossible to achieve the latter (morally informed actual agreements) unless people are skilled in making the former (morally relevant hypothetical agreements). Moreover, since morally informed actual agreements by large numbers of people are hard to come by, monological thinking with its morally relevant hypothetical agreements is frequently our best guide for determining what is morally right for us to do. Frequently, the conditions necessary for reaching morally informed actual agreements do not exist, as would be the case when not all the would-be participants to an agreement are trying to do what is morally right. In such cases, in order to determine what we should morally do, we need to rely on monological thinking to determine what people would agree to under fair conditions, and here is where Rawls's hypothetical contractualism can prove helpful.

Jaggar, however, has still other objections to using hypothetical agreements that we need to consider. In a later article, Jaggar objects to the claim, made earlier, that in an unjust society some people will not be able to do original position-type thinking, either through improper moral education or their own fault. She claims that such a view is elitist (Jaggar 1995). But why is claiming, e.g., that in an unjust society some men may not have the sympathetic imagination to put themselves in the place of women, elitist? Surely this claim should not sound strange to most feminists aware of the many problem facing women today. Why then should Jaggar object to it?

Jaggar claims that her major objection to hypothetical consent theory is that it mistakenly assumes that one person can speak authoritatively for everyone else. But claiming that we need to imaginatively put ourselves into the position of others in determining what is right is perfectly consistent with allowing that people should speak for themselves or through their chosen representatives. Yet in allowing that people should speak for themselves or through their chosen representatives, we must also recognize that we will sometimes be morally justified in opposing what people say and do, as, for example, when they deny basic rights to others. In order to know when we are justified in so acting in opposition to others, we need to be able to put ourselves imaginatively in their position and in all other related positions and determine what would be acceptable to all parties given that, in such circumstances, no morally informed actual agreement is possible. In such circumstances, which, from a feminist perspective, will be prevalent in existing societies, the use of Rawls's hypothetical contractualism should turn out to be quite helpful. Of course, this is not to deny that we should push for morally informed actual agreements, but a feminist, like Jaggar, should recognize that when we cannot get them, we have no moral alternative but to rely on morally relevant hypothetical consent in determining what is right for us to do.

As you will recall, my main objective in this section was to examine in detail at least some of the feminist criticisms of traditional ethics which Jaggar cites in her contribution to this volume. To that end, I have focused on the objections that Benhabib, Okin, Friedman, Young, and Jaggar herself have raised about the adequacy of Rawls's hypothetical contractualism. I have argued that once Rawls's theory is given its most favorable interpretation, it can be shown to be compatible with what is morally defensible in these feminist objections.

Conclusion

I have approached the contributions of this volume with the habits of a reconciler or a peacemaker, looking for ways of bringing apparently conflicting views together.

To bring libertarians and their opponents together, I have argued that the libertarian's own ideal supports the same sort of welfare institutions favored by welfare liberals and socialists. To bring utilitarians and their opponents together, I have appealed to the common ground of contemporary social contract theory to argue for the need to place certain constraints on the pursuit of utilitarian goals. Finally, to bring feminists and their opponents together, I have argued that once Rawls's hypothetical contract theory is given its most favorable interpretation, it is compatible with what is morally defensible in a number of feminist objections to traditional ethics.[7] Of course, I have not argued for the superiority of a peacemaking over the dominant warmaking way of doing philosophy, which seeks to defeat and put down opposing views by whatever means are available, although I have done so elsewhere (Sterba 1998, ch. 1). In ethics, however, the desirability of reaching at least some type of practical reconciliation should be more than evident. If ethics cannot reasonably establish what we should do and be, what good is it? If ethical theorists cannot assist the process of reasonably establishing what we should do or be, what good are they?

Notes

1   In general, Narveson does recognize the possibility of conflicts of liberty. He writes: "In general, anyone's desire to do anything is potentially in conflict with someone else's desired course of action. Your combing your hair is incompatible with my shaving it all off; my going to the opera is incompatible with your burning down the opera house; and so on. . . . Can this idea . . . generate any . . . coherent rules?" (308) So, in principle, he is committed to recognizing these conflicts of liberty between the rich and the poor.

2   It is unclear whether Narveson accepts the "ought" implies "can" principle as I have formulated it. He says that the proper principle must be the one "that can be most expected . . . to enable each of us to live the better lives that we envisage to be achievable, given our various interests" (323) which may lead one to think that he does accept the principle, but the fact that he claims that a society without a right to welfare would be acceptable to all, including the poor, leads one to think that he does not really accept this principle after all.

3   If this reconciliation argument is correct, it drastically narrows the distance between the libertarian view and the other views discussed in this paper.

4   I say it only goes somewhat to meeting this objection to utilitarianism because in Hooker's theory, fairness is only one consequence among others and it is not clear how it is to weigh against those other consequences. By contrast, the standard of fairness in contemporary social contract theory operates more as a constraint on the pursuit of other consequences.

5   This interpretation, or at least the first part of it, is similar to the way Marilyn Friedman proposes to understand impartiality. Unfortunately, she sees herself as opposing Rawls's view rather than interpreting it (see Friedman 1993, ch. 1).

6   There is a problem, however, determining when these conditions obtain. In 1971, Rawls did not think that it was biased to regard existing family structures as just, thereby failing to apply his original position decision procedure to them, but it was. Similarly, today

Rawls presumably does not think that it is biased not to extend his original position decision-procedure to all living things. But I have argued elsewhere that it is (see Sterba 1994).

7   It might be objected that my argument for reconciliation might be more effectively carried out if the reconciliation I favor could be shown to require concessions from all sides. But, in fact, concessions *are* required from all sides for my reconciliation arguments to go through, although in setting out my argument I have tended to focus on only the major concessions that are required. Thus, in my argument between libertarians and their opponents, while I focus on the concessions that libertarians must make concerning the practical requirements of their view, the opponents of libertarians must also concede that only the deserving poor have a right to welfare. Similarly, in the debate between utilitarians and their opponents, while I focus on the need for utilitarians who are committed to contemporary social contract theory to constrain the pursuit of utility in their critical/ theoretical thinking, opponents of utilitarianism would also have to concede that this constraint is not absolute. Finally, in the debate between feminists and their opponents while I argue for certain concessions that feminists, like Benhabib, should make to social contract theorists, opponents of feminism must concede that the best interpretations of social contract theory favor feminism as well. I owe this objection and other valuable comments on my essay to Hugh LaFollette.

References

Benhabib, Seyla: *Situating the Self* (New York: Routledge, 1992).

Friedman, Marilyn: *What Are Friends For?* (Ithaca: Cornell University Press, 1993).

Hare, R. M.: "Justice and Equality," in James P. Sterba (ed.), *Justice: Alternative Political Perspectives*, 3rd edn. (Belmont, CA: Wadsworth, 1999).

——: "Rawls' Theory of Justice," *Philosophical Quarterly* (1973).

Harsanyi, John: *Rational Behavior and Bargaining Equilibrium in Games and Social Situations* (Cambridge: Cambridge University Press, 1977).

Jaggar, Alison: *Morality and Social Justice* (Lanham: Rowman and Littlefield, 1995).

——: "Taking Consent Seriously: Feminist Practical Ethics and Actual Moral Dialogue," in Earl Winkler and Jerrold Coombs (eds.), *Applied Ethics: A Reader* (Oxford: Blackwell, 1993).

Okin, Susan: *Justice, Gender and the Family* (New York: Basic Books, 1989).

Rawls, John: "Fairness as Goodness," *Philosophical Review* (1975).

——: *A Theory of Justice* (Cambridge, MA: Harvard University Press, 1971, 1975)

Sterba, James P.: *Justice for Here and Now* (Cambridge: Cambridge University Press, 1998).

——: "Rawls's Hypothetical Contractualism," *New German Critique* (1994).

——: "A Rational Choice Theory of Punishment," *Philosophical Topics* (1990).

——: *How To Make People Just* (Totowa: Rowman and Littlefield, 1988)

——: "Is There a Rationale for Punishment?" *The American Journal of Jurisprudence* (1984).

——: *The Demands of Justice* (Notre Dame, IN: Notre Dame University Press, 1980).

——: "Contractual Retributivism Defended," *Political Theory* (1979).

——: "Retributive Justice," *Political Theory* (1977).

Young, Iris: *Justice and the Politics of Difference* (Princeton: Princeton University Press, 1990).

Index